gustinian Heritage Institute, Inc.

D1563179

THE WORKS OF SAINT AUGUSTINE
A Translation for the 21st Century

Part II – Letters
Volume 1:
Letters 1- 99

Michael
Joseph
Thomas

Gerald
Allan
Joseph

Au

Le

THE WORKS OF SAINT AUGUSTINE
A Translation for the 21st Century

Letters 1 - 99

II/1

translation and notes by
Roland Teske, S.J.

editor
John E. Rotelle, O.S.A.

New City Press
Hyde Park, New York

Published in the United States by New City Press
202 Cardinal Rd., Hyde Park, New York 12538
©2001 Augustinian Heritage Institute

Library of Congress Cataloging-in-Publication Data:

Augustine, Saint, Bishop of Hippo.
    The works of Saint Augustine.
    "Augustinian Heritage Institute"
    Includes bibliographical references and indexes.
    Contents: — pt. 3, v .15. Expositions of the Psalms, 1-32
—pt. 3, v. 1. Sermons on the Old Testament, 1-19.
— pt. 3, v. 2. Sermons on the Old Testament, 20-50 — [et al.] — pt. 3,
v. 10 Sermons on various subjects, 341-400.
    1.   Theology — Early church, ca. 30-600.   I. Hill,
Edmund.   II. Rotelle, John E.   III. Augustinian
Heritage Institute.   IV. Title.
BR65.A5E53 1990   270.2   89-28878
ISBN 1-56548-055-4 (series)
ISBN 1-56548-163-1 (pt. 2, v. 1)

We are indebted to Brepols Publishers, Turnholt, Belgium,for their use of the Latin critical text
of *Enarrationes in Psalmos I-CL,* ed. D. Eligius Dekkers, O.S.B. et Johannes Fraipont,
Corpus Christianorum Latinorum XXXVIII-XL (Turnholt, 1946) 1-2196.

Nihil Obstat:John E. Rotelle, O.S.A., S.T.L., Censor Deputatus
Imprimatur: + Robert A. Brucato, D.D., Vicar General
                Archdiocese of New York, May 31, 2001

Printed in the United States of America

For the Reverend

Francis Paul Prucha, S.J.

Priest, Scholar, and Friend

Contents

General Introduction

The Letters of Saint Augustine are an invaluable source of information for the study of Church history, of dogma and liturgy, and of social history in late antiquity.[1] All told, the correspondence of Augustine includes 308 letters, 252 that he himself wrote, 49 that others sent to him and seven letters that others sent to a third party.[2] In addition to the 270 letters in the Maurist edition, Migne's *Patrologia Latina* added three new letters and a fragment of another, inserting the new letters in chronological order, to the extent this was possible, and adding an "A" to the number of the previous letter. Goldbacher's critical edition added three more letters: 92A, 173A, and 185A. Two more letters, 212A and 215A, were added earlier in the century. Finally, in 1981 Johannes Divjak added 29 more letters which he numbered 1* to 29*, without any attempt to fit them into the chronology, which was already dubious in many cases.

The critical edition of Letters 1-270, with nine additional letters added in, was done by A. Goldbacher and published in CSEL 34, 44, 57, and 58 (Vienna, 1895-1923). The critical edition of Letters 1*-29* was done by J. Divjak in CSEL 88 (Vienna, 1981). The French edition and translation in BA 46^B includes valuable notes. Letters 1 to 270 have been translated into French by F. Poujoulat in *Saint Augustin: Lettres* (Paris, 1858), into Italian by T. Alimonti and L. Carrozzi in *Sant'Agostino: Le Lettere* I, I, and III (Rome: Città Nuova Editrice, 1969-1974), and into Spanish by Lope Cilleruelo in *Obras Completas de San Agustín* 8, 11a, and 11b (Madrid: Biblioteca de Autores Cristianos, 1951, 1958, and 1986). The Spanish bilingual text also includes in the last volume the Divjak letters. Seventy-eight letters have been translated into German by A. Hoffmann in *Des heiligen Augustinus ausgewählte Briefe* I. Bibliothek der Kirchenväter 29 and 30 (Munich, 1917). All the letters have been translated into English in the Fathers of the Church series, Letters 1 to 270 by W. Parsons in volumes 12, 18, 20, 30, and 32 (New York, 1951-1956), as well as the Divjak letters by Robert Eno in volume 81 (Washington, D.C., 1989). There are also English translations of selected letters in *A Select Library of the Nicene and Post-Nicene Fathers of the Christian Church*, Series 1, Volume 1, ed. Philip Schaff (New York, 1886; reprinted, Grand Rapids, 1956), in *Selected Letters*, translated by J. H. Baxter,

---

1. See Frank Morgenstern, *Die Briefpartner des Augustinus von Hippo: Prosopograhische, sozial- und indeologiegeschichtliche Untersuchung* (Bochum: Universitätsverlag Dr. N. Brochmeyer, 1993) 1. This volume is a very valuable resource for studying Augustine's letters.
2. *Ibid.* 3.

Loeb Classical Library 239 (Cambridge, 1953), and in *Letters of Saint Augustine*, translated and edited John Leinenweber (Tarrytown, N.Y., 1992).

The Text and the Translation

I have translated the text of the Goldbacher edition, though I at times departed from it in favor of a wording found in Migne or in either the NBA or BAC texts. Augustine's epistulary style is generally clear and quite straightforward, especially in contrast to that of some of his correspondents, such as Licentius, Paulinus of Nola, and Pope Innocent—not to mention letters to and from the imperial court. I have tried to preserve the literal sense of the text without losing readability. The formal terms of address that Augustine and his correspondents used will undoubtedly strike the modern reader as stilted. Though modern English uses Your Holiness or Your Excellency for addressing a pope or a bishop and Your Majesty for a king or queen, Augustine uses a much wider range of such terms of respect, ranging from Your Charity and Your Benevolence to Your Fraternity and even Your Amplitude. Though I have retained most of these, I found some of these expressions all but impossible to render literally in English. I have retained the Latin endings on proper names, except for names such as Cyprian where the omission of "us" seems more natural and for names that are already used in English such as Valentine. For the dating of the letters, which in very many cases is hardly more than a guess, I have relied on the BAC and NBA editions, as well as the book by Morgenstern.

Introduction to Letters 1 to 99

The first volume of the Letters of Saint Augustine covers the period from his retreat at Cassiciacum in Italy in the fall of 386 or the spring of 387 to height of the Donatist controversy in 408 or 409. The volume contains a total of 100 letters.[3] Sixteen of these were written by others: three by Nebridius, five by Paulinus of Nola, five by Jerome of Bethlehem, one by Nectarius, a citizen of Calama in Numidia, one by Maximus of Madaura, and one by Publicola, a Catholic lay man and Roman senator. One Letter was written by Paulinus of Nola to Romanian, Augustine's wealthy patron, on the occasion of Augustine's being ordained coadjutor bishop of Hippo. Another was written by Paulinus to Augustine's close friend, Alypius, who is also listed as coauthor with Augustine of six of the letters.

Some of the letters naturally belong together as parts of a correspondence continued over the years, such as Augustine's early exchange of letters with

---

3. Letter 92A was not included in the Maurist numbering.

Nebridius, or the eleven letters of correspondence with Paulinus of Nola and his wife, Therasia, or the stormy exchange of another eleven letters between Augustine and Jerome. Many letters deal with problems related to the Donatist schism, either appealing to the Donatists to return to the unity of the Catholic Church, or attempting to strengthen the Catholic faithful against the violent attacks of the Circumcellions, or invoking the power of the state to suppress the Donatist heresy. According to the *Revisions* Letters 54 and 55 constitute a work entitled *Two Books for the Questions of Januarius.*[4] Many of the letters can only be dated in a general fashion, and at times Augustine's correspondent is scarcely identifiable. I have added a short introduction before each letter in which I have tried to offer the reader information about the addressee of the letter and its content and background.

---

4. See *Revisions* II, 20.

Letter 1

At the end of 386 or the beginning of 387, Augustine wrote from Cassiciacum to Hermogenian, a Catholic Milanese layman, explaining his theory about why the Academics concealed the truth in a manner suited to their times (paragraph 1). But now, Augustine argues, such a practice leads to an abandonment of all search for the truth (paragraph 2). Hence, Augustine asks Hermogenian to reconsider what Augustine wrote about the Academics at the end of the third book of his *Answer to the Skeptics*, where he had first proposed his theory (paragraph 3).

Augustine sends greetings to Hermogenian.

1. Not even in joking would I dare to attack the Academics. After all, how would the authority of such great men fail to disturb me, if I did not believe that they stood for a far different view than is commonly believed?[1] Hence, to the extent I could, I imitated them rather than attacked them, something I could never do. For it seems to me that it had been quite appropriate to those times that, if anything pure flowed from the Platonic spring, it should wind through shady and thorny thickets for the nourishment of very few human beings rather than that it should run through open country with cattle rushing in here and there, so that it could not be kept at all clear and pure. For what is more appropriate for an animal than to think that the soul is a body?[2] Against such human beings I think that the art and method of concealing the truth was usefully devised. In this age, however, when we now see no philosophers except perhaps those wearing the philosopher's mantle—and those I, of course, hardly deem worthy of so venerable a name—human beings must, it seems to me, be recalled to the hope of finding the truth, if the view of the Academics has deterred any from a grasp of reality by the cleverness of their words. Otherwise, what was suited at the time for eradicating the deepest errors might begin to be an obstacle for inculcating knowledge.

2. For at that time the enthusiasm of the various sects was ablaze with such passion that nothing was to be feared except the assent to something false. But driven by those arguments from what each had believed that he held as solid and unshakeable, he sought something else with greater constancy and caution to the extent that there was greater concern for morals and it was thought that the truth lay hidden mostly deeply and most obscurely in the nature of the world and of minds. But now there is so great a shrinking from toil and so great a lack of

---

1. At the end of *Answer to the Skeptics* III, Augustine claimed that the Academics hid their true convictions from the masses under skepticism, while they in fact held the teachings of Plato.
2. Such was the common philosophical position in the Latin West, except for the few Neoplatonists whom Augustine encountered in Milan.

interest in the fine arts that, as soon as people hear that the most intelligent philosophers thought that nothing can be grasped as true, they cease to use their mind and leave it in the dark for eternity. For they do not dare to believe that they have keener minds than those philosophers so that they might see clearly what Carneades[3] could not discover with such great desire, talent, and leisure, with such great and diverse learning, and finally even over a very long life. But if people go against their own laziness even a little and read the same books by which it is supposedly proven that knowledge is denied to human nature, they fall into so deep a sleep that they do not wake up even at the heavenly trumpet.[4]

3. Hence, because I regard your sincere judgment about my writings most pleasing and hold you in such high esteem that, in my opinion, error cannot be found in your wisdom, nor pretense in your friendship, I ask that you consider that point more carefully and write back to me whether you agree with what at the end of the third book I thought one should hold, perhaps more as a conjecture than as something certain, but as something more useful, I think, than improbable. But whatever may be the case with those writings, I am not as pleased that, as you put it, I have defeated the Academics—for you write this with more affection perhaps than truth—as that I have broken for myself that most odious snare by which I was held back from the breast of philosophy out of a despair of finding the truth, which is the food of the soul.

---

3. Carneades (214/213—129/128 B.C.), a renowned skeptic, was the founder of the New Academy; he taught that no certitude at all was possible and developed a theory of probability.

4. That is, not even at the last judgment.

Letter 2

In 386 or 387 Augustine wrote from Cassiciacum to Zenobius, a friend and Milanese Catholic layman, the brother of Dioscorus.[1] He explains that, though the true philosophy, namely, Christianity, teaches us to control our desire for passing things, Augustine still longs for the presence of Zenobius and complains that he has been avoiding him.

Augustine sends greetings to Zenobius.

1. We are in full agreement, I think, that everything that a sense of the body attains cannot remain in the same way even for a moment of time, but slips away, flows off, and holds onto nothing actual, that is, to speak Latin, it does not exist. The true and divine philosophy[2] warns us to rein in and to quiet the most destructive love of these things, which abounds with punishments, in order that, even while the mind governs this body, it may by its whole self be borne toward and ardently desire those things that always exist without change and are not pleasing because of a transient beauty. Though this is so and though my mind sees in itself that you are a true and simple man, the sort of person who can be loved without any worry, we, nonetheless, admit that, when you depart from us in terms of the body and are separated by place, we seek this contact with and sight of you to the extent that brothers are permitted to desire it. If I know you well, you, of course, are fond of this defect in us, and though you desire for your dearest and closest friends everything good, you are afraid that they will be healed of this defect. But if you are so strong of mind that you can recognize this snare and laugh at those caught in it, you are truly a great and different man. As for myself, when I long for someone who is absent, I want to be longed for too. I am, nonetheless, as vigilant as I can be and strive to love nothing that can be absent from me against my will. And out of duty I in the meanwhile warn you, whatever your disposition may be, that it is necessary to finish the conversation I began with you if we have any care about ourselves. For I would never allow you to finish it with Alypius,[3] even if he wanted to. He does, however, not want to. It is, after all, not typical of his humanity to fail to make the effort with me to hold you with us by as many letters as possible, though you try to escape on the pretext of some necessity or other.

---

1. See Letters 117 and 118 from and to Dioscorus.
2. Augustine means the Christian religion.
3. Augustine's friend from his youth and throughout his life, Alypius was baptized with Augustine in Milan and became bishop of Augustine's hometown, Thagaste, in 395.

The Correspondence with Nebridius: Letters 3-14

Twelve Letters are extant from the correspondence between Augustine and Nebridius; they reveal the deep friendship between these two men and cast light upon Augustine's philosophical and theological development during the period from before his return from Rome to Africa until the death of Nebridius in approximately 391.[1] After his return to Africa Augustine settled in his hometown, Thagaste, where he was undertaking to live a life of leisure and contemplation in a monastic community of sorts. Nebridius, a wealthy Carthaginian and friend from their student days, had followed Augustine to Milan, and, as the *Confessions* recount, he was baptized after his return to Africa, perhaps on his deathbed. It was Nebridius who presented Augustine with the decisive argument against the Manichees and with the arguments against the claims of the astrologers.[2] After their return to Africa, Nebridius remained in Carthage, where he died around 391.

---

1. For a study of this correspondence, see Georges Folliet, "La correspondence entre Augustin et Nebridius," in *L'opera letteraria di Agostino tra Cassiciacum et Milano: Agostino nelle terre di Ambrogio (1-4 ottobre 1986)*. Ed. Giovani Reale, et al. Palermo: Edizioni Augustinus, 1987, 191-215.
2. See *Confessions* VII, 2, 3 and 6, 8.

Letter 3

In early 387 Augustine replies from Cassiciacum to a letter of Nebridius that has not survived. He tells his friend that he does not deserve to be called happy (paragraph 1). He explores where one may find the happy life (paragraphs 2 and 3) and appeals to a favorite argument to show that happiness is to be found in the immortal mind (paragraph 4). Finally, Augustine wonders whether his friendship with Nebridius should not be counted as a good of fortune, the sort of good a wise man should not desire (paragraph 5)—a topic that raises a point of Latin grammar.

Augustine sends greetings to Nebridius.

1. I remain uncertain whether I should think it the effect, so to speak, of your persuasive words or whether it really is the case. For it came upon me suddenly, and I did not sufficiently consider to what extent I ought to believe it. You are waiting to find out what this is. What do you think? You almost convinced me, not, of course, that I am happy—for that is the lot of the wise man alone—but that I am at least like someone happy, as we say that a man is like a man in comparison with that true man whom Plato knew, or that those things that we see are like something round or something square though they are far distant from those that the mind of the few sees.[1] For I read your letter after supper by lamplight; it was almost time for bed, but not also time to go to sleep. Once having gotten into bed, I long considered with myself and had these conversations, Augustine with Augustine: Is what Nebridius holds not true, namely, that we are happy? No, of course not. For even he does not dare to deny that we are still foolish. Well, then, do the foolish also attain the happy life? That is hard to accept. As if folly itself is a small unhappiness or as if there is any other unhappiness but folly. Why, then, did he think this? Did he, after reading those writings of mine, dare to believe that I was happy? He is not reveling in premature joy, especially since we well know the ponderousness with which his thoughts proceed. This, then, is the answer: He wrote what he thought would be most pleasing to us. Because whatever we put in those writings was also pleasing to him, he wrote filled with joy, and he was not concerned about what he should have committed to his joyous pen. What if he read the *Soliloquies*?[2] He would have rejoiced much more exuberantly, and he would not have found anything

---

1. Augustine alludes to the Platonic doctrine that things in this sensible world are merely copies or images that resemble their true archetypes, the Ideas, which are seen only by the minds of the few.
2. Augustine wrote the two books of the *Soliloquies* in 387; *The Immortality of the Soul* was intended as a draft for a third book.

better to call me but happy. He, therefore, quickly bestowed that title on me, and he did not hold back anything that he might say of me if he were even more joyous. See the effects of joy!

2. But where is this happy life? Where? Where is it? Oh, if only it consisted in rejecting the atomism of Epicurus! Oh, if only it consisted in knowing that there is nothing below but the world! Oh, if only it consisted in knowing that points on the top and bottom of a sphere turn more slowly than those around the middle! And other similar things that we know. But now, how am I happy or what sort of a happy person am I who do not know why a world this great exists? For the intelligible patterns of the shapes that cause it to exist do not in any way prevent its being greater to the extent anyone might wish. Or would it not be objected to me—in fact, would we not be forced to admit that bodies are divisible to infinity so that from a given base, so to speak, we would get a determinate number of bodies of a determinate quantity? Hence, since no body is permitted to be the smallest, how shall we allow one to be the largest than which there cannot be one larger? Unless perhaps what I once said to Alypius[3] in complete secrecy has great force, namely, the intelligible number increases to infinity, but is not, nonetheless, decreased infinitely, for it is not possible to break it down past the monad.[4] A sensible number, on the other hand, can decrease infinitely, but cannot increase infinitely. For what else is a sensible number but the quantity of bodily things or of bodies? And perhaps for this reason philosophers rightly assigned riches to intelligible things and neediness to sensible ones. After all, what is more wretched than always to become less and less? What is better than to increase as much as you wish, to go where you wish, to return when you wish, as far as you wish, and to love very much that which cannot be decreased? For whoever understands those numbers loves nothing so much as the monad, nor is this surprising since it is what makes the other numbers loveable. But why, nonetheless, is the world this great? For it could be larger or smaller. I do not know; for it is this way. And why is it in this place rather than in that? We should not raise a question on this point, for whatever the answer to it might be, there would still be a question. That one idea bothered me much, namely, that bodies should be infinitely divisible. And I have perhaps got an answer to it from the contrary power of intelligent numbers.

3. But wait a minute; let us see what this idea is that comes to mind. Certainly the sensible world is said to be the image of an intelligible one. What we see, however, in the images reflected by mirrors is surprising. For, though the mirrors are huge, they do not reflect images larger than the bodies set before them, even if the bodies are very small. But in small mirrors, such as in the pupils

---

3. Alypius was a friend of Augustine from boyhood; he became the bishop of Thagaste.
4. The monad here seems to be the intelligible One of Plotinian thought; see *True Religion* 32, 60—34, 63, where Augustine uses similar language in speaking of the One.

of the eyes, a very small image is formed in accord with the size of the mirror, even if a large face is set opposite it. Hence, the images of bodies may become smaller if the mirrors are smaller, but they cannot become larger if the mirrors are larger. There is surely something hidden here, but now I must go to sleep. I do not, after all, seem happy, even to Nebridius, when I am seeking something, but I do perhaps when I find something. But what is that something? Is it perhaps that little argument which I often cherish as my sole resource and in which I take too much delight?

4. Of what are we composed? Of soul and body. Which of these is better? The soul, of course. What is praiseworthy in the body? I see nothing else but beauty. What is beauty in the body? The harmony of the parts along with a certain pleasing color. Is this form better where it is true or where it is false? Who has any doubt that it is better where it is true? Where is it true? In the soul, of course. The soul, therefore, should be loved more than the body. But in what part of the soul is the truth found? In the mind and intelligence. What is opposed to this? The senses. Must, then, one resist the senses with all the strength of the mind? Obviously. What if sensible things cause too much delight? Let them stop causing delight. How does this come about? By the habit of doing without them and of desiring better things. What if the soul dies? The truth, therefore, dies, or the intelligence is not truth, or the intelligence is not in the soul, or something can die in which there is something immortal. But none of these is possible. Our *Soliloquies* already contain this, and it has been sufficiently proven. But because of our familiarity with evils we are frightened and wavering. Finally, even if the soul dies, something that I see cannot happen in any way, it has been sufficiently shown in this period of leisure that the happy life does not consist in the enjoyment of sensible things. For these and similar reasons I perhaps seem to Nebridius to be happy or at least somewhat happy. I wish that I seemed so to myself as well. What do I lose from this, or why should I refrain from having a good opinion of myself? I said these things to myself; then, I prayed as was my habit and went to sleep.

5. I wanted to write these things to you. For I am delighted that you thank me when I conceal from you nothing that crosses my mind, and I am happy that I please you in that way. In whose eyes, then, should I more willingly write nonsense than in the eyes of him whom I cannot fail to please? But if it lies in the power of fortune that one person loves another, see how happy I am who find so much joy in goods of fortune, and I desire, I admit, that such goods of mind richly increase. But the most truly wise men, whom alone one may call happy, wanted that the goods of fortune neither be feared nor desired—you worry about whether "desired" should be *cupi* or *cupiri*.[5] This is fortunate. For I want you to inform me about the conjugation of this verb. For when I conjugate similar

---

5. Augustine is apparently puzzled over whether the present passive infinitive of "*cupio*" should be formed as a verb of third or fourth conjugation.

verbs, I become uncertain. After all, *"cupio"* is like *"fugio,"* like *"sapio,"* like *"jacio,"* and like *"capio,"* but I do not know whether the infinitive mood is *"fugiri"* or *"fugi,"* *"sapiri"* or *"sapi."* I could have followed *"jaci"* and *"capi,"* if I were not afraid that someone would catch me and throw me where he might want,[6] as if in a game, if he proved that the supines *"jactum"* and *"captum"* are different from *"fugitum,"* *"cupitum,"* and *"sapitum."* Likewise, I do not know whether these three should be pronounced with a long and accented penultimate syllable or with a short and unaccented one. I would like to provoke you to write a longer letter. I beg that I may read your writing for a little longer. For I cannot say how great a pleasure it is to read your letter.

---

6. The infinitives *"capi"* and *"jaci"* are from verbs that mean "to catch" and "to throw."

Letter 4

Again writing to Nebridius from Cassiciacum, most probably in early 387, Augustine explains the slow progress he has made in distinguishing sensible and intelligible natures (paragraph 1) and appeals to a short argument from the superiority of the mind or intelligence to the eyes of the body and their gaze, an argument that convinces him that eternal things are as present to us as we are to ourselves (paragraph 2).

Augustine sends greetings to Nebridius.

1. It is at least surprising how unexpectedly it happened that, when I asked which of your letters was left for me to answer, I found only one that still holds me indebted to you. In it you ask that, with our leisure, a leisure as great as you think you have or desire that we have, we indicate to you the progress we have made in distinguishing sensible nature and intelligible nature. But I do not think that you are unaware of the fact that, if anyone is more deeply immersed in false opinions to the extent that he is involved with them longer and with greater familiarity, the same thing happens much more readily to the mind with the truth. In that way, nonetheless, we gradually make progress with age. Though there is, of course, a great difference between a boy and a young man, no one who is asked daily from boyhood on will on a certain day say that he is now a young man.

2. I do not want you to interpret this in the sense that you think that we have come by the strength of a more solid intelligence, as it were, to a certain manhood of the mind. For we are boys, but, as it is often said, good boys and not bad ones. For the troubled eyes of my mind are filled with the concerns of wounds inflicted by the senses, but they are often revived and raised up by that little argument, which you know so well, that the mind and intelligence are better than the eyes and this ordinary looking. This would not be the case, unless those things that we understand had more being than these things which we see. I ask that you consider with me whether there is any strong opposition to this argument. Meanwhile, refreshed by this argument and having implored God's help, I begin to be raised up both to him and to those things that most truly are true, and I am at times filled with so great a foretaste of imperishable things that I am surprised that I at times need that argument in order to believe that those things exist that are in us with as much presence as each of us is present to himself. Please check for yourself—for I admit that you are more cautious about this matter than I am—lest, without knowing it, I am still owe you answers. For the sudden release from so many burdens, which I had at one point counted, does not make me confident about this, though I do not doubt that you have received letters from me for which I do not have replies.

Letter 5

Writing to Augustine between 388 and 391, perhaps from his estate near Carthage, Nebridius laments the demands of the citizens of Thagaste upon Augustine that distract him from contemplation. Nebridius invites him to come and find rest at his country home near Carthage.

Nebridius sends greetings to Augustine.

1. Is it true, my dear Augustine? Do you devote such energy and patience to the affairs of your fellow citizens, while you do not receive in turn that repose that you desire so much? Please, who are these people who make demands upon your goodness? I believe that they do not know what you love and what you long for. Have you no friend who will convey to them your desires? Do you have neither Romanian[1] nor Lucinian? Let them at least hear me. I cry out, I testify that you love God and desire to serve him and cling to him. I would like to invite you to my country home and have you rest there. For I am not afraid of being labeled your seducer by your fellow citizens whom you love too much and by whom you are loved too much.

---

1. Romanian was a wealthy citizen of Thagaste, Augustine's patron, and the father of Licentius.

Letter 6

Between 388 and 391 Nebridius writes to Augustine, probably from his country home, and expresses his appreciation for Augustine's letters, filled as they are with Christ, Plato, and Plotinus. He claims that in his opinion there cannot be memory without imagination (paragraph 1) and wonders whether we do not derive images from the imagination itself rather than from sensation. He asks Augustine for his views (paragraph 2).

Nebridius sends greetings to Augustine.

1. I am as delighted to have your letters as I am to have my own eyes. For they are great, not in size, but for the things they contain, and they contain great proofs and proofs of great things. They speak to me of Christ, of Plato, of Plotinus. They will, therefore, be delightful for me to hear because of their eloquence, easy to read because of their shortness, and salutary to understand because of their wisdom. You will, therefore, take care to teach me what your mind has found holy and good. But you will answer this letter when you discuss something more subtle with regard to imagination and memory. For it seems to me that, though not every image involves memory, there can be no memory without an image. But you say: What about when we recall that we understood or thought about something? To this I reply and state that this happened because, when we understood or thought of something bodily and temporal, we produced something that belongs to imagination. For we either have joined words to understanding and thoughts, and these words involve time and pertain to sensation or imagination, or in thinking our intellect has experienced something of the sort that could have produced a memory in the imaginative soul. I have said this, as usual, without consideration and in a confused manner; you will examine it and, after having rejected what is false, you will present the truth in a letter.

2. Listen to another idea. Why, I ask you, do we not say that the imagination receives all images from itself rather than from sensation? For, just as the intellectual soul is admonished by sensation to see its own intelligible objects rather than to receive something from sensation, so the imaginative soul can be admonished by sensation to contemplate its own images rather than to receive something. After all, this may perhaps be the reason that it can, nonetheless, see those things that sensation does not see. This is a sign that it has in itself and from itself all images. You will also reply what you think on this topic.

Letter 7

Between 388 and 391 Augustine replied to Nebridius' previous letter; he explains how there can be memory without images (paragraph 1). He appeals to the Platonic doctrine that intellectual learning is only remembering to show that we remember present intelligible things, though, he insists, our original vision of them was in the past (paragraph 2). He argues against Nebridius' idea that we can form images of sensible things without having previously used our senses (paragraph 3). The images we have can be divided into three kinds: those derived from previous sensations, for example, the image of a person I have seen; those we make up, for example, my image of Aeneas or of Medea; and those arrived at by reason, such as the image we form when reasoning with numbers and mathematical figures (paragraph 4). Augustine then shows that the soul has none of these kinds of images before it makes use of the senses of the body (paragraph 5). We can imagine things that we have never sensed because the soul has a power of diminishing and increasing images of things we have seen and of combining them in new ways, but we could never imagine the taste of strawberries or cherries before tasting them, just as someone born blind has no idea of colors (paragraph 6). Augustine tells Nebridius that he should not be surprised at how we can imagine things that we have never experienced through the senses since the soul has many activities that are free from images. Finally, he warns him to avoid entering into friendship with the shadowy images of sensible things (paragraph 7).

Augustine sends greetings to Nebridius.

1, 1. I shall refrain from any introduction and immediately begin what you impatiently want me to say, especially since I am not going to come to an end soon. You think that there can be no memory without images or representations of the imagination, which you chose to call "fantasies." I disagree. First, then, we must see that we do not always remember things that pass away, but very often things that last. Hence, though memory claims for itself a hold on past time, it is clear that memory, nonetheless, is in part memory of those things that leave us and in part memory of those things that we leave. For, when I remember my father, I, of course, remember someone who has left me and is no more, but when I remember Carthage, I remember something that still is and that I have left. In both of these kinds of things, however, memory holds onto the past time. For I remember both that man and this city from what I have seen, not from what I see.

2. Here you perhaps ask, "Where is this going?" especially since you observe that each of these can enter memory only by that representation of the imagination. It is, however enough for me for the time being to have shown that one can say that there is also memory of those things that have not yet perished. But make

yourself more attentive in order to hear how this helps me. Some speak falsely against that truly remarkable discovery of Socrates by which he maintains that those things that we learn are not impressed upon us as new, but are recalled into memory by recollection. These objectors say that memory is of past things, but that these things that we learn by understanding, on the authority of Plato himself,[1] last forever and cannot perish and, for this reason, are not past. They do not notice that this vision is past, because we once saw these things by the mind. And since we have flowed down from them and have begun to see other things in another way, we see them again by remembering them, that is, through memory. Hence, if—to leave other things aside—eternity itself lasts forever and does not require any products of the imagination upon which, as if upon vehicles, it might enter the mind and cannot, nonetheless, come into the mind unless we have remembered it, there can be a memory of certain things without any imagination.

2, 3. But your idea that the soul can imagine bodily things without having used the senses of the body is shown to be false in this way: If, before the soul uses the body for sensing bodily things, it can imagine the same bodily things and if—as no one in his right mind doubts—the soul was in a better state before it was entangled in these deceptive senses, the souls of the sleeping are in a better state than the souls of those awake, the souls of madmen are in a better state than those who are free from this plague. For the sleeping and the insane are affected by these images by which they were affected before having used the senses, these most deceptive messengers. And either the sun that they see will be truer than the sun that the sane and the awake see, or false things will be better than true ones. If these ideas are absurd, as they in fact are, that imagining, my dear Nebridius, is nothing but a wound inflicted by the senses, and they do not, as you write, produce a certain reminder so that such images are formed in the soul, but they cause the very introduction or, to put it more clearly, the impression of this falsity into or upon the soul. It, of course, bothers you how it happens that we think of those faces and shapes that we have never seen, and you are right to be bothered. I shall, therefore, do what will extend this letter beyond the usual limit, but not for you, for whom no page is more pleasing than one which brings you more words from me.

4. I see that all these images, which you call "fantasies" along with many people, are most suitably and truthfully divided into three kinds. One of these is impressed by things we sense; the second by things we think of; the third by things we reason to. Examples of the first kind are found when my mind pictures in itself for me your face or our late friend, Verecundus,[2] and anything else of

---

1. See Plato, *Phaedrus* 72E and 75C.
2. Verecundus was a Milanese teacher of grammar who lent to Augustine and his friends his villa at Cassiciacum where Augustine composed the earliest of his dialogues. See *Confessions* IX, 3 5-6.

lasting or mortal things that I have, nonetheless, seen and sensed. Those fall under another kind that we suppose to have been or to be in a certain way, for example, when for the sake of argument we imagine certain things that in no sense are an obstacle to the truth, the sort of things we picture when we read histories and when we hear or compose or invent myths. For I picture for myself the face of Aeneas,[3] as I want and as it comes to my mind, the face of Medea[4] with her winged serpents bound to the yoke, the faces of Chremes and a certain Parmenon.[5] In this kind there are also included those that were substituted for the truth either by the wise who disguise a truth in such figures or by the foolish who found various superstitions, such as Phlegethon of the underworld, the five caves of the nation of darkness, the North Pole that holds up the heaven, and a thousand other portents of the poets and heretics.[6] We say even in the midst of an argument: Suppose that there are three worlds, one on top of the other, such as this one world is; suppose that a square shape encloses the earth, and the like. We frame and think of all these as the mood of our thought would have them. For with regard to the things that pertain to the third kind of images we deal most of all with numbers and dimensions. In part we do this in the real world, for example, when we discover the shape of the whole world, and there follows upon this discovery an image in the mind of the thinker. In part we do this in the disciplines, for example, in geometrical figures, musical rhythms, and the endless variety of numbers. Though they are in my opinion grasped as true, they, nonetheless, give rise to false imaginings, which reason itself scarcely resists. And yet it is not easy even for the discipline of logic to be free of this evil, since we imagine certain tokens,[7] as it were, in distinctions and conclusions.

5. In this whole forest of images I do not believe that you think that the first kind belongs to the soul before it is joined to the senses, nor is there need to discuss this further. With regard to the other two kinds one could still correctly pose the question, if it were not evident that the soul is less subject to falsity when it has not been exposed to the deceptiveness of sensible things and of the senses. But who has any doubt that these images are less true than these sensible things? For those things that we suppose and believe or invent are in every respect absolutely false, and those things that we see and sense are certainly far more true, as you recognize. Now in that third kind whatever bodily space I picture, though thought seems to have given birth to it by the principles of scientific disciplines, which involve no deception, I prove it to be false by arguments

---

3. Aeneas is the hero of Virgil's epic poem, the *Aeneid*, on the founding of Rome.
4. In Greek mythology Medea helped Jason steal the golden fleece from her father.
5. Chremes and Parmenon are characters in a comedy of Terence.
6. Phlegethon is one of the rivers of the underworld; see Virgil, *Aeneid* VI, 551. The five caves are part of the Manichean myth.
7. Pebbles were used as tokens on a counting-board as a means of calculation in somewhat the same way the beads are used on an abacus.

from the same principles. As a result of this, I do not by any means believe that the soul lay in such a great ignominy of falsity, when it was not yet sensing by means of the body, when it was not yet pummeled through the deceptive senses by a mortal and fleeting substance.

3, 6. How, then, does it come about that we think of things we have not seen? What do you suppose but that there is a certain power implanted in the soul for decreasing or increasing, a power that the soul carries with it wherever it goes? This power can be especially observed in the case of numbers. It, for example, causes the image of a raven set, as it were, before our eyes, which is, of course, familiar to our sight, to be transformed by adding and subtracting certain elements and to be turned into any image whatever that has absolutely never been seen before. It brings it about that shapes of this sort spontaneously, as it were, invade the thoughts of souls that habitually indulge in such things. By subtracting from or adding to, as was said, what sensation has brought to it, the soul that uses the imagination may, therefore, bring forth those things that it attains by no sense in their totality. But it had attained parts of them in this or that thing. In that way we children who were born and raised inland could already imagine seas just from seeing water in a small cup, though the taste of strawberries or cherries would never have entered our mind before we tasted them in Italy. This is the reason why those blind from infancy do not find anything to answer when they are questioned about the light and colors. For they never experience any colored images if they have not sensed any.

7. Do not be surprised at how those things that are formed in the nature of reality can be imagined, though the soul which is present in all does not first ponder them within itself, since it never perceived them externally. For, when in anger or joy or any of the other emotions of the mind we form in our body many expressions and hues, our thought does not first conceive that we can produce such images. These follow upon our emotions in those marvelous ways that are to be left to your consideration, when numbers hidden in the soul are brought on stage without any shape of bodily falsity. From this I would like you to understand that, since you experience so many acts of the mind free from all the images about which you are now asking, the soul acquires the body by any action other than by thinking of sensible forms, for I do not think it experiences these in any way before it has use of the senses of the body. Hence, by our friendship and by our very fidelity to the divine law I earnestly warn you, my very dear and most delightful friend, not to enter into friendship with these shadows of the lower world and not to hesitate to break off that friendship you have begun. For in no way do we resist the senses of the body, which is for us a most sacred duty, if we show fondness for the blows and wounds they inflict.

Letter 8

Again in the years between 388 and 391 Nebridius writes from Carthage to Augustine in Thagaste and asks for help in understanding how the heavenly powers produce dreams and images in someone who is sleeping.

Nebridius sends greetings to Augustine.

1. Since I am in a hurry to get to the point, I want no introduction, no beginning. How does it happen, my dear Augustine, and what means is it that the higher powers, by which I want you to understand the heavenly powers, use, when they want to make us see some dreams when we are sleep? What means, I ask, is this? That is, how do they do it? By what art, by what devices, by what instruments or drugs? Do they shove our mind by their thoughts so that we also imagine them in our thinking? Or do they offer and present to us what they produced in their body or imagination? But if they produce them in their body, it follows that, when we sleep, we also have within us other bodily eyes by which we see those things that they have formed in their body. But if they are not helped by their body to produce these things, but arrange them in their imagination and in that way reach our imaginations and produce the vision that is a dream, why, I ask you, do I not by my imagination force your imagination to generate those dreams that I first formed in it for myself? Surely, I too have a power of imagination, and it is able to picture what I want, though I produce absolutely no dream for you. Rather, I see that our body itself generates dreams in us. For, when the body is in bad shape, it forces us by the disposition by which it is tied to the soul to represent this in marvelous ways through the imagination. Often when we are thirsty while sleeping, we dream that we drink, and when hungry, it seems as if we are eating, and there are many other things that are transferred by imagination from the body to the soul as if by a sort of exchange. Do not be surprised if these ideas are less elegantly and less subtly expressed, given their obscurity and our lack of experience. You will work at doing this to the extent you are able.

Letter 9

Replying to Nebridius' previous letter, Augustine assures his friend that they will be together, not in place, but in the Lord, if Nebridius enters into his mind and raises it to the Lord (paragraph 1). Turning to Nebridius' question about how heavenly spirits produce our thoughts and dreams, Augustine agrees to offer some guidelines for thinking about the question (paragraph 2). He suggests that, since every mental activity produces its effect upon the body, though we may not notice it, the airy or ethereal spirits may perceive effects in the body that we do not and may use them to produce ideas in our minds (paragraph 3). As a example, he shows that the emotion of anger produces bile in the body and that bile in turn can cause further anger (paragraph 4). Finally, Augustine suggests that Nebridius should combine the present letter with Letter 7 in order to have a fuller answer.

Augustine sends greetings to Nebridius.

1. Although you know my mind, you perhaps do not, nonetheless, know how much I would like to enjoy your presence. But God will some day grant this great benefit. I read your most recent letter in which you complained about your loneliness and a certain abandonment by your friends, with whom life is most pleasant. But what else should I tell you but what I have no doubt you already do? Enter into your mind, and raise it up to God as much as you can. For there you have us as well in a more certain way, not by means of bodily images, which we must now use in our recollection, but by means of that thought by which you understand that it is not by place that we are together.

2. When I consider your letters to which I replied at length when you were asking for something free from doubt, that letter deeply frightened me in which you asked how it happens that certain thoughts and dreams are implanted in us by higher powers or by demons. For it is an important issue, and given your prudence you too see that one ought not to reply to it by a letter, but by a face-to-face conversation or by a treatise. Having become familiar with your talents, I shall, nonetheless, try to set forth some guidelines on this question in order that you may either put together the rest by yourself or not give up hope that one can come to a probable explanation of a matter so important.

3. For I think that every activity of the mind produces some effect in the body, but that it reaches our senses, which are so obtuse and so slow, only when the activities of the mind are more intense, such as when we are angry or sad or joyful. From this one can conjecture that, even when we think something and it is not apparent to us in our body, it can, nonetheless, be apparent to the airy or ethereal living beings, which have very keen senses, and in comparison with their senses our senses should not be considered senses. Those traces, so to speak, of

31

its activity that the mind can impress upon the body can, therefore, remain and produce a certain habit, as it were, and when these have been unconsciously stirred up and touched in accord with the will of the being that stirs them up and touches them, they produce in us thoughts and dreams, and this is done with a surprising ease. For, if it is evident that the exercise of our earthly and very sluggish bodies is able to attain certain incredible feats in playing musical instruments or walking a tightrope and in countless other spectacles of this sort, it is by no means absurd that those beings that produce something with an airy or ethereal body in bodies that they naturally penetrate enjoy a much greater ease in moving whatever they want, while we perceive nothing and yet are modified in some way by them. For we also do not perceive how an abundance of bile forces us to more frequent anger, and it, nonetheless, does force us, though this very abundance I mentioned was produced because we were angry.

4. But if you are, nonetheless, unwilling to accept from us in passing this likeness, ponder it in thought to the extent you can. For, if the mind constantly meets with some difficulty in doing and accomplishing what it desires, it is constantly angry. But anger, in my opinion, is nothing but a passionate desire to remove those things that impede ease in acting. We are, therefore, generally angry, not only at human beings, but at a pen in writing when we shatter and break it, and gamblers become angry at the dice, artists at their pencil, and anyone at any instrument whatever as the result of which he meets with difficulty. But physicians also claim that bile increases with this constancy in being angry. Because of an increase of bile, however, we in turn become angry both readily and when there is almost no reason. In that way what the mind produced in the body by its activity will in turn be able to disturb it.

5. These issues can be treated very extensively and be brought to a more certain and fuller knowledge by many testimonies to such facts. But add to this letter the one which I recently sent you concerning images and memory,[1] and consider it with greater care. For from your reply it was clear to me that you did not fully understand it. Hence, when you add to this letter you are now reading from that other one what was said in it concerning a certain natural ability of the mind to diminish and to increase something by thought, it will perhaps not trouble you how it comes about that even the shapes of bodies that we have never seen are formed in us either by thinking or by dreaming.

---

1. That is, Letter 7.

Letter 10

Sometime after the previous letter Augustine again wrote from Hippo to Nebridius in Carthage. He acknowledges that Nebridius' complaint that Augustine has neglected to provide for their living together disturbed him very much, but sees no way that they can achieve life together (paragraph 1). He argues that journeys back and forth between Hippo and Carthage would preclude the leisure needed for contemplating the journey that is death and for becoming godlike in leisure (paragraph 2). He claims that we at times have foretastes of a life free from fear that assure us of the possibility of attaining such a union with God (paragraph 3).

Augustine sends greetings to Nebridius.

1. Never has any of your questions kept me in as much turmoil in my thinking as that one which I read in your most recent letter, in which you blame us because we neglect to provide for how we might be able to live together. That would be a grave wrong and one filled with danger, were it not false. But since solid reason seems to show that we can live here in accord with our purpose rather than at Carthage or even in the country, I am quite uncertain about what I am to do with you, my Nebridius. Should I send to you a most comfortable means of transport? For our Lucinian claims that you could be carried without harm in an enclosed sedan chair. But I think that your mother, who scarcely endured your absence when you were healthy, will endure it much less easily, now that you are ill. Shall I come to you? But here there are those who could not come with me and whom I think it would be wrong to abandon. You, after all, can dwell comfortably in the chambers of your mind. But it demands hard work for these to be able to do the same. Should I frequently go and return and be now with you and now with them? But this is neither to live together nor according to our purpose. After all, the journey is not short, but so utterly long that to undertake often the task of making it would mean not to have arrived at the leisure we hoped for. In addition, there is the bodily infirmity because of which I too, as you know, cannot do what I want, unless I utterly cease to want anything more than I can do.

2. To ponder, therefore, throughout the whole of life journeys, which can be neither peaceful nor easy for you, is not the mark of a man who ponders that one last journey, which is called death, the only one, as you understand, that we should truly ponder. God, of course, granted to a certain few men whom he wanted to be rulers of churches that they not only look forward to that last journey courageously, but also eagerly desire it and undertake without any anguish the labors of making these other journeys. But neither to those who are swept off to such administrative positions by the love of temporal honor nor to

those who seek a life of busyness, when they are not holding office, do I think this great good is granted, namely, that amid uproar and restless comings and goings they achieve the familiarity with death that we are seeking. For in leisure both of them would be permitted to become godlike. Or, if this is not true, I am, if not the most stupid, certainly the laziest of all men, for I cannot taste and love that pure good unless I enjoy a certain carefree repose. Believe me, there is a need of a great withdrawal from the tumult of perishing things in order to produce in a human being a freedom from fear that is not due to insensitivity, boldness, the desire for vainglory, or superstitious credulity. This also produces that solid joy that is absolutely not to be compared with any delight in the smallest degree.

3. But if such a life is not the lot of human nature, why does this freedom from worry come about at times? Why does it come about more frequently, the more anyone worships God in the sanctuary of his mind? Why does that tranquility often remain even amid human actions, if anyone leaves that shrine for the purpose of action? Why do we, however, at times not fear death when we speak of it, but even desire it when we do not speak of it? I tell you, for I would not say this to just anyone. To you, I repeat, I say this, for I know well your journeys upward. Since you have often experienced the pleasure of the life of the mind when it dies to a love that is bodily, will you, then, deny that the whole of human life can become free from fear so that it is rightly called wise? Or will you dare to claim ever to have experienced this disposition, which reason supports, except when you are confined in your innermost self? Since this is the case, you see that one point remains, namely, that you also consider with me how we may live together. For you know much better than I do what should be done with your mother, whom your brother, Victor, will not abandon in any case. I do not want to write other things for fear that I may distract you from thinking of this.

Letter 11

Sometime after the previous letter, Augustine again wrote to Nebridius. After setting aside the question of how they might be able to live together, Augustine turns to Nebridius' many and difficult questions and begs him not to ask new ones for a time (paragraph 1). He takes up the very difficult question of why only the Son is said to have assumed a human nature, though the three persons are said to do everything they do in common. Augustine first insists upon the inseparability of the works of the three persons according to the Catholic faith (paragraph 2). He uses as an example the fact that every nature exists, is this or that, and remains to the extent it can, pointing out that one of these is never found without the other (paragraph 3). Then he tries to show that the assumption of human nature is proper to the Son, though it brings with it the knowledge of the Father and the sweetness of the Holy Spirit. He claims that, though the persons do everything together, we had to be shown this distinctly on account of our weakness (paragraph 4).

Augustine sends greetings to Nebridius.

1. The question deeply disturbed me that you posed some time ago with a certain somewhat friendly reproach, namely, on what basis we might be able to live together, and I had decided to write back to you on this point alone and to demand a response from you and not to turn our pen aside to any other issue pertinent to our studies until this one was brought to an end between us. But the very brief and very true observation in your recent letter quickly relieved my concern. For you said that we should not think about this, since, as the situation demands, either we will come to you when we can or you will come to us when you can. Relieved, as I said, by this, I considered all your letters to see which answers I owed you. In them I found so many questions that, even if they could be easily resolved, they would overwhelm the talent and free time of anyone by their sheer number. But they are so difficult that, even if only one of them were laid upon me, I would not hesitate to confess that I was overburdened. This introduction, however, aims to make you stop asking new questions for a while until we are completely free of our debt and to make you write back to me on the basis of your own judgment. And yet, I know how it will be to my disadvantage since I am putting off my sharing in your sublime thoughts, even if for only a short while.

2. Listen, then, to what I think about the mystical assumption of the man,[1] which the religion in which we have been initiated teaches was done on account of our salvation as something we are to believe and to know. I have not chosen

---

1. Augustine uses the more concrete expression, "the assumption of the man," where we would use "the assumption of human nature," or the reverse expression, "the incarnation of the Word."

this question in order to reply to it rather than the rest because it is the easiest of them all, but I thought it deserved more than the rest that I should devote my efforts to it. For those questions that concern this world do not seem to me to be sufficiently relevant to the attainment of the happy life, and if they produce some pleasure when they are investigated, we still ought to fear that they may take up time that we should spend on better ones. Hence, with regard to the question presently under discussion, I am first of all surprised that you are disturbed at why not the Father, but the Son is said to have assumed the man, and are not also disturbed about the Holy Spirit. For the Catholic faith teaches and believes that this Trinity is so inseparable—and a few holy and blessed men also understand this—that whatever this Trinity does must be thought to be done at the same time by the Father and by the Son and by the Holy Spirit. The Father does not do anything that the Son and the Holy Spirit do not do, nor does the Son do anything that the Father and the Holy Spirit do not do, nor does the Holy Spirit do anything that the Father and the Son do not do. From this it seems to follow that the whole Trinity assumed the man. For, if the Son assumed the man and the Father and Holy Spirit did not, they do something apart from one another. Why, then, is the assumption of the man ascribed to the Son in our mysteries and sacred rites? This huge question is so difficult and concerns so important a matter that it is not possible here to state it with sufficient clarity nor to prove it solidly. I, nonetheless, dare, since I am writing to you, to convey what I have in mind rather than to explain it. In that way you can by yourself conjecture the rest in accord with your talents and your friendship with us, because of which you know me very well.

3. There is no nature, Nebridius, and no substance whatsoever that does not have in itself and does not display these three elements: first, that it exists; second, that it is this or that; and third, that it remains as it was to the extent it can. That first element reveals the very cause of the nature from which all things come; the second reveals the form by which all things are fashioned and somehow or other formed;[2] the third reveals a certain permanence, so to speak, in which all things exist. But if it is possible that something exists that is not this or that and does not remain in its kind, or if it is possible that it is this or that, but does not exist and does not remain in its kind to the extent it can, or if it is possible that it does in fact remain in its kind in accord with the powers of its kind, but does not, nonetheless, exist and is not this or that, then it is possible that in that Trinity some person does something apart from the others. But if you see that it is necessary that whatever exists is immediately this or that and remains in its kind to the extent it can, those three do nothing apart from one another. I see that I have up to now dealt with the part of this question that makes the solution difficult. But I wanted briefly to show you, at least if I did what I wanted to do,

2. The CSEL edition indicates a lacuna here.

the subtlety and the great truth with which the inseparability of this Trinity is understood in the Catholic Church.

4. Now listen to how it is possible that what troubles you might not be a problem. That form that is properly ascribed to the Son also pertains to a certain discipline and skill, if we are correct to use this term in these areas, and to the understanding by which the mind itself is informed by thought. And so, since that assumption of the man has brought it about that we are taught a certain discipline for living and given an example of doing what we have been commanded under the majesty and clarity of certain principles, all of this is not without reason attributed to the Son. For in many matters, which I leave to your thought and wisdom, though many things are present, one, nonetheless, stands out and claims for itself quite reasonably a certain character of its own. For example, in those three questions, even if one asks whether something exists, there is also present the question of what it is, for it cannot exist unless it is something. In that case we must also either approve or disapprove, for whatever it is, it deserves some evaluation. And so, when one asks what it is, it is necessary that it exist and that it be weighed by some evaluation. In this way too, when one asks of what sort it is, it is also, of course, something. And so, though all these are inseparably joined to one another, a question does not take its name from all of these, but from the intention of the one who asks it. Hence, human beings needed a discipline by which they might be suitably taught and formed. We cannot, nonetheless, say that what is produced in human beings by this discipline does not exist or should not be desired. But we, first of all, desire to know both the means by which we might attain some knowledge and that in which we might remain. We had first, therefore, to be shown a certain norm and rule of discipline. This was done through that divine dispensation of the assumed man, which is properly to be ascribed to the Son, so that there follows through the Son both a knowledge of the Father, that is, of the one principle from whom all things come, and a certain interior and ineffable tenderness and sweetness of remaining in this knowledge and of scorning all mortal things, which gift and function is properly attributed to the Holy Spirit. Though all these actions, then, are done with the highest unity and inseparability, they still had to be shown to us distinctly on our account, for we have fallen from that unity into multiplicity. No one, after all, raises anyone up to where he is unless he goes down a little toward where that other is. You have my letter, not one that will end your concern about this question, but one that will perhaps begin to place your thoughts on a certain foundation in order that you may follow up the other points with your talent, which is well known to me, and may obtain them with the piety, upon which one must above all take a stand.

Letter 12

In this fragment of a letter to Nebridius written between 389 and 391 Augustine again touches on the question of the incarnation, which was raised in the previous letter.

Augustine sends greetings to Nebridius.

1. You write that you sent more letters than we have received. But I am neither able not to believe you, nor are you able not to believe me. For, even if I am not able to be equal in my replying, your letters are, nonetheless, kept with no less care by me than they are frequently sent by you. We, however, agree that you have not received more than two longer letters from us, for we did not send a third. Now, having examined the letters themselves, I notice that I have replied to approximately five of your questions, except that the one question, which was touched upon in passing as it were, still did not perhaps satisfy your desire, though I was not rash in leaving it to your intelligence. You must rein that desire in a little and be willing to put up with some summaries. But, if I cheat you of the understanding of anything when I am sparing in the use of words, do not, of course, spare me. Rather, demand everything that I owe you by that right of friendship, which might perhaps have more influence upon me if it could in any respect be more pleasant. You, therefore, will count this letter among my shorter letters, but I have not granted[1] you that it in no way takes anything from the pile of letters I owe you. After all, you send me shorter ones that add to the same pile. Hence, you will quite easily grasp the question you asked about the Son of God, namely, why he rather than the Father is said to have assumed the man, though the two of them are inseparable, if you recall our conversation, in which we tried to explain[2] to the extent we could—for it is something ineffable—who is the Son of God by whom we are united. To touch on this briefly here, the very teaching and form of God through whom all things that have been made were made is called the Son of God. But whatever has been done through that man he assumed has been done for our instruction and information.

---

1. The text of the Letter has several lacunae; I have followed the conjecture of *"sivi"* found in the NBA text in place of *"sibi."*
2. I have followed the suggestion of the NBA edition which fills in what seems to be a lacuna.

Letter 13

Within the same years, 389 to 392, Augustine wrote to Nebridius about the difficulty of finding the leisure to discuss new ideas (paragraph 1). He returns to the subject of the body or quasi-body which, according to some, is the vehicle by which the soul moves in place (paragraph 2). While bodies cannot be known through the intellect, various characteristics of bodies can be (paragraph 3). There are two ways in which we understand something, but without sharper senses than we have, the question of the soul's vehicle cannot be settled (paragraph 4).

Augustine sends greetings to Nebridius.

1. I do not like to write to you the same old things, but I am not permitted to write new ones. For I see that the first is not suitable for you and that I am not free to do the other. From the time I left you, after all, I have not had the opportunity, I have not had the leisure to raise and ponder those questions that we used to discuss among ourselves. The winter nights are, of course, very long, and I do not sleep through the whole of them. But when I have leisure, things come up that require more thought and necessarily destroy my leisure.[1] What am I to do? Am I to be mute or silent before you? You want neither of these, nor do I. Hence, come now, and hear what the last stretch of the night was able to draw from me when I wrote this letter while it dragged on.

2. You must remember the topic that we frequently tossed back and forth in conversation and that tossed us about breathless and heated with excitement, namely, that concerning a certain perpetual body or quasi-body of the soul, which you recall some people call the vehicle of the soul. It is clear that this thing is certainly not intelligible if it is moves in place. But whatever is not intelligible cannot be understood. We are not, however, absolutely prevented from coming to some judgment that approximates the truth regarding something that escapes the intellect, at least if it does not escape the senses. But what can neither be understood nor sensed begets an extremely rash and childish opinion. And this thing with which we are dealing is something of that sort, if it exists at all. Why, then, I ask you, do we not declare a holiday for this little question and, after calling upon God, raise our whole selves to the supreme quiet of the highest living nature?

3. Here you may perhaps say that, although bodies cannot be perceived, we can, nonetheless, perceive by way of intelligence many things that pertain to the body, such as that we know that there is a body. Who, after all, would deny this or

---

1. The text here is problematic.

who would say that this is like the truth rather than the truth itself? Thus, though a body is like the truth, it is absolutely true that there is something of the sort in nature. A body, therefore, is judged to be sensible, but the existence of a body intelligible, for, otherwise, it could not be perceived. Thus, that body of whatever sort it is concerning which we are inquiring and upon which the soul is thought to rely in order to pass from place to place, though it is not sensible to our senses, may be sensible to certain senses that are far more sharp. But whether it exists can be known by way of the intelligence.

4. If you are going to say this, realize that what we call understanding takes place in us in two ways, either internally by the mind itself on its own and by reason, as when we understand that the intellect itself exists, or by an admonition from the senses, as that which we have already mentioned, when we understand that a body exists. In these two cases we understand that first through ourselves, that is, by consulting God concerning what is within us, but we understand the second, again by consulting God, but concerning what is reported by the body and the senses. If this holds true, no one can understand with regard to that body whether it exists, except someone whose senses have reported something concerning it. And if there is any such being in the number of living beings, for we see that we ourselves are not in that number, I think that what I began to say above has also been brought to an end. That is, this question does not pertain to us. I would like you to think of this repeatedly and to take care that I come to know what results you derive from your thinking.

Letter 14

Again between 389 and 391, Augustine wrote to Nebridius about how busy he is (paragraph 1). Nebridius raised a question about how he and Augustine are individuals, though they so often do the same things. Augustine argues that bodily things never do the same actions (paragraph 2). Augustine shifts the discussion from the difference between the sun and the other stars to the even greater difference between Christ and other human beings (paragraph 3). Finally, he argues that in the wisdom of God there is one idea of a human being according to which he creates the many human beings, but that God also has knowledge of the many human beings (paragraph 4).

Augustine sends greetings to Nebridius.

1. I preferred to reply to your most recent letter, not because I belittled your earlier questions or found less delight in them, but because in replying to it I am undertaking something more important than you suppose. For, although you directed that I send you a letter that is longer than the longest of them, we do not, nonetheless, have as much leisure as you think and as much as you know we desired and do desire. Do not ask why this is so, for it would be easier for me to set forth the difficulties by which I am prevented than the reasons why I am.

2. You ask why, though you and I are individuals, we do many things that are the same, while the sun does not do the same thing as the other stars. I wish I could state the reason for this fact. For, if we do the same things, the sun also does many actions with other things; if it does not, nor do we. I walk, and you walk; it moves, and they move. I am awake, and you are awake; it shines, and they shine. I argue, and you argue; it revolves, and they revolve. The act of the soul, nonetheless, is in no way comparable to those things that we see. But if you compare soul to soul, as is fair, you should consider that, if there is any soul present in them, the stars either think or contemplate the same thing—or whatever else they might more suitably be said do—more than human beings. But if you pay careful attention, as you usually do, nothing absolutely the same can be done by two of them in terms of the movements of their bodies. Or, when we are walking together, do you immediately think that we are doing the same thing? That should be far from your wisdom. For it is necessary that one who walks further to the north either moves ahead of the other by an equal stride or walks more slowly. Neither of these, nonetheless, can be perceived by the senses. But, unless I am mistaken, you are looking for what we understand, not what we sense. If, however, we move from the north to the south in unison, sticking to each other's side as much as possible, and walk on smooth and level marble or even ivory, the two of us still cannot have the same motion anymore than we have the same

pulse in the veins, the same shape, and the same countenance. Take us away, and put in our place the offspring of Daucus;[1] you still will accomplish nothing. In these identical twins there is the same necessity of their moving by their own motions as there was of their being born as individuals.

3. But, you will say, this is evident only to reason; that the sun differs from the stars is also clear and evident to the senses. If you force me to focus on largeness, you know how many things are said about the spaces between them and the great uncertainty to which this clarity is reduced. But to grant that things are as they appear, for that is what I believe, whose senses were deceived by the tallness of Naevius,[2] who was a foot taller than the tallest men at six feet? And I believe that you have searched too much for someone his equal in height, and since you did not find anyone, you wanted to stretch out our letter to his stature. Hence, since something of this sort exists even on earth, I do not think one should be surprised at the sky. If, however, it bothers you that apart from the sun the light of no star fills the day, who, I ask you, appeared among human beings as great as that man whom God assumed far differently than other holy and wise men? If you compare him with other human beings, they are kept at a greater distance than the other stars in comparison with the sun. Look at this likeness with care. For by the mind with which you excel it is possible that we have resolved in passing a certain question that you proposed concerning the man Christ.

4. You likewise ask whether that highest truth and highest wisdom and form of things through which all things were made, which our holy religion professes to be the only Son of God, contains the idea of man in general or that of each one of us. That is an important question. But it seems to me that insofar as it concerns the creation of a human being there is present there the idea of man alone, not that of me or of you. But insofar as it concerns the course of time, various ideas of human beings live in that purity. But since this is most obscure, I do not know by what likeness it can be made clear, unless we perhaps have recourse to those arts that are present in our soul. For in the knowledge of geometry there is one idea of an angle and one of a quadrangle. Hence, as often as I want to point out an angle, only one idea of an angle comes to mind. But I would never describe a quad-rangle unless I looked upon the idea of four angles at the same time. In the same way each man was created according to the one idea by which a man is under-stood. But for there to be a people, although the idea itself is one, still it is an idea not of a man, but of men. If, then, Nebridius is a part of this universe, as he is, and the whole universe is made up of its parts, God the creator could not have failed to have an idea of the parts. Hence, the fact that there is present in him the idea of many human beings does not have to do with a particular human being, though

---

1. See Virgil, *Aeneid* X, 391; the sons of Daucus were said to be as similar as two drops of water.
2. A Roman renowned for his height; see Pliny the Elder, *Natural Histories* VII, 16.

again in marvelous ways all are reduced to a unity. But you will ponder this more extensively. Meanwhile, I ask that you be content with this, although I have already gone beyond the measure of Naevius.

Letter 15

Writing in 390 or 391 to Romanian, his wealthy friend and fellow citizen of Thagaste, Augustine promises to send him his book, *True Religion*, which he dedicated to him, and exhorts him to use the time of prosperity he is enjoying for the acquisition of eternal goods.

Augustine sends greetings to Romanian.[1]

1. This letter does not indicate so much my lack of paper as it bears witness to my abundance of parchment. I sent the ivory tablets I have along with a letter to your uncle. After all, you will more readily excuse this scrap of hide because what I wrote to him could not be postponed, and I thought it also most inappropriate not to write to you. But I beg you, if any of our tablets are there, to send them on account of such needs. I have written something on the Catholic religion,[2] to the extent that the Lord deigned to give his help, which I want to send to you before my arrival, if I am not lacking paper in the meanwhile. For you will tolerate any sort of writing from the workroom of Majorinus. As for the manuscripts, apart from the books, *On the Orator*,[3] I had lost them all. But I could make no other reply than that you should take those you want, and I now remain of the same mind. For in my absence I do not know what more I might do.

2. I was most pleased that in your last letter you wanted me to share in your family's joy. But

> Do you ask me to be ignorant of the face of the tranquil sea
> And its quiet waves?[4]

though you neither ask that of me nor are you yourself ignorant of it. Hence, if some period of peace has been granted you for thinking of what is better, make use of God's gift. For, when these things happen, we ought not to congratulate ourselves, but ought to be grateful to him through whom they come about. After all, an administration of temporal goods that is just, in accord with duty, and rather peaceful and tranquil for something of its nature, merits the reception of eternal goods, if it does not take possession of a man when he possesses it, does

---

1. Romanian was a wealthy citizen of Thagaste, friend and patron of Augustine, and the father of Licentius, Augustine's student at Cassiciacum. Augustine drew Romanian into Manicheism and dedicated to him, *Answer to the Skeptics* and *True Religion*, in an endeavor to win him over to Catholicism. Eventually Romanian did become a Catholic. See Letter 32 in which Paulinus of Nola writes to him to congratulate him on Augustine's consecration as bishop.
2. That is, his work, *True Religion*.
3. Cicero's famous work.
4. Virgil, *Aeneid* V, 848-849; these are the words of Palinurus, the helmsman of Aeneas' ship, just before the goddess of sleep puts him to sleep so that he falls from the ship.

not entangle him when it increases, and does not completely absorb him when things become peaceful.[5] For it was said by the lips of the Truth himself, *If you were not faithful in another's property, who will give you what is your own?* (Lk 16:12). When, therefore, worries over temporal goods have been eased, let us seek stable and certain goods; let us soar above our earthly wealth. It is not, after all, without reason that amid an abundance of honey a bee has wings, for it kills one who clings to it.

---

5. The CSEL edition has "*putatur*" preceded by a lacuna; the editions, which I have followed, have "*pacatur*" with no indication of a lacuna.

Letter 16

Most likely in 390 Maximus of Madaura in Numidia, a pagan grammarian, probably known to Augustine from his student days, wrote to Augustine. He explains that the one highest God is worshiped under many names and in many ways (paragraph 1). The Christians, on the other hand, he claims, worship their martyrs, who are mere humans, in place of the gods of Rome. Maximus also mocks the odd-sounding names of some of the Punic martyrs (paragraph 2). He asks Augustine who this God of the Christians is whom they worship in secret (paragraph 3) and warns Augustine that he is keeping a copy of his letter (paragraph 4).

Maximus of Madaura[1] sends greetings to Augustine.

1. Desiring to be frequently cheered by your letters and by the stimulus of your words with which you have quite recently knocked me about in a most pleasant way without damage to our friendship, I did not hold back from returning similar words for fear that you might call my silence resentment. But I ask you that, if you consider these words to be like my old limbs, you receive them with the forgiveness of kindly ears. Greece tells the story with an uncertain reliability that Mount Olympus is the home of the gods. But we see and approve that the forum of our city is inhabited by a crowd of salutary deities. In fact, who is so demented, so mentally incapacitated as to deny that it is most certain that there is one highest God, without beginning, without natural offspring, the great and magnificent father, as it were? With many names we call upon his powers spread through the created world, since we all are ignorant of his proper name. After all, "god" is a name common to all religions. And so it is that, while we as suppliants grasp certain of his members, as it were, piece by piece, in various supplications, we seem to worship him as a whole.

2. But I cannot pretend that I am not impatient with so great an error. Who, after all, would tolerate that Mygdo[2] should be preferred to Jupiter brandishing his thunderbolts or that Sanaes and the martyr of martyrs, Namphamo, should be preferred to Juno, to Minerva, to Venus, to Vesta—and horror!—to all the immortal gods? Among them Lucitas is honored with scarcely less worship, as well as others to an indefinite number—names hateful to the gods and to men!

---

1. Maximus was a pagan grammarian from Madaura or Madauros, a city of Numidia near Thagaste, where Augustine went as a young man to study. See *Confessions* II, 3, 5. It is possible that he knew Maximus from those days.
2. Mygdo, Sanaes, Namphamo, and Lucitas were Punic names of Christian martyrs. Maximus found the names ugly and interpreted the cult of the martyrs as the worship of members of the one God.

Defiled by the consciousness of their wicked crimes, heaping outrages upon outrages, under the guise of a glorious death, they have met with an end suited to their characters and actions. Foolish people frequent their tombs, if it is worth mention, while the temples are abandoned and the shades of their ancestors neglected, so that the prediction of that prophet who treats them in contempt might be clearly seen,

In the temples of her gods Rome will swear by shades.[3]

But it almost seems to me at this time that the war of Actium has arisen again in which Egyptian monsters, which are not going to last, dare to shake their spears at the gods of Rome.

3. But I ask you, O man of great wisdom, that, having set aside and abandoned the power of eloquence, having also omitted the arguments of Chrysippus,[4] by which you usually fight, and having abandoned for a time the dialectic which strives in a struggle with all its might to leave nothing certain, show me concretely who this god is, whom you Christians claim as your own and whom you pretend to see as present in hidden places.[5] For we worship our gods with pious prayers openly in the daylight before the eyes and ears of all mortals and render them propitious to us by sweet victims, and we insist that this is seen and approved by all.

4. But as an old and ailing man, I withdraw myself from this battle for the future and gladly enter upon the view of the poet from Mantua,

Each person is guided by his own pleasure.[6]

After this I do not doubt, excellent sir, who have wandered off from my religion, that this letter will be stolen by some people and will perish by the flames or in some other manner. And if that happens, there will be a loss of paper, but not of our words, a copy of which I shall forever retain among all those who are truly religious. May the gods keep you! Through them all of us mortals, whom the earth sustains, venerate and worship in a thousand ways in a harmonious discord their father and the father of all mortals.

---

3. Lucan, *Pharsalia* 7, 459.
4. Chrysippus of Soli (c. 280-206 B.C.) was a Stoic philosopher who systematized the teaching of that school.
5. Maximus alludes to the Christian celebration of the Eucharist.
6. Virgil, *Bucolics* II, 65.

Letter 17

Probably before the law prohibiting the worship of idols on 28 February 391, Augustine replies to the previous letter from Maximus. He first rejects Maximus' idea that the many gods are members of the one God (paragraph 1) and then points out that the names of the gods of Rome are far more ridiculous than the Punic names of certain Christian martyrs (paragraph 2). Roman authors in fact reveal that their gods are human (paragraph 3), and the Bacchic revels are hardly preferable to the Christian mysteries (paragraph 4). Finally, Augustine prays that Maximus will agree to enter upon a serious conversation (paragraph 5).

Augustine sends greetings to Maximus of Madaura.

1. Are we carrying on a serious conversation, or do you want to joke? For, from the tenor of your letter, I am unsure whether it is because of the weakness of your case or because of the geniality of your character that you prefer to be clever rather than better prepared. For you first draw a comparison between Mount Olympus and your town's forum. I do not know how that comparison is relevant, except to remind me that Jupiter pitched camp on that mountain when he waged war against his father, as that history teaches which your people call sacred, and that in your forum there are two statues, one of Mars in the nude, the other of him in armor, while in front of them a statue of a human being was placed with three fingers extended to hold in check the demonic power most hostile to the citizens. Would I, then, ever have believed that by making mention of that forum you wanted to refresh my memory of such deities, unless you preferred to joke rather than to be serious? But clearly with regard to that claim by which you said that such gods are certain members of the one great God, I warn you, if you permit, to refrain with great care from such sacrilegious conceits. If you are really speaking of the one God about whom, as the ancients said, the learned and unlearned agree, do you say that the members of this God are the deities whose cruelty or, if you prefer, power is confined in the image of a dead man? I could say many things on this topic; you see, after all, given your wisdom, how wide open the door stands for your refutation. But I hold myself in check so that I am not thought to be using rhetoric rather than speaking the truth.

2. Now, as for the fact that you have gathered certain Punic names of the dead because of which you thought that witty insults, as you see them, ought to be cast upon our religion, I do not know whether I ought to refute this or pass it over in silence. For, if these matters seem as frivolous to your august self as they really are, I do not have much time for joking. But if they seem important, I am surprised that, if you were bothered by the absurdity of these names, you did not

recall that you have among your priests Eucaddires and among your deities Abaddires. I suspect that you did recall these when you were writing your letter, but that because of your friendly and charming character you wanted, by way of a diversion, to remind us of the many things in your religion at which one should laugh. After all, as an African writing to Africans, for we are both living in Africa, you could not forget yourself to such an extent that you thought that Punic names should be criticized. For, if we translate those names, what else does "Namphamo" mean but a man with a good foot, that is, one whose arrival brings some happiness, just as we are accustomed to say that someone started off on the right foot when some success followed upon his arrival? If you disapprove of that language, deny that many words of wisdom have been committed to memory in Punic books, as is disclosed by very learned men. You should, of course, regret that you were born in the place where the cradle of that tongue is still warm. But if it is not reasonable that the sound of the language is displeasing to us and if you recognize that I have correctly translated that name, you have reason to be angry at your Virgil, who invites your Hercules to the sacrifices that Evander offered him in this way:

> Come to us and to the sacred rites in your honor;
> Come favorably disposed with a propitious foot.[1]

He wants him to come with a propitious foot. He, therefore, wants Hercules to come as Namphamo, about whom you choose to insult us so much. If, nonetheless, you want to laugh, you have lots of material for laughing in your own religion: a god of manuring, a god of the toilet, bald Venus, the god Fear, the god Pallor, the goddess Fever, and countless others of this sort for whom the ancient Romans, worshipers of images, constructed temples and whom they thought they should worship. If you neglect them, you neglect the gods of Rome, and as a result it is understood that you are not initiated into the rites of Rome, and yet you scorn and despise the Punic names, as if you were extremely dedicated to the altars of the Roman deities.

3. It seems to me that, perhaps even more than we do, you regard those sacred rites as of absolutely no value, but that you derive some sort of pleasure from them for the journey through this life, since you also did not hesitate to have recourse to Maro, as you write, and to defend yourself by his verse in which he says,

> Each person is guided by his own pleasure.[2]

For, if the authority of Maro pleases you, as you indicate that it does, then this verse, of course, also pleases you:

1. Virgil, *Aeneid* VIII, 302.
2. Virgil, *Bucolics* II, 65.

> Saturn was first to come down from ethereal Olympus, fleeing
> From the arms of Jupiter, an exile deprived of his kingdom,[3]

and the other lines by which he wants us to understand that Saturn and such gods of yours are human beings. For Virgil read much history that rested upon ancient authority, just as Tully also had read it who mentions the same point in his dialogues[4] more than we would have dared to ask, and he endeavors to bring it to the knowledge of human beings to the extent that those times permitted.

4. But as for your statement that your sacred rites are preferable to ours because you worship the gods publicly, while we make use of more hidden assemblies, I first ask you how you have forgotten that illustrious Liber, who you think ought to be entrusted to the eyes of only a few initiates.[5] Second, you yourself recognize that, when you mentioned the public celebration of your sacred rites, you wanted to achieve nothing but that we should set before our eyes as spectacles the city counselors and leading men reveling madly through the streets of your city. If a deity comes to dwell in you during that celebration, you surely see what sort of deity it is that deprives you of your mind. But if you are pretending, what do these mysteries of yours amount to, even in public? Or to what does so shameful a lie pertain? Finally, why do you not predict the future if you are prophets? Or why do you rob bystanders if you are of sound mind?

5. And so, since your letter made us recall these and other points, which I think should now be passed over, why should we mock your gods when no one who knows your mind and has read your letter can fail to understand that they are subtly mocked by you yourself? And so, if you want us to discuss something in these matters that is appropriate to your age and wisdom and that in accord with our purpose could be rightfully demanded of us by our friends, seek for something worthy of our discussion and speak with such care on behalf of your gods that we may not suspect that you have abandoned their cause, for you remind us of what can be said against them rather than say something in their defense. Above all, nonetheless, in order that this point may not escape your notice and unwisely lead you to sacrilegious charges, you should know that Catholic Christians, who also have a church in your town, do not worship any of the dead and adore nothing as a god that has been created and established by God, but adore the one God himself, who has created and established all things. These topics will be treated more fully with the help of the one and true God, when I have come to know that you want to have a serious discussion.

3. Virgil, *Aeneid* VIII, 319-320.
4. See Cicero, *The Nature of the Gods* (*De natura deorum*) I, 42, 119.
5. The cult of Liber, or Bacchus, was restricted to those who were initiated.

Letter 18

During 390 or 391 Augustine wrote this letter to Celestine, possibly the same deacon and future pope to whom he wrote Letter 192. He asks Celestine to return his books on the Manichees and sums up in a nutshell his view of the hierarchy of being and the task of the Christian life in relation to it.

Augustine sends greetings to Celestine.

1. How I wish I could constantly say one thing to you! But that one thing is that we should strip ourselves of empty worries and clothe ourselves in useful ones. For, with regard to a freedom from all worries, I do not know whether we should hope for any in this world. I wrote to you, and I did not receive a reply. I sent the books against the Manichees that I could send once they were ready and corrected, but nothing of your judgment or of your impression of them has been conveyed to me. It is now time for me to ask them back and for you to return them. I beg, therefore, that you do not delay to send them back with your reply from which I want to know what you are doing with them or what weapons you think you still need to defeat that error.

2. Since I, of course, know you well, receive this small, but important idea. There is a nature mutable in terms of places and of times, such as a body. There is also a nature mutable in no way in terms of places, but only in terms of times, such as the soul. And there is a nature which cannot be changed either in terms of places or in terms of times; this is God. What I have here said is mutable in some way is called a creature; what is immutable is the creator. But since we say that everything that we say is existing exists insofar as it lasts and insofar as it is one, and since unity is the form of all beauty, you, of course, see what exists in the highest manner, what exists in the lowest, but still exists, and what exists in an intermediate manner, greater than the lowest and less than the highest. That highest being is happiness itself; the lowest is what can be neither happy nor unhappy. That in the middle lives unhappily by turning to the lowest, but lives happily by conversion to the highest. One who believes in Christ does not love the lowest, is not proud over the intermediate, and thus becomes fit to cling to the highest. And this is the whole of what we are commanded, admonished, and set afire to do.

Letter 19

In 390 or 391 Augustine wrote to Gaius, a Catholic layman of Africa, whom he may have converted to the Catholic Church. He sends Gaius copies of all his writings and explains how we recognize in ourselves the truth of what we read. He urges Gaius to continue his search for the truth and to cling to the truth he has attained.

Augustine sends greetings to Gaius.

1. It is impossible to say the amount of pleasure with which we were filled and are often filled at the remembrance of you since we left you. For we recall that, though the ardor of your search for knowledge was remarkable, it did not exceed the bounds of moderation in argument. I would, after all, not easily find anyone who poses questions with greater passion and who listens with greater calm. I would, therefore, like to speak much with you, for it would not be too much, no matter how much it was, if I was speaking with you. But it is difficult. What need is there to ask the reasons? It is indeed difficult. Perhaps at some point it will be much easier. May that be God's will; now it is certainly something else. I, therefore, gave to the brother through whom I sent the letter the task of presenting to your most prudent charity all our writings to read. For he will not force upon you anything of mine against your will; I know, after all, the good will you bear in your heart toward us. If, nonetheless, after having read them, you give them your approval and see their truth, do not think that it is ours except in the sense that they were given to us, and you may turn yourself toward that source from which it has also been given to you to approve them. No one, after all, sees in the book itself or in the author he reads that what he reads is true, but sees it rather in himself, if a certain light of truth is impressed upon his mind, a light which is not bright in the ordinary way and is most far removed from the impurity of the body. But if you find some things false and deserving of your disapproval, know that they were dampened by human cloudiness, and regard them as truly ours. I would, however, urge you to seek the truth, if I did not think that I see the mouth of your heart gasping, as it were, after it. I would also urge you manfully to hold onto the truth you already know, if you did not reveal so clearly the strength of your mind and purpose. For everything that is alive in you has been revealed to me in a short time, almost as if the covering of the body had been torn open. Nor will the most merciful providence of our Lord in any way allow that a man so good and so outstandingly intelligent be apart from the Catholic flock of Christ.

Letter 20

In 390 or 391 Augustine wrote from Thagaste to Antoninus, a Catholic layman in Africa. He expresses his satisfaction at Antoninus' Christian attitude (paragraph 1). Augustine explains that it is not dangerous to be mistaken about a particular human being, but only to be mistaken about what is the good of a human being (paragraph 2). Finally, Augustine prays that Antoninus' son may grow up as a Christian and that his wife may be brought into the Church (paragraph 3).

Augustine sends greetings to Antoninus.

1. Since two of us owed you letters, part of the debt has been paid in great abundance inasmuch as you see one of us present, and since from his lips you also hear me, I could have skipped writing back to you, if I had not done so at his command, for with his setting out to see you what I have done seemed to be superfluous. Hence, I perhaps speak more fruitfully with you than if I were present before you when you both read this letter and hear him in whose heart you very well know that I dwell. With great joy I considered and digested the letter of Your Holiness, since it presents a Christian mind without any stain from this wicked age and most friendly to us.

2. I congratulate you, and I thank our God and Lord for your hope and faith and love, and I thank you in his presence that you think so well of us that you believe us to be faithful servants of God and that you love that in us with a most pure heart, and yet on this too we ought to congratulate your good will rather than give thanks to you. For it benefits you to love goodness itself, which he certainly loves who loves someone whom he believes to be good, whether that other person is such or is other than he is believed to be. In this area only one error must be avoided, namely, that anyone thinks, not of a human being, but of the good of a human being otherwise than the truth demands. But, my dearest brother, you are in no way mistaken in believing or knowing that it is a great good to serve God willingly and chastely. When you love anyone because you believe him to be a partaker of such a good, you have the fruit of your love, even if he is not such a person. Hence, you are to be congratulated over this, but we should congratulate the other, not if he is loved for this reason, but if he is such a person as that one thinks who loves him on this account. And so, what sort of persons we may be and how far we have advanced toward God is God's concern, whose judgment cannot be mistaken, not merely about the good of a human being, but about the very human being. It is enough for you in relation to the reward of beatitude, so far as it concerns this point, that you embrace us with the whole bosom of your heart, believing that we are such persons as servants of God ought to be. But we thank you greatly because, when you praise us as if we

53

were such persons, you exhort us in a wonderful way to want to be such persons. We also thank you even more if you not only commend yourself to our prayers, but also do not neglect to pray for us. Prayer for a brother, after all, is more pleasing to God when it is offered as a sacrifice of love.

3. I greet your little son, and I pray that he grows up in accord with the salutary commandments of the Lord. I desire and pray that the one faith and true devotion, which is the Catholic faith alone, may also come to your house. If you perhaps think further effort on our part is necessary for this purpose, do not hesitate to claim it for yourself, relying upon our common Lord and the law of love. I, of course, counsel you, with your most religious wisdom, to implant or to nourish a reasonable fear of God in your spouse[1] by reading the word of God and by serious conversation. For there is hardly anyone concerned about the state of his soul and, for this reason, intent upon seeking the will of the Lord without any stubbornness who by using a good guide does not distinguish the difference between some sect and the one Catholic Church.

---

1. Literally, "weaker vessel"; see 1 Pt 3:7.

Letter 21

Augustine wrote to Valerius, the bishop of Hippo, a little before Easter of 391 and shortly after Valerius ordained him to the priesthood. He explains to his bishop that he is unprepared for the office of priest with all the perils it involves (paragraph 1). He claims that the tears he shed, when he was forcibly ordained, were due to his lack of preparation for the office (paragraph 2), and he begs Valerius for a period of time in which he may study the scriptures (paragraph 3). Though he admits to knowing enough for his own salvation, he pleads ignorance of how best to minister to others (paragraph 4). He reminds Valerius of the severity of God's judgment if the bishop does not grant Augustine's request (paragraph 5) and sums up his ardent plea for time off (paragraph 6).

To my most blessed and venerable lord and most sincerely beloved father, Bishop Valerius,[1] Augustine, a priest, sends greetings in the Lord.

1. Before all I beg you that with your devout wisdom you bear in mind that in this life, and especially at this time, nothing is easier, more pleasant, and more attractive for men than the office of bishop, priest, or deacon, if the task is carried out perfunctorily or in a self-serving manner, but that before God nothing is more miserable, more sad, and more worthy of condemnation. Likewise, nothing in this life, and especially at this time, is more difficult, more laborious, and more dangerous than the office of a bishop, priest, or deacon. But before God nothing is more blessed if one soldiers as our emperor commands![2] But I did not learn either from my boyhood or young manhood what this manner of service is, and at the time when I had begun to learn, I suffered violence because of the merit of my sins—I do not, after all, know what else I should think—so that the second post at the helm was handed to me who did not yet know how to hold an oar.

2. But I think that my Lord wanted to correct me in that way precisely because I dared, as if I were more learned and better, to reprimand the mistakes of many sailors before I had experienced what is involved in their work. And so, after I was launched into the middle of the sea, I began to feel the rashness of my reprimands, though even earlier I judged this ministry to be filled with perils. And this was the reason for those tears that some of the brothers noticed that I shed in the city at the time of my ordination, and not knowing the reasons for my sorrow, they, nonetheless, consoled me with a good intention with what words they could, though with words having absolutely nothing to do with my wound. But I

---

1. Valerius was the bishop of Hippo; he ordained Augustine a priest and would soon make him his coadjutor bishop.
2. See 1 Tm 1:18-19 and 2 Tm 2:4.

have experienced this much more, very much more extensively than I thought, not because I saw some new waves or storms about which I had previously had not known, heard, read, or thought. Rather, I had not at all known my skill and strength for avoiding or enduring them, and I thought them to be of some value. The Lord, however, laughed at me and chose to reveal me to myself by this experience.

3. If he did this, not in condemning me, but in showing me mercy—for I certainly have this hope even now that I know my illness—I ought to examine carefully all the remedies of his scriptures and, by praying and reading, work that he may grant my soul health suited for such dangerous tasks. I did not do this before because I did not have the time. For I was ordained at the time when we were planning a period of retreat for gaining knowledge of the divine scriptures and wanted to arrange our affairs in order that we could have the leisure for this task. And the truth is that I did not yet know what I lacked for such work as now torments and crushes me. But if I learned through actual experience what a man needs who ministers to the people the sacrament and word of God with the result that I am now not permitted to pursue what I have learned that I lack, you are asking, Father Valerius, for my death. Where is your love? Do you really love me? Do you really love the Church that you wanted me to serve in this way? And yet I am certain that you love both me and the Church. But you think that I am well prepared, while I know myself better, and I would, nonetheless, not have known myself if I had not learned by experience.

4. But Your Holiness perhaps says, "I would like to know what is lacking in your instruction." There are so many things lacking that I could more easily list what I have than what I desire to know. For I would dare to say that I know and hold with complete faith what pertains to our salvation. But how am I to exercise this ministry for the salvation of others, *not seeking what is beneficial for me, but for many, that they may be saved* (1 Cor 10:33)? There are perhaps some counsels recorded in the holy books—in fact there is no doubt about this—and by the knowledge and grasp of these a man of God can minister to the more ordinary affairs of the Church or at least live with a sounder conscience among the bands of the wicked or die so that he does not lose that one life for which humble and gentle Christian hearts sigh. But how is this possible except as the Lord himself said: By seeking, by asking, and by knocking?[3] That is, by praying, by reading, and by weeping. For this task I wanted to obtain through the brothers from your most sincere and venerable love a short time for myself, say, up to Easter, and I now ask this through these prayers.

5. For what am I going to reply to the Lord, my judge? That I could not investigate these things since I was prevented by church business? If, then, he says to me, "Wicked servant, if some land of the church were being subjected to some-

---

3. See Mt 7:7-8 or Lk 11:9-10.

one's false accusations—land on which great effort is being spent to harvest its fruits—and if you could do something on its behalf before an earthly judge, would you not, having left the field which I watered with my own blood, proceed to plead the case with the agreement of everyone and even under commands and compulsion from some people? And if the judgment came down against you, would you not also appeal overseas? And in this case no complaint would recall you, even if you were absent for a year or more, for fear that someone else might own the land necessary, not for the soul, but for the body of the poor, though my living trees would more easily satisfy their hunger and do so in a way more pleasing to me, if they were carefully cultivated. Why, then, do you claim that you lacked leisure time to learn how to cultivate my field?" Tell me what I should reply, I beg you. Or perhaps you want me to say, "Since old Valerius believed that I was instructed in all these matters, he allowed me less time to learn these things, the more he loved me."

6. Consider all these things, old Valerius; I beg you by the goodness and severity of Christ, by his mercy and judgment, by him who has inspired you with such great love for us that we do not dare to offend you, not even for the benefit of our soul. For me, however, you make the Lord and Christ witness of the innocence and love and sincere affection that you have for us, as if I myself could not swear to all these things. I implore your love and affection that you may be merciful to me and grant me as much time as I have requested for the purpose for which I requested it and help me by your prayers that my desire may not be unfulfilled and that my absence may not be without fruit for the Church of Christ and for the benefit of my brothers and fellow servants. I know that the Lord does not scorn that love that prays for me, especially in such a case, and accepting it as a sacrifice of sweetness, he will in perhaps less time than I asked return me instructed in the most salutary counsels of his scriptures.

Letter 22

Between 391 and 393 Augustine as a priest in Hippo wrote to Aurelius, the bishop of Carthage and primate of Africa, thanking him for his goodness toward him and his brethren (paragraph 1). Augustine laments the feasting and drunkenness in the cemeteries throughout Africa where the martyrs are supposedly honored and the dead remembered (paragraph 2). He points out the difficulty of banning such feasting and drinking in private when its public celebration is thought to honor the martyrs (paragraph 3). These practices are no longer carried on except in the churches of Africa, and Augustine suggests that Aurelius should lead the way in banishing them from Africa (paragraph 4). He urges Aurelius to use teaching and advice rather than commands and threats (paragraph 5).

Augustine, a priest, sends greetings to Bishop Aurelius.[1]

1, 1. I hesitated a long time and did not find words of gratitude with which I might reply to your letter. For everything I might say was surpassed by the love of my heart, which the reading of your letter has stimulated to greater ardor, though it was already surging upward of its own accord. I, nonetheless, entrusted myself to God, who works in me in accord with my abilities, that I might write in reply those things that are fitting for the zeal of each of us in the Lord and in our care for the Church, given your position of authority and mine of obedience. And as for that first point, namely, that you believe that you are helped by my prayers, I not only do not try to deny this, but even gladly embrace it. For in that way our Lord will hear me, even if not because of my prayers, certainly because of yours. You have accepted with great good will that our brother, Alypius,[2] has remained in our company in order to be an example to the brothers desiring to avoid the cares of this world, and I am grateful for this in a way I cannot explain in words. May the Lord reward your soul for this. The whole company of brothers, therefore, which has begun to come together with us, is indebted to you for so great a favor in that you take care of us, like someone most present in spirit, though we are so far distant in terms of places of the earth. Hence, we devote ourselves to prayers to the extent we can that the Lord may graciously sustain with you the flock entrusted to you and may never abandon you, but be present as *a helper in time of need* (Ps 9:10), showing to his Church through your priesthood the mercy[3] that spiritual men beseech him with tears and groans to show.

---

1. Aurelius became bishop of Carthage in 393 and presided over that church until his death in 429 or 430.
2. Augustine's close friend from boyhood who will soon become bishop of Thagaste, Augustine's hometown.
3. See Ps 18:51.

2. You should, therefore, know, my most blessed lord who are venerable with the fullest love, that we do not give up hope. In fact, we hope intensely that our Lord and God can by the authority of your person, which we are confident was impressed not upon the flesh, but upon the spirit, heal by the heavy sword of councils[4] and by your earnestness the many carnal diseases and illnesses that the African church suffers in many, but bemoans only in a few. For, though the apostle briefly mentioned in one passage three kinds of vices that are to be detested and avoided and from which there arises a crop of countless vices, one of these vices that he put in the second place is severely punished in the church, while the other two, that is, the first and the last, seem tolerable to human beings, and in that way it can slowly come about that they are no longer thought to be vices. For the vessel of election says, *Not in feasting and drunkenness, not in fornication and impurity, not in strife and jealousy; rather, put on the Lord Jesus Christ, and do not provide for the flesh with its desires* (Rom 13:13-4).

3. Of these three, then, fornication and impurity are considered so great a crime that no one is thought worthy, not merely of ministry in the Church, but even of sharing in the sacraments, who stains himself by this sin, and that is perfectly correct. But why that sin alone? Feasting and drunkenness, after all, are considered permissible and licit to the point that they are committed even at celebrations in honor of the blessed martyrs, not only on feast days, but even daily. Who does not see that this is something deplorable if he sees it with the eyes not of the flesh? If this foulness were only shameful and not also sacrilegious, we might think that it was to be tolerated with whatever ability for tolerance we have. And yet what do we do with that passage in which, after the same apostle listed many vices among which he mentioned drunkenness, he ended by saying that one should not take bread with such people?[5] But let us tolerate these practices in matters of sex and domestic corruption and even in those banquets that are held within private homes, and let us receive the body of Christ with those people with whom we are forbidden to eat bread. At least let this great disgrace be kept from the tombs of the bodies of the saints; at least let it be kept from the places for the sacraments, from houses of prayer. For who dares to forbid privately what is called the honor of the martyrs when it is celebrated in public?

4. If Africa were first to try to eliminate these practices, it would deserve to be worthy of imitation by the other lands, but since through the greater part of Italy and in all or almost all the churches across the sea—in part because they were never practiced, in part because, when they had just sprung up or when they had been established, they were destroyed and wiped out by the diligence and attention of holy bishops who truly had the life to come in mind[6]—how can we hesi-

---

4. The CSEL edition indicates a lacuna; I have followed the Maurist conjecture of *"conciliorum."*
5. See 1 Cor 5:11.
6. The text is here corrupt and has a lacuna.

tate to correct so great a moral defect, at least with so widespread an example set before us? And we, of course, have as bishop a man from those parts, something for which we thank God.[7] And yet he is a man of such modesty and gentleness and also of such prudence and solicitude in the Lord, that, even if he were African, he would quickly be convinced from the scriptures that he must cure the wound that had been inflicted by a custom that is unbridled and free in a bad sense. But the plague of this evil is so great that it cannot, in my opinion, be completely healed except by the authority of a council. Or, if the healing must begin from one church, just as it seems bold to try to change what the church of Carthage holds, so it involves great impudence to want to keep what the church of Carthage has corrected. But for this purpose what other bishop should we desire but the one who as a deacon condemned these practices?[8]

5. What was deplorable then must now be eliminated, not harshly, but in a spirit of gentleness and kindness,[9] as scripture says. For your letter, a proof of most genuine love, gives me confidence that I may speak with you as with myself. These practices, then, are eliminated, in my opinion, not with harshness, not with toughness, not in an imperious manner, but by teaching rather than commanding, by warning rather than threatening. For one has to deal with a large number in that way, but severity should be applied to the sins of the few. And if we use any threat, let it be done with sorrow, by threatening from the scriptures punishment in the future, not so that we ourselves are feared in our power, but so that God is feared in our words. In that way the spiritual people or those close to spiritual people will first be moved, and by their authority the remaining multitude will be subdued by even the gentlest, but most insistent admonitions.

6. But since carnal and ignorant folks often regard these drinking bouts and dissolute banquets in the cemeteries as not merely honors paid to the martyrs, but also as consolations for the dead, it seems to me to be easier to dissuade them from this foul and shameful practice if it is also forbidden by the scriptures and if sacrifices for the spirits of the dead, which we should believe can truly help them, are at their tombs not sumptuous and are offered, not sold, without pride and with readiness to all who ask. But should some wish to offer some money out of devotion, let them give it immediately to the poor. In that way they will not seem to abandon the commemorations of their own dear ones, something that can produce no slight sadness of heart, and they will celebrate in the church what they celebrate with piety and goodness. Let these words suffice for the time being with regard to feasting and drunkenness.

---

7. Augustine refers to Valerius, the bishop of Hippo, who was Greek.
8. Aurelius was a deacon in Carthage between 390 and 393 when he was ordained bishop.
9. See Gal 6:1 and 1 Cor 4:21.

2, 7. But with regard to strife and jealousy why should I say anything? For these vices are more serious, not in the people, but in our own number. The mother of these vices is pride and the eagerness for human praise, which also often leads to hypocrisy. One does not resist this unless the fear and love of God is inculcated by frequent testimonies from the books of God, at least if he who does this presents himself as an example of patience and humility, taking less for himself than is offered, but in any case accepting from those who honor him neither everything nor nothing. And let him accept whatever praise or honor he accepts, not on account of himself who ought to live entirely in the presence of the Lord and scorn human honors, but on account of those whose interests he cannot take care of, if he loses respect because of too much abasement. After all, the words of scripture apply here, *Let no one hold your youth in contempt* (1 Tm 4:12), since he said this who in another passage says, *If I wanted to please human beings, I would not be a servant of Christ* (Gal 1:10).

8. It is a great thing not to rejoice over the honors and praises of human beings, but to remove all vain pomp, and if anything is retained from it as necessary, to refer the whole of it to the benefit and salvation of those who bestow the honor. For it was not said in vain, *God will crush the bones of those who want to please human beings* (Ps 53:6). For what is more feeble, what is so without the stability and strength, which bones signify, as a man who is weakened by the tongue of those who speak evil, though he knows that the things they say are false? Sorrow over their action would in no way tear at the bowels of his soul if the love of praise did not crush his bones. I am confident of the strength of your soul, and so I say to myself these ideas I share with you. Still, you are, I believe, so gracious as to consider with me how serious and difficult they are. For only one who has declared war on this enemy feels its strength, because, even if it is easy for someone to do without praise when it is denied, it is difficult not to take delight in it when it is offered. And yet, we ought to have our mind so lifted up to God that, if we are praised undeservedly, we correct those we can so that they do not think there is in us something that is not there or that something is our own that belongs to God. We should correct them so that they do not praise those things that, even if we do not lack them or even if they abound, are, nonetheless, not at all praiseworthy, such as all the goods that we have in common with the animals or with impious human beings. But if we are deservedly praised on account of God, we congratulate those who are pleased by a true good, not ourselves because we are pleasing to human beings, and only on the condition that we are before God the sort of men they believe we are and that this is not attributed to us, but to God. For all things that are truly and deservedly praised are his gifts. I daily repeat these things to myself, or rather he does whose salutary precepts they are, wherever they are found in the divine readings or are suggested interiorly in our hearts. And yet, when mightily struggling with the

enemy, I often receive wounds from him, when I cannot remove the delight from the praise offered me.

9. I have written these things in order that, if they are not now necessary for Your Holiness, either because you yourself have more such thoughts and more useful ones or because Your Holiness has no need of this medicine, you may at least know my sins and may know why you should deign to pray to God for my weakness. By the humanity of him who commanded that we should bear one another's burden,[10] I beg you to do this in the greatest abundance. There are many things concerning our life and conduct over which I would shed tears, but which I would not want to come to you by letter. Rather, I wish that there were no other means of communication between my heart and your heart but my lips and your ears. But if old Saturninus, a man venerable in our eyes and most dear to all of us because of his complete sincerity, a man whose fraternal love and zeal toward you I observed when I was present, would deign, when he shall see it is opportune, to come to us, whatever we could speak of with that man filled with holiness and spiritual love will differ either not at all or not very much from what we would have done with Your Reverence. I beg with prayers so great that no words suffice to express them that you deign to ask and obtain this from him. For the people of Hippo deeply and excessively fear my absence at so great a distance. They do not even trust me so that I may see the field which was given to the brothers by your foresight and generosity, as we learned prior to your letter through our holy brother and fellow servant, Parthenius, from whom we heard many other things we desired to hear. The Lord will grant that the other things that we still desire will also be realized.

---

10. See Gal 6:2.

Letter 23

Between 391 and 395, while still a priest, Augustine wrote from Hippo to Maximinus, the Donatist bishop on Siniti in Numidia. He first explains the reverential mode of address that he used in writing to Maximinus (paragraph 1). Then he explains the sinfulness of rebaptizing and his reluctance to believe that Maximinus has rebaptized a Catholic (paragraph 2). He asks Maximinus to reply to him and to state whether he rebaptizes or not (paragraph 3). Augustine argues against the repetition of Christian baptism (paragraph 4) and points out that Maximinus has it in his power to set an example for the rest of Donatist Africa (paragraph 5). Augustine suggests that both parties set aside past wrongs and deal with the present case (paragraph 6). He even proposes that his letter and Maximinus' reply be read to the people when the military is not present (paragraph 7). Finally, Augustine explains that the urgency of the case demanded that he take action in the absence of his bishop (paragraph 8).

To my most beloved lord and honorable brother, Maximinus, Augustine, a priest of the Catholic Church, sends greetings in the Lord.

1. Before I come to the point about which I wanted to write to Your Benevolence, I shall give an account of the salutation of this letter lest it disturb you or anyone else. I wrote, "lord," because scripture says, *You have been called to freedom, brothers; only do not use your freedom as an opportunity for the flesh, but rather serve one another through love* (Gal 5:13). Since, then, I am serving you through love by this very duty of writing a letter, I call you "lord" without any absurdity on account of our one and true Lord who gave us these commands. But as for the fact that I wrote, "most beloved," God knows that I not only love you, but love you as myself, since I am quite conscious to myself that I desire the same goods for you as for myself. But as for "honorable," which I also added, I did not add this to honor your episcopacy. After all, you are not my bishop, nor should you take this as spoken with contempt, but in that spirit by which we ought to have on our lips, *Yes, yes; no, no* (Mt 5:37 and Jas 5:12). For you are not unaware, nor is any human being who knows us unaware, that you are not my bishop and that I am not your priest. I, therefore, willingly call you "honorable" on the basis of that rule by which I know that you are a human being and know that a human being has been made to the image and likeness of God[1] and placed in a position of honor by the very order and law of nature, if by understanding what he should understand he preserves his honor. For scripture says, *Though placed in a position of honor, man did not understand; he has been made equal to mindless animals and has become like them* (Ps 49:21). Why, then, should I

---

1. See Gn 1:27.

not call you "honorable" insofar as you are a human being, especially since I dare not to give up hope concerning your salvation and correction as long as you are in this life? But you are not unaware that we are commanded by God to call you, "brother,"[2] so that we say even to those who deny that they are our brothers, "You are our brothers," and this holds especially true for the case on account of which I have wanted to write to Your Fraternity. For, now that I have given an account of why I made such an introduction for this letter, listen in complete calmness to what follows.

2. Though I express in the strongest words I can my hatred for the lamentable and deplorable custom of people in this region who, though they boast of the Christian name, do not hesitate to rebaptize Christians, there were some people who praised you and who said to me that you do not do that. I admit, at first I did not believe them. Then, considering that it is possible that fear of God entered the human soul reflecting on the future life so that it held itself back from a most evident crime, I gratefully believed that with such an intention you refused to be so far removed from the Catholic Church. I was, of course, seeking an occasion to speak with you in order that, if it were possible, that small disagreement that had remained between us might be removed, when, you see, a few days ago it was reported that you rebaptized our deacon in Mutugenna.[3] I was deeply saddened both over his wretched fall and over your unexpected crime, my brother. After all, I know which is the Catholic Church. The nations are the heritage of Christ, and the possession of Christ is the ends of the earth.[4] You also know this, or if you do not know, pay attention. It can be easily learned by those who are willing. To rebaptize, then, a heretical person who has already received these signs of holiness that the Christian discipline has handed down is a sin without a doubt. To rebaptize a Catholic is, however, a most grievous sin. And yet, not believing this report since I held a good opinion of you, I myself went to Mutugenna, and I could not see the poor man, but I heard from his parents that he has now also become your deacon. And I still think so well of your disposition of heart that I do not believe that he was baptized again.

3. Hence, I beg you, most dear brother, by the divinity and the humanity of our Lord Jesus Christ, to be so good as to write back to me what has happened and to write back in such a way that you bear in mind that I want to read your letter to our brothers in the Church. I have written this so that I would not offend Your Charity, when I later do something that you hoped I would not do, and so that you would not raise a just complaint about me before our common friends. I do not see, then, what keeps you from writing back. For, if you do rebaptize, there is nothing that you should fear from the men of your company, since you will write back that you do

---

2. See Is 66:5.
3. A town in Numidia.
4. See Ps 2:8.

what they command that you do, even if you do not want to. But when you maintain that this should be done with as many proofs as you can, they will not only not be angry, but will even praise you. If, however, you do not rebaptize, seize the freedom of Christ, brother Maximinus; seize it, I beg you. In the sight of Christ do not fear the reproach or do not be terrified at the power of any human being. The honor of this world is passing; its pride is passing. In Christ's future judgment neither pulpits with flights of steps nor thrones with canopies nor flocks of processing and chanting nuns will be called to our defense when our consciences begin to accuse us and the judge of our conscience begins to pass judgment. Those things which are here honors will there be burdens; those things which here buoy us up will then pull us down. These honors which are shown to us for a time on account of the good of the Church will perhaps be defended by a good conscience, but they will not be able to defend a bad conscience.

4. With regard, then, to what you do with so pious and so religious a mind, if you do in fact act in this way—I mean, if you do not repeat the baptism of the Catholic Church, but rather approve it as the baptism of the one truest mother, who offers her breast to all the nations for their rebirth and who, as the one possession of Christ that stretches out to the ends of the earth,[5] pours out in them her milk after their rebirth—if you really act in this way, why do you not burst forth in a cry that is exultant and free? Why do you cover the very useful brightness of your lamp under a bushel?[6] Why have you not torn and cast aside the old skins of timid servitude and instead put on the confidence of Christ? Why do you not go out and say, "I know of only one baptism consecrated and sealed by the name of the Father and of the Son and of the Holy Spirit? Where I find this form, I must approve. I do not destroy what I recognize as the Lord's; I do not spit[7] at the standard of my king." Those who divided the clothing of the Lord did not destroy it.[8] And they still did not believe that Christ would rise, but they saw him dying. If his clothing was not torn by his persecutors when he was hanging on the cross, why is his sacrament destroyed by Christians when he is seated in heaven? If I were a Jew in the time of the old people when I could not be anything better, I would certainly have received circumcision. That sign of the righteousness of faith[9] was at that time so powerful, before it was rendered void by the coming of Christ, that an angel would have suffocated the infant son of Moses if his mother had not taken a piece of stone and circumcised the boy and by this sacrament warded off imminent death.[10] This sacrament also held back the River Jordan

---

5. See Ps 2:8.
6. See Mt 5:15, Lk 11:33, 8:16, and Mk 4:21.
7. Literally: "I do not subject to exsufflation the standard of my king," that is, to the baptismal rite by which the priest "blows out" the devil from the candidate for baptism.
8. See Jn 19:24.
9. See Rom 9:11.
10. See Ex 4:24-26.

and turned it back toward its source.[11] The Lord himself received this sacrament when he was born, although he emptied it of meaning when he was crucified. For those signs were not condemned; rather, they departed when more timely ones took their place. For, just as the first coming of the Lord took away circumcision, so his second coming will take away baptism. After all, just as now after the freedom of faith has come and the yoke of servitude has been removed, no Christian is circumcised in the flesh, so then when the righteous are reigning with the Lord and the wicked have been condemned, no one will be baptized, but what they signified, that is, the circumcision of the heart and purity of consciousness, will remain for eternity. If, then, I were a Jew at that time and if a Samaritan came to me and wanted to become a Jew after abandoning that error, which the Lord condemned when he said, *You worship what you do not know; we worship what we know for salvation comes from the Jews* (Jn 4:22)--if this Samaritan, then, whom the Samaritans had circumcised, wanted to become a Jew, he would certainly be exempt from the audacity of a repetition, and we would be forced not to repeat, but to approve that action commanded by God, though performed in a heresy. But if in the flesh of a circumcised man I would not find a place to repeat the circumcision because that member is only one, much less is a place found in one heart where the baptism of Christ might be repeated. And so, you who want to have a twofold baptism necessarily require a duplicitous heart.

5. Cry out, then, that you act correctly, if you do not rebaptize, and write back to me about this, not only without trepidation, but even with joy. Let none of your councils frighten you, my brother. For, if they are displeased with this, they do not deserve to have you, but if they are pleased, we trust in the mercy of the Lord, who never abandons those who fear to displease him and try to please him, that there will soon be peace between you and us. In that way, our dignities, a dangerous burden for which we shall give an account, will not cause the poor people who believe in Christ to take food together in their homes, but not to share together the table of Christ. Do we not deplore the fact that a husband and wife swear to one another, in most cases by Christ, that they are uniting their bodies in fidelity, and yet they tear apart the body of Christ by their different communion? If by your moderation and prudence and by the love that we owe to him who shed his blood for us, this great scandal, this great triumph of the devil, this great destruction of souls were eliminated in these regions, who would describe in words the palm of victory that the Lord would prepare for you because, in order to heal the other members that lie miserably wasting away through the whole of Africa, you set an example of a remedy so easily imitated? Since you cannot see my heart, how I fear that I may seem to speak to you with insults rather than with love! But I at least find nothing more that I might do but to offer for examination my words to you and my mind to God.

---

11. See Ps 114:3.5.

6. Let us remove from the center stage those empty objections that are often hurled at one another by ignorant parties. You should not raise as an objection the era of Macarius,[12] nor should I do the same with the violence of the Circumcellions,[13] if this latter problem does not apply to you, nor those earlier events to me. The threshing floor of the Lord has not yet been winnowed; it cannot be free from straw. Let us pray and do as much as we can that we may be the wheat. I cannot be silent about our deacon who was rebaptized, for I know how dangerous for me such silence is. After all, I do not plan to pass my time in the vanity of ecclesiastical honors; rather, I bear in mind that I will give an account to the prince of all pastors about the sheep entrusted to me. If you perhaps do not want me to write these things to you, you must, my brother, pardon my fear. For I fear very much that, if I am silent and pretend nothing is wrong, others will also be rebaptized by you. I have, therefore, determined to pursue this cause to the extent that the Lord offers me the strength and ability, in order that all who are in communion with us may know from our peaceful discussions how much the Catholic Church differs from heresies and schisms and how much one should avoid the destruction to come for either the weeds or the branches that have been cut off from the vine of the Lord.[14] If you enter upon this discussion with me willingly so that by our agreement the letters of both of us are read out to our peoples, I shall rejoice with unexpressible joy. But if you do not accept this calmly, what shall I do, brother, even though you are unwilling, but read our letters to the Catholic people in order that they may be better instructed? But if you refuse to reply by letter, I have decided to read at least my letter in order that, when people recognize your lack of confidence, they may at least be ashamed to be rebaptized.

7. And I will not do this when the army is present for fear that someone of yours might think that I wanted to do this with more violence than the cause of peace requires. I will do it after the departure of the army in order that all who hear us may understand that it is not part of my purpose that people be forced against their will into communion with anyone, but that the truth may become known to those who seek it most peacefully. Terror from temporal authorities will cease on our side; let there also cease on your side terror from bands of Circumcellions. Let us deal with the facts; let us deal with reason; let us deal with the authorities of the divine scriptures; as quiet and peaceful as we can be, let us

---

12. Macarius and Paul were commissioners sent by the emperor, Constantius, to Africa in 347 to settle the Donatist controversy; in the following years Macarius so mistreated and persecuted the Donatists that his name became legendary among them. "In Numidia the 'Time of Macarius' was remembered by the Donatists, in the same way as the 'Time of Cromwell' was remembered in Ireland" (Peter Brown, *Augustine of Hippo: A Biography* (Berkeley: University of California Press, 1967) 215.

13. The Circumcellions were an extremist group of the Donatists, roaming bands of men and women, who often practiced savage violence against their Catholic opponents.

14. See Mt 13:24-30 and Jn 15:1-8.

ask; let us seek; let us knock that we may receive and find and have the door opened for us.[15] For it may perhaps be possible that, with the Lord helping our single-hearted efforts and prayers, this great deformity and impiety may begin to be wiped out from our lands. If you do not believe that I want to do this after the departure of the soldiers, write back to me after the departure of the soldiers. For, if I choose to read my letter to the people when the army is present, you can produce my letter to prove that I violated my word. May the mercy of the Lord keep this from my conduct and from the aim with which he has deigned to inspire me through his yoke.

8. If he had been here, my bishop would perhaps have rather sent a letter to Your Benevolence, or I would have written at his command or with his permission. But in his absence I did not allow this issue to cool off because of delay when the rebaptism of the deacon is or is said to be a recent occurrence, since I was aroused by the tortures of the bitterest sorrow over the true death of a brother. By the help of the Lord's mercy and providence, some compensation will perhaps soothe this pain of mine. May our God and Lord deign to inspire you with a peaceful mind, my lord and most beloved brother.

---

15. See Mt 7:7-8 or Lk 11:9-10.

The First Correspondence with Paulinus of Nola: Letters 24-27 and 30-32

Twelve letters of the correspondence with Paulinus of Nola are included in this volume. Unlike the correspondence with Nebridius, these letters are scattered over the period from before Augustine's consecration as coadjutor bishop up to the end of the Donatist crisis in 411, and further letters between Augustine and Paulinus, then the bishop of Nola, are found in the second volume of the Letters. In this volume we have the first letters from Paulinus to Alypius and Augustine as well as the letter of Augustine to Licentius, whom he commended to Paulinus' care, Augustine's first two letters to Paulinus, and Paulinus' reply to Augustine and his letter to Romanian, Licentius' father.

Letter 24

Before the winter of 394 Paulinus and his wife, Therasia, wrote from Nola in Italy to Augustine's close friend, Alypius, who was by that time bishop of Thagaste. After prefatory words about the love of God (paragraph 1), Paulinus acknowledges the receipt of Augustine's works against the Manichees and sends to Alypius his spiritual father's copy of Eusebius' work on the history of the Church (paragraphs 2 and 3). He expresses his desire to know Alypius' background and his relations with Ambrose (paragraph 4). He asks that the correspondence with Alypius may be continued (paragraphs 5 and 6).

To our rightly honorable and most blessed father, Alypius,[1] Paulinus and Therasia,[2] sinners, send greetings.

1. It is true charity; it is perfect love that you have proven that you have for our lowly selves, my truly holy lord, who are rightly most blessed and most lovable. For we have received through our servant, Julian, returning from Carthage, a letter bringing so great a light from Your Holiness that we seem not to come to know, but to recognize once again your love for us. For this love has, of course, flowed from him who predestined us for himself from the beginning of the world,[3] and in him we were created before we were born, because he *created us and not we ourselves* (Ps 100:3), God who *made what will be* (Is 45:11 LXX). And so, formed by his foreknowledge and work into this similarity of our desires and into the unity of faith or into the faith that brings unity, we have been united by a love that precedes knowledge. As a result we can recognize each other by the revelation of the Spirit prior to any bodily glimpse of each other. We are, therefore, grateful and boast in the Lord who, one and the same everywhere on earth, produces in his own people his love by the Holy Spirit, whom he poured out over all flesh,[4] making his city joyous by means of the stream of the river.[5] Among its citizens he has rightly placed you as a leader along with the leaders of his people[6] in the chair of an apostle. He also willed that we be counted in your lot, for he raised us up after we had fallen and lifted up the poor from the earth.[7]

---

1. Augustine's friend from boyhood who followed him to Milan, was baptized with him by Ambrose, and had become the bishop of their hometown, Thagaste.
2. Paulinus, a wealthy aristocrat, and his wife, Therasia, renounced their riches and began to reside in Nola in Italy in 395 after he was ordained a priest in Barcelona the previous year. He later became bishop of Nola.
3. See Eph 1:4-5.
4. See Jl 2:28.
5. See Ps 46:5.
6. See Ps 113:8.
7. See Ps Ps 113:7 and 146:8.

But we are more grateful for that gift of the Lord by which he placed us in the chamber of your heart and by which he has also deigned to insert us into your innermost self. As a result we can claim for ourselves a special confidence in your love, since we have been challenged by these services and gifts so that we are not permitted to love you hesitantly or slightly.

2. For we have received as a special sign of your love and concern the work consisting of five books of the holy and perfect man in the Lord Christ, our brother Augustine.[8] We admire and esteem that work so much that we believe its words were dictated by God. And so, with the confidence in your oneness of heart which we cannot but esteem, we have also dared to write to him. For we trust that through you we will be excused in his eyes of our ignorance and commended to his love, as well as to all the saints by whose services, though they are absent, you have deigned to protect us. And you will undoubtedly take care with an equal love that through Your Holiness we may in turn pay our respect to the companions of Your Holiness in the clergy and to your imitators in faith and virtue in the monasteries. For, though you live among the people and rule over them, governing the sheep of the Lord's pasture, you have, nonetheless, created a desert for yourself by abandoning the world and rejecting your own flesh and blood, a man who is hidden from the many, but who is called among the few.

3. As in some sense a gift in return, though everything is less than you, I have procured, as you commanded, that universal history by the venerable Eusebius, the bishop of Constantinople.[9] There was, however, a delay in complying with this. For, since I myself did not have this volume, at your instruction I found it at Rome in the home of our truly most holy father, Domnio, who undoubtedly obeyed me more promptly in this favor because I indicated that it was to be sent on to you. Because, nonetheless, you were so good as to convey to me the addresses where you might be found, we wrote, as your yourself advised, to your venerable companion in the episcopacy, our father, Aurelius,[10] so that, if you are now living in Hippo Regius, he might deign to forward to you our letter and the manuscript after it was copied at Carthage. We have also asked of the holy men, Comes and Evodius,[11] whom we know from your words that are proofs of their love, that they themselves take care to write so that my father, Domnio, is not

---

8. These books were *True Religion*, the two books of *Genesis in Answer to the Manichees*, and the two books of *The Catholic Way of Life and the Manichean Way of Life*. In Letter 25, 2, Paulinus refers to them as Augustine's "Pentatuch against the Manichees."

9. *The History of the Church* (*Historia ecclesiastica*) written by Eusebius of Caesarea covering events up to the Council of Nicea. Paulinus is mistaken in speaking of him as the bishop of Constantinople, though he did write a life of Constantine.

10. Aurelius, the bishop of Carthage since 393.

11. Evodius, a friend of Augustine's since childhood, who followed him to Milan and returned with him to Africa where he would soon become bishop of Uzalis in Africa Proconsularis. With Comes Evodius was setting up a monastery in Carthage.

deprived for too long of the manuscript and that the copy sent to you may remain without any need of returning it.

4. But because you have shown me your great love, though I did not deserve or expect it, I especially ask this favor of you, namely, that in return for this history of the times you recount for me the whole history of Your Holiness. Set forth in words the history of your family, of the house[12] from which you have been called by so great a Lord, and of the beginnings from which you were set aside from the womb of your mother so that, after giving up the family of your flesh and blood, you were transferred to the mother of the children of God, who nurses them with milk, and you were brought into a royal and priestly people.[13] For, since you indicated that you learned of the name of our lowly selves at Milan when you received the sacraments of initiation there, I admit that I was more curious and wanted to learn about you in order that I might know you in every respect in order that I may congratulate you more if you were either called to the faith or consecrated to the priesthood by Ambrose,[14] our father. For in that way we would both be seen to have the same man as our father in the faith. For, though I was baptized by Delphinus at Bordeaux[15] and consecrated at Barcelona in Spain by Lampius[16] at the demand of the people suddenly ablaze with that desire, I was, nonetheless, always nurtured in the faith and am now sustained in the order of priesthood by the love of Ambrose. Finally, he wanted to claim me for his clergy so that, though I live elsewhere, I would be judged his priest.

5. But so that you may not be ignorant of me, you should know that this old sinner, drawn from darkness and the shadow of death,[17] has not long ago drawn in the breath of life and has not long ago set my hand to the plow[18] and taken up the cross of the Lord. May we be helped by your prayers in order that we may be able to carry it to the end. This reward will be added to your merits if you lighten our burdens by your intercession. For a holy man helping a laborer—for I do not dare to call myself "brother"—will be exalted like a great city.[19] And you are indeed a city built upon a mountain, or like a lighted lamp on a stand[20] you shine

---

12. See Virgil, *Aeneid* VIII, 114.
13. See 1 Pt 2:9. P. Courcelle suggested that Paulinus' request to know about the life of Alypius led to Augustine's writing the sections about Alypius in *Confessions* VI, 7, 11-10, 16 and thus to the whole of the *Confessions*. See James O'Donnell, *Augustine: Confessions* (Oxford: Clarendon Press, 1992) II, 360-362, for a discussion of the evidence.
14. Ambrose was bishop of Milan from 373 or 374 until his death in 397; he baptized Augustine at the Easter Vigil in 387.
15. Delphinus was bishop of Bordeaux from 380 to 404.
16. In the late fourth century Lampius was the successor to Pacian, who was a prominent theologian and author.
17. See Ps 107:14, Lk 1:79, and 1 Pt 2:9.
18. See Lk 9:62.
19. See Prv 18:19.
20. See Mt 5:14-15.

with a sevenfold brightness,[21] while we are hiding under the bushel basket of our sins. Visit us with your letters, and bring us out into the light in which you live, seen by the eyes of all on a golden stand. Your words will be a light for our paths,[22] and our head will be anointed with the oil of your lamp.[23] And our faith will be kindled when we receive from the breath of your lips food for the mind and light for the soul.

6. May the peace and grace of God be with you, and may the crown of righteousness remain for you on that day, my lord and father, who are rightly most beloved, venerable, and deeply longed for. We ask you to greet with much love and salutary deference the blessed companions and imitators in the Lord of Your Holiness, our brothers, if we may call them this, who are serving the Lord in the Catholic faith in the churches and monasteries of Carthage, Thagaste, and Hippo Regius, and in all your parishes and in all the places known to you throughout Africa. If you receive the manuscript of the saintly Domnio, be so good as to send us a copy. And I ask that you write and tell me which hymn of mine you know. We have sent to Your Holiness as a sign of unity a single loaf of bread in which is also contained the solidity of the Trinity. You shall make this loaf a bread of blessing if you deign to accept it.

---

21. See Is 11:2 for the seven gifts of the Holy Spirit to which Paulinus alludes.
22. See Ps 119:105.
23. See Ps 23:5.

Letter 25

Paulinus and Therasia also wrote, most probably in 394, from Nola to Augustine in Hippo. Paulinus thanks Augustine for the five books of Augustine that Alypius had brought to Nola and praises the books highly for the benefit they bring to the Church (paragraph 1). Continuing his high praise for Augustine's works, which he calls his "Pentateuch against the Manichees," Paulinus asks Augustine to send him any further works he produces (paragraph 2). Paulinus pleads for help for his own spiritual growth through both Augustine's prayers and learning, reminding Augustine that, though they are about the same age, Paulinus is only an infant in the spiritual life (paragraph 3). Paulinus describes his abandonment of public office and his entry upon a life of asceticism, while continuing to ask for Augustine's guidance (paragraph 4). Paulinus expresses his hope that their mutual friendship, which has begun through Alypius, may grow more and more (paragraph 5).

Paulinus and Therasia, sinners, send greetings to Augustine, their lord and venerable brother, with whom they are one in heart.

1. The love of Christ, which urges us[1] and binds us together in the unity of faith, despite the distance between us, has itself banished any feeling of reticence, given us the confidence to write to you, and made you known to my heart through your writings, which I have at present in five books.[2] These books, which are rich with the learning of the schools and sweet with heavenly honey, provide medicine and nourishment to my soul. We received these books with the help of our blessed and venerable bishop, Alypius,[3] not for our instruction only, but also for the benefit of the Church in many cities. I now have those books at hand for reading; I am delighted by them; I take from them food, not that food which perishes,[4] but that which produces the substance of eternal life through our faith, by which we are incorporated into Christ Jesus, our Lord. For our faith, which cares not for visible things, but longs for those that are invisible,[5] is strengthened by the writings and examples of the faithful through the love that believes all things[6] in accord with the truth of almighty God. O truly the salt of the earth,[7] by which our hearts are seasoned so that they cannot become vain with the error of the world! O lamp worthy to be set upon the lampstand of the

---

1. See 1 Cor 5:14.
2. See the note to the previous letter for the identity of these books.
3. Alypius, Augustine's friend from boyhood, was by this time bishop of Thagaste.
4. See Jn 6:27.
5. See 2 Cor 4:18.
6. See 1 Cor 13:7.
7. See Mt 5:13, Lk 14:34.

Church,[8] widely spreading about in Catholic cities the light fed by the oil of gladness from the sevenfold lamp, you scatter the clouds of heretics, dense though they are, and bring out the light of the truth from the confusion of darkness by the splendor of your brilliant words.

2. You see, my admirable brother, with whom I am one in heart, who are to be loved in Christ the Lord, how I acknowledge you as a friend, with what great awe I admire you, with what great love I embrace you, I who daily enjoy the conversation of your writings and am fed by the spirit of your mouth. For I would be right to call your mouth a pipe of living water and a vein of eternal truth because Christ has become a fountain of living water springing up in you unto eternal life.[9] Out of a desire for him my heart has thirsted for you,[10] and my earth has desired to be inebriated by the richness of your river.[11] Since you have so well armed me with this Pentateuch[12] of yours against the Manichees, if you have prepared any defenses against other enemies of the Catholic faith—for our enemy, who has a thousand "tricks by which to do us harm,"[13] must be fought by weapons as varied as the ambushes by which he attacks—I beg you to bring them forth from your armory, and do not refuse to give us the weapons of righteousness. For I am a sinner, even now laboring under a great burden, an old soldier in the number of sinners, but a new recruit in the incorporeal army of the eternal king. I have up to now wretchedly admired the wisdom of the world, and I was a fool and speechless before God because of a literature without benefit and a wisdom that was false. But after *I grew old among my enemies* (Ps 6:8) and became foolish in my thoughts,[14] *I raised my eyes to the mountains* (Ps 120:1), looking to the precepts of the law and the gifts of grace. From there help has come to me from the Lord,[15] who, not repaying us in accord with our iniquities,[16] gave sight to the blind, released the fettered,[17] and brought down the man wrongly standing upright in order to raise up the man who has piously humbled himself.

3. I follow, therefore, still not with equal paces, the great footprints of the righteous if only I might be able by the help of your prayers to grasp the extent to which I have been grasped by the mercies of God. Guide, then, this little one as he creeps uncertainly, and teach him to walk in your footsteps. For I do not want

---

8. See Mt 5:15, Mk 4:12, Lk 8:16 and 11:33.
9. See Jn 4:14.
10. See Ps 63:2.
11. See Ps 36:9.
12. Paulinus compares Augustine's five books against the Manichees to the first five books of the Bible.
13. Virgil, *Aeneid* VII, 338.
14. See Rom 1:21.
15. See Ps 120:1-2.
16. See 103:10.
17. See Ps 146:7

you to consider me in terms of the age of my bodily rather than of my spiritual birth. My age according to the flesh is, of course, now that at which that man at the Beautiful Gate was healed by the apostles through power of the word.[18] But in terms of the birthday of the soul, I still am at the age of those infants who, sacrificed by blows aimed at Christ,[19] anticipated by their pure blood the sacrifice of the Lamb and foreshadowed the Lord's Passion. And so, by your words teach me like someone still an infant with regard to the word of God and like someone still a nursling in terms of spiritual age as I reach for your breasts filled with faith, wisdom, and love. If you consider our common office, you are a brother. If you consider the maturity of your mind and thoughts, you are for me a father, if even you are perhaps younger in years, for gray-haired wisdom has advanced you even as a young man to the maturity in merit and to the honor due to the elders. Hold me close to you, then, and strengthen me in the sacred writings and spiritual pursuits, for I am, as I said, a newcomer in terms of time and, for this reason, inexperienced in their use after long dangers and after many shipwrecks, and scarcely emerging from the waves of the world. You, who are already settled on the solid shore, welcome me into a safe cove in order that we may sail together, if you think me worthy, in the harbor of salvation. Meanwhile, with your prayers, like a life raft, support me as I strive to emerge from the dangers of this life and the depth of sins in order that I may leave this world, stripped of everything as if from a shipwreck.

4. Hence, I have taken care to lift myself up from the burdens of office and to strip myself of weighty clothing in order that, at Christ's command and with his help, I might, unimpeded by the garments of the flesh and worry over tomorrow,[20] climb out of this stormy sea of the present life, which separates God and us with our sins crying out in between. I do not boast that I have achieved this, but even if I could boast, I would boast in the Lord,[21] for he is able to bring to completion what we can will,[22] but my soul still longs to desire the judgments of God.[23] Imagine when he who still longs to desire him will actually attain the realization of what God wills! To the extent, however, that I can, I have loved the beauty of his holy house,[24] and to the extent that I could, I had chosen to be the least in the house of the Lord.[25] But he who chose to set me aside from the womb of my mother[26] and to draw me from the love of flesh and blood to his grace has

18. See Acts 3:2-10; 4:22.
19. See Mt 2:16.
20. See Mt 6:34.
21. See 2 Cor 10:17.
22. See Rom 7:18.
23. See Ps 119:20.
24. See Ps 26:8.
25. See Ps 84:11.
26. See Gal 1:15.

also chosen to raise me up from the earth,[27] though I am without any positive merit, and to lead me forth from the pit of miseries and from the mire of the dregs,[28] to seat me with the princes of his people[29] and to give me a share in your rank, in order that, though you surpass me in merits, I may be your equal in sharing the same office.

5. Not, therefore, out of presumption on my part, but because the Lord has chosen and arranged it in his providence, I claim for myself the bonds of brotherhood, and though I am unworthy, I consider myself worthy of so great an honor, for I certainly know that in accord with your holiness—for you are truly wise—you do not think proud thoughts, but adapt yourself to the lowly.[30] And so, I hope that you will readily welcome in the depth of your heart the love of our lowly selves, which I trust that you have already received through the most blessed priest, Alypius, our father, since he agreed. After all, he undoubtedly has made himself an example for you of loving us before knowing us and beyond what we deserve. By the Spirit of true love, who both penetrates and is poured out everywhere, he was able to see us by loving us and to touch us by conversation, though we were unknown to him and separated from him by a long stretch of the land or of the sea. He gave us the first proofs of his affection and pledges of your love in the previously mentioned gift of books. And with as much zeal as he desired that we might love Your Holiness not just in a middling way, once you were known not merely by his words, but also more fully by your own eloquence and faith, we believe that he took care that you would love us very much in return in imitation of him. We pray that the grace of God may remain with you, as it is now, for eternity, our brother and lord who are one of heart with us in Christ and venerable and most longed for. With very much affection stemming from our brotherly oneness of heart, we greet your whole house and all those who follow and imitate your holiness in the Lord. We ask that you bless by accepting it the one loaf of bread we sent you as proof of our oneness of heart.

---

27. See Ps 113:7.
28. See Ps 40:3.
29. See Ps 113:8.
30. See Rom 12:16.

Letter 26

In 394 or 395 Augustine wrote to Licentius, the son of Romanian, Augustine's wealthy patron. Licentius had been present with Augustine at Cassiciacum and plays important roles in several of the Dialogues dating from that period. Obviously Licentius remains somewhat of a disappointment for Augustine. After apologizing for not having written sooner, Augustine hopes that Licentius will find the path to God (paragraph 1), but fears that his former student is shackled to mortal things and points to reasons for concern that he finds in Licentius' letters (paragraphs 2 and 3). Licentius had sent Augustine a lengthy poem, which is appended to this letter. Augustine challenges Licentius, who had reminisced about the good days that he had spent at Cassiciacum as Augustine's student, to listen to his own poetry and to give himself to God (paragraph 4). He pleads with Licentius to heed Christ's call and suggests that he visit Paulinus and learn from him how to abandon the world (paragraph 5). He warns Licentius that the pleasure and honors of the world lie to us and urges him to cling to Christ, the Truth (paragraph 6). Licentius' poem to Augustine, his teacher, is filled with odd things to come from a Christian. He, for example, speaks of Christ as our Apollo and of his Father as the father of the gods! He blends together the language of Roman mythology and of the bible; he, for example, refers to Christ as "the Son of thundering Jove, smoothing the rough areas into level fields," where he alludes to Luke 3:5. All told, Licentius' poem must have given Augustine good reason to be concerned about the soul of his former student.

Augustine sends greetings to Licentius.

1. I have hardly found the opportunity to write to you. Who would believe it? Licentius, nonetheless, has to believe me. I do not want you to search out the causes and reasons; even if they could be given, I do not owe them to the trust with which you believe me. For I did not receive your letter by means of persons by whom I could send back a reply. But as for what you asked that I ask, I have taken care to do so by a letter to the extent that it seemed opportune, but it is for you to judge what I have accomplished. If, however, it has not yet been done, either I will act more insistently when I come to know this or when you yourself remind me again. Up to now I have spoken with you regarding the chains of this life, which continue to clang; now in a few words accept the concerns of my heart over my hope for you that is not merely passing, namely, that in some way the path to God may open up for you.

2. I am afraid, my Licentius, that you, who again and again reject and fear the shackles of wisdom, are most strongly and most fatally shackled to mortal things. For wisdom will afterwards set loose those whom it has first bound and tamed by certain laborious exercises, and she gives herself to them for their enjoyment once they have been set free. And those she has first trained by

78

temporal bonds she will later wrap in eternal embraces, a chain than which nothing can be imagined either more pleasant or solid. I admit that these first chains are hard for a while, but I would not call the latter ones hard because they are most sweet nor soft because they are most strong. What are they, then, but what we cannot express, but what we can, nonetheless, believe, hope for, and love? But the chains of this world have true harshness and false pleasantness, certain pain and uncertain pleasure, hard labor and fear-filled rest, a reality full of misery and a hope empty of happiness. You place your neck and hands and feet in these chains when you long to be under the yoke of such honors, think that your actions are otherwise not fruitful, and strive to remain where you not only ought not to go, if you were invited, but not even if you were compelled.[1]

3. Here will you perhaps give me the reply of Terence's servant, "Whoa, you are here spouting words, O wisdom"?[2] Accept them, then, in order that I may pour them forth rather than throw them out. Or, if I sing, but you dance to another voice, even so I do not regret it. After all, singing also has its funny moments, even if one for whom the song is sung with melody full of love does not move his limbs in relation to it. Certain words in your letters have disturbed me, but I thought it inappropriate to deal with them when concern for your actions and whole life has me boiling.

4. If your verse was spoiled by disordered rhythm, if it did not stand by its own laws, if it offended the ear of the listener by its unequal measures, you would surely be ashamed and you would not delay or stop until you put your verse in order, corrected it, fixed it, and made it regular by learning and practicing the art of meter with the keenest desire and at the cost of any labor. When you yourself are spoiled by disorder, when you do not stand by the laws of God, and when in living your life you are not in harmony with the good wishes of your family and with this learning of yours, why do you think that all this should be cast behind you and neglected? As if you were of less value in your own eyes than the sound of your tongue and as if the fact that you offend the ears of God by your disordered conduct is less bad than if a grammatical authority became angry at your disordered syllable. You write:

Oh may tomorrow's[3] dawn bring back for me
With her joyous chariot those past days
We spent in the high mountains in the midst of Italy,
Where we enjoyed with you the freedom of leisure
And the spotless laws of good men. May the harsh cold
Not prevent me with its grey ice, nor the fierce storms
Of the Zephyrs and the roar of the north wind

---

1. I have changed the sentence from a question to a statement.
2. Terence, *Adelphoi* 769.
3. I have followed here and in Licentius' poem the reading "*crastina*" in place of "*pristina*."

Keep me from following your footsteps at a careful pace.

This is all I need: that you give the command.

What a wretch I am if I do not give the command, if I do not compel and order, if I do not beg and plead. But if your ears are closed to my words, let them be open to your own lips; let them be open to your own poetry. Listen to yourself, you who are most stubborn, most cruel, and most deaf. What good is it to me that you have a tongue of gold and a heart of iron? With what, not poetry, but lamentations, shall I be able to mourn your poems, in which I see the sort of soul, the sort of mind that I may not take and offer to our God? You wait for me to give the command: be good, be quiet, be happy, as any day could dawn for me more pleasantly than that I might enjoy your good mind in the Lord, or do you really not know how I hunger and thirst for you, or do you not admit it by this very poem of yours? Recall the intention with which you wrote these lines. Give yourself to me; now say to me, "This is all you need: that you give the command." Here is my command: Give yourself to me if this is all you need; give yourself to my Lord, who is the Lord of us all, who gave you that fine mind. For what am I but your servant through him and your fellow servant under him?

5. Does he not give the command? Listen to the gospel; it says, *Jesus stood and cried out, "Come to me, all you who labor and are burdened, and I shall refresh you. Take my yoke upon you, and learn from me that I am meek and humble of heart, and you will find rest for your souls. For my yoke is easy, and my burden light* (Mt 11:28-30). If you do not hear these words or if they do not reach your ears, do you, Licentius, expect Augustine to command his fellow servant and not rather to mourn that the Lord commands him in vain? In fact, he does not command, but invites and begs in a sense that he may refresh those who labor. But, of course, to your strong and arrogant neck the yoke of the work is more pleasant than the yoke of Christ. If Christ forces us to labor, see who it is who forces us and the reward by which he forces us. Go to Campania; get to know Paulinus,[4] an outstanding and holy servant of God; learn how he unhesitatingly shrugged off the great pride of this world with a more generous neck to the extent it was more humble in order to make it subject to the yoke of Christ, as he did in fact make it subject. And now, he exults quietly and humbly with Christ in control of his journey. Go, learn the richness of his mind by which he offers sacrifices of praise to him, restoring to him whatever good he has received from him, for fear that he might lose everything if he does not restore it to him from whom he has this.

6. Why are you troubled? Why do you waver? Why do you turn your ear to imagining deadly pleasures and turn it away from us? They lie; they die; they lead to death. They lie, Licentius. "In this way may reason disclose the truth for

---

4. Paulinus, a priest and the future bishop of Nola in Campania, renounced his great wealth and power to live a simple Christian life.

us," as you desire; "in this way may it flow more abundantly than the Eridanus."[5] Only the truth speaks the truth; Christ is the truth.[6] Let us come to him in order that we may not labor. In order that he may refresh us, let us take his yoke upon us, and let us learn from him that he is meek and humble of heart, and we shall find rest for our souls. For his yoke is easy, and his burden is light.[7] The devil is seeking to have you as one of his jewels. If you had found a gold chalice in the earth, you would give it to the Church of God. You have received from God a mind that is spiritually gold, and you serve your passions with it and in it make yourself a toast to Satan! Do not, I beg you; may you at some point realize the sorrowful and pitiful heart with which I wrote this, and may you have pity on me, if you have become worthless in your own eyes.

Licentius' Poem for Augustine, His Teacher[8]

In searching the mysterious journey of the profound Varro,[9] the mind grows dull and flees in fright at the light it faces. Nor is it a surprise; all my desire for reading, after all, collapses, when you do not give a hand, and it fears to rise on its own. For, as soon as love persuaded me to read the puzzling volumes of so great a man and to grasp their sacred meanings in which he presented the harmony of numbers and explained that the world sings to the thundering Jove and sets in motion regular dances, the difficulty of the matter wrapped our heart in varied gloom and introduced a cloud into our mind.

Hence, I frantically ask for figures drawn in the dust and stumble upon other darkness: in short, the causes and the bright paths of the stars, whose obscure location he points out through the clouds. I lay, so hesitating that neither a person relying on the caverns of the dead nor one who keeps us from knowing the hidden places of the sky has met with such a complete collapse.[10]

For the myths of the Greeks report that Proteus, when he refuses to disclose the future to worried questioners, foams like a wild boar, flows like a river, roars like a lion, hisses like a snake, but was finally caught for minor functions usually done with birds. But I, who am tormented excessively by graver worries, seek

---

5. See Licentius' poem.

6. See Jn 5:6 and 14:6.

7. See Mt 11:29-30.

8. The CSEL edition places the poem at the end of the Letter rather than before paragraph 4. See Danuta Schanzer, "'Arcanum Varronis iter': Licentius' Verse Epistle to Augustine," *Revue des études augustiniennes* 37 (1991) 110-143, for an analysis and translation of the poem from which I have benefited greatly. I have not attempted to put Licentius' dactylic hexameters into verse.

9. Probably a reference to M. Terentius Varro Reatinus (116-27 B.C.), though possibly to the poet, M. Terentius Varro Atacinus (82-36 B.C.)

10. The previous sentence is extraordinarily difficult to interpret and is probably corrupt in the Latin.

certain sweet or sweetish nourishment for my soul. Varro's replies remain hidden. What help or nymph should I ask with song of a suppliant? What rivers shall I call upon? Or should I with my voice call upon you, for the ruler of Olympus set you in charge of the fountains to nourish children and ordered hidden streams to burst forth far and wide from the richness of your mind?

Bring help immediately, my teacher; do not abandon my feeble abilities, and begin to turn over with me the sacred soil; for, unless mortal things mislead me, time is slipping by and dragging me toward old age. Our Apollo[11] fills your heart and makes propitious his Father and the Father of the gods, and reveals a good law and a peace won by blood,[12] and by the removal of the veil he discloses every secret. For you had counted perhaps twenty[13] great cycles of the sun, when you were snatched up by fairest reason, richer than kingdoms of the world, sweeter than all nectar; it gave you stability after your wandering and put you in the middle from where you can turn your vision toward all things.

O my good friend, take up the journey of your years, ever finding new heights to the extent that wisdom increases with being loved.[14] Continue on the path that the Son of thundering Jove leads you, smoothing the rough areas into level fields.[15] And when evening has brought your preaching[16] to light-filled dawn and you have blessed the holy fire, remember me. You who apply your thirsting ear to the eternal laws, beat your breast with your hands, prostrate your limbs on the ground, and remember the pains you merited, and forbid wrongdoing. God commands one thing for all, our priest reminds us, and the coming bolts of lightning terrify us.

Oh may tomorrow's[17] dawn bring back for me with her joyous chariot those past days that we spent in the high mountains in the midst of Italy, where we enjoyed with you the freedom of leisure and the spotless laws of good men. The harsh cold would not prevent me with its grey ice, nor would the fierce storms of the Zephyrs and the roar of the north wind keep me from following your footsteps at a careful pace. This is all I need: that you give the command and that blood still flow in my limbs. We will follow you to the Moroe[18] in the heat of summer and to the Danube in winter. Though an unknown Garamantian offers

---

11. That is, Jesus Christ.
12. "*Cruenta*: blood-spattered" is odd if taken, as I have, in reference to the redemption. Shanzer suggests "*incruenta*: without bloodshed," but admits that it does not scan.
13. Shanzer suggests "*trigenta*: thirty" which would be closer to Augustine's age at the Cassiciacum period. But "twenty" would fit with the age at which Augustine read Cicero's *Hortensius* and first fell in love with philosophy. See *Confessions* III, 4, 7-8.
14. See Wis 9:9.
15. See Lk 3:5.
16. I have followed Shanzer and others in reading "*praeconia*" in place of "*praecordia*." I take Licentius to be referring to the Easter vigil.
17. Again I followed Shanzer and others who read "*crastina*" in place of "*pristina*."
18. I have followed the reading by Shanzer and others of "*Meroen*" in place of "*Neuros*."

me hospitality, and the river, Hypanis, fleeing the Exampaean lake, resounds with foam at the Scythian wave of the Callipides, we will even go to the Leuci where Leucia stretches to the risings of the sun and to the deserted peaks of the vast Mount Cassus by which Cassia equals the mountains of Epidaphe. With your encouragement I will seek the place from where I might see Aurora at rest with her chariot unharnessed and the day asleep in the middle of the night. For no labor or fear will frighten me off when God hears the innocent with their sincere prayers.

And now I would give up the chairs of the sons of Romulus, peaks empty of righteousness,[19] houses filled with revelry, and vain uproars, and I would at once wholly come to your heart, if a mind bent on marriage did not hold me back as I go. Believe me, O learned friend, about my woes and true sorrow because the sails promise no harbors without you, and we wander far through the troubled seas of life, sailors rushing headlong as if in dense fog, whom the fury of the south wind and the blast from the east has struck and whom the whirlwind has deprived of guides who have been swept away. Suddenly, we poor wretches are tossed about in heavy seas. Neither the deck nor the prow nor finally the sails can withstand the storms, and the whole idea of controlling the helm lies there, over-whelmed. In that way the wind drives me, and the turmoil of desire tosses me into the deadly sea, and land is not near.[20]

But when I ponder your clear words, my teacher, I think that I am more able to believe you. "The situation is tricky; it is deceptive and sets nets to trap our minds." For, having forgotten the past, I offer the present, my dear friend. We have not fallen from your heart, have we?

Alas for me! Where am I to go where I might open my mind to you? Sooner will doves seek safe shelter under the Aegean, and seagulls build nests in trees contrary to their custom; sooner will the hungry lioness feed the cattle that follow her, and the long-starved wolf nourish the tender lambs. Changing the world divided between them, either let the Barcaean plow Taurus, or the Isaurian plow Hyrcania. Sooner will the interrupted day, frightened by Thyestean feasts, disappear in fleeting dawn; sooner will rain produce the Nile; sooner will does wander through the skies;[21] sooner will the mountains sing and the rivers applaud than your gifts, my teacher, will be forgotten and rejected by me. Love prevents this and maintains the bond of our shared honesty.

Here, here let the beauty of friendship reign with the enemy put to flight. For we do not join our minds in agreement on account of either fragile riches or gold that causes rebellion. Nor has the favor of the crowd joined us which, when it

---

19. I have followed the reading by Shanzer and others of "*recti*" in place of "*Remi*."
20. I follow Shanzer and others in reading "*adsunt*" in place of "*absunt*."
21. Shanzer accepts the reading of "*aequora*" instead of "*aethera*." I have retained the latter because it echoes Virgil, *Eclogues* I, 59: "*ante leves pascentur in aethere cervi.*"

collapses, separates those who were previously lofty, but the labor that reads interior ideas divulged in books and discovered by your mind and a noble teaching you presented and answers to good questions.

And though my Calliope may shrink from your loftiness at close quarters and hide her face as she deals with useless things, this bond of the mind, nonetheless, and faithful ties not even he would break, nor would he diminish in any way our strength, he who broke through the Alps guarded by mountainous cliffs and besieged Italian cities with their walls.[22]

Flow on, you waters sprung from swollen streams, to separate either the Ripheans from the Arimphaeans or the towns of the Caspian from the Cimmerian homes, and let regions that the sea of Azov and the Hellespont touch set afar the boundary between Europe and Asia. Does not Dodona as she tires cattle on both slopes cut off the Molopes from the boundary of Talarus and related Arabs?[23] Nor did the friendly pact of peace last between the Sidonians and the sacrilegious Phrygians, although for a time all had in common the privileges of guests. Why, then, shall I sing of the discord and fighting of brothers? Why shall I sing of the good beatings of parents, of the furies of mothers, and of proud children? Even in the world above there is a peaceful discord, and there are as many rites as laws given by opinion. One love binds us. Not even if Boreas should give me a hundred voices, and if a tongue rigid with steel should emit as many breaths through a hundred mouths, could we recall the things that, once united by the nature of their old places, glory has separated and you removed from the round world.[24]

But besides the fact that we come from one city, that one house raised us, that we are dipped in one blood of the world, the Christian faith unites us, and as for the facts that an immense journey separates us and that the shore of the sea spread out between us holds us apart—love scorns both of these, for it overlooks the joys the eyes bring us and ever enjoys an absent friend because it depends upon a deep heart and searches for nourishment for its inner fiber.

Meanwhile, whatever future writings shall come forth with the salutary conversation of good men and as equals in sweetness to those earlier ones, which you pondered and have poured forth into the light as honey like nectar that was conceived deep in your heart, they will make you present to me if you are good to me and hand on to me the book in which music resides after having been understood.[25] For I am wholly ablaze for those. Grant this; in this way may reason disclose the truth for us; in this way may it flow more abundantly than the Eridanus, and may the contagions of the world by no means fly about the fields of our farmer.

---

22. Licentius refers to Hannibal.
23. Shanzer suggests that there is a lacuna in the text.
24. Along with Shanzer I find the last clause baffling.
25. I have followed the conjecture by Shanzer and others of *"intellecta"* in place of *"in te lenta."*

Letter 27

In 396 Augustine replied to Paulinus, first expressing his love for him and his desire to see him (paragraphs 1 to 3). Then he commends to Paulinus Romanian, his friend and wealthy patron, Alypius, his friend from boyhood, who is now the bishop of Thagaste, and finally, Licentius, the son of Romanian, about whose welfare Augustine is deeply concerned. (paragraphs 4 to 6).

To Paulinus, my truly holy and venerable lord and my brother worthy to be celebrated in Christ with the highest praise, Augustine sends greetings in the Lord.

1. O my good man and good brother, you were hidden from my soul, and I tell it that it should tolerate the fact that you are still hidden from my eyes, but it hardly listens to me; in fact, it does not listen to me. But should it tolerate this? Why does the longing for you torture me interiorly within my very soul? For, if I were suffering bodily pains and if they did not disturb the tranquility of my mind, I would be said to tolerate them rightly. But when I do not calmly bear the fact that I do not see you, it is intolerable to call that tolerance. But since you are the sort of person you are, it would perhaps be more intolerable that I tolerate being without you. It is good, then, that I cannot calmly bear that which, if I were bearing it calmly, I myself ought not to be calmly borne with. What has happened to me is strange, but true. I am in pain because I do not see you, and my pain itself consoles me. For I do not like the courage by which one patiently bears the absence of good persons, like yourself. For we, of course, also long for the Jerusalem to come, and we long for it more impatiently to the extent that we more patiently put up with all things for its sake. Who, then, can refrain from joy when he sees you in order that he may be able not to feel pain when he does not see you? Hence, I can do neither one, and since, if I could, I could do so only inhumanly, I am delighted at my inability, and there is some consolation in the fact that I am delighted. My pain consoles me, not because it has subsided, but because I considered it. Do not, I beg you, reprehend me because of the holier earnest sincerity you possess, and do not say that I am not rightly pained over my still not knowing you since you have revealed yourself, that is, your interior self, for me to see. What then? If I had learned either anywhere or in your earthly city of you as my brother and friend —and a man so great and so good in the Lord—do you think that I would feel no pain if I were not allowed to come to know your home? How, then, should I not feel pain that I do not as yet know your face, that is, the home of your soul, as I know my own face?

85

2. For I read your letter flowing with milk and honey.[1] It reveals the simplicity of your heart with which you seek the Lord, as you think well of him,[2] and it offers him glory and honor.[3] The brothers have read it, and they rejoice tirelessly and ineffably over your good qualities, which are rich and excellent gifts of God. All who have read it seize upon it, because they are seized by it when they read it. I cannot express how sweet is the scent of Christ[4] and how it radiates from it. How that letter rouses us to seek you when it presents you to our sight! For it makes you both visible and desirable. After all, the more it in some sense reveals your presence, the less does it allow us to endure your absence. All of us love you in it and long to be loved by you. God is praised and blessed by whose grace you are such a person. In it Christ is awakened in order that he might graciously calm the winds and the seas[5] for you as you move toward his solid ground. In it the readers see your wife, not introducing her husband to a life of softness, but bringing strength back into the heart of her husband. She has been returned and restored to oneness with you and is united to you with spiritual embraces, which are stronger to the degree they are more chaste.[6] In you who are one with her we greet her with all the reverence due to Your Holiness. In your letter the cedars of Lebanon,[7] which were brought down and then raised up to fashion the ark with a framework of love, cut the waves of this world without corruption. In it glory is held in scorn in order to be won, and the world is abandoned in order to be gained. In it the little children or even the tiny babes of Babylon are dashed against the rock,[8] that is, vices coming from confusion and worldly pride.

3. Your letter offers these and similar very pleasing and very holy vistas to your readers; that letter is a letter of faith unfeigned, a letter of good hope, a letter of pure love. How it creates a thirst for you and a longing and fainting of the soul in the courts of the Lord![9] What a most holy love it breathes forth! With what richness of a sincere heart it boils over! What thanks it gives to God! What favors it obtains! Is it more soothing or more ardent, more filled with light or more fruitful? Why, after all, is it that it so calms us, so inflames us, so drenches us with rain, and brings us such fair weather? Why is it, I ask you, or what shall I give you to repay you for it, if not that I am wholly yours in him to whom you wholly belong? If that is not enough, I certainly do not have anything more. But you have made me think that it is enough. For you were so good as to honor me in that letter with such great praises that I am proven guilty of not having believed

---

1. See Ex 3:8.
2. See Wis 1:1.
3. See Ps 29:2.
4. See 2 Cor 2:15.
5. See Mt 8:26.
6. Paulinus and Therasia lived together in a marriage without sexual relations.
7. See 1 Kgs 5:6.9.
8. See Ps 137:8-9.
9. See Ps 83:3.

you, if I think it not enough when I give myself to you. I am indeed ashamed to believe that I have so much goodness, but I am more reluctant not to believe you. Here is what I shall do. I shall not believe that I am as good as you think because I do not recognize such goodness, and I shall believe that you loved me because I feel and clearly see that. In that way I shall be neither rash with regard to myself nor ungrateful toward you. And when I offer myself wholly to you, it is not too little, for I offer one whom you love intensely. And if I do not offer you someone as good as you think I am, I do, nonetheless, offer you someone for whom you may pray that I may merit to be so good. I, after all, now beg that you do this more for fear that you may wish that less be added to what I am, because you suppose that I already am what I am not.

4. May I present a very dear friend of mine, and a very close friend of mine from the beginning of my boyhood, who carries this letter to Your Excellency and most eminent Charity. His name is found in my book on religion,[10] which Your Holiness has read with great pleasure, as you indicate by your letter. He has, after all, also become someone more pleasing to you by reason of the commendation of the great man who sent him to you. I would not want you to believe this man, who is so close a friend of mine, about what he may perhaps say in praise of me. For I have also noticed that he is often misguided in his judgment, not out of a desire to lie, but out of his propensity to love, and he thinks that I have already received certain gifts that I long to receive from the Lord with the mouth of my heart wide open. And if he does this to my face, who would not guess at the extent to which he happily proclaims about me in my absence things that are better rather than true. He will, however, furnish a supply of our books for the study of Your Reverence. For I know of nothing that I have written, either for those outside the Church of God or for the brothers, that he does not have. But when you read them, my holy Paulinus, do not let those things that the truth speaks through our weakness hold you so rapt that you are less careful to notice what I myself say. Otherwise, in eagerly drinking in the good and correct things that were given to me as his minister, you may not pray for the sins and mistakes that I myself make. For in these points that you rightly find displeasing, if you pay attention, you see me myself, but in those points in my books that you rightly find pleasing through the gift of the Spirit that you have received, you should love and praise him, with whom there is the fountain of life and in whose light we shall see the light,[11] not in an enigma, but face to face, though now we see it in an enigma.[12] In these things, then, that I have belched forth from the old leaven, when I recognize them as I read, I condemn myself with sorrow, but in those

---

10. Augustine dedicated to Romanian his book, *True Religion*, by which he tried to win Romanian back from the Manicheism to which he had converted him.
11. See Ps 36:10.
12. See 1 Cor 13:12.

things that by the gift of God I spoke from the unleavened bread of sincerity and truth,[13] I rejoice with trembling. For what do we have that we have not received?[14] But a person is, after all, better who is rich with greater and more gifts of God than with smaller and fewer ones. Who would deny this? But it is again better to thank God for a small gift of his than to want to be thanked oneself for a great one. Pray for me, my brother, that I may always confess this from the heart and that my heart may not be out of harmony with my tongue. Pray, I beg, that I may call upon the Lord, not wanting to be praised, but praising him, and I shall be saved from my enemies.[15]

5. There is another reason why you should love this brother of mine more, for he is a relative of the venerable and blessed bishop, Alypius,[16] whom you embrace with your whole heart and rightly do so. For whoever thinks well of that man thinks of the great mercy of God and of the marvelous gifts of God. And so, after he had read your request by which you indicated that you desire that he should write his life's story for you, he both wanted to do it because of his good will toward you and did not want to because of his modesty. When I saw him wavering between his love and his modesty, I took the burden from him onto my own shoulders. For he also ordered me to do this by letter. If, then, the Lord gives his help, I shall quickly introduce the whole of Alypius into your heart. For I was especially afraid that he would be afraid to reveal everything that the Lord bestowed upon him for fear that someone with less understanding—for you would not be the only reader—might think that he did not praise God's gifts to human beings, but himself. Then you, who know how to read these pages, would be cheated of the knowledge of your brother which was owed to you on account of his watching out for the weakness of others. I would have done that, and you would now be reading of him, if my brother, Romanian, had not suddenly decided on a departure we had not foreseen. I commend him to your heart and to your tongue that you may offer yourself to him in as friendly a manner as if you were not now making his acquaintance, but came to know him before with me. For, if he does not hesitate to open himself to your heart, he will be healed by your tongue either in every respect or to a large extent. I, after all, want him to be more frequently reproved by the words of those who love a friend in a non-worldly manner.

6. But as for Romanian's son, our son too, whose name you will also find in some of our books,[17] I had decided, even if he did not come to the presence of Your Charity, to entrust him by letter to your hands to be consoled, exhorted, and instructed, not so much by the sound of your voice as by the example of your

13. See 1 Cor 5:8.
14. See 1 Cor 4:7.
15. See Ps 18:4.
16. Alypius was the bishop of Thagaste.
17. Romanian's son, Licentius, appears in *Answer to the Skeptics*, *The Happy Life*, and *Order*.

strength. I, of course, ardently desire that, while his age is still a field green with youth, he may change its weeds into grain and believe those who have experience with regard to what he desires to experience with danger to himself. Now, then, from his poem and from the letter that I sent to him, you understand, given your most benevolent and gentle wisdom, why I sorrow over him, what I fear, and what I desire. Nor do I give up hope that the Lord will be there to help in order that I may be set free by you, his minister, from such fevers of worry. Since you intend to read many of our writings, I will surely find your love more pleasing to me if, because of those things that you have found displeasing, you as a righteous man correct me with mercy[18] and reprehend me. For you are not the sort of man with whose oil I should fear to have my head anointed. The brothers, not only those who live with us and those who, wherever they live, likewise serve God, but almost all those who are happy to know us in Christ, greet, reverence, and long for Your Brotherhood, Your Beatitude, and Your Humanity. I do not dare to ask it, but if you have time free from your ecclesiastical duties, you will see what all of Africa along with me is thirsting for.

---

18. See Ps 141:5.

The Correspondence between Augustine and Jerome

This volume contains the beginning of the correspondence between Augustine of Hippo and Jerome of Bethlehem, six letters to Jerome and five from him. Letter 28, the first letter from Augustine to Jerome, reached Jerome only many years later after it had circulated in Rome and elsewhere and after Jerome had heard reports of a book that Augustine had written against him. The heart of the controversy centers around the interpretation of Galatians on the part of Jerome who, as Augustine saw it, claimed that Paul told a lie when he wrote that Peter was not living correctly in relation to the gospel, though Augustine also thought that Jerome would do better to translate the Greek scriptures rather than the Hebrew into Latin.[1]

---

1. See Robert J. O'Connell, S.J., "When Saintly Fathers Feuded: The Correspondence between Augustine and Jerome," *Thought* 54 (1979) 344-364, for an informed and readable account of the exchange between the two saints.

Letter 28

Between 394 and 395 Augustine wrote from Hippo to Jerome in Bethlehem this first letter, which reached Jerome only nine years later after it had circulated among others in Rome and elsewhere. As result, Jerome came to hear that Augustine had written a book to attack him long before he saw the actual letter. Subsequent letters between the two saints reveal a spirited and at times angry debate, though by the time of the Pelagian controversy Jerome and Augustine are close friends and collaborators. In the present letter, after praising Jerome whom he has come to know better through the report of Alypius, he commends Brother Profuturus to Jerome (paragraph 1). Augustine urges Jerome to translate the scriptures from the Greek Septuagint rather than from the Hebrew (paragraph 2). He warns Jerome against the view that Paul used a useful or advantageous lie in rebuking Peter in Galatians (paragraph 3) and argues that to admit any sort of lie in the scriptures completely undermines their authority (paragraph 4). Hence, Augustine begs Jerome to avoid appealing to useful lies in interpreting the scriptures (paragraph 5) and sends to Jerome some of his own writings for criticism (paragraph 6).

To my most beloved lord, Jerome, a brother and fellow priest, who should be served and embraced with the most sincere devotion of love, Augustine sends greetings.

1, 1. Never has physical presence made anyone as well known to someone else as your peaceful joy and truly liberal pursuit of your studies in the Lord has made you known to me. Hence, although I desire very much to know you in every respect, there is, nonetheless, a certain aspect of you of which I have less, namely, your physical presence. After brother Alypius,[1] now a most blessed bishop, but then already worthy of the episcopacy, saw you and, returning here, was seen by me, I cannot deny that your physical appearance was to a large extent impressed upon me by his report. And before his return, when he saw you there, I saw you, but with his eyes. For one who knows us would say that we are two, not in mind, but in body, at least in terms of our harmony and most trustworthy friendship, not in merits by which he surpasses me. Since, then, you already love me, first, because of the communion of the Spirit by which we strive for unity, second, because of his words, I am by no means acting impudently, as if I were someone unknown, in commending to you, my brother, Brother Profuturus,[2] whom we hope will truly profit[3] from our efforts and your help, and

---

1. Alypius had traveled to Palestine where he met Jerome; upon his return to Africa he was consecrated bishop of Thagaste.
2. Profuturus did not carry this letter, but was consecrated bishop of Cirta in Numida. For this reason Letter 28 was not delivered to Jerome, but circulated in Rome and elsewhere before Jerome saw it.
3. Augustine puns on Profuturus' name and the verb for profiting.

yet he is perhaps such a good man that he will rather commend me to you than I will commend him to you. I ought perhaps to have written only this far if I wanted to be content with the type of letter one usually writes, but my mind bubbles over to share ideas with you concerning our studies, which we undertake in Christ Jesus, our Lord, who also graciously provides to us in no small amount through your love many benefits and provisions for the journey that he himself has shown us.

2, 2. We, therefore, beg you, and the whole zealous society of the African churches begs you along with us, not to hesitate to devote your careful effort to translating the books of those who have so excellently commented on our scriptures in Greek. For you can bring it about that we too have those fine men, and that one especially, whom you preferably cite in your writings.[4] But I do not want you to labor over translating the canonical holy books into the Latin language, except in the way in which you translated Job so that it may be seen by the use of signs what is the difference between your translation and the Septuagint[5] which has the very weightiest authority. I, however, cannot say how astonished I would be if there were still something found in the Hebrew texts that has escaped so many expert translators of that language. For I leave aside the seventy; concerning the harmony of either their mind or spirit, which is greater than if there were only one man, I do not pass a certain judgment for some side except that I think that they should be given a preeminent authority in this task without any controversy. Those men bother me more who, though they have translated later and have clung tooth and nail, as they say, to the method and rules of Hebrew words and expressions, not only do not agree with one another, but have left many points that need to be dug out and disclosed so much later. For, if they are obscure, we believed that you too can also be mistaken on them. But if they are evident, we do not believe that they could have been mistaken in them. By explaining, therefore, the reasons for this in accord with your love, I beg you to assure me about this.

3, 3. I also read certain writings on the Letters of Paul the apostle, which were said to be yours. When you wanted to explain the Letter to the Galatians from among them, you took up that passage where the apostle Peter is called back from his deadly pretense. There, I admit, the fact that a man as fine as you are or someone else undertook the defense of a lie leaves me in more than a little in pain, until those points that trouble me are refuted, if they can perhaps be refuted. For I regard it as absolutely disastrous to believe that there is a lie in the holy books, that is, that those men who gave us and put into writing that scripture lied

---

4. Augustine means Origen of whom Jerome was quite fond before the crisis a few years later over his thought.
5. The Greek translation of the Hebrew scriptures that was made in the third and second centuries before Christ, supposedly by seventy-two translators who, though working separately, each produced the same translation.

in their books. It is, of course, one question whether good men ought to lie at some time, and it is another question whether a writer of the holy scriptures ought to lie. In fact, it is not another question; it is no question at all! For, if a useful lie has once been admitted into so lofty a peak of authority, no section of those books will remain that will not, as soon as anyone finds it either difficult in terms of conduct or incredible in terms of faith, be attributed by the same most deadly rule to the plan and purpose of a lying author.

4. After all, suppose that the apostle Paul lied when he said, in reproaching Peter, *If, though you are a Jew, you live like a Gentile and not like a Jew, why do you force the Gentiles to live like Jews?* (Gal 2:14); suppose that he thought that Peter acted correctly and both said and wrote that he had not acted correctly in order to mollify, as it were, the minds of those in an uproar. What, then, shall we reply when wicked men arise, forbidding marriage, the very men whom he foretold?[6] They might say that everything that the same apostle said in upholding the law of marriage[7] was a lie he told on account of persons who could have been upset because of the love of their spouses. That is, he did not hold this, but spoke to calm their opposition. There is no need to mention many examples. For lies can be seen as useful even in the praises of God in order that the sluggish might be set afire with love for him, and in that way the authority of holy and pure truth will nowhere be certain in the holy books. Do we not see that the same apostle says with great concern for teaching the truth, *But if Christ has not risen, our preaching is empty, your faith is also empty. We, however, are found to be false witnesses of God, since we have given testimony against God that he raised up Christ whom he has not raised up* (1 Cor 15:14-15)? If anyone says to him, "Why are you horrified at this lie since you have said something that, even if it is false, pertains very much to the praise of God?" Would the apostle not detest the insanity of this man, and would he not, by whatever words and ideas he could, open the inner chambers of his heart to the light, crying out that false praise for God is no less a crime or perhaps even a greater crime than finding fault with the truth about him. Our aim must, therefore, be that a man occupies himself with the knowledge of the scriptures who regards them as so holy and so true that he refuses to find satisfaction in any part of them through useful lies and rather passes over what he does not understand than prefers his own ideas to that truth. For, when he appeals to such lies, he wants us to believe him, and he tries to make us not believe the authorities of the divine scriptures.

5. With all the strength that the Lord has supplied me, I myself would, of course, prove that all those testimonies that have been used to defend the usefulness of a lie must be interpreted in some other way in order that we may teach that the truth of those books is solid in every respect. For, just as testimonies

---

6. See 1 Tm 4:1-3.
7. See 1 Cor 7:10-16.

ought not to be lies, so they ought not to favor a lie. But I leave this point to your intelligence. Once you have given more careful consideration to the passage, you will perhaps see this more readily than I. But your piety will force you to this consideration, for because of it you recognize that the authority of the divine scriptures is crumbling so that each person believes in them what he wants and does not believe what he does not want, once one is convinced that those men from whom we have received them could have told useful lies in their writings. Or are you perhaps going to give us some rules by which we might know where it is necessary to lie and where it is not. If this is possible, please, do not in any way explain it with lying and dubious reasons, and I beg you by the most true humanity of our Lord, do not judge me burdensome and impudent. For, to be brief, it is surely not a great fault by which my error favors the truth, if in your case the truth can correctly favor a lie.

4, 6. I would like to say many other things and discuss Christian studies with your most sincere heart, but no letter suffices for this desire of mine. I do this more fully through the brother whom I am happy to have sent to be exposed to and nourished with your sweet and profitable conversations. And, nonetheless, even he perhaps does not absorb as much as I would like—something I say without offense to him—though I in no sense hold myself superior to him. For I admit that I have more capacity for taking you in, but I see that he is becoming fuller—and in that respect he undoubtedly surpasses me. And after he returns, as I hope he will do successfully with the Lord's help, and after I have become a sharer in his heart that you have filled, he will not fill up my still remaining emptiness and eagerness for your thoughts. Thus it will turn out I will even then have a greater need and he a greater abundance. The same brother, of course, carries with him some of our writings; if you do me the kindness of reading them, please, also apply to them the sincere, but severe judgment of a brother. For I understand the words of scripture, *The righteous man will correct me with mercy and reproach me, but the oil of the sinner will not anoint my head* (Ps 141:5), to mean that one who heals with his reproaches shows more love than a flatterer who anoints the head. I, however, find it very difficult to read as a good judge what I myself have written, for I am either more cautious or more enthusiastic than is correct. I also at times see my defects, but I prefer to hear of these from my betters for fear that, after I have correctly found fault with myself, I do not again go easy on myself and think that I have judged myself meticulously rather than justly.

Letter 29

In 395, Augustine wrote from Hippo to Alypius, bishop of Thagaste, telling him how he preached against the practice of the African churches of celebrating the feast days of the saints with drunken banquets in the churches (paragraphs 1 to 11). Finally, he asks for Alypius' prayers for his efforts against the Circumcellions (paragraph 12).

A letter of a priest of Hippo Regius to Alypius, bishop of Thagaste, concerning the birthday of Leontius, once bishop of Hippo.[1]

1. In the absence of Brother Macarius, I could for the moment write to you nothing certain about problem about which I could not fail to be concerned. It is said that he will return soon, and I will do what can be done with the help of God. With regard to our concern about them, although our fellow citizens, the brothers who were present, could have assured you, the Lord has, nonetheless, offered us a topic worthy of a discussion by letter, by which we console each other. In meriting this we believe that we were helped very much by your concern, which, of course, could not have existed without your prayer for us.

2. And so, we shall not omit telling Your Charity what happened in order that you may thank God along with us over the benefit we have received, since you poured forth prayers along with us for obtaining it. After your departure it was reported to us that people were in an uproar and were saying that they could not tolerate the prohibition of that solemnity. In calling it "joy," they try in vain to hide the term "drunkenness," as was already reported even when you were present. By the hidden providence of almighty God it turned out opportunely for us that on the fourth day of the week this passage in the gospel was to be commented on in sequence, *Do not give what is holy to dogs, and do not cast your pearls before swine* (Mt 7:6). I commented, therefore, on dogs and pigs in such a way that those arguing against the commandments of God with an obstinate barking and devoted to the filth of carnal pleasures were forced to be ashamed, and my sermon came to such a conclusion that they saw how wicked it is to do something in the name of religion within the walls of the church that, if they continued to do it in their homes, it would be necessary to exclude them from what is holy and from the pearls in the church.

3. But though these ideas were favorably accepted, it did not, nonetheless, do enough for so great a problem since few people had come. When, however, this sermon was discussed outside by those who were present in accord with the

---

1. The priest is, of course, Augustine. The heading was added by the Maurist editors in place of the missing salutation; the birthday of Leontius was the date of his death.

ability and desire of each person, it met with many who spoke against it. But after the day of Lent had dawned and a large crowd came for the hour of preaching, that passage in the gospel was read in which, after driving out the sellers of animals from the temple and after overturning the tables of the money changers, the Lord said that the house of his Father had become a den of thieves instead of a house of prayer.[2] After having made them attentive by raising the question of drunkenness, I myself also read out that passage, and I added an argument to show with how much more anger and forcefulness our Lord would have expelled from the temple drunken banquets, which are shameful everywhere, since he expelled from there licit commerce. For they were selling things necessary for the sacrifices, which were licit at that time. I asked them whom they thought a den of thieves resembled more, those selling necessities or those drinking immoderately.

4. And since I had the readings prepared to support this, I added next that in that temple, in which the body and blood of the Lord was not yet offered, the people of the Jews, who were at that time still living according to the flesh, not only never celebrated drunken banquets, but not even sober ones. I said that in their history they were never found publicly drunk in the name of religion, except when they celebrated a feast after fashioning an idol.[3] After I said this, I also took up the book and read out the whole passage. I also added with as much sorrow as I could that, in order to distinguish the Christian people from the hardheartedness of the Jews, the apostle said that his Letter was written *not on tablets of stone, but on the tablets of hearts of flesh* (2 Cor 3:3). Since Moses, the servant of God, smashed the two tablets of stone on account of those leaders,[4] how could we fail to smash the hearts of these men of the new testament who want annually to display in celebrating the days of the saints the same behavior that the people of the old testament displayed once and for an idol.

5. Then, after the volume of Exodus was returned, having emphasized the crime of drunkenness as much as the time allowed, I took up the apostle Paul and showed the sins among which it was listed. I read the passage, *If any brother is called a fornicator or worshiper of idols or greedy or slanderous or a drunk or a thief, do not even eat with such a person* (1 Cor 5:11), warning them with groans of the great danger faced when one banquets with those who become drunk even in their homes. I also read what follows shortly after, *Make no mistake. Neither fornicators, nor idoltators, nor adulterers, nor the effeminate, nor sodomites, nor thieves, nor the greedy, nor the drunken, nor slanderers, nor robbers will possess the kingdom of God. And you were such, but you have been washed; you have been made righteous in the name of the Lord Jesus Christ and in the Spirit*

2. See Mt 21:12-13.
3. See Ex 32:6.
4. See Ex 32:19.

of our God (1 Cor 6:9-11). After this was read, I said that they should consider how believers could have heard, *But you have been washed*, who still tolerate in their heart, that is, in the interior temple of God, such filth of concupiscence, against which the kingdom of the heavens is closed. From there we came to this passage, *When, therefore, you gather together, it is not in order to celebrate the Lord's supper, for, when eating, each of you takes his own supper. And one goes hungry, while another is drunk. Do you not have homes for eating and drinking? Do you take no account of the Church of God?* (1 Cor 11:20-22). After this was read, I stressed with greater care that no dinners, not even decent and sober ones, ought to be held in church, since the apostle did not say, "Do you not have homes for becoming drunk?" as if it were only forbidden to become drunk in church. Rather, he said, *For eating and drinking*, which can be done decently, but outside of church, by those who have homes where they can be refreshed by needed nourishment. And yet, we have come to these difficulties of corrupt times and relaxed morals so that we do not now desire decent dinners, but the reign of drunkenness within our homes.

6. I also mentioned the passage of the gospel on which I commented yesterday where it was said of the false prophets, *From their fruits you will know them* (Mt 7:16). Then I recalled to mind that "fruits" in that passage meant nothing but "works," and I then asked among which fruits drunkenness was mentioned. And I read out the passage from Galatians, *But the works of the flesh are evident; they are fornication, impurity, licentiousness, idolatry, sorcery, hostility, strife, jealousy, anger, dissensions, divisions, hatred, drunkenness, orgies, and the like. I warn you regarding them, as I warned you before, that those who do such things will not inherit the kingdom of God* (Gal 5:19-21). After these words I asked how we Christians, whom the Lord commanded to be recognized from their fruits, were to be recognized from the fruit of drunkenness. I also added to the reading what follows, *But the fruits of the Spirit are love, joy, peace, patience, kindness, goodness, faithfulness, gentleness, and continence* (Gal 5:22-23). And I made them consider how shameful and deplorable it was that they wanted not only to live privately with those fruits of the flesh, but also to bring honor to the Church with them and, if they were given the power, to fill the whole area of so large a basilica with crowds of banqueting drunks, while they refuse to bring gifts to God from the spiritual fruits, to which they are invited by the authority of the holy scriptures and by our groans, and to celebrate the feasts of the saints especially by them.

7. After I did this, I returned the book, and having enjoined prayer as much as I could and to the extent that the very danger of the situation forced me and the Lord graciously provided strength, I set before their eyes the common danger both of those who were entrusted to us and of those of us who were going to have to give an account concerning them to the chief pastor. I begged them by his humility, his extraordinary mistreatment, the slaps, the spit on the face, the

blows, his crown of thorns, his cross and blood that, if they were not[5] somewhat displeased with themselves, they would at least take pity on us and think of the inexpressible love of the venerable, old Valerius[6] toward me. For he did not hesitate to lay upon my shoulders the very dangerous burden of commenting on the words of the truth on their account, and he often said to them that his prayers were answered when we arrived. And he rejoiced that we had come to him, not, of course, for our common death or for the sight of their death, but for the common struggle for eternal life. Finally, I also said that I was certain and trusted in him who cannot lie and who promised through the mouth of his prophet concerning our Lord Jesus Christ, *If his children abandon my law and do not walk in my commandments, if they profane my ordinances, I shall visit their crimes with the rod and their sins with scourges, but I shall not take away my mercy* (Ps 89:31-34). I said, therefore, that I trusted in him that, if they scorned all these words that were read and spoken to them, he would visit them with the rod and scourge, but would not allow them to be condemned along with this world. In this appeal I acted as our protector and ruler gave me the energy and power for the magnitude of the problem and the danger. I did not evoke their tears with my tears, but when I said such things, I admit, I was caught up in their weeping and could not hold back my own. And when we had both equally wept, I brought my sermon to an end with the fullest hope of their correction.

8. On the following day, when the day had dawned for which the mouths and bellies were accustomed to prepare themselves, it is reported to me that some of them, even of those who were present at the sermon, had not yet stopped their complaining and that the force of a very bad habit had such power over them that they spoke with its voice alone and said, "Why now? After all, it is not the case that those who earlier did not forbid this were Christians." When I heard this, I absolutely did not know what mightier devices I might prepare for influencing them; I was, nonetheless, planning, if they thought that they should persist, to read that passage from the prophet Ezekiel, *The lookout is acquitted if he reported the danger, even if those to whom it is reported refuse to beware* (Ez 33:9),[7] to shake the dust from my clothes, and to leave.[8] But then the Lord showed that he does not abandon us and showed how he exhorts us to place our trust in him. For an hour before we climbed into the pulpit, those same persons approached me who I had heard had complained about the attack on their long-standing custom. After receiving them politely, I brought them by a few words to a sound opinion, and when the time came for the sermon, I omitted the reading which I had prepared because it did not now seem necessary, and I said a

---

5. I have conjectured the negative.
6. Valerius was bishop of Hippo; he had consecrated Augustine as his coadjutor bishop in 395.
7. The Latin text which Augustine used differs from the Vulgate.
8. See Mt 10:14.

few things about this question, namely, that we could say nothing more brief or more true in answer to those who say, "Why now?" than, "Now at least."

9. Nonetheless, for fear that the ignorant crowd might think that we treated with a certain contempt those who before us either permitted or did not dare to forbid such obvious crimes, I explained to them what caused these practices to arise in the Church, that is, once peace was established after the persecutions, which were so many and so intense, the crowds of pagans who wanted to become Christians were held back by the fact that they were accustomed to spend feast days with their idols in an abundance of feasting and drinking. And since they could not easily give up these most harmful and yet such long-standing pleasures, our predecessors decided to tolerate an aspect of their weakness for the time being and to allow them to celebrate other feast days, after those that they gave up, in honor of the martyrs, at least without a similar sacrilege, though with similar unrestraint. For, once they were gathered together in the name of Christ and subject to the yoke of such great authority, they would receive salutary commandments about sobriety, which they would not be able to oppose on account of their respect and reverence for the source of the commandments. Hence, it is now time, I concluded, that those who do not dare to deny that they are Christians should begin to live according to the will of Christ in order that, now that they are Christians, they may reject those practices that were permitted in order that they might become Christians.

10. Then I exhorted them that we should want to be imitators of the Church across the sea in which these practices were in part never accepted and in part corrected by good pastors with the obedience of the people. And because examples of daily drunkenness in the basilica of the blessed apostle Peter were brought forth, I first said that we had heard that this had often been forbidden, but that the place was distant from the residence of the bishop and in so large a city there is a great multitude of people who live according to the flesh, especially since travelers, when they first arrive there, retain that custom with more insistence, the more ignorant they are. Hence, so great a plague could not as yet be brought under control and quieted down. If, nonetheless, we wanted to honor the apostle Peter, we ought to heed his commandments and to look with more devotion at his Letter, in which his will is seen, rather than at his basilica, in which it is not seen. And having immediately taken up the book, I read out where it says, *For, since Christ suffered for us in the flesh, arm yourselves also with the same thought, for he who has suffered in the flesh has renounced the flesh, so that he now lives for the remaining time in the flesh, not by the desires of human beings, but by the will of God. For the past time is enough for your having acted in accord with the will of human beings, living in lusts, desires, drunkenness, orgies, and the wicked worship of idols* (1 Pt 4:1-3). After I did that, I saw that all were with singleness of heart beginning to have a good will and had rejected their bad habit, and I urged them to be present in the afternoon for the readings

and psalms. For I thought that the day should be celebrated more purely and more sincerely in that way. And I said that surely from the crowd of those gathering one could easily see who followed his mind and who his belly. In that way, after all the readings, the sermon came to an end.

11. In the afternoon a larger crowd was present than in the morning, and up to the hour at which we came out with the bishop, readings alternated with psalms. After we came out, two psalms were read. Then, though I was reluctant, since I now wanted so perilous a day to be over with, old Valerius forced me under an order to say something to them. I gave a short sermon in which I thanked God. And since we heard that the customary banquets were being celebrated by the heretics in their basilica, for they were still drinking at the very time when we were doing this, I said that the beauty of the day stands out in comparison with the night and that the color white is more pleasing by reason of its nearness to black. So too, our gathering with its spiritual celebration would perhaps have been less pleasing if the carnal binge did not stand in contrast with it, and I exhorted them constantly to desire such feasts as ours if they had tasted how sweet the Lord is. I warned that those who pursue as primary what will at some point perish must be afraid, since each of us becomes a companion of what he loves, and the apostle mocked such people when he said, *Their god is their belly* (Phil 3:19), for the same apostle said in another passage, *Food is for the belly, and the belly for food, but God will destroy both the one and the other* (1 Cor 6:13). Therefore, we must follow what is not destroyed, but what is kept most distant from the longing of the flesh by the sanctification of the Spirit. And after I had said what the Lord was so good as to suggest along those lines for the time, vespers, which are daily celebrated, were completed, and as we left with the bishop, the brothers sang a hymn, with no small crowd of both men and women remaining and singing until the darkness fell.

12. I summarized for you as briefly as I could what you undoubtedly wanted to hear. Pray that God may deign by our efforts to turn aside all scandals and all offenses. To a large extent, of course, we are at rest along with you in the liveliness of fervor because we so often receive reports of the gifts of the spiritual church of Thagaste. The ship with the brothers has not yet come. At Hasna where our brother, Argentius, is priest, the Circumcellions invaded the basilica and smashed our altar. The case is now being heard; we ask you to pray much that it may be settled peacefully and as is proper for the Catholic Church in order to subdue the tongues of the restless heretics. We sent a letter to Asiarcha. My most blessed brothers, may you persevere in the Lord, while keeping us in mind. Amen.

Letter 30

Late in 394 Paulinus and Therasia write from Nola a second letter to Augustine, since they did not receive a reply to their previous letter. They send the second letter in the hands of Romanus and Agilus and ask Augustine to send a reply through them (paragraphs 1 to 3).

Paulinus and Therasia,[1] sinners, send greetings to Augustine, their lord and venerable brother with whom they are one in heart.

1. I have known you in your holy and pious labors, my brother in Christ and my lord, with whom I am one in heart, though you did not know me. I have seen you, though you were absent. Hence, I long ago embraced you with my whole mind and also hastened to approach you by letter in a friendly and brotherly conversation. And I believe that my words had been brought to you by the gracious help of the Lord. But since the servant, whom we had sent to greet you and others equally dear to God before winter, has still not appeared, we were unable further to put off our duty and control our most ardent desire for word from you. We have, therefore, written a second time, if our earlier letter has been so fortunate as to reach you. Or we write for the first time, if it has not had the good fortune of coming into your hands.

2. But you, my spiritual brother, who judge all things,[2] do not estimate our love for you only by our duty or by the date of our letters. For the Lord is my witness who, though one and the same, produces his love everywhere in those who are his own, that already from the moment when through the gift of the venerable bishops, Aurelius and Alypius,[3] we have come to know you through your works against the Manichees,[4] a love for you was implanted in us to so that it does not seem that we are beginning a new friendship with you, but resuming an old one, as it were. Finally, even if we now write without experience of your words, we do not, nonetheless, write as if we were without experience of you, and we, as it were, recognize you in turn in the spirit through the interior man. Nor is it surprising if we are present to one another, though we are absent, and that we know one another, though we are unknown, since we are members of one body,[5] have one head, are filled with one grace, live by one bread, walk one way, and dwell in the same house. Finally, in everything that we are, with all the hope

---

1. Paulinus was the future bishop of Nola in Italy; Therasia was his wife.
2. See 1 Cor 2:15.
3. Aurelius was bishop of Carthage, and Alypius bishop of Thagaste.
4. See Letter 24, note 8, for the books in question.
5. See Rom 12:4, 1 Cor 12:12, 10:17, Gal 6:10.

and faith by which we at present are supported and strive for the future, we are one both in the Spirit and in the body of the Lord for fear that we should be nothing if we fall away from the One.

3. How small a part of us it is that our bodily absence denies each other! It is, of course, only this fruit by which those eyes are fed that look for temporal rewards. And yet, the grace of bodily presence ought not to be called temporal in spiritual persons to whom the resurrection will also bestow eternity on their bodies, as we dare to presume because of the power of Christ and the goodness of God the Father, though we are unworthy. Hence, I wish that the grace of God would also grant us this gift through our Lord Jesus Christ that we might see your face even in the flesh! It would not only grant a great joy to our desires, but it would also increase the light for our minds and enrich our neediness from your abundance. And this is something you can grant to us even while we are absent, especially on this occasion on which our sons, Romanus and Agilus,[6] are returning in the name of the Lord, after having completed their work of charity. They are one in heart with us and most dear to us in the Lord, and we commend them to you like our other selves. We ask that they may specially enjoy the love of Your Charity because of their work. For you know what lofty rewards the Most High promises to a brother who helps a brother.[7] If you should wish through them to recompense me with some gift of the grace that has been given to you, you will do so safely. For they are, I would have you believe, one heart and one soul with us in the Lord.[8] As the grace of God is with you, so may it remain for eternity, my brother in Christ the Lord, with whom I am one in heart and who are venerable, most beloved, and longed for. Greet for us all the saints in Christ, for there is no doubt that such men cling to you. Commend us to all the saints in order that they may deign to pray for us along with you.

---

6. The two men carried Letter 30 to Augustine.

7. See Prv 18:19.

8. See Acts 4:32.

Letter 31

In late 396 or 397 Augustine replied from Hippo to Paulinus and Therasia in Nola. Augustine thanks them for their second letter and tells them of his pleasure over meeting Romanus and Agilus, the bearers of their letter (paragraphs 1 to 2). He complains about their somewhat hasty departure (paragraph 3) and explains that his having been consecrated coadjutor to Valerius prevents his traveling to Nola (paragraph 4). He invites Paulinus to visit him in Africa (paragraph 5) and praises his poverty and humility (paragraph 6). Augustine commends to Paulinus a troubled young man and sends him a copy of his three books entitled: *Free Will* (paragraph 7). Augustine asks Paulinus for a copy of his *Against the Pagans* (paragraph 8) and sends on the greetings of his own bishop, Valerius, and of Severus, now bishop of Milevis (paragraph 9).

To Paulinus and Therasia, his most beloved and most sincere lord and lady, his brother and sister, who are truly blessed and outstanding in the most abundant grace of God, Augustine sends greetings in the Lord.

1. Though I wanted my letter by which I replied to your earlier letter—if it is in any way possible for me to reply to your letter—to come into the hands of Your Charity as quickly as possible in order that, though absent in one sense, I might be able quickly to be with you, my slowness bestowed on me the benefit of your second letter.[1] The Lord is good who often does not give what we want in order to give what we should have preferred. For it is one thing that you were going to write after receiving my letter; it is another thing that you have written without receiving mine. Though we read your letter with great joy, this joy would certainly have been lacking to us if our letter had quickly found its way to Your Holiness, as we desired and especially wanted. But now to have in hand this present letter and to hope for that other one delights me with a grander joy. In that way our negligence cannot be blamed, and the more generous kindness of the Lord has brought about what he judged more conducive to our desire.

2. We have welcomed with great joy in the Lord the holy brothers, Romanus and Agilus,[2] like another letter of yours, a letter that hears my words and replies and is like the sweetest part of your presence, but which makes us desire more avidly to see you. Why or when or how could you offer or could we demand that you teach us about yourselves as much as we have learned from their lips? There was also present—something which could be present on no page—so great a joy in them as they told us of you that from their very faces and eyes as they spoke we read with an inexpressible joy you yourselves, who were written in their hearts.

---

1. Letter 30 from Paulinus and Therasia arrived before Augustine answered Letter 25 from them.
2. Romanus and Agilus carried Letter 30 to Augustine.

There was also this greater benefit. No page—no matter how much good the written page contains—itself derives any profit although it is opened up for the profit of others. But we read this letter of yours, namely, the soul of the brothers, in conversation with them so that their soul appeared more blessed in our eyes to the extent that it had been more fully written by you. Therefore, I copied it into our hearts in order to imitate the same blessedness by most eagerly asking everything about you.

3. For this reason we were reluctant to allow them to leave so quickly, though they were returning to you. See, after all, I beg you, the loves between which we were torn. They should, of course, have been sent off more rapidly to the extent that they desired to obey you more urgently. But to the extent that they wanted this more, they made you more present to us. By that desire they, of course, showed how dear your heart was to them. We, therefore, wanted less to send them off to the extent that they more justly insisted on being sent off. Oh, what an intolerable situation, were it not that we would not be separated from one another by this departure, were it not that "we are members of one body, have one head, are filled with one grace, live by one bread, walk one way, and dwell in the same house."[3] After all, why should we not use the same words? For you recognize, I believe, that these are taken from your letter. But why are these your words rather than mine? For, just as they are true, so they come to us from our union with the same head. And if they had something personal that was given to you, I loved them much more so that they occupied the road of my heart and did not allow words to pass from my heart to my tongue until your words came first, more pure to the extent that they were yours. My holy brother and sister, whom God loves, members with us of one body, who would doubt that we are kept alive by one Spirit except someone who does not experience the love by which we are bound to one another?

4. I would, nonetheless, like to know whether you endure this bodily absence more patiently and more easily than we do. If that is the case, I admit, I am not fond of this courage of yours, unless it is perhaps because of the fact that I am the sort of person whom you should long for less than we should long for you. Surely if I had the patience to endure your absence, I would be displeased with it. For I would be lazy about getting to see you. But what is more absurd than to become lazier because of courage? But Your Charity ought to consider the care for the Church by which I am bound because my most blessed father, Valerius,[4] who greets you heartily along with us and longs for you much, as you will hear from the brothers, did not allow me to be his priest without imposing upon me the greater burden of being his coadjutor in the episcopacy. Because of his great love and because of the great desire of the people I believed that the Lord willed

---

3. Letter 30, 2.
4. Valerius was bishop of Hippo, and Augustine was his coadjutor.

this, and I greatly feared to excuse myself since some precedents closed off every excuse I had. But though the yoke of Christ is by itself gentle and the burden light,[5] if this chain bites into me in some respect and this load weighs upon me on account of my own recalcitrance and weakness, the consolation of your presence would in a way I cannot express render it somewhat more endurable and bearable for me. I hear, however, that you live less encumbered by such cares and freer from them.[6] Hence, it is not impudent for me to ask and request and demand that you be so good as to come to Africa, which labors with a greater thirst for such persons than from its well-known dryness.

5. God knows that we also long for your bodily presence in these lands, not only on account of my desire, nor only on account of those who have learned of your choice of a way of life either from us or from rumors spreading the word everywhere, but also on account of the others who in part do not hear of it and in part do not believe what they have heard, but are able to love what they have come to discover.[7] For, though you are living your life with sincerity and mercy, *let your works*, nonetheless, *shine forth* also in the sight of the human beings of these lands *that they may see your good deeds and glorify your Father who is in heaven* (Mt 5:16). Those fishermen abandoned their boats and nets at the Lord's call, and they also rejoiced in remembering that they abandoned everything and followed the Lord.[8] He truly gives up everything who gives up not only as much as he was able to have, but also as much as he wanted to have. God's eyes are witnesses of one's desires, while human eyes are witnesses of one's possessions. Somehow or other, when superfluous and earthly goods are loved, they have a tighter hold on us when we have acquired them than when we desired them. For why did that man who was asking the Lord's advice for obtaining eternal life depart in sadness when he heard that, if he wanted to be perfect, he should sell all that he had and distribute it to the poor and that he would have treasure in heaven, if it was not that he had, as the gospel says, great wealth?[9] For it is one thing to be unwilling to absorb into our bodies what we do not have; it is quite another to tear away what we have already taken in. The former things are rejected like food; the latter are cut off like members. With what great and with what marvelous joy Christian love sees that people in our times do with joy through the gospel of the Lord what the rich man heard with sadness from the lips of the Lord!

6. Though I can find no words to explain what my heart has conceived and labors to bring to birth, you, nonetheless, prudently and piously understand that

---

5. See Mt 11:30.
6. Paulinus consented to be ordained a priest in Barcelona in 394 on the condition that he would not be obliged to reside there; in 395 he returned to Nola in Campania and was consecrated bishop there probably in 409.
7. Paulinus and his wife renounced their great wealth in order to live in poverty and to embrace the monastic life
8. See Mt 19:27 and Lk 18:23.
9. See Mt 19:21-22 and Lk 18:22-23.

this is not your glory, that is, human glory, but the glory of the Lord in you. For you both eye the enemy with great caution and work with great devotion to be meek and humble of heart as disciples of Christ.[10] It is, after all, better to retain earthly wealth with humility than to abandon it with pride, because, then, you correctly understand that this is not your glory, but the glory of the Lord, will see how poor and inadequate are my words. For I spoke of the praises of Christ, for which the tongues of angels are not equal. We desire, then, that this glory of Christ be also brought before the eyes of our people, that is, that examples be set before us of each sex in one marriage trampling down pride and not giving up the hope of perfection. I do not know whether you could do anything more merciful than if you refuse to conceal that you are the sort of people you have chosen to be.

7. I commend to Your Goodness and Charity Vetustinus, a youth pitiful even in the eyes of non-believers; you will hear from him the reasons for his disaster and journey abroad. For his resolution in accord with which he promises that he will be a servant of God will be proven with more certainty by a longer time, a more robust age, and the passing of his present fear. I sent to Your Holiness and Charity three books, and I wish they resolved as big a question as they are themselves big, for the question they examined is free choice.[11] I fear less in your case the labor involved in reading them, the more I perceive the ardor of your love. But I know that our brother, Romanian, does not have these books or does not have all of them; I gave to him almost all the works that I was able to write and that were suited for the ears of anyone. I did not give them to him to carry to you because of your love for me, but through him I indicated that you should read them. For he already had them all and carried them with him; through him I sent you my first reply.[12] I believe that, with the spiritual wisdom that the Lord has given you, Your Holiness has already experienced the goodness that the man has in his mind and the aspect in which he still limps out of weakness. Hence, you have read, I hope, of the concern with which I commended both him and his son to Your Goodness and Charity and the close relationship that ties them to me. May the Lord build them up through you. I should rather ask this of him, for I know how much you want this.

8. I learned from the brothers that you wrote a work called, *Against the Pagans*; if we deserve anything from your heart, send it without delay in order that we may read it. For your heart is such an oracle of the Lord that we presume that we will be given from it replies that are both pleasing and most exhaustive for the wordiest of questions. I believe that Your Holiness has the books of the most blessed bishop, Ambrose, but I desire greatly to have those that he wrote

---

10. See Mt 11:29.
11. These were Augustine's three books on *Free Will* (*De libero arbitrio*).
12. That is, Letter 27.

with great care and fulsomeness against certain very ignorant and proud persons who claim that the Lord profited from the books of Plato.[13]

8. Our most blessed brother, Severus, once my fellow disciple, but now the bishop of Milevis, who is well known to the brothers of the same city, greets Your Holiness with due respect along with us. All the brothers with us, who are with us serving the Lord, also do this just as they long for you; they long for you just as they love you, and they love you just as you are good. The bread that we sent will become a richer blessing by reason of the love of Your Goodness in receiving it. May the Lord protect you from this generation for eternity, my most beloved and most sincere lord and lady, my truly kind brother and sister, who are most excellent because of the most abundant grace of the Lord.

---

13. These books of Ambrose are no longer extant.

Letter 32

After the previous letter Paulinus and Therasia wrote to Augustine's friend and patron, Romanian. Paulinus first expresses his joy at the arrival of the brothers and of letters from Africa (paragraph 1). He is particularly pleased to hear that Augustine has been consecrated coadjutor bishop of Hippo (paragraph 2). He expresses his concern about Romanian's son, Licentius, who is filled with worldly ambition (paragraph 3). Paulinus turns to words of exhortation to Licentius himself, urging him to listen to his teacher, Augustine (paragraph 4), and explaining that he is adding to the letter a poem of exhortation for Licentius, who he knows is taken with poetry (paragraph 5). Paulinus' poem warns Licentius against the deceptive attraction of honor and power and urges him to commit himself to Christ.

To their rightly esteemed lord and honorable brother, Romanian,[1] *Paulinus and Therasia*[2] *send greetings.*

1. The day before we wrote this, our brothers returned from Africa. You saw that we eagerly awaited their arrival, O most beloved of the saints and most dear friend. We received through them letters from Aurelius, Alypius, Augustine, Profuturus, and Severus,[3] who are now equally all bishops. Grateful for such recent words from so many and such holy men, we have hastened to tell you of our joy in order that by these cheerful reports we might also share with you the joy that we awaited in our worrisome journey. If you have perhaps come to know the same reports about these venerable and beloved men through the arrival of other ships, receive them a second time from us as well, and exult again as if the reason for joy were renewed. But if this messenger from us will be the first to come to you, rejoice that we have in your land met with such great love through the gift of Christ that we are either the first or among the first to know whatever God's providence accomplishes there, which is always, as scripture says, marvelous in his saints.[4]

2. But we have not written this only to rejoice because Augustine has received the episcopacy, but because the churches of Africa have merited this care from God so that they hear the heavenly words from the lips of Augustine who was

---

1. Romanian was a wealthy man from Thagaste, Augustine's patron, and the father of Licentius. Augustine dedicated to him *Answer to the Skeptics* and *True Religion*.
2. Paulinus was the future bishop of Nola, and Therasia was his wife.
3. Aurelius was bishop of Carthage; Alypius bishop of Thagaste; Augustine bishop of Hippo; Profuturus bishop of Cirta; and Severus bishop of Milevis.
4. See Ps 68:36.

promoted in a novel manner[5] to a greater grace in the service of the Lord and consecrated not to take the place of the bishop in his see, but to be his assistant. For Valerius, the bishop of the church of Hippo, is in good health, and Augustine is his coadjutor bishop. And that blessed old man, whose most pure mind has never been touched by any stain of jealous envy, now gathers from the Most High fruits worthy of the peace of his heart, for he has now merited to have as a colleague the man whom he simply desired to have as his successor in the priestly office. Could anyone have believed this before it happened? But those words of the gospel can also be applied to this work of the Almighty, *For human beings these things are difficult, but for God all things are possible* (Lk 8:27, Mt 19:26, Mk 10:27). Let us, therefore, rejoice and be glad in him *who alone produces wonders* (Ps 72:18) and *who makes those who are of one heart dwell together in a house* (Ps 68:7). For *he has looked upon our lowliness* (Dt 26:7) and visited his people with benefits.[6] He has raised up a man of strength[7] in the house of David, his servant,[8] and now he has raised up a man of strength in his Church among his elect in order to break the strength of sinners, that is, of the Donatists and the Manichees, as he promises through the prophet.[9]

3. I wish that this trumpet of the Lord by which he sounds forth through Augustine would strike the hearing of our son, Licentius, but in such a way that he may hear with that ear by which Christ enters and from which the enemy does not snatch the seed of God.[10] Then Augustine will truly seem to himself to be Christ's high priest because he will then feel that he has also been heard by the Most High, if he brings to birth in Christ as a son worthy of himself this lad whom he begot in literature as worthy of you. For, I want you to believe, he has even now written to us with a burning concern for him. We trust in Christ almighty that the spiritual desires of Augustine may prevail over the carnal desires of our young man. He will be conquered even against his will—believe me! He will be conquered by the faith of his most devout father so that he may not conquer by a bad victory, if he prefers to conquer unto his own destruction rather than to be overcome for his own salvation. Lest the duty of brotherly love should seem devoid of content, we sent to you and to our son, Licentius, five loaves from the provisions of the army of Christ, in whose battle dress we fight daily for a frugal subsistence. After all, we were not able to exclude from our blessing Licentius, for we desire to unite him intimately to us by that same grace. Let us, nonetheless, speak to him in a few words so that he may not say that I did

---

5. Augustine was consecrated bishop in 395 against the directives of the Council of Nicea which neither Valerius nor he knew, but which forbade that a priest be ordained bishop in a diocese in which another bishop was living.
6. See Lk 1:68.
7. I have translated "*cornu*: horn" and "*cornua*: horns" as "man of strength" and "strength."
8. See Lk 1:69.
9. See Ps 75:11.
10. See Mt 13:4.19, Mk 4:4.15, and Lk 8:5.12.

not write to him what I wrote to you about him. For we say to Aeschinus what Micio hears.[11] But why should I say this in the words of others since I can express everything in our own, and to use the words of others is generally not the mark of a sound head? By the grace of God we have a head that is safe and sound, for our head is Christ. May you be ours in Christ, as we desire, in good health to a ripe old age and always blessed along with your whole house, my lord and brother, who are rightly most deserving of honor and love.

4. Hear, then, my son, the law of your father, that is, the faith of Augustine, and do not reject the counsels of your mother,[12] for the parental love of Augustine equally and rightly claims that name in your regard. For he carried you as a little one in his arms, and he nourished you from childhood with the first milk of worldly wisdom. And he now desires to suckle and nourish you for the Lord with spiritual food. For he sees that you are adult in terms of bodily age, but still an infant for the word of God, still wailing in the cradle in terms of spiritual things, hardly taking your first steps in Christ with unsteady feet, even if the teaching of Augustine like the hand of a mother and the arm of a nurse guides the tottering little one. If you hear and follow him, to use once again the words of Solomon to attract you, *My son, you will receive a crown of graces for your head* (Prv 4:9). Then you will be truly consul and pontiff,[13] not that one you dreamed of in your imagination, but one formed by the very Truth, that is, by Christ, who will replace the empty images of your dreams with the solid results of his action. For you will, Licentius, be truly pontiff and truly consul, if you cling to the prophetic footsteps and apostolic discipline of Augustine, as blessed Elisha clung to Elijah and as the young Timothy clung to the illustrious apostle, as an inseparable companion on the roads of God in order that you may learn to merit the priesthood with a perfect heart and to provide for the salvation of peoples with the lips of a teacher.

5. This is enough of admonitions and exhortations; I believe, after all, that by a few words and a little labor, my Licentius, you can be made enthusiastic for Christ, since you have already been set afire from your boyhood by the spirit and words of the venerable Augustine for the pursuit of truth and wisdom, for Christ is truly both of these, and for the highest good of every good. If he does not have enough influence with you for your good, what can I do, who follow after him at so great a distance and am so poor compared to all his wealth? But I have confidence in the power of his talents and the fineness of your mind, and I hope that fuller and greater results have been produced in you than still need to be produced. And so, I have dared to speak of a twofold grace in that I might with due love be compared to that man in my concern for you and might, at least by

---

11. See Terence, *The Brothers* I, 2, 96-98, where one brother says to another, "When I say this to him, Micio, I am saying it to you."
12. See Prv 1:8.
13. Licentius has ambitions for these high politcal and religious offices in the empire.

my proven affection, be counted among those who long for your salvation. For I know that the palm for the completion of this result in your case is above all destined for Augustine. I fear, my son, to offend your ears by the harshness of my inconsiderate language and to inflict through the ears an annoying wound upon your mind as well. But I recall your letter from which I have understood that you are familiar with poetic rhythms, and at your age I myself was fond of that study. And so, in recalling your letter, I discovered a remedy for soothing your mind, if I have wounded it in any way, that is, by poetic rhythm to call you to the Lord, the creator of every sort of harmony. I beg you to give it a hearing and not to spurn in my words the issue of your salvation. Rather, willingly accept my loving concern and fatherly attitude even in these humble words, for the fact that they include the name of Christ, which is above every name,[14] makes them worthy of respect so that no believer can hold it in contempt.

Paulinus' Elegiac Poem for Licentius

Come now, break off the delays and the tight bonds of the world,
Do not fear the gentle yoke of the good Lord.
Present things are, of course, beautiful, but marvelous only
To flighty minds. A wise mind, however, is not awed by them.
Now Rome with her ill advice attracts you by her various
Beauties; alas, she is able to seduce even the strong.
But, my son, I beg you, keep Father Augustine always
Before your mind as you face all the allurements of the city.
Gazing upon him and holding him in your heart, you will be safe
Amid such great dangers of this fragile life.
I will warn you of this, repeating it again and again:[15]
Flee the pitfalls of hard military service.
The word, "honor," is attractive; serving it is evil;
the result is full of affliction.
One now happy to choose it will soon regret having done so.
It is a joy to climb to the heights,
But to come down from them is filled with fear.
If you stumble, you fall with greater injury from the highest pinnacle.
Now false goods please you; now ambition carries you off
With every breeze, and hollow fame holds you in her glassy bosom.
But once you have put on the belt of a soldier

---

14. See Phil 2:9.
15. See Virgil, *Aeneid* III, 436.

That leads to losses and great turmoil, and
Once fruitless labor from it has broken you,
You will blame your empty hopes too late and in vain, and
You will want to break the chains that you are now fashioning.[16]
Then you will recall the truthful warnings of Father Augustine,
And you will grieve because you held them in contempt.
Hence, if you are wise and if you are good, my son, listen, and
Welcome the words of your fathers, the counsel of your elders.
Why do you withdraw your wild neck from the yoke?
My burden is light; my yoke is gentle.[17] These are Christ's
Loving words. Believe God. And put your head under the yoke;
Take the gentle bit in your mouth;
And bend your shoulders under the light burden.[18]
You can do this now when you act as a free man held back
By no chains, no worry about a wife, no high honor.
This is a good freedom: to serve Christ and in him
To be above all; only a man who has given himself
To Christ the Lord is not a slave to
Human masters or vices or proud kings.
Do not regard the nobles as free whom you now see
Carried on high before the awe-stricken city.
For you see that they think they have such great freedom
That they refuse to bow their heads to God.
Pitiful in the eyes of many mortals,[19] he both serves
His servants and buys serving girls to be his masters.
They who have suffered eunuchs and great palaces know,
Along with any wretch who suffers Rome willingly,
The great price of sweat and the loss of dignity by which one
Has the mantle of a soldier or the honor of office.
Nor does that powerful man who merits to be the highest of all
Attain such a position that he serves no one.
Though he boasts that he is truly master of the whole city,
He serves demons if he worships idols.
Alas! On account of these men you delay in the city,
Licentius, and you scorn Christ's kingdom to please them.
You call them your masters and greet with bowed head
Men who you see are servants of wood and stone!
They reverence silver and gold with the name of God.

---

16. See Mt 11:20.
17. See Mt 11:30.
18. See Virgil, *Georgics* III, 188.
19. See Horace, *Odes* I, 24, 9.

Their god is what the disease of greed longs after.
I deplore that a man who does not love Augustine
Loves these people and that a man who chooses
To worship them does not worship Christ.
For this reason God himself says that one cannot serve
Two masters,[20] for oneness of mind is pleasing to God:
Since there is one faith, one God,[21] and Christ,
Who is the only Son of the Father, the service
Of the one Lord can hardly be divided.
For the possessions and empires of Caesar and Christ
Are as far apart as heaven and earth.
Rise up from the earth, but now while the spirit rules
These limbs,[22] and penetrate the heaven with your mind.
The weight of the flesh is no hindrance.
Die now to bodily actions, and contemplate the goods
Of the life of heaven with a clear mind.
You are a spirit, although you are confined in the body,
If only, as a conqueror, you destroy the work of the flesh
With a devout mind. I have written these words to you,
Dear lad, because I was compelled by a confident love;
If you accept them, you will be accepted by God.
Believe that Augustine has a double in me for your sake;
Accept us two fathers with a single filial piety.
Scorn us, and we both lose you with greater pain.
Listen to us, and we both have a sweet reward.
The happy care of two fathers has toiled over you,
And you can have the great honor to have made both happy.
But when I link myself with Augustine, I do not boast
That I am his equal in merits, for I only compare myself
To him in terms of my love for you.
For why should I pour out my meager dew to water you?
Besides me you have two rivers to bathe you:
Alypius, your brother, and Augustine, your teacher.
The first, a relative, the latter, the father of your mind.
With so great a brother and teacher you have the ability.
Do you still hesitate to aim for the stars on such wings?
Whatever you do--for the world should not hope for you
As a friend--you will not be given to the earth,

---

20. See Mt 6:24 and Lk 16:13.
21. See Eph 4:5-6.
22. See Virgil, *Aeneid* IV, 336.

O soul, who are owed to Christ.
Though you contemplate marriage and high honors,
You will one day be restored to the Lord.
Two just men, I believe, will conquer one sinner,
And the prayers of your brothers will banish your desires.
Hence, return to the path on which a father by his words
And a brother by his blood, both priests, bid you to walk.
They pull you back to what is yours, for now you seek
What belongs to others; these kingdoms which your father
And brother possess are rather yours.
Seek them; long for them; waste no time on external goods.
If you do not want what is yours,
Who will give you what belongs to others?
You yourself will not be your own man, and sent
By the senses far off through the external world,
You will live, alas!, an exile from your own heart.
It is enough that a worried father has composed
These verses for his son, since I either want or fear
For you what I want or fear for myself.
If you accept it, this page will one day bring you life.
If you reject it, it will be as a witness against you.
May Christ, my dearest son, grant that I may see you
Safe and sound, and may he make you his servant forever.
Live, I beg, but live for God. For to live for the world
Is a work of death. But to live for God is a life really alive.

Letter 33

In 396 or earlier Augustine wrote to his counterpart, Proculeian, the Donatist bishop of Hippo from 395 to 410. Augustine explains why he addresses Proculeian with such titles of respect (paragraph 1) and expresses his joy at hearing that he is willing to enter into a discussion of their differences (paragraph 2). He apologizes for Evodius' language, which may have unintentionally given offense (paragraph 3). Augustine spells out the conditions of a fruitful conference between them (paragraph 4) and pleads for an end to the destructive schism (paragraph 5). Finally, he pleads that they may come to an agreement for the sake of the people (paragraph 6).

To his honorable and most beloved lord, Proculeian, Augustine sends greetings.

1. I ought not to argue longer with you over the salutation on my letter on account of the vanities of ignorant human beings. For we are trying to recall each other from error, and before a complete discussion of the case some people could think that it is uncertain which one of us is in error. We, nonetheless, do each other a service if we deal sincerely with each other in order that we may be set free from the evil of discord. Even if it is not evident to many people that I do this with a sincere heart and with a fear inspired by Christian humility, he, nonetheless, sees for whom no hearts are closed. You, however, readily understand what it is in you that I do not hesitate to honor. For I do not consider the error of schism worthy of any honor; rather, I desire that all human beings be healed of it as far as this lies in my power. But without any uneasiness caused by doubt I think that I should treat you with honor, especially because you are bound to us by the bond of human society itself and because some indications of a more agreeable attitude are evident in you, because of which we should by no means give up hope that you could readily embrace the truth, once it has been shown to you. I, however, owe you as much love as he commanded who loved us up to the ignominy of the cross.

2. But do not be surprised that I have long kept my silence before Your Benevolence. I did not think that you held the view that Brother Evodius, whose reliability I cannot fail to trust, joyfully reported to me. For, when it happened by chance that you gathered in one house and a discussion emerged between you about our hope, that is, about the heritage of Christ, he said that Your Grace said that you wanted to confer with us in the presence of good men. I am very happy that you have deigned to offer this to my lowly self, nor can I in any way ignore such a great opportunity afforded by your good will, namely that, to the extent that the Lord will deign to provide strength, I may seek with you and discuss the cause, the origin, and the reason for such a sad and deplorable division in the

Church of Christ, to which he said, *I give my peace to you; I leave my peace with you* (Jn 14:27).

3. I heard, of course, that you complained about the brother I mentioned because he said something offensive to you in reply. I beg you not to hold that offensiveness against him, for I am certain that it did not arise from a proud heart. After all, I know my brother, but if with too much zeal in arguing for his faith and the love of the Church he perhaps said something that Your Reverence did not want to hear, it should not be called arrogance, but confidence. For he wanted to engage in a discussion with arguments, not simply to offer flattering agreement. This, after all, is the oil of the sinner with which the prophet does not want his head to be anointed. For he speaks as follows, *The righteous man will correct me with mercy and rebuke me, but the oil of the sinner will not anoint my head* (Ps 141:5). For he prefers to be corrected by the severe mercy of the righteous man rather than to be praised by the smooth unction of flattery. Hence, there is also the statement of the prophet, *Those who declare you happy lead you into error* (Is 3:12). For this reason it is also a correct and common saying, "He has a swollen head." For it was fattened by the oil of the sinner, that is, not by the harsh truth of correction, but by the smooth falsity of praise. Nor do I ask that you interpret this in the sense that I want you to understand that you were corrected by my brother, Evodius, as if by a righteous man. For I fear that you may think that I am also saying something offensive to you, something that I am trying to avoid very much. But he is righteous who said, *I am the truth* (Jn 14:16). And so, when any human being utters the truth from his lips with some harshness, we are corrected, not by that human being, who is perhaps a sinner, but by the very Truth, that is, by Christ, who is righteous, in order that our head may not be anointed by the unction of sweet, but harmful flattery, that is, by the oil of the sinner. And yet, even if Brother Evodius, a little excited in defense of his ecclesial communion, said something rather haughty because of his more agitated state, you should excuse his age and the importance of the issue.

4. I beg you to remember what you graciously promised, namely, that in the presence of those whom you choose we would investigate in harmony an issue so important and pertaining to the salvation of all. Only let our words not be futilely carried off by the breeze, but rather set down in writing in order that we may hold our conference with more tranquility and orderliness, and if something we said should slip from our memory, it may be recalled by being read back to us. Or, if you prefer, let us first confer with each other without any intermediary either by letters or by conversation and reading, wherever you wish. Otherwise, some unrestrained listeners might prefer to see a battle, as it were, between us rather than to ponder their own salvation during our discussion. The people could be informed afterward by us of the conclusion we have come to. Or, if you prefer to use letters, let them be read out to our peoples in order that we may at some point say, not "peoples," but "one people." I, of course, gladly accept what

you want, what you command, what you prefer. And I promise with full confidence concerning the mind of my most blessed and venerable father, Valerius,[1] who is absent at the moment, that he will learn of this with great joy. For I know how much he desires peace, and he is not tossed about by the inanity of vain pride.

5. I ask you: Of what concern to us are the old quarrels? Granted, those wounds have lasted up to the present that the hot tempers of proud men inflicted upon our members. Because these wounds have become gangrenous, we have lost the pain on account of which one usually calls in a physician. You see the great and miserable foulness that defiles Christian homes and families. Husbands and wives agree with each other about the bed, but disagree about the altar of Christ. They swear to each other by him in order to have peace with each other, and they cannot have peace in him. Children and their parents have one house of their own, but do not have one house of God. They desire to be heirs of their parents with whom they quarrel about being heirs of Christ. Servants and masters divide their common Lord *who took up the form of a servant* (Phil 2:7) in order that he might set all free by his servitude. Your people honor us; our people honor you. Your people appeal to us because of our priestly attire; our people appeal to you because of your priestly attire. We welcome the words of all; we want to offend no one. Why has only Christ, whose members we tear apart, offended us? When men need us because they want to settle their lawsuits over worldly matters before us, they call us holy men and servants of God so that they may accomplish their earthly business. Let us at last ourselves carry out the business of our salvation and theirs, not about gold, not about silver, not about estates and cattle. On account of these things we are greeted every day with heads bowed in order that we may bring the disputes of human beings to an end. But there exists between us so shameful and destructive a dispute about our head. Let those who greet us lower their heads as much as they want in order that we may bring them into agreement on earth; our head, in whom we are not in agreement, has lowered himself from heaven even to the cross.

6. I ask and beg you, if you have some of that humanity that many praise, let your goodness be seen in this case, if it is not a pretense for the sake of passing honors. May the deepest feelings of mercy be stirred in you, and may you choose that the issue be discussed, persisting along with us in prayers and discussing everything together peacefully, so that the poor people who are obedient to our positions may not cause us trouble at the judgment of God because of their obedience. May they, rather, be called back from errors and disagreements by our genuine love, and may they be guided onto the paths of truth and peace. I pray that you may be blessed in the eyes of God, my honorable and most beloved lord.

---

1. Valerius was the bishop of Hippo; Augustine was his coadjutor until Valerius' death in 396.

Letter 34

In 396 or 397 Augustine wrote to Eusebius, a Roman official in Hippo and a Catholic layman. Though he desires and prays for the unity of Christians (paragraph 1), something terrible has happened, namely, a young man who was rebuked by his Catholic bishop for beating and threatening to kill his mother has gone over to the Donatists and has been rebaptized (paragraph 2). As the young man injured his mother in the flesh, so he has tried to injure his spiritual mother, the Church (paragraph 3). The crime of the young man is too great to pass over in silence (paragraph 4). Augustine urges Proculeian, the Donatist bishop of Hippo, to hold with him the sort of discussion he promised (paragraph 5). Finally, Augustine proposes that another less learned bishop take his own place in the discussion with Proculeian (paragraph 6).

To his excellent and rightly esteemed and honorable brother, Eusebius,[1] *Augustine sends greetings.*

1. God, who sees the secrets of the human heart, knows that, as much as I desire peace among Christians, I am troubled by the sacrilegious actions of those who persevere in its disruption in an unworthy and impious fashion. God knows that this attitude of my mind is directed toward peace and that I am not trying to force anyone involuntarily into the Catholic communion, but to reveal the plain truth to all who are in error. Then, once our ministry has made it evident with God's help, the very truth may be enough to persuade them to embrace and follow her.

2. After all, what is more terrible, I ask you, than what has now happened —not to mention other things? A young man is rebuked by his bishop because in his madness he constantly beats his mother and does not, even on those days when the severity of the laws pardons even the most wicked,[2] hold back his impious hands from the body from which he was born. He threatens the same mother that he will go over to the sect of Donatus and that he will kill her whom he is accustomed to beat with an incredible furor. He threatens her, goes over to the sect of Donatus, is rebaptized in his madness, and is clothed in white garments,[3] while clamoring for his mother's blood. He is placed within the altar rail where he stands conspicuously, and the eyes of all the groaning faithful have set before them, as if he were reborn in Christ, a man plotting to kill his mother.

3. Do you, then, a man of sound judgment, approve of these goings-on? I would never believe this of you; I know how carefully you consider things. A

---

1. Eusebius was a Catholic layman and Roman official in Hippo.
2. All criminal suits ceased during Holy Week.
3. The newly baptized were clothed in white at the Easter Vigil.

mother according to the flesh is struck in the members by which she bore and nourished her ungrateful child; our spiritual mother, the Church, forbids this, and she is struck in the sacraments by which she bore and nourished her ungrateful child. Does he not seem to have said, grinding his teeth for the blood of his mother, "What shall I do to the Church that forbids me to strike my mother? I have found what I shall do. I shall also strike her with whatever injuries I can. I shall do something to myself from which her members will suffer. I shall go to those who know how to drive out[4] the grace in which I was born in her and to destroy the form that I received in her womb. I shall torture both of my mothers with savage torments. Let the mother who bore me later be the first to bury me. For her sorrow I shall die spiritually; for the other's death I shall continue to live carnally." What else should we expect, my honorable Eusebius, but that, now secure as a Donatist, he is armed against the poor woman, worn down by old age and all alone as a widow, whom he was forbidden to beat by the Catholic Church? For what else did he conceive in his crazed heart when he said to his mother, "I shall go over to the Donatist sect, and I shall drink your blood"? See, now bloody in his conscience, but white in his garment, he fulfills a part of his promise; there remains the other part, namely, that he will drink his mother's blood. If, then, you approve these actions, let his clerics and sanctifiers[5] urge him to fulfill within his eight days all that he vowed.[6]

4. The right hand of the Lord is, of course, powerful to hold back the fury of that man from the poor and desolate widow and to frighten him from so wicked a plan in ways he knows. What was I, nonetheless, when stricken by so great a grief of mind, to do if I did not at least speak out? Or do those men do these actions, while I am told, "Be silent"? May the Lord turn aside from me such madness! When he himself commands me through his apostle and says that a bishop ought to refute *those who are teaching what should not be taught* (Tt 1:11), should I be silent, because I am frightened by their indignation? I wanted that a crime as sacrilegious as that should be recorded in the public records. I wanted this precisely so that no one, especially in other cities, would think that, because I deplored these actions, I made up something when it was advantageous, since even at Hippo it is now said that Proculeian did not give the order that the public record reported.

5. But how can we act with more moderation than by dealing with so serious an issue through you, a man endowed with a most illustrious office and at peace

---

4. Augustine alludes to the rite of exsufflation in which the devil was "blown out" of the candidate for baptism; when the Donatists rebaptized someone, they used this rite against the grace of the previous baptism.

5. Augustine uses "sanctifier" rather than "minister" since the Donatists held that the effect of the sacrament depends on the holiness of the minister.

6. The eight days from the Easter Vigil when the newly baptized received a white garment which they wore until White Sunday (*Dominica in albis*).

because of a most thoughtful disposition of will? I ask, therefore, as I have already asked through our brothers, good and honest men, whom I have sent to Your Excellency, that you deign to investigate whether Victor, the priest of Proculeian, did not receive this order from his bishop that he reported to the public authorities or whether, though Victor himself said something different, they charged him with falsehood in the proceedings, though they belong to the same communion. Or if he agrees that we peacefully deal with this whole question of our division, in order that the error, which is already evident, may become more evidently known, I gladly agree. For I heard what he proposed, namely, that without turmoil among the people ten serious and honest men from each side be present with us and that we investigate in accord with the scriptures where the truth is to be found. For that suggestion that some men have again reported to me that he made as to why I should not go to Constantina since there were more of them there or that I ought to go to Milevis because they were, as they say, about to hold a council there, is ridiculous to mention, as if I personally have the care of any church but that of Hippo. For me the whole point at issue in the present question has to do especially with Proculeian. But if he perhaps thinks that he is not up to it, let him implore the help of any colleague he chooses. For in other cities we only deal with what pertains to the Church to the extent that the bishops of the same cities, our brothers and fellow priests, either permit us or ask us.

6. And yet I fail to understand what this man, who says that he has been a bishop for so many years, is afraid of in me, a mere beginner, that he does not want to hold a discussion with me. If he is afraid of my learning in fine literature, which he has not studied or has studied less, how does this pertain to this question, which must be examined either from the holy scriptures or from the ecclesiastical or public documents in which he has been well versed for so many years that he ought to be the more learned in them? Finally, there is my brother and colleague, Samsucius, the bishop of the church of Turris, who has acquired no literary learning of the sort this man fears. Let him be present and deal with him. I shall ask him, and he will, I trust in the name of Christ, readily grant me my request to take my place in this matter, and the Lord will, we trust, help him as he fights for the truth, a man, though not refined in his speech, learned in the true faith. There is, then, no reason why Proculeian should refer the question to any others so that we do not continue between ourselves what pertains to us. Nor, as I said, will I avoid those others if he asks their help.

Letter 35

Shortly after the previous letter, that is, in 396 or 397, Augustine again wrote to Eusebius, asking him to pose several questions to Proculeian for him (paragraph 1). He also asks Eusebius to inform the Donatist bishop of the case of the subdeacon, Primus, who was rebaptized after abandoning the Catholic side because of penalties imposed for his improper conduct with certain nuns (paragraph 2). Augustine states his rule of not accepting into the Catholic Church someone who is under penalties from his own communion except in the status of a penitent. He also points to his own practice of not accepting back into the Catholic communion someone who is unwilling to return (paragraph 4). He again urges Eusebius to bring these incidents to the attention of Proculeian (paragraph 5).

To his excellent lord and rightly honorable and most beloved brother, Eusebius,[1] *Augustine sends greetings.*

1. I have not by my bothersome exhortations and pleas imposed upon your reluctant will, as you claim, that you undertake the function of judge between bishops. Even if I had, in fact, wanted to persuade you to do this, I could perhaps have easily shown how you could judge between us in such an open and shut case, and I could have shown you what it is that you are doing, namely, that, without having heard both sides, you, who are fearful of the role of judge, do not hesitate to declare your decision for one side. But, as I said, I let this go for the time being. I had, however, asked nothing else of Your Honor and Grace but this one request, and I ask in this letter that you at least deign to give it your attention. Ask Proculeian whether he said to his priest, Victor, what the public records reported that he said to him. Or did those who were sent to do this not write down in the records what they heard from Victor, but what was false? And, finally, what would he think about discussing the whole question at issue between us? I, however, think that I do not make a man a judge if I ask him to question someone and to deign to write back the response he received. I, therefore, again ask this now, namely, that you do not hesitate to question him, because he refuses to receive my letter, as I have also learned. If he were willing to do this, I would, of course, not act through Your Excellency. But when he is unwilling, how can I proceed in a more peaceful fashion than by posing through you, a good man and a friend of his, the question that the burden of my office does not allow me to pass over in silence? A man of your character was displeased that a mother was

---

1. The same Roman official to whom the previous letter was addressed.

beaten by her son, but you said, "If he[2] had known, he would have banished so wicked a young man from his communion." I reply briefly: He knows now; let him now banish him.

2. I also add another point: After a subdeacon once belonging to the church of Spanianum, by the name of Primus, was forbidden an access to the nuns that was contrary to good discipline and after he showed contempt for the sound rules and commandments, he was removed from the rank of clerics. And angered at the discipline of God, he went over to those others and was rebaptized. Either he also brought with him two nuns, fellow tenants with him on an estate of Catholic Christians, or they followed him. They too were, nonetheless, rebaptized. And now along with gangs of Circumcellions[3] amid roving bands of women who have shamelessly refused to have husbands for fear of having any discipline, he proudly exults in orgies of detestable drunkenness, happy that the freedom for an evil way of life has been opened up most widely for him, the very reason why he was excluded from the Catholic Church. Perhaps Proculeian is also unaware of this. Let it, therefore, be brought to his attention by earnestness and moderation; let him command that Primus be removed from his communion since he chose that communion only because he had lost clerical status in the Catholic Church on account of his disobedience and depraved conduct.

3. For, if the Lord is willing, I myself am going to observe this norm, namely, that whoever wants to come over to the Catholic Church after having been lowered in rank for disciplinary reasons will be received in the humble status of a penitent, to which they too would perhaps have forced him if he had chosen to remain among them. But consider, I beg you, how detestably they act when they persuade those whom we rebuke with ecclesiastical discipline for living bad lives to come to a second bath and to answer that they are pagans in order that they may deserve to receive it. So much blood of the martyrs has been shed so that those words would not come from the lips of Christians! And then, as if they were renewed and as if they were made holy, they mock the discipline that they could not bear, having, in fact, become worse under the appearance of new grace by the sacrilege of a new madness. Or, if I am wrong in my concern that these matters be corrected by Your Benevolence, let no one complain about me if I have these matters brought to the attention of Proculeian by the public records, which, I think, cannot be denied to me in a Roman city. For, since God commands that we speak and preach the word, that we refute *those who teach what they ought not* (Ti 1:11), and that we persist *in time and out of time* (2 Tm 4:3), as I prove from the words of the Lord and of the apostles, let no human being think that I should be persuaded to be silent about these matters. But if they

---

2. That is, Proculeian, the Donatist bishop of Hippo. See the previous letter for the Catholic lad who beat his mother and fled to the Donatist church where he was rebaptized.
3. The Circumcellions were roving bands of Donatists who in the fever of piety robbed and attacked Catholics and destroyed their churches.

think that they should try something in the line of violence and robbery, the Lord will not fail to protect his Church, for he has subjected all earthly kingdoms to his yoke in his embrace that extends over the whole earth.

4. For the daughter of a tenant farmer of the Church who had been one of our catechumens was won over to those people against the will of her parents, and she also donned the habit of a nun where she had been baptized. Though her father wanted to recall her by fatherly severity to the Catholic communion, I had refused that the woman, whose mind had been corrupted, should be taken back unless she were willing and desired by free choice what is better. That farmer began to insist even with blows that his daughter agree with him. I immediately and absolutely forbade that he should do this. Meanwhile, when we were passing through Spanianum, a priest of Proculeian, standing in the midst of the estate of a Catholic and praiseworthy woman, shouted out after us with a most impudent cry that we were traditors[4] and persecutors. He even hurled this abuse at that woman who belongs to our communion and in the midst of whose estate he was standing. When I heard these shouts, I not only held myself back from a fight, but also quieted the crowd that was traveling with me. And yet, if I should say, "Let us examine who are or were traditors or persecutors," they answer me, "We do not want to argue, but we want to rebaptize. We would, like wolves, prey upon your sheep, biting from ambush; if you are good shepherds, be silent." For what else did Proculeian command if it was really he who gave this command: "If you are a Christian, save it for God's judgment, but if we do this, be silent"? The same priest also dared to threaten a farmer, a man who manages the estate of the Church.

5. Let Proculeian, I beg you, also be informed by you of all these happenings. Let him restrain the insanity of his clerics, about which, honorable Eusebius, I have not kept silent before you. Please be so good, therefore, as to write back to me, not what you hold on all these matters, for I do not want you to think that I have placed upon you the burden of being a judge, but about what they reply to me. May the mercy of God keep you safe, my excellent lord and rightly honorable and most beloved brother.

---

4. The traditors were those who handed over the sacred books or vessels during the time of persecution.

Letter 36

After April 397 Augustine wrote to the priest Casulanus to refute the treatise of a certain Roman, referred to as "Urbicus" or "the city fellow," in which he most ineptly argued in favor of the obligation to fast on the Sabbath (paragraphs 1 to 9). Augustine shows the absurdity of the author's argument through a discussion of fasting or not fasting on the Lord's Day (paragraphs 10 to 15). He discusses the fasts of Elijah and of Daniel, Paul's view of the various manners of fasting and their relation to Christian love of the neighbor (paragraphs 16 to 26). Finally, having mentioned the errors of the Manichees and of the Priscillianists with regard to fasting, Augustine states the view that Ambrose, the bishop of Milan, taught with regard to the observance of the different practices of different churches, namely, that one ought to follow the practice of the Church in which one is (paragraphs 30-32).

To his most beloved brother and fellow priest, for whom we long, Casulanus,[1] Augustine sends greetings in the Lord.

1, 1. I do not know how it has happened that I have not replied to your first letter, and I do, nonetheless, know that I did not do that out of contempt for you. For I am very pleased by your studies and by your words themselves, and I desire that you make progress at this young age and abound in the word of God in order to build up the Church, and I exhort you to this. But now, having received your second letter, in which by the fraternal and most just law of love that unites us you demand that I at long last reply to you, I thought that I should not put off any longer the gratification of your desire that stems from love, and I have undertaken to free myself of my debt to you amid my most pressing occupations.

2. Regarding the point, then, about which you consult me, namely, whether it is permitted to fast on the Sabbath, I reply that, if it were in no way permitted, certainly neither Moses nor Elijah nor the Lord himself would have fasted for forty days in a row.[2] But this argument leads to the conclusion that it is not forbidden to fast even on the Lord's Day. And yet, whoever thinks that this day should be set aside for fasting, as certain people observe the Sabbath by fasting, will be a cause of no small scandal to the Church and with good reason. For in these questions on which the divine scripture has determined nothing certain, the custom of the people of God or the practices of our ancestors are to be taken as law. If we want to argue about them and find fault with some people on the basis of the custom of others, there will arise an endless struggle that should be avoided, since it produces no certain proofs of the truth through the labor of

---

1. Casulanus was a Catholic priest, probably from Africa.
2. See Ex 34:28; 1 Kgs 19:8; Mt 4:2 and Mk 4:2.

argumentation. Otherwise, it might cloud over the fair skies of love with the storm of contention. That man has not taken care to avoid this danger whose long discourse you thought that you should to send to me along with your previous letter in order that I might reply to him.

2, 3. I do not, however, have such long periods of time that I should use them to refute his views one by one, for I need those periods of time for finishing off other more urgent works. But use that fine mind, by which you reveal yourself to me in your letter and which I love in you as God's gift, to consider a little more attentively the words of a certain man of the city,[3] as you call him, and you will see that he has been not at all afraid to wound by his injurious language almost the whole Church of Christ *from the rising of the sun to its setting* (Ps 50:1). Nor should I say, "Almost the whole," but "clearly the whole Church of Christ." For he is not found to have spared even the Romans, whose custom he thinks he defends. But he does not understand how the brunt of his insults overflows upon them as well, because he does not pay attention. For, when arguments fail him by which to prove that one ought to fast on the Sabbath, he inveighs insolently against the luxury of banquets, against drinking parties, and wicked drunkenness, as if not fasting is equivalent to being drunk. For, if this is the case, what good, then, does it do the Romans to fast on the Sabbath, since on other days when they do not fast, in accord with this man's argument they must be considered drunks and belly-worshipers? But, if it is one thing to weigh down the heart by overeating and drunkenness, something that is always wrong, it is something else to ease up on fasting, while observing moderation and temperance. When that is done on the Lord's Day, it certainly does not have a Christian as its critic. Let this man first distinguish the dinners of the saints from the excessive eating and drinking of those whose God is their belly; otherwise, he makes the Romans themselves such worshipers of the belly when they do not fast. And then let him ask, not whether it is permitted to be drunk on the Sabbath, something which is not also permitted on the Lord's Day, but whether one should also refrain from fasting on the Sabbath, as one usually does on the Lord's Day.

4. Would that he would ask or assert this in such a way that he would not most openly speak evil against the Church spread throughout the whole world, except for the churches of Rome and a few Western churches. But now who is going to tolerate it that throughout all the Eastern and also many Western Christian peoples he says of so many and such great men and women, servants of Christ, who eat soberly and moderately on the Sabbath that they are given over to the flesh and cannot please God?[4] Who is going to tolerate it that he says that scripture says of them: Let the wicked depart from me; I do not want to know their

---

3. Casulanus used "*Urbicus*: man of the city" to refer to the author of the views on fasting, apparently unwilling to name the individual.
4. See Rom 8:8.

way?[5] Who is going to tolerate it that he says that they are worshipers of the belly, preferring Judaism and the children of the slave girl to the Church, taking care of the belly, not by a law of justice, but of pleasure,[6] and not yielding to obedience, and that they are flesh and have their mind set on death,[7] and such other things? If he said these things of any one servant of God, who ought to listen to him, who ought not to avoid him? But when with these insults and slanders he attacks the Church that is bearing fruit and growing throughout the whole world and that eats dinner on the Sabbath almost everywhere, I warn whoever this is to control himself. After all, you certainly did not want me to condemn the man since you do not want me to know his name.

3, 5. *"The Son of Man,"* he says, *"is Lord of the Sabbath* (Mt 12:8), on which it is especially permitted to do good rather than evil."[8] If, then, we do evil when we eat dinner, we do not live well on any of the Lord's Days. But he admits that the apostles ate on the Sabbath, and he says that it was not time for them to fast, for which reason the Lord says, *The days will come for the bridegroom to be taken from them, and then the friends of the bridegroom will fast* (Mt 9:15), for there is a time for joy and a time for grief.[9] He ought, first of all, to have noticed that the Lord spoke there about fasting, not about fasting on the Sabbath. Secondly, when he wants us to understand that grief should be linked to fasting and joy to food, why does he not think that whatever it was that God wanted to signify by the words of scripture that *on the seventh day he rested from all his works* (Gn 2:2), he did not there signify grief, but joy? Or is he perhaps going to say that by that respose of God and sanctification of the Sabbath he signified joy for the Jews, but grief for the Christians? And still, when God sanctified the seventh day because on it *he rested from all his works*, he did not say anything about fasting or eating on the Sabbath. Nor afterward, when he gave to the Hebrew people commandments about the observance of this day,[10] did he speak about taking or not taking nourishment. He only commands human beings to abstain from their own work, at least from servile work. The earlier people interpreted this as foreshadowing what was to come[11] and abstained from works in the way in which we now see that the Jews abstain, not, as it is supposed, like the carnal Jews who do not understand what the Christians correctly understand. Nor, after all, do we understand these things better than the prophets who at that time, when it was necessary that they do so, observed the same abstention from work on the Sabbath that the Jews think should still be observed. This is the reason that God

---

5. See Mt 7:23 or Lk 13:27; it does not seem to be a quotation from scripture despite what Augustine says.
6. See Gal 4:31.
7. See Rom 8:5-6.
8. See Mt 12:12.
9. See Eccl 3:4.
10. See Dt 5:12-15.
11. See Col 2:17.

commanded that the man be stoned who had gathered wood on the Sabbath.[12] But we never read that someone was stoned or judged worthy of some punishment for either fasting or for eating dinner on the Sabbath. Let that man figure out which of these two fits with rest and which with toil. For he linked joy to those who eat and grief to those who fast, or he understood the Lord to have linked them when he said in his response about fasting, *The friends of the bridegroom cannot mourn as long as the bridegroom is with them* (Mt 9:15).

6. He, however, said that the apostles ate on the Sabbath because it was not yet time for them to fast on the Sabbath, something which the old tradition, of course, forbade. Was it, therefore, not yet time for them to abstain from work on the Sabbath? Did not the tradition of the elders forbid this? And yet on the very day of the Sabbath on which we read that the disciples of Christ ate, they, of course, plucked ears of corn, something that was not permitted on the Sabbath, because the tradition of the elders forbade it. Let him, then, see whether one would not perhaps more appropriately reply to him that the Lord wanted his disciples to do these two things on that day: one, to gather the ears and, two, to take nourishment, so that the former action would count against those who want to abstain from work on the Sabbath, while the latter would count against those who force people to fast on the Sabbath. For, with the change in times, the Lord signified that abstinence from work was a superstitious practice, but he wanted that fasting on the Sabbath to be an option for both times. I do not want to state this as something certain, but I want to point out what could be said to him in response much more aptly than what he says.

4, 7. "How," he asks, "will we not be condemned with the Pharisee if we fast only twice in a week?" as if the Pharisee should be condemned because he fasts twice in a week and not because he raised himself up in pride above the Publican.[13] This fellow can, however, say that those who give a tenth of all their harvest to the poor are condemned with the Pharisee, because he also boasted of this among his works, something which we desire that many Christians would do and we find scarcely a very few who do. Or will someone who is not unjust, not an adulterer, or not a robber, be condemned with the Pharisee, because he boasted that he was none of these? Anyone who thinks that is certainly insane. But if these qualities that the Pharisee says that he had are undoubtedly good, though we should not have them with the proud boastfulness that was seen in him, but should have them with the humble piety that he did not have, so fasting twice in a week is without benefit in a man such as the Pharisee was, but is an act of devotion in someone humbly faithful or faithfully humble. And yet, the words of the gospel do not say that the Pharisee was condemned, but rather that the Publican was declared righteous.

---

12. See Nm 15:35.
13. See Lk 18:11-12.

8. But if he thinks that we should understand the Lord's words, *Unless your righteousness is more abundant than that of the scribes and the Pharisees, you shall not enter the kingdom of heaven* (Mt 5:21), in the sense that, unless we fast more than twice in a week, we cannot fulfill this command, it is a good thing that there are seven days, which recur again and again as time unfolds. After we have, then, subtracted two days from these so that we do not fast on the Sabbath and the Lord's Day, there remain five days on which we can surpass the Pharisee who fasts twice in a week. For I think that, if someone fasts three times in a week, he already surpasses the Pharisee who fasted twice in a week. But if someone fasts even four times or even five times in a week so that he omits no day except for the Sabbath and the Lord's Day, something many people do for their whole life, especially those who live in monasteries, they surpass in the labor of fasting not only the Pharisee, who fasts twice in a week, but also the Christian, who is accustomed to fast on the fourth and the sixth days and on the Sabbath, as the Roman people often do. And this fellow whoever he is, this thinker from the city, as you refer to him, calls a person carnal, even if the person fasts five continuous days aside from the Sabbath and the Lord's Day without taking refreshment for his body at all on any of these days, as if food and drink taken on the other days do not pertain to the flesh. And he condemns him as a worshiper of the belly, as if dinner on the Sabbath alone enters his belly.

5, 9. What is enough to surpass the Pharisee, namely, to fast three times in the week, is, of course, not enough for this man. Rather, with the exception of the Lord's Day, he forces people to fast on the six other days, when he says, "After the ancient stain is removed,[14] as two in one flesh, those who remain under the discipline of Christ ought not to hold banquets filled with delights with those people outside the law and with the leaders of Sodom and of Gomorrah, but with those who dwell in holiness and are consecrated to God they ought in accord with the solemn law of the Church to fast lawfully more and more. In that way at least a minor mistake committed over the six days may be washed away by the fountains of fasting, prayer, and almsgiving, in order that, refreshed by the *'alogia'*[15] of the Lord's Day, we can all sing worthily with equal heart, *You have satisfied, O Lord, the hungry soul, and you have given drink to the thirsty soul"* (Ps 107:9). When he says these things and exempts only the Lord's Day from continued fasting, he accuses not only the Christian peoples of the East and of the West, among whom no one fasts on the Sabbath, but also blindly and carelessly accuses the church of Rome. For he says, "Those who remain under the discipline of Christ ought not to hold banquets filled with delights with those people without the law and with the leaders of Sodom and of Gomorrah, but with

---

14. That is, after baptism, which removes original sin.
15. Literally, the term signified "irrationality" or "bestiality." Apparently Sunday dinner knew no bounds after a week of fasting; see paragraph 11 where Augustine interprets the terms, though undoubtedly in a rather pejorative sense.

those who dwell in holiness and are consecrated to God they ought in accord with the solemn law of the Church to fast lawfully more and more," and then, to define what it is to fast lawfully, he goes on to say, "In that way at least a minor mistake committed over the six days may be washed away by the fountains of fasting, prayer, and almsgiving." He, of course, thinks that those who fast fewer than six days in the week do not practice fasting lawfully, are not consecrated to God, and do not wash away the stains of error that are contracted from this mortality. Let the Romans, then, figure out what they should do, because this man's line of argument also treats them very contemptuously. For how many are found among them, apart from a very few clerics or monks, who fast daily on all these six days, especially since it seems that one is not supposed to fast there on the fifth day of the week?

10. Next I ask: if even a minor mistake committed on any day is removed or washed away by the fast of that day, since he says, "In that way at least a minor mistake committed on the six days may also be washed away by the fountains of fasting," what shall we do about the error that sneaks up on us on the Lord's Day, on which it is a scandal to fast? Or if no error sneaks up on Christians on that day, let this fellow, who as a great devotee of fasting accuses the worshipers of their belly, see how much honor and benefit he attributes to the belly, if one does not do wrong on that day when one eats. Or does he perhaps locate so much good in the fast on the Sabbath that the fast on the Sabbath can alone wipe away even a minor mistake, as he says, of the other six days, that is, even of the Lord's Day? And does one avoid doing wrong on that day alone on which one fasts the whole day? Why is it, then, that he prefers the Lord's Day to the Sabbath, as if by Christian law? Look, according to him, the day of the Sabbath is found to be much holier. For on it one does not do wrong when one fasts on it all the day long, and by the same fast he washes away the mistakes of the other six days and thus of the Lord's Day itself. I suspect that you do not approve this presumption.

11. And now, since he wants to be seen as a spiritual man and accuses those who eat on the Sabbath of being carnal, notice how on the Lord's Day he is refreshed by no modest repast, but takes delight in "irrationality (*alogia*)." But what is "*alogia*," a word taken from the Greek language, but to indulge in feasts to the point of departing from the path of reason? Hence, animals that lack reason are called "irrational (*aloga*)," and those people given over to the belly are like them. On this account, an excessive banquet, at which the mind, where reason rules, is somehow overwhelmed by the consumption of food and drink, is called an "*alogia*." Moreover, it is on account of food and drink, not of the mind, but of the belly, that he says that we should sing because of the irrationality of the Lord's Day: *You have satisfied, O Lord, the hungry soul, and you have given drink to the thirsty soul* (Ps 107:9). Oh what a spiritual man! Oh what a man to reprehend the carnal! Oh what a great devotee of fasting and no worshiper of the belly! See who it is who admonishes us not to corrupt the law of the Lord by the

law of the belly, not to sell the bread of heaven for earthly food, and who adds, "For because of food Adam lost paradise; because of food Esau lost his birthright." See who it is who says, "For the temptation of the belly is a familiar attack of Satan; he persuades one to yield a little in order to take away everything. And the interpretation of these precepts," he adds, "does not yield to the worshipers of the belly."

12. Does he not by these words seem to aim at having us fast even on the Lord's Day? Otherwise, the day of the Sabbath, on which the Lord rested in the tomb, will be holier than the Lord's Day, on which he rose from the dead. For the Sabbath is certainly holier if, according to the words of this man, by fasting all sin is avoided on the Sabbath and the sin contracted on other days is wiped away. But by food for the belly one does not avoid temptation on the Lord's Day, but makes room for the devil's attack, and paradise is lost, and one's birthright is lost. Why is it, then, that he again tells us, contradicting himself, that we should take refreshment on the Lord's Day, not by a modest, sober, Christian dinner, but that, rejoicing and clapping in "*alogia*," we should sing, *You have satisfied, O Lord, the hungry soul, and you have given drink to the thirsty soul*" (Ps 107:9)? If, of course, we do not sin on that day when we fast and if we wash away the mistakes of the other six days when we fast on the Sabbath, no day will be worse than the Lord's Day, no day will be better than the Sabbath. Believe me, my dearest brother, no one understands the law, as this fellow does, except for someone without understanding. For, if it was not food, but forbidden food that destroyed Adam[16] and if it was not a meal, but a meal desired to the point of contempt for the sacrament contained in his birthright that condemned Esau, the nephew of holy Abraham,[17] then holy and faithful people eat piously, just as sacrilegious and unbelieving people fast impiously. But the Lord's Day is preferred to the Sabbath because of faith in the resurrection, not because of the custom of eating or even because of the abandon of drunken singing.

6, 13. "Moses," he says, "did not eat bread or drink water for forty days."[18] But he goes on to say why he said this: "See, Moses, a friend of God, who dwelled in the cloud, gave the law, and led the people, in celebrating thrice two Sabbaths with fasting did not offend God, but earned merit." Does he not notice what can logically be said against this? For, if he sets forth the example of Moses' fasting because in those forty days he fasted on thrice two Sabbaths, as he puts it, and if from this he wants to persuade people to fast on the Sabbath, he should, therefore, persuade people to fast on the Lord's Day, because in those forty days Moses, nonetheless, fasted on thrice two days of the Lord. But he goes on and says, "And yet the Lord's Day was reserved along with Christ for the coming

16. See Gn 2:17 and 3:1-6.
17. See Gn 25:29-34.
18. See Ex 24:18.

Church." I do not know why he said this. For, if he said it because one should fast much more after the Lord's Day came with Christ, then one should—heaven forbid!—fast even on the Lord's Day. Suppose, however, that he was afraid that on account of his fast of forty days it might be objected that one should fast on the Lord's Day, and suppose that he added for this reason, "Yet the Lord's Day along with Christ is reserved for the Church to come," Then Moses may be understood to have fasted even on the day that follows the Sabbath for that reason, namely, that Christ had not yet come, though whom the Lord's Day itself came to be, on which one should not fast. Why, then, did Christ himself likewise fast for forty days?[19] Why during those forty days did he not break his fast on those thrice two days that followed the Sabbath, in order that he might teach even before his resurrection that we should eat on the Lord's Day, just as he gave his blood for us to drink before his Passion? You certainly see that the fast of forty days that this fellow mentions does not pertain to the issue of whether we should fast on the Sabbath, just as it does not pertain to the issue of whether we should fast on the Lord's Day.

14. He, of course, does not notice what can be said against it regarding the Lord's Day when, just as we should blame drunken banquets and all gluttonous and drunken debauchery, he blames eating dinners on the Sabbath, though they can be the dinners of moderate and sober people. And, therefore, we do not have to reply to him on each point since he says the same things again and again in criticizing the vices of debauchery instead of eating dinner on the Sabbath, for he does not find anything else to say except the foolish and irrelevant things he says. The question is whether or not one should not fast on the Sabbath, not whether or not one should indulge in debauchery, something that those who fear God do not do even on the Lord's Day, though they do not, of course, fast on that day. Who, however, would dare to say what this fellow has said? "How," he asks, "will actions that force us into sin on a day that has been made holy be for us either approved by us or worthy of God?" He admits that the day of the Sabbath was made holy and says that human beings are forced into sin because they eat. And for this reason either the Lord's Day was not made holy according to this man and the Sabbath begins to be the better, or, if the Lord's Day was made holy, we are forced into sin because we eat.

7, 15. And he tries to prove by divine testimonies that we should fast on the Sabbath, but he does not find any means to prove this. He says, "Jacob ate and drank wine, and he was satisfied, and he withdrew from God, his salvation,[20] *and there fell on one day twenty-three thousand*" (Ex 32:28), as if it said, "Jacob ate on the Sabbath, and he withdrew from God, his salvation." And when the apostle mentioned that so many thousands fell, he did not say, "Let us not eat on the

19. See Mt 4:2, Lk 4:2.
20. See Ex 32:1-8.28.

Sabbath as those people ate." Rather, he said, *Let us not commit fornication, as some of them have committed fornication, and on one day there fell twenty-three thousand* (1 Cor 10:8). What else does it mean when it says, *But the people sat down to eat and to drink, and they got up to play* (Ex 32:6; 1 Cor 10:7)? The apostle also cited this testimony, but in order to keep them from the worship of idols, not from eating on the Sabbath. This fellow does not prove that this was done on the Sabbath, but makes a guess, as he pleased. But just as it is possible that people fast and that, when they break their fast, if they are inclined to drink, they become drunk, so it is possible that people do not fast and, if they are temperate persons, they eat moderately. Why is it, then, that, in wanting to persuade people to fast on the Sabbath, he uses the apostle as witness when he says, *Do not become drunk with wine, for there are all sorts of debauchery in this* (Eph 5:18), as if he said, "Do not eat on the Sabbath, for there are all sorts of debauchery in this"? But just as this precept of the apostle not to become drunk with wine, in which there are all sorts of debauchery, is observed by Christians who fear God when they eat dinner on the Lord's Day, so it is observed when they eat dinner on the Sabbath as well.

16. "In order to speak more clearly against those in error," he says, "no one offends God by fasting, even if he does not earn merit." Who would say this except someone who does not consider what he says? When the pagans fast, therefore, do they cease to offend God for this reason? Or if he wanted us to understand what he said as referring to Christians, who will not offend God if he should choose to fast on the Lord's Day to the scandal to the whole Church, which is spread out everywhere? Then he adds testimony from the scriptures that are of no avail for the cause that he took up. He says, "Because of fasting Elijah was given paradise and reigns in his body,"[21] as if those who do not fast on the Sabbath do not preach fasting, just as those who do not fast on the Lord's Day do, nonetheless, preach fasting, or as if Elijah fasted at a time when the people of God also fasted on the Sabbath. But I think that we should reply concerning the forty days of Elijah the same thing we replied concerning the forty days of Moses' fast. "By fasting," he says, "Daniel escaped unharmed from the jaws of lions dry with frenzy,"[22] as if he read that he fasted on the Sabbath or that he was also with the lions on the Sabbath. We do, nonetheless, read there that he also ate.[23] "By fasting," he says, "the faithful brotherhood of the three conquered their prison blazing with fire and adored the Lord, whom they welcomed as a guest on their pyre." These examples of the saints are unable to persuade one to fast on any day; how much less are they able to do so on the Sabbath? For we not only do not read that the three men were sent into the furnace blazing with fire on

21. See 1 Kgs 19:8 and 2 Kgs 2:11.
22. See Dn 6:16-23.
23. See Dn 3:23-93.

the Sabbath, but we do not even read that they were there long enough that anyone could say that they fasted. In fact, it hardly takes the length of one hour to sing their confession and hymn, nor did they walk about amid those harmless flames for a longer time than it took to finish that song, unless this fellow counts the length of even one hour as fasting. If that is so, he has no reason to be angry at those who eat on the Sabbath; up to the time of dinner, after all, one fasts for a much longer time than they did in that furnace.

17. He also uses that testimony of the apostle where he says, *The kingdom of God is not food and drink, but righteousness and peace and joy in the Holy Spirit* (Rom 14:17), and he wants us to understand that the kingdom of God is the Church in which God reigns. I ask you, when he said these words, was the apostle trying to get Christians to fast on the Sabbath? Rather, he was not talking about fasting on any day when he said this. He said this against those who in the manner of the Jews thought that purity consisted in abstinence from certain foods in accord with the old law and as an admonition to those brethren whose indiscriminate taking of food and drink was scandalizing the weak. For this reason, after he had said, *Do not destroy by your food one for whom Christ has died* (Rom 14:15), and, *Do not let our good be the object of blasphemy* (Rom 14:16), he then added, *The kingdom of God is not food and drink*, and the rest. But in the way in which this fellow understands these words of the apostle, namely, that the kingdom of God, which is the Church, is not found in food and drink, but in fasting, I tell you that we ought not to fast only on the Sabbath, but ought never take food and drink at all so that we do not ever withdraw from this kingdom of God. But I think that, as this fellow admits, we belong to the Church somewhat more devoutly on the Lord's Day when we, nonetheless, eat, as he himself grants.

8, 18. "Why," he asks, "do we complain at offering a sacrifice dear to the principal Lord, a sacrifice that the Spirit desires and the angel praises?" Then he adds that testimony of the angel saying, *Prayer along with fasting and almsgiving is good* (Tb 12:8). Why he said, "the principal Lord," I do not know, unless the writer perhaps made a mistake and it escaped your notice so that you did not correct what you sent me to read. He wants us to understand that fasting is a sacrifice dear to the Lord, as if this question was about fasting and not about fasting on the Sabbath. For the Lord's Day does not go by without a sacrifice that is dear to the Lord, because we do not fast. He still goes on and adds testimonies completely foreign to the cause that he undertook to defend. He says, *Offer to God a sacrifice of praise* (Ps 50:14), and wanting somehow or other to connect these words of the psalm to the present issue, he says, "Not, of course, a banquet of blood or drunkenness in which there are multiplied, not praises owed to God, but blasphemies coming from the devil's instigation." Oh the blind presumption! A sacrifice of praise is, therefore, not offered on the Lord's Day because we do not fast, but we have a "banquet of drunkenness" and "there are multiplied blasphemies coming from the devil's instigation." If it is wicked to say this, let him understand that the words of scripture, *Offer to God a sacrifice of praise*, do not signify fasting. Fasting is, of course, not practiced on certain days, especially on feasts, but the sacrifice of praise is offered on all days by the Church, which is spread throughout the whole world. Otherwise, those fifty days after Easter up to Pentecost, on which people do not fast, will be, according to this man, without any sacrifice of praise, something that no one, even a madman, would dare to say, not to mention a Christian. For on these days alone in many churches, but especially on these days in all churches, there is sung the Alleluia, the cry of praise that no Christian, no matter how ignorant, fails to know.

19. He, nonetheless, also admits that we eat on the Lord's Day, not in drunkenness, but in rejoicing, when he says that we, coming from the Jews and from the Gentiles, many with the Christian name, but few chosen ones with the faith, ought to offer to God with praise a fast pleasing to the Lord with the evening incense of the Sabbath in place of the sacrifices of animals, and by its fervor the works of sins will collapse as if consumed by fire. "And in the morning," he says, "because we obeyed him, he will hear us, and we will have homes for eating and drinking, not in drunkenness, but in rejoicing, once the Lord's celebration is over." And so, one then celebrates with "*eulogia*," not, as he said above, with "*alogia*."[24] But I do not know why the day of the Sabbath, which the Lord made holy, so offends him that he thinks that one cannot eat and drink on it with the sort of rejoicing that is free from drunkenness, since we could fast before the Sabbath in the same way as he says one should fast on the Sabbath before the Lord's Day. Or does he think that it is forbidden to eat for two consecutive days? Let him, therefore, see the great reproach that he heaps, even upon the church of Rome, where, even in these weeks in which they fast on the fourth, sixth, and Sabbath days, the people eat for three consecutive days, namely, on the Lord's Day and on the second and third days of the week.

20. "It is certain," he says, "that the life of the sheep depends on the choice of the shepherds, but, *Woe to those who say that what is good is evil, that darkness is light and light darkness, that bitter is sweet and sweet bitter*" (Is 5:20). I do not understand well enough what these words of his mean. For, if you write these things just as the "city fellow" says them, in the city the people who depend on the decision of their pastor fast on the Sabbath with their bishop. But if he writes these things to you because you yourself wrote something of the sort in your letter, let him not persuade you that the Christian city praises one who fasts on the Sabbath in such a way that you are forced to condemn the Christian world when it eats. For, when he says, *Woe to those who say that what is good is evil,*

---

24. See above, paragraph 11, for an explanation of the "*alogia*"—the feast without rational limits that the "city fellow" would have people celebrate on the Lord's Day. The term, "*eulogia*," simply means "blessing" here.

that darkness is light and light darkness, that bitter is sweet and sweet bitter, wanting us to understand that fasting on the Sabbath is good, light, and sweet, but that eating is evil, dark, and bitter, who has any doubt that he condemns the whole world in all Christians who eat on the Sabbath? He neither looks at himself nor attends to those to whom he speaks in order that he might be held in check by his own writings from this rash boldness. He, of course, immediately added, *Let no one judge you in food or in drink* (Col 2:16), which he, of course, does who in this way accuses those who take food and drink on the Sabbath. How great it would have been if this also brought into his mind the words that the same apostle says elsewhere, *Let not the one who eats hold the one who does not eat in contempt, and let not the one who does not eat condemn the one who eats* (Rom 14:3)! In this way he would have maintained this balanced view by which he would avoid scandals between those who fast on the Sabbath and those who eat. As a result, no one who eats would hold in contempt someone who does not eat, and no one who does not eat would condemn someone who eats.

9, 21. "Peter too," he says, "the chief of the apostles, the doorkeeper of heaven, the foundation of the Church, taught the Romans this same thing, after the death of Simon,[25] who was merely a symbol of the devil to be conquered by fasting, and the faith of the Romans is proclaimed to the whole orb of the earth." Did the other apostles, then, in opposition to Peter teach Christians throughout the whole world to eat? Just as, then, Peter and his fellow disciples lived in harmony with one another, so let those who fast on the Sabbath, the people whom Peter planted, and those who eat, the people whom his fellow disciples planted, live in harmony with one another. It is, of course, the opinion of very many, though most Romans say that it is false, that, when the apostle Peter was about to do battle with Simon Magus on the Lord's Day, he fasted along with the church of the same city on the day before on account of the danger of that great trial, and that, after he obtained such favorable and glorious success, he kept that practice, and some churches of the East imitated it. But if, as this man says, Simon Magus was a symbol of the devil, the devil is clearly not a tempter for the Sabbath or for the Lord's Day, but for every day. And yet people do not on every day fast against him since they eat on all days of the Lord and for the fifty days after Easter and, in different places, on the solemnities of the martyrs and certain feasts, and yet the devil is conquered if *our eyes are always turned to the Lord* in order that he *may rescue our feet from the snare* (Ps 25:15), and whether we eat or drink, or whatever we do, let us do all for the glory of God, and let us, to the extent we can, be without offense to the Jews and the Greeks and to the Church of God.[26] Those who give scandal by eating or give scandal by fasting do not pay

---

25. Simon Magus; see Acts 8:21 and *Heresies* I.
26. See 1 Cor 10:31-32.

enough attention to this, and through both forms of intemperance they stir up scandals by which the devil is not overcome, but overjoyed.

22. But suppose he replies that James taught in Jerusalem, that John taught in Ephesus, and the rest taught in other places the same thing that Peter taught in Rome, that is, that one should fast on the Sabbath, but that the other lands have departed from this teaching and Rome has stood firm in it. And suppose, on the contrary, that it is reported that some places in the West, including Rome, have not preserved what the apostles handed down, but that the lands of the East where the gospel itself began to be preached remained without any variation in that view that was handed down at the same time by all the apostles, along with Peter himself, namely, that one should not fast on the Sabbath. This contention, then, is endless, generating quarrels, not settling questions. Let there, then, be one faith for the universal Church that is spread everywhere, interiorly, as it were, in the members, even if the unity of the faith itself is celebrated with some different observations that in no way hamper what is true in the faith. For *all the beauty of the daughter of the king is within*; those observations, however, that are practiced in various ways are understood to lie in her clothing; hence, it is said there, *Clothed in garments of many colors with gold fringes* (Ps 45:14-15). But let that clothing also be varied for diverse celebrations in such a way that it is not torn by hostile strife.

10, 23. "Finally," he says, "if a Jew denies the Lord's Day by celebrating the Sabbath, how can a Christian observe the Sabbath? Let us either be Christians and celebrate the Lord's Day, or let us be Jews and observe the Sabbath. For *no one can serve two masters*" (Mt 6:24). Does he not speak as if there is one Lord of the Sabbath and another of the Lord's Day? And he does not listen to the words he himself quoted, *For the Son of Man is Lord of the Sabbath* (Lk 6:5). But insofar as he wants us to be as far removed from the Sabbath as the Jews are from the Lord's Day, is he not so greatly mistaken that he could also say that we ought not to accept the law and the prophets, just as the Jews do not accept the gospel and the apostles? You, of course, understand the evil that he thinks when he thinks this. But he says, *All the old things have passed away, and they have become new in Christ* (2 Cor 5:17); this is true. For on this account we do not abstain from work on the Sabbath like the Jews, even if we relax the obligation of fasting to mark the rest signified by that day. And if some of our brothers do not think that the rest of the Sabbath should be marked by a relaxation of the fast, we by no means quarrel over the variety of the royal clothing for fear that we might disturb the interior members of the queen herself, where we hold one faith, even concerning that rest itself. For, even if, because the old things have passed away, the carnal observance of the Sabbath has passed away with them, it is, nonetheless, not true that we serve two masters because we eat on the Sabbath and on the Lord's Day without any superstitious absence from work, for there is one Lord of the Sabbath and of the Lord's Day.

24. But this fellow who says that the old things have passed away in the sense that "in Christ the sacrificial table has yielded to the altar,[27] the sword to fasting, fire to prayers, animals to bread, and blood to the cup," does not know that the term "altar" is used more frequently in the writings of the law and the prophets and that an altar to God was first set up in the tabernacle that Moses erected. "Sacrificial table" is also found in the apostolic writings where the martyrs cry out beneath the sacrificial table of God.[28] He says that the sword has yielded to fasting, not recalling that sword of the gospel with which the soldiers of both testaments are armed, a sword with a double edge.[29] He says that fire has yielded to prayers, as if prayers were also then not offered in the temple and as if fire has not now been sent into the world by Christ.[30] He says that animals have yielded to bread, as if he did not know that even then the loaves of proposition used to be put on the Lord's table[31] and that now he partakes of the body of the immaculate Lamb.[32] He says that blood has yielded to the cup, not thinking that even now he receives blood in the cup. How much better and more appropriately would he say that the old things have passed away and new ones have come to be in Christ in such a way that altar yields to altar, the sword to the sword, fire to fire, bread to bread, animal to animal, and blood to blood. We, of course, see that the carnal old condition yields in all of these to the spiritual new condition. In that way, then, we should understand that on this passing seventh day whether people eat or some also fast, the carnal Sabbath has yielded to the spiritual Sabbath. When in this latter we desire everlasting and true rest, we scorn in the former the temporal abstinence from work, which is now superstitious.

11, 25. The other points that follow by which he brought his discussion to an end, just like certain others that I did not think should be mentioned, are much more irrelevant to the question discussing fasting or eating on the Sabbath. But I leave them for you to consider and to judge, especially if you are helped in some respect by what I have said. I think I have replied sufficiently to this man in accord with my ability. If, however, you ask my view on this matter, I see, when I carefully reflect on it, that fasting is commanded in the Gospels and the Letters of the apostles and in the whole volume called the New Testament. But I do not find it settled by a command of the Lord or of the apostles on which days one ought not to fast and on which days one ought to. And for this reason I feel that it is more suitable to be less strict rather than more strict, not for obtaining eternal rest, which is obtained by faith and righteousness, in which is found *the beauty of*

---

27. The Latin uses two terms "*ara*" and "*altare*" both of which mean "altar." I have translated the former as "sacrificial table" to differentiate them.
28. See Rv 6:9-10.
29. See Eph 6:17 and Heb 4:12.
30. See Lk 12:49.
31. See Ex 25:30.
32. See 1 Pt 1:19, Mt 26:26-28, Mk 14:22-24, Lk 22:17-20, 1 Cor 11:23-25.

the king's daughter within (Ps 45:14), but for signifying that eternal rest where there is the true Sabbath.

26. In fasting or eating on this Sabbath, nonetheless, nothing seems to me more safe and more peaceful to observe than this: *Let the one who eats not look down on one who does not eat, and let the one who does not eat not judge the one who does* (Rom 14:3). *For we shall not have more if we have eaten, nor shall we be in need if we have not eaten* (1 Cor 8:8), that is, having in these matters preserved intact our fellowship with those among whom we live and with whom we live for God. For, as the apostle's words are true, *It is bad for a man who gives scandal by eating* (Rom 14:20), so it is bad for a man who gives scandal by fasting. We are not, therefore, like those who saw John not eating and not drinking and said, *He has a devil.* But we are also not like those who saw Christ eating and drinking and said, *Look, the man is a glutton and a drunkard, a friend of tax collectors and sinners* (Mt 11:18-19; Lk 7:33-35). To these sayings, of course, the Lord himself added a very important point; he said, *And wisdom is justified by her children* (Mt 11:19). If you ask who these are, read the scripture: *The children of wisdom are the church of the righteous* (Sir 3:1). These are those who, when they eat, do not scorn those who do not eat and those who, when they do not eat, do not judge those who eat, but who clearly scorn and judge those who give scandal whether they eat or do not eat.

12, 27. And the situation is simpler with regard to the day of the Sabbath because the Roman Church fasts as well as some others, even if they are few, whether near to it or far from it. But it is a great scandal to fast on the Lord's Day, especially after the heresy of the Manichees emerged,[33] which is detestable and most clearly very opposed to the Catholic faith and the divine scriptures, for they established for their hearers this day as a lawful day for fasting. And as a result of this to fast on the Lord's Day is regarded as more abominable, unless perhaps someone might be able to extend a fast beyond a week without taking any meal in order to approximate a fast of forty days as far as one can, as we know some people have done. For some brothers who are thoroughly reliable have maintained that a certain man attained the fortieth day. For, just as in the times of the patriarchs of old, Moses and Elijah did nothing against the Sabbath dinners when they fasted for forty days, so one who is able to spend seven days in fasting did not choose the Lord's Day for his fast, but found that day among those many days during which he vowed that he would fast. If, nonetheless, a continued fast is to be broken in a week, it is broken more appropriately on no other day than the Lord's Day. If, however, the body is given refreshment only after a week, the Lord's Day is not, of course, chosen for fasting, but is found in the number of days that one chose to include in his vow.

---

33. For the Manichees, see *Heresies* 46.

28. Do not let it bother you that the Priscillianists,[34] who are very similar to the Manichees, often appeal for fasting on the Lord's Day to the testimony from the Acts of the Apostles, when the apostle Paul was in Troas. For scripture says, *But when we were gathered together on the first day of the week to break bread, Paul spoke to them, since he was going to leave the next day, and he extended his talk to the middle of the night* (Acts 20:7). Then, when he came down from the dining room where they were gathered to raise back to life the young man who, overcome by sleep, had fallen from the window and was found dead, scripture speaks of the apostle as follows: *But when he went up, after he had broken bread and tasted it, he spoke to them for a long while until daybreak, and so he departed* (Acts 20:11). Heaven forbid that one should interpret this in the sense that the apostles were accustomed regularly to fast on the Lord's Day. For the day that we now call the Lord's Day was then called the first day of the week. For the day of the Lord's resurrection is called *the first day of the week* (Mt 28:1) by Matthew, but *day one of the week* (Mk 16:2, Lk 24:1, and Jn 20:1) by the other evangelists. And it is clear that it is the day that was afterwards called the Lord's Day. Either, then, they gathered together after the end of the day of the Sabbath at the beginning of the night, the night that, of course, pertained to the Lord's Day, that is, to day one of the week, and thus, being about to break bread on the same night, as we break bread in the sacrament of the body of Christ, he extended his discourse up to the middle of the night. Then, after the celebration of the mysteries, he again addressed those who were gathered there up until daybreak, because he was in a great rush to depart at dawn on the Lord's Day. Or surely, if they had gathered together on day one of the week, not during the night, but during the day at the hour of the Lord's supper, then the words, *Paul spoke to them since he was going to leave the next day* (Acts 20:7), expressed the reason for extending his talk, for he was going to leave and he wanted to give them sufficient instruction. They did not, therefore, regularly fast on the Lord's Day, but the apostle thought that the sermon that they needed and listened to with the ardor of most fervent zeal should not be interrupted for the sake of bodily refreshment. For he was about to leave, and because of his other journeys hither and yon he would visit them never again or very seldom, especially since he was then about to leave those lands, as the following paragraphs teach, so that he might not see them again in the flesh. And in this way we are rather shown that they were not accustomed to fast on the Lord's Day. For, so that no one would believe that, the writer of the book took care to explain the reason for extending the discourse in order that we might know that, if some necessity should arise, eating should not take preference over some more urgent action. For those most eager listeners who thought that the very fountain was about to leave them and

---

34. See *Heresies* 72, as well as the Introduction to Orosius' *Memorandum to Augustine* and Augustine's *To Orosius*.

who, therefore, were drinking in whatever he poured forth with so great and insatiable a thirst, not for water, but for the word, passed up, not only a carnal dinner, but also such a supper.

29. But though fasts on the Lord's Day were not at that time customary for them, it was not, nonetheless, so obvious a scandal for the Church, if for some such necessity as the apostle Paul had they did not take care to take refreshment for their bodies for the whole of the Lord's Day up to midnight or even up to dawn. But now after heretics, especially the most wicked Manichees, began to practice fasting on the Lord's Day, not when some need arises, but to teach this as if it were established as a sacred practice, and after they became known to the Christian peoples, I do not think that one should do what the apostle did, even with the sort of necessity he had, for fear that one might incur a greater evil with scandal than the good one derives from the preaching. And yet, whatever cause or necessity exists that leads a Christian to fast on the Lord's Day, such as that which we find in the Acts of the Apostles at the danger of shipwreck, when the apostle himself was sailing for fourteen days and, for this reason, fasted on two of the Lord's Days,[35] we ought not to have the least doubt that the Lord's Day should not be included among the days of fast when one has not vowed to continue for more days without any food.

13, 30. But the reason why the Church fasts especially on the fourth and sixth days seems to be that, if one considers the Gospel, on the fourth day of the week, which is commonly called Wednesday,[36] the Jews are found to have plotted to kill the Lord. But if we pass over one day, on the evening of which the Lord ate the Paschal dinner with his disciples, which was the end of the day which we call the fifth day of the week, he was then betrayed on that night, which already pertained to the sixth day of the week, which is clearly the day of his Passion. This day was the first day of the unleavened bread, beginning from evening.[37] But the evangelist, Matthew, says that the fifth day of the week was the first day of unleavened bread, because on the evening following it, there would be the Paschal supper, the supper at which the unleavened bread and the sacrifice of the lamb began to be eaten. From this we infer that it was the fourth day of the week when the Lord said, *You know that in two days it will be the Passover, and the Son of Man will be handed over to be crucified* (Mt 26:2), and for this reason this day is assigned for fasting, because, as the evangelist goes on to say, *Then the chief priests and elders of the people gathered in the courtyard of the high priest, who was called Caiaphas, and they made a plan to arrest Jesus by deceit and to kill him* (Mt 26:3-4). But there intervened one day, of which the Gospel says, *But on the first day of unleavened bread the disciples approached Jesus and said,*

---

35. See Acts 27:33.
36. Literally, "the fourth ferial day."
37. See Mt 26:17.

"Where do you wish that we should prepare to eat the Passover?" (Mt 26:17). After the intervention of this day, the Lord suffered on the sixth day of the week, a point which no one doubts. Hence, the sixth day is also correctly assigned for fasting. Fasting, of course, signifies humility. For this reason scripture says, *And I humbled my soul in fasting* (Ps 35:13).

31. There follows the Sabbath, the day on which the flesh of Christ rested in the tomb, just as in the first production of the world God rested from all his works on that day.[38] From this there has arisen that variety in the garment of the queen, namely, that some, especially the people of the East, prefer to relax their fast in order to mark that rest, while others prefer to fast in order to mark the humility of the death of the Lord, as the Roman church and some other churches of the West do. But on the one day on which the Pasch is celebrated in order to renew the memory of the event, the death of the Lord which the disciples mourned in a human manner, all fast so that even those who eat on the other Sabbaths throughout the year observe the fast with great devotion; they, of course, signify two things on the one day: both the grief of the disciples on the anniversary and the good of rest on the other Sabbaths. There are, of course, two things that cause us to hope for the beatitude of the righteous and the end of all misery: death and the resurrection from the dead. In death there is the rest of which the prophet says, *My people, enter into your chambers, and hide a little while until the anger of the Lord passes by* (Is 26:20). But in the resurrection there is perfect happiness in the whole human being, that is, in the flesh and in the spirit. This is the reason that it was thought that both of these should not be signified by the work of fasting, but rather by the joy of refreshment, except for that one Paschal Sabbath on which the grief of the disciples, as we said, was to be marked by a longer fast on account of the memory of what happened.

14, 32. But, as I mentioned above, we do not find in the gospels and the letters of the apostles, which properly pertain to the revelation of the new testament, that it was clearly commanded that fasts should be observed on certain days. And for this reason this matter also, as do very many others, which it would be difficult to enumerate, finds a place in the garment of the variety that belongs to the daughter of the king, that is, to the Church. Hence, I shall tell you what the venerable Ambrose, the bishop of Milan, by whom I was baptized, replied to me when I asked him about this. For my mother was with me in the same city, and though while still catechumens we cared very little about these topics, she was deeply concerned about whether she should fast on the Sabbath according to the custom of our city or should eat in accord with the custom of the church of Milan. And so, in order to free her from this hesitation, I asked this of the previously mentioned man of God. But he said, "What more can I teach on this than what I myself do?" At this I thought that he gave no command by this response except

---

38. See Gn 2:2-3.

that we should eat on the Sabbath, for I, of course, knew that he did this. But he went on and added, "When I am here, I do not fast on the Sabbath; when I am in Rome, I fast on the Sabbath. And to whatever church you come," he said, "observe its custom, if you do not want to be scandalized or to give scandal." I took this response back to my mother, and it was enough for her, nor did she doubt that she should obey. We also have followed this. But since it happens, especially in Africa, that one church or the churches of one region have some who eat on the Sabbath and others who fast, it seems to me that one should follow the custom of those to whom the congregation of those peoples has been entrusted to be governed. Hence, if you willingly accept my advice, especially since I have probably said more than enough on this topic, at your request and under pressure from you, do not oppose your bishop on this matter, and follow what he himself does without any worry or quarrel.

Letter 37

In approximately 397 Augustine wrote from Hippo to Simplician, who succeeded Ambrose as bishop of Milan in 397. Augustine expresses his gratitude for Simplician's letter (paragraph 1) and his delight over the fact the Simplician is pleased with his writings (paragraph 2). He promises to answer the set of questions Simplician has posed for him (paragraph 3), a promise he fulfilled with the work, *A Miscellany of Questions in Response to Simplician.*

To Simplician,[1] his most blessed lord and his father who deserves to be reverently embraced with most sincere love, Augustine sends greetings in the Lord.

1. I have received the letter that Your Holiness kindly sent me. It is filled with reasons for true joy because you are mindful of me, because you love me as always, and because whatever of his gifts the Lord has deigned to bestow on me by his mercy, not by my merits, is a source of great pleasure for you. In your letter I have drunk in from your most loving heart your fatherly affection for me, not as something recent and new; rather, I rediscovered it as something I had experienced and known well, my most blessed lord, who deserve to be reverently embraced with most sincere love.

2. But how have our literary efforts, over which we have sweated in the composition of certain books, met with such good fortune that you have deigned to read them? It must be that the Lord, to whom my soul is subject, has wanted to comfort my concerns and relieve me of the worry by which I am necessarily troubled in such works for fear that I may perhaps stumble out of ignorance or carelessness, even in the perfectly level field of truth. After all, when what I write pleases you, I know whom it pleases, for I know who it is who dwells in you. The same one who distributes and gives all spiritual gifts has, of course, strengthened my obedience through your approval. For whatever those writings have worthy of your approval, it was God who said in my ministry, "Let it be made, and it was made." But in your approval *God saw that it was good* (Gn 1:10.12.18.21.25).

3. Even if I were trapped in my slowness and did not understand the short questions that you were so good as to ask me to untangle, I would resolve them with the help of your merits.[2] I have only this request: that you pray to God on

---

1. Simplician was chosen as the successor to Ambrose as bishop of Milan upon the latter's death in 397; Augustine had met him during his stay in Milan from 384 to 387. In fact, it was Simplician who told Augustine the story of the conversion of Marius Victorinus; see *Confessions* VIII, 2, 3-5.

2. It seems probable that Augustine sent this letter to Simplician along with his work, *Miscellany of Questions in Response to Simplician* (*De diversis quaestionibus ad Simplicianum*).

behalf of my weakness. And whether in the case of these questions by which in your kindly and fatherly fashion you wanted to provide me with exercise or in the case of any other of our writings that might perhaps come into your holy hands, not only take the care to read them, but also assume the role of censor to correct them, because, as I recognize God's gifts, so I know my own mistakes. Goodbye.

Letter 38

In the middle of 397 Augustine wrote to Profuturus, formerly a priest of Hippo and now bishop of Cirta in Numidia, telling him about the ill health he was suffering (paragraph 1). He mentions the death of Bishop Megalius and warns against allowing anger to turn into hatred (paragraph 2). He closes with greetings and a request for a favor (paragraph 3).

Augustine sends greetings to his brother, Profuturus.

1. In terms of the spirit, to the extent it pleases the Lord and he himself deigns to give us strength, we are doing fine, but as far as the body goes, I am in bed. For I can neither walk nor stand nor sit from the pain and swelling of fissures and hemorrhoids. But even so, since it is the Lord's will, what else should we say but that we are doing fine? For we should be blamed if we do not want what he wills rather than think that he either does or permits something that is not right. You know all this, but because you are for me like another me, what would I more willingly say to you than what I say to myself? We, therefore, commend to your holy prayers our days and nights. Pray for us that we do not spend the days intemperately and that we tolerate the nights calmly in order that, even if *we walk in the midst of the shadow of death*, the Lord may be with us *so that we fear no evil* (Ps 23:4).

2. I have no doubt that you have already heard that the primate Megalius[1] has died. For almost twenty-four days have passed since the burial of his body as I write this. We wish to know, if possible, whether you have already seen, as you planned, his successor in the primacy. There are scandals, but there is also a refuge. There are sorrows, but there are also consolations. And you very well know, best of brothers, how amid these trials we must be on guard for fear that hatred for anyone should take hold of the depths of our heart and not allow us to *pray to God in our room with the door shut* (Mt 6:6), but should rather close the door on God himself. But it sneaks up on us since no one who is angry thinks that his anger is unjust. For, when it takes root in that way, anger becomes hatred while the sweetness added as if from righteous resentment holds it longer in the cask until the whole becomes sour and spoils the cask. Hence, it is much better to become angry at someone, even unjustly, than to slip, as if we were justly angry, into a hatred for someone with a hidden ease coming from anger. In receiving unknown guests, after all, we usually say that it is much better to put up with an evil man than perhaps to turn away a good man through ignorance, while we are trying to avoid receiving a bad man. But in the dispositions of the soul the oppo-

---

1. Megalius was bishop of Calama and primate of Africa who consecrated Augustine bishop.

site is the case. For it is incomparably more salutary not to open the sanctuary of the heart when anger comes knocking with righteousness than to admit an anger that will not easily withdraw and will grow into a tree from a sapling. It impudently dares to grow even more quickly than one thinks. For it does not blush in the dark when the sun has set over it.[2] You certainly realize the care and concern with which I write these words if you recall what you spoke about with me recently on a certain journey.

3. We greet our brother, Severus[3], and those who are with him. We would perhaps have also written to them if the haste of the courier had permitted. But I ask that you help our Victor with the same brother. I express my gratitude to him before Your Holiness that he notified us when he set out for Constantina. I ask that he be sure to return through Calama on account of the business which he knows and because of which I suffer the most heavy burden of old Nectarius[4] with his many pleas about this matter. For that is what he promised me. Goodbye.

2. See Eph 4:26.
3. Severus was the Catholic bishop of Milevis in Numidia from 395 to 426.
4. Nectarius was a pagan and a prominent citizen of Calama; he wrote Letters 90 and 103 to Augustine and received Letters 91 and 104 in reply.

Letter 39

In approximately 397 Jerome wrote from his monastery in Bethlehem to Augustine in Hippo. He commends to Augustine the deacon, Praesidius, the bearer of the letter, and asks that his greetings be passed on to Alypius.

To Augustine, his truly holy lord and most blessed bishop, Jerome sends greetings in the Lord.

1, 1. Last year, by our brother, Asterius, a subdeacon, I had sent a letter to Your Grace to fulfill promptly the duty of repaying your greeting, and I think you received it.[1] Now I also beg through my holy brother, the deacon Praesidius, first that you be mindful of me and second that you regard the bearer of the letter as recommended by me and know that he is someone very close to me. And in whatever his needs demand, take care of him and provide for him, not because he lacks something under Christ's providence, but because he desires most eagerly friendships with good men and believes that he has obtained the greatest benefit in forming such friendships. But as to why he sailed to the West you will be able to learn from his own account.

2, 2. We who dwell in the monastery are buffeted by waves from this side and that, and we endure the troubles of our earthly pilgrimage. But we believe in him who said, *Have confidence; I have overcome the world* (Jn 16:33), for by his grace and protection we shall obtain victory against the devil, our enemy. I beg that you greet the holy and venerable brother, Bishop Alypius,[2] with respect for me. The holy brothers who zealously serve the Lord in the monastery greet you with great enthusiasm. May Christ our omnipotent God keep you safe and sound as well as mindful of us, my truly holy lord and esteemed bishop.

---

1. The letter to which Jerome refers is no longer extant; hence, this is the first letter we have from Jerome to Augustine.
2. Alypius was by this time bishop of Thagaste.

Letter 40

Toward the end of 397 Augustine wrote this letter to Jerome; the letter did not immediately arrive, but was found on an island in the Adriatic in 398, copied, and readdressed to Jerome. Augustine thanks Jerome for his letter and invites him to a more extended correspondence (paragraph 1). He thanks him for his book on ecclesiastical writers and their works (paragraph 2). Augustine expresses his concern about Jerome's interpretation of the dispute between Peter and Paul in the Letter to the Galatians and warns against admitting any lies into the scriptures (paragraph 3). He explains Paul's view of the role of the Jewish sacraments (paragraph 4) and the reasons why Paul reprimanded Peter (paragraph 5). Augustine explains what Paul rejected in the Jewish observances (paragraph 6) and invites Jerome to recant his position (paragraph 7), while insisting that he himself is only seeking the truth (paragraph 8). Augustine finally complains about Jerome's having provided so little information about the views of Origen and suggests how Jerome might usefully expand his work on Christian writers and their works (paragraph 9).

To his most beloved lord and brother who are worthy to be respected and embraced with the most sincere display of love, his fellow priest, Jerome, Augustine sends greetings.

1, 1. I am grateful that, in return for the greeting I wrote to you, you have replied with a full letter, though a much shorter one than I would have liked to receive from you, for you are such a man that from you no amount of words is too long, no matter how much time it takes. Although we are beset by great worries over the affairs of others and worldly ones at that, I would not readily excuse the brevity of your letter, if I did not bear in mind that it replies to even fewer words of my own. Hence, enter into this conversation by letter with us so that we do not allow bodily absence to do much to keep us apart, though we are united in the Lord *by oneness of the Spirit* (Eph 4:3), even if we rest our pen and are silent. After all, the books that you produced from the granary of the Lord present almost the whole of you to us. For, if we do not know you because we have not seen the face of your bodily person, you do not know even yourself in this way. For you also do not see it. But if you are known to yourself for no other reason than that you know your mind, we too know it to no small extent in your writings, for which we bless the Lord that he has given you who are such a fine person to yourself and to us and to all the brethren who read your writings.

2, 2. It is not long ago that a certain book of yours among others came into our hands; we still do not know what its title is, for the manuscript does not, as is usual, have the title on the first page. The brother with whom it was found, nonetheless, said it was called the "Epitaphs."[1] We would believe that you chose to give it this name if we had read in it only of either the lives or the writings of those already dead. But since it mentions the works of many who were living at the time it was written or are still living now, we are puzzled why you would either have given or be believed to have given it this title. We fully agree that you wrote the same book with great usefulness.

3, 3. In the explanation of the Letter of the apostle Paul to the Galatians we also found something that bothers us much. For, if so-called useful lies are admitted in the holy scriptures, what authority will remain in them? What statement, finally, could be found in those scriptures whose weight would crush the wickedness of stubbornly defended error? For, as soon as you produce the statement, if your opponent holds another view, he will say that the writer falsified the statement you produced for some good purpose. For where would he be unable to do this, if in that narrative that the apostle began by saying, *But as for what I write to you, look, before God I do not lie* (Gal 1:20), one could believe and maintain that Paul lied in that passage where he said of Peter and Barnabas, *When I saw that they were not walking correctly with respect to the truth of the gospel* (Gal 2:14)? For, if they were walking correctly, he lied, but if he lied there, where did he speak the truth? Or will he be thought to have spoken the truth where he says what the reader holds, but when something turns up contrary to the view of the reader, it will be ascribed to a useful lie? For there will be plenty of reasons why he should be thought not only to be able to lie, but also to be obliged to lie, if one makes room for this rule. It is not necessary to press this argument with many words, especially with you, for enough has been said for someone with wisdom and foresight. But I would never claim that I am trying to enrich with my few coins your fine mind, which by God's gift is solid gold, nor is there anyone better suited than you to correct that work.

4, 4. I, after all, should not instruct you how to understand the words of the same apostle, *I have become to the Jews like a Jew in order that I might gain the Jews* (1 Cor 9:20) and the other things that are said there out of merciful compassion, not out of false pretense. For he who cares for a sick person becomes like someone sick, not when he falsely states that he has a fever, but when with the mind of someone compassionate he thinks of how he would want to be cared for if he were ill. He was, after all, a Jew, but having become a Christian, he had not abandoned the sacraments of the Jews, which that people had suitably and legitimately received at the time when they were necessary. Therefore, he undertook their observance when he was already an apostle of Christ, but he did this in order to teach that they were not dangerous for those who wanted to observe them, as they had received them from their parents, even though they had come to believe in Christ, but that they should no longer place the hope of salvation in

---

1. The book was Jerome's *Famous Men* (*De viris illustribus*).

them. For the salvation that was signified by those sacraments had arrived through the Lord Jesus. And for this reason he judged that they should in no way be imposed upon the Gentiles because by their heavy and unnecessary burden they would hold them back from the faith insofar as they were not used to them.[2]

5. Hence, he did not correct Peter because he was observing the traditions of his forefathers. If he had wanted to do that, he would neither have lied nor acted inappropriately, for practices that, though now superfluous, were customary would not, nonetheless, do harm. But he corrected Peter because he was forcing the Gentiles to live like Jews,[3] something that he could in no way accomplish unless he himself carried out those practices in that way, as if they were still necessary for salvation after the coming of the Lord. That was something from which the truth strongly dissuaded him through the apostleship of Paul. Nor was the apostle Peter unaware of this; rather, he was doing this, *in fear of those who were from the circumcision* (Gal 2:12). And so he was truly corrected, and Paul reported the truth so that the entire holy scripture, which was published for the faith of those to come, would not waver and become unsteady with doubt once the justification of a lie has been accepted. It is not, after all, possible or necessary to explain in writing the great and inexplicable evils that follow if we grant this. It could, however, suitably and less dangerously be demonstrated if we were speaking directly to one another.

6. Paul had, then, abandoned the evil that the Jews held, first of all, that, *not knowing the righteousness of God and wanting to establish their own righteousness, they were not subject to the righteousness of God* (Rom 10:3); secondly, that, after the Passion and resurrection of Christ, when the sacrament of grace had been given and revealed *according to the order of Melchizedek* (Heb 6:20), they still thought that they should observe the old sacraments, not because of the habit of celebrating them, but because of their necessity for salvation. And yet, if they never had been necessary, the Maccabees would have become martyrs for them without purpose and without benefit.[4] Finally, the Jews persecuted the Christian preachers of grace as enemies of the law. He says that he considered *as losses and rubbish in order that he might gain Christ* (Phil 3:8) these and other such errors and vices, not the ceremonies of the law, if they are observed following the custom of the fathers. In that way he himself observed them, not because of their being necessary for salvation, as the Jews thought they should be observed, or because of false pretense, something he reprehended in Peter. For, if he observed those sacraments because he pretended that he was a Jew in order to gain them, why did he not also offer sacrifice with the Gentiles since he became like someone without the law for those who were without the law in

2. See Acts 15:28.
3. See Gal 2:4.
4. See 2 Mc 7:1.

order that he might gain them too? Rather, he did that like someone who was a Jew by birth, and he said all this, not in order that he might deceitfully pretend that he was what he was not, but because he thought that he should mercifully help them in that way, as if he were laboring under the same error, not, of course, out of the cunning of a liar, but out of the love of someone compassionate. Just as in the same passage he introduced the general statement, *For the weak I became weak in order that I might gain the weak*, so we should understand the following conclusion, *For all I have become all things in order to gain all* (1 Cor 9:22), to refer to this aim, namely, that he would be seen to have shown pity for the weakness of each person as if for something in himself. For, when he said, *Who is weak and I am not weak?* (2 Cor 11:29), he did not want us to understand that he pretended to have the weakness of another, but that he had compassion for him.

7. Hence, I beg you, take up genuine and truly Christian severity with love to correct and emend that work, and sing, as they say, a παλινῳδίαν.[5] The truth of Christians is incomparably more beautiful than the Helen of the Greeks.[6] On behalf of it our martyrs have fought against this Sodom more bravely than those heroes fought against Troy. Nor do I say this in order that you may receive eyes for your heart; heaven forbid that you have lost them! But I say that in order that you may turn back those healthy and watchful eyes that you have, eyes that you have by some deliberate disregard turned them away so that you do not see what bad effects result if we in one case believe that a writer of the books of God can with a good and pious intention lie in some part of his work.

5, 8. I had on this topic written a letter to you some time ago, but it was not delivered to you because the man to whom I had entrusted it did not himself arrive.[7] As a result there occurred to me, when I was dictating this one, something that I also ought not to have omitted in this one, namely that, if your view is different and better, you should readily pardon my fear. For, if you hold a different view and you hold the truth, and unless it is true, it cannot be better, I do not want to say it is with no fault, but certainly it is with no great fault that my error favors the truth, if the truth can in any case correctly favor a lie.

6, 9. But with regard to what you deigned to write back about Origen, I already had known that I should approve and praise the correct and true ideas we find, not only in ecclesiastical writings, but also in all writings, and disapprove and reprehend false and incorrect ideas. But I desired, and I still desire, from your wisdom and learning that you inform us of his mistakes by which that great man is proved to have withdrawn from the true faith. In the book in which you mentioned all the ecclesiastical writers and their writings that you could remember,[8] it would be better, I think, if, when you named those who you knew

---

5. Literally, a recantation. Augustine is asking Jerome to formally disavow his error.
6. The Trojan War was fought over the legendary beauty of Helen.
7. That is, Letter 28, which was carried by Profuturus.
8. That is, *Famous Men*.

were heretics, since you did not want to pass over even these, you would add the points on which they are to be avoided. And yet, you did pass over some, and I would like to know why you did that. Or if you did not want to overly extend that volume so that, having mentioned heretics, you did not add the points on which Catholic authority condemns them, I have a request that brotherly love points out to you through my lowly self. I hope that it will not place too heavy a burden on your literary labors, through which you have by the grace of the Lord our God both kindled and fostered sacred studies no small amount in the Latin language. I ask that, if your work load allows, you publish in one book a short digest of the mistaken teachings of all the heretics who have up to this time tried to spoil the rectitude of the Christian faith either by impudence or by stubbornness. This would contribute to the knowledge of those who either do not have time because of other tasks or do not have the ability because of the foreign language to read and to come to know so much. I would ask you at length if this were not usually a sign of someone who counts less on the other person's love. Meanwhile, I commend Paul, this brother of ours in Christ, very highly to Your Grace, and we testify before God to the good opinion of him in our regions.

Letter 41

Soon after his ordination as bishop, Augustine, along with Alypius, the bishop of Thagaste, wrote to Aurelius, the bishop of Carthage and primate of Africa. They congratulate him for allowing priests to preach (paragraph 1), and they ask that copies of some of these sermons be sent to them (paragraph 2).

To Bishop Aurelius,[1] their most blessed lord, their most dear brother, who is to be reverently and most sincerely embraced, and their fellow priest, Augustine and Alypius[2] send greetings in the Lord.

1. *Our mouth is filled with joy and our tongue with exultation* (Ps 125:2), when your letter reports that your holy thought has, with the help of the Lord who inspired it, been realized concerning all our ordained brothers and especially concerning the sermons of priests, which are delivered to the people in your presence. By their tongues Your Charity cries out with a louder voice in the hearts of human beings than they cry out in their ears: "Thanks be to God!" For what better words do we bear in mind and utter with our lips and write with a pen than, "Thanks be to God." Nothing can be said more briefly than this, nothing heard more gladly, nothing understood of more grandeur, and nothing done more fruitfully. Thanks be to God, who has endowed you with so faithful a heart toward your sons and has brought out into the light what you had in the inner chamber of the mind where the human eye does not penetrate. For he has granted to you, not only the possession of a good will, but also those in whom your good will can be seen. So be it; clearly, so be it; *let* these works *shine forth before men in order that they may see*, rejoice, *and glorify the Father who is in heaven* (Mt 5:16). In such priests may you find delight in the Lord; may he graciously hear you as you pray for them, for you do not refuse to hear him as he speaks through them. Let us go; let us walk; let us run in the way of the Lord; may the little ones be blessed along with the great; *may they be pleased with them who say to them, We shall go to the house of the Lord* (Ps 122:1). Let those go first, and let these follow, having become imitators of them as they are of Christ.[3] May the route of holy ants be fervent; may the activity of holy bees spread its perfume; may their fruit be borne in patience with salutary perseverance up to the end. *Nor does the Lord allow us to be tempted beyond what we can bear, but with temptation he also produces a way out in order that we can endure* (1 Cor 10:13).

---

1. Aurelius became bishop of Carthage in 393 and presided over that see until his death in 429 or 430.
2. Augustine's friend from boyhood, now bishop of their hometown, Thagaste.
3. See 1 Cor 11:1.

153

2. Pray for us, you who are worthy to be heard when you approach God with a truly great a sacrifice of most pure love and praise for him in your works. Pray that these works may also shine forth in us, because he to whom you pray knows how great is our joy that they shine forth in you. These are our desires; these multitudes of consolations *bring joy to our soul in accord with the multitude of our sorrows* (Ps 94:19). This is so because it was promised in that way; what remains will also be that way, just it has been promised. We beseech you, through him who has given you these gifts and has through you showered the people you serve with this blessing, that you command that individual sermons of these men, ones that you choose, be written out, corrected, and sent to us. For I am not neglecting to do what you have commanded, and, as I have already often written, I await to know what you think concerning Tychonius' seven rules or keys.[4] We commend highly Brother Hilary, the chief and principal doctor of Hippo. For concerning Brother Romanus we know what you are trying to do, and we should ask nothing but that the Lord help you on his behalf. Amen.

---

4. Tychonius, an older contemporary of Augustine, was a Donatist whose seven principles of scriptural interpretation Augustine adopted and commented on in *Teaching Christianity*.

Letter 42

In the fall of 398 Augustine wrote to Paulinus and Therasia. He complains that he had not heard from them for the past two summers and asks again that Paulinus send him his *Against the Pagans*, if it is finished.

To his praiseworthy lord and lady and most holy brother and sister in Christ, Paulinus and Therasia, Augustine sends greetings in the Lord.

Could one have supposed or expected that we would through our brother, Severus, have demanded a reply that Your Charity has not yet sent, though we have desired it so long and so ardently? Why is it that we are compelled to go thirsty for two summers and for summers in Africa? What more should I say? O you people, who daily give away your possessions, pay your debt. Or have you perhaps postponed letters to us for so long a time because I had heard that you were writing a work against the worshipers of demons and had shown that I intensely desired that work, since you wanted to complete and send it?[1] Oh, I wish that from your rich table you would at least relieve my hunger during so many years for anything penned by you. If the table is not yet prepared, we shall not cease to complain unless you give us some refreshment while you in the meanwhile bring it to perfection. Greet the brothers, especially Romanus and Agilis. Those who are here with us greet you, and they are along with us not impatient enough only if they do not love you enough.

---

1. See Letter 31.

Letter 43

At the end of 396 or early in 397 Augustine wrote to a group of Donatist leaders with an appeal for unity. He writes to them, not as to heretics, but as to men ready to be corrected (paragraph 1). He desires to be a peacemaker (paragraph 2). He recalls the beginning of the schism at which a council of seventy bishops condemned Caecilian, the bishop of Carthage (paragraph 3), which was followed by the ordination of Majorian and the councils at Rome and at Arles, which condemned the Donatists (paragraph 4). The perfidy of Secundus of Tigisi completes the picture (paragraph 5). Augustine reminds his addressees that eternal life is at stake (paragraph 6), points out the injustices involved in the Donatist councils (paragraph 7), and explains why the Donatists rejected councils held overseas to hear their case against Caecilian (paragraphs 8 and 9). The Donatist council that condemned Caecilian was in fact composed of bishops who had themselves handed over the scriptures (paragraph 10). In any case the council should not have condemned bishops who were not present (paragraph 11).

The case of Felix of Aptungi, who was condemned by the Donatists, but later proved innocent, shows how the Donatists could have condemned the innocent Caecilian (paragraph 12). Donatist complaints about the emperor's hearing the case against them are inconsistent (paragraph 13). They should at least listen to the decision handed down by the bishops whom the emperor appointed (paragraph 14). Augustine compares the calm judiciousness of the judges with the perversity of the Donatist accusers (paragraph 15) and points to the impartial and peaceful judgment of Pope Melchiades (paragraph 16). Augustine reminds his readers of the influence exerted by the wealthy woman, Lucilla, whom Caecilian had offended by rebuking her when he was still a deacon and who bribed the Donatist bishops (paragraph 17). Since Caecilian knew what the situation was, he wisely refused to submit to the judgment of the Donatists (paragraph 18). Furthermore, since the overseas churches remained in communion with Caecilian, the Donatists chose to take their case against him overseas where they lost at Rome (paragraph 19). Then the Donatists again appealed to the emperor who granted them another episcopal hearing at Arles where they again lost. Unwilling to give up, they forced the emperor to hear their case in Milan, where he acquitted Caecilian (paragraph 20).

Despite their crimes, the Donatists complain about the use of civil powers to correct them (paragraph 21). Augustine produces scripture texts to show how the early Church and the people of Israel tolerated sinners in their midst (paragraphs 22 and 23). The Donatists, in fact, tolerate in their midst the criminal Circumcellions (paragraph 24). Even if the Donatists cannot agree with the Catholics about the facts at the time of Caecilian, they have the present fact of the Catholic Church's being spread throughout the world, as scripture had promised (paragraph 25). Augustine points to the similarities between the Donatists' breaking away from the rest of the Church and the Maximianists' breaking away from the Donatists (paragraph 26). Finally, Augustine urges the Donatists to return to the unity of the Catholic Church and insists that "no one wipes out from the earth the Church of God" (paragraph 27).

To his most beloved lords and his brothers who are rightly to be praised, Glorius, Eleusius, the two Felixes, Grammaticus,[1] *and all the others to whom this is pleasing, Augustine sends greetings.*

1, 1. The apostle Paul, of course, said, *Avoid a heretical man after one rebuke, knowing that such a man is perverse and a sinner and has been condemned by himself* (Ti 3:10). But people like yourselves should by no means be considered to be heretics. For you defend your view, though false and erroneous, without any stubborn animosity, especially since you did not give rise to it by the brazenness of presumption, but have received it from your parents, who were seduced and fell into error, and you seek the truth with a cautious concern, ready to be corrected when you find it. If I did not believe that you were such people, I would perhaps not be sending you a letter. And yet, just as we are warned that we should avoid the heretic swollen with odious pride and insane with the stubbornness of evil strife for fear that he may deceive the weak and the little ones, so we do not deny that we should correct him in whatever ways we can. This is the reason why we have written even to some leaders of the Donatists, not letters of communion that they now no longer accept on account of their having turned away from the Catholic unity, which is spread through the whole world, but such private letters as we are permitted to send even to pagans. And though they have at some point read these, they, nonetheless, either refused to reply to them or, as is more believable, they could not. In this way we thought that we had sufficiently fulfilled the duty of love, which the Holy Spirit teaches that we owe, not only to our people, but also to all peoples. He speaks to us through the apostle, *But may the Lord give you increase and make you abound in love for one another and for all* (1 Thes 3:12). He also warns in another place that those who hold different views should be rebuked with moderation, *in case,* he says, *God may perhaps give them repentance to know the truth and they may escape from the snares of the devil, after have been held captive by him to do his will* (2 Tm 2:26).

2. I said this in the beginning so that no one would think that I sent this letter to you with more impudence than prudence in that I wanted to deal with you in this way about the business of your soul, since you do not belong to our communion. And yet, if I wrote something to you about the business of a farm or of settling some other financial dispute, perhaps no one would find fault. This world is so dear to human beings, and they themselves have grown worthless in their own eyes! This letter, then, will be a witness for my defense in the judgment of God,

---

1. These are all Donatist laymen from Thiave in Numidia.

who knows with what intention I acted and who said, *Blessed are the peacemakers because they will be called the children of God* (Mt 5:9).

2, 3. Be so good as to recall, then, that, when we were in your city and dealt with you about some matters concerning the communion of Christian unity, certain records were brought forth by your side from which it was read out that almost seventy bishops condemned Caecilian, then bishop of the Carthaginian church, who belonged to our communion, along with his colleagues and those who ordained him. In those records the case of Felix of Aptungi was reported as much more hateful and criminal than the others. When they were all read, we replied that one should not be surprised if the persons who at that time produced that schism thought that those against whom they were stirred up by jealous and wicked persons should be hastily condemned in their absence without a hearing of their case, but not without compiling the proceedings. We, however, said that we had other ecclesiastical records in which Secundus of Tigisi, who then held the primacy in Numidia, left the traditors,[2] who were present and had confessed, to the judgment of God and allowed them to remain in their episcopal sees as they were. Their names are counted among those who condemned Caecilian, since Secundus himself presided over the same council, in which he condemned those who were absent as traditors by the votes of those whom he pardoned when they were present and confessed.

4. Then we said that, at some point after the ordination of Majorinus, whom by their wicked crime they elevated to the episcopacy in opposition to Caecilian, when they erected altar over against altar and destroyed the unity of Christ by frenzied discord, they asked Constantine, who was then emperor, for episcopal judges to act as arbitrators and to pronounce judgment on their questions that had arisen in Africa and destroyed the bond of peace. After this was granted, when Caecilian and those who had sailed from Africa in opposition to him were present, Melchiades,[3] who was then bishop of Rome, acted as judge along with his colleagues, whom the emperor had sent at the request of the Donatists. But nothing could be proved against Caecilian, and for this reason, after he had been confirmed in his episcopacy, Donatus,[4] who was at that time his opposite number, was found guilty. After this happened, since they all remained in the stubbornness of their most wicked schism, the same emperor later had the same case examined more carefully and brought to an end at Arles.[5] But they appealed the ecclesiastical judgment in order that Constantius would hear their case. After

---

2. The traditors were those bishops who in the persecution of Diocletian handed over the sacred books or vessels. I have transliterated the term to avoid a longer paraphrase.
3. Melchiades was pope from 311 to 314; he condemned Donatism and upheld Caecilian at the Lateran Council of 313.
4. Donatus, the bishop of Casae Nigrae in Numidia, from whom the schism took its name.
5. The Council of Arles met on 1 August 314.

this came about, with both sides present, Caecilian was judged innocent,[6] and they left defeated and, nonetheless, remained in the same error. Nor was the case of Felix of Aptungi overlooked, but at the order of the same emperor he was acquitted in the proconsular proceedings.

5. But since we were only saying all this, not also reading it, you surely thought that we were doing less than you expected, given our insistence. When we perceived this, we did not delay to send for those records, which we promised to read. All these records arrived after an interval of less than two full days while we hastened off to the Church of Gelizi in order to return to your town from there. And, as you know, they were read out to you on one day to the extent that time allowed. First there was read the part where Secundus of Tigisi did not dare to remove from the college of bishops the traditors who confessed, though afterward with them he dared to condemn Caecilian and his other colleagues, who had not confessed and who were absent. Then we read the proconsular proceedings where Felix was proved innocent by a most careful examination. You remember that these were read to you in the morning. But in the afternoon we read their petitions to Constantine and, after he appointed judges, the ecclesiastical proceedings held in the city of Rome in which they were condemned, while Caecilian was retained in his episcopal dignity. Finally, we read the letter of the emperor, Constantine which showed that everything was fully attested to the highest degree.

3, 6. What more do you want, you people? What more do you want? We are not dealing with your gold and silver. It is not your land and estates, not even the health of your body that is at stake. We are challenging your souls about acquiring eternal life and escaping eternal death. Wake up at long last! We are not dealing with some obscure question; we are not searching out some hidden secrets for the penetration of which either no human hearts or very few are capable. The issue lies in the open. What stands out more clearly? What is seen more quickly? We say that innocent and absent people were condemned by a council that acted in haste, though it was one with large numbers. We prove this by the proconsular proceedings by which he was pronounced free from every crime of handing over the sacred books, though the proceedings of the council that your people brought forth declared him a criminal. We say that sentences were passed by confessed traditors upon those who were said to be traditors. We prove this by the ecclesiastical proceedings in which they are mentioned by name. Among them Secundus of Tigisi pardoned, as if with a view to peace, their crimes that he knew, and later, when the peace was destroyed, he condemned with them those he did not know. From this it is clear that he even at first was not concerned about peace, but was afraid for himself. For Purpurius, the bishop of Limate, had objected to him that, when Secundus himself was also arrested by an

---

6. The judgment was pronounced by the emperor at Milan in 316.

officer and his troops in order that he would hand over the scriptures, he was released, not, of course, without reason, but because he handed them over or ordered that something be handed over. Fearing that this suspicion could easily enough be proven, having received advice from a younger Secundus, a relative of his, and having consulted others bishops who were with him, he left the most obvious crimes to be judged by God. In that way he was thought to have had an eye out for peace, but that was false since he had an eye out for himself.

7. For, if the thought of peace dwelled in his heart, he would not have later at Carthage, along with those who surrendered the books, men whom he had dismissed when they were present and had confessed, condemned for the crime of surrendering the sacred books those men who were absent and whom no one had proven guilty before. He ought to have feared more that the peace of our unity would be violated to the degree that Carthage was a large and famous city, from which the evil that arose there might pour down, as if from its head, over the whole body of Africa. It was also close to the overseas regions and renowned for its very distinguished reputation. For this reason it had a bishop of more than average authority who could disregard a number of enemies conspiring against him since he saw that he was united by letters of communion to the Roman church, in which the primacy of the Apostolic See always thrived, and to the other lands from which the gospel came to Africa. He was ready to state his case there if his opponents tried to separate those churches from him. Because he refused to come to the gathering of his colleagues, for he saw or suspected or, as they claim, pretended that they had been turned against the truth of his case by his enemies, Secundus ought all the more, if he wanted to be a protector of the peace, to have avoided condemning in their absence those who absolutely refused to appear for the judgment. For he was not dealing with priests or deacons or clerics of lower rank, but with his colleagues who could keep their case intact for the judgment of other colleagues, especially of the apostolic churches, where judgments pronounced against them, when they were absent, would be absolutely without effect. After all, they did not later leave a court that they first approached, but they never wanted to approach the court that they always held suspect.

8. This fact especially ought to have drawn the attention of Secundus, then the primate, if he was presiding over the council in order to preserve peace. For he would perhaps have keep quiet and bridled the mouths rabid against the absent, if he said, "You see, brothers, that after so great a slaughter of persecution peace has been granted through the mercy of God by the rulers of the world; we Christians and bishops ought not to destroy the Christian unity that the pagan enemy no longer attacks. And so, either let us leave to the judgment of God all these cases that the scourge of the time of unrest inflicted upon the Church, or if there are some among you who know the crimes of these men for certain so that they can easily prove them and convict those who deny them and if they are afraid to

be in communion with such people, let them go to our brothers and colleagues of the churches across the sea, and let them there first complain about the actions and contempt of these bishops, because, conscious of their guilt, they refused to come to a court of their African colleagues. In that way they might be ordered from overseas to come and reply there to the objections raised against them. But if they do not do this, their wickedness and perversity will be seen there also, and after a letter to all the churches with their name has been sent through the whole world, wherever the Church of Christ has spread, they will be cut off from communion with all the churches to prevent some error from arising in the chair of the Carthaginian church. Then we shall at last safely ordain another bishop for the people of Carthage when these people have been separated from the whole Church. Otherwise, when another has already been ordained, the new bishop might not be accepted into communion by the church across the sea, because they will not see that the present bishop has been deposed from his office, for rumor has declared him already ordained, and the church across the sea has sent letters of communion to him. And thus there might arise the great scandal of schism in the unity of Christ in a time of peace, when we wish too hastily to cast our judgments and dare to erect another altar, not over against Caecilian, but over against the world, which is in communion with him out of ignorance."

9. If any wild man refused to obey this sound and correct counsel, what was he going to do? Or how was he going to condemn some of his absent colleagues when he did not have control of the proceedings of the council since the primate was opposed? But if such a great rebellion had arisen and against the primatial see that some now wanted to condemn those whom the primate wanted to refer elsewhere, how much better would it be to disagree with such bishops who were plotting unrest and upheaval than with the communion of the whole world! But since the charges were not such that they could be proven in an overseas court against Caecilian and those who ordained him, they did not, for this reason, want the case to be brought there before they had passed sentence against him. And after they had passed sentence, they did not work with perseverance to bring to the notice of the church across the sea the traditors condemned in Africa, with whom that church ought to avoid communion. For, if they had tried that, Caecilian and the others would have defended themselves and would have won their case with a most careful examination of the issue against their false accusers before the overseas judges.

10. That perverse and wicked council, then, was, as is believed, composed mostly of traditors, whom Secundus of Tigisi pardoned when they confessed. For, since the rumor of the surrender of the books had spread about, they tried to turn suspicion away from themselves by denouncing others, and since people who believed the bishops were saying false things about the innocent throughout Africa, namely, that they were condemned at Carthage as traditors, those bishops who really handed over the scriptures were hiding as if in a cloud of the

falsest rumor. From this you see, my friends, that what some of your people said was improbable to have happened, namely, that those very same ones who had confessed their surrender of the books, and had ensured that their case should be left to God, afterward sat to judge and condemn as traditors bishops who were absent. For they rather grasped the chance to be able to pour out false charges upon the others and in this way to turn aside from an investigation of their own crimes the tongues of human beings, once they were turned against those others. Otherwise, if it were not possible that anyone condemn in another the sins which he himself committed, Paul the apostle would not say to certain people, *For this reason you are without excuse, every one of you who judges. For in that act by which you judge another you condemn yourself. For you do the same things that you condemn* (Rom 2:1). Those bishops did precisely this so that these words of the apostle apply to them fully and properly.

11. When Secundus left their crimes to God's judgment, he was, therefore, not aiming at peace and unity. Otherwise, he would have taken more care at Carthage that a schism not arise where no one was present whose admitted crime he was forced to pardon. Rather, as would have been most easy, the whole preservation of peace would have involved only the refusal to condemn those who were absent. And so, they would have done injustice to the innocent, even if they had chosen to pardon those who were not convicted, who had not confessed, and who were not even present. A person, of course, accepts a pardon if his wrongdoing is absolutely certain. How much more inhuman and blind were those who thought that they could condemn those crimes that they could not even have pardoned since they were unknown! But in the former case the crimes that were known were left to God in order that no others might be looked for; in this case unknown crimes were condemned in order that those former crimes might be concealed. But someone will say, "They knew those crimes." Even if I should grant this, they ought, of course, to have spared those who were absent. For they had not fled from the court where they had never been present, nor did the Church consist of those African bishops alone so that they would seem to have avoided all ecclesiastical judgment if they refused to present themselves to their court. There were thousands of colleagues across the sea where it was evident that those bishops could be tried who seemed to hold their African or Numidian colleagues suspect. What has happened to the cry of scripture, *Before you question him, do not blame anyone, and after you have questioned him, rebuke him justly* (Sir 11:7). If, then, the Holy Spirit wanted no one blamed or rebuked if he had not been questioned, how much more of a crime is it that bishops were not only blamed and rebuked but completely condemned who, as absent, could not have been questioned about their crimes at all?

12. But these, nonetheless, say that they condemned the known crimes of those who were absent, who had not fled from the court since they were never present, and who stated that they held suspect that group of judges. How, I ask

you, my brothers, did they know those crimes? You answer, "We do not know, since this knowledge was not explained in those proceedings." But I shall show you how they knew. Pay attention to the case of Felix of Aptungi, and first read how they were more severe toward him. They, therefore, knew the case of the others in the same way they knew the case of this man, who was later proven utterly innocent by a careful and frightening inquest. When that man has been found innocent against whom they raged much more inhumanly, how much more justly and safely and quickly ought we to judge those bishops innocent since these men accused their crimes less severely and condemned them with a milder reproach!

4, 13. Or, as someone said—and you were perhaps displeased at it when it was said to you, but it still should not be passed over. For he said, "A bishop ought not to be tried by a proconsular court," as if he himself arranged this for himself and the emperor did not order that the inquest be conducted in this way. For that issue especially pertains to his care, and he will give an account to God about it. Those men made him the arbiter and judge of a case involving the surrender of the sacred books and schism when they sent petitions to him to whom they later appealed, and they, nonetheless, refused to abide by his judgment. And so, if he is to be blamed whom an earthly judge has acquitted, though he did not himself ask for this, how much more are they to be blamed who wanted an earthly king to be the judge of their case! But if it is not criminal to appeal to the emperor, it is not criminal to have one's case heard by the emperor. And it is not, therefore, criminal to have it heard by one to whom the emperor delegates the case. That friend wanted charges to be brought because in the case of Bishop Felix one witness was suspended on the rack and because another was also tortured with tongs. Was Felix able to oppose this so that the inquest was not carried out with such great diligence or severity, when the judge was acting to discover the facts of that case? For what else is it to refuse such an inquest but to confess to the crime? And yet amid the terrible cries of the bailiffs and the bloody hands of the executioners that proconsul himself would never condemn an absent colleague who refused to present himself to his court since he had another court where he could be heard. Or, if he did condemn him, he would certainly pay the just and due punishments even in accord with the laws of the world.

5, 14. But if you are not happy with the proconsular proceedings, yield to the ecclesiastical ones. They have all been read out to you in order. Or ought perhaps Melchiades, the bishop of the Roman church, along with his colleagues, the bishops from across the sea, not to have taken over for themselves a case that was ended by seventy Africans where the primate of Tigisi presided? What about the fact that Melchiades did not himself take it over? When asked, the emperor sent bishops as judges to preside with him and to determine what seemed just concerning that whole case. We prove this by the petitions of the Donatists and by the words of the emperor himself. For you remember that both were read to you, and you now have the freedom to inspect and copy them. Read and examine them all. See the great concern for preserving or restoring peace and unity with which everything was examined, the treatment of the legal standing of the accusers, the defects by which certain of them were disqualified, and the clear proof from the words of those present that they had nothing to say against Caecilian. Rather, they wanted to transfer the whole case to the people on the side of Majorinus, that is, to the rebellious multitude alienated from the peace of the Church. And in that way Caecilian would be accused by that crowd that they thought could turn the minds of the judges to their will by disorderly outbursts alone, without the production of any proof and without an investigation of the truth. As if an angry mob drunk from the cup of error and corruption would bring true charges against Caecilian, when seventy bishops, as it is clear concerning Felix of Aptungi, condemned their absent and innocent colleagues with such great madness! After all, they wanted Caecilian once again to be accused by the sort of mob with which they agreed in order to pronounce their sentences against innocent men who had not been questioned. But they had clearly not found the sort of judges whom they might persuade to such madness.

15. In accord with your wisdom, after all, you can note their perversity on this point and the sober sincerity of the judges who were unable up to the very end to be persuaded that Caecilian should be accused by the people on the side of Majorinus, who had no certain legal standing, and how the judges demanded of them either accusers or witnesses or people in some way necessary to the case who had come with them from Africa, and how it was said that they were present, but were withdrawn by Donatus. The same Donatus promised that he would produce them, and after he had promised that not once, but often, he refused further to approach that court where he had already confessed so much that by not approaching thereafter he seemed to want to avoid nothing else but being condemned when present. And yet, the crimes that ought to have been condemned were revealed when he was present and questioned. In addition, certain people presented a list of charges denouncing Caecilian. After this was done, you know how the inquest was reopened against Caecilian, who the people were who brought the charges, and how nothing could be proved against Caecilian. What shall I say, since you have heard all this and you can read it as often as you wish?

16. Concerning the number of seventy bishops, however, you remember what was said, since it was brought up against us as the weightiest authority, and yet very sober and sincere persons preferred to refrain from judgment about endless questions tied together as if by an inextricable chain. They did not care about how many those bishops were or from where they were assembled, since they saw that they were blinded by such great rashness that they dared to pass such precipitous sentences upon absent colleagues who had not been questioned. And yet how different was the final sentence pronounced by blessed

Melchiades, how innocent, how impartial and peaceful. By that judgment he did not dare to remove from his company colleagues against whom nothing had been established, and after Donatus alone, whom he had found to be the source of the whole evil, was found especially guilty, he left to the others the free option of recovering their good health. He was ready to send letters of communion even to those who had been clearly ordained by Majorinus so that in whatever places there were two bishops as a result of the dissension, he wanted to confirm the one who had been first ordained, but to provide for the other another people to rule. Oh what a fine man! Oh what a son of Christian peace and what a father of the Christian people! Compare this handful with that mob of bishops, and compare, not the one number with the other, but the one authority with the other—in the one case moderation, in the other rashness, in the one vigilance, in the other blindness. And in this case gentleness did not destroy integrity, nor was integrity opposed to gentleness. But in the other case fear is cloaked with fury, and fury is aroused by fear. For these bishops had come together to reject false crimes by the investigation of true ones, while those had come together to conceal true crimes by the condemnation of false ones.

6, 17. Should Caecilian have handed himself over to those men to have them hear his case and to pronounce judgment when he had such judges that, if his case were brought before them, he would most easily prove his innocence? He should absolutely not have surrendered himself to them, not even if, as coming from elsewhere, he were recently ordained bishop of the Carthaginian church and did not know what a certain very wealthy woman at that time, Lucilla, could do to corrupt the minds of the evil and ignorant. For he had offended her by a rebuke in defense of church discipline when he was a deacon. This evil too contributed to carrying out that wickedness. For in that council in which the absent and innocent bishops were condemned by confessed traditors, there were a certain few who desired to cover over their own crimes by blackening the reputation of others in order that people would be distracted by false rumors and turned away from the investigation of the truth. They were, then, few in number who made this their special goal, though they had greater authority because of their fellowship with Secundus, who had spared them out of fear. But the rest, it is reported, were bought and stirred up against Caecilian especially by Lucilla's money. The proceedings exist in the possession of the governor, Zenophilus; in them a certain Nundinarius, a deacon deposed by Sylvanus, the bishop of Cirta, as the proceedings show, when he tried in vain to satisfy them by letters from other bishops, disclosed many things in anger and made them public in court. Among these we read that they mention that, after the bishops were bribed in the church of Carthage, the capital of Africa, by Lucilla's money, altar was erected over against altar. I know that we did not read these proceedings to you, but you remember that there was not enough time. There was also present some mental anguish from the swelling of pride because they themselves had not ordained him bishop of Carthage.

18. Since by all these means Caecilian learned that they had come together, not as true judges, but as enemies and bribed men, how could it have happened that either he himself would choose or the people over whom he presided would permit that, having left his church, he should go to a private home, not to be examined by a hearing of his colleagues, but to be slaughtered by the forces of the faction and by a woman's hatred? How could this have happened, especially since he saw that before the church across the sea, which was free from private hostilities and from both sides of the disagreement, the hearing of his case remained undamaged and unimpaired? And if the opponents refused to present a case there, they would cut themselves off from the perfectly innocent communion of the rest of the world. But if they had tried to accuse him there, then he would have been present and would have defended his innocence against all their plots, just as you learned that he did later, after they had far too late asked for an overseas trial, when they were already guilty of schism and defiled by the horrendous outrage of erecting another altar. For they would have done so in the first place if they were relying on the truth, but they wanted to come to court when false rumors had become strong with the length of time, as if the age of the rumor were the decisive factor. Or, what is more believable, after Caecilian was condemned as they wanted, they thought that they were secure, trusting in their number and not daring to present so bad a case elsewhere where, without any bribery at work, the truth could be found out.

7, 19. But after they learned by the facts that the rest of the world remained in communion with Caecilian and that the churches across the sea sent letters of communion to him and not to the bishop they had wickedly ordained, they were ashamed to continue to remain silent. For it could be asked of them as an objection why they allowed the church among so many nations to maintain through ignorance communion with those who were condemned and why they cut themselves off from communion with innocent bishops of the world, when by remaining silent they permitted the whole world to be out of communion with the bishop whom they ordained for the people of Carthage. They chose to lodge a case, as is said, with two possible outcomes,[7] against Caecilian before the churches across the sea prepared for either of them. Thus, if they could by any trickery whatsoever of false accusation have defeated him, they would have most completely satisfied their desire; if, however, they could not, they would have persisted in the same perversity, but now as if they had gotten what they were saying, namely, that they had suffered from bad judges. That is the cry of all those who have a weak case when they have been defeated by even the most obvious truth, as if we could not also most justly say this to them, "Look, let us

7. The Latin has simply "*ad duas,*" where one manuscript adds "*fraudes.*"

consider those bishops who judged the case in Rome not to be good judges; there still remained the plenary council of the universal Church where the case could be brought even against these judges so that, if they were proven guilty of having judged wrongly, their judgments would be set aside." Let them prove that they did this, for we easily prove that they did not from the fact that the whole world is not in communion with them. Or if they did do this, they were defeated even there, as their separation itself reveals.

20. But what they did afterward is, nonetheless, sufficiently shown by the letter of the emperor. For they dared to accuse of judging wrongly ecclesiastical judges of such great authority, the bishops whose judgment declared Caecilian's innocence and their wickedness, not before other colleagues, but before the emperor. He granted them another trial at Arles, that is, by other bishops, not because it was now necessary, but because he yielded to their perversity and desired to restrain such impudence by all means. For a Christian emperor did not dare to take up their troublesome and false complaints in order that he himself might pronounce judgment on the judgment of the bishops who heard the case at Rome. Rather, as I said, he gave them other bishops, and they again preferred to appeal from them to the emperor, for you have heard how he warded them off on this matter. And I wish that at least by his judgment they had put an end to their most unhealthy animosity, and I wish that, as he himself yielded to them, he would have pronounced judgment concerning this case after the bishops, with an aim of seeking pardon afterward from the holy prelates. In that way, they would have nothing further to say, if they did not obey the judgment of him to whom they appealed, and in that way they would at some point yield to the truth. For he ordered that the parties meet him at Rome for handling the case. When for some reason or other Caecilian did not come there, the emperor commanded, after having been requested by them, that they follow him to Milan. Then some of them began to withdraw, perhaps angered because Constantine did not imitate them so that he right away and quickly condemned Caecilian in his absence. When the foresighted emperor learned of this, he made the rest come to Milan, escorted by guards. And after Caecilian also came, he also presented himself, as the emperor wrote, and having heard the case with the diligence, care, and foresight that his letter indicates, he judged Caecilian innocent and the Donatists most wicked.

8, 21. And they still baptize outside of the Church and, if they could, they would rebaptize the Church; they offer sacrifice in dissension and schism, and they greet with the term "peace" people whom they remove from the peace of salvation. The unity of Christ is torn in two; the heritage of Christ is blasphemed; the baptism of Christ is subjected to the rite of exsufflation.[8] And they do not

---

8. That is, that part of the baptismal rite in which the devil is blown out of the candidate for baptism by the breathing upon him of the minister.

want these crimes to be corrected in them by temporal scourges through ordinary human powers in order that they might not be destined for eternal punishments for such great sacrileges. We raise as objections to them the madness of schism, the insanity of rebaptizing, and the wicked separation from the heritage of Christ, which is spread through all nations. We read out, not merely from our books, but also from theirs, the names of the churches that they read today and with which they are today not in communion. When those names are read out in their gatherings, they say to their readers, "Peace be with you," and they do not have peace with those peoples to whom that letter was written. And they raise as objections to us the false crimes of those now dead and, even if they are true, they are still the crimes of others. For they do not understand that they are all caught in those objections we make against them, whereas, in the objections they make against us, they reprehend the straw or the weeds in the Lord's harvest, but the charge does not pertain to the wheat. Nor do they consider that those who are pleased with the bad people in the unity are themselves in communion with bad people. But those who find them displeasing and cannot correct them and do not dare to uproot the weeds before the time of the harvest, *for fear that they might also uproot the wheat* (Mt 13:24-3), are in communion, not with their actions, but with the altar of Christ. In that way they are not only not defiled by them, but even deserve to be praised and lauded by the words of God. After all, they endure for the good of the unity what they hate for the good of justice in order that the name of Christ might not suffer the blasphemy of horrible schisms.

22. *If they have ears, let them hear what the Spirit says to the churches* (Rv 2:7). For in the Revelation of John we read as follows; he says, *Write to the angel of the church of Ephesus: He who holds the seven stars in his right hand, he who walks in the midst of the seven candlesticks of gold, says this: I know your works and your labor and patience and that you cannot tolerate evil persons, and you have tested those who say that they are apostles and are not, and you have found them to be liars. And you have patience, and you have put up with them on account of my name, and you have not failed* (Rv 2:1-3). If he wanted us to understand this of an angel of the higher heavens and not of heads of the church, he would not go on to say, *But I hold against you that you have abandoned your first love. Recall, then, from where you have fallen, and do penance, and do the works you did at first. If not, I shall come to you, and I shall move your candlestick from its place unless you do penance* (Rv 4:5). This cannot be said to the higher angels who always retain their love; those who have fallen from there are the devil and his angels.[9] He, therefore, says, "first love," because the church endured the false apostles on account of the name of Christ, and he commands that she seek again that love and do her earlier works. And there are raised against us as objections the crimes of sinful men, not our own, but those of

_____

9. See Mt 25:41; Rv 12:9.

others, and these in part unknown. If we saw them even as true and present and tolerated them for the sake of unity, sparing the weeds on account of the wheat, whoever hears the holy scriptures without being deaf at heart would say that we are worthy, not only with no rebuke, but even with no small praise.

23. Aaron tolerates the many people who demand, build, and worship an idol.[10] Moses tolerates so many thousands who murmur against God and sin against his name so many times.[11] David tolerates Saul who persecutes him, who abandons the things of heaven with his wicked conduct and seeks the things below by the arts of magic; he avenges him when he is slain, and even calls him the anointed of the Lord on account of the mystery of his holy anointing.[12] Samuel tolerates the wicked sons of Eli and his own evil sons; because the people would not tolerate them, the people were accused by divine truth and rebuked by divine severity. Samuel, finally, tolerates the people who are proud and contemptuous of God.[13] Isaiah tolerates those whom he accuses of many true crimes. Jeremiah tolerates those from whom he suffers so much. Zechariah tolerates the Pharisees and scribes who scripture testifies existed at that time. I know that I have passed over many; let those who want read; let those who are able read the heavenly words; they will find that all the holy servants and friends of God always had those whom they needed to tolerate in their people. Sharing with them, nonetheless, in the sacraments of that time, they were not only not defiled, but they also endured them in a praiseworthy manner, *eager*, as the apostle says, *to preserve the unity of the Spirit in the bond of peace* (Eph 4:3). Let them also take note of the time after the coming of the Lord when we would find many more examples of this toleration throughout the world if they could have all been written down and verified. But take note of those we have. The Lord himself tolerates Judas, a devil, a thief, and a man who betrays him for money; he allows him to receive along with the innocent disciples what the faithful know is our ransom. The apostles tolerate the false apostles,[14] and among those who seek *what is their own, not what pertains to Jesus Christ* (Phil 2:21), Paul, not seeking what is his own, but what pertains to Jesus Christ, lives a life of most glorious tolerance. Finally, as I mentioned a little before, the ruler of the church is praised by the word of God under the name of an angel because, though he hated evil persons, he tolerated them on account of the name of the Lord, after having tested and found them out.

24. In short, let them ask themselves: Do they not tolerate the slaughters and fires of the Circumcellions, those people who venerate the bodies of others who willingly throw themselves over a cliff, and the groaning of the whole of Africa

---

10. See Ex 32:6.
11. See Ex 14:11; 15:24; 16:2.8; 17:2-3; Nm 14:2; 16:41.
12. See 1 Sm 28:7-20.
13. See 1 Sm 2:27-29; 3:21; 8:1-5.
14. See 2 Cor 11:13.

under the incredible evils of the one Optatus?[15] I will not now mention the tyrannical powers of single regions, cities, and estates throughout Africa and the robberies in public view. For it is better that you yourselves mention these things either privately or openly, as you please. For wherever you turn your eyes, you will see what I am saying or rather what I pass over in silence. Nor, after all, do we accuse on this account those individuals whom you love. For they are not displeasing to us because they tolerate evil persons, but because they are intolerably evil on account of the schism, on account of their altar over against our altar, on account of their separation from the heritage of Christ spread throughout the world, as it was promised so long ago.[16] We deplore and grieve over the violated peace, the sundered unity, the repeated baptisms, and the abused[17] sacraments, which are holy even in wicked persons. If they consider these of little importance, let them look at the examples that show how important God considers them. Those who fashioned an idol were slain by the customary death of the sword,[18] but the leaders of those who chose to cause a schism were swallowed by the earth, and the crowd who agreed with them were consumed by fire.[19] The difference in their punishments reveals the difference of their merits.

9, 25. The holy books are handed over in the persecution; those who handed them over confess, and they are left to God's judgment. The innocent are not questioned and are condemned by rash human beings. The one who among those who were innocent and absent was accused much more intensely than the rest is proven free of guilt by reliable judges. The judgment of the bishops is appealed to the emperor. The emperor is chosen as judge; when he judges, the emperor is scorned. You have read what was done then; you see what is being done now. If you are in the least bit of doubt about those past events, look at these present ones. Let us, of course, not deal with old papers, nor with public archives, nor with judicial or ecclesiastical proceedings. Our book is greater—the world; in it I read the fulfillment of the promise I read in the book of God. It says, *The Lord said to me, "You are my son; this day I have begotten you. Ask of me, and I shall give you the nations as your heritage and the ends of the earth as your possession"* (Ps 2:7-8). Let whoever does not share in this heritage, whatever books he may possess, know that he has been disinherited. Whoever fights against this heritage proves quite well that he is a stranger to the family of God. The question, of course, centers around the handing over of the books of God in which this heritage is promised. Let that person, then, be believed to have handed over the

---

15. The Donatist bishop of Thamugadi, the successor of Gaudentius; see *Answer to Gaudentius* 1, 18, *Answer to the Letter of Parmenian* 2, 2, and Letter 53, 6.
16. See Ps 2:8.
17. Literally, "sacraments subjected to the rite of exsufflation," that is, sacraments from which the devil was expelled.
18. See Ex 32:1-28.
19. See Nm 16:1-35, 41:49.

testament to the flames who brings suit against the will of the testator. What has the church of the Corinthians done to you, O sect of the Donatists, what has it done to you? But what I say of this church I want you to understand regarding all such churches that are located so far off. What have they done to you? They were utterly unable to know either what you did or whom you slandered. Or has the world lost the light of Christ because Caecilian offended Lucilla in Africa?[20]

26. Let them finally realize what they have done. It is only right that after a certain period of years their action has come back to their eyes. Investigate the woman through whom Maximian,[21] who is said to be a relative of Donatus, cut himself off from communion with Primian and how, after gathering a group of bishops, he condemned Primian in his absence and was ordained bishop in opposition to him, just as, having gathered a group of bishops with the help of Lucilla, Majorinus condemned Caecilian in his absence and was ordained bishop in opposition to him. Or do you perhaps want it to count that Primian was acquitted by the other African bishops of his communion in opposition to the sect of Maximian, but you do not want it to count that Caecilian was acquitted by the bishops in unity across the sea against the sect of Majorinus? I ask you, my brothers, what do I ask that is so great? What do I want you to understand that is so difficult? There is, of course, a big difference, and the African church is incomparably less in authority and in number if it is compared to the others of the world. And it is far smaller, even if there were unity here, far smaller compared to all the other Christian peoples than the sect of Maximian compared to the sect of Primian. I ask, nonetheless, and I think it is just that the council of Secundus of Tigisi, which Lucilla aroused against the absent Caecilian and against the apostolic sees and the whole world in communion with Caecilian, should have as much validity as the council of the Maximianists has, which some woman or other likewise aroused against the absent Primian and the remaining multitude in Africa who were in communion with Primian. What is clearer to see? What is more just to ask?

27. You see all this, and you know it, and you groan, and yet God sees that nothing forces you to remain in so deadly and sacrilegious a schism, if in order to attain a spiritual kingdom you would overcome your carnal affection and if in order to avoid everlasting punishments you would not be afraid to offend the friendships of human beings, which are of no help in God's courtroom. There you are, go and consult; learn what can be said against these views of ours. If they produce papers, we produce papers; if they say that ours are false, let them not be angry that we say this of theirs. No one wipes out from heaven the decree of God; no one wipes out from the earth the Church of God. He promised the

---

20. See above paragraph 17 above for more on Lucilla.
21. Maximian was a Donatist deacon of Carthage who, angered at his bishop, Priamian, in 393 broke away from the Donatists and formed the Maximianists.

whole world; she has filled the whole world. And she contains both evil and good, but on earth she loses only the evil, while in heaven she admits only the good. But this discourse which we have drawn from the grace of God with a great love of peace and of you—as he knows—will be for you a source of correction, if you are willing, but a witness against you, if you are not.

Letter 44

In 396 or 397 Augustine wrote to a group of Donatist laymen about his encounter with Fortunius, the Donatist bishop of Thiave (Thubursicum Numidarum), of whom they had spoken highly. Augustine recounts his friendly meeting with Fortunius amid a turbulent crowd who were hoping to see a fight (paragraph 1). Despite Donatist opposition, some notes were taken, and Augustine has written them up in this letter (paragraph 2). The issue of the true Church is raised (paragraph 3). The Donatists claim that their being persecuted proves that they are the true Christians (paragraph 4). Augustine points out that the Donatists are not in communion with the churches overseas (paragraph 5). The Donatist appeal to the Council of Sardica to show that they were in communion with the churches overseas fails, once it is shown to be an Arian council (paragraph 6). Furthermore, persecution alone is not proof of righteousness (paragraph 7). Fortunius mentions the killing by Catholics of the administrator who was set in place by the Donatists before the ordination of Majorinus and asks how such killers can fail to be evil (paragraph 8).

Augustine argues that killings in the name of Christianity, whether by Catholics or by Donatists, are wrong, though in the Old Testament era Elijah rightly killed the false prophets (paragraph 9). In the new testament period, however, we should follow, rather, the example of Jesus with respect to Judas, his "traditor" (paragraph 10). To the Donatist complaint that they are still suffering persecution, Augustine replies that they themselves created a schism because of their intolerance (paragraph 11). As time ran out, Fortunius mentioned with apparent regret that the practice of rebaptizing Catholics who come to the Donatists has been established. Augustine urges both sides to forget past wrongs and to end the schism (paragraph 12). He insists on the importance of the pursuit of Christian unity (paragraph 13) and proposes means to continue the discussion with Fortunius or other Donatists (paragraph 14).

To his most beloved lords and esteemed brothers, Eleusius, Glorius, and the two Felixes,[1] *Augustine sends greetings.*

1, 1. When I was traveling to the church of Cirta, I made the acquaintance of Fortunius, whom you have as bishop of Tubursicum, though most hurriedly, while passing through his city. And I found him to be exactly as you usually and most kindly promise him to be. When we reported to him your conversation regarding him, he did not refuse us who wanted to see him. We, therefore, went to him, for it seemed that we ought to offer that to his age rather than to demand that he first come to us. We set out, therefore, with no small number of companions whom the circumstances had by chance found gathered around us. But after we had settled down in his home, no small crowd also assembled because of the

---

1. Some of the same Donatist laymen to whom the previous letter was addressed.

rumor spread about. We, however, saw that there were very few in that whole crowd who desired that the issue be treated in a useful and salutary manner and that so important a question on so important an issue be discussed with wisdom and piety. But the rest had assembled for the spectacle of our quarrel, as it were, almost in manner of the theater rather than for instruction toward salvation with Christian devotion. Hence, they could neither offer us silence nor hold a discussion with us attentively or at least in modest and orderly fashion, except, as I said, for those few whose intention was seen to be religious and undivided. Therefore, everything was thrown into confusion by the noise of those speaking freely and without control in accord with the impulse of the mind of each person, and neither he nor we were able to obtain, either by asking or even at times by threatening, that they offer us a polite silence.

2. The discussion somehow got under way, and we continued for several hours in dialogue to the extent we were permitted by the voices of the uproarious when they fell silent. But we saw at the beginning of the discussion that what was said immediately slipped from memory, whether ours or that of those whose salvation we were most concerned with. Hence, in order that our discussion might be more careful and moderate and also in order that you and the other brothers who were absent might come to know by reading what we accomplished, we asked that our words be taken down by stenographers. For a long time he or those who agreed with him were opposed to this; afterward, he, nonetheless, agreed. But the stenographers who had been present and could have quickly done this refused for some reason or other to take it down. We at least got the brothers who were with us to take it down, though they could do this only rather slowly, and we promised that we would leave there the same records. They agreed. Our words began to be taken down, and some words were spoken by each side for the records. Afterward, the stenographers gave up, unable to put up with the disorderly interruptions of the uproarious and with our discussion, which was also more disorderly on this account, though we, of course, did not stop and said many things, as each of us was given the opportunity. I did not want to deprive Your Charity of all these words of ours to the extent that I could recall the discussion of the whole issue. For you can read my letter to Fortunius in order that he may agree that I have written the truth or may convey without delay anything he remembers better.

2, 3. After all, he was the first who was so good as to praise our life, which he said that he discovered from you, who perhaps recounted it with more benevolence than truth, and he added that he said to you that we could have done well all those things that you mentioned regarding us if we had done them in the church. Then we began to seek which was that church in which one ought to live, whether that one which, as the holy scriptures foretold so long ago, would spread over the whole earth[2] or that one which a small part of Africa or of the Africans

---

2. See Ps 2:7-8.

would contain. Here he first tried to claim that his communion was everywhere on earth. I asked whether he could give me letters of communion, which we call "patent," for wherever I wanted, and I stated that it was evident to all that the question could most easily be brought to an end in this way. I was, however, ready, if he agreed, that such letters be sent by us to those churches which we both read in the authoritative writings of the apostles were already founded at that time.

4. But because the claim was clearly false, he quickly left the point in a confusion of words. Among these words he mentioned that gospel warning of the Lord in which he said, *Beware of false prophets; many will come to you in sheep's clothing, but within they are ravenous wolves. From their fruits you will know them* (Mt 7:15.16). When we said that the same words of the Lord can be recited by us with reference to them, he turned from there to exaggerating the persecution that he said his side often endured, wanting to show from this that their followers are Christians because they suffer persecution. When during these words I was preparing to reply from the gospel, he was the first to mention the passage from it where the Lord said, *Blessed are those who suffer persecution on account of justice because theirs is the kingdom of heaven* (Mt 5:10). Grateful for that passage, I immediately added that we must, therefore, inquire whether they have suffered persecution on account of justice. I wanted a discussion on this question because it was, of course, clear to everyone whether the time of Macarius[3] found them situated in the unity of the Church or already divided from it by schism. Thus those who want to see whether they suffered persecution on account of justice should consider whether they rightly cut themselves off from the unity of the whole world. If they were found to have done so unjustly, it would be evident that they suffered persecution on account of injustice rather than on account of justice and, for that reason, cannot be added to the number of the blessed, of whom it was said, *Blessed are those who suffer persecution on account of justice.* Then there was mention of that surrender of the books, which is more talked about than it is certain. But our side replied that their leaders were rather all traditors, and that, if they did not want to believe our documents on this point, we ought not to be forced to believe their documents.

3, 5. But having set aside this doubtful question, I asked how these people had justly separated themselves from the innocence of other Christians who preserve throughout the world the order of succession from the apostles and are established in the most ancient churches, though they were utterly ignorant about who were traditors in Africa. For they certainly could only be in communion with those who they heard held the chairs of bishops. He answered that the churches

---

3. Macarius, an imperial commissioner sent in 347 to Africa along with Paul to settle the Donatist dispute, sided with the Catholics. The harshness of his methods made the time of Macarius legendary among the Donatists.

of the regions across the sea long remained innocent until they consented to the shedding of the blood of those who, he said, suffered the persecution of Macarius. There I could have said that the innocence of the churches across the sea could not have been destroyed by the hatred of the time of Macarius, since it could in no way be proved that he did what he did under their instigation. But as a shortcut I preferred to ask whether, if the overseas churches lost their innocence by the savagery of Macarius from the time when they were said to have consented to it, it is proven that the Donatists remained in unity with the Eastern churches and the other parts of the world at least up to those times.

6. Then he brought forth a certain volume in which he wanted to show that the Council of Sardica[4] had issued a letter to the African bishops who were in the communion of Donatus. When it was read, we heard the name of Donatus among the other bishops to whom they had written. And so we began to ask that we be informed whether this was the Donatus from whose sect these people take their name, for it is possible that they had written to a Donatus who was a bishop of another sect, especially since in those names there was not even a mention made of Africa. How, therefore, could he prove that we should understand by that name "Donatus" the bishop of the sect of Donatus, since he could not even prove whether that letter was sent to bishops of the African churches in particular. For, though the name "Donatus" is usually African, it would not be impossible that either someone from those regions have an African name or that some African be made bishop in those regions. After all, we did not find in it either a date or the consul so that something clear might emerge from a consideration of its date. We had certainly heard that, after they had split from the Catholic communion, the Arians[5] at some time or other tried to make the Donatists their allies in Africa: my brother, Alypius, whispered this idea into my ear. Then, having accepted that volume, I considered the statutes of that council and read that the Council of Sardica condemned Athanasius, the Catholic bishop of Alexandria, whose conflict against the Arians in highly passionate debates is well known, and Julius, the bishop of the Roman church, who was just as Catholic. Hence, it was clear to us that it was a council of Arians, whom these Catholic bishops most strongly opposed. And so, we wanted to receive and to take with us the volume for a more careful examination of the times. But Fortunius refused to hand it over, saying that we have it there when we might want to consider something in it. I also asked that he would permit me to mark it by my handwriting, for I was afraid, I admit, that another volume might perhaps be produced in its place when I had to ask for it because the situation demanded, but he refused that too.

---

4. The Council of Sardica was convoked by Pope Julius (342-343). The Arian bishops withdrew from the council and sent the letter mentioned as if from the council.

5. The Arians originated in Alexandria with the priest, Arius, in the early fourth century; though condemned at the Council of Nicea in 325, they continued to be influential well into the next century. See *Heresies* XLIX.

4, 7. Then he began to insist that I reply briefly to his questions, asking me whom I would consider just—the one who persecutes or the one who suffers persecution. To which I replied that he did not correctly pose the question in that way, for it is possible that both are unjust and it is also possible that the more just persecutes the more unjust. It does not, therefore, follow that anyone is more just because he suffers persecution, though that is generally the case. Then, when I saw that he was delaying much on this point because he wanted the justice of his side to be seen as certain because it suffered persecution, I asked him whether he thought Ambrose, the bishop of the Milanese church,[6] a just man and a Christian. He was, of course, forced to deny that the illustrious man was Christian and just. For, if he admitted that he was, we would immediately object that Fortunius judged that he had to be rebaptized. Since he was, therefore, forced to state those reasons why he was not to be considered Christian and just, I mentioned the great persecution he endured, when his church was surrounded even by armed troops.[7] I asked him also whether he considered Maximian,[8] who produced a schism from them at Carthage, both just and Christian. He could only say that he did not. I also mentioned that he suffered such persecution that his church was destroyed to its foundations. I was, therefore, trying by these examples to persuade him, if I could, that he should now stop saying that to suffer persecution is the most certain proof of Christian justice.

8. He also explained that in the very beginning of the schism, when his predecessors thought that they wanted in some way to hush up the guilt of Caecilian in order to avoid a schism, they gave a certain administrator[9] to the people of his community located in Carthage before Majorinus[10] was ordained in opposition to Caecilian. Hence, he said that this administrator was killed by our people in his church. I admit that I had never heard of this before, though our side rejects and refutes so many charges raised by them and hurls more and greater charges at them. But, all the same, after he told us of this, he again began to ask whom I thought to be just—the one who killed or the one who was killed, as if he had already proven to me that the crime was committed, as he had reported it. I said, therefore, that we must first ask whether it was true; for one ought not rashly to believe whatever is said, and it could, nonetheless, have been the case either that both were equally bad or even that someone bad killed someone worse. For it is really possible that the rebaptizer of the whole person is more criminal than a slayer of the body alone.

---

6. Ambrose was bishop of Milan from 374 to 397; he baptized Augustine in 387.

7. See *Confessions* IX, 7, 15.

8. Maximian, a deacon in Carthage, split away from the Donatists in 397 in anger at his bishop, Primian.

9. An "*interventor*" administered or governed a diocese during a period when there was no bishop of it.

10. Majorinus, the first Donatist bishop of Carthage, was consecrated in 313.

9. For this reason he also ought not to have asked me what he later asked me. For he said that a bad person ought not to be killed by Christians and just people, as if we would call those in the Catholic Church who do this just persons. They usually state these charges against us with more ease than they can prove them. For many of them, even bishops and priests and other clerics, gather crowds of highly enraged people and do not stop inflicting so much violent killing and destruction, not upon Catholics alone, but even at times upon their own people when they can. Since this is so, he feigned ignorance, nonetheless, of the most criminal deeds of his own people that he knows better than I, and he urged me to say whether a just person would kill even a bad man. Even though this had nothing to do with the present issue, for we admitted that, wherever these actions were done in the name of Christ, they were not done by good persons, we, nonetheless, replied in order to make him realize the question that should be asked. We asked whether he thought that Elijah was just, something he could not deny. Then we added how many false prophets he slew by his own hand. Here he really saw what he needed to see, namely, that such actions were then permitted to the just.[11] For they did such acts with their prophetic spirit and by the authority of God who undoubtedly knows for whom it is good even to be killed. He demanded, therefore, that I show that now in the time of the new testament any of the just killed someone, even a criminal and wicked person.

5, 10. Then we returned to the previous discussion by which we wanted to show that we ought not to raise as objections against them their crimes, nor ought they to raise as objections against us such actions of ours, if they find any. For it cannot, of course, be shown from the new testament that any just person killed someone, but it can be proved by the example of the Lord that innocent people tolerated criminals. After all, he allowed his betrayer,[12] who had already accepted payment for him, to be with him among the innocent up to the last kiss of peace. He did not conceal from them that there was a great criminal among them, and he, nonetheless, for the first time gave the sacrament of his body and blood to all in common, when the betrayer had not yet been excluded.[13] Since almost all were moved by this example, Fortunius tried to say that before the Passion of the Lord such communion with the criminal was not a hindrance to the apostles because they had not yet received the baptism of Christ, but the baptism of John. After he said this, I began to ask him how scripture had, then, said that Jesus baptized more than John, though he himself did not baptize, but his disciples did, that is, he baptized through his disciples.[14] How, then, did they give what they had not received, as the Donatists themselves so often say? Did

---

11. I followed the CSEL reading of "*alia licuisse tunc*" instead of "*talia eum licuisse.*"

12. The Latin for "betrayer" is "*traditor.*" Augustine is really pointing out that Jesus tolerated his traditor, though the Donatists did not tolerate the traditors of the sacred books.

13. See Mt 26:14-16.20-28.

14. See Jn 4:1-2.

Christ perhaps baptize with the baptism of John? Next I was going to ask him many questions along these lines, for example, how John was then asked about the baptism of the Lord and how he replied that the Lord had the bride and was the bridegroom.[15] Was it then permitted that the bridegroom should baptize with the baptism of John, that is, with the baptism of a friend and servant? Finally, how were they able to receive the Eucharist when they were not yet baptized? Or how did he reply to Peter who wanted him to wash all of him, *One who has once bathed does not need to be washed again, but is entirely clean* (Jn 13:10)? For the perfect cleansing is not the baptism in the name of John, but that in the name of the Lord, if the one who receives it presents himself as worthy of it. But if he is unworthy, the sacraments still remain in him, not for his salvation, but for his destruction. Though I was going to ask these questions, he himself saw that he should not ask about the baptism of the disciples of the Lord.

11. Then we came to another topic on which many on each side spoke as they were able. Among the things said was that our people still were going to persecute them, and he said to us that he wanted to see what sort of people we would show ourselves to be in that persecution, whether we were going to assent to such savagery or were not going to give it our consent. We said that God sees our hearts, which they could not see, and that they are too ready to fear these events which, if they do come about, come from evil persons, though they themselves have worse ones than these. Nor ought we, nonetheless, to separate ourselves from the Catholic communion if anything should perhaps happen when we were unwilling or even opposed to it, if we were able, since we learned peaceful toleration from the lips of the apostle, *Bear with one another in love; strive to preserve the unity of the Spirit in the bond of peace* (Eph 4:2-3). We said that those who produced the schism did not have this toleration and peace, while now those who are more meek among their own people tolerate more serious evils for fear that what has already been split may be further split, if they are unwilling to tolerate less serious evils for the sake of unity. We also said that in the times of the old testament the peace of unity and toleration was not preached with such a strong commendation as by the example of the Lord and the love of the new testament, and yet those prophets and holy men often charged the people with crimes when they tried to remove themselves from the unity of that people and from the communion in receiving those sacraments that then existed.

12. From there we somehow or other came to mention Genethlius of blessed memory, the bishop of Carthage before Aurelius,[16] because he suppressed a decree directed against them and did not allow its implementation. They all praised him and spoke of him with great affection. Among those praises we

---

15. See Jn 3:22-29.
16. Genethlius died in 391 or 392; he was followed by Aurelius, a close ally of Augustine, who remained in office until his death in 430 or 431.

added that, if Genethlius himself had fallen into their hands, they would have judged that he also needed to be rebaptized. And we said these things when we were already standing because the time for departure was near. Then that old man clearly said that the rule had already been made that whoever of the faithful comes to them from us is baptized, and it was evident that he said this with as much reluctance and sorrow as possible. He, of course, very clearly deplored the many wrongs of his people and showed how removed he was from such actions, as was proven by the testimony of his whole city, and he brought forth those points that he was accustomed to say in a mild complaint to his people. Hence, we mentioned that passage of the prophet, Ezekiel, where scripture clearly says that the sin of the child will not be held against the parent, nor the sin of the parent against the child. It says there, *For, just as the soul of the parent is mine, so the soul of the child is also mine. Only the soul which sins will die* (Ez 18:4.20). Everyone agreed that in such discussions we ought not to hurl at one another as objections the violent actions of bad persons. There remained, therefore, the question of the schism. And so, we exhorted him to strive with us again and again with a calm and peaceful mind that so important an investigation might by a careful examination come to an end. At this point he was so kind as to say that it is only we who seek these goals, but that our people refuse to seek them. We departed after having promised that we would present to him many colleagues, certainly at least ten, who want to investigate the issue with such great good will and mildness and with such pious zeal as we felt that he already noticed in us and approved. He also promised this concerning the number of their bishops.

6, 13. Hence, I exhort and implore you by the blood of the Lord that you remind him of his promise and diligently insist that the task begun should be carried to completion, for you already see that it has nearly come to an end. For, in my opinion, it will be very difficult for you to find among your bishops so helpful a mind and will as we saw in this old man. On the following day, after all, he came to us, and we began to investigate these matters again. But because the necessity of ordaining a bishop was already tearing us away from there, we could not stay with him a longer time. For we had already sent to the head of "the worshipers of heaven,"[17] whom we had heard had instituted a new baptism among them, and led many astray by that sacrilege, in order that we might speak with him to the extent that the restrictions of the time permitted. After Fortunius learned that that man was coming and saw that we had taken up some other business, he left us with good will and in peace, since some necessity to depart constrained him.

14. It seems me that, in order that we may completely avoid the disturbing crowds that are a hindrance rather than a help and that we may with God's help continue in a truly friendly and peaceful spirit the important a task that we have

---

17. The "*caelicolae*" were an heretical group mentioned in a decree of Honorius against heretics.

undertaken, we ought to meet in a village where neither of us has a church, a village which people of our communion and of his share in common, such as the village of Titiana. Whether, then, such a place is in the territory of Tubursicum or in that of Thagaste, whether with the man I mentioned or someone else is found, let us have the canonical books present and any documents that can be produced by the two sides. Having set aside all other concerns, let us, with no disturbances interfering, if it pleases God, devote as many days as we can to this. Let each of us pray to the Lord in the home of his host, and with the help of God, to whom Christian peace is most pleasing, let us bring so important a matter, which was begun with such good spirit, to a successful end of this inquiry. Write back, of course, what you and Fortunius think about this proposal.

Letter 45

Early in 398 Alypius and Augustine wrote to Paulinus of Nola and his wife, Therasia. They complain about not having received a letter from Paulinus for two years (paragraph 1). They also ask for a copy of Paulinus' work, *Against the Pagans*, which they heard Paulinus was writing. Finally, they commend to Paulinus the bearer of the letter and his business (paragraph 2).

Alypius and Augustine send greetings in the Lord to Paulinus and Therasia,[1] *their lord and lady, their most dear brother and sister, who are praiseworthy in Christ.*

1. The fact that you have for some reason or other stopped writing has by no means made us slow to write you, though, look, it is two whole years since our most dear brothers, Romanus and Agilis,[2] traveled to you, and we have received no letter from you. For, though in other matters the more anyone is loved, the more he seems worthy of imitation, in this case the opposite is true. For the more ardently we love you, the less well do we bear with your not writing to us, nor do we want to imitate you in this. See, then, we greet you, if not replying to your letter, for none has come to us, at least asking for one, and with no slight sorrow, though perhaps Your Charity also complains in a like manner, if you know of letters you sent that have not reached us and, in turn, of letters sent by us that were not delivered to you. If that is so, let us turn our complaints into prayers to the Lord that he may not deny us such great consolations.

2. We had heard that you were writing a work against the pagans; if it is finished, we ask that you do not delay to send it by the bearer of this letter. He is someone dear to us, and we can in all seriousness offer good testimony to his reputation in our regions. He asks through us that Your Holiness may be so good as to commend him to those with whom he has business and before whom he fears that his good case may be defeated. He himself will better explain what the issue is; he can also be questioned about the particulars, which may perhaps cause confusion. We regard him most favorably, and we thank your most sincere goodness before the Lord our God if through your effort we may rejoice over the security of a Christian brother.

---

1. Paulinus was the future bishop of Nola, and Therasia was his wife. Alypius was Augustine's friend from his youth and was at this time bishop of Thagaste.
2. Romanus and Agilis carried Letter 30 from Paulinus to Augustine and returned to Paulinus with Letter 31.

Letter 46

Between 396 and 399 Publicola, a Catholic layman and Roman senator,[1] wrote to Augustine, raising a series of questions to which Augustine replies in the next letter. The questions concern the taking of oaths (paragraphs 1 to 5), the eating or sale of foods offered to idols (paragraphs 6 to 11 and 17 to 18), and self-defense and foreseen losses or harm (paragraph 12 and 13), drinking from springs or wells sacred to the gods (paragraph 14), and the use of the baths or sedan chairs used by pagans (paragraph 15 and 16).

Publicola sends greetings to Bishop Augustine, his beloved and venerable father.

Scripture says, *Ask your father, and he will tell you; ask your elders, and they will speak to you* (Dt 32:7). For this reason I decided that I must investigate the law in such a case from the lips of a priest; by this letter I explain the nature of the case in order that I may at the same time also be instructed on various other cases. I have marked the individual different questions by chapters. Please reply to them individually.

1. It is the custom, as I have heard, among the Arzuges[2] that the barbarians swear to the decurion who governs the frontier or to the tribune, swearing by their demons, when they have been hired to carry baggage or for protecting the crops, and that the individual landowners or stewards hire them for protecting the crops as thereby trustworthy, when the decurion sends a letter, or individual travelers who must pass through them hire them. But a doubt has arisen in my heart whether the landowner who has hired a barbarian whose reliability is thought to be solid because of his swearing by demons is not either himself defiled or whether those things guarded by the barbarian are defiled or whether the person guided by the barbarian guide is defiled. But you must know that the barbarian who swears this oath receives money from the landowner for protecting the crops or that the guide receives money from the traveler. But along with this so-called reward, which is usually given by the landowner or traveler, that gravely sinful oath given to the decurion or tribune also is obvious to everyone, and it bothers me for fear that it may defile the person who accepts the oath of the barbarian or the things that the barbarian protects. For under whatever condition, even when money and hostages have been given, a wrongful oath is involved, as I have heard, as a means. Please, write back to me with a

---

1. Publicola was the husband of Albina and the father of Melania the Younger; he owned large estates in Byzacena.
2. The Arzuges were a barbarian people living to the south of Byzacena.

definitive answer, not with doubts. If you yourself write in a doubtful manner, I can fall into greater doubts than before I asked.

2. I also heard that those stewards who run my estate accept an oath from barbarians who swear by demons to protect the crops. If, then, they swear by their own demons to guard the crops, do they not defile those crops so that, if a Christian knowingly eats from them or uses the price received for them, he is rendered impure? Explain this please.

3. Likewise, I heard from someone that a barbarian does not swear to a steward, and someone else said that he does swear to a steward. If the one who told me that a barbarian swears to the steward also spoke falsely to me, should I only on the basis of what I heard not use these crops or the income from them on account of what I heard alone, since it is written, *But if someone says that it has been offered to idols, do not eat on account of the person whom I have indicated* (1 Cor 10:28)? Is this case like the case concerning food offered to idols? But if it is, what ought I to do with the crops or the income from them?

4. Ought I to question each of the two persons who said to me that an oath is not sworn to my steward or who said that an oath is sworn to my steward and ought I to test the statement of each by witnesses in order to discover which of the two spoke the truth? And ought I not to touch these crops or the income until I have tested whether he who said that an oath was not sworn to the steward spoke the truth?

5. If a barbarian who swears by a sinful oath made that Christian steward or tribune who rules over the frontier to swear to him for the sake of keeping faith with him for protecting the crops by the same gravely sinful oath by which he swore, is only that Christian rendered impure? Are not those things also rendered impure for the sake of which he swore? Or if a pagan who rules over the frontier swears to a barbarian for the sake of keeping faith with him by a gravely sinful oath, does he not render unclean the things on behalf of which he swears? If I send someone to the Arzuges, is it permissible for him to accept that gravely sinful oath from a barbarian? And is a Christian not rendered impure if he accepts such an oath?

6. Is it permissible for a Christian knowingly to eat wheat or another food from a threshing floor or from a winepress from which an offering has been made to a demon?

7. Is it permissible for a Christian knowingly to take wood from a sacred grove for some use of his own?

8. If someone goes to a butcher and buys meat that has not been offered to idols and has two ideas in his heart, namely, that it was and was not offered to idols, and clings to his belief that it was not offered to an idol, does he sin if he eats it?

9. If someone does something good about which he doubts whether it is good or bad, if he does it while thinking that it is good, though he had also thought it bad, is the sin attributed to him?

10. If someone lied in saying that food was offered to idols and afterwards again said that he lied and had truly lied, is it permissible for a Christian to eat it or to sell it and to use the income from it because of what he has heard?

11. Suppose a Christian while on a journey meets with necessity, overcome by the hunger of a day or two days or more days so that he cannot survive, and suppose that it happens that in the dire condition of hunger, from which he sees that his death is already drawing near, he finds food set before an idol where there are no human beings and he cannot find other food. Ought he to die or eat from it?

12. If a Christian sees that he is going to be killed by a barbarian or a Roman, should the Christian himself kill them so that he is not killed by them? Or is it permissible to fight them or repel them without killing, since scripture says, *Do not resist someone evil* (Mt 5:39)?

13. Should a Christian build a wall for his land on account of an enemy? And is that Christian who built the wall the cause of murder when some begin to fight and kill the enemies from it?

14. Is it permitted to drink from a spring or from a well into which something from a sacrifice has been thrown? May a Christian drink from a well that is located in a temple, if the temple is abandoned? If in a temple in which an idol is worshiped there is a well or a spring of the idol and if no rite has been performed in the same well or spring, may a Christian draw water from it and drink?

15. May a Christian bathe in the baths or hot springs in which sacrifice is offered to idols? May a Christian bathe in the baths in which the pagans have bathed on their feast day, either with them or without them?

16. May a Christian ride in the same sedan chair in which pagans rode, coming from their idols on their feast day, and they committed something sacrilegious there in the sedan chair and a Christian knows this?

17. Does a Christian sin if, when invited by someone, he has meat set before him for dinner about which it was said to him that it was offered to idols and he did not eat it, but afterwards by some chance he finds the meat for sale that had been taken to some merchant and he buys it? Or does he sin if it is served to him when he is invited by someone else and he does not recognize it and eats it?

18. Should a Christian knowingly buy and eat vegetables or some fruit from a garden or from the land belonging to idols or their priests?

In order that you may not labor too hard in investigating about oaths or about idols, I wanted, of course, to set before your eyes what we have found with the Lord's help. But if you find anything else clearer or better in the scriptures, please indicate it to me. Hence, the passages we found are those in which Laban said to Jacob, *The God of Abraham and the God of Nachor* (Gn 31:53), but the scripture did not indicate which God this was. And again, there is the passage where Abimelech came to Isaac when he swore or those did who were with him,[3] but scripture does not indicate what sort of oath they swore. Again, scripture speaks of idols when the Lord said to Gideon in the Book of Judges that he should offer a holocaust of the calf which he had killed.[4] And it says in the case of Joshua son of Nun that with regard to Jericho all the gold, silver, and bronze was brought into the treasuries of the Lord, and everything from the city was called holy, that is, dedicated to the Lord.[5] And what do the words in Deuteronomy mean: *You shall not bring an abomination into your house; otherwise, you shall be accursed just as it is* (Dt 7:26)?

May the Lord keep you; I send you my greetings; pray for me.

---

3. See Gn 26:26-31.
4. See Jdg 6:26.
5. See Jos 6:16-19.

Letter 47

Sometime after the preceding letter, Augustine wrote in answer to Publicola. He points out the difficulty involved in satisfying his friend's request (paragraph 1), but goes on to discuss various moral questions, for example, whether Christians can make use of an oath which pagans swear, since they swear by false gods (paragraph 2), or whether it is permissible to use things offered to false gods (paragraph 3) and whether it is permissible to eat food offered to idols (paragraph 4). On the question of killing, Augustine distinguishes between killing in defense of one's country as a soldier and in defense of oneself (paragraph 5). Finally, he considers whether a starving traveler may eat food that he finds in the shrine of an idol (paragraph 6).

To his honorable and most beloved son, Publicola, Augustine sends greetings in the Lord.

1. After I learned from your letter of the turmoil of your mind, it immediately became mine as well, not that all such problems that you told me were disturbing you also disturbed me, but I admit that I was perplexed over how this turmoil might be taken from you, especially since you ask that I write back to you with a definitive answer so that you would not fall into greater doubts than before you asked me. For I see that this does not lie in my power. After all, no matter how I write what I regard as most certain, if I do not persuade you, you will undoubtedly be more uncertain. For I am not able also to persuade anyone in the same way that I can urge him. Nonetheless, in order that I might not refuse my little effort to Your Charity, after some deliberation I thought that I should reply.

2. It certainly perplexes you whether one should rely on the fidelity of someone who swears by demons to keep faith. Here I want you to consider first whether, if someone swears by false gods that he will keep faith and does not keep it, you do not think that he has sinned twice. For, if he kept the faith promised by such an oath-taking, he would be judged to have sinned only because he swore by such gods. No one, however, would rightly find fault with the fact that he kept faith. But now, because he both swore by gods, something which he should not have done, and because contrary to the fidelity he promised he did what he ought not to have done, he, of course, sinned twice. And for this reason someone who relies on the fidelity of that man who has clearly sworn by false goods and relies on it, not for something evil, but for something licit and good, does not link himself with that sin of his of swearing by demons, but with his good agreement in which he kept faith. Nor do I here say that he kept that faith because of which those baptized in Christ are called faithful. For that faith is far different and far removed from the faith of human accords and agreements. Without any doubt it is, nonetheless, less evil to swear truthfully by a false god

187

than to swear falsely by the true God. For perjury is more blameworthy to the extent that the name by which one swears is more holy. It is, therefore, another question whether one does not sin who makes someone swear to him by false gods, because the man who swears to him worships false gods. Those testimonies that you mentioned concerning Laban and Abimelech can be of help for this question, at least if Abimelech swore by his gods and Laban by the god of Nachor. This, as I said, is another question that would perhaps bother me if those examples concerning Isaac and Jacob had not come to mind and any others that there are. Perhaps, nonetheless, that statement in the New Testament that we should not swear at all[1] still presents a problem. It seems to me that this was said, not because it is a sin to swear to the truth, but because to commit perjury is a very great sin, and he who warned us not to swear at all wanted us to be far removed from that sin. But I know that you have another opinion, but we ought not to argue about it now in order that we may rather do that about which you thought that you should consult me. Hence, as you do not swear, so do not force someone else to swear, if you want. Although it said that we should not swear, I do not remember reading in the holy scriptures that we should not receive an oath from someone. But it is another question whether we ought to enjoy that peace that is produced between others who swear oaths to one another. If we do not want this, I do not know whether we shall be able to find anywhere to live on earth. For not only at the frontier, but in all the provinces peace is won by the oaths of barbarians. Hence, it will follow that not only the crops that are guarded by those who have sworn by false gods, but all things that are protected by the peace maintained by that oath are everywhere defiled. But if it is utterly absurd to say this, do not let those questions that were disturbing you disturb you.

3. Likewise, if with the knowledge of a Christian something is taken from the threshing floor or the winepress for sacrifices to the demons, he sins if he permits it to be done where he has the power to forbid it. But if he finds that it has been done or did not have the power to forbid it, he uses the remaining uncontaminated fruits from which those were taken, just as we use fountains from which we know with full certitude that water is drawn for the use of the sacrifices. The same consideration applies to the baths. Nor do we hesitate to draw breath from the air into which we know smoke arises from all the altars and incense of demons. Hence, it is clear that we are forbidden to use or to be thought to use something for the honor of other gods, when we take it in such a way that, though we hold it in contempt, we induce those who do not know our mind to pay honor to these gods. And when we destroy temples, idols, groves, and anything else of this sort because we have been given the power, though it is evident that, when we do this, we do not honor them, but rather detest them, we ought, nonetheless, not to take anything from them, at least for our private and personal use. In that

---

1. See Mt 5:34.

way it will be clear that we destroy them out of piety, not out of greed. But when they are turned to common use, not to personal and private uses, or to the honor of the true God, the same thing happens to them that happens to the human beings themselves when they are converted from the unbelieving and sacrilegious people to the true religion. We understand that God taught this in those testimonies that you yourself quoted when he ordered that wood from the groves of alien gods be used for the holocausts[2] and with regard to Jericho that all the gold, silver, and bronze be brought into the treasuries of the Lord.[3] This is also the reason why it is written in Deuteronomy, *You shall not desire their silver or gold, nor shall you take some of it for yourself for fear that you transgress on account of it, for it is an abomination to the Lord your God. And you shall not bring something abominable into your home; otherwise, you will become accursed like it, and you will also commit a grave offense and you will be thoroughly defiled by that abomination because it is accursed* (Dt 7:25-26). It is quite clear that it is forbidden to make private use of such things and also to take something from them into one's house in order to show it honor, for it is then an abomination and something accursed, but not when the sacrilegious honor of such things is eliminated by their perfectly clear destruction.

4. But with regard to food offered to idols you can be certain that we need observe nothing more than what the apostle commanded. And for this reason recall his words on this subject; if they were obscure, we would explain them in accord with our capacity. But he does not sin who afterwards eats in ignorance food that he earlier rejected as having been offered to the gods. Every vegetable and fruit in whatever field it is grown belongs to him who created it, for *The Lord's is the earth and its fullness* (Ps 25:1 and 1 Cor 10:26), and *every creature of God is good* (1 Tm 4:4). But if what is grown in the fields is consecrated to an idol or offered in sacrifice, it must then be reckoned among the food offered to an idol. We must, after all, beware that, if we think that one should not eat a vegetable that was grown in the garden of the temple of an idol, it does not follow that we think that the apostle ought not to have taken food among the Athenians because it was the city of Minerva and consecrated to her godhead. I would answer this same thing concerning a well or a fountain that is in a temple. It really disturbs me more, however, if something from the sacrifices is thrown into the fountain or well. But the same reasoning holds for the air that receives all that smoke of which we spoke above. Or perhaps this case is thought to differ because that sacrifice from which the smoke is mixed with the air is not offered to the air, but to some idol or demon, but sacrifices are sometimes put into water in such a way that sacrifice is offered to the water itself. But we do not, of course, abstain from using the light of this sun because those sacrilegious people do not

---

2. See Jgs 6:26.
3. See Jos 6:19.

cease to offer it sacrifice where they can. Sacrifice is also offered to the winds, which we use, nonetheless, for such great advantages of ours, though they seem in a sense to draw in and devour the smoke from the same sacrifices. Suppose that someone has doubts about whether some meat has been offered in sacrifice, and it is not meat offered in sacrifice. If he has the idea that it was not offered in sacrifice and eats it, he does not, of course, sin, because the meat was not offered in sacrifice and he did not think that it was, even if it was earlier thought to have been. After all, it is not forbidden to correct one's beliefs from false to true. But if someone thinks what is evil is good and does it, he, of course, sins by thinking this. And these are all sins of ignorance when anyone thinks that something is a good action that is a bad one.

5. I do not approve of the advice about killing human beings for fear that one might be killed by them, unless one is perhaps a soldier or is obligated by public office so that he does this, not for himself, but for others or for the city where he himself also lives, after he has received lawful authority, if it is appropriate to his person. Perhaps, however, those who are deterred by fear from doing something evil also receive some benefit. But the reason it was said, *Let us not resist someone evil* (Mt 5:39), is so that we do not take delight in vengeance that feeds the soul with the evil of another, not so that we neglect the correction of human beings. Hence, he who has constructed a wall around his land is not guilty of the death of another if someone dies after having been struck by its collapse.[4] Nor, after all, is a Christian guilty if his bull kills someone by goring him or his horse by throwing a shoe! Ought the bulls of a Christian not to have horns or his horse not have hoofs or his dog not have teeth? But the apostle Paul took care to bring it to the notice of the tribune that ambushes were being prepared for him by certain wicked persons and, for this reason, he received an armed escort. If criminals threw themselves upon their weapons, would Paul have acknowledged a crime on his part in the shedding of their blood? Heaven forbid that what we do or have for a good and licit purpose should be imputed to us if some evil happens to someone apart from our intention! Otherwise we ought not to have metal tools for the home or field for fear that anyone might kill himself or another by them. Nor should we have a tree or a rope for fear that someone might hang himself. Nor should we make a window for fear that someone may throw himself out of it. Why should I mention more examples since I cannot come to an end in mentioning them? What, after all, is there in the good and licit use of human beings that cannot also be used to procure death?

6. There remains, if I am not mistaken, for us to say something about that Christian traveler whom you mentioned who was overcome by dire straits of hunger, if he nowhere found anything except food set before an idol, where there was no other human being. Is it better for him to die of hunger than to take it as

---

4. I have followed Migne rather than the CSEL edition which indicates a lacuna here.

food? On this question it does not follow that the food was offered to an idol. For it could have been left there out of forgetfulness or deliberately by people who broke their journey there and took refreshment or put it there for any other reason. I shall reply briefly. Either it is certain that it was offered to an idol, or it is certain that it was not, or it is not known whether it was. If it is certain that it was, it is better to reject it out of Christian virtue. But if it is known not to have been or it is not known whether it was, one can eat it without any worry of conscience in the case of necessity.

Letter 48

In 398 Augustine wrote to Eudoxius, the abbot of the monks on the island of Capraria.[1] Augustine first recalls the oneness he shares with Eudoxius and his monks in the body of Christ (paragraph 1). He then urges them to steer a middle path between the contemplative and the active life (paragraph 2) and exhorts them to do whatever they do for the glory of God (paragraph 3). Finally, he expresses the hope that his exhortation will lead them to keep him in their prayers, and he tells Eudoxius of the death of one of his brothers (paragraph 4).

To his beloved lord, most desired brother, and fellow priest, Eudoxius,[2] and to those brothers who are with you, Augustine sends greetings in the Lord.

1. When we think of the peace that you enjoy in Christ, we too find rest in your love, even though we are caught up in the midst of various difficult labors. For we are one body under one head in such a way that you are also busy in us and we are at leisure in you. Because *if one member suffers, all the members suffer with it, and if one member receives glory, all the members rejoice with it* (1 Cor 12:26). Let us admonish, then, and ask and implore through Christ's deepest lowliness and most merciful height that you be mindful of us in your holy prayers for we believe that your prayers are more vigilant and attentive. The dark tumult of worldly courtroom procedures, after all, often wounds and weakens our prayers. Even if we do not have such cases of our own, those who force us to go one mile, and with whom we are commanded to go another two,[3] impose upon us such great burdens that we can scarcely catch our breath. We believe, nonetheless, that, with the help of your prayers, he into whose sight the groaning of prisoners enters[4] will set us free from every difficulty, as we persevere in that ministry in which he has deigned to place us with the promise of a reward.

2. But we exhort you in the Lord, brothers, that you keep to the way of life you have undertaken and that you persevere in it up to the end,[5] and if your mother, the Church, desires any services from you, do not undertake them with an eager burst of pride or reject them because of the attraction of indolence. Rather, obey God with a meek heart, submitting yourselves with gentleness to him who rules you, who guides the meek in justice, who teaches the meek his ways.[6] Do not prefer your leisure to the needs of the Church. If no good men were willing to

---

1. It is disputed whether this island is the one located to the north of Corsica or the one of the same name in the Balearics.
2. Eudoxius was a Catholic priest and abbot of a monastery from the island of Capraria.
3. See Mt 5:41.
4. See Ps 79:11.
5. See Mt 24:13 and 10:22.
6. See Ps 25:9.

minister to her as she brings to birth new children, you would not have found a way to be born in Christ. But just as we must hold to the path between fire and water so that we are neither burned nor drowned, so we ought to steer our journey between the peak of pride and the whirlpool of indolence, as scripture says, *Do not turn aside either to the right or to the left* (Dt 17:11 and Prv 4:27). For there are some who, while too afraid of being filled with pride and carried off, as it were, to the right, are drowning because they have fallen to the left. And again there are some who, while restraining themselves too much from the left for fear of being swallowed up by the torpid softness of idleness, disappear in ashes and smoke, corrupted and consumed by the pride of boastfulness. So, my brothers, love leisure in such a way that you hold yourselves back from all earthly delight and that you remember that there is no place where he who fears our flying back to God cannot set his snares. Let us condemn the enemy of all good persons, for we were once his captives. Let us consider that we have no complete rest *until iniquity passes away* and *justice is turned into judgment* (Ps 57:2 and 94:15).

3. Likewise, when you eagerly do something strenuous and work unstintingly, whether in prayers or in fasting or in almsgiving, when you give something to the needy or forgive injuries, *as God has also forgiven us in Christ* (Eph 4:32; Col 3:13), when you subdue harmful habits and chastise the body, subjecting it even to servitude,[7] when you bear with tribulation and, above all, bear with one another in love—for what does one bear with who does not bear with his brother?—or when you are guarding against the cleverness and ambushes of the tempter and are repelling and extinguishing his fiery darts with the shield of faith,[8] then, *singing and chanting in your hearts to the Lord* (Eph 5:19), or with words in harmony with your hearts, *do all for the glory of God who does all things in all* (1 Cor 10:31, 12:6). And be so fervent in spirit[9] that your soul may receive praise in the Lord.[10] For this is the action of someone on the straight road who always has his eyes on the Lord, because the Lord rescues his feet from the snare.[11] Such action is not broken because of work, and it is not cold because of leisure. It is neither turbulent nor flagging, neither too bold nor cowardly, neither too hasty nor idle. Do all this, and the God of peace will be with you.[12]

4. Let not Your Charity regard me as forward because I wanted to speak to you, at least by means of a letter. For I do not admonish you about this matter because I think that you are not now acting in this way, but I believed that you

---

7. See 1 Cor 9:27.
8. See Eph 6:16.
9. See Rom 12:11.
10. See Ps 34:3.
11. See Ps 25:15.
12. See Phil 4:9 and 2 Cor 13:11.

would commend me to God to no small degree, if you do those actions that you do by his grace with a recollection of our words. For your reputation came to our attention even before, and now the brothers who have come from you, Eustasius and Andrew, have brought to us from your holy way of life the good odor of Christ.[13] Of these Eustasius has gone on to that peace that is not battered, like an island, by the waves, nor does he long for Capraria because he now no longer desires to don his shirt of a penitent.

---

13. See 2 Cor 2:15.

Letter 49

Probably in 398, but between 396 and 410, Augustine wrote to Honoratus, a Donatist bishop. He expresses his pleasure over the plan to discuss the schism by letters apart from the disturbance of crowds (paragraph 1). Augustine points out that the Catholic Church is now spread throughout the whole world as scripture had predicted it would be (paragraph 2). Augustine challenges Honoratus to explain how Christ has lost his Church throughout the world and has come to have only the Donatist church in Africa (paragraph 3).

To Honoratus, a bishop of the Donatist sect,[1] *Augustine, a bishop of the Catholic Church, sends greetings.*

1. We are very much pleased by your plan that you kindly presented to us through our brother, Herotes, a man most dear to us and praiseworthy in Christ, namely, that we deal with each other by letters where no uproar from the crowds can disturb our agenda that we should take up and deal with in all gentleness and peace of soul, just as the apostle says, *A servant of Lord should not be quarrelsome, but meek toward all, docile, patient, rebuking in moderation those who think differently* (2 Tm 2:24). We shall, therefore, briefly state the questions to which we desire your answers.

2. Because we see that the Church of God that is called Catholic is spread throughout the world, as it was foretold that it would be, we think that we ought not to doubt about so very evident a fulfillment of the holy prophecy, which the Lord also confirmed in the gospel and the apostles, through whom the same Church was spread, as it was foretold that it would. For in the beginning of the most holy Book of Psalms it is written about the Son of God, *The Lord said to me, "You are my Son; today I have begotten you. Ask of me, and I shall give you the nations as your inheritance and the ends of the earth as your possession"* (Ps 2:7-8). And the Lord Jesus Christ says that his gospel will be preached among all nations.[2] And before the word of God arrived in Africa, the apostle Paul wrote in the beginning of the Letter to the Romans, *Through whom we have received grace and apostleship to bring about obedience to the faith in all nations for the sake of his name* (Rom 1:4). Then he himself preached the gospel from Jerusalem in the surrounding territory through all of Asia up to Illyricum.[3] He established and founded churches, not he himself, but the grace of God with him,[4] as

---

1. Honoratus was a Donatist bishop in Numidia. The Letter may have be written as late as 410 and as early as 396.
2. See Mt 24:14.
3. See Rom 15:19.
4. See 1 Cor 15:10.

he himself bears witness. But how can anything be seen with greater evidence than when we find the names of regions and of cities in his letters? He writes to the Romans, to the Corinthians, to the Galatians, to the Ephesians, to the Philippians, to the Thessalonians, and to the Colossians. John also writes to seven churches,[5] which he mentions were established in those parts, and we understand that the universal Church is also indicated in these by the number seven, namely, Ephesus, Smyrna, Sardis, Philadelphia, Laodicea, Pergamum, and Thyatira. And it is evident that we are today in communion with all these churches, just as it is evident that you are not in communion with these churches.

3. We ask, then, that you not delay to reply to us with the reason—which you perhaps know—why it has come about that Christ lost his inheritance spread throughout the world and suddenly remained only among the Africans, and not in all the Africans? For the Catholic Church is also in Africa because God willed and foretold that it would be present through all lands. But your sect, which is called the sect of Donatus, is not present in all these places to which the writings and the words and deeds of the apostle had come. But do not say that our Church is not called Catholic, but Macarian,[6] as you call it. You ought to know, since it is most easy to know, that in all those areas from which the gospel of Christ flowed into those lands neither the name of Donatus nor that of Macarius is known. But you yourselves cannot deny that your sect is called the sect of Donatus, and this is known to all wherever your communion exists. Please, then, write back to us in order that we may know how it is possible that Christ lost his Church in the whole world and began to have it among you alone. For it is up to you to show this. For us, after all, it is enough for our case that we see the prophecy and the holy scripture fulfilled throughout the world. But I, Augustine, have dictated this because I have long wanted to speak with you about this. For I think that we can, on account of our nearness, discuss this issue by letters without any uproar, if God helps to the extent that necessity demands.

---

5. See Rv 1:11.
6. The Donatists called the Catholic Church Macarian after the Roman official who harshly persecuted the Donatists in the middle of the fourth century.

Letter 50

After the summer of 399, Augustine wrote to the leaders of the colony of Sufes in Africa Byzacena where a statue of Hercules was torn down by Christians who were implementing Honorius' law of 10 July 399, which ordered the destruction of the pagan temples. In retaliation the pagans of the town massacred sixty Christians. Augustine denounces their horrible crime, promises the restoration of their statue, and with bitter irony asks them to restore the lives they have taken.

To the leaders and chiefs or to the elders of the colony of Sufes, Augustine, the bishop, sends greetings.

The most notorious crime and unexpected cruelty of your savagery has rocked the earth and struck at the sky so that blood shines and murder is decried in your streets and temples. Among you the laws of Rome have been buried, and the fear of righteous courts has been spurned. There is certainly no respect and no reverence for the emperors. Among you the innocent blood of brothers sixty in number has been shed, and if anyone has killed more, he has done so with praise and holds first place in your government. Come on, let us get to the principal issue. If you say that it was your Hercules, we shall then give him back: metal is at hand; rocks are not lacking; there are also various kinds of marble; an abundance of workmen are present. But your god is sculpted, turned, and adorned with diligence. We also add some red to depict the shame with which your sacred rites can resound. For, if you say that it was your Hercules, we have collected coins one by one and have bought your god for you from the artist. Restore, then, the lives that your bloody hand has torn away, and just as we restore to you your Hercules, so also restore the lives of so many people!

Letter 51

In either 399 or 400 Augustine wrote to Crispinus, the Donatist bishop of Calama, a town in Numidia to the south and east of Hippo. Augustine invites Crispinus to discuss by an exchange of letters the schism that divides them, reminding his counterpart that schism was punished in scripture more severely than idolatry and the burning of a sacred book (paragraph 1). Turning Donatist objections back against them, Augustine asks why they accepted back into their communion the bishops who broke away from them in the schism of Maximian (paragraph 2) and why they persecuted the members of that sect (paragraph 3). Why too did the Donatists accept the baptism of the Maximianists, though they do not accept the baptism of the Catholics (paragraph 4)? Augustine insists that baptism belongs to Christ, not to the Donatists or to the Catholics, and asks why the Donatists separate themselves from the rest of the world by a greater schism than that of Maximian (paragraph 5).

1. Because your people criticize our humility, I added this form of salutation to this letter,[1] and I might seem to have done this in contempt for you, if I do not await your reply to me. Why should I remind you at length about your promise in Carthage or our insistence? Regardless of how we acted, let those things be in the past so that they do not impede what remains. Now, unless I am mistaken, there is no excuse if God grants his help; we are both in Numidia and are near to each other in terms of locality. Rumor has reached me that you still want to examine while debating with me the question that divides our communion. See how quickly all the evasions are removed; reply to this letter if you will, and perhaps it will suffice, not only for us, but also for those who desire to hear us. Or if it will not suffice, let us continue with letters and replies until it does suffice. What greater advantage, after all, could such great nearness of the cities we inhabit offer us? For I have decided to do nothing with you on this issue except by letters so that what is said may not slip from the memory of either of us or so that interested persons, who perhaps cannot be present, may not be deprived of such information. You are accustomed to toss about false statements about past events, perhaps not because you want to lie, but because you are mistaken. Hence, if you agree, let us measure those events by present ones. You are surely aware that in the times of the people of the old testament the sacrilege of idolatry was committed[2] and a contemptuous king burned the book of a prophet.[3] The sin of schism would not be punished more harshly than each of these crimes unless it

---

1. Though this letter to Crispinus, the Donatist bishop of Calama in Numidia, lacks the usual salutation, Augustine often addressed the Donatists as brothers and as most dear, terms which he explained and justified in Letter 33.
2. See Ex 32:1.6.
3. See Jer 36:23.

were considered more serious. For you, of course, recall how the earth opened up and swallowed alive the authors of schism and how fire poured down from heaven and consumed those who had sided with it.[4] Neither the construction and worship of an idol nor the burning of a sacred book deserved to be punished in such a way.

2. You are often raise as objections to us charges that are not only not proven against our people, but that are rather proven against your people who were driven by fear of persecution and handed over the sacred books to be burned in the fire. Why, then, have you received back those whom you condemned for the crime of schism "by the true words of" your "plenary council," as it is recorded there, into the very same episcopacy in which you condemned them? I refer to Felician of Musti and Praetextatus of Assuri. After all, these men were not, as you often say to the ignorant, from that number for whom your council had given a postponement and fixed a date beyond which they would be bound by the same sentence if they had not returned to your communion. They were rather from that number whom you condemned without delay on that day on which you granted a delay to those others. I shall prove this if you deny it; your council is explicit. We have the proconsular acts in our hands in which you affirmed this more than once. Prepare another defense if you can so that we do not cause delays while you deny what I prove. If Felician and Praetextatus were innocent, why were they condemned in that way? If they were criminals, why were they taken back in that way? If you prove them innocent, why should we not believe that innocent men could have been condemned on the false charge of surrendering the books by a much smaller number of your predecessors if three hundred and ten of their successors were able to condemn innocent men on the false charge of schism "by the true word of a plenary council," as it was so pompously stated? But if you prove that they were rightly condemned, what defense remains for why they were received back into the same episcopacy except that, by emphasizing the benefit and salutariness of peace, you show that even these crimes should be tolerated to maintain the bond of unity? I wish you would do this, not with the strength of the word, but with that of the heart! You would, of course, see how the peace of Christ should not be violated by any slanders throughout the world, if it is permissible in Africa that men condemned even for sacrilegious schism are received back in the very same episcopacy to maintain the peace of Donatus.

3. You likewise often raise as an objection to us that we persecute you by earthly powers. On this point I do not want to discuss either what you deserve for the terribleness of so great a sacrilege or how much Christian kindness restrains us. This is what I say: If this is a crime, why did you fiercely attack the same

---

4. See Nm 16:31-35.

Maximianists[5] through judges sent by those emperors, whom our communion begot through the gospel, and why did you by the roar of controversies, by the power of ordinances, and by the assault of troops drive them from the basilicas which they had and in which they were at the time of the division? What they suffered in individual places during that conflict is attested to by recent traces of events. The records show what orders were given; the lands in which the holy memory of that notorious Optatus, your tribune,[6] is venerated cry out what was done.

4. You are also accustomed to say that we do not have the baptism of Christ and that it exists nowhere outside of your communion. I could on this issue speak somewhat more at length. But in opposition to you there is no need, for you have accepted the baptism of the Maximianists along with Felician and Praetextatus. For they baptized many when they were in communion with Maximian, though, as the records testify, you tried by a long judicial conflict to expel by name from their basilicas those very men, that is, Felician and Praetextatus. As many, then, as they baptized at that time, they now have with them and with you, not only during times of critical illness, but during the solemnities of Easter, in so many churches that belong to their cities, and even in large cities. They have those people who were baptized outside their sect in the crime of schism, and for none of these was baptism repeated. And I wish that you could prove that those whom Felician and Praetextatus baptized, as if with no benefit, outside your sect in the crime of schism were baptized again, as if to their benefit, by them when they were received back within your sect. For, if these people had to be baptized again, those bishops had to be ordained again. After all, they lost their episcopacy in withdrawing from you if they were not able to baptize outside of your communion. For, if in departing they did not lose their episcopacy, they were, of course, able to baptize. But if they lost it, they, then, ought to have been ordained upon their return in order that what they had lost might be restored to them. But have no fear. Just as it is certain that they returned with the same episcopacy with which they left, so it is certain that they reconciled to your communion without any repetition of baptism along with themselves all whom they baptized in the schism of Maximian.

5. With what tears, then, will we be able sufficiently to deplore the fact that the baptism of the Maximianists is accepted and that the baptism of the whole world is subjected to exsufflation?[7] Whether after a hearing or without a hearing, whether justly or unjustly, you condemned Felician, you condemned Praetextatus. Tell me, which bishop of the Corinthians has been heard or

---

5. The Maximianists were a schismatic group that broke away from the Donatists.

6. Optatus was the Donatist bishop of Thamugadi; he was also called Gildonian after Count Gildo whose rule from 395 to 397 brought persecution against the Maximianists.

7. Exsufflation was part of the rite of baptism; it symbolized the expulsion of the devil from the candidate.

condemned by one of yours? Which bishop of the Galatians, of the Ephesians, of the Colossians, of the Philippians, of the Thessalonians, and of all the other cities of which scripture says, *All the families of the nations shall worship in his sight* (Ps 22:28)? The baptism, then, of the Maximianists is accepted, and the baptism of those apostolic churches is subjected to exsufflation, though baptism belongs neither to these nor to those, but to him of whom it was said, *This is he who baptizes* (Jn 1:33). But I am not talking about this; turn to those matters that are at hand; look at those that strike even blind eyes. Those who were condemned have baptism, and those who have not had a hearing do not! Those explicitly named in the crime of schism and cast out have baptism, and those who are unknown, far away, never accused, never brought to trial do not! Those who were cut off from part of Africa that was already cut off from the Church have baptism, and those from whom the gospel itself came to Africa do not have it! Why should I burden you with more? Reply to these questions. Consider the sacrilege of schism with which your council charged the Maximianists; consider the persecutions through judicial powers that you brought upon them. Consider their baptism that you accepted along with those whom you condemned, and answer, if you can, if you have some means to throw the ignorant into confusion, why you are separated from the world by a far greater crime of schism than that which you boast to have condemned in the Maximianists. May the peace of Christ win out in your heart.

Letter 52

In 399 or 400 Augustine wrote to Severinus, a relative and a Donatist, about abandoning his criminal schism. Augustine reminds Severinus that their true relationship must be in the body of Christ (paragraph 1). The sect of Donatus, Augustine explains, is a branch that does not bear fruit (paragraph 2). On the other hand, all the other churches apart from the Donatist churches are in communion with one another (paragraph 3). Finally, Augustine reminds his relative that their blood relationship is of no account toward everlasting salvation in Christ (paragraph 4).

To his much loved lord and very dear brother, Severinus, Augustine sends greetings.

1. Though the letter from you, my brother, was very late, and though it was apart from what I expected, I, nonetheless, was happy to receive it, and I was especially flooded with greater joy when I learned that your servant came to Hippo for this reason alone, that is, to bring to me your letter, my brother. I thought, after all, not without reason that the idea entered your mind to recall our blood relationship, only because you perhaps see—just as I know the considerable weight of your wisdom—how we should feel sorrow that we, who are brothers according to the flesh, do not live in the body of Christ in one society. This is especially true since it is easy for you to observe and see the city built upon a mountain, of which the Lord says in the gospel that it cannot be hidden.[1] For it is the Catholic Church; the reason it is called καθολική in Greek is that it is spread throughout the whole world. No one is permitted to be unaware of this; for this reason it cannot be hidden, according to the word of our Lord Jesus Christ.

2. The sect of Donatus, however, found only in Africans, slanders the world and does not consider that by that sterility, because of which it refuses to bear the fruits of peace and love, it is cut off from that root of the Eastern churches, from which the gospel came to Africa. If a bit of soil is brought to them from those lands, they reverence it, but if a believer comes to them from there, they subject him even to exsufflation[2] and rebaptize him. The Son of God who is the truth, after all, foretold this[3] when he said that he was the vine, his children the branches, and his Father the farmer.[4] He said, *My Father will destroy the branch*

---

1. See Mt 5:14.
2. Exsufflation was part of the rite of baptism which symbolized the expulsion of the devil from the candidate.
3. See Jn 14:6.
4. See Jn 15:1.

that does not bear fruit in me, but he will trim the branch that does bear fruit in me in order that it may bear more fruit (Jn 15:2). It is, therefore, not surprising if they who refused to bear the fruit of love were cut off from that vine which grew and filled all the lands.[5]

3. If the Donatists had raised as objections to their colleagues true crimes, when their predecessors created a schism, they themselves would have won their case before the church overseas, from which the authority of the Christian faith came to these parts. The result would have been that those men were excluded against whom they raised as objections those same crimes. But now when the accused are found to be on the inside in communion with the apostolic churches, whose names they have and read in the holy books, while their accusers are located outside and separated from that communion, who would fail to understand that they had a good case who were able to win it before impartial judges? Or if the Donatists had a good case and could not prove it to the churches overseas, how did the world do them harm since the bishops could not have rashly condemned their colleagues who had not been proved guilty before them of the crimes with which they were charged? Therefore, innocent people are rebaptized, and Christ is subjected to exsufflation in innocent people. If, however, the same Donatists knew true crimes of their African colleagues and neglected to point them out and to prove them to the churches overseas, they cut themselves off from the unity of Christ by a most wicked schism. They have no excuse, and you know it well, especially since so many criminals emerged among them and they tolerated them for so many years for fear of sundering the sect of Donatus. And they did not hesitate at that time to break up the peace and unity of Christ by hurling their false suspicions, as you yourselves see.

4. But some sort of carnal habit, brother Severinus, holds you there, and long have I grieved, long have I groaned, and long have I desired to see you in order to speak to you about this topic. After all, what good does temporal health and relationship do if we scorn in our thinking the eternal heritage of Christ and everlasting salvation? For the time being let it suffice for me to have written these ideas, which for hard hearts are very few and almost none at all, but for your mind, which I know well, they are quite many and very important. After all, they do not come from me, for I am nothing apart from what I await, namely, the mercy of God; rather, they come from God almighty, and anyone who in this age will contemn him as Father will find him as judge in the age to come.

---

5. See Ps 80:10.

Letter 53

In approximately 400 Augustine, Alypius, and Fortunatus wrote to Generosus, a Catholic of Constantina in Numidia, whom a Donatist priest had tried to convert by a letter that Generosus forwarded to the Catholic bishops. Augustine writes with his colleagues that, if the Donatist priest claims to have a revelation from an angel about the order of his church aimed to making Generosus leave the Catholic Church, he should regard such an angel as anathema (paragraph 1). If the succession of bishops is the order in question, Augustine points out that in the whole succession of the bishops of Rome there is no Donatist (paragraph 2). If in that succession from Peter to Anastasius there has been a traditor, there is still no grounds for schism (paragraph 3). In fact, there were traditors among the bishops of Constantina, Generosus' own city (paragraph 4). The Donatists invoked the authority of the emperor, but refused to abide by his judgment (paragraph 5). If the Donatists are not defiled by the Maximianists, whom they themselves condemned, but took back into their communion, the rest of the world could not be defiled by the sins of a few Africans (paragraph 6). Though the author of the letter claims to have been taught by an angel, Saint Paul has warned us against Satan who can transform himself into an angel of light (paragraph 7).

To Generosus, their most beloved and honorable brother, Fortunatus, Alypius,[1] *and Augustine send greetings in the Lord.*

1, 1. You wanted us to know of the letter that a priest of the Donatists sent to you, and although you also laugh it to scorn with the mind of a Catholic, we, nonetheless, ask that you bring to him this reply in order that you may rather do him some good if he is not hopelessly stupid. He, after all, wrote that an angel commanded him to inform you of the practice of the Christianity of your city, though you hold onto the Christianity, not of your city, nor only of Africa or of the Africans, but that of the whole world, which has been and is being announced to all the nations. Hence, it is not enough that the Donatists are not ashamed to have been cut off and that they do not help themselves in order to return to the root when they can, but they try also to cut others off along with them and to prepare them for the fire, like dried branches. In his clever vanity, as I see it, he pretends on your account that an angel stood before him. Hence, suppose that there stood before you that same angel. And if that angel said these things to you that this man says he conveys to you at the angel's command, you must bear in mind the words of the apostle who says, *Even if we or an angel from heaven should proclaim a gospel to you apart from what we have proclaimed to you, let him be anathema* (Gal 1:8). For it has been proclaimed to you by the words of the

---

1. Generosus was a Catholic layman and consul of Numidia; Fortunatus was the Catholic bishop of Cirta in Numidia; Alypius was now bishop of Thagaste, his and Augustine's hometown.

Lord Jesus Christ that his gospel will be announced to all the nations and that then the end will come.[2] It has been proclaimed to you through the writings of the prophets and of the apostles that the promises were made to Abraham and to his descendant, that is, to Christ,[3] when God said to him, *In your descendants all the nations will be blessed* (Gn 12:3, 22:18). Even if, then, an angel from heaven said to you who have these promises, "Abandon the Christianity of the whole world, and hold onto that of the sect of Donatus," whose practice is explained to you in the letter of the bishop of your city, that angel ought to be anathema, because he tried to cut you off from the whole, shove you into a part, and separate you from the promises of God.

2. If, after all, we must consider the order of bishops in succession, how much more certainly and in a way truly conducive to salvation would we begin from Peter himself, who symbolized the whole Church and to whom the Lord said, *Upon this rock I shall build my Church, and the gates of hell will not conquer it* (Mt 16:18). For Linus came after Peter; Clement after Linus; Anacletus after Clement; Evaristus after Anacletus; Sixtus after Evaristus; Telesphorus after Sixtus; Hyginus after Telesphorus; Anicetus after Hyginus; Pius after Anicetus; Soter after Pius; Alexander after Soter; Victor after Alexander; Zephirinus after Victor; Calixtus after Zephirinus; Urbanus after Calixtus; Pontian after Urbanus; Antherus after Pontian; Fabian after Antherus; Cornelius after Fabian; Lucius after Cornelius; Stephan after Lucius; Sixtus after Stephan; Dionysius after Sixtus; Felix after Dionysius; Eutychian after Felix; Gaius after Eutychian; Marcellus after Gaius; Eusebius after Marcellus; Miltiades after Eusebius; Sylvester after Miltiades; Marcus after Sylvester; Julius after Marcus; Liberius after Julius; Damasus after Liberius; Siricius after Damasus; Anastasius after Siricius. In this order of succession no Donatist bishop is found. But the Donatists unexpectedly sent an ordained priest from Africa; he presided over a few Africans in Rome and originated the name of the Montenses or Cutzupits.[4]

3. Even if during those times some traditor crept into the order of bishops that runs from Peter himself to Anastasius,[5] who now occupies that see, it would not bring any harm to the Church or to the innocent Christians, to whom the Lord in his foresight said concerning bad superiors, *Do what they say, but do not do what they do. For they speak, but they do not act accordingly* (Mt 23:3). He said this in order that the hope of the believer might be certain and that such hope, not placed in a human being, but in the Lord, would not be blown away by the storm of sacrilegious schism, as these Donatists are blown away who read in the holy books about the churches to which the apostles wrote and who themselves have

---

2. See Mt 24:14.
3. See Gal 3:16.
4. The Roman Donatists were called "Montenses" or "hill people," because of their lack of culture. It is not known why they were called Cutzupits.
5. Anastasius began his pontificate in 398.

no bishop in them. But what is more perverse and insane than to say to readers who read the same letters, "Peace be with you," while being separated from the peace of those churches to which the letters were written?

2, 4. And yet, so that no one is fooled concerning the order of bishops of Constantina, that is, of your city, read out for him the record of the proceedings held before Munatius Felix, the perpetual priest, the supervisor at that time of the same city of yours, on May 22 during the eighth consulate of Diocletian and the seventh of Maximian.[6] It is crystal-clear from them that Paul, the bishop, handed over the sacred books and that Sylvanus, who was then his subdeacon, also brought forth and handed over with him certain vessels of the Lord, even ones that had been carefully concealed, namely, a silver box and a silver lamp. Then a certain Victor said, "You were a dead man if you had not found them." The author of the letter mentions as a great man in the letter that he wrote to you this Sylvanus, who was most clearly a traditor and who was then ordained bishop by Secundus of Tigisi, the bishop primate. Let their proud tongue fall silent and acknowledge their crimes in order that it may not rave with madness and mention the crimes of others. Read for him, if he wants, records of the ecclesiastical proceedings of Secundus of Tigisi that were held in the house of Urbanus the Donatist, in which he left to God as their judge the traditors who had confessed: Donatus of Masculi, Marinus of Aquae Tibilitanae, Donatus of Calama. Along with these confessed traditors he ordained for them as bishop Sylvanus, the traditor whom we mentioned. Read for him the records of the proceedings before Zenophilus, the governor, in which a certain deacon, Nundinarius, angry at Sylvanus because he was excommunicated by him, disclosed to the courts all these events that are established clearer than daylight by certain documents, by the answers of witnesses, and by the recitation of the records and of many letters.

5. There are many other documents that you might read to him if he was willing to avoid being quarrelsome and to listen with wisdom. There are the petitions of the Donatists to Constantine that he send episcopal judges from Gaul to end this dispute between the bishops of Africa. There is also the letter of the same emperor when he sent bishops to the city of Rome. There are also the proceedings in the city of Rome where the case was heard and examined by the bishops whom he had sent. Likewise, there is another letter in which the emperor we mentioned states that the Donatists complained before him about the judgment of their colleagues, that is, of the bishops whom he sent to the city of Rome. In this letter he decided that other bishops should sit in judgment at Arles, where the Donatists also appealed from the judgment of these bishops to the same emperor, and, finally, he himself heard the case between the two sides; there he testifies with very great force that the Donatists were defeated by the innocence

---

6. The proceedings took place in 303. See *Answer to Cresconius* III, 29, 33.

of Caecilian. If he is willing, he will listen to this and will be silent and cease plotting against the truth.

3, 6. And yet, we do not rely upon those documents as much as we do upon the holy scriptures in which it was promised that the inheritance of Christ would extend to the ends of the earth in all nations.[7] Hence, these people who have been separated by wicked schism hurl accusations against the straw in the Lord's harvest, which is mixed with the wheat and must be tolerated up to the end when the whole threshing floor will be winnowed at the last judgment.[8] Hence, it is clear that these charges, whether true or false, do not pertain to the Lord's grain, which must continue to grow through the whole field, that is, through the world, up to the end of the world, as the Lord says in the gospel,[9] not as a false angel says in the error of this fellow. For this reason God has rightly repaid these wretched Donatists who throw many false and empty accusations against innocent Christians, who are throughout the world mixed in with bad Christians as if with their straw or weeds. For in their universal council at Carthage they condemned their own schismatic Maximianists who had condemned Primian, had baptized outside of communion with Primian, and had rebaptized after Primian. And yet, from their number they accepted after no short time certain men into the dignity of their episcopacy, namely, Felician of Musti and Praetextatus of Assuri, when Optatus the Gildonian[10] forced them to do so, along with all those whom they baptized when they were in schism and condemned. But if they are not defiled by those whom they condemned with their own lips as criminal and sacrilegious and whom they compared to those first schismatics whom the earth swallowed alive,[11] when they are again in communion with them after they have been taken back into their own episcopal dignity, let them at long last wake up. Let them realize the great blindness and great insanity with which they say that the world was defiled by the crimes of Africans, which it did not know, and that the inheritance of Christ, which was shown to have been promised to exist in all the nations, had been wiped out by the sins of Africans through the infection of communion with them, though they do not want to be thought to be wiped out and defiled when they are in communion with those whose crimes they knew and condemned.

7. For this reason, since the apostle Paul again says that Satan transforms himself into an angel of light, it is no surprise that his ministers transform them-

---

7. See Ps 2:8.
8. See Mt 13:20 and 3:12.
9. See Mt 13:30.
10. Optatus preceded Gaudentius as Donatist bishop of Thamugadi. See *Answer to Gaudentius* I, 38. He was called Gildonian because he shared in the tyrannical plundering of Count Gildonian. He was killed in prison for his wrongdoings. See *Answer to the Letters of Petilian* II, 92.
11. See Nm 15:31-33.

selves into ministers of justice.[12] If he really saw some angel, a messenger of error and desirous to separate Christians from Catholic unity, he himself has experienced an angel of Satan transforming himself into an angel of light. But if he is lying and saw nothing of the sort, he is himself a minister of Satan transforming himself into a minister of justice. And yet, if, when he considers all these facts, he does not choose to be exceedingly perverse and stubborn, he can be set free from every seduction to error whether stemming from another or his own. For using the opportunity you provided we have addressed him without any hatred, observing in his regard the rule of the apostle, *A servant of the Lord should not be quarrelsome, but meek toward all, docile, patient, rebuking with moderation those who think otherwise. For perhaps God may grant them repentance in order to come to know the truth, and they may come to their senses from the snares of the devil, after having been captured by him to do his will* (2 Tm 2:24-26). If, then, we said anything harsh, let him realize that it is not intended to provoke bitterness in disagreement, but correction in love. May you live safe and sound in Christ, my most beloved and honorable brother. Amen.

---

12. See 2 Cor 11:14-15.

Letter 54

In approximately 400 Augustine wrote to Januarius, a Catholic layman, in answer to his questions about differing religious practices. Augustine distinguishes sacraments found in the New Testament and in the universal tradition and practice of the Church (paragraph 1) from other observances (paragraph 2). He recalls Saint Ambrose's advice that Augustine had sought for Monica, namely, that one should follow the practice of the church to which one comes (paragraph 3). Whether one receives the eucharist daily or not so frequently is not as important as receiving the sacrament worthily (paragraph 4). So too, in different places the sacrifice is offered on Holy Thursday both in the morning and in the evening (paragraph 5). In some places the Lenten fast is continued on Holy Thursday and in others it is broken (paragraph 6). The Lord's having given communion to the apostles after dinner does not amount to an argument for the evening celebration on Holy Thursday (paragraph 7) or against the eucharistic fast, which is universally observed in the Church (paragraph 8). Augustine suggests an explanation for the morning and evening celebration of the eucharist on Holy Thursday (paragraph 9) and for the custom of bathing on the same day (paragraph 10).

In his *Revisions*, Augustine lists Letters 54 and 55 as books entitled: *Two Books of Answers to the Questions of Januarius.*

Revisions II, 20

The two books whose title is the *Questions of Januarius* contain much discussion of the sacraments that the Church observes either everywhere or in particular places, that is, not equally in all places. The books were not, nonetheless, able to mention all of them, but they replied sufficiently to what was asked. The first of these books is a letter; it has at the top the writer and the addressee. But this work is counted among my books because the following book, which does not have our names, is much lengthier, and many more topics are treated in it. In the first book, then, as for what I said about the manna, namely, that it tasted in the mouth of each person as the person wanted, I have no idea what could prove this except the Book of Wisdom, which the Jews do not accept as having canonical authority.[1] This effect could, nonetheless, have come about for believing Jews, not for those who murmured against God, for they would not have desired other food if the manna tasted the same as what they desired. This work begins: "To those questions you asked me."

---

1. See Wis 16:20.

Answers to the Questions of Januarius

Book One

To his most beloved son, Januarius, Augustine sends greetings in the Lord.

1, 1. I would have preferred to know first what you yourself would answer to those questions that you asked me if you were asked them. For, in that way I could have answered much more briefly by either approving or correcting your replies, and I would either agree with you or correct you. This, as I said, is what I would have preferred. But in order that I might answer now, I chose to produce a longer discussion rather than to cause a delay. First of all, then, I want you to hold onto what is the principal point of this discussion, that our Lord Jesus Christ, as he himself says in the gospel, has made us subject to his gentle yoke and light burden.[2] For this reason he bound together the society of the new people by sacraments very few in number, very easy in their observance, and most excellent in what they signify. They are, for example, baptism made sacred by the name of the Trinity, the partaking of his body and blood, and any other that is mentioned in the canonical scriptures, with the exception of those about which we read in the books of Moses and which imposed a heavy servitude upon the old people, such as was suitable to their heart and to a prophetic time. But we are given to understand that those practices we observe which are not in scripture, but in tradition, and which are observed throughout the whole world, are maintained as taught and established either by the apostles themselves or by plenary councils, which have an authority in the Church most conducive to salvation: for example, the passion and resurrection of the Lord, his ascension into heaven, and the coming of the Holy Spirit from heaven that are celebrated solemnly each year, and any other occurrence that is observed by the universal Church wherever it is spread.

2, 2. But there are other practices that vary from place to place and region to region. For example, some fast on Saturday and others do not; some receive daily the body and blood of the Lord in communion, while others receive only on certain days; in some places no day passes without the Sacrifice being offered, while in other places it is offered only on Saturday and Sunday, and in still others only on Sunday. And whatever else of the sort one notices, this whole kind of practice is open to differing observation according to choice, nor is there any discipline in these matters better for a serious and prudent Christian than to act in the way he sees the church acts to which he may have come. For what is proved to be neither contrary to the faith nor contrary to good morals should be regarded

---

2. See Mt 11:30.

as indifferent and should be observed in accord with the society of those with whom one is living.

3. I believe that you once heard this from me,[3] but I, nonetheless, repeat it now as well. My mother, who followed me to Milan, discovered that the Milanese church did not fast on Saturday; she began to be upset and to be in doubt about what to do. At that time I was not concerned about such things, but on her account I consulted Ambrose, a man of blessed memory, on this point. He replied that he could teach me nothing but what he himself did, since, if he knew a better rule, he would follow it instead. I had thought that he meant to advise us not to fast on Saturday without giving any reason, but by his own authority alone; yet he went on and said to me, "When I go to Rome, I fast on Saturday; when I am here, I do not fast. So to whatever church you go, observe its custom if you do not want to be a scandal to anyone or anyone to be a scandal to you." When I reported this rule to my mother, she willingly made it her own. But I thought of this statement again and again, and I always regarded it as if I had received it from a heavenly oracle. For I often saw with sorrow and grief that many of the weak are upset by the quarrelsome stubbornness or superstitious timidity of certain brothers. For they stir up such quarrelsome questions in matters of this sort that cannot be brought to a definite end by the authority of holy scripture or by the tradition of the universal Church or by the benefit of amending one's life. At the basis of their opinion, after all, there is only some sort of argument on the part of the thinker either that he has grown accustomed to it in his homeland or that he saw it elsewhere and thinks that he has become more learned the further he is from home in his travels. As a result such people judge nothing correct but what they themselves do.

3, 4. Someone might say that the eucharist should not be received daily. Why? "Because," he says, "one should choose the days on which one lives with more purity and self-control in order to approach so great a sacrament worthily. *For one who eats unworthily eats and drinks to his own condemnation*" (1 Cor 11:29). Another will say the opposite; he says, "On the contrary, if the wound of sin and the attack of the disease is in fact so great that such medicines need to be postponed, one ought to be removed from the altar by the authority of the bishop in order to do penance, and one ought to be reconciled by the same authority. For this is what it is to receive unworthily: if one receives at that time when he ought to be doing penance. But one should not by his own judgment abstain from or return to communion, as he pleases. On the other hand, if the sins are not so great that a person should be judged to deserve excommunication, he ought not to withdraw from the daily medicine of the Lord's body." One perhaps settles the dispute between them more correctly who warns them above all to remain in the peace of Christ, but let each do what he piously believes according to his faith

---

3. See Letter 36, 14, 32.

should be done. For neither of them dishonors the body and blood of the Lord; rather, they strive with each other to honor the most salutary sacrament. After all, Zacchaeus and that centurion did not quarrel with each other, nor did one of them prefer himself to the other, when one of them received the Lord into his home[4] and the other said, *I am not worthy that you should enter under my roof* (Mt 8:8). They both honored the savior, though in a different and almost contrary way; both were in misery because of their sins; both obtained mercy. It also serves as a comparison that in the earlier people the manna tasted in the mouth of each one as the individual wanted,[5] just as that sacrament by which the world is conquered has a different taste in the heart of each Christian. For one person does not dare to receive every day out of respect, and another does not dare to skip any day out of respect. This food only refuses to tolerate contempt, just as the manna refused to tolerate boredom. The apostle, after all, says that it is received unworthily by those who do not distinguish this food from other foods by the veneration due to it alone. For, after he had said, *He eats and drinks to his own condemnation*, he immediately went on to say, *not recognizing the body of the Lord* (1 Cor 11:29). This is quite clear from this whole passage in the First Letter to the Corinthians, if one pays careful attention.

4, 5. Suppose that someone is perhaps traveling in that place where people who persevere in the observance of Lent do not bathe or break their fast on Thursday.[6] He says, "I will not fast today." He is asked why. "Because," he says, "it is not done in my homeland." What else does he try to do but to prefer his own custom to that of another? After all, he is not going to read this to me out of the book of God, nor will he quarrel at the top of his voice with the universal Church wherever it is extended. Nor will he show that the other acts against the faith, but that he himself acts in accord with it and in accord with the best morals, nor will he prove that the other violates them or that he observes them. They, of course, violate their own quiet and peace in arguing over a superfluous question. I would prefer, nonetheless, in cases of this sort that both the former in the country of the latter and the latter in that of the former would not refuse to do what the others do. But suppose that, when traveling in a foreign country where the people of God are more numerous or assemble more often or are more fervent, one saw, for example, that the eucharist is offered twice on Thursday of the last week of Lent, both in the morning and in the evening. And if, upon coming back to his own country where it is the custom that it be offered at the end of the day, he contends that this is illicit and wrong, because he saw a different practice elsewhere, this idea is childish; it is to be avoided in ourselves and tolerated and corrected in our people.

---

4. See Lk 19:6.

5. See *Revisions* II, 20, where Augustine says that he no longer knows where he got this idea.

6. Presumably on Holy Thursday.

5, 6. Notice, then, to which of these three kinds the first question of yours that you put in your memorandum belongs. For these are the words of your question: "What should one do on the Thursday of the last week of Lent? Should one offer the sacrifice in the morning and again after supper on account of the words, *In a like manner after they had eaten supper* (Lk 22:20 and 1 Cor 11:25)? Or should one fast and offer the sacrifice only after supper? Or should one also fast and eat supper after offering the sacrifice, as we are accustomed to do?" To these questions, then, I reply that, if the authority of the divine scripture prescribes whichever of these we should do, we should have no doubt that we ought to do what we read in it so that we now no longer argue about how we should act, but how we should understand the mystery. The situation is the same if the whole Church throughout the world follows one of these practices. For in this case too it is a sign of most insolent madness to doubt that we should act in that way. But neither the former nor the latter holds for what you are asking. It remains, then, that it belongs to that third kind of practice that varies from place to place and region to region. Let each person, then, do what he finds in the church to which he comes. For whichever of these practices one follows, it is not against the faith nor against morals, which are not better with this practice or that. For these reasons, that is, on account of faith or on account of morals, one must correct what was being done wrongly or begin to do what was not being done. The very change of a custom, even one that is helpful in its benefit, causes a disturbance by its novelty. Hence, a change that is not of help by its benefit is, as a result, useless and harmful because of its disturbance.

7. Nor should one suppose that the practice arose in many places of offering the sacrifice on Holy Thursday after the meal because scripture says, *In a like manner he took the cup after the supper* (Lk 22:20 and 1 Cor 11:25) and so on. For scripture could have called "supper" the meal in which they just received his body so that they next received the cup. The apostle, after all, says elsewhere, *When you come together, it is not, therefore, to eat the Lord's supper* (1 Cor 11:20), where he calls this reception of the eucharist the Lord's supper. The words of the gospel could have caused more confusion about whether, already having eaten on that day, they should offer the sacrifice or receive the Eucharist; it says, *But when they had eaten, Jesus took bread and blessed it* (Mt 26:26), though he had also said above, *But since it was late, he reclined with the twelve, and as they were eating, he said to them, "One of you will betray me"* (Mt 26:20). For afterward he gave them the sacrament. And it is perfectly clear that, when the disciples first received the body and blood of the Lord, they did not receive while fasting.

6, 8. Should the whole Church, nonetheless, be made the subject of slander because it always receives when fasting? After all, it was on this account that the Holy Spirit decided that in the honor of so great a sacrament the body of the Lord should enter the mouth of a Christian before other food. For this custom is observed throughout the world for this reason. Nor does it follow that just because the Lord distributed the eucharist after the apostles had eaten, it does not follow that the brethren ought to assemble to receive that sacrament after having had dinner or supper or that they ought to confuse the Lord's supper with their ordinary meals, as they did whom the apostle rebukes and corrects. For, in order to teach more emphatically the depth of that mystery, the savior wanted to fix this last gift in the hearts and memory of the disciples, whom he was about to leave to enter upon his passion. And he gave no command about the order in which the eucharist should thereafter be received in order to leave the decision about its place to the apostles, through whom he was going to govern the Church. For, if he had directed them that the Eucharist should always be received after other food, I am confident that no one would have changed that practice. But when the apostle says, in speaking of this sacrament, *Hence, brothers and sisters, when you come together to eat, wait for one another. If someone is hungry, let him eat at home in order that you may not come to condemnation*, he immediately added, *But I shall regulate the other matters when I come* (1 Cor 11:33-34). From this we can understand that he had established the Eucharistic fast that does not vary by any difference in its practice. For it would have taken too long for him to teach them in that letter the whole order to follow that the entire Church observes throughout the world.

7, 9. But some find attractive a certain probable argument that on one specific day in the year on which the Lord gave this supper it is permitted that the body and blood of the Lord be offered and received after eating as if to have a more striking commemoration. I, however, think that it is better to offer the sacrifice at that hour so that one who has also fasted could attend the sacrifice after the meal that is taken at the ninth hour. Hence, we do not force anyone to eat before that supper of the Lord, but we also do not dare to contradict anyone. I do not, none-theless, think that this practice was instituted except because many or almost all had the custom of bathing on that day in many places. And because some also observe the fast, the sacrifice is offered in the morning on account of those who take food, for they cannot tolerate fasting and bathing together, but on account of those who fast the sacrifice is offered in the evening.

10. But if you ask why the custom of also bathing has arisen, nothing more probable comes to my mind as I think of this than that the bodies of those to be baptized, unwashed throughout the observance of Lent, would come to the font with offense to the senses unless they were bathed on some day. But this day was especially chosen for this on which the anniversary of the Lord's supper is cele-brated. And because this was permitted to those who were going to be baptized, many wanted to bathe along with them and to break their fast.

After having discussed these points as well as I could, I advise you to observe what I have said as well as you can, as is fitting for a prudent and peaceful son of the Church. If the Lord is willing, I shall at some other time answer the other questions you asked.

Letter 55

As we saw in the introduction to Letter 54, in his *Revisions* II, 20, Augustine considered this and the previous letter as a work and not as a letter. Soon after Letter 54, Augustine replied to another letter from Januarius, which had reminded him of the remaining questions to be answered (paragraph 1). Januarius had asked why Easter is not celebrated on the same day every year as Christmas is; in his answer Augustine points out that the birth of the Lord is not celebrated as a sacrament, while the Pasch is celebrated as a sacrament, for it not merely recalls the past event, but symbolizes our own passing from death to life (paragraph 2). Though in faith we have passed from death to life (paragraph 3), our resurrection is still to come (paragraph 4). Augustine explains why the Pasch is celebrated in the month of the new harvest (paragraph 5) and flatly rejects the Manichean account of the moon's waxing and waning (paragraph 6). He offers a more scientific account of the phases of the moon (paragraph 7) and, after explaining the symbolism of the sun and the moon (paragraph 8), he shows why the Pasch is celebrated, beginning from the twenty-first day of the month of the new harvest (paragraph 9). For the moon is a symbol of the Church militant (paragraph 10). He warns that, though creatures are used as symbols of divine realities, they must never be worshiped (paragraph 11). He insists that Christians do not make observations of the heavenly bodies for the purpose of astrology (paragraphs 12 and 13) and argues for legitimate uses of creatures as symbols and of observations of the weather (paragraphs 14 and 15).

Augustine explains why the Christian celebration of the Pasch includes the Sabbath (paragraph 16) and how the Sabbath symbolizes our eternal rest in heaven (paragraphs 17 through 19). For the aim of all our actions is directed toward that eternal rest (paragraph 20). Augustine shows the usefulness of allegories for setting the soul aflame with love (paragraph 21) and points out that for Christians the commandment to rest on the Sabbath is to be interpreted figuratively, that is, in terms of a spiritual rest (paragraph 22). Christians observe the eighth day as the Lord's day, the day Christ rose (paragraph 23).

Augustine explains the significance of the Easter triduum (paragraph 24) and of the four directions in which the cross is extended (paragraph 25). Augustine reminds Januarius that we are now saved only in hope and will attain perfect rest only after this life (paragraph 26). Augustine sums up what he has said about the Paschal sacrament (paragraph 27) and turns to the topic of the forty days of fasting and the symbolism of the number forty (paragraph 28). So too, he explains the symbolism of the number fifty, the days after Easter to the Ascension, and finds a parallel in the old testament (paragraphs 29 to 31). He discusses the singing of the Alleluia during Eastertide, the washing of the feet, and other customs, such as singing, where he remarks in passing that the Donatists criticize the lack of vigor in the Catholics' singing (paragraphs 32 to 34).

Augustine discusses some Church customs that he thinks should be abolished (paragraph 35), answers a question about abstinence from meat on the grounds of its impurity (paragraph 36), and comments on the use of the gospels for telling one's fortune (paragraph 37). Finally, Augustine reminds Januarius that love of God and of the neighbor contains the essence of the scriptures (paragraph 38) and warns that knowledge without love is useless (paragraph 39).

Answers to the Questions of Januarius

Book Two

1, 1. Having read your letter in which you reminded me to pay my debt by resolving the remaining questions that you had asked so long ago, I could not tolerate it that your eager desire, which is most pleasing and most dear to me, should be further put off, and although I was in the midst of my many tasks, I made it most important that I answer you with respect to those questions you asked. I do not want to discuss your letter any longer for fear that this may itself prevent me from now at last repaying the debt I owe.

2. You ask what is the reason "why the anniversary for the celebration of Lord's passion does not recur on the same day of the year, as the day does on which he is said to have been born," and then you add, "If this is on account of the Sabbath and the moon, what significance does the observation of the Sabbath and the moon have in this matter?" Here you must first realize that the birthday of the Lord is not celebrated as a sacrament, but we only recall to memory that he was born, and for this reason there was no need to do anything else but mark with festive devotion the day of the year on which the event occurred. But there is a sacrament in a celebration when the commemoration of the event is carried out in such a way that it is understood also to signify something that must be received in a holy manner. In that way, therefore, we celebrate the Pasch, that is, we not only recall to memory what was done, namely, that Christ died and rose, but we also do not omit other things that bear witness concerning him, such as the signification of the sacraments. Because, as the apostle says, *He died on account of our sins, and he rose on account of our justification* (Rom 4:25), a certain passage from death to life is marked off as holy in that passion and resurrection of the Lord. For the very word we use, "Pasch," is not Greek, as is often supposed by people, but those who know the language say that it is Hebrew. After all, the event does not take its name from "suffering," because in Greek "to suffer" is πάσχειν, but from the Hebrew word because there is a passage, as I said, from death to life. In the Hebrew language "Pascha" means "a passage," as those who know the language tell us. The Lord himself wanted to express this when he said, *One who believes in me passes from death to life* (Jn 5:24). And the same evangelist is understood to have wanted to express this, especially when he said about the Lord who was about to celebrate with his disciples the Pasch in which he gave them the mystical supper: *When Jesus saw that his hour had come to*

pass from the world to the Father (Jn 13:1). We, therefore, are instructed concerning the passing from this mortal life to another immortal life, that is, after all, from death to life, in the passion and resurrection of the Lord.

2, 3. This passage is something we now accomplish through faith that leads to the remission of sins in the hope of eternal life for us who love God and the neighbor, for *faith works through love* (Gal 5:6), and *the righteous live because of faith* (Hab 2:4). *But hope that is seen is no longer hope, for why does one hope for what one sees? If, however, we hope for what we do not see, we wait for it in patience* (Rom 8:24). In accord with the faith, hope, and love by which we began to be under grace, we have already died along with Christ and were buried with him through baptism into death,[1] as the apostle says, *Because our old self has been crucified together with him* (Rom 6:6), and we have risen with him, *because he has raised us with him and made us sit with him in heavenly places* (Eph 2:6). This is the reason for that exhortation: *Bear in mind the things that are above, not those that are on earth* (Col 3:2). But what he goes on to say, *For you have died, and your life is hidden with Christ in God. When Christ, your life, appears, then you also will appear with him in glory* (Col 3:3-4), clearly indicates what he wants us to understand, namely, that our present passage from death to life, which takes place through faith, is accomplished in the hope of the future resurrection and glory in the end *when this corruptible body*, that is, this flesh in which we now groan, *puts on incorruptibility and this mortal body puts on immortality* (1 Cor 15:53). For now we do indeed have through faith *the first fruits of the spirit*, but still *we groan in ourselves, awaiting the adoption, the redemption of our bodies. For we are saved in hope* (Rom 8:23). When we are living in this hope, *the body is indeed dead on account of sin, but the spirit is life on account of righteousness*. But see what follows; he says, *If, however, the Spirit of him who raised up Jesus from the dead dwells in you, he who raised up Christ from the dead will also bring to life your mortal bodies through his Spirit dwelling in you* (Rom 8:10-11). The universal Church, then, which is now found on the pilgrimage of mortality, awaits at the end of the world what has already been revealed in the body of Christ, who is the firstborn from the dead,[2] because his body, of which he is the head, is also none other than the Church.

3, 4. Some people, after all, who consider the words which the apostle frequently uses, namely, that we have also died with Christ[3] and have risen with him, and who do not understand in what sense he says them, have thought that the resurrection has already taken place and that no further resurrection is to be hoped for at the end of time. He says, *Among these is Hymenaeus and Philetus who have gone astray with regard to the truth, saying that the resurrection has*

---

1. See 2 Tm 2:12 and Rom 6:4.
2. See Col 1:18.
3. See Rom 6:8, Col 2:20, and 2 Tm 2:11.

already taken place, and they have upset the faith of some (2 Tm 2:17). The same apostle refutes and abhors them, though he, nonetheless, says that we have risen with Christ. Why does he say this except because this has taken place in us through faith, hope, and love in accord with the first fruits of the Spirit? But hope that is seen is not hope, and if we, therefore, hope for what we do not see, we await it with patience.[4] There, of course, remains the redemption of our body, and while we await it, we groan within ourselves. This is the reason for his words: *Rejoicing in hope, patient in tribulation* (Rom 12:12).

5. This renovation of our life, therefore, is indeed a passage from death to life that first takes place through faith in order that we may rejoice in hope and may be patient in tribulation as long as our exterior self is still being corrupted, but our interior self is renewed from day to day.[5] On account of the very beginning of a new life, on account of the new self that we are commanded to put on, while we take off the old self,[6] we throw out the old yeast in order that we may be new dough, for Christ, our Pasch, has been immolated.[7] On account of this renewal of life, then, the first month in the months of the year was assigned for this celebration. For it is also called *the month of the new harvest* (Ex 23:15). But because in the whole time of the world the third era has appeared, the resurrection of the Lord is on the third day. For the first time is that before the law; the second that under the law; the third that under grace, in which there is now revealed the sacrament hidden before in the obscurity of prophecy. This, therefore, is signified by the number of the moon; because the number "seven" usually is seen in scripture as symbolic of a certain perfection, the Pasch is celebrated in the third week of the moon, the day that falls between the fourteenth and the twenty-first.

4, 6. Another sacrament is also found there, and if it is obscure for you because you are less well trained in such investigations, do not be sad. And do not think that I am better because I learned this in the studies of my boyhood. After all, *let him who boasts boast in knowing and understanding that I am the Lord* (Jer 9:24). Some who have studied such matters have searched out many things about the numbers and motions of the stars. And those who have examined them more carefully have conjectured that the waxing and waning of the moon comes from the revolution of its sphere, not because something is added to its substance when it waxes or is taken away when it wanes. The Manichees who held such an opinion in their insane ignorance said that the moon becomes full, just as a ship becomes full, from an escaping portion of God, and they do not hesitate to believe and to say with their sacrilegious heart and lips that this portion of God was mingled with the princes of darkness and defiled with their filth. They say, then, that the moon is full when the same part of God, after it has been purified

4. See Rom 8:23-24.
5. See 2 Cor 4:16.
6. See Col 3:9-10.
7. See 1 Cor 5:7.

from defilement by great efforts, fleeing from the whole world and every sewer, is restored to God who mourns until it returns. They say that it is filled during half of the month and in the other half is poured into the sun as if into another ship. But amid these damnable blasphemies they could, nonetheless, never invent an explanation of why either in beginning or ceasing to shine the moon glows with crescent-shaped light or why it begins to diminish from the middle of the month and does not become full to the point of overflowing.

7. But some men studied these matters with exact numbers so that they not only explained why eclipses of the sun and the moon occurred, but also predicted long in advance when they were going to occur and determined in advance the set intervals of their occurrence by precise calculations and committed them to writings, and those who read them now and understand them predict them just as well, nor do these events occur other than they predict. Such men do not deserve pardon, as the holy scripture says, because *though they were so capable that they were able to form a judgment of the universe, they did not find its Lord with greater ease* (Wis 13:9), though they could have found him with humble piety. These men conjectured from the horns of the moon, which are turned away from the sun, whether the moon is waxing or waning, that the moon receives its light from the sun and that it receives its rays more on the side that is seen by the earth to the extent that it recedes more from the sun. But to the extent that it draws nearer to the sun after the middle of the month in the other half of its orbit, to that extent it receives light from above and cannot receive rays from the side that it has turned to the earth and, for that reason, seems to wane. Or, if the moon had its own light, they say that it has it on one side of the sphere, and it shows this side that it gradually reveals to the earth as it recedes from the sun until it has shown the whole as if there were increases, while there is no addition of what was lacking, but there is only a disclosure of what was present there. And it again gradually hides what was revealed, and in that way it seems to wane. But whichever of these two hypotheses are true, it is certainly evident and easily known by anyone who pays attention that the moon does not increase for our eyes except by receding from the sun and is not decreased except by drawing near to the sun on the other side.

5, 8. Notice now what we read in Proverbs, *The wise man lasts like the sun, but the fool is changed like the moon* (Sir 27:12). And who is this wise man who lasts but that sun of justice of which scripture says, *The sun of justice has risen for me* (Mal 4:2)? And the wicked will mourn on the last day that this sun has not risen for them, and they will say: *And the light of justice has not shone upon us, and the sun has not risen for us* (Wis 5:6). For God makes this sun visible to the eyes of the flesh rise over the good and the evil, just as he also makes rain to fall on the just and the unjust.[8] Suitable comparisons, however, are always drawn

---

8. See Mt 5:45.

from visible things for invisible ones. Who, then, is that fool who *is changed like the moon* but Adam *in whom all sinned* (Rom 5:12)? The human soul withdrawing from the sun of justice, that is, from that internal contemplation of the immutable truth, turns all its powers to earthly things and is more and more darkened by this in its interior and higher powers, but when it begins to return to that immutable wisdom, the more it draws close to it with the disposition of piety, the more the exterior self is corrupted, while the interior self is renewed more from day to day,[9] and all that light of the mind that was turned toward lower things turns back to higher ones and is in some way removed from the things of earth in order that it may die more and more to this world and that its life may be hidden with Christ in God.[10]

9. It is, therefore, changed for the worse in going forth to exterior things and in casting forth its inner parts in its life,[11] and this seems better to the earth, that is, to those who *have earthly thoughts* (Phil 3:19), when the sinner is praised for the desires of his soul and he who acts unjustly is blessed.[12] But it is changed for the better when it gradually turns its attention and its glory away from the things of earth, which are seen in this world, and turns them toward higher and interior things, and this seems worse to the earth, that is, to those who *have earthly thoughts*. Hence, those wicked people who in the end do fruitless penance are also going to say this among many things: *These are the ones we considered as objects of mockery and as deserving reproach; in our madness we considered their lives as insanity* (Wis 5:3-4). And in this way the Holy Spirit, in taking a likeness from visible things for invisible ones and from bodily things for spiritual ones, wanted that passage from one life to another, which is called Pasch, be observed between the fourteenth and twenty-first day of the moon—after the fourteenth day in order to take a likeness from the moon, not only on account of the third time that I mentioned above because the third week begins from it, but also on account of the conversion from exterior to interior things. The Holy Spirit wanted the Pasch observed by the twenty-first day on account of the number "seven," which is often a symbol of the universe and which is also attributed to the Church on account of its likeness to the universe.

6, 10. And so, John the apostle in the Apocalypse writes to seven churches.[13] But the Church, which is still situated in this mortality of the flesh, is designated by the term "moon" in the scriptures on account of this mutability. This is the reason for the words: *They have prepared their arrows in their quivers in order to strike the righteous of heart in the darkness of the moon* (Ps 10:3, LXX). For, before what the apostle said is realized, *When Christ, your life, appears, then you*

---

9. See 2 Cor 4:16.
10. See Col 3:3.
11. See Sir 10:9.
12. See Ps 10:3.
13. See Rv 1:4.

will also appear with him in glory (Col 3:4), the Church seems dark in the time of
its exile, as it groans amid many injustices, and then we must fear the plots of
deceitful attackers that he referred to by the term "arrows." Hence, in another
passage it says on account of the most faithful messengers of the truth whom the
Church brings to birth everywhere, *The moon is a faithful witness in the sky* (Ps
89:38). And when the psalmist sang about the kingdom of the Lord, he said, *In
his days there will arise justice and an abundance of peace until the moon is
destroyed* (Ps 72:7). That is, an abundance of peace will increase to the point that
it does away with all the mutability of mortality. *Then the last enemy, death, will
be destroyed* (1 Cor 15:26), and whatever resists us from the weakness of the
flesh, because of which we do not yet have perfect peace, will be entirely
consumed when *this corruptible body puts on incorruptibility and this mortal
body puts on immortality* (1 Cor 15:53-54). This is the reason why the walls of
that city called Jericho, which in the Hebrew language is said to mean "moon,"
fell when the ark of the covenant was carried around them the seventh time.[14]
After all, what else is done by the announcement of the kingdom of the heavens,
which the carrying of the ark around Jericho symbolized, but to destroy all the
defenses of mortal life, that is, to destroy through free choice by the sevenfold
gift of the Holy Spirit all the hope of this world that is opposed to the hope of the
world to come? For on this account, when the ark went around them, those walls
fell, not by a violent attack, but of their own accord. There are also other testimonies of the scriptures that teach us by the mention of the moon the meaning of the
Church, which in this mortality is in pain and labor on a journey away from that
Jerusalem whose citizens are the holy angels.

11. The foolish who refuse to change for the better ought not for this reason to
think that those sources of light should be adored because there is at times drawn
from them a likeness for symbolizing the divine mysteries, for such a likeness is
drawn from every creature. Nor ought we to incur the sentence of condemnation
that the lips of the apostle utter concerning certain people *who worshiped and
served the creature rather than the creator, who is blessed forever* (Rom 1:25).
For, just as we do not adore farm animals, though Christ is said to be both a
lamb[15] and a calf,[16] or a wild animal because he is said to be the lion of Judah,[17] or
a stone because Christ was the rock,[18] or Mount Sion because it symbolizes the
Church, so we do not adore either the sun or the moon, though from that heavenly creation, as from many earthly creatures, symbols are taken for mystical
teachings.

---

14. See Jos 6:16.20.
15. See Jn 1:29.
16. See Ez 43:19.
17. See Rv 5:5.
18. See 1 Cor 10:4, Mt 21:42.

7, 12. Hence, the ravings of the Manichees deserve to be mocked and detested. When we raise as objections to them the empty lies by which they hurl human beings down into the error into which they have first been cast down, they think that they are saying something when they ask us, "Why do you celebrate the Pasch in accord with calculations of the sun and the moon?" as if we criticize the positions of the stars or the changes of seasons, which were created by the sovereign and most good God, and not their perversity, which misuses things that were created most wisely to support the most empty opinions of their folly. For, if an astrologer is going to forbid our taking from the stars and the heavenly sources of light likenesses to symbolize mystically the sacraments, let the augurs forbid that it be said to us, *Be simple like doves*; let the Marsi forbid that it be said to us, *Be shrewd like serpents* (Mt 10:16),[19] and let the actors forbid that we mention the harp in the psalms. Or because we take from these things signs to represent the mysteries of the word of God, let them say, if they want, that we take the auspices or prepare poisons or imitate the immorality of the theater, something that it is sheer madness to say.

13. We do not, therefore, conjecture the outcomes of our actions from the sun and the moon or from the times of the year or of the month in order that in the most perilous storms of this life we may not suffer the shipwreck of our free choice, dashed as it were upon the rocks of wretched servitude. Rather, we take from them with religious devotion suitable likenesses for signifying something in a sacred manner. Thus with the freedom of Christians we use the rest of creation, the winds, the sea, the earth, birds, fishes, animals, trees, and human beings in many ways for speaking, but for the celebration of the sacraments we use only a very few, such as water, wheat, wine, and oil. In the servitude, however, of the old people they were commanded to celebrate many sacraments that are handed on to us only to be understood. We do not, therefore, observe the days and years and months and seasons[20] for fear that we should hear from the apostle, *I fear for you that I may perhaps have labored for you in vain* (Gal 4:11). For he blames those who say, "I shall not set out today because it is an unlucky day or because the moon is in such a phase," or "I shall set out in order that things may go well, for the position of the stars is favorable," or "I shall not do business this month because that star rules the month for me," or "I shall do it because my star begins the month," or "I shall not plant a vineyard this year because it is leap year." No wise person, however, would think that those who observe the seasons should be blamed when they say, "I shall not set out today because a storm has begun," or "I will not set sail because there are still the remnants of winter," or "It is time to plant because the earth is soaked from the autumn rains," or any other natural effects that are noted in the perfectly ordered rotation of the stars

---

19. Augurs practiced divination by the observation of birds, while the Marsi were snake-charmers.
20. See Gal 4:10.

concerning the movement of the air and the humors for causing changes in the seasons. Of these scripture said when they were created, *And let them be for signs and for seasons and for days and years* (Gn 1:14). But if any symbolic likenesses are taken not only from the heavens and the stars, but also from the lower creation for the presentation of the mysteries, the result is a certain eloquence of a teaching conducive to salvation that is suited to turn the affections of the learners from visible things to invisible ones, from bodily things to non-bodily ones, and from temporal things to eternal ones.

8, 14. Nor does anyone of ours pay attention to the fact that at the time when we celebrate the Pasch, the sun is in the position of the Ram (Aries), as they call a certain position of the stars at which the sun is truly found in the month of the new harvest.[21] But whether they want to call that same part of the sky the Ram or something else, we have learned from the holy scriptures that God created all the stars and arranged them in the heavenly places that he chose. Let them divide those places differentiated and ordered by the stars into whatever sections they want, and let them designate them by whatever names they want. Wherever the sun might be in the month of the new harvest, this celebration would find it there on account of the likeness of the sacrament of renewing life, about which we have said enough above. But if that position of the stars could also be called the Ram on account of some appropriateness of its shape, the word of God would not be afraid to draw some likeness of a sacrament from such a source, just as it has drawn mystical likenesses of the realities it wants to present in figures from other not merely heavenly, but also earthly creatures, such as Orion and the Pleiadaes, Mount Sinai, Mount Zion, such as the rivers called Geon, Phison, Tigris, and Euphrates, or such as the River Jordan, which is mentioned so many times in the holy mysteries.

15. It is one thing to observe the stars to test the weather conditions, as farmers and sailors do, or to locate parts of the world and to direct a course there and back, as navigators of ships do or those who cross through sandy deserts in interior regions to the south without any certain path, or to make mention of some stars to signify something symbolically in a useful instruction. But who can fail to understand what a difference there is between these useful observations and those follies of human beings who observe the stars to learn, not about the weather, nor about the ways to travel, nor about the calculation of the seasons, nor about spiritual comparisons, but about the outcomes of actions supposedly determined by fate?

9, 16. Let us now, however, go on to see why the celebration of the Pasch includes the Sabbath; this, after all, is characteristic of the Christian religion. For the Jews observe the month of the new harvest and the moon from the fourteenth day to the twenty-first. But because that Passover of theirs on which the Lord

---

21. Aries, or the Ram, marks the first month and runs approximately from 21 March to 19 April.

suffered occurred so that the day of the Sabbath fell between his death and his resurrection, our forefathers thought that they should make this addition in order that our feast might be distinguished from the feast of the Jews and that it might be observed by the following generations on the anniversary of his passion. And we should believe that the Lord did this with good reason. For he who is before all times, by whom times were made, who came in the fullness of time, and who had the power to lay down his life and to take it up again[22] was not awaiting a hour set by fate, but an hour appropriate to the sacrament he had begun to teach us, when he said, *My hour has not yet come* (Jn 2:4).

17. For we are now, as I said above, living in exile in faith and hope, and what we are striving to attain by love is a certain holy and perpetual rest from all the toil of all our troubles. We have a passage from this life into it, a passage that our Lord Jesus Christ deigned to show us in advance and to make holy by his passion. In that rest, however, there is not a lazy idleness, but a certain ineffable tranquility of leisurely action. After all, we shall in the end rest from the works of this life so that we rejoice in the action of the next life. But because such action is carried out by the praise of God without the labor of our limbs and the worry of cares, we do not pass into that life through rest in such a way that toil takes its place, that is, so that the action of the next life does not begin so that our rest ceases. For we do not return to labors and cares, but there remains in that action what belongs to rest—neither toil at work nor wavering in thought. Because then we return through rest to the first life, from which the soul has fallen into sin, that rest is signified by the Sabbath. But that first life that is restored to those returning from exile and receiving their original robe is symbolized by the first day of the week, which we call the Lord's Day. Search for the seven days; read Genesis, and you will find that the seventh day has no evening because it signifies rest without end. The final rest, however, is everlasting, and for this reason the eighth day will have everlasting happiness because that rest, which is everlasting, starts on the eighth day and is without end. Otherwise, it would not be everlasting. And in that way, then, the first day will be the eighth in order that the first life may be restored, but restored as eternal.

10, 18. The Sabbath was, nonetheless, given to the earlier people as a day to be celebrated in leisure of the body in order that it might be a symbol of sanctification in the rest of the Holy Spirit. For in Genesis we never read of any sanctification on any of the previous days; rather, it was said only of the Sabbath: *And God made holy the seventh day* (Gn 2:3). For souls love rest, whether pious or wicked souls, but for the most part they do not know the way to attain what they love. Nor do bodies seek anything by their weights but what souls seek by their loves. For, just as a body strives to move by its weight, either upward or downward, until it comes and rests in the place toward which it was striving—the

---

22. See Jn 10:18.

weight of oil, of course, if released in the air, pushes downward, but in water rises upward—so souls strive toward those things that they love in order that they may rest in them when they arrive. And many things delight us through the body, but there is no eternal rest in them, nor even a long rest, and for this reason they rather soil the soul and weigh it down so that they impede its pure weight by which it is carried to higher things. When, therefore, the soul finds delight in itself, it does not yet find delight in an immutable reality, and for this reason it is still proud because it regards itself as the highest, though God is higher. Nor is it left unpunished in such a sin because *God resists the proud, but gives grace to the humble* (1 Pt 5:5, Jas 4:6). But when the soul finds delight in God, it finds in him the true, certain, eternal rest that it was seeking in other things and was not finding there. Hence, it is admonished in the psalm, *Take delight in the Lord, and he will grant you the wishes of your heart* (Ps 37:4).

19. Because, then, *the love of God is poured out in our hearts through the Holy Spirit who has been given to us* (Rom 5:5), our sanctification is commemorated on the seventh day on which rest is commended to us. But because we cannot do good works unless helped by his gift, as the apostle says, *For it is God who produces in you both the will and the action in accord with good will* (Phil 2:13), we shall not be able to rest after all our good works that we do in this life unless we have been made holy and perfect for eternity by his gift. Hence, scripture says of God himself that, after he had made *all things very good, he rested on the seventh day from all the works which he made* (Gn 1:31 and 2:2). For that day signified the future rest that he was going to give us human beings after our good works. After all, just as when we do good works, he by whose gift we do good works is said to work within us, so when we rest, he by whose gift we rest is said to rest.

11, 20. This is the reason that the third commandment about the observation of the Sabbath is also found in the first three commandments of the decalogue, which pertain to God, for the remaining seven pertain to the neighbor. For the whole law depends on two commandments.[23] Thus we understand the Father in the first commandment where we are forbidden to worship the likeness of God in some handiwork of human beings, not because God does not have an image, but because no image of him ought to be worshiped except that Image that is what he is, and that Image ought not to be worshiped in place of him, but along with him. And because a creature is mutable and, for this reason, scripture says: *Every creature is subject to vanity* (Rom 8:20) and because the nature of the whole is revealed even in a part, lest anyone should think that the Son of God, the Word through whom all things were made,[24] is a creature, there follows the second commandment, *You shall not take the name of the Lord your God in vain* (Ex

---

23. See Mt 22:40.
24. See Jn 1:3.

20:7 and Dt 5:11). But the third commandment of the law speaks of the Holy Spirit in whom that rest is given to us that we love everywhere, but do not find except in loving God, when his love is poured out in our hearts through the Holy Spirit who has been given to us,[25] because God made holy the seventh day[26] on which he rested. That commandment speaks of the observation of the Sabbath, not in the sense that we should think that we are now at rest in this life, but in the sense that all the good works we do have no other goal but the everlasting rest to come. Remember, after all, especially what I mentioned above, namely, that *we have been saved in hope, but hope that is seen is no longer hope* (Rom 8:24).

21. All these things, however, that are presented to us in figures pertain somehow to nourishing and fanning the fire of love by which we are carried upward or inward to rest as if by a weight. For they arouse and kindle love more than if they were set forth bare without any likenesses of the sacraments. The reason for this fact is difficult to state. But it is, nonetheless, a fact that something presented in an allegorical meaning arouses more, delights more, and is appreciated more than if it were said in full openness with the proper terms. I believe that, as long as it is still involved with the things of earth, the feeling of the soul is set afire rather slowly, but if it is confronted with bodily likenesses and brought from there to spiritual realities that are symbolized by those likenesses, it is strengthened by this passage, and is set aflame like the fire in a coal when stirred up, and is carried with a more ardent love toward rest.

12, 22. Hence, among all those ten commandments we are commanded to observe symbolically only that one set forth there concerning the Sabbath, and we have taken up that symbol to understand it, not to celebrate it in bodily leisure. For the Sabbath signifies the spiritual rest of which the psalm says, *Rest and see that I am the Lord* (Ps 46:11) and to which human beings are called by the Lord himself when he says, *Come to me, all you who labor and are burdened, and I shall refresh you. Take my yoke upon you, and learn from me that I am meek and humble of heart, and you will find rest for your souls* (Mt 11:28-29). We, nonetheless, observe the other commandments in the proper sense as they are commanded without any symbolic meaning. For we have clearly learned that not to worship idols, not to take the name of the Lord our God in vain, not to honor our father and mother, not to commit adultery, not to kill, not to steal, not to bear false witness, not to desire our neighbor's wife, and not to desire any property of the neighbor[27] do not symbolize something else and signify something else mystically. Rather, they are observed just as they sound. We are not, nonetheless, commanded to observe the Sabbath literally in terms of leisure from bodily work, as the Jews observe it. And unless their observation of it,

---

25. See Rom 5:5.
26. See Gn 2:3.
27. See Ex 20:1-17 and Dt 5:6-21.

which is commanded in that way, signifies another spiritual rest, it should be judged as worthy of being laughed at. Hence, it is not without reason that we understand that everything that is said symbolically in the scriptures is meant to arouse the love by which we tend toward rest, since that commandment alone in the decalogue is commanded as a symbol since it commends to us that rest that is loved everywhere, but is found to be certain and holy only in God.

13, 23. The Lord's day was made known, not to the Jews, but to Christians, by the resurrection of the Lord, and from then it began to have its own celebration. The souls of all the saints are, of course, at rest before the resurrection of the body, but they do not have that activity which enlivens the bodies they received. Such action is, of course, signified by the eighth day, which is also the first, for it does not take away that rest, but glorifies it. For we will not get back along with the body difficulties from the body because we also will not get back corruption. *For this corruptible body must put on incorruptibility and this mortal body immortality* (1 Cor 15:53). Hence, before the resurrection of the Lord the mystery of the eighth day, by which the resurrection is signified, was not unknown to the holy patriarchs filled with the prophetic spirit. For a psalm is entitled "for the eighth,"[28] and on the eighth day infants were circumcised,[29] and in Ecclesiastes it says in order to distinguish the two testaments, *Give to these seven and to those eight* (Eccl 11:2). But its meaning was held back and hidden, and they were only taught to celebrate the Sabbath, because there was previously the rest of the dead, but there was the resurrection of no one who, in rising from the dead, would die no more and over whom death would no longer have dominion.[30] Hence, after such a resurrection took place in the body of the Lord so that what the body of the Church hopes for in the end might come first in the head of the Church, the Lord's day, that is, the eighth day, which is also the first, has now begun to be celebrated. We also understand the reason why, though the observance of the Pasch at which the Jews were commanded to kill and eat the lamb most clearly prefigures the passion of the Lord, they were not ordered to wait for the occurrence of the Sabbath and its falling in the third week of the moon in the month of the new harvest. In that way the Lord also showed the meaning of the same day by his passion for he had come to reveal the Lord's day, that is, the eighth day which is also the first.

14, 24. Consider, therefore, the most sacred three days of the crucified, buried, and risen Lord. Of these three the cross signifies what we are doing in the present life, but what the burial and resurrection signify we have only in faith and hope. For at present we are told, *Take up your cross and follow me* (Mt 16:24). But the flesh is crucified where we put to death our earthly members: fornica-

28. See Ps 7:1.
29. See Gn 17:12.
30. See Rom 6:9.

tion, impurity, wantonness, greed,[31] and the other things of this sort of which the same apostle says, *If you live according to the flesh, you will die, but if you put to death the deeds of the flesh by the spirit, you will live* (Rom 8:13). Hence, he also says of himself, *The world is crucified to me, and I to the world* (Gal 6:14). And in another place he says, *Knowing that our old self has been nailed to the cross along with him in order that the body of sin might be destroyed so that we no longer are slaves to sin* (Rom 6:6). As long, therefore, as our works strive to destroy the body of sin, as long as our exterior self is being corrupted in order that our interior self may be renewed from day to day,[32] it is the time of the cross.

25. These are, of course, also good works, but they are, nonetheless, still full of toil, though their reward is rest. But scripture says, *Rejoicing in hope* (Rom 12:12), in order that, when we think of our future rest, we may work at our labor with joy. The breadth of the cross in the transverse beam, to which the hands are nailed, symbolizes this joy. For we understand the works in the hands and the joy of the worker in the breadth, because sadness causes narrowness. In height of the cross, which the head touches, we understand the expectation of reward from the lofty justice of God. For he *will reward each one according to his works, eternal life, of course, to those who by patience in doing good seek glory, honor, and incorruptibility* (Rom 2:6-7). Therefore, the length of the cross, by which the whole body is stretched out, signifies patience because of which those who are patient are called long-suffering. But the depth of the cross, which is inserted into the earth, symbolizes the secret of the mystery. You recall, after all, if I am not mistaken, the words of the apostle that I used in this description of the cross, where he says, *Rooted in and founded upon love in order that you may be able to comprehend along with all the saints what is the length and breadth and height and depth* (Eph 3:17-18). But those things that we do not yet see and do not yet possess are symbolized by the other two days. Those things, after all, that we now do when we have been fastened as if by the nails of the commandments to the fear of God, as scripture says, *Attach my flesh by nails to a fear of you* (Ps 119:120), are counted among what is necessary; they are not among those things that are to be sought and desired for their own sake. For this reason he says that he desires that greatest good, namely, *to be dissolved and to be with Christ, but to remain in the flesh is necessary on your account* (Phil 1:23-24). He says, *to be dissolved and to be with Christ*; from this moment there begins the rest that is not interrupted, but glorified by the resurrection. It is, nonetheless, now possessed by faith *because the righteous live from faith* (Hab 2:4). *Or do you not know*, he asks, *that whoever of us have been baptized in Christ Jesus have been baptized in his death? We have, therefore, been buried along with him into death through baptism* (Rom 6:3). How except by faith? For it has not yet been carried to fulfill-

31. See Col 3:5.
32. See 2 Cor 4:16.

ment in us who are still groaning in ourselves and awaiting the adoption, the redemption of our body.[33] *For we have been saved in hope, but hope that is seen is no longer hope. For why does one hope for what he sees? But if we hope for what we do not see, we await it through patience* (Rom 8:24-25).

26. Keep in mind how often I mention this so that we do not suppose that we ought now to become happy and free from all problems already in this life and, for this reason, murmur against God with sacrilegious lips in the trials of temporal existence, as if he is not giving what he promised. He, of course, promised what is necessary for this life, but the consolations of the wretched are not the same as the joys of the blessed. The psalmist said, *O Lord, in accord with the multitude of the sorrows in my heart your exhortations have brought joy to my soul* (Ps 94:9). Let us, then, not murmur amid difficulties so that we do not lose the breadth of joy of which scripture says, *Rejoicing in hope*, for there follows, *suffering in tribulation* (Rom 12:12). The new life, then, is now begun in faith and lived in hope, for it will then reach perfection when death will be swallowed up in victory,[34] when that last enemy, death, is destroyed,[35] when we shall be changed and made equal to the angels. For the apostle says, *We, after all, shall all rise, but not all will be changed* (1 Cor 15:51), and the Lord says, *They will be equal to the angels* (Lk 20:36). For we have now been grasped by God in fear through faith, but we shall then grasp him in love through vision. *For, as long as we are in the body, we are away from the Lord. We now, after all, walk by faith, not by vision* (2 Cor 5:6). The apostle himself, who says *that I may grasp as I have been grasped*, admits that he himself has not grasped the goal, *Brothers, I do not think that I have grasped it* (Phil 3:12-13). But the hope that we have from the promise of the truth is certain, and so, after he said, *We, therefore, have been buried along with him through baptism into death*, he went on to say, *in order that, as Christ rose from the dead through the glory of the Father, so we also may walk in the newness of life* (Rom 6:4). We, therefore, walk in the reality of toil, but in the hope of rest, in the flesh of our old self, but in the faith of our new self. For he says, *The body is indeed dead on account of sin, but the spirit is life on account of righteousness. But if the Spirit of him who raised up Jesus Christ from the dead dwells in you, he who raised Jesus Christ from the dead will give life to your mortal bodies through his Spirit who dwells in us* (Rom 8:10-11).

15, 27. These events are celebrated at the annual recurrence of the Pasch on the authority of the divine scriptures and by the agreement of the universal Church spread throughout the world. It is celebrated, as you now understand, as a great sacrament. And in the old scriptures the time for celebrating the Pasch is prescribed only in the month of the new harvest from the fourteenth day to the

---

33. See Rom 8:23.
34. See 1 Cor 15:54.
35. See 1 Cor 15:26.

twenty-first day of the moon. But because it is clear from the gospel on which day the Lord was crucified and was in the tomb and rose, the observance of those days was joined together by the councils of the fathers, and the whole world was persuaded that it is necessary to celebrate the Pasch in that way.

28. The forty days of fasting, of course, takes its origin both in the old books from the fasting of Moses[36] and of Elijah[37] and in the gospel because the Lord fasted for that many days[38] in order to show that the gospel is not in disagreement with the law and the prophets. In the person of Moses, of course, the law is repre-sented; in the person of Elijah the prophets, for between them the Lord also appeared in glory on the mountain[39] in order to emphasize more clearly what the apostle says of him, *Having the testimony of the law and the prophets* (Rom 3:5). In what part of the year, then, would the forty-day fast be more suitably observed than in that near to and adjoining the passion of the Lord? For it signifies this life full of toil, for which we need self-control in order to fast from friendship with the world. For the world, of course, does not cease to charm us by her deceptions and to scatter and toss before us the deceits of her snares. But I think that the number "forty" signifies this life because the number "ten" expresses the perfec-tion of our beatitude. Just as the number "eight" does because it comes back to the first, so this number expresses, it seems to me, that the creature, which is symbolized by seven, should cling to the creator, in which the oneness of the Trinity is revealed. In time the creator is preached through the whole world, because the world is marked off by the four winds, is constructed out of the four elements, and is changed by the succession of the four seasons. Ten taken four times equals forty, but when its parts are counted in, forty adds "ten,"[40] and they become fifty as the reward of toil and self-control. For it was not in vain that the Lord himself remained for forty days after the resurrection on this earth and in this life with his disciples, and after he ascended into heaven, he sent the Spirit he promised after an interval of ten days, when Pentecost arrived. This fiftieth day contains another mystery because seven times seven are forty-nine, and when one comes back to the beginning, which is the eighth day, as well as the first, the number "fifty" is reached. And fifty days are now celebrated after the resurrec-tion of the Lord not as symbolic of toil, but of rest and joy. On this account we stop our fasting, and we pray standing up, which is a sign of the resurrection. For this reason this practice is observed on all Sundays at the altar, and the Alleluia is sung, which signifies that our action in the future will be nothing but to praise

---

36. See Ex 34:29.
37. See 1 Kgs 19:8.
38. See Mt 4:2.
39. See Mt 17:1-13, Mk 9:2-13, and Lk 9:28-36.
40. The calculation here is unclear unless "its parts" refers to the parts of ten, that is, seven and three.

God, as scripture says, *Blessed are they who dwell in your house, O Lord; they will praise you forever* (Ps 84:5).

16, 29. But fifty days are also emphasized in the scriptures, and not only in the gospel because the Holy Spirit came on the fiftieth day, but also in the old books. For in them, after the Jews celebrated the Pasch with the sacrifice of the lamb, fifty days are counted off up to the day on which the law, which was written by the finger of God, was given on Mount Sinai to Moses the servant of God,[41] but in the books of the gospel it is stated with full clarity that the finger of God signifies the Holy Spirit. For, when one evangelist said, *I cast out demons by the finger of God* (Lk 11:20), another said this same thing in this way, *I cast out demons by the Spirit of God* (Mt 12:28). Who would not prefer to all the empires of this world, even if they were at peace with extraordinary happiness, this joy of the divine mysteries when they shine forth with the light of sound doctrine? Do the two testaments not faithfully and harmoniously chant the sacred truth, just as the two Seraphim cry out to each other, singing the praises of the Most High, *Holy, holy, holy, Lord God of hosts* (Is 6:3)? The lamb is slain; the Pasch is celebrated, and after an interval of fifty days the law is given that was written by the finger of God to instill fear.[42] Christ is slain who was led like a lamb to sacrifice, as Isaiah testifies;[43] the true Pasch is celebrated, and after an interval of fifty days the Holy Spirit, who is the finger of God, is given to arouse love. The Holy Spirit is opposed to human beings who are seeking their own interests and, for this reason, carrying a harsh yoke and a heavy burden and not finding rest for their souls. *For love does not seek what is its own* (1 Cor 13:5). This is the reason that the quarrelsomeness of heretics is always restless; the apostle states that they have the stubbornness of Pharaoh's magicians. He says, *For, just as Jannes and Jambres resisted Moses, so these people resist the truth, corrupted in their mind, reprobates regarding the faith, but they will not get very far. For their madness will be evident to everyone, as that of those men was* (2 Tm 3:8-9). After all, because they were most restless on account of this corruption of their mind, they failed in the third miracle, admitting that the Holy Spirit who was in Moses was against them. For, when they failed, they said, *The finger of God is here* (Ex 8:19). But just as, when the Holy Spirit has been won over and placated, he offers rest to the meek and humble of heart, so when he is opposed and hostile, he stirs up the haughty and proud with disquiet. Those tiny flies because of which the magicians of Pharaoh failed when they said, *The finger of God is here*, symbolized this disquiet.

30. Read Exodus, and see how many days after they celebrated the Pasch the law was given. God speaks to Moses in the desert of Sinai on the third day of the

41. See Ex 12:6; 19:1-2; 31:18.
42. See Ex 31:18.
43. See Is 53:7.

third month. Note, then, the first day after the beginning of the third month, and see what he says among other things. He says, *Go down to bear witness to the people, and purify them today and tomorrow. Let them wash their clothes, and let them be ready for the third day. For on the third day the Lord will come down upon Mount Sinai in the presence of all the people* (Ex 19:20). Then the law was given, that is, on the third day of the month. Count, then, from the fourteenth day of the first month, on which the Pasch was celebrated, up to the third day of the third month, and you will find seventeen days of the first month, thirty days of the second month, and three of the third month, which equal fifty. The law in the ark signifies the sanctification of the body of the Lord; through the resurrection of his body the rest to come is promised us, and love is breathed into us by the Holy Spirit for receiving that rest. *But the Spirit was not yet given because Jesus had not yet been glorified* (Jn 7:39). This is the reason why that prophecy was sung, *Rise up, O Lord, into your rest, you and the ark of your sanctification* (Ps 132:8). Where there is rest, there is also sanctification. Hence, we have now received the pledge in order that we may love and desire it. But *in the name of the Father and of the Son and of the Holy Spirit* (Mt 28:19) all are called to the rest of the next life to which we pass from this life, and this is what the Pasch signifies.

17, 31. For this reason the number "fifty" multiplied by three, with the addition of the number "three" to indicate the eminence of the mystery, is found in those great fish the Lord commanded should be pulled up on the right side, when he was revealing his new life after the resurrection. Nor were the nets torn,[44] for then the restlessness of heretics did not yet exist. Then a perfect and peaceful man, purified in soul and in body by the chaste words of the Lord, like silver from the earth refined by fire and purified sevenfold,[45] will receive the reward of a denarius,[46] so that there are ten and seven. For in this number, as in others that offer many symbols, an amazing mystery is found. Not without reason is the seventeenth psalm alone found in its entirety in the Books of the Kings,[47] for it signifies that kingdom where we will have no enemy. After all, its title is: *On the day on which the Lord rescued him from the hand of all his foes and from the hand of Saul* (Ps 18:1 and 2 Sm 22:1). For, who is symbolized by David if not he who came from the seed of David according to the flesh?[48] In his body, of course, which is the Church, he still suffers from foes. Hence, that persecutor whom he struck down by his voice and whom he incorporated into his body by eating him, as it were, heard his words from heaven, *Saul, Saul, why are you persecuting*

---

44. See Jn 21:6-11.
45. See Ps 12:7.
46. See Mt 20.2.9-10.13. The denarius was a silver Roman coin originally worth ten copper coins; the name is analogous to the expression "a tenner" for a ten dollar bill.
47. See 2 Sam 22:2-51. The Second Book of Samuel is also known as the Second Book of Kings. According to the Hebrew numbering of the psalms Psalm 17 of the Vulgate is numbered 18.
48. See Rom 1:3.

me? (Acts 9:4). But when will this body of his be rescued from the hand of all his foes except when that last enemy, death, will be destroyed?[49] That number of the one hundred and fifty-three fishes pertains to this time. For this number "seventeen" rising in a triangle adds up to the sum of one hundred and fifty-three. Rising from one to seventeen, add all the numbers in between, and you will find that number; that is, add two to one, they become three; add three, and they become six; add four, and they become ten; add five, and they become fifteen; add six, and they become twenty one; add the rest in the same way, and the seventeenth number will become one hundred and fifty-three.[50]

32. We hold these, that is, the Pasch and Pentecost, most firmly on the basis of the scripture. The agreement of the Church has supported the observance of those forty days before the Pasch, as well as the distinction of the eight days of the newly baptized from the rest, that is, so that the eighth day coincides with the first. But the singing of the Alleluia only during these fifty days is not observed everywhere. For on other days it is also sung at different times in different places, but it is sung on those days everywhere. I do not, however, know whether standing both on those days and on all Sundays is observed everywhere. I stated, nonetheless, as well as I could, the rule the Church follows on this, and I think it is evident.

18, 33. But with regard to the washing of the feet, since the Lord commended this on account of the kind of humility that he came to teach, as he himself later explained,[51] you asked at what time so great a virtue should most of all be taught also by action, and that time comes to mind to which this teaching would fit more religiously. But many have refused to accept this as a custom for fear that it should seem to belong to the sacrament of baptism. Some have also not hesitated to remove it as a custom. But in order to practice this at a less public time and to distinguish it from the sacrament of baptism, some have chosen to do this action either on the third day of the octave, because the number "three" has a very important place in many sacraments, or on the eighth day itself.

34. I am quite puzzled over why you wanted me to write something for you about those practices that are different in different places, since it is not necessary to know this, and only one most salutary rule is to be observed in these matters: Wherever we see that there are being instituted or know that there have been instituted practices that are not against the faith and not contrary to good morals and have some value for encouraging a better life, we not only do not find fault with them, but we also follow them by praising and imitating them, if the weakness of some does not stand in the way so that there might be a greater loss.

---

49. See 1 Cor 15:26.
50. The number 153 is a triangular number; if one starts with one dot at the bottom and adds a line with two and then a line with three, the sum at the seventeenth line will be one hundred fifty-three.
51. See Jn 13:14.

For, if their weakness stands in the way so that greater gains are to be hoped for in those who want it than losses are to be feared in those who object, we should by all means certainly do what can also be defended from the scriptures, such as with regard to the singing of hymns and psalms, since we have the examples and precepts of the Lord himself and the apostles. Regarding this practice, which is so useful for piously stirring the mind and for kindling the heart with love of God, the custom varies, and generally members of the Church in Africa are unenthusiastic to the point that the Donatists find fault with us because in church we sing without feeling the divine canticles of the prophets, while they set aflame their revelries by the singing of songs that are merely human compositions, as if with rousing blasts of a trumpet. But when the faithful are gathered in church, what time is not right for singing holy songs, except during the readings or the homily or when the priest prays aloud or when the voice of the deacon calls for common prayer?

19, 35. But at other periods of time I absolutely do not see what Christians gathered together could do that would be better, or more useful, or more holy. I cannot, however, approve what is introduced contrary to custom in order supposedly to observe a mystery, even though I do not dare too readily to disapprove many such practices in order to avoid offending some persons who are either holy or easily offended. But I am extremely saddened that many things that are commanded in the books of God for a most salutary purpose are neglected, and so many false opinions are in the air that a person who touches the ground with a bare foot during the octave of the Pasch is rebuked more severely than one who buries his mind in drunkenness. All such practices, then, that are not contained in the authorities of the holy scriptures and are not found to have been established by the councils of bishops and are not supported by the custom of the universal Church, but vary in countless ways in accord with the customs[52] of different places so that the reasons that led people to establish them can hardly or cannot at all be found, should undoubtedly, I think, be eliminated when the opportunity presents itself. For, even if one cannot discover how these practices are contrary to the faith, they do, nonetheless, oppress with servile burdens the religion that the mercy of God willed to be free and to have very few and very evident sacraments to celebrate. Thus it turns out that the condition of the Jews is more tolerable, for, though they have not recognized the era of freedom, they are subjected to the burdens of the law, not to human opinions. But the Church of God that is situated amid much straw and many weeds tolerates many things, and yet she does not approve, does not pass over in silence, and does not do those things that are opposed to the faith or to a morally good life.

---

52. I have followed the reading "moribus" that is found in the old editions in place of "motibus" that is found in the CSEL.

20, 36. And so, what you wrote, namely, that certain brothers abstain from eating meat inasmuch as they consider it impure, is most clearly opposed to the faith and sound doctrine. But if I chose to discuss this point at greater length, some people could suppose that the apostle's commandment on this was obscure. Among the many things that he said on this topic, he also detested the impious opinion of the heretics so that he said, *But the Spirit clearly says that in the last times certain people will withdraw from the faith by paying attention to deceitful spirits and the doctrines of demons with the hypocrisy of liars. Having a conscience that is seared, they forbid marriage and abstain from food that God created to be received with thanksgiving by the faithful and those who know the truth. For every creature of God is good, and nothing that is received with thanksgiving is to be rejected. It is, after all, made holy by the word of God and prayer* (1 Tm 4:1-5). And in another passage he says of these matters, *All things are pure for the pure, but for the impure and for non-believers nothing is pure, but their mind and conscience are defiled* (Ti 1:15). You yourself, go, read the rest, and read it aloud to those to whom you can so that they do not make the grace of God ineffective in themselves, for we have been called into freedom.[53] Only let them not use that freedom as an opportunity for the flesh and refuse to hold back from any food for the sake of reining in concupiscence of the flesh, just because they are not permitted to act in a superstitious and unbelieving manner.

37. But as for those who read their fortunes in the pages of the gospels, though it is preferable that they do this rather than run to consult the demons, I still do not like this custom of wanting to use for worldly affairs and for the vanity of this life the words of God that speak of the next life.

21, 38. If you do not think that these answers are enough for you for the questions you asked, you are too unaware of my abilities and occupations. For I am so far from being ignorant of nothing, as you supposed, that I read nothing in your letter that caused me more sadness, because it is most patently false. And I am surprised that you do not realize that there are many things I do not know, not only in countless other areas, but that even in the holy scriptures themselves there are more things that I do not know than I know. I have a hope in the name of the Lord that will not be fruitless, because I have not only believed my God who said that the whole law and the prophets depend on those two commandments, but I also have learned this by experience and experience it every day, since no sacrament or any more obscure passage of the sacred writings is disclosed to me where I do not find the same commandments, *For the end of the commandment is love from a pure heart, a good conscience, and unfeigned faith* (1 Tm 1:5), and, *the fullness of the law is love* (Rom 13:10).

---

53. See Gal 5:13.

39. And so, my dear friend, whether these passages or others, read them, learn them so that you remember that it was said with perfect truth, *Knowledge puffs up, but love builds up* (1 Cor 8:1). But *love is not jealous and does not puff up* (1 Cor 13:4). Let knowledge, then, be used as a certain scaffolding by which the building of love may arise to remain for eternity, even when knowledge is destroyed.[54] Used for the purpose of love, knowledge is highly beneficial, but of itself without such an end, it is proven to be not only superfluous, but also dangerous. I know, however, the holy thoughts that guard you under the shadow of the wings[55] of the Lord your God. But I warned you of these matters, though only briefly, because I know that this same love of yours, which is not jealous, will give or read this letter to many others.

---

54. See 1 Cor 13:8.
55. See Ps 17:8 and 57:2.

Letter 56

Between 396 and 410, perhaps around 400, Augustine wrote to Celer, a wealthy landowner of Hippo Regius. He encouraged him in the pursuit of the knowledge of Christian wisdom (paragraph 1). While congratulating Celer for having a good mind and for escaping the clutches of the Donatists, he warns him that it is a more difficult task to break with bad moral habits and lead a good Christian life (paragraph 2).

To his excellent and rightly honorable and most dear son, Celer, Augustine sends greetings.

1. I have not forgotten my promise and your desire. But because I was gone due to the need to visit the churches that fall under my care, I could not by myself immediately repay my debt, yet I nonetheless did not want to owe you for a longer time what I could have repaid since I had it. Hence, I appointed my dearest son, the priest Optatus, to read with you at those hours that you thought more convenient those materials that I promised. He thinks that he can do all this, and Your Excellency will persuade him to do it more promptly and quickly, the more you welcome it with gratitude. But I believe that you understand full well how much I love you and want you to be trained in the studies leading to salvation in the knowledge of things human and divine.

2. If you do not reject the love of my services, I am confident that you will make such progress in the Christian faith and in moral conduct fitting a person in a position such as yours that you will look forward to the last day of this temporal smoke or fog, which is called human life, a day no mortal may avoid. I am confident that you will look forward to this day either eagerly or securely or at least not hopelessly worried, not in the vanity of error, but in the solidity of truth. After all, just as it is certain that you are alive, let it be that certain that this life that is spent in temporal delights should by the doctrine of salvation be reckoned not as life, but as death, in comparison with the eternal life that is promised us through Christ and in Christ. But I would have no doubt, given the fine quality of your mind, that you will very easily free yourself from this attachment to the Donatists if you appreciate Christian purity in a fully religious manner. For it is not a difficult task, even for those who are mentally slow, if they only listen patiently and attentively, to see clearly the unshakable foundations of the proofs that refute that error. But it requires greater strength to break the chain of sinfulness, which has become habitual and like a friend, in order to pursue an unfamiliar rectitude. And in no case should we abandon hope regarding your noble-spirited freedom and clearly virile heart since the Lord our God is your help and encouragement. May the mercy of the Lord our God keep you safe, my excellent and rightly honorable and most dear son.

Letter 57

Soon after the previous letter Augustine again wrote to Celer. He argues that the Donatists departed from the Catholic Church without just cause (paragraph 1) and informs Celer that he wants to confer with a certain friend of the Donatist sect who is a subject of Celer (paragraph 2).

To my most dear lord and rightly honorable and estimable son, Celer, Augustine sends greetings in the Lord.

1. I believe that, upon further consideration of the matter, Your Wisdom very easily understands that there is no just reason why the sect of Donatus tore itself from the whole world, throughout which the Catholic Church has spread in accord with the promises of the prophets and of the gospel. If a more careful discussion of this matter is needed, I recall that I gave to Your Benevolence a book to read when your son, who is most dear to me, my Caecilius, conveyed to me that you were asking for it. The book was at your house for more than a few days. If you either wanted or were able to read it out of a desire to know about this question, even among your many occupations, I have no doubt that in your wisdom you would have discovered that the Donatists have nothing that they can say against it with any probability. And if anything still perhaps troubles you, we could perhaps, to the extent that God grants and permits, reply to your questions or also give you something to read.

2. For this reason I ask that you more earnestly commend the Catholic unity in the region of Hippo to your men, especially to Paternus and Maurusius. I know the vigilance of your heart, and there is no need, I believe, to write more, since, if you want, you can very easily learn what others care for or avoid in your possessions and what is being done on your estate. I have been heartily assured that there is a friend of yours on your estate with whom I desire to be in accord; I ask that you foster this cause in order that you may have great praise among men and a great reward before God. For he had conveyed to me through a certain Carus, our common friend, that he feared doing this on account of certain violent men of his party whom he will not be able to fear on your estate and under your protection. Nor should you love in him what is not constancy, but clearly stubbornness. It is, after all, shameful to change one's view, but only when it is true and correct; it is praiseworthy and salutary to change a view that is foolish and harmful. Just as, however, constancy does not permit one to become worse, so stubbornness does not permit one to be corrected. Hence, as the former should be praised, so that latter should be corrected. The priest whom I sent will convey the rest more clearly to Your Wisdom. May the mercy of God keep you safe and happy, my most dear lord and rightly honorable and estimable son.

Letter 58

Not after 410, most probably in 401, Augustine wrote to Pammachius, an illustrious Roman senator, who had large estates in Numidia. He congratulates him for having brought his tenant-farmers in Numidia into the unity of the Catholic Church by his exhortation (paragraph 1) and expresses his deep love for Pammachius because of what he has done (paragraph 2). Finally, he urges the senator to read this letter to others in order to encourage them to follow Pammachius' example (paragraph 3).

To my excellent and rightly estimable lord and most dear son in the heart of Christ, Pammachius, Augustine sends greetings in the Lord.

1. Your good works blossoming by the grace of Christ have made you someone among his members worthy of honor and clearly most well-known and beloved. Not even if I saw your face daily would you be better known to me than when through the brilliance of this one action of yours I looked into your interior that is fair with the beauty of peace and radiant with the light of the truth. I looked and I recognized you; I recognized you and I fell in love. To this dear friend I now speak; to him I write who became known to me despite his bodily absence. We were, nonetheless, already together, and we were living, united under one head; unless you were rooted in his love, the Catholic unity would not be so dear to you. You would neither have admonished with such language your African tenant-farmers living in that part of the world where the fury of the Donatists arose, that is, in the midst of Numidia Consularis, nor would you have roused them with such a fervor of spirit that they chose with such prompt devotion to follow the course that they believed so fine and great a man as you would only follow because he knew the truth. And in that way, though separated from you so far in terms of spatial distances, they came under the same head and were counted for eternity along with you among the members of him by whose commandment they serve you.[1]

2. In this action of yours, then, I embraced you as someone I know, and I rejoiced to congratulate you in Christ Jesus our Lord and to send you this letter of congratulations as some sign of my heartfelt love for you, nor could I do any more. But I ask that you do not measure by it all my love for you. Pass beyond this letter, once you have read it, by an invisible and interior passage, and by thought continue on into my heart, and see what my heart feels about you. For there will lie open to the eye of love the chamber of love that we close to tumultuous trivialities of the world when we adore God in it, and you will see in it the

---

1. See Eph 6:5 and 1 Pt 2:18.

239

delights of my joy over your action, which is so good that I am not able to utter by my tongue or express by my pen those delights ardent and aflame in a sacrifice of praise for him by whose inspiration you willed this and by whose help you were able to do it. *Thanks be to God for his ineffable gift* (2 Cor 9:15).

3. Oh, from how many other senators like you and sons of the Church like you we in Africa desire the sort of action that we rejoice over in your case! But it is dangerous to exhort those men; it is safe to congratulate you. They, after all, will perhaps not do it, and the enemies of the Church will plot to deceive the weak as if they conquered us in their mind. But you have already acted, and as a result the enemies of the Church are confounded at the fact that the weak have been set free from their clutches. Hence, it seemed to me to suffice that you read this letter to those men you can on the basis of their being Christian, with confidence in their friendship. For in that way they will believe from your action that there can be done in Africa what they are perhaps slow to do because they think that it cannot be done. Nor did I want to write about the ambushes that the heretics construct with their twisted heart, because I laughed at them for having thought that they could achieve anything in the estate of Christ, which is your soul. You will, nonetheless, hear these things from my brothers whom I commend most highly to Your Excellency in order that you may not spurn them, even if their fears are needless in the case of so great and so unexpected a conversion of human beings, over whom our Catholic mother rejoices because of you.

Letter 59

At the end of 402 Augustine wrote to Victorinus, a claimant to the primacy of Numidia, who had summoned a council. Augustine excuses himself from attending because of his many other occupations, but points out several irregularities in Victorinus' letter and urges him to settle the question of the primacy of Numidia with Xantippus, who also lays claim to it (paragraph 1). Augustine suggests that Victorinus and Xantippus summon a small group of senior bishops to settle the claim to the primacy and only afterward to summon all the bishops for a council (paragraph 2).

To his most blessed lord and venerable father and fellow priest, Victorinus, Augustine sends greetings in the Lord.

1. The circular letter reached me on the ninth of November when the day was already over and found me very indisposed so that I was absolutely unable to come. It is up to Your Holiness or Your Honor to judge whether this letter disturbed me because of my inexperience or whether I was right to be disturbed. I read in the same letter that you wrote to the two provinces of Mauretania,[1] which we know have their own primates. But if a council of those bishops had to be convoked in Numidia, the names of some Mauretanian bishops who were more senior certainly ought to have been included in your letter; when I did not find this in your letter, I was very surprised. Next, the letter was written to the Numidians with such a disruption and confusion of proper order that I found my name in the third place, though I know I became a bishop after many others. This circumstance is both quite unjust to others and odious to me. Besides our venerable brother and colleague, Xantippus of Thagura,[2] says that the primacy belongs to him, and he is regarded as such by many bishops, and he sends letters of this sort. This mistake can also be easily recognized and corrected between the two of you, but his name, nonetheless, ought not to have been omitted in the letter that Your Reverence sent. If his was written among the other names and not put in the first place, I would be very surprised. How much more ought one to be surprised that you made no mention of the man who ought most of all to have come to the council in order to deal first of all with the rank of primacy, a question that concerns the bishops of all the churches of Numidia!

---

1. That is, Mauretania Sitifensis and Mauretania Caesariensis. Besides the primate of Africa Proconsularis, who as bishop of Carthage was the primate for the whole of Africa, there were primates for each of the other provinces, namely, Numidia, the two Mauretanias, and Byzacena.
2. Xantippus was called the primate of Numidia in the synod of Milevis on 27 August 402.

2. For these reasons I would also have hesitated to come for fear that the circular letter, in which such a disorder was found, might be a fake, although the limits on my time and other grave necessities would have prevented me in many ways. Hence, I ask Your Beatitude to forgive me and to deign to strive first of all that Your Holiness and old Xantippus settle harmoniously which of you ought to convoke a council. Or at least, and I think this would be better, without prejudice to anyone, let both of you convoke our colleagues, especially those who are close to you in seniority as bishops. They can easily recognize which of you is speaking the truth in order that the same question may be settled among the few of you before any others. Then, once the error has been remedied, let the younger bishops be convoked by the rest, for on this question they can and ought to believe only you inasmuch as you are the more senior bishops, and they do not now know which of the two they should most believe. I have sent this letter sealed with the seal that imprints the face of a man looking sideways.

Letter 60

At roughly the same time as the previous letter, Augustine wrote to Aurelius, the bishop of Carthage and primate of Africa, about a certain Donatus and his brother who had left the monastery. Augustine counsels Aurelius against allowing monks who have abandoned the monastery to be readily chosen as clerics, since even a good monk does not necessarily make a good priest (paragraph 1). Augustine points out that Donatus and his brother did not leave the monastery with his authorization and that the case of Donatus, who was ordained before any decision of a council, is different from that of his brother, who has not yet been ordained (paragraph 2).

To his most blessed lord and truly most dear brother worthy of reverence with due obedience, his fellow priest, Bishop Aurelius, Augustine sends greetings in the Lord.

1. I received no letter from Your Reverence since we physically parted from each other. But I have now read the letter of Your Grace concerning Donatus and his brother, and I have wavered back and forth for a long time about what reply I should make. But as I pondered again and again what would be conducive to the salvation of those whom we serve in Christ by providing them with spiritual nourishment, nothing else occurred to me but that we should not open this path to the servants of God so that they suppose that they are more likely to be chosen for a better position if they have become worse men. And it is, after all, easy for them to fall, and a most shameful injury is done to the clerical order if those who abandon their monastery are chosen for the army of the clergy since from those who remain in their monastery we usually choose only the more tested and better to be members of the clergy, unless as the common folk say, "A bad flute player makes a good singer." In the same way the common folk joke about us and say, "A bad monk makes a good cleric." It is something highly deplorable if we raise monks up to such ruinous pride and think that clerics, among whom we are counted, are worthy of grave abuse. After all, at times even a good monk does not make a good cleric if he has sufficient continence and, nonetheless, lacks the necessary instruction and the personal integrity required.

2. But I am sure that Your Beatitude has thought concerning these men that they withdrew from the monastery by our decision in order that they might be more useful to the people of their region, but that is not true. They left of their own accord; they went off of their own accord while we resisted as much as we could for the sake of their salvation. And with regard to Donatus, since his ordination had already taken place before we determined anything about this in a

council,[1] if he has perhaps been corrected from the perversity of his pride, let Your Wisdom do as you see fit. But with regard to his brother, who was the main reason why Donatus himself left the monastery, I do not know what answer I should give, since you understand what I think. I do not dare to speak in opposition to Your Wisdom, Your Honor, and Your Charity, and I, of course, hope that you will do what you see will be salutary for the members of the Church.

1. In the Council of Carthage on 1 September 401.

Letter 61

At the end of 401 or early in 402 Augustine wrote to Theodore, a deacon of Carthage, and explained his policy regarding the reception of Donatists into the Church. Augustine gives Theodore a letter in his own hand in which he testifies that he demands only the removal of their dissent and error and welcomes them back with the sacraments they have received (paragraph 1). He assures the Donatists that he will acknowledge any other gifts of God in them and urges Theodore to give them this letter in his own hand waiting as proof if they want it (paragraph 2).

To his dearest brother, Theodore,[1] Augustine sends greetings.

1. When Your Benevolence spoke with me about how we receive clerics from the sect of Donatus if they want to become Catholics, I decided to express[2] what I replied to you also by sending you this letter in order that, if anyone questions you on this topic, you may also show by a letter in my handwriting what we hold or do with regard to this question. You should know, then, that we disapprove in them only of their dissent by which they became heretics or schismatics. For they do not hold onto the unity and truth of the Catholic Church, insofar as they do not maintain peace with the people of God who are spread throughout the whole world and insofar as they do not recognize the baptism of Christ in human beings who have received it. We, therefore, blame the evil error that they hold, but we recognize, venerate, and embrace in them the good name of God, which they have, and his sacrament. But we grieve over them because they are in error, and we desire to gain them for God through the love of Christ in order that in the peace of the Church they might have for their salvation the holy sacrament that outside of the Church they have for their destruction. If, then, the sins of human beings are removed and God's gifts are honored in human beings, there will be brotherly harmony and amiable peace so that the love of Christ conquers the persuasions of the devil in the hearts of human beings.

2. And so, when anyone comes to us from the sect of Donatus, we do not accept their sins, that is, their dissent and error; rather, these are removed as impediments to harmony. And we embrace our brothers, standing with them, as the apostle says, *in oneness of the Spirit, in the bond of peace* (Eph 4:3), and acknowledging in them the gifts of God, whether holy baptism, the blessing of ordination, the profession of continence, the vow of virginity, the faith in the

---

1. Theodore was a Catholic layman of Hippo; PL adds the usual salutation to a Catholic "in the Lord."
2. The CSEL edition indicates a lacuna here; I have followed the reading in PL.

Trinity, or any other gift. Even if all of these were present, they, nonetheless, did no good if love was not there.[3] But who truly claims to have the love of Christ when he does not embrace his unity? And so, when they come to the Catholic Church, they do not receive here what they had, but they receive here what they did not have in order that what they had may begin to benefit them. For here they receive the root of love in the bond of peace and in a society that is one in order that all the sacraments of the truth, which they have, may not contribute to their damnation, but to their deliverance. After all, branches ought not to boast because they are not thorn trees, but vines.[4] For, if they were not living from the root, they will be cast into the fire with all their kind. But of certain branches that had been broken off, the apostle said that *God is able to graft them back again* (Rom 11:23). And so, my dearest brother, if you see any of them in doubt over the rank in which we might receive them, show them this letter, which you know well is written in my own hand, and if they want to have it in their own possession, let them have it, for I make God the witness of my soul that I will receive them so that they have not only the baptism of Christ that they received, but also the income and sustenance they agreed upon.[5]

---

3. See 1 Cor 13:3.
4. See Rom 11:18.
5. I have followed the reading "*honorem patrimonii et continentiam*" in place of "*honorem sanctimonii et continentiae.*" The NBA edition cites Du Cange as saying "but it seems that we should read 'patrimonii' so that it indicates that they would receive back 'patrimonium et continentiam,' that is, their income and what is necessary for the maintenance of their condition" (VI, p. 86; my translation).

Letter 62

Before autumn of 402, Alypius, Augustine, and Samsucius wrote to Severus, bishop of Milevis, about problems with a cleric, Timothy. Augustine reports that, when the three bishops arrived at Subsana, they corrected the situation, but were lied to (paragraph 1). Timothy appears to have refused a transfer because of an oath he took, but Augustine persuaded him that he would not be committing perjury since he could not swear to what someone would choose to do. Timothy finally agreed to follow the decision of the bishops (paragraph 2).

To his most blessed lord and his venerably most dear and most sincere brother and fellow priest, Severus,[1] and to the brothers who are with you, Alypius, Augustine, Samsucius,[2] and those brothers who are with us, send greetings in the Lord.

1. After we had come to Subsana and investigated what was done there against our will while we were absent, we found that some things had happened as we had heard of them, but other things had happened otherwise, though all had to be deplored and endured. To the extent that the Lord helped, we corrected them, in part by admonition, in part by prayer. We ask that you pardon that action that, of course, saddened us very much after the departure of Your Holiness, namely, that the brothers were sent off from there without a guide for their journey, and we ask that you realize that it was done out of fear rather than out of malice. For the people thought that the brothers were sent by our son, Timothy, especially to provoke Your Charity to anger against us, while they themselves wanted to keep everything intact for our arrival, which they were hoping would be with you. They thought that the brothers would not leave if they did not receive a guide for the journey. But who would doubt that this was a mistake? For this reason it also happened that Fossor was told that Timothy had already left with the brothers. That was certainly false, but it was not a priest who said it. And that the brother, Carcedonius, was unaware of all this was explained to us most clearly, to the extent that such things usually are made clear.

2. But why should we delay over more points? Our son, Timothy, whom I mentioned, was very deeply upset because he felt quite against his will an unexpected perplexity. He indicated to us that, when you dealt with him about being a servant of God at Subsana, he burst out and swore that he would not leave you under any condition. And when we asked his intention, he answered that he was prevented by an oath from being in the place where we wanted him to be even

---

1. Severus was the Catholic bishop of Milevis in Numidia from 395 to 426.
2. Alypius was bishop of Thagaste, and Samsucius was bishop of Turris; see Letter 34, 6.

before, though he was now at peace, especially over the revelation of his freedom. And we showed him that he would not be guilty of perjury if, in order to avoid a scandal, it came about, not by his doing, but by yours, that he could not be with you, since he could not swear concerning your will, but only concerning his own, and he admitted that you had not in turn made an oath to him. In the end he said what a servant of God, a son of the Church, ought to say, namely, that whatever we decided along with Your Holiness to do with him, he would certainly go along with it. Hence, we ask and beseech Your Wisdom by the love of Christ that you remember everything we have said and make us happy by your reply. *For we stronger ones*—if amid such great dangers of temptations one should dare to say this—*ought to bear the burdens of the weak* (Rom 15:1), as the apostle says. Brother Timothy has not written to Your Holiness because your holy brother has conveyed to you everything that has been done. Mindful of us, may you boast in the Lord, my most blessed lord and venerably most dear and most sincere brother.

Letter 63

Soon after the previous letter, Augustine again wrote to Severus of Milevis about the cleric, Timothy. Severus had written Augustine, expressing surprise that the latter tolerated what could have been corrected. Augustine tells him to stop being surprised because Timothy's ordination to the subdiaconate cannot be undone (paragraph 1). Augustine also points out that he has corrected many things about the incident by reprimands, admonitions, and prayers (paragraph 2). Furthermore, Timothy has been returned to Severus (paragraph 3), but Augustine points out that, since Timothy became a lector in one of his churches, he ought to have stayed in Augustine's diocese.

To his most blessed lord and venerable brother and fellow priest, Severus, who is to be loved with the most sincere love, and to the brothers who are with you, Augustine and the brothers who are with me send greetings in the Lord.

1. If I should say what this situation forces me to say, what will happen to my concern for preserving love? But if I do not say these things, what will happen to the freedom of our friendship? Though wavering back and forth for a time, I, nonetheless, chose to excuse myself rather than to accuse you. You wrote that you were surprised that we chose to tolerate, though with sorrow, what we could have remedied by correction, as if we should not feel sorrow over wrongdoing, even if it is afterward corrected insofar as possible, or as if we should not in particular tolerate what cannot be undone, though the wrongdoing is evident. And so, stop being surprised, my most sincere brother. For Timothy was ordained a subdeacon at Subsana apart from my advice and desire when the deliberation as to what should be done about him was still leaning now this way, now that between our different views. Look, I am still sad, though he has already returned to you, and on this point we do not regret having obeyed your will.

2. Listen as well to what we corrected by reprimands, by admonitions, and by prayers, even before he left here; otherwise, it might seem to you that we corrected nothing because he had not yet returned to you. By reprimands we corrected him, first of all, because he did not obey you in that he set out to return to Your Holiness before having consulted Brother Carcedonius; this disobedience was the origin of our disturbance. Then we reprimanded the priest and Verinus who we found out were the causes for his being ordained. For, when we reprimanded them, they all admitted that they wrongly did all these things and asked to be forgiven in what would have been far too proud a fashion if we did not believe that they had been corrected. After all, they could not bring it about that those actions had not been done, but we were trying to do nothing else by our reprimands than to make them know that they had acted wrongly and to be sorry

for that. By admonitions, however, we first corrected all of them so that they would not dare to do such things again lest they experience the wrath of God. Then we admonished Timothy in particular, for he was saying that he was compelled only by his oath to go to Your Charity. We told him that Your Holiness, considering, as we hoped would be the case, what we had said when together, would not want him to be with you on account of the scandal to the weak for whom Christ died and on account of the discipline of the Church that they neglect to their danger, since he had here already become a lector.[1] We admonished him that, free from the obligation of an oath, he should with a mind completely at peace serve God, to whom we are going to give an account of our actions. By admonitions we also brought, as best we could, Brother Carcedonius, to the point that he also would most patiently accept whatever the provident need of maintaining ecclesiastical discipline would demand that there be done with regard to Timothy. But by prayers we have corrected ourselves in order to commend to the mercy of God both our governance and the outcomes of our counsels and to ask that, if we had been smitten by some indignation, we might take flight under his soothing right hand and be healed. See how many things we have corrected, in part by reprimands, in part by admonitions, and in part by prayers.

3. And now, considering the bond of love in order that Satan may not have dominion over us, for we are not unaware of his intentions,[2] what else ought we to have done but obey your will? For you did not think that what was done could have been corrected unless he, with regard to whom you complain that you have suffered injury, were restored to you. Brother Carcedonius himself has also done this with peace of mind, considering Christ in you, though after no slight mental anguish, because of which I beg that you pray for him. And when I was still thinking that I should consider sending a different letter to Your Fraternity since Timothy was lingering with us, Carcedonius feared your fatherly anger and cut off my deliberation, not only permitting, but even insisting that Timothy be returned to you.

4. But I leave my case, Brother Severus, to your judgment. For I am certain that Christ dwells in your heart, and by him I beg you to consult him, for he presides over your mind that is subject to him. Consult him about whether a man who had begun to serve as a lector at Subsana in a church entrusted to my governance—and not one time, but a second and a third time—and had read, as a companion of the priest of the church of Subsana, at Turris, Ciza, and Verbalis, can or ought to be judged not to have been a lector. And just as at God's

---

1. In the Council of Milevis of 27 August 402 it was decreed that "if a cleric has exercised even just one time the office of lector in one church, he ought not to be transferred to another church in order to be ordained a cleric." Mansi, *Sacrorum Conciliorum Collectio* (Paris: H. Welter, 1901-1927), III, 787.
2. See 2 Cor 2:11.

command we have corrected what was done against our will, so you too likewise correct at God's command what was previously done without your knowledge. For I do not fear that you will fail sufficiently to understand how wide a door is opened for the destruction of the order of ecclesiastical discipline if a cleric of another church swears to anyone that he will not leave him, while the other allows him to stay with him, claiming that he is acting in that way in order to avoid being the cause of the other's perjury. And yet, surely the one who does not allow this, and does not permit him to stay with him, himself observes the rule in peace without any blame, because the cleric could take an oath about himself, not about someone else.

Letter 64

Soon after Christmas of 401, Augustine wrote to Quintian, a priest of Carthage. Augustine urges Quintian to be patient in seeking reconciliation with his bishop, Aurelius (paragraph 1). He expresses his willingness to have him visit if Quintian comes to Hippo, though he suggests that there are other bishops who are more senior and nearer at hand through whom he might more easily plead his case (paragraph 2). He admonishes Quintian about using non-canonical writings and corrects his understanding of another conciliar decree (paragraph 3). Finally, he commends the people of Vigesilit for refusing to accept a bishop deposed by a plenary council of Africa (paragraph 4).

To his most beloved lord, brother, and fellow priest, Quintian, Augustine sends greetings in the Lord.

1. We do not disdain to look at bodies that are less beautiful, especially since our souls are not yet beautiful, as we hope that they will be when he who is ineffably beautiful shall appear to us, in whom we now believe, but do not see. Then *we shall be like him, because we shall see him as he is* (1 Jn 3:2). We admonish you to think the same thing yourself about your soul, if you are willing to hear me as a brother, and not to presume that it is beautiful. Rather, as the apostle commands, rejoice in hope, and do what follows. For he speaks this way: *Rejoice in hope, but be patient in tribulation* (Rom 12:12). *For we have been saved in hope*, as the same apostle also says. *After all, hope that is seen is not hope. For who hopes for what he sees? But if we hope for what we do not see, we await it in patience* (Rom 8:24-25). Let not this patience fail in you, and in a good conscience *wait for the Lord, and act courageously. Let your heart be strong, and wait for the Lord* (Ps 27:14).

2. It is, of course, evident that, if you came to us, while not in communion with the venerable bishop, Aurelius, you could not be in communion with us either, but we would act with the same charity with which we have no doubt that he acts. Nor would your arrival be burdensome to us because you must act in a calm manner to preserve the discipline of the Church, especially if your conscience is clear, something which you and God know. For, if Aurelius postponed the discussion of your case, he did not do so out of hatred for you, but because of other demands upon him; if you knew them, as you know your own, you would not be surprised or saddened at the delay. We ask that you believe the same thing about the demands upon us, because you likewise cannot know them. There are bishops older than we are and more worthy of authority and nearer in place through whom you could more easily pursue the cases of the church belonging to your administration. Nor have I been silent before old Aurelius, my venerable

252

brother and colleague, a man who deserves to be treated with all the respect due to his merits, about your tribulation and the complaint of your letter; rather, I have taken care to make known to him your innocence by a copy of your letter. But I received your letter either a day before or two days before Christmas when you informed me that he would go to the church of Badesilit where you fear that the people of God are going to be disturbed and harmed. For this reason I certainly do not dare to address your people by letter, but I could write back to those who write to me. How could I, however, on my own initiative write to a people that has not been entrusted to my governance?

3. Nonetheless, let what I say to you alone, who have written me, reach through you those who need to hear it said. As for you, do not first throw the Church into a scandal by reading to the people writings that the canon of the Church has not accepted. After all, heretics, and especially the Manichees, often use these writings to throw the minds of the unlearned into confusion, and I hear that they like to hide out in your territory. I am, therefore, surprised that Your Wisdom admonishes me to order that those men who come from you to us to enter the monastery should not be received in order that what we have decided in council might remain in effect. And at the same time you do not remember that the council determined which are the canonical writings that ought to be read to the people of God.[1] Reexamine, then, the council, and commit to memory everything that you read there, and you will also find that the council decided only regarding clerics, not also concerning lay persons, that those coming from elsewhere should not be received into a monastery.[2] For the reason is not that there was any mention of a monastery, but because it was decided that no one should receive a cleric from elsewhere. But in a recent council[3] it was decided that those who left a monastery or were thrown out should not become clerics elsewhere or superiors of monasteries. If, then, something bothers you with regard to Privation, realize that we have not yet accepted him into the monastery, but I sent his case to the primate, Aurelius, in order that I may do what he decides in his regard. After all, I wonder whether he can be counted as a lector who has only once read the scriptures, and those were non-canonical ones. For, if he is a lector in the church for this reason, then those scriptures are, of course, ecclesiastical. But if those scriptures are not ecclesiastical, whoever reads them, even in church, is not a lector of the church. With regard to that young man, nonetheless, I must observe what that bishop whom I mentioned decides.

4. But if the people of Vigesilit, who along with you are most dear to us in the heart of Christ,[4] refuse to accept a bishop deposed in a plenary council of Africa,

---

1. In the Council of Hippo of 393, canon 38, and in the Council of Carthage of 397, canon 47.
2. See the Council of Carthage of 397, canon 21.
3. In the Council of Carthage of 13 September 401.
4. See Phil 1:8.

they will be acting wisely, and they neither can nor should be forced to do so. And whoever uses violence to force them reveals what sort of man he is, and he will cause us to understand what sort of a man he was before when he wanted no one to believe anything evil of him. No one so clearly reveals the sort of case he has as one who tries with turmoil and complaints to recover by means of secular powers or by any violent means a dignity he lost. For he does not want to serve Christ as Christ wills, but to lord it over Christians against their will. Brother, be careful; the devil is very clever, but *Christ is the wisdom of God* (1 Cor 1:24).

Letter 65

Late in 401 or in the beginning of 402 Augustine wrote to Xantippus, the primate of Numidia, about the priest, Abundantius. Augustine informs Xantippus that Abundantius was ordained a priest in a small town under Augustine's care, that he developed a poor reputation, that upon investigation Augustine discovered that he embezzled money, broke his fast on the eve of Christmas, and spent the night in the house of a woman of ill repute (paragraph 1). Abundantius has the right to appeal his case, but must do so within a year. Augustine has meanwhile removed him from the office of the priesthood and sent him back to his home, fearing to entrust a parish to the man, though he will abide by the decision of an episcopal court if Abundantius appeals his case (paragraph 2).

To his most blessed lord and father worthy of veneration and fellow priest, old Xantippus,[1] Augustine sends greetings in the Lord.

1. I greet Your Excellency with the devotion that a man of your merits deserves, commending myself very much to your prayers, and I inform Your Wisdom that a certain Abundantius had been ordained a priest in the rural town, Strabonia, which belongs to our diocese. Since he was not living the life of the servants of God, he had begun to have a reputation that was not good. I was very worried about that, but, nonetheless, did not believe anything rashly. When, however, I clearly became more worried, I made an effort to see if I could somehow attain some certain evidence of his evil way of life. And I first found out that he embezzled the money of a certain peasant that was entrusted to him for religious purposes and that he could provide no credible account of it. Then he was proved guilty and confessed that on the fast day before Christmas, on which the church of Gippi, like all the rest, fasted, he remained in the same rural town after he had said farewell to his colleague, the priest of Gippi, a little before noon, as if he were about to set out for his own church. And without any cleric with him, he ate dinner and supper at the house of a certain woman of ill repute and stayed the night in the same house. In the inn of this woman a certain cleric of ours from Hippo had stayed and was removed from his position for this reason. And since Abundantius knew this perfectly well, he could not deny it. For what he denied, I left to God's judgment, while I pronounced judgment on what he was not permitted to conceal. I feared to entrust a church to him, especially one situated amid the rabidness of the heretics who go about barking. He asked me to give him a letter for the priest of the rural town of Armemano in the territory of Bulla from where he had come to us and to explain his situation. In that way the

---

1. Xantippus was the Catholic bishop of Thagura and primate of Numidia.

priest would not think something worse of him, and he might live there, if possible, a better life without the office of the priesthood. I did so, moved by compassion. It was necessary, however, that I made this known, especially to Your Wisdom, for fear that he might surprise you by some deception.

2. I, however, heard his case when it was one hundred days before Easter Sunday, which was going to fall on the sixth of April. On account of the council I have taken care to make this known to Your Reverence, and I did not conceal this from him, but faithfully disclosed to him what the council decided,[2] namely that, if he neglects to pursue his case within a year, but later perhaps thinks he has a case worth pursuing, no one would thereafter hear his plea. But, most blessed lord and father worthy of veneration, if we think that these proofs of bad conduct on the part of clerics, especially when they begin to have a reputation that is not good, have to be punished only in the way in which the council had decreed, we begin to be forced to desire to know what cannot be known and either to condemn what is uncertain or to pass over what is truly unknown. I certainly thought that a priest should be removed from the office of the priesthood who on a day of fast on which the church of the same place also fasted, after saying goodbye to his colleague, a priest of the same place, dared to stay and to have both dinner and supper in the house of a woman of ill repute, without being accompanied by a cleric, and to sleep in the same house, for I was afraid to entrust to him thereafter a church of God. But if the judges of the church think otherwise, since the council decided that the case of a priest is to be settled by six bishops, let a bishop who is willing entrust to him a church entrusted to his care. I am afraid, I admit, to entrust any people to such priests, especially when no good reputation comes to their defense in order that they might be forgiven this. Otherwise, if something more harmful occurs, I would be sick at heart and blame myself.

---

2. Augustine refers to the Council of Carthage held on 13 September 401.

Letter 66

Shortly after 400 Augustine wrote to Crispinus, the Donatist bishop of Calama in Numidia. The letter lacks a salutation.[1] Augustine reprimands Crispinus for having rebaptized approximately eighty tenant farmers of an estate that he bought. He points out that Christ bought by his blood those whom Crispinus has bought by money (paragraph 1). He challenges Crispinus to have their discussion recorded and translated for the people of Mappala and to let them choose which communion they want (paragraph 2).

1. You should, of course, fear God, but since in rebaptizing the people of Mappala you wanted to be feared as a man, why should an imperial order not have such force in a province if a provincial order has such force in a town? If you compare the persons, you are only a landowner; he is the emperor. If you compare the places, you are in charge of a rural town; he is in charge of an empire. If you compare the causes, he was acting to mend a division; you were acting to divide a unity. But we do not want to cause you fear of a man. For we could have had you pay ten pounds of gold in accord with the imperial orders. Do you perhaps not have the means to pay what those who rebaptize are ordered to pay, while you spend a lot to buy those whom you rebaptize? But we are not, as I said, going to cause you fear of a man. Let Christ rather cause you fear. I want to know what you would reply to him if he should say to you, "Crispinus, was it a high price you paid to buy the fear of the people of Mappala, and was my death to buy the love of all the nations a low price? Was what you counted out of your purse for rebaptizing your tenant farmers more effective than what flowed from my side for baptizing my peoples?" I know that you could hear much more if you would turn your ear to Christ and could be admonished by the people you bought about how impiously you speak against Christ. For, if you believe that you securely own by human law what you bought with your money, how much more securely does Christ own by divine law what he bought by his blood! He, of course, indisputably will own the totality of which scripture says, *He will be lord from sea to sea and from the river to the ends of the earth* (Ps 72:8). But how can you be certainly confident that you will not lose what you think that you have bought in Africa when you say that Christ lost the whole world and remains only in Africa?

2. Why should I say more? If the people of Mappala went over to your communion of their own will, let them hear both of us so that what we say is written down and, after it has been signed by us, let it be translated into Punic.

---

1. The letter bears no salutation; the oldest manuscript has: "The beginning of the booklet of Saint Augustine, the Catholic bishop, against Crispinus, the schismatic."

Then, with fear of any master removed, let them choose what they want. After all, from what we shall say it will be clear whether they remain in error under compulsion or hold onto the truth willingly. For, if they do not understand these issues, how rashly you have dragged off people who do not understand! But if they do understand, let them, as I said, hear both of us, and let them do what they choose. If any people, who you think were coerced by their masters, came over to us from you, let the same thing be done in this case too. But if you do not want this to happen, who does not see that you are not confident of having the truth? The wrath of God, however, is to be avoided both here and in the world to come. I call upon you in the name of Christ to reply to these points.

Letter 67

Probably in 403, Augustine wrote to Jerome in Bethlehem. Augustine tells Jerome that he has heard that Jerome has received his letter, and he begs for a reply (paragraph 1). Augustine denies the truth of the rumor that he wrote a book against Jerome and asks Jerome to correct him if he has said something wrong in other writings (paragraph 2). Finally, Augustine expresses the wish that they could converse together regularly and again pleads for a reply to his letter (paragraph 3).

To his most dear and most beloved lord and honorable brother in Christ and fellow priest, Jerome, Augustine sends greetings in the Lord.

1, 1. I heard that my letter has come into your hands, but I have not held it against Your Charity that I have not merited an answer; there has undoubtedly been some obstacle. Hence, I realize that I should rather pray to the Lord that he may grant to your will the ability of sending your reply. For he already gave you the ability to reply since, when you choose to, you can do so most easily.

2, 2. I also doubted whether I should believe this matter that was, of course, reported to me, but I ought not also to have doubted whether I should write to you something about this. I was, however, told in brief that some brothers reported to Your Charity that I wrote a book against you and sent it to Rome. Know that this is not true; I call God to witness that I have not done this. But if some things are found in some of my writings in which I am found to hold some position different from yours, I think that you ought to know that I did not say it against you, but that I wrote what I thought, or if you cannot know this, believe it. I would say this, of course, in the sense that I am not only fully prepared to hear as a brother what you hold to the contrary, if something disturbs you in my writings, but I also beg and demand this of you. For I will rejoice either over my correction or over your good will.

3. Oh, if I were only permitted, even if not living in the same house, at least nearby, frequently to enjoy in the Lord a pleasant conversation with you. But since God has not granted this, I ask that you strive to preserve, increase, and make perfect our being together in the Lord as much as we can be and not disdain to reply, however rarely. Greet with respect from me the holy brother, Paulinian, and all the brothers who are with you and rejoice over you in the Lord. May you be mindful of us and be heard by the Lord in every holy desire, my dearest and most beloved lord and honorable brother in Christ.

Letter 68

In 402 Jerome wrote to Augustine from Bethlehem, having finally received Augustine's letter in which the bishop of Hippo warned Jerome about his interpretation of Galatians. Jerome complains about the letter in which Augustine had called upon him to recant his views (paragraph 1). He warns Augustine not to provoke him lest the young Augustine be beaten as the young boxer, Dares, was beaten by old Entellus in the *Aeneid* (paragraph 2). Finally, Jerome complains about the writings of Rufinus (paragraph 3).

To the truly holy lord and most blessed bishop, Augustine, Jerome sends greetings in the Lord.

1. At the very moment of the departure of our holy son, Asterius, the subdeacon,[1] the letter of Your Beatitude arrived in which you assure me that you did not send a book against my humble self to Rome.[2] I had not heard that you did this either, but copies of a certain letter seemingly written to me arrived here through our brother, the deacon, Sysinnius.[3] In it you admonish me that I should sing a παλινῳδίαν [4] over a certain chapter of the apostle and that I should follow the example of Stesichorus who wavered between blaming and praising Helen, so that he lost his eyes by finding fault with her and received them back by praising her.[5] I simply say to Your Reverence that, though the style and kinds of argument[6] seemed to me to be yours, I did not, nonetheless, think I should rashly believe copies of a letter, for fear that you might be offended at my reply and justly demand that I ought to have verified the authenticity of your words and then written back. There added to the delay the long illness of the holy and venerable Paula.[7] For, while we spent much time at her side when she was ill, we almost forgot your letter or that of him who had written it under your name. There came to mind that verse, *Inopportune talk is like music at a time of mourning* (Sir 22:6). And so, if it is your letter, write openly, or send better copies so that we can enter upon the discussion of the scriptures without any rancor in the heart, and let us either correct our error or learn that we have blamed the other without grounds.

---

1. The CSEL edition omits *"mei necessarii,"* which the Maurists had added.
2. See Letter 67, II, 2.
3. See Letter 40.
4. That is, Augustine had asked Jerome to recant his views on the Letter to the Galatians.
5. See Isocrates, 10, 64, where it is claimed that Helen blinded the poet Stesichorus for speaking of her in a disparaging way; he recovered his sight when he composed his recantation.
6. Jerome uses the Greek term ἐπιχειρήματα: kinds of argument.
7. Paula was a wealthy Roman lady who with her daughter Eustochium moved to Bethlehem in 385 where she founded a monastery; she died on 1 January 404.

2. But God forbid that I should dare to tamper with anything in the books of Your Beatitude. It is enough for me to show that mine are correct without picking away at someone else's. Besides, Your Wisdom knows very well that everyone is convinced of his own opinion[8] and that it is the mark of childish boasting—something that children were once in the habit of doing—to seek a reputation for one's own name by attacking illustrious persons. Nor am I so foolish as that I should think that I am injured by the different ways in which you explain things, because you would not be injured if we held ideas contrary to yours. But it is a real reason for reproach among friends if we do not see our own satchel and fix our eyes on the knapsack of others, as Persius says.[9] There remains for you only that you love one who loves you and that you, a youth in the field of scripture, do not challenge an old man. We have had our great moments, and we have run as best we could. Now when you are running and covering long distances, we deserve some rest. And at the same time—if I may say this with your pardon and with respect for you—so that you do not think that you alone have alluded to a passage from the poets, recall Dares and Entellus[10] and the popular proverb, "The tired ox puts his foot down with more force." In sadness have we dictated these things. Would that we deserved your embraces and that by conversation with each other we either learned something or taught something!

3. With his usual temerity Calphurnius, with the surname, Lanarius,[11] sent me his accursed writings, which I learned have reached Africa by his efforts. I replied to them briefly in part, and I have sent you copies of that little book and will send you a lengthier work when it is opportune. In it I avoided doing injury to anyone in terms of their good reputation as a Christian, but only refuted the lies and derangement of an ignorant madman. Remember me, holy and venerable bishop. See how much I love you in that, not even after having been provoked, do I want to reply, nor do I believe that the fault is yours, which I would perhaps reprehend in another. Our common[12] brother humbly greets you.

---

8. See Rom 14:5.
9. See Persius, *Satires* (*Saturae*) 4, 24.
10. See Virgil, *Aeneid* 5, 368-484. The old Entellus beats the younger boxer to a pulp, before Aeneas stops the fight.
11. Jerome refers to Rufinus of Aquilea. In his *Defense against Jerome* (*Apologia in Hieronimum*) Rufinus defended his translation of Origen's *Principles* (*De principiis*), which Jerome had criticized.
12. Goldbacher regards "*communis*" as a proper name; the NBA editors suggest that Jerome is referring to Paulinian.

Letter 69

After 27 August 402 Alypius and Augustine wrote to Castorius, a Catholic layman of Bagai in Numidia. They explain that the abdication of Castorius' brother, Maximian, bishop of Bagai, was a good and praiseworthy act for the sake of the peace of the church (paragraph 1). They go on to urge Castorius to succeed his brother as bishop and to use his many gifts in the service of the church (paragraph 2).

To their deservedly most beloved lord and rightly honorable and esteemed son, Castorius, Alypius and Augustine send their greetings in the Lord.

1. The enemy of Christians has endeavored through our most dear and charming son, your brother,[1] to stir up a most dangerous scandal for our Catholic mother who has welcomed you to her motherly bosom as you fled from a disinherited sect into the heritage of Christ. This enemy desires, of course, to cloud over with dark sadness the clear skies of our joy, which we have derived from the good of your conversion.[2] But the Lord our God, who is merciful and full of pity,[3] consoling the afflicted, feeding the little ones, and curing the sick, permitted him to hold a position of power in order that we might rejoice much more over a situation that has been corrected than we grieved over the damage to it. It is, of course, far more glorious to set aside the burden of the episcopacy for the sake of avoiding dangers to the Church than to have taken it up for the sake of directing its course. He, of course, shows that he could have worthily received the honor, if the interests of peace permitted, since he defends it not unworthily after having received it. God, then, willed to show to the enemies of the Church through your brother, our son, Maximian, that those who do not seek their own interests, but those of Jesus Christ[4] are close to his heart. For he did not abandon the ministry of dispensing the mysteries of God[5] because he was conquered by some worldly desire, but he renounced it[6] because he was motivated by a pious

---

1. Castorius' brother, Maximian, had been a Donatist bishop and, hence, was received into the Catholic Church as a bishop. He resigned the office to preserve the unity of the Church.
2. I have followed the reading in the editions which have "*conversionis*" in place of "*conversationis*," which is found in the CSEL.
3. See Psalms 86:15; 103:8; 111:4; 112:4; 144:8; Jas 5:11.
4. See Phil 2:21.
5. See 1 Cor 4:1.
6. The Council of Milevis on 27 August 402 dealt with the abdication of Maximian. In the Acts of the Council it says, "With regard to Maximian of Bagai it is decided to send to him and to his faithful a letter from the council that authorizes him to renounce the episcopacy and then to choose another bishop." Mansi, *Sacrorum Conciliorum Collectio* (Paris: H. Welter, 1901-27), III, 787A.

love for peace. He did not want that there should arise in the members of Christ an ugly and dangerous or perhaps even destructive dissension because of his position of honor. What, after all, would be more blind and more worthy of detestation than to abandon a schism on account of the peace of the Catholic Church and to disturb the Catholic peace itself by a question over his position of honor? For what would be more praiseworthy and more suited to Christian love than, having abandoned the insane pride of the Donatists, to cling to the heritage of Christ in order to demonstrate by testimony to humility his love of unity? And so, with regard to him, just as we rejoice to have found him to be such a man that the storm of this trial did not by any means overthrow what the word of God built up in his heart, so we hope and pray from that Lord that in the rest of his life and in his conduct he may make it clear how he would have done well what he would certainly do if it had been necessary. May God grant the eternal peace that is promised to the Church to this man who understood that it was not good for him to do what was not good for the Church.

2. As for you, however, my dearest son, our no small joy, who are prevented from accepting the episcopacy by no such necessity, it would be fitting that you dedicate to Christ the natural abilities in yourself, something that he gave to you. Your talent, prudence, eloquence, seriousness, sobriety, and the other virtues, by which your character is adorned, are gifts of God. Whom do they serve better than him by whom they were given in order that they may be preserved, increased, perfected, and rewarded? Let them not be used to serve this world; otherwise, they will fade away and disappear with it. There is no need to urge this point with you at length; we know the great ease with which you consider the hopes, empty desires, and uncertain life of vain human beings. Cast, then, out of your mind whatever it had conceived from the expectation of earthly and false happiness. Work in the field of God[7] where the harvest is certain, where so many promises made so long ago have been fulfilled that it would be most insane to give up hope about those that remain. We beseech you by the divinity and humanity of Christ, by the peace of that heavenly city from which we are away from home on a journey and are earning eternal rest by our temporal labor. Take the place of your brother in the bishopric of the church of Bagai; he did not fall from it in shame, but yielded gloriously. We have hopes of very rich growth for that people through your mind and tongue, which have been enriched and adorned by God's gifts. Let them understand through your own self that your brother has not done what he did for the sake of his own ease, but for the sake of their peace. We have ordered that this letter not be read to you except when those people who need you already possess you. For we already have possession of you by the bond of spiritual love because you are much needed by our college of bishops. But you will know afterward why we have not come to you with our bodily presence.

---

7. See Mt 21:28.

Letter 70

After 397 or 400 Alypius and Augustine wrote to Naucelio, a Donatist lay man. They point out that Felician, the Donatist bishop of Musti, was condemned and then reinstated in his bishopric and argue that, if his condemnation was unjust, then the condemnation of the earlier traditors could have been unjust (paragraph 1). They also point out that, when Felician was in communion with the Maximianists, a splinter group which broke away from the Donatists, he baptized many and those whom he baptized were received back into the Donatist communion without being rebaptized (paragraph 2).

To their most beloved lord and honorable brother, Naucelio,[1] Alypius and Augustine send greetings.

1. You reported to us the reply of your bishop, Clarence, that is, that he did not deny that Felician of Musti was condemned by them and afterward received back into his position of honor,[2] but had been condemned as an innocent man, since he was not present and proved that he was not present. We are saying this in order that he may reply to it. For it was wrong to condemn without a hearing the man whom those people who condemned him now themselves declare to have been innocent. Therefore, if he was innocent, he ought not to have been condemned, or if he was guilty, he ought not to be taken back. If he was taken back as innocent, he was condemned though innocent; if he was condemned because he was guilty, he was taken back though guilty. If those who condemned him did not know whether he was innocent, they are to be blamed for their rashness because they dared to condemn an innocent man whose case was not heard and about whom they were ignorant, and from the present case we understand that they condemned with the same rashness those earlier bishops whom they accused of the crime of handing over the sacred books. For, if they could have condemned Felician though he was innocent, they could have called traditors those earlier bishops though they did not surrender the books.

2. Second, the same Felician whom they condemned was in communion with Maximian[3] for a long time. If he was innocent when he was condemned, why did he at a later time, when in communion with the criminal Maximian, baptize many outside their communion? They themselves are witnesses to this who brought the case before the proconsul in order that the same Felician might be

---

1. Naucelio was a Donatist layman from Thabraca in Africa Proconsularis where Clarence was the Donatist bishop.
2. This was done in 397.
3. Maximian was a Donatist deacon of Carthage who broke away from the Donatists to form his own sect. See Letter 43, 9, 26.

excluded from the basilica on the grounds that he was involved with Maximian. It was, therefore, not enough to have condemned someone not present, to have condemned a man without a hearing, to have condemned, as they admit, an innocent man; they also brought a case against him before the proconsul in order to expel him from the church. Let them admit that even when they were expelling him from the church, they counted him among the condemned and criminals and Maximianists. And so, when he baptized people while in communion with Maximian, did he administer a true or a false baptism? But if he who was in communion with Maximian administered a true baptism, why do they accuse the baptism given throughout the world? But if he administered a false baptism when he was in communion with Maximian, why were those whom he baptized in the schism of Maximian received back along with him in that way without anyone in your sect rebaptizing them?

Letter 71

Perhaps in 403, Augustine wrote to Jerome. He pleads with Jerome to take advantage of the courier, the deacon Cyprian, to reply to his letters (paragraph 1). Augustine mentions the three previous letters to Jerome to which Jerome has not replied (paragraph 2). He tells Jerome that he has learned of his translation of Job from the Hebrew and expresses regret that Jerome has omitted from the Greek text the indications of the variant readings (paragraph 3). Augustine also expresses his preference for the Greek Septuagint text over the Hebrew (paragraph 4) and recounts a problem that arose in one congregation when the bishop introduced Jerome's translation of Jonah from the Hebrew (paragraph 5). Augustine compliments Jerome on his translation of the gospel and asks for Jerome's opinion on passages where the Septuagint differs from the Hebrew (paragraph 6).

To his venerable lord and lovable holy brother and fellow priest, Jerome, Augustine sends greetings in the Lord.

1, 1. From the time I began to write to you and to long for your replies, I have never had a better opportunity than to have my letter brought to you by a servant and most faithful minister of God and someone very dear to me, such as our son, Cyprian, the deacon. Through his hands I so certainly hope for a letter from you that we could not hope for anything more certain in this sort of matter. For our son whom I mentioned will not lack zeal in seeking a reply; he will not lack charm in gaining one, nor carefulness in guarding it, speed in carrying it, and reliability in delivering it. If I somehow merit so much, may the Lord grant his help and be present in your heart and in my desire so that no more important desire may hinder your brotherly good will.

2. And so, since I already sent two letters, but afterward received none from you, I chose to send the same letters again in the belief that they have not arrived. Even if they did arrive and your letters rather were perhaps unable to reach me, send once again those letters that you already sent if you perhaps kept copies. If not, dictate again something for me to read, provided that you do not, nonetheless, delay to answer this letter because it has already been a long time that I am waiting for it. When I was still a priest I had prepared my first letter to be sent to you by the hands of a certain brother of ours, Profuturus,[1] who later became a colleague of ours and has already left this life. He was not able at that time to deliver it because, right when he was arranging to leave, he was prevented by the burden of the episcopacy and then soon died. I have decided to send this letter now as well in order that you may know how ardently I then desired to converse

---

1. See Letter 28.

with you and how much I suffer because the senses of your body are so far distant from me by which my mind might have access to your mind, my most charming brother worthy of honor among the members of the Lord.

2, 3. In this letter, however, I add what I learned later, namely, that you translated Job from the Hebrew, though we already have your translation of the same prophet made from the Greek language into Latin in which you marked with asterisks what is found in the Hebrew and is missing in the Greek and marked with obelisks what is found in the Greek and is not in the Hebrew. You did this with such a wonderful care that in certain passages we see stars for every word, signifying that those words are in the Hebrew, but not in the Greek. Now, however, in this later version that was made from the Hebrew, I do not find the same fidelity to the words, and it disturbs me no small amount as I ponder why in the first translation asterisks are inserted with such great care that they indicate that even the smallest particles of speech that are present in the Hebrew are lacking in the Greek or why in this second translation made from the Hebrew less care was used in order that these same particles might be found in those passages. I wanted to cite something from it as an example, but the book that was translated from the Hebrew was not available to me at the time. Because, nonetheless, you soar ahead of me in natural talents, you understand well enough, I think, not merely what I said, but also what I wanted to say, so that you may reply to what bothers me once the reason has been presented.

4. I would, of course, prefer that you translate for us the canonical Greek scriptures, which are said to have had seventy translators.[2] It will, after all, be extremely annoying if your translation begins to be read more frequently in many churches because the Latin churches will be out of harmony with the Greek churches, especially since, when the Greek book is produced, that is, in a widely known language, your translation will easily be proven to be in opposition to it. But if anyone is upset by something unfamiliar in the translation from the Hebrew and raises the charge of falsification, he will rarely or never have access to the Hebrew texts by which your translation might be defended against the objection. But even if one had access to the Hebrew, who would tolerate the condemnation of so many Latin and Greek authorities? In addition, even the Hebrews, when consulted, can offer a different response so that you alone seem indispensable since you can prove even them wrong. But who will be the judge? I would be surprised if you can find one.

3, 5. For, when a certain brother bishop of ours began to have your translation read in the church over which he presides, a particular passage in the prophet Jonah caused a disturbance because it was presented in far different language than had become familiar to the senses and memory and had been chanted for so many ages. There was produced so great an uproar among the people, especially

---

2. The Septuagint version is so named because of the seventy translators.

when the Greeks brought accusations and stirred up the charge of falsification, that the bishop—this took place in the city of Oea[3]—was forced to demand the testimony of Jews. But, whether out of ignorance or out of malice, they replied that what both the Greek and Latin texts had and said was in the Hebrew books. What then? The man was forced to correct the text as if it were incorrect, since he did not want to be left without any people after the grave crisis. Hence, it seems to us as well that you could have been mistaken at times on some points. And see what a problem this presents in those writings that cannot be corrected by a comparison with the texts in familiar languages.

4, 6. So then, we offer to God no small thanks for your work by which you translated the gospel from Greek because there is no problem in almost all the passages when we compare it with the Greek scripture. Hence, if anyone for the sake of argument favors the old incorrect version, he will be either easily instructed or refuted when the books are brought out and compared. Even if certain very rare passages rightly trouble someone, who is so hardhearted that he will not readily pardon a work so useful that he is not able to praise it as it deserves? I wish, however, you would be so good as to explain to me what you think as to why in many passages the authority of the Hebrew book is quite different from the Greek books that are called the Septuagint. For that version has no small authority; it has deservedly, after all, been widely used and was used by the apostles. Not only does the text itself indicate this, but I also remember that you testified to it. And for this reason you will do very much good if you render that Greek scripture, which the seventy produced, into correct Latin, for the Latin we have is so different in different manuscripts that it is barely tolerable. And it rouses such suspicions that something else may be found in the Greek that one hesitates to quote or to prove something from it. I thought this letter would be short, but somehow or other it became very pleasant for me to go on with it as if I were conversing with you. But I beg you by the Lord not to delay in answering all these questions and in offering me your presence as far as possible.

---

3. The modern city of Tripoli in Lybia.

Letter 72

Toward the end of 403 or at the beginning of 404 Jerome wrote to Augustine. Jerome expresses his amazement over how a letter that Augustine claims not to have written against Jerome has had so wide a circulation (paragraph 1). He points out that there should be no suspicion among friends and explains why he did not want to reply to a letter that may not have come from Augustine (paragraph 2). Jerome admonishes Augustine for attacking an old man, a veteran who is no longer a solider (paragraph 3). He points out how Augustine has injured their friendship by what he has written (paragraph 4). Again Jerome warns that Augustine is provoking an old man, claims that he has not read Augustine's other writings, and counsels Augustine to see to it that letters addressed to Jerome arrive in Jerome's hands first (paragraph 5).

To his truly holy lord and most blessed bishop, Augustine, Jerome sends greetings.

1, 1. You send me frequent letters, and you often push me to respond to a certain letter of yours, copies of which, as I have already written before, came into my hands without your signature through Sysinnius, the deacon. You indicate that you first sent the letter by Brother Profuturus and secondly through some other person, and that Profuturus was held back from the journey and was made a bishop and died soon thereafter,[1] while the other man, whose name you do not mention, feared the dangers of the sea and changed his plans to set sail. Since that is so, I cannot sufficiently express my amazement at how this letter is said to be in the hands of many at Rome and in Italy and has not come to me alone to whom it was sent, especially since the same brother, Sysinnius, said that he found it among your other treatises, not in Africa, not in your home, but on an island of the Adriatic, nearly five years ago.

2. All suspicion should be removed from a friendship, and one should speak with a friend just as with another self. Some of my close friends and vessels of Christ, of whom there are a great many in Jerusalem and in the holy places, suggested that you did not act with a pure intention, but with a mind seeking praise, scandal, and distinction among the people. In that way you might win greatness at our expense so that many would know that you challenged me and I was afraid, that you wrote like someone learned and I was silent like someone uneducated and had finally found someone to set a limit to my garrulousness. To speak frankly, I did not at first, however, want to reply to Your Reverence, above all because I believed that the letter was not clearly yours or that it was a sword coated with honey, as the common proverb says of some people. Secondly, I

---

1. See Letters 71, 2 and 82, 4 and 30.

wanted to avoid seeming to reply to a bishop of my communion impudently and to criticize some things in a letter of someone who criticizes me, especially since I judged that certain points in it are heretical.

2, 3. Finally, I did not want to reply to you for fear that you would make the just complaint and say, "Why then have you done this? Had you seen my letter and in the signature had you recognized the writing of a hand familiar to you? Was it in order readily to injure a friend and to turn the malice of another into scorn for me?" Hence, as I have already written, either send the same letter under your own signature,[2] or stop pestering an old man hiding in his cell. But if you want to practice or to display your learning, seek young, eloquent, and noble men; there are said to be very many of these at Rome who could and would dare to do battle with you and to hold their own with a bishop in a discussion of the holy scriptures. I was once a soldier, but am now a veteran, and now I ought to praise your victories and those of others; I ought not myself to fight again with my worn-out body.[3] Otherwise, if you push me frequently to reply, I would remind you of the famous story of how by his patience Quintus Fabius Maximus crushed Hannibal who was exulting in his youth.[4]

Time takes away everything, even the mind. I remember
That as a boy I often passed long days in singing.
Now I have forgotten so many songs; even the voice itself
Abandons Moeris now.[5]

And to speak rather of the holy scriptures, in transferring all the benefits and delights he had received from King David to his young son, Barzillai the Gileadite showed that old age ought neither to desire such things nor to accept them when offered.[6]

4. But you swear that you have not written a book against me nor sent to Rome one that you have not written.[7] And you add that, if some things are perhaps found in your writings that disagree with my interpretation, you did not injure me, but wrote what you thought correct. I ask you to listen to me with patience. You have not written a book; how then did others bring to me writings filled with your criticisms of me? Why does Italy have what you did not write? With what reason do you demand that I reply to those writings that you deny that you have written? I am not so dense that, if you hold different views, I would think that you did me an injustice. But if you criticize my statements close up, demand an account of my writings, compel me to correct what I wrote, challenge me to sing

2. Jerome had not yet received Letter 71 which was accompanied by Letters 28 and 40.
3. See Horace, *Letters* 1, 1, 3.
4. See Livy, XXII, 12-18. Fabius defeated Hannibal by his tactics of stalling for which he earned the epithet "Cunctator."
5. Virgil, *Bucolics* IX, 51-54.
6. See 2 Sm 19:31-38.
7. See Letter 67, 2, 2.

a παλινῳδίαν,[8] and restore my sight,[9] in this you do injury to our friendship, in this you violate the laws of our relationship. I write these things so that we do not seem to battle in a childish manner and to give material for arguments to our respective followers and foes, for I desire to love you in a sincere and Christian manner and not to hold back anything in my mind that differs from what is on my lips. For it is not proper that I, who have sweated with toil in the monastery with my holy brothers from youth to this age, should dare to write something against a bishop of my communion and against that bishop whom I began to love before I began to know him, who first invited me to friendship, and over whom I rejoiced as he rose up after me in the learning of the scriptures. Therefore, either deny that the book is yours if it perhaps is not yours and stop demanding a reply to what you have not written, or if it is yours, honestly confess it in order that, if I write something in my own defense, the blame may lie with you who have provoked it, not with me who have been compelled to reply.

3, 5. You add that you are ready to accept it in a brotherly fashion if anything disturbs me in your writings or if I want to correct anything, and that you will not only rejoice over my benevolence toward you, but you ask that I do this. Again I say what I feel; you provoke an old man; you goad a silent one; you seem to boast of your learning. But it is not befitting my age to be thought to bear ill will toward one whom I ought rather to take under my wings. And if the misguided find in the gospels and the prophets what they try to criticize, are you surprised if in your books and especially in the explanation of the scriptures, at least those that are most obscure, certain ideas seem to depart from full correctness? And I say this, not because I judge that certain ideas in your works deserve to be criticized. For I have never spent any effort on reading them, nor do we have many copies of them apart from your books of the *Soliloquies* and certain commentaries on the psalms.[10] If I wanted to examine them, I would not say that they disagreed with me, who am a nobody, but that they differed from the interpretations of the ancient Greeks.

Farewell, my most dear friend, my son in terms of age, but my father in terms of dignity, and since I ask this of you, take care that whatever you write to me comes into my hands first.

---

8. That is, to recant his view of Galatians.
9. See Letter 40, 7.
10. The *Soliloquies* were written in 397; the Expositions of the Psalms were begun in 391.

Letter 73

In 404 Augustine again wrote to Jerome in an effort to resolve the misunderstanding that had arisen between them. Augustine tells Jerome that he is both consoled by his most recent letter and also pained by it (paragraph 1). Augustine points out that he too is offended by some implications of Jerome's letter (paragraph 2). In any case he asks pardon of Jerome for having offended him (paragraph 3). Augustine assures Jerome that he welcomes his criticism, though human weakness is bound to feel pain, even at just correction (paragraph 4). Augustine tells Jerome that he wishes that they lived closer to each other so that they could exchange letters more frequently (paragraph 5). He acknowledges that he received and read some writings from Jerome in reply to the attacks of Rufinus, and he deplores the destruction of the friendship between the two (paragraph 6). Again Augustine urges Jerome to write to him (paragraph 7), and again he deplores the loss of the friendship between Jerome and Rufinus (paragraph 8). Augustine argues that there should be a freedom on the part of both Jerome and himself so that each can express his views and his criticism of the other (paragraph 9). Augustine points out that the evil that someone does is a far worse evil than the evil that someone else says about him and that the latter is to be borne with patience (paragraph 10).

To his venerable lord and most beloved brother, his fellow priest, Jerome, Augustine sends greetings in the Lord.

1, 1. I think that my letter that I sent by the servant of God, our son, Cyprian,[1] came into your hands before you received this letter. By the former letter you recognized with complete certainty that it was my letter of which copies reached you there, as you mentioned. On its account I now think that, like the brazen Dares, I began to be pounded and turned about by your replies as if by the heavy and hard gloves of Entellus.[2] Now, however, I am replying to that letter of yours that you were so good as to send me by our holy son, Asterius.[3] In it I found many signs of your most benevolent love for me and also certain signs of some ways in which I have offended you. And so, where I found comfort in reading it, I was immediately slapped in the face. I was certainly amazed, perhaps most of all, that, though you say that you did not think that you should rashly believe copies of my letter for fear that I would be offended by your response and justly complain that you ought first to have verified the authenticity of my words and then written back,[4] you later command that, if it is my letter, I should write

---

1. That is, Letter 71.
2. See *Aeneid* V, 387-484, where the old boxer, Entellus, wears down and beats the young Dares.
3. Asterius carried Letter 68.
4. See Letter 68, 1.

openly or send better copies so that we can enter upon a discussion of the scriptures without any rancor in the heart.[5] How, after all, can we enter upon this discussion without rancor if you are ready to offend me? Or, if you are not ready, how would I be offended by you, if you have given no offense, and how would I justly demand that you ought first to have verified the authenticity of my words and to reply in that way, that is, so as to offend me in that way. For, unless by writing back you had offended me, I could not have justly demanded that. Hence, when you reply so that you give offense, what room is left for us to enter upon the discussion of the scriptures without rancor. Heaven forbid, of course, that I should take offense if you wanted and were able to show me by a certain argument that you understood more correctly than I that passage from the letter of the apostle or any other passage of the holy scriptures. On the contrary, heaven forbid that I should not gratefully count it among my gains if I should be instructed by your teaching or corrected by your criticism.

2. Nonetheless, my very dear brother, unless you thought that you were offended by my writings, you would not think that I could be offended by your replies. For I would never have thought it of you that, though you do not think that you were offended, you, nonetheless, write back in order to offend me. Or, if, though you did not reply in that manner, you thought that I was able to be offended because of my excessive stupidity, you have clearly offended me by this very fact that you thought that of me. But in no way would you rashly believe that I, whom you have never experienced to be such a fool, was such a fool, for you were unwilling rashly to believe the copies of my letter, even though you knew my style. After all, if with good reason you saw that I would have a just complaint if you rashly believed that a letter that was not mine was mine, how much more would I justly complain that someone unjustly thought me to be such a person as he who had thought this never found me to be? In no way, then, should you go so far that, though you do not reply in such a way that I might be offended, you, nonetheless, think that I am terribly foolish and could have been offended even by such a reply of yours.

2, 3. It remains, then, that you were planning to offend me by your reply if you knew by a certain proof that the letter was mine. And so, since I do not believe that you thought that I should be unjustly offended, there remains that I recognize my fault, namely, that I offended you first by the letter that I cannot deny is mine. Why, then, do I try to go against the current of the river and not rather ask pardon? I beseech you, therefore, by the goodness of Christ[6] that, if I have offended you, you forgive me and do not repay evil with evil by offending me in turn. You will, however, offend me if you remain silent about an error of mine, which you may perhaps find in my words or actions. For, if you criticize in me

---

5. See Letter 68, 1.
6. See 2 Cor 10:1.

those things that do not deserve criticism, you do harm to yourself rather than to me. Far be it from your conduct and holy way of life that you should do this with the will to offend, while blaming in me with a slanderous tongue something that you know in your truthful mind does not deserve blame. And for this reason either you will kindly reprimand a person, even if he lacks the fault that you think deserves reprimand, or you will soothe with fatherly love him whom you cannot win over to your view. For it is possible that you think something other than what is the truth, provided that you do not do anything other than what love demands. For I too shall accept most gratefully a reprimand given out of great friendship, even if an action that can be correctly defended does not deserve to be reprimanded. Or I shall at the same time acknowledge both your benevolence and my fault, and to the extent that the Lord grants, may I be found grateful for the one and corrected by the latter.

4. Why, then, should I fear your words, which are perhaps harsh, but are certainly salutary, as if they were the gloves of Entellus? Dares was pummeled, not cured, and he was, therefore, defeated, not healed. But if I accept your healing rebuke in tranquility, I shall not suffer from it; if, however, human weakness, at least mine, cannot but be a little saddened, even when I am truthfully accused, it is better that the swelling of the head hurt while it is cured than that it not be healed when it is spared. This is, after all, what he clearly saw who said that enemies who rebuke us are generally more beneficial than friends who are afraid to rebuke us.[7] For, when the former quarrel with us, they at times mention true faults that we should correct, but when the latter are afraid to spoil the sweetness of friendship, they manifest less freedom than they should with respect to just judgment. Hence, even if you are, as you suppose, an ox tired perhaps in the age of the body, but not, nonetheless, in the vigor of your mind, as you sweat on the threshing floor of the Lord in fruitful labor,[8] look, here I am; if I have said something wrong, put your foot down on me with more force. After all, the weight of your age ought not to be bothersome to me, provided that the chaff of my fault is being crushed.

5. Accordingly, I either read or recollect the words that you put at the end of your last letter with a sigh of great desire. You say, "Would that we deserved your embraces and that by conversation with each other we either learned something or taught something."[9] But I say, "Would that we at least dwelled in nearby regions of the earth in order that, if we could not engage in conversations, we could send our letters more frequently. But now we are so far from the eyes and ears of each other in terms of distance of place that I remember that I as a youth wrote to Your Holiness about those words of the apostle to the Galatians.[10] And

---

7. See Cicero, *Friendship* (*De amicitia*) 24, 90.
8. See Letter 68, 2.
9. Letter 68, 2.
10. See Letter 28, which was written in 394 or 395.

now, you see, I am already an old man, and I have not yet merited a reply." Due to some interference, copies of my letter more easily reached you than the letter itself, despite my care. For the man who had then accepted it neither delivered it to you nor returned it to me. But in your letters that were able to come into my hands I saw such great learning that I would prefer none of my own studies to being at your side, if only I could be there. But because I cannot, I have it in mind to send to you one of our sons in the Lord whom you can educate for us, if I merit a reply about this matter as well. For I do not have, nor could I have, such great knowledge of the divine scriptures as I see that you have. And if I have some ability in this area, I use it completely for the people of God. But on account of my work for the Church I cannot at all have the leisure for training scholars in more details than the people will listen to.

3, 6. We do not know of any slanderous writings against your name that have come to Africa. We have, nonetheless, received what you were so kind as to send, when you replied to those slanders. When I had read through it, I admit, I was much saddened that so great an evil of discord had emerged between persons so dear and close, who were joined by a bond of friendship known to almost all the churches.[11] And we see quite clearly in your letter how much you control yourself, how much you restrain the barbs of your indignation so that you do not repay slander with slander. If, nonetheless, when I read it, I was melted by sorrow and frozen with fear, what would those writings that he wrote against you do to me, if they had perchance have come into my hands? *Woe to the world because of scandals* (Mt 18:7). See, it is coming true; what the Truth says is certainly taking place, *Because sinfulness will abound, the love of many will grow cold* (Mt 24:12). What trusting hearts will safely pour themselves out to one another? To whose minds will love wholly entrust itself in security? Finally, what friend should not be feared as a future enemy if there could arise between Jerome and Rufinus this hostility we deplore? Oh, our wretched and pitiable state! Oh, how unreliable is our knowledge of the wills of present friends where there is no foreknowledge of their future! But why should I suppose that I should lament this to one person about another when a man's own future is not even known to himself. For each of us knows somehow, perhaps hardly at all, the person he now is, but he does not know what he will be afterward.

7. And yet, if the holy and blessed angels have not only the knowledge of what each of them is at present, but also the foreknowledge of what each will be, I do not at all see how the devil was ever happy, though he was still a good angel, since he knew his future sinfulness and his everlasting punishment. I would like to hear from you what you think about this matter, if there is any need to know it. See what the lands and seas that physically separate us do. If I were this letter of

---

11. Augustine refers to the friendship between Jerome and Rufinus of Aquilea, which had broken up over their views of Origen.

mine that you are reading, you would already have told me what I asked for. But now when will you write back? When will you send it? When will it arrive? When shall I receive it? And yet, would that we would receive it at some point, and how patiently we endure the fact that we cannot receive it as soon as we want! Hence, I return to those most sweet words of your letter, which were full of your holy desire, and I make them mine in turn, "Would that we deserved your embraces and that by conversation with each other we either learned something or taught something,"[12] if it were in any way possible that I should teach you.

8. Over these words, which are now not yours alone, but also mine, I am delighted and refreshed, and by our mutual desire, though it hangs in the air without reaching its goal, I am consoled in no small part, but over these words I am again stabbed with the sharpest swords of pain when I think that there developed the damage of such great bitterness between you, to whom God had granted so generously and extensively that very thing that the two of you[13] longed for, namely, that you might as the closest of friends savor together the honey of the scriptures! When, where, and for whom must we not fear, since this was able to happen to you, men mature in age and living by the word of the Lord at that time when you had already laid worldly burdens aside and were already following the Lord without their encumbrance? And you were living together in that land on which the Lord walked with human feet and where he said, *My peace I give to you; my peace I leave with you* (Jn 14:27). Truly *human life on earth is a temptation* (Jb 7:1). Alas for me that I cannot find you together somewhere! Perhaps in my upset, my pain, and my fear, I would cast myself at your feet; I would weep as much as I could; I would plead as much as I loved, now with each one of you for himself, now with both of you for each other—and for others, especially for the weak for whom Christ has died,[14] since they watch you on the stage of this life, as it were, with great danger to themselves. Do not spread about concerning yourselves in writing those issues on which you refuse to be in harmony. After all, you will not be able to destroy them by being in harmony. And you would be afraid to read them, once you are in harmony, for fear that you might go back to quarreling.

9. But I say to Your Charity that nothing has frightened me more than this example when in your letter to me I read certain indications of your indignation, not so much those concerning Entellus and the tired ox,[15] where you seemed to me to joke with a light heart rather than to threaten me in anger, as that which it is quite clear that you wrote seriously. I spoke about this above, perhaps more than

12. Letter 68, 2.
13. I have followed the reading "*vestrum*," which is found in at least one manuscript, rather than "*nostrum*," which does not fit the context.
14. See 1 Cor 8:11.
15. See Letter 68, 2.

I should have, but not more than I feared. There you said, "For fear that I would be offended and justly complain."[16] I ask you, if it is possible, that we investigate and discuss something between us in order that our hearts may be nourished without the bitterness of discord. But if I cannot say what I think needs correction in your writings and if you cannot do the same with mine except with a suspicion of hatred and an injury to our friendship, let us cease from this and spare our life and salvation. Let the knowledge that puffs up be less surely attained, provided that the love that builds up is not harmed.[17] I myself perceive that I am far from that perfection of which scripture speaks, *If anyone does not offend in words, he is a perfect man* (Jas 3:2). But clearly by the mercy of God I think that I can easily ask pardon of you, if I have offended you in some way, and you ought to disclose this to me in order that, when I have heard you, you may gain your brother.[18] After all, you ought not to allow me to be in error because you cannot do this to my face because of the distance between us. Certainly, with regard to the very things that we want to know, if I know or believe or think that I have some truth about which you hold something different, I shall try to defend it, to the extent that the Lord grants, without any offense to you. But with regard to your being offended, when I see that you are angry, I shall ask for nothing but your pardon.

10. I by no means think that you could have become angry unless I either said what I ought not to have or did not say it as I ought to have, for I am not surprised that we know each other less well than we are known by our closest and most intimate friends. I admit that I find it easy to abandon my whole self to the love of them, especially when I am wearied by the scandals of the world, and I find rest in that love without any worry. I, of course, feel that God is in that person to whom I abandon myself with security and in whom I find rest in security. And in that security I do not at all fear that incertitude of tomorrow stemming from the human fragility that I lamented above. For, when I perceive that a man is aflame with Christian love and has become my loyal friend with that love, whatever of my plans and thoughts I entrust to him I do not entrust to a human being, but to him in whom he remains so that he is such a person. For *God is love, and he who remains in love remains in God, and God in him* (1 Jn 4:16). And if he abandons God, he necessarily causes as much sorrow as he had caused joy when he remained in him. After he has changed from a close friend into an enemy, it is better, nonetheless, that he seek to make up lies in his cleverness rather than that he find anything to make public in his anger. Each of us can easily obtain this result, not by hiding what he has done, but by not doing what he wishes to remain

---

16. Letter 68, 2.
17. See 1 Cor 8:2.
18. See Mt 18:15.

hidden. The mercy of God grants to good and pious people that they may live in freedom and security among any enemies[19] to come, without making public the sins of others committed against them and without committing any sins that they fear may be made public. For, when a slanderer makes up something false, people either do not believe it at all, or one suffers injury only to his reputation, while his salvation remains secure. But a sin that one commits is an enemy within, even if the gossip or accusation of someone close does not make it public. Hence, who among the wise would not see how you ought to bear with patience and with the consolation of a good conscience the present incredible hostility of someone who was once a very close and intimate friend? And you ought to count among the weapons on the left what he hurls about or what some perhaps believe, for one does battle against the devil with those weapons no less than with those on the right.[20] I would, nonetheless, prefer that he were somehow more gentle rather than that you were better armed in this way. It is a great and sad source of wonder that you have come from such friendship to such hostilities; it will be reason for joy and for much greater joy if you return from such hostilities to your original oneness of heart.

---

19. Many manuscripts have "*amicos*," though CSEL has "*inimicos*," the reading that I have followed.
20. See 2 Cor 6:7.

Letter 74

In 404 Augustine wrote to Praesidius, a bishop of Numidia, the same man to whom he wrote Letter 39 when Praesidius was a deacon. Augustine asks the bishop to forward his letter to Jerome, but he also asks Praesidius to correct him as a brother if he has said anything that he should not have in his letters to Jerome.

To his most blessed lord and rightly venerable brother and fellow priest, Praesidius, Augustine sends greetings in the Lord.

1. Just as, when I was present, I asked Your Sincerity, so I now also admonish you not to hesitate to send my letter to our holy brother and fellow priest, Jerome. In order, however, that Your Charity may know how you ought to write to him on behalf of my cause, I sent copies of my letter to him and of his to me[1] in order that, once you have read them, Your Wisdom may easily see both my moderation, which I thought I must observe, and his reaction, which I did not fear without reason. Or if I wrote something that I ought not to have or in a way in which I ought not to have, do not write to him about me, but rather write to me myself out of fraternal love in order that, having been corrected, I may ask his forgiveness if I myself recognize my fault.

---

1. That is, Letter 73 to Jerome and Letter 72 from Jerome.

Letter 75

Finally, in 403 or 404, Jerome replies to Augustine's questions from Letters 28, 40, and 71. He mentions that he is replying in a hurried state to Augustine's questions or rather criticisms of his works (paragraph 1). Comparing himself to David about to fight proud Goliath, Jerome passes over Augustine's words of flattery (paragraph 2) and takes up the question of the title of his work, *Famous Men*, which Augustine says should not have been called *Epitaphs*, as he had heard it was called (paragraph 3). The heart of the letter focuses upon Augustine's admonition to Jerome about holding that Paul lied in rebuking Peter. Jerome points out that he was simply following the interpretation of other authors and that he had not presented this interpretation as a definitive one, as Augustine should have noticed (paragraph 4). He then turns to attack Augustine for holding that Jewish converts to Christianity are obliged to obey the Mosaic law (paragraph 5). Jerome points out that Origen introduced the interpretation that Paul only pretended to rebuke Peter to defend Peter from that attack of Porphyry and that Chrysostom followed it (paragraph 6). Jerome then cites extensively from scripture to show that even the books of scripture favor his interpretation (paragraph 7). He argues that Paul knew that Peter was the source of the decree of the Council of Jerusalem regarding the abrogation of the dietary laws and that Paul showed great deference for the authority of Peter (paragraph 8). Peter approved of the abolition of the Mosaic law, but was forced into observation of it out of fear, and Paul himself did the same thing (paragraphs 9 and 10). Since both Peter and Paul observed the law out of fear of the Jews, Paul could hardly reprehend in Peter what he himself did; his reprimand was rather a useful lie (paragraph 11).

Augustine's interpretation, which Jerome takes to be that Jewish converts should still obey the law, is both dangerous and favors the position of the heretical Ebionites (paragraphs 12-13). Jerome insists that the gospel has abolished the law and that the observance of the law is perilous for anyone (paragraph 14). Jerome reprimands Augustine for his view that it was all right for converts from Judaism to observe the traditions of their forefathers, not because they were necessary for salvation, but simply as part of their tradition (paragraph 15). Jerome argues that to observe the ceremonies of the law is wrong and again claims that Augustine verges on the heresy of Ebion (paragraph 16). Jerome charges that according to Augustine Peter pretended to observe the law, while Paul who criticized him brazenly observed the law (paragraph 17). Finally, Jerome insists that he is not a teacher of lies and asks Augustine to stop stirring people up against him (paragraph 18).

Jerome expresses surprise that Augustine prefers the Latin translation of the Septuagint to his own "humble translation of a Christian" (paragraph 19) and defends his making a translation from the Hebrew against Augustine's argument that he should translate from the Greek (paragraph 20). Jerome defends his translation of the passage from Jonah where his translation of "ivy" instead of "gourd plant" had created a disturbance in an African church to the point that a bishop was almost deposed. Finally, Jerome tells Augustine to find some young men with whom to fight, but to leave him, now an old man, in peace (paragraphs 21 and 22).

To his truly holy lord and most blessed bishop, Augustine, Jerome sends greetings in Christ.

1, 1. By means of the deacon, Cyprian, I received at the same time three letters or rather short works of Your Excellency that contain various questions, as you call them, but are criticisms of my works, as I see them. If I want to reply to them, I will need the size of a book. I shall, nonetheless, try, to the extent I can, not to exceed the size of a longer letter and not to cause a delay for the brother, who is in a hurry. He demanded letters from me three days before he was going to depart so that I am compelled to blurt these ideas out on the run and to reply with a disorderly discourse, not with the seriousness of a writer, but with the haste of someone dictating. And such a discourse generally does not lead to solid doctrine, but to chance results, as when sudden outbreaks of war throw even the bravest soldiers into confusion, and they are forced to flee even before they can snatch up their arms.

2. On the other hand, our weaponry is Christ, and it is the teaching of the apostle Paul who writes to the Ephesians, *Take up the weapons of God in order that you may be able to resist on the evil day* (Eph 6:13). And again he says, *Stand firm, having girded your loins with the truth and having donned the breastplate of righteousness and having shod your feet in preparation for the gospel of peace. Above all, take up the shield of faith by which you can extinguish all the fiery darts of the evil one, and take the helmet of salvation and the sword of the Spirit, which is the word of God* (Eph 6:14-17). Armed with such weapons King David once went into battle, and having taken five smooth stones from the stream,[1] he showed that amid the whirlwinds of this world there was nothing harsh or filthy in his thoughts, as he drank from the stream on the way, and for this reason, he held his head high,[2] and he decapitated the most proud Goliath with his own sword, striking the blasphemer in the forehead and wounding him in that part of the body in which Uzziah, who assumed the role of a priest, was also stricken with leprosy.[3] And the holy man boasts in the Lord, saying, *The light of your countenance has been sealed over us, O Lord* (Ps 4:7). Let us, therefore, also say, *My heart is ready, O God; my heart is ready; I shall sing and make music in my glory. Raise up the harp and the lyre. I shall rise up at dawn* (Ps 58:8-9). In that way there will be fulfilled in us the words, *Open your mouth, and I shall fill it* (Ps 81:11), and, *The Lord will give his word to those who bring good news with much strength* (Ps 68:12). I have no doubt that you yourself also pray that the truth may win out among us as we do battle. For you do not seek your own glory, but Christ's,[4] and when you conquer, I shall also conquer if I have

1. See 1 Sam 17:40-51.
2. See Ps 110:7.
3. See 2 Chr 26:19.
4. See Jn 7:18.

learned of my mistake, and on the contrary, when I conquer, you win out, because it is not children who save for their parents, but parents for their children.[5] And in the Book of Chronicles we read that the sons of Israel went forth to fight with a peaceful mind even amid swords and bloodshed and the bodies of the slain, thinking not of their own victory, but of the victory of peace. Let us, then, reply to everything, and let us resolve the many questions with a few words, if Christ commands this. I pass over the greetings and signs of respect by which you soothe my mind, and I am silent about the flattery by which you strive to soften your criticism of me. I shall go right to the issues.

2, 3. You say that you received from a certain brother my book, which did not have a title and in which I listed both Greek and Latin writers of the Church. And when you asked him—to use your words—why the first page was without a title or by what name it should be called, he replied that it is called *"Epitaphs,"* and you argue that it would be correctly named in that way if you had read in it only about the lives and writings of those who had already died. But since the works of many who were alive at the time it was written and are still alive now are mentioned in it, you wonder why I gave it this title. I think that Your Wisdom can understand the title from the work itself. After all, you have read Greek and Latin authors who have described the lives of famous men. You know that they would never have entitled this work *"Epitaphs,"* but *"Famous Men,"* for example, leaders, philosophers, orators, historians, poets, and authors of epics, tragedies, and comedies. But a book of epitaphs is properly written only of the dead, something I know that I once did at the passing of the priest, Nepotanus, of blessed memory.[6] Hence, this book should be called either *"Famous Men,"* or *"Writers of the Church,"* though it is said to have been entitled, "Authors," by many ignorant people trying to correct the title.[7]

3, 4. In the second place you ask why I said in the commentary on the Letter to the Galatians that Paul could not have criticized in Peter what he himself did[8] and could not have rebuked the pretense in another of which he himself was held guilty. And you state that the rebuke of the apostle was not feigned, but genuine, and that I ought not to teach a lie, but that everything that is found in the scriptures is just as it says.[9] To these points I reply, first of all, that Your Wisdom ought to have recalled the brief preface to my commentaries where I say in my own name, "What follows then? Am I so foolish or rash as to promise what he could not do? By no means! Rather, on this point I think I am more cautious and

---

5. See 2 Cor 12:14.
6. Jerome's "Epitaph for Nepotianus," the nephew of Eliodorus, the bishop who ordained Jerome, is Letter 60 among the Letters of Jerome.
7. *Famous Men* (*De viris illustribus*) was written in 392 and contains a summary of Latin Christian literature from the beginning up to the time of Jerome.
8. See Gal 2:11.
9. See Letter 40, 3, 3.

timid, because, feeling the feebleness of my own powers, I followed the commentaries of Origen.[10] For that illustrious man wrote five volumes in the proper sense on the Letter to the Galatians and completed the tenth book of his *Miscellany*[11] with a summary explanation of his commentary. He also composed various treatises and excerpts that could suffice by themselves alone. I omit Didymus, for me a man of vision,[12] and the man from Laodicea,[13] who recently left the Church, and Alexander, the old heretic,[14] Eusebius of Emesa,[15] and Theodore of Heraclea,[16] who have also left us some commentaries on this. If I took even a few ideas from them, they would amount to something not to be completely scorned. And to state it simply, I read all these, and gathering very many ideas in my mind, I summoned the secretary and dictated to him either my own ideas or those of others without paying attention to the order either of the words at times or of their meanings. It is a gift of divine mercy that what others have said well is not lost through our ignorance and that what pleased their own people is not displeasing to foreigners."[17] If, then, you had thought anything in our exposition worthy of criticism, it was up to a man of your learning to investigate whether those things that we wrote are contained in the Greek authors in order that, if they did not say them, you might then rightly condemn my view, especially since I frankly admitted in the preface that I followed the commentaries of Origen and dictated either my own ideas or those of others, and at the end of the same chapter that you criticize, I wrote: "If anyone is displeased by this interpretation which shows that Peter did not sin nor did Paul impudently accuse his elder, he ought to explain the logic by which Paul criticizes in another what he himself committed."[18] From this I showed that I did not defend the view that I read in the Greek authors as definitive, but that I stated what I had read in such a way that I left it to the choice of the reader whether those ideas should receive approval or disapproval.

---

10. Origen, born in Alexandria in 185, died in 253/254 in Tyre, where he founded a school. He was probably the greatest theologian in the Church up to his time, though after his death various alleged teachings of his were condemned.
11. That is, his Στρωματεῖς.
12. Didymus the Blind was a close follower of Origen.
13. Apollinaris of Laodicea died circa 390; he denied that Christ had a human soul and mind. See *Heresies* 55.
14. Jerome probably refers to Alexander of Jerusalem who was a friend and defender of Origen; he died in 250 or 252.
15. Eusebius became bishop of Emesa in Macedonia circa 339. See Jerome's *Famous Men* (*De viris illustribus*) XCI, where he says that Eusebius wrote ten books on the Letter to the Galatians.
16. Theodore, bishop of Heraclea in Thrace, was an influential semi-Arian. The writings of Diodorus of Tarsus were once attributed to him.
17. Jerome, *Commentary on Paul's Letter to the Galatians* (*Commentariorum in epistolam ad Galatas libri tres*), Prologue: PL 26, 308-309.
18. *Ibid.* I, at 2:14: PL 26:342.

5. You, then, in order to avoid doing what I had asked, have found a new argument so that you claim that the Gentiles who believed in Christ were free from the burden of the law, but that those who became believers from among the Jews were subject to the law. In that way through the person of each of them Paul as the teacher of the nations correctly criticized those who observed the law, and Peter is criticized, who as the leader of the circumcised[19] commanded the Gentiles to do what only those who were from the Jews ought to have observed. If you want this, in fact, because you want that all who come to believe from the Jews *have the obligation of obeying the law* (Gal 5:3), you as a bishop renowned in the whole world ought to promulgate this view and bring all the bishops to agree with you. In my small cell with the monks, that is, my fellow sinners, I do not dare to decide important issues except to admit honestly that I have read the writings of my predecessors and have set forth various explanations in my commentaries in accord with the custom of all of them in order that each person may follow the view he wants from the many. I certainly think that you have read and approved this in worldly literature and in the books of God.

6. Origen first introduced this interpretation in the tenth book of his *Miscellany* where he explained Paul's Letter to the Galatians, and the other commentators followed him. They introduce it at least principally for the purpose of replying to the blaspheming Porphyry, who blamed the impudence of Paul for daring to criticize Peter, the leader of the apostles, and to accuse him to his face and to restrain him by argument, because he acted wrongly, that is, because he who accused the other of sinning was in the same error as he was. What shall I say of John who long ruled the church of Constantinople as bishop and composed a very lengthy book on this very chapter in which he followed the view of Origen and the ancients?[20] If you criticize me for being in error, allow me, please, to be in error with such men, and when you see that I have many companions in my error, you ought to produce at least one supporter of what you claim as the truth. This should suffice concerning the exposition of one chapter of the Letter to the Galatians.

7. But so that I do not seem to rely on the number of witnesses against your argument and to dodge the truth by help of illustrious men and not to dare to engage in a fight, I shall briefly set forth some examples from the scriptures. In the Acts of the Apostles *a voice spoke to Peter, saying, "Get up, Peter, kill and eat,"* that is, *all kinds of animals and reptiles and birds* (Acts 10:13.12). By that statement it is shown that no man is unclean by nature, but that all are equally called to the gospel of Christ. To this Peter replies, *"Heaven forbid! For I have never eaten anything common and unclean."* A second time a voice said to him, *"Do not call common what God has purified."* And so, he went to Caesarea and, having entered the house of Cornelius, he opened his mouth and said, *Truly I find*

---

19. See Gal 2:7-8.
20. See John Chrysostom, *Commentary on the Letter to the Galatians:* PG 61, 611-682.

that God shows no partiality, but in every nation one who fears him and acts righteously is acceptable to him (Acts 10:34-35). Then *the Holy Spirit descended upon them, and believers from among the circumcised, who had come with Peter, were astonished because the grace of the Holy Spirit had been poured out upon the Gentiles. Then Peter replied, "Can anyone deny us water to keep us from baptizing these people who have received the Holy Spirit, as we have?" And he ordered that they be baptized in the name of Jesus Christ. The apostles and the brethren who were in Judea, however, heard that the Gentiles had received the word of God. But when Peter went up to Jerusalem, those who came from the circumcision argued against him, saying, "Why have you entered the house of people who have not been circumcised and eaten with them?"* (Acts 10:44-45.47-48; 11:1-3). After he had explained to them the whole reason, finally he ended his speech with these words, *If, then, God has given the same grace to them as to us who believed in the Lord Jesus Christ, who am I to say no to God?" After they heard this, they were silent and glorified God, saying, "God, then, has given to the Gentiles repentance that they may have life"* (Acts 11:17-18). Again, much later when Paul and Barnabas came to Antioch, they reported after the church had gathered *the great things that God had done with them and that he had opened the doorway of faith for the Gentiles. But some coming from Judea taught the brethren and said, "Unless you are circumcised in accord with the custom of Moses, you cannot be saved." And so, after they had raised no small rebellion against Paul and Barnabas,* both the accused and their accusers *decided to go up to Jerusalem to the apostles and elders about this question, and when they had arrived in Jerusalem, certain of those from the sect of the Pharisees who had come to believe in Christ stood up and said, "They must be circumcised and commanded to observe the law of Moses,"* and a great dispute arose over this statement. *Peter,* with his usual frankness, *said, "Brothers, you know that in the early days God chose among us that the Gentiles should hear the word of the gospel through my lips and should believe and that God who knows hearts bore witness to them in giving the Holy Spirit to them, just as to us, and he made no distinction between them and us, purifying their hearts by faith. Now, then, why do you tempt God by imposing a yoke upon the neck of the disciples that neither our fathers nor we could carry? But we believe that we are saved through the grace of our Lord Jesus Christ, just as they are." The whole crowd, however, fell silent* (Acts 14:26; 15:1-2.4-5.7-12). And the apostle James and all the elders came over to his view at the same time.

8. It should not be troublesome to the reader, but useful to him and to me, that we prove that the apostle Paul was not previously ignorant that Peter was even the source of this decree that the law was not to be observed after the coming of the gospel.[21] Secondly, Peter had such great authority that Paul had written in his

---

21. See Acts 15:6-7, for the decision of the Council of Jerusalem.

letter, *Then after three years I came to Jerusalem to see Peter, and I remained with him for fifteen days* (Gal 1:18). And again in the following lines he said, *After fourteen years I again went up to Jerusalem with Barnabas and took Titus along as well, but I went up in accord with a revelation and explained to them the gospel that I preach among the Gentiles* (Gal 2:1-2). He showed that he did not have confidence in preaching the gospel until it was confirmed by the statement of Peter and of the others who were with him. There immediately follows: *Privately with those who seemed the leaders for fear that I was perhaps running or had run in vain* (Gal 2:2). Why privately and not in public? For fear of producing a scandal for the believers from the number of the Jews who thought that the law must be observed and that they should believe in the Lord and savior in that way. And so, even at the time when Peter came to Antioch,[22] though the Acts of the Apostles do not record this, but we have to believe Paul's statement, Paul writes that he resisted him to his face because he deserved a reprimand. *For, before certain men came from James, he ate with Gentiles, but after they had come, he withdrew and kept separate, fearing those who were from the circumcision. And the other Jews agreed with him so that Barnabas too was led astray by them in that hypocrisy. But when I saw*, he says, *that they were not acting correctly in relation to the truth of the gospel, I said to Peter in the presence of all: "If you live like a Gentile and not like a Jew, though you are a Jew, how do you force the Gentiles to live like Jews?"* (Gal 2:11-14), and so on. No one, then, has any doubt that the apostle Peter was the original author of this view that he is accused of violating. But the reason for the violation is the fear of the Jews; the scripture says, after all, that at first *he ate with the Gentiles, but after certain men had come from James, he withdrew and kept separate, fearing those who were from the circumcision* (Gal 2:12). He feared that the Jews, whose apostle he was, might abandon the faith of Christ because of the example of the Gentiles and that the imitator of the good shepherd might lose the flock entrusted to him.

9. Just as, then, we have shown that Peter approved of the abolition of the Mosaic law, but was forced by this fear to the pretense of observing it, let us see whether Paul who accused the other did something of the sort. We read in the same book: *But Paul traveled through Syria and Cilicia, building up the churches, and he came to Derbe and Lystra. And, look, a certain disciple was there by the name of Timothy, the son of a believing Jewish woman and a Gentile father. The brethren who were in Lystra and Iconium gave testimony to this man. Paul wanted him to go with him, and he took him and circumcised him on account of the Jews who were in those places. For everyone knew that his father was a Gentile* (Acts 15:41-16:3). O blessed apostle Paul, you who blamed the pretense in Peter because he withdrew from the Gentiles on account of fear of the

---

22. See Gal 2:11.

Jews who had come from James, why are you forced to circumcise Timothy, the son of a Gentile father and himself a Gentile, contrary to your view? After all, he was not a Jew who had not been circumcised. You will answer me: *On account of the Jews who were in those places.* You, therefore, who pardon yourself for the circumcision of a disciple coming from the Gentiles, pardon Peter as well, your predecessor, for having done some things out of fear of the Jewish believers. Again scripture says, *But after Paul had stayed many days, he said goodbye to the brethren and sailed to Syria, and Priscilla and Aquila went with him. And he shaved his head at Cenchreae, for he had made a vow* (Acts 18:18). Granted that he was forced in the former case to do some things that he did not want to do, why did he let his hair grow because of a vow and later shave it off according to the law, something that Nazarites were accustomed to do according to the law of Moses?[23]

10. But these things are minor in comparison with what follows. Luke, the author of the sacred history, reports: *When we had come to Jerusalem, the brethren welcomed us gladly,* and on the next day James and all the elders who were with him *approved his gospel and said to him, "You see, brother, how many thousands there are in Judea who have believed in Christ, and all these are zealous for the law. But they have heard about you that you teach the abandonment of Moses on the part of those Jews who live among the Gentiles, saying that they should not circumcise their sons nor live according to our custom. What is this, then? A large number must, of course, gather, for they will hear that you have come. Do, then, what we tell you. We have four men who have taken a vow about themselves. Take them with you, and sanctify yourself with them, and pay their expenses for shaving their heads, and all will know that what they have heard about you is false, but that you also live, observing the law." Then Paul took those men, and having purified himself with them on the next day, he entered the temple, announcing the completion of the days of purification until the sacrifice was offered for each of them* (Acts 21:17-18.20-24.26). O Paul, I ask you again about this. Why did you shave your head? Why did you process barefooted in the ceremonies of the Jews? Why did you offer sacrifices, and why were victims sacrificed for you according to the law? You will, of course, reply: "For fear that those who came to believe from the Jews might be scandalized." You pretended, therefore, to be a Jew in order to gain the Jews, and James and the other elders taught you this pretense. But you still could not escape. For after a disturbance arose when you were going to be killed, you were rescued by a tribune and sent by him to Caesarea under the careful guard of soldiers for fear that the Jews might kill you as someone who pretends to observe the law and who destroys it. And coming to Rome from there, in the inn where they brought

---

23. See Nm 6:18.

you, you preached Christ to the Jews and the Gentiles, and your sentence was upheld by the sword of Nero.[24]

11. We have learned that on account of fear of the Jews Peter and Paul both equally pretended to observe the commandments of the law. With what effrontery, then, with what audacity can Paul reprehend in another what he himself did? I, or rather others before me, explained the reason that they had in mind, not defending a useful lie, as you write, but teaching an honest form of diplomacy, in order to demonstrate the wisdom of the apostles and to hold in check the impudence of the blaspheming Porphyry. For he says that Paul and Peter fought with each other in a childish struggle and that Paul even burned with hatred for the virtues of Peter and boastfully wrote things that he either did not do or that, if he did do them, he did them impudently, since he reprimanded in Peter what he himself did. Those authors interpreted the passage as well as they could. How do you explain this passage? You will surely say something better since you have found fault with the view of the earlier writers.

4, 12. You write to me in the letter: "I, after all, should not instruct you how to understand the words of the same apostle, *I have become to the Jews like a Jew in order that I might gain the Jews* (1 Cor 9:20) and the other things that are said there out of merciful compassion, not out of false pretense. For he who cares for a sick person becomes like someone sick, not when he falsely states that he has a fever, but when with the mind of someone compassionate he thinks of how he would want to be cared for if he were ill. He was, after all, a Jew, but having become a Christian, he had not abandoned the sacraments of the Jews, which that people had suitably and legitimately received at the time when they were necessary. Therefore, he undertook their observance when he was already an apostle of Christ, but he did this in order to teach that they were not dangerous for those who wanted to observe them, as they had received them from their parents, even though they had come to believe in Christ, but that they should no longer place the hope of salvation in them. For the salvation that was signified by those sacraments had arrived through the Lord Jesus."[25] The sense of your whole discourse, which you dragged out with a very long argument, is that Peter did not make a mistake insofar as he thought that those who came to believe from the Jews should observe the law, but that he deviated from the right path because he forced the Gentiles to live like Jews. But he forced them, not by the command of a teacher, but by the example of his life. And Paul did not speak contrary to what he did, but wanted to know why Peter was forcing those who were from the Gentiles to live like Jews.

13. This is the essence of the question, in fact of your view, namely, that after the coming of the gospel of Christ Jewish believers act correctly if they observe

---

24. See Acts 23:23-24.
25. Letter 40, 4, 4.

the commandments of the law, that is, if they offer the sacrifices that Paul offered, if they circumcise their sons, if they keep the Sabbath, as Paul with Timothy and all the Jews have observed them. If this is true, we slip into the heresy of Cerinthus and of Ebion;[26] though they believed in Christ, they were condemned by our fathers for the sole reason that they mixed the ceremonies of the law with the gospel of Christ and professed the new teaching without giving up the old. What shall I say about the Ebionites who pretend that they are Christians? Up to the present there exists among the Jews in all the synagogues of the East a heresy that is called the heresy of the Minaei, and it is condemend by the Pharisees up to the present. They are commonly called Nazareans;[27] they believe that Christ, the son of God, was born of the Virgin Mary, and they say that he is the one who suffered under Pontius Pilate and rose, in whom we also believe. But insofar as they want to be both Jews and Christians, they are neither Jews nor Christians. I, therefore, beg you, who think that our little wound, an opening made by a pinprick, a mere nick, needs to be healed, to heal the wound of this opinion, which was inflicted by a lance of great weight.[28] After all, it is not the same crime to set forth the different views of the ancients in the explanation of the scriptures and to reintroduce into the Church a most criminal heresy. But if the necessity is imposed upon us to accept the Jews with their legal observances and if it will be permissible for them to observe in the churches of Christ what they practiced in the synagogues of Satan—I am going to say what I think—they will not become Christians, but will make us Jews.

14. After all, who among the Christians will patiently listen to what is contained in your letter: "Paul was a Jew, but having become a Christian, he had not abandoned the sacraments of the Jews, which that people had suitably and legitimately received at the time when they were necessary. Therefore, he undertook their observance when he was already an apostle of Christ, but he did this in order to teach that they were not dangerous for those who wanted to observe them, as they had received them from their parents."[29] Again I beg you that you hear my sorrow without becoming angry. Paul observed the ceremonies of the Jews though he was already an apostle of Christ, and you say that they are not dangerous for those who wanted to observe them as they received them from their parents. I, on the contrary, shall say and proclaim quite frankly, even if the whole world shouts against me, that the ceremonies of the Jews are dangerous and deadly for Christians and that whoever, whether from the Jews or from the Gentiles, observes them has descended into the pit of the devil. *For Christ is the end of the law for the justification of every believer* (Rom 10:4), that is, of the

---

26. For the heresies of Cerinthus and Ebion, see *Heresies* 8 and 10.
27. On the Nazareans, see *Heresies* 9.
28. Literally "with the weight of a phaleric lance." These were large javelins hurled down through the openings in towers.
29. Letter 40, 4, 4.

Jew and of the Gentile. For he will not be the end of the law for the justification of every believer if the Jew is an exception, and in the gospel we read: *The law and the prophets existed up to John the Baptist* (Lk 16:16; Mt 11:13). And in another passage we read: *On this account, then, the Jews sought the more to kill him, because he not only violated the Sabbath, but said that God was his father, making himself equal to God* (Jn 5:18). And again it says, *Of his fullness we have all received, grace in place of grace, because the law was given through Moses, but grace and the truth came through Jesus Christ* (Jn 1:16-17). Instead of the grace of the law, which is past, we have received the grace of the gospel, which remains, and instead of the shadows and images of the old testament the truth has come through Jesus Christ. Jeremiah also prophesied, speaking in the name of God: *Behold, the days will come, says the Lord, and I shall establish with the house of Judah and with the house of Israel a new testament, not according to the testament that I made with their fathers on the day when I took their hand to lead them out of the land of Egypt* (Jer 31:31-32). Notice what he says, for he does not promise the new testament of the gospel to the people of the Gentiles, with whom he had not made a testament, but to the people of the Jews, to whom he had given the law through Moses. He promises them a new testament in order that they might no longer live in the old condition of the law, but in the new condition of the spirit.[30] Paul, however, around whom this whole question centers, frequently sets forth statements of this sort, and for the sake of brevity I shall add only a few of them: *Look, I, Paul, say to you that, if you have yourselves circumcised, Christ does you no good* (Gal 5:2). Again he says, *You who are trying to justify yourselves by the law have been removed from Christ; you have fallen from grace* (Gal 5:4). And further on he says, *If you are led by the Spirit, you are no longer under the law* (Gal 5:18). From this it is clear that he who is under the law, not as matter of diplomacy, as our predecessors intended, but really, as you understand it, does not have that Holy Spirit. But we shall learn from God who teaches us the nature of the commandments of the law; he says, *I have given them commandments that were not good and ordinances by which they do not live* (Ex 20:25). We say these things, not in order to destroy the law like Mani and Marcion,[31] for we know that it is holy and spiritual, as the apostle says,[32] but because, after there came faith *and the fullness of time, God sent his own Son, born of a woman, born under the law, to redeem those who were under the law, in order that we might receive the adoption of children* (Gal 4:4-5) and in order that we might live, not under the schoolmaster,[33] but under an adult who is Lord and heir.

---

30. See 2 Cor 3:6.
31. For Mani and Marcion, see *Heresies* 46 and 22. Mani and Marcion both rejected the Old Testament.
32. See Rom 7:12.14.
33. See Gal 3:25.

15. There follows in your letter: "Hence, he did not correct Peter because he was observing the traditions of his forefathers. If he had wanted to do that, he would neither have lied nor acted inappropriately."[34] Again I say, "You are a bishop, a teacher of the churches of Christ; prove that what you say is true. Take one of the Jews who, after having become Christian, has his newly born son circumcised, who observes the Sabbath, who abstains from *foods that God created to be used with thanksgiving* (1 Tm 4:3), who sacrifices a lamb in the evening on the fourteenth day of the first month. When you do this, or rather when you do not do this—for I know that you are a Christian and will not do something sacrilegious—whether you want to or not, you will condemn your view, and then you will learn by hard work that it is more difficult to defend one's own views than to criticize those of others. And lest we perhaps might not believe or rather might not understand what you say—after all, a discourse dragged out in length often lacks intelligibility, and the ignorant criticize it less when they do not perceive its meaning—be persistent and explain this: "Paul had, then, abandoned the evil that the Jews held." What is the evil of the Jews that Paul abandoned? It is, of course, what follows: "That, *not knowing the righteousness of God and wanting to establish their own righteousness, they were not subject to the righteousness of God* (Rom 10:3); secondly, that, after the Passion and resurrection of Christ, when the sacrament of grace had been given and revealed *according to the order of Melchizedek* (Heb 6:20), they still thought that they should observe the old sacraments, not because of the habit of celebrating them, but because of their necessity for salvation. And yet, if they never had been necessary, the Maccabees would have become martyrs for them without purpose and without benefit.[35] Finally, the Jews persecuted the Christian preachers of grace as enemies of the Law. He says that he considered these and other such errors and vices *as losses and rubbish in order that he might gain Christ*" (Phil 3:8).[36]

16. We have learned from you the evils of the Jews that the apostle abandoned; again, from your teaching, let us learn what he held were their benefits. You say: "They are the ceremonies of the law, if they are observed following the custom of the fathers. In that way he himself observed them, not because of their being necessary for salvation."[37] I do not understand well enough what you want to say by, "Not because of their being necessary for salvation." After all, if they do not contribute to salvation, why are they observed? But if they should be observed, they, of course, contribute to salvation, especially those whose observance has produced martyrs. They would not be observed unless they contrib-

---

34. Letter 40, 4, 5.
35. See 2 Mc 7:1.
36. Letter 40, 4, 6.
37. *Ibid.*

uted to salvation. Nor are they some things that are indifferent between good and evil, as the philosophers argue. Self-control is good; dissoluteness is evil; something indifferent between them is walking, emptying the bowels, sneezing, spitting phlegm. These are neither good nor bad, for whether you do or do not do these actions, you have neither justice nor injustice. Observing the ceremonies of the law, however, cannot be something indifferent, but is either good or bad. You say that it is good; I say that it is bad, and bad not only for those who come from the Gentiles, but also for those who have come to believe from the Jews. Unless I am mistaken, while you avoid one problem in that passage, you fall into another. For, while you are afraid of the blasphemy of Porphyry,[38] you rush into the snares of Ebion, when you decree that these people who have come to believe from the Jews should observe the law. And because you understand that what you say is dangerous, you again try to moderate it with needless verbiage, "Not because of their being necessary for salvation, as the Jews thought they should be observed, or because of false pretense, something he reprehended in Peter."[39]

17. Peter, therefore, pretended to observe the law, but Paul, who reprimanded Peter, brazenly observed the practices of the law, for there follows in your letter: "For, if he observed those sacraments because he pretended that he was a Jew in order to gain them, why did he not also offer sacrifice with the Gentiles since he became like someone without the law for those who were without the law in order that he might gain them too?[40] Rather, he did that like someone who was a Jew by birth, and he said all this, not in order that he might deceitfully pretend that he was what he was not, but because he thought that he should mercifully help them in that way, as if he were laboring under the same error, not, of course, with the wiles of a liar, but with the feeling of compassion."[41] How well you succeed in defending Paul! For he did not pretend to be in the error of the Jews, but was really in that error. And he did not want to imitate Peter who was lying in order that he might hide what he was out of fear of the Jews, but stated with complete frankness that he was a Jew. Oh, the novel mercy of the apostle! While he wants to make Jews Christians, he himself became a Jew. After all, according to you, he could not have brought the dissolute to frugality unless he had proved himself to be dissolute, and he could not have mercifully come to the aid of the wretched unless he himself felt wretched. After all, they are truly wretched and to be wept over with mercy who make the apostle a Jew out of their stubbornness and out of their love for the law that has been abolished. Nor is there a great difference between my view and yours, for I say that out of fear of Jewish believers both Peter and Paul carried out, but only as a pretense, the command-

---

38. Porphyry, the great Neoplatonic philosopher, wrote *Against the Christians* (*Contra Christianos*), a work no longer extant.
39. Letter 40, 4, 6.
40. See 1 Cor 9:21.
41. Letter 40, 4, 6.

ments of the law. You, however, claim that they did this mercifully, "not with the wiles of a liar, but with the feeling of compassion."[42] Fine, as long as it is clear that they pretended to be what they were not. That argument that you use against us, namely, that he ought to have become a Gentile for the Gentiles, if he became a Jew for the Jews, works rather in our favor. For, just as he was not really a Jew, so he was not really a Gentile, and just as he was not really a Gentile, so he was not really a Jew. He was, however, an imitator of the Gentiles because he received the uncircumcised into the faith of Christ and permitted the indiscriminate eating of the foods that the Jews condemn, not, as you suppose, as part of the worship of idols.[43] *For in Christ neither circumcision nor the lack of circumcision counts for anything* (Gal 5:6 and 6:15), but the observance of the commandments of God.

18. I ask, therefore, and I beseech you again and again to pardon my little discussion and to blame yourself, if I have gone beyond the limit I set. For you forced me to reply and took away my eyes like those of Stesichorus. Do not suppose that I am a teacher of lies, for I follow Christ who said: *I am the way and the truth and the life* (Jn 14:6). Nor is it possible that, as a worshiper of the truth, I bend my neck to a lie. Do not stir up against me a crowd of the ignorant who reverence you as bishop and welcome you with the honor due to the priesthood as you preach in the church, but who look down on me as someone at the end of his years and almost decrepit, a man who pursues the privacy of the monastery and the countryside. Seek for yourself people to teach or to criticize. For the sound of your voice has hardly reached us who are separated from you by such great stretches of land and sea, and if you write a letter, let it be delivered to me to whom it should be sent before Italy and Rome receives it.

5, 19. In the other letters you ask why my first translation of the canonical books had asterisks and bars set before certain words, though I later published another translation without these signs.[44] I do not want to offend you, but you seem not to understand what you asked. For the former is the translation of the seventy translators,[45] and wherever there are bars, that is, obelisks, it means that the seventy said more than there is found in the Hebrew, but where there are asterisks, that is, bright stars, something was added by Origen from the edition of Theodotion.[46] And in that case we translated from the Greek, but in this case we expressed what we understood from the Hebrew, preserving at times the truth of the meaning rather than the order of the words. I am also surprised that you read the books of the seventy translators, not as they were originally published, but as

---

42. Letter 40, 4, 6.
43. See 1 Cor 8:1-2.
44. See Letter 71, 2-3.
45. The Septuagint version is so called because it was supposedly made by seventy translators.
46. Theodotion was a second century Jewish scholar who translated the Hebrew scriptures into Greek. Origen published his version in the sixth column of his *Hexapla*.

they were emended or corrupted by Origen with the obelisks and asterisks, while you do not follow the humble translation of a Christian, especially since Origen took those things that he added from the edition of a Jew and a blasphemer who came after the passion of Christ. If you want to be a true devotee of the seventy translators, do not read those words under the asterisks; rather, erase them from your volumes in order that you may show that you are a real fan of the old version. And if you do this, you are forced to condemn all the libraries of the churches. For we find scarcely one or two books that do not have them.

6, 20. Now, you say that I ought not to have made another translation after those old versions, and you use a novel syllogism: "The books that the seventy translated were either obscure or clear; if they were obscure, we have to believe that you also could be mistaken in them, but if they were clear, it is obvious that they could not have been mistaken in them."[47] I reply to you with your own argument: All the old commentators, who came before us in the Lord and who translated the holy scriptures, translated either what was obscure or what was clear. If they translated what was obscure, how do you dare to explain after them what they were not able to explain? But if they translated what was clear, it is needless for you to have wanted to explain what they could not have missed, especially in the explanation of the Psalms.[48] Among the Greeks they were explained in many volumes, first by Origen, secondly by Eusebius of Caesarea, thirdly by Theodore of Heraclea, fourthly by Asterius of Scythopolis, fifthly by Apollinaris of Laodicea, sixthly by Didymus of Alexandria.[49] There are also said to be works of others on a few psalms, but we are now speaking of the entire book of the psalms. Among the Latins, however, Hilary of Poitiers and Eusebius, the bishop of Vercelli, have translated Origen and Eusebius, and our Ambrose has followed Origen in certain of the psalms.[50] Let Your Wisdom answer me why after such great and so many commentators on the psalms you have different ideas. For, if the psalms are obscure, we have to believe that you also could be mistaken in them, but if they are clear, we believe that they could not have been mistaken about them. And in this way your commentary will be superfluous on both counts, and by this rule no one will dare to speak after earlier writers, and a writer will not have the freedom to write on anything on which another author has

---

47. Jerome takes the argument from Letter 28, 2, 2; he slightly changes Augustine's words.
48. Augustine was composing his *Expositions of the Psalms* and had sent some examples to Jerome.
49. For Origen's *Homilies on the Psalms*, see PG 12, 1053-1685; for Eusebius' *Commentaries on the Psalms*, see PG 23 65-1396. The work of Didorus of Tarsus was first attributed to Theodore of Heraclea. For Asterius, see G. Bardy, "Aristerius le sophiste," *Revue d'historie ecclesiastique* (1926) 221-272, for some fragments. For Didymus, see PG 39, 1155-1616, for various fragments. There are no extant writings of Apollinaris.
50. For Hilary's *Treatise on the Psalms*, see PL 9, 231-908; the translation of Eusebius of Caesarea's commentary on the Psalms by Eusebius of Vercelli has been lost. For Ambrose, see his *Homilies on Twelve Psalms* and *Explanation of Psalm 118* in PL 14:921-1526.

worked. On the contrary, it ought to be a mark of your humanity also to pardon others on a point on which you pardon yourself. For I have not so much tried to do away with the older works, which I corrected and translated from the Greek into Latin for people of my tongue, as to bring into the open those testimonies that the Jews passed over or corrupted, in order that our people might know what the original Hebrew contains. If anyone does not want to read it, no one is going to force him against his will. Let him drink the old wine with its sweetness and reject our new wine, which has been published to explain the earlier translations. In that way, where those are not understood, they may become clearer as a result of our works. The sort of commentary to be followed with the holy scriptures is explained by the book I wrote on the best kind of commentary and by the short prefaces to the books of God that we put at the beginning of our edition. I think that the wise reader ought to be referred to them. And if, as you say, you accept my work in the emendation of the New Testament and explain the reason why you accept it, namely, because very many who have the knowledge of the Greek language can judge my work, you ought to have believed that there is the same integrity in the Old Testament, because we have not made up any words of our own, but have translated the words of God, as we found them in the Hebrew. If you have doubts, ask the Hebrews.

21. You will object: What if the Hebrews either refuse to reply or choose to lie? Will all the Jews, as numerous as they are, remain silent about my translation? Will we be able to find no one who has knowledge of the Hebrew language? Or will they all imitate those Jews who, you say, were found in Africa and conspired to slander me? For in your letter you weave together a story of this sort. "For, when a certain brother bishop of ours began to have your translation read in the church over which he presides, a particular passage in the prophet Jonah caused a disturbance because it was presented in far different language than had become familiar to the senses and memory and had been chanted for so many ages. There was produced so great an uproar among the people, especially when the Greeks brought accusations and enkindled the charge of falsification, that the bishop—this took place in the city of Oea[51]—was forced to demand the testimony of Jews. But, whether out of ignorance or out of malice, they replied that what both the Greek and Latin texts had and said was found in the Hebrew books. What then? The man was forced to correct the text as if it were incorrect, since he did not want to be left without any people after the grave crisis. Hence, it seems to us as well that you could have been mistaken at times on some points."[52]

7, 22. You say that I incorrectly translated a passage in Jonah and that a bishop almost lost his priesthood because of the rebellion of the people who were crying

---

51. The modern city of Tripoli in Lybia.
52. Letter 71, 3, 5.

out on account of the discrepancy of one word. And you hold back what it is that I mistranslated, taking from me the chance to defend myself out of fear that whatever you say may be demolished by my response. But after many years "gourd plant" turned up when a Cornelius and an Asinius Pollio[53] of that time stated that I translated "ivy" instead of "gourd plant." We replied quite extensively on this point in the commentary on Jonah and are content now to say only that in that passage where the seventy translators translated "gourd plant" and Aquila along with the others translated "ivy," that is, Κιττόν, it has "*ciceion*" written in the Hebrew text, which the Syrians commonly call "*ciceiam*." It is a type of bush having wide leaves like a vine, and when it is planted, it quickly grows into a small tree, holding itself up by its own trunk without the help of any stakes or poles that gourd plants and ivy need. If I had chosen to translate it as "*ciceion*," rendering the word literally, no one would understand; if I translated it as "gourd plant," I would say what is not found in the Hebrew. I used "ivy" in order to be in agreement with the other translators. But if your Jews, as you claim, said out of malice or ignorance that this is found in the Hebrew books, it is evident that they either do not know the Hebrew language or wanted to lie in order to mock the gourd-lovers. At the end of this letter I beg you not to force an old man now at rest and a former veteran to go to war and again to risk his life. You, who are a young man and have been raised to the height of the episcopacy, go, teach the peoples and enrich the houses of Rome with the new harvest from Africa. For me it is enough to whisper in a corner of the monastery with a poor fellow who listens and reads.

---

53. That is, descendants of these men who were severe critics in Roman history.

Letter 76

At the end of 403 Augustine wrote to the Donatists this letter, which lacks a salutation and in which he spoke to them in the name of the Catholic Church. He first exhorts them to return to the unity of the Catholic Church (paragraph 1). He accuses the Donatists of trying to separate the grain from the weeds before the harvest, while he points out the inconsistency in the Donatist practice (paragraph 2). For the Donatists have accepted back into their communion the Maximianists whom they had previously condemned (paragraph 3). In closing, he again emphasizes the inconsistency of the Donatists' schism (paragraph 4).

1. To you, Donatists, the Catholic Church says, *Sons of men, how long will you be heavy of heart? Why do you love vanity and search for a lie?* (Ps 4:3). Why have you divided yourselves from the unity of the whole world by your wicked sacrilege of schism? You pay attention to false statements, which human beings who are either lying or in error speak to you, concerning the handing over of the divine books so that you die in your heretical separation. And you do not pay attention to what those books say to you so that you might live in the Catholic peace. Why do you open your ears to the words of human beings who say what they could never prove, while you are deaf to the words of God who says, *The Lord said to me, "You are my son; this day I have begotten you. Ask me, and I shall give you the nations as your inheritance and the ends of the earth as your possession"* (Ps 2:7)? *The promises were made to Abraham and to his descendant. It does not say: To his descendants, as if to many, but as if to one: To his descendant, that is, to Christ* (Gal 3:16). He says, *In your descendant all the nations will be blessed* (Gn 22:18). Raise up the eyes of your heart, and consider the whole world and see how all the nations are blessed in the offspring of Abraham. Then people believed about that one offspring what they did not yet see; now you yourselves see him, and still you refuse to see him. The Passion of the Lord is the price paid for the world; he redeemed the whole world, and you are not in agreement with the whole world to your gain, but rather argue to your loss for your sect in order to destroy the whole. Hear in the psalm of the price by which we have been redeemed; it says, *They have pierced my hands and my feet; they have counted all my bones. But they have looked at me and gazed upon me; they have divided my clothes and cast lots over my coat* (Ps 22:17-19). Why do you want to divide the clothes of the Lord? Why do you not want to hold along with the whole world onto that tunic of love woven from the top down? In the psalm itself we read that the whole world holds onto it; it says, *All the ends of the earth will remember and turn to the Lord, and all the families of the nations will adore before his eyes, because his is the kingdom and he will be lord over the nations* (Ps 22:28-29). Open the ears of your heart and hear, because *the God of*

gods, the Lord, has spoken and has called the earth from the rising of the sun to its setting; from Zion has gone forth the perfection of his beauty (Ps 50:1-2). If you refuse to understand this, listen to the gospel where the Lord now speaks by his own lips and says, *For it was necessary that all the things written about Christ in the law and the prophets be fulfilled and that penance and the forgiveness of sins be preached in his name through all the nations, beginning from Jerusalem* (Lk 24:44.47). The words of the psalm, *He called the earth from the rising of the sun to its setting*, correspond to those in the gospel, *Through all the nations*, and the words in the psalm, *From Zion has gone forth the perfection of his beauty*, correspond to the words of the gospel, *Beginning from Jerusalem*.

2. You imagine that you escape the weeds before the time of the harvest, because you are nothing but weeds. For if you were grain, you would tolerate the weeds that are mixed in and would not split yourselves off from the crop of Christ. Of the weeds it was, of course, said, *Because injustice will abound, the faith of many will grow cold*, and of the wheat it was said, *The one who perseveres up to the end will be saved* (Mt 24:12-13). Why do you believe that the weeds have increased and filled the world, but that the wheat has decreased and remains only in Africa? You say that you are Christians, and you contradict Christ. He said, *Allow them both to grow until the harvest* (Mt 13:30); he did not say, "Let the weeds increase, and let the grain decrease." He said, *The field is the world*; he did not say, "The field is Africa." He said, *The harvest is the end of the world*; he did not say, "The harvest is the time of Donatus." He said, *The harvesters are the angels*; he did not say, "The harvesters are leaders of the Circumcellions."[1] And because you accuse the wheat in defense of the weeds, you have proved that you are weeds, and what is worse, you have separated yourselves from the wheat ahead of time. For some of your predecessors, in whose sacrilegious schism you continue to be, handed over the holy books and vessels of the Church as we read in the municipal records, and some of your predecessors forgave them when they admitted it and were in communion with them. And both groups assembled at Carthage in a splinter council filled with fury; they condemned people without a hearing for the crime of surrendering the books, about which they had already come to an agreement among themselves. They ordained a bishop over against a bishop, and they raised up an altar against an altar.[2] Afterward they sent a letter to the emperor, Constantine, in order that bishops from across the sea might decide the case between Africans. When they were granted the judges for whom they asked and who decided the case at Rome, they did not obey them, and they accused the bishops before the emperor as if

---

1. The Circumcellions were bands of Donatist fanatics, who wandered from one shrine to another, often causing destruction and serious harm to Catholics.
2. The council was held in 312 under Secundus, bishop of Tigisi in Numidia; in it Majorinus was elected as the Donatist bishop in opposition to Caecilian, the Catholic bishop.

they decided the case wrongly.[3] They again appealed to the emperor from the decision of other bishops who had been sent to Arles,[4] and having had their case heard by him and found to be liars, they remained in their same crime. Be on watch for your salvation; love peace; return to the unity. When you are willing, we will read out for you all these things as they were done.

3. They are in communion with evil persons who consent to the action of evil persons, not those who tolerate the weeds in the Lord's field up to the harvest or the chaff until the last winnowing. If you hate evil persons, remove yourselves from the crime of schism. If you feared being mingled with the evil, you would not have for so many years kept Optatus living among you in perfectly obvious sinfulness.[5] Now you call him a martyr; it only remains for you to call him Christ, who died on his account. Finally, how has the Christian world offended you from which you have cut yourselves off in your wicked fury? And how have the Maximianists merited so well from you?[6] They were condemned by you, and they were forced from their basilicas through the civil courts. But you again received them back in their dignities. How did the peace of Christ offend you so that in opposition to it you separate yourselves from those whose reputation you blacken? And how did the peace of Donatus merit so well from you that in defense of it you welcome back those whom you condemn? Felician of Musti is now with you. We read in the municipal records that he was previously condemned in your council and was afterwards accused by you in the court of the proconsul and attacked by you in the city of Musti.[7]

4. If the surrender of the books is criminal, because God punished with death in war the king who burned the book of Jeremiah,[8] how much more criminal is the sacrilege of schism, whose authors, to whom you compare the Maximianists, the earth opened for and swallowed alive![9] How, then, do you charge us with the crime of surrendering the books, a charge that you do not prove, while you condemn and receive back your own schismatics? If you are righteous because you suffered persecution through the emperors, the Maximianists are more righteous than you, for you yourselves persecuted them through the judges sent by the Catholic emperors. If you alone have baptism, what effect does the baptism of the Maximianists have among you upon those whom Felician baptized after having been condemned and with whom he was afterwards welcomed back to you? Let your bishops reply to these questions, at least to your lay persons, if

---

3. The council was held under Pope Mechiades on 10 February 313.
4. The synod of Arles on 8 January 314 upheld the acquittal of Caecilian.
5. Optatus was the Donatist bishop of Thamugadi from 388 to 398; he died in prison soon after the suppression of the revolt of Gildo.
6. For the Maximianists who broke away from the Donatists in 393, see Letter 43, 9, 26.
7. Felicianus of Musti broke away from the Donatists with the Maximianists, but was received back by the Donatists.
8. See Jer 36:23-30.
9. See Nm 16:31-33.

they do not want to speak to us, and for your own salvation consider what it means that they are unwilling to speak with us. If the wolves held a council in order not to reply to the shepherds, why have the sheep lost their good sense so that they enter the lairs of the wolves?

Letter 77

Between 401 and 408 Augustine wrote to Felix and Hilarinus, two Catholic laymen of Hippo, concerning the scandal that had arisen concerning the priest, Boniface, and the monk, Spes. Augustine urges Felix and Hilarinus not to be disturbed by scandals in the Church since the Lord has foretold that they would occur (paragraph 1). He further explains that he will not remove the name of Boniface from the list of his priests since he has not been proven guilty and since the case has been referred to the judgment of God (paragraph 2). The following letter adds further information about the case.

To his most beloved lords and rightly honorable brothers, Felix and Hilarinus, Augustine sends greetings in the Lord.

1. I am not surprised that Satan disturbs the hearts of the faithful; resist him, while remaining in the hope of the promises of God, who cannot deceive. He not only has deigned to promise eternal rewards to us who believe and hope in him and persevere in his love up to the end, but also foretold that there will be temporal scandals by which our faith must be exercised and tested. For he says, *Because injustice will abound, the love of many will grow cold*, but he immediately adds, *But whoever perseveres up to the end will be saved* (Mt 24:12). Why, then, is it surprising that human beings speak evil of the servants of God, and since they cannot ruin their life, they try to destroy their reputation, for they do not cease daily to blaspheme against their very God and Lord, when they are displeased by whatever he does against their will by his just and hidden judgment? For this reason I exhort Your Wisdom, my most beloved lords and rightly honorable brothers, that you ponder with a fully Christian heart the scripture of God, who has foretold to us that all these things would happen and warned us to be strong in opposition to them and in opposition to the slanderous gossip and rash suspicions of human beings.

2. In brief, then, I say to Your Charity that I have not discovered the priest Boniface to be in any sin and that I by no means believe or have believed anything of the sort about him. How, then, could I order that his name be removed from the list of the priests since the gospel causes us deep fear where the Lord says, *In the judgment by which you have judged you will be judged* (Mt 7:2)? For, since the case that has arisen between him and Spes[1] is pending upon God's judgment in accord with their decision, which can be read out to you, if you wish, who am I that I should dare to anticipate the judgment of God by removing or suppressing his name? I as a bishop ought not rashly to have

---

1. Spes was a monk from Augustine's monastery; see the following Letter.

suspected anything evil about him, and I as a human could not clearly judge about the hidden actions of human beings. After all, in secular cases when the judgment is referred to a higher authority, we await that decision, while everything else remains as it was. For this reason it is not now permitted to challenge it for fear that an injustice may be done to the higher judge, if something were changed while his judgment was pending. And there is, of course, a big difference between divine authority and even the very highest human authority. May the mercy of the Lord our God never abandon you, my most beloved lords and honorable brothers.

Letter 78

Between 401 and 408 Augustine wrote to his monks, the clergy, and the faithful of Hippo. A monk from Augustine's monastery by the name of Spes, when accused of a sexual sin by Boniface, a priest of the same monastery, in turn accused Boniface. Somehow the charges became public knowledge. Hence, Augustine wrote to his flock that the Lord had foretold that scandals would arise in order that people would not give up hope when they see them occurring (paragraph 1). Augustine tells his people that they should grieve over such a scandal, but not so that their love grows cold (paragraph 2). He explains that, since he could not determine the truth of the matter, he is sending the two to the shrine of Felix of Nola where God has in the past made known the truth of such situations (paragraph 3). He explains that God may have permitted the case to become public in order that the people might join him in praying for its proper resolution; meanwhile, he does not want to remove the name of Boniface from the list of the clergy (paragraph 4). Augustine warns his people against believing rumors and judging ahead of time (paragraph 5). He asks his people not to add to his sorrow by believing that all priests and monks sin because one has sinned, if he in fact has sinned (paragraph 6). He explains that he had tried to keep the matter quiet to spare them sorrow and temptation (paragraph 7). He admonishes some of his people who boasted that no Catholics had fallen away like two Donatist deacons who had committed apostasy, and that they should not boast in that manner (paragraph 8). He closes by pointing out that he has nowhere found better men than in the monasteries and that he has also found none worse than monks who fell (paragraph 9).

Augustine sends greetings in the Lord to his most beloved brothers, the clergy, the elders, and all the people of the church of Hippo, whom I serve in the love of Christ.

1. I wish that you had your mind carefully intent upon the scriptures and did not need the help of our words over any scandals and that he who also consoles us might rather console you. He foretold not only the good things with which he was going to repay his holy and faithful people, but also the evils with which this world was going to abound. And he took care that they were written down beforehand in order that we might look forward to the good things that are going to follow after the end of the world with more certitude than we experience the evils that were similarly foretold as coming before the end of the world. For this reason the apostle says, *For whatever was written before was written for our instruction in order that through patience and the consolation of the scriptures we might have hope in God* (Rom 15:4). But what need was there for the Lord Jesus himself not only to say, *Then the righteous will shine like the sun in the kingdom of their Father* (Mt 13:43), something that will be realized after the end of the world, but also to cry out, *Woe to the world because of scandals* (Mt 18:7)?

303

He said this so that we would not fool ourselves into thinking that we can come to the thrones of eternal happiness in any other way than by not giving up when we are tried by temporal evils. What need was there to say, *Because injustice will become abundant, the love of many will grow cold* (Mt 24:12)? He said this only so that those of whom he was speaking when he added, *But whoever perseveres up to the end will be saved* (Mt 24:13), would not be upset when they saw love growing cold because of the abundance of injustice and would not become frightened and would not give up, because they were saddened as if by events that were unexpected and unforeseen. Rather, when they see that those events that he predicted would come before the end are taking place, they would patiently persevere up to the end in order that they might in confidence merit to reign after the end in that life that does not have an end.

2. Hence, my dearest people, in this scandal because of which some are disturbed about the priest, Boniface, I do not say to you that you should not grieve. For the love of Christ is not present in those who do not grieve over these things. But the malice of the devil abounds in those who rejoice over such things. It is not that we see something in the priest we mentioned that should be judged worthy of condemnation; rather, it is that two men from our house have such a case that one of them is considered to be undoubtedly wicked, and the reputation of the other is bad among certain people and doubtful among others, even if his conscience is not blackened. Grieve over these things because they should be grieved over, still not so that because of that grief your love grows cold in living well, but so that it is inflamed to beseech the Lord. In that way, if your priest is innocent, as I am inclined to believe, because, when he perceived the impure and unclean passion of the other, he wanted neither to consent nor to remain silent, the judgment of God may quickly restore him to his ministry, once he has been proven to be innocent. But if he has some sin on his conscience, something I do not dare to suspect, and wanted to injure the reputation of the other, since he could not defile his chastity, as the other with whom he has this case says, the Lord will not permit him to conceal his wickedness. Rather, what human beings cannot discover will be made manifest by God's judgment concerning one or the other of them.

3. For this case tormented me for a long time, and I did not find a way to prove one of the two guilty, though I was more inclined to believe the priest. I had thought first of all to leave both of them to God's judgment until something should emerge in the one of them whom I had suspected because of which he would be thrown out of our house with just and clear reason. But he was most insistently trying to be raised to the clerical state either here by me or elsewhere by my letters, and I was by no means inclined to impose hands in ordination on that man whom I suspect of so great a sin or to present him to some brother of mine with my recommendation. Hence, he began to act in a more unruly manner in order that, if he were not raised to the clerical state, the priest, Boniface, would

not be allowed to remain in his office. At this provocation I saw that Boniface did not want to cause a scandal to any persons who were weak and inclined to suspicion concerning the doubtfulness of his life and was ready to suffer the loss of his office before human beings rather than uselessly to go on to disturb the church in that struggle in which he could not prove his good conscience to people who were ignorant and doubtful and more inclined toward suspicion. Hence, I chose a middle path, namely, that both of them should bind themselves by a firm agreement to go to a holy place where the awesome acts of God might more readily disclose the bad conscience of anyone and might compel him to confession because of punishment or fear. God is, of course, everywhere, and he who created all things is not contained or enclosed by any place, and he must be adored by his true adorers in spirit and in truth,[1] in order that, hearing in secret, he may also justify and crown them in secret. With regard, nonetheless, to these actions of God that are visibly known to human beings, who can search out his plan as to why these miracles occur in some places and do not occur in others? For the holiness of the place where Blessed Felix of Nola's body is buried, where I wanted them to go, is very well known to many. For whatever God made manifest there about one of them could more easily and more faithfully be recorded for us. For we knew at Milan at the tomb of the saints, where the demons confessed in a miraculous and terrifying way, that a certain thief, who had come to that place in order to deceive by swearing falsely, was forced to confess his theft and to return what he had taken. Is not Africa filled with the bodies of holy martyrs? And, nonetheless, we know that such things do not happen anywhere here. As the apostle says, *Not all* the saints *have the gift of healing, nor do all have the discernment of spirits* (1 Cor 12:30.10); in the same way God, who distributes his gifts as he wills,[2] did not want that these things should occur at all the tombs of the saints.

4. Hence, though I did not want this most heavy grief of my heart to be brought to your attention for fear that I might upset you by saddening you terribly and uselessly, God did not want this to be concealed from you, perhaps in order that you might devote yourselves to prayer along with us in order that he might deign to make known to us too what he himself knows in this case, but we cannot know. I have, however, not dared either to cancel or to remove the name of the priest from the number of his colleagues for fear that I might seem to do injury to the authority of God under whose scrutiny the case is still pending, if I wanted to anticipate his judgment by my own prior judgment. Nor do judges do this in worldly concerns when a doubtful case is referred to a higher authority, not daring to make any change while a decision is pending. And it was decided in the council of bishops that no cleric who had not been proven guilty ought to be

---

1. See Jn 4:23.
2. See 1 Cor 12:11.

suspended from communion unless he does not present himself for the examination of his case.[3] Boniface, nonethless, has accepted this humiliation to the point that he has not received letters by which he might ask for the respect due to his office on his journey in order that in that place where they are both unknown equality might be preserved with regard to both. And now, if you do not want his name to be read out in the list of priests for fear that we give a pretext to those who do not want to enter the Church—as the apostle says, to those who are looking for a pretext[4]—that action will not be due to us, but to those because of whom it was done. For what harm does it do a man if human ignorance does not want his name to be read out from that list, provided a bad conscience does not remove him from the book of the living?[5]

5. Hence, my brothers who fear the Lord, remember what Peter says, *For your enemy, the devil, goes around like a roaring lion, seeking whom he may devour* (1 Pt 5:8). He tried to ruin the reputation of one whom he cannot devour by leading him into wickedness in order that, if possible, he may lose courage because of the insults of human beings and the detraction of wicked tongues and in that way fall into his jaws. But if he cannot spoil even the reputation of an innocent person, he tries to persuade him to judge his brother through evil suspicions in order that the devil may swallow him up once he has been ensnared in that way. And who is able to grasp or to list all his wiles and deceits? Against these three that pertain to the present case, first, so that we may not be led into wickedness by imitating bad examples, God speaks to us through the apostle, *Do not carry the yoke with unbelievers, for what does justice have in common with injustice? Or what share does light have with darkness?* (2 Cor 6:14). He likewise says in another passage, *Do not be misled; evil conversations corrupt good morals. Be sober and righteous; do not sin* (1 Cor 15:33-34). But in order that you might not lose courage because of the tongues of detractors, God said through the prophet, *Listen to me, you who know justice, my people, in whose heart is found my law. Do not fear the insults of human beings, and do not be overcome by their detraction. Do not consider it important that they scorn you. For they will be worn out through time like a garment, and they will be eaten like wool by a moth. But my righteousness remains forever* (Is 41:7-8). But now so that you do not perish because of an evil heart by having false suspicions concerning servants of God, bear in mind those words of the apostle where he says, *Do not judge anything ahead of time before the Lord comes and illumines what is hidden in darkness, and he will reveal the thoughts of the heart, and then each one will have praise from God* (1 Cor 4:5). Also bear in mind the words of

---

3. See the Third Council of Carthage, canons 7 and 8, held in 397.
4. See 2 Cor 11:12.
5. See Ps 69:29.

scripture, *The things that are evident belong to you, but those that are hidden belong to God* (Dt 29:29).

6. It is evident, of course, that these things do not happen in the Church without grave sadness on the part of the saints and the faithful. May he, nonetheless, console us who foretold all these things and admonished us not to grow cold because of the abundance of injustice, but to persevere up to the end in order that we might be saved.[6] For, as far as I am concerned, if there is in me the least love of Christ, *who of you is weak and I am not weak? Who of you is scandalized and I do not burn?* (2 Cor 11:29). Do not, therefore, increase my torments by losing courage either over false suspicions or over the sins of others. Do not, I beg you, for fear that I should say of you, *And they added to the pain of my wounds* (Ps 69:27). For we bear much more easily those who rejoice over these sorrows of ours, which the psalmist foretold so long ago in the person of the body of Christ, when he said: *Those who sat in the gate have spoken insults against me, and those who drank wine have sung songs against me* (Ps 69:13), and we have learned to pray even for them and to will what is good for them. After all, for what else do they sit there and what else do they aim at but that, when any bishop or cleric or monk or nun has fallen, they believe that all of them are like that, spread it about, and argue that it is true, though all of them cannot be shown to be like that? And, nonetheless, when some married woman is found to be an adulteress, they do not throw out their own wives, nor do they accuse their mothers. But when some crime, even if it is not true, is spoken of or when a real crime is revealed concerning some of those who make a profession of holiness, they insist, make every effort, and strive that people believe this about all of them. It is easy, then, to compare those who seek pleasure for their evil tongue from our sorrows to those dogs—if they are perhaps to be understood in a bad sense—who licked the wounds of that poor man who lay before the door of the rich man and who endured all sort of toil and indignities until he came to rest in the bosom of Abraham.[7]

7. Do not torment me anymore, you who have some hope in God; do not multiply those wounds that they lick, you for whom we are in peril at every moment, having battles on the outside and fears within, perils in the city, perils in the desert, perils from the pagans, perils from false brethren.[8] I know that you feel sorrow, but do you feel more bitter sorrow than I do? I know that you are upset, and I fear that amid the tongues of the detractors the weak will fail and perish, the weak for whom Christ died.[9] Let not our sorrow be increased because of you, because your sorrow was not produced by our sin. After all, this is what I

6. See Mt 24:12 and 11:22.
7. See Lk 16:20-22.
8. See 2 Cor 7:5 and 11:26.
9. See 1 Cor 8:11.

tried to avoid, namely, that, if it were possible, we should neither neglect nor bring to your attention this evil to be avoided over which the strong are uselessly tormented and the weak are dangerously disturbed. But may he who has permitted that you be tested by this knowledge give to you the strength to endure it and may he educate you by his law; may he teach you and make less difficult these evil days until the pit is dug for the sinner.[10]

8. I hear that some of you are saddened over this more than over the apostasy of those two deacons who had come to you from the sect of Donatus. You acted as if they brought disgrace upon the school of Proculeian,[11] when you boasted of us that nothing of the sort had come about in the clerics from our school. Whoever of you did this, I tell you, you did not act correctly. Look, God taught you *that he who boasts should boast in the Lord* (1 Cor 1:31). You should raise as objections to the heretics only that they are not Catholics. Otherwise, you will be like those who, since they do not have any defense in the issue of their separation, try only to gather up the crimes of human beings and spread about more of them in lies. Since they cannot accuse or obscure the truth of the divine scripture, which teaches that the Church of Christ is spread everywhere, they portray the men who preach this as hateful and make up about them whatever comes into their mind. But you did not come to know Christ in that way, if you listened to him and were taught in him.[12] He, of course, makes his faithful secure even from evil ministers who commit their own sins, but speak of his gifts, where he says, *Practice what they say, but do not do what they do. For they preach, but they do not practice* (Mt 23:3). Pray, of course, for me for fear that I may perhaps be found to be rejected after preaching to others,[13] but when you boast, boast not in me, but in the Lord. For however vigilant may be the discipline of my monastery, I am human, and I live among human beings. Nor do I dare to claim for myself that my monastery is better than the ark of Noah where among eight persons one was found to be rejected[14] or better than the house of Abraham where it was said, *Cast out the handmaid and her son* (Gn 21:10) or better than the house of Isaac of whose twins it was said, *I have loved Jacob, but I hated Esau* (Mal 1:2). Nor is my monastery better than the house of Jacob himself where a son defiled with incest the bed of his father,[15] nor better than the house of David whose son slept with his sister[16] and whose other son rebelled against the holy gentleness of his father,[17] nor better than the dwelling of the apostle Paul. For, if he dwelled only

---

10. See Ps 94:12-13.
11. Proculeian was the Donatus bishop of Hippo.
12. See Eph 4:20-21.
13. See 1 Cor 9:27.
14. See Gn 7:13 and 9:22-27.
15. See Gn 49:4.
16. See 2 Sm 13:14.
17. See 2 Sm 15:12.

among the good, he would not have said, *Fights on the outside, fears on the inside* (2 Cor 7:5), nor would he have said when he was speaking of the holiness and faith of Timothy, *I have no one who is genuinely concerned about you. Everyone is seeking his own interests, not those of Jesus Christ* (Phil 2:20-21). Nor is my monastery better than the dwelling of the very Lord Christ in which eleven good men put up with the disloyal and thieving Judas, nor better finally than heaven from which the angels fell.

9. I, however, simply confess to Your Charity before the Lord our God, who is witness to my soul, that from the time I began to be a servant of God, just as I have with difficulty come to know any better persons than those who have made progress in monasteries, so I have not come to know worse people than those who have fallen in monasteries. As a result I think that the Apocalypse says of this, *The righteous will become more righteous, and the impure will further become impure* (Rv 22:11). Hence, even if we are saddened by some filth, we are, nonetheless, also consoled by many jewels. Do not, then, because of the watery waste that offends your eyes despise the olive press which fills the medicine chest of the Lord with the fruit of clear oil. May the mercy of the Lord our God guard you, my most beloved brethren, in his peace against all the attacks of the enemy.

Letter 79

In 404 Augustine wrote this letter, which lacks a salutation, to a certain unidentified Manichean priest. From 7 to 12 December 404 Augustine debated with Felix the Manichee, and it is possible that the present letter was addressed to Felix. He challenges his addressee either to resolve the question that Augustine had proposed to Fortunatus in the debate held with him or to leave Hippo and not return.

In vain do you hang back since from a distance it is clear what sort of person you are. The brothers have indicated to me what they discussed with you. It is good that you do not fear death, but you ought to fear that death that you bring upon yourself by blaspheming against God. You understand that this visible death, with which all human beings are familiar, is the separation of the mind from the body. It is not a great achievement to understand that. But you add on your own that it is a separation of good from evil. If the mind is something good and the body something evil, he who joined them together is not good. He, therefore, is either evil or was afraid of evil. Do you boast that you do not fear human beings, though you fashion for yourself such a god who was so afraid of the darkness that he joined good and evil together? Do not, however, be proud of heart because, as you wrote, we consider you important because we want to ward off your poisons so that your plague does not spread to more people. After all, the apostle did not consider those people important whom he called dogs, when he said, *Beware of the dogs* (Phil 3:2). Nor did he consider those people important whose words he said spread like a cancer.[1] And so I order you in the name of Christ that[2]. . . if you are prepared, resolve the question over which your predecessor, Fortunatus, failed.[3] And he left here on the condition that he would not return unless, after having had a discussion with his people, he found something that he could reply to the contrary in discussion with our brothers. But if you are not prepared for this, depart from here, and do not pervert the ways of the Lord and lay snares to kill weak souls with poisons. Otherwise, with the help of the right hand of our Lord you will be ashamed as you had never dreamed.

---

1. See 2 Tm 2:17.
2. There is a lacuna in the text.
3. Augustine debated Fortunatus at Hippo on 29 August 392.

Letter 80

Toward the end of 404 or the beginning of 405 Augustine wrote to Paulinus, the future bishop of Nola, and his wife, Therasia. Augustine apologizes for the brevity of the letter, which is due to imminent departure of the courier, Celsus, and promises a longer letter (paragraph 1). He asks Paulinus to explain to him how we can know the will of God for us in the less obvious cases (paragraph 2). Since it is often difficult to know God's will for us, he again asks Paulinus to share with him what he usually does in ambiguous cases or has learned that one should do (paragraph 3).

To his holy brother and sister, Paulinus and Therasia, who are beloved of God and rightly venerable and much longed for, Augustine sends greetings in the Lord.

1. Since our dearest brother, Celsus, asked for a response, I hurried to pay my debt, and I really hurried. For, though I thought that he was still going to remain with us for several more days, when the opportunity of setting sail suddenly presented itself, he announced to me, when it was already night, that he would depart on the next day. What was I to do, since I could not detain him? And since he was hastening to you with whom he is better off, I ought not to have, even if I could have. Hence, at that moment I grabbed a few ideas to dictate and send, while confessing that I owe you a lengthier letter, when after the return of our venerable brothers, our colleagues, Theasius and Evodius,[1] I shall have first been satisfied in your regard. For we hope in the name of Christ and by his help that you will at any time now come to us more fully in their hearts and on their lips. Though I am writing these lines, I had sent another letter a few days ago through our dear son, Fortunatian, a priest of the church of Thagaste, who was about to sail for Rome. Now, then, I ask for what I usually ask, namely, that you do what you usually do. Pray for us that God may see our humility and our labor and may pardon all our sins.[2]

2. If you are willing, however, I desire to discuss with you by letter such ideas as we could discuss if we were present face to face. See, you resolved with a Christian mind and devotion that little question that I had recently posed, as if we were present to one another in sweet conversation, but much too hastily and briefly. The charm of your lips could have, of course, dwelled on it a little longer and more amply, if you wanted to explain this point somewhat more clearly. For

---

1. These bishops were sent to the court of the emperor, Honorius, in order to explain the letter of the Council of Carthage held on 26 June 404, which had asked for the implementation of the law of 392 against the schismatics.
2. See Ps 25:18.

you said that you had decided to continue in that place that you happily enjoy with such a disposition that, if the Lord wants something else of you, you would prefer his will to yours. How do we know the will of God, which we must prefer to our own will? Is it only in something that we ought to endure willingly, because we are being forced even against our will? For in that case there happens what we do not want, but we correct ourselves so that we want it, because he wants, and it is wrong to reject the excellence of his will and it is not possible to escape it. In that way someone else bound Peter and took him where he did not want to go; he, nonetheless, went where he did not want to, and he willingly underwent a cruel death.[3] Or is the will of God also found in a case where there is the possibility of not changing one's mind, though something else occurs in which we instead see the will of God calling us to change our mind, not because our intention was bad; rather, it was one in which it would have been right to remain if he had not called us to another. For it was not wrong for Abraham to nurture and educate his son to the extent he could and insofar as it was up to him up to the end of his life. But when he was suddenly ordered to kill him, he did not, of course, change a previous evil intention, but an intention that would have been evil if he had not changed it after the command.[4] On this too I have no doubt that you have the same view.

3. But generally we are forced to recognize that the will of God is other than our will had been, not by a voice from heaven, not by a prophet, not by a revelation in a dream or in a rapture of the mind, which is called ecstasy, but by events that happen and call us to something other than we had decided—for example, if we decided to depart and something arose that a careful reflection on our duty forbids us to abandon, or if, when we decide to remain there, something is reported to us that forces us to depart because of the same careful reflection. With regard to this third kind of reason for changing one's mind, I ask that you discuss with me more fully and clearly what you think. It, of course, often bothers us, and it is difficult not to pass up something that we ought by preference to do, as long as we do not want to change our decision with which we earlier decided to remain. It is not that the decision was bad, but it now is bad because something that we should do instead has come up and is being neglected. And if it had not come up, we would have stayed with the earlier decision, not only without blame, but even with praise. In this case it is not difficult to be deceived. Here the words of the prophet have their application, *Who understands his sins?* (Ps 19:13). For this reason, I ask that you share with me your thoughts about what you usually do in such cases or what you find should be done.

---

3. See Jn 21:18-19.
4. See Gn 22:2.10.

Letter 81

Jerome wrote this letter to Augustine, perhaps in 404 or 405, and excuses himself for not replying to Augustine sooner, coming close to an apology for his reply to Augustine in Letter 75. He asks that from now on they put aside their quarreling and write cordial and friendly letters, playing on the field of the scriptures without injuring each other.

To his truly holy lord and most blessed bishop, Augustine, Jerome sends greetings in Christ.

I anxiously asked our holy brother, Firmus, how you were doing, and I was happy to hear that you were safe and sound. Again, though I do not say that I was hoping for a letter from you, but demanding one, he said that he left Africa without your knowledge. I, therefore, send through him my dutiful greetings, and at the same time I beg you to pardon my embarrassment, which I could not deny before you who long commanded that I write back. Nor did I reply to you, but one side of the issue replied to the other. And if it is wrong to have replied, I ask that you listen with patience; it is much worse to have given provocation. Let such complaints be banished from here; let there be between us sincere brotherhood, and from now on let us send each other letters filled, not with questions, but with love. The holy brothers who serve the Lord with us greet you amply. I ask that you give my humble greetings to the holy men who with you bear Christ's light yoke, especially to the holy and venerable Alypius. May Christ, our omnipotent God, keep you safe and sound and mindful of me, my truly holy lord and most blessed bishop. If you have read the book of my explanations of Jonah, I trust that you do not pay much attention to the silly question about the gourd plant. But if the friend who first came at me with the sword has been repulsed with the pen,[1] let it be a mark of your humanity and justice to find fault with the one making an accusation, not with the one giving a response. If you want, let us playfully exercise on the field of the scriptures without causing injury to each other.

---

1. Jerome refers to Rufinus of Aquilea with whom he was in a bitter dispute.

Letter 82

In 404 or 405 Augustine again wrote to Jerome after having received from him Letters 72, 75, and 81. He begins by asking Jerome's pardon (paragraph 1). Then he turns to Jerome's invitation to "playfully exercise on the field of the scriptures without causing injury to one another"—a phrase that does not fit with Augustine's serious concern about the inerrancy of the canonical books (paragraphs 2 and 3). The issue is whether Paul spoke the truth in Galatians 2:14 when he said that Peter and Barnabas *were not living correctly in relation to the gospel*, especially since Paul had earlier in Galatians 1:20 called upon God as his witness that he was not lying (paragraph 4). It is worse, Augustine insists, to think that Paul did not write the truth than to suppose that Peter acted wrongly (paragraph 5). Though the Manichees reject many parts of the scriptures as false, they at least do not attribute lies to the apostles (paragraph 6).

The question is not about what Paul did, but about what he wrote (paragraph 7). Paul observed some of the Jewish laws, not because he considered it necessary for salvation, but in order not to seem to hold in contempt that law God had given (paragraph 8) and in order to show that Christ's teaching did not condemn as sacrilegious the law of Moses, which prefigured Christ (paragraph 9). The Council of Jerusalem forbade the imposition of the Jewish law on the Gentiles; it did not forbid Jews from living according to the law out of reverence for the words of God (paragraph 10). Paul rebuked Peter because he was observing the law as a pretense, as if its observation was necessary for salvation, though he knew that was not true (paragraph 11). Paul circumcised Timothy to avoid giving the Jews the impression that Christians despised circumcision like idolatry (paragraph 12). Augustine defends his view that the observation of the law can be an indifferent action, neither good nor bad (paragraphs 13 and 14). The Jewish rites, such as circumcision, prefigured Christ, and after his coming they are not observed as necessary for salvation, though they were not immediately abolished (paragraph 15). If Jerome's view is that Christian converts from Judaism are correct in observing the law as a pretense, he has fallen into a heresy worse than Ebionism (paragraph 16). Augustine admits that he should have added to his statement that Paul's observance of the law was not dangerous the phrase: "at least at that time when the Christian faith was first revealed" (paragraph 17). Augustine continues to argue that the first Christians and even Christ himself did not observe the Mosaic law as a pretense (paragraphs 18 and 19) and explains the sense in which being under the law is blameworthy (paragraph 20).

Augustine turns to the issue of lies of expediency or of useful lies (paragraph 21) and argues that, regardless of the question of expedient lies in general, at least the authors of scripture must be absolutely free of lies (paragraph 22). Augustine undermines Jerome's claim to have earlier commentators on his side (paragraph 23) and appeals to Ambrose and Cyprian as well as to Paul's own claim that in Galatians he is not lying (paragraph 24), for he prefers to believe Paul rather than anyone else (paragraph 25). Augustine explains further what he meant by Paul's acting out of compassion and argues that his compassion involved no deceit (paragraphs 26 to 29).

Augustine expresses his pleasure at finding in Jerome's letter expressions of love and friendship (paragraph 30) and insists that sincerity and truthfulness is the basis of friendship (paragraph 31). Augustine explains how his previous letter had come to be circulated in Rome long before it reached Jerome (paragraph 32) and insists that he did not intend to offend Jerome (paragraph 33). Augustine grants the wisdom of Jerome's translating the scriptures from the Hebrew and asks for a copy of his translation of the Septuagint (paragraphs 34 and 35). Finally, Augustine promises to make a greater effort to have his letters delivered directly to Jerome and again expresses his love for Jerome (paragraph 36).

To his most beloved lord and holy brother and fellow priest, Jerome, who is worthy of honor in the heart of Christ, Augustine sends greetings in the Lord.

1, 1. I had already sent a lengthy letter to Your Charity, replying to that letter of yours to me that you mention that you sent through your holy son, Asterius, who is now not only my brother, but my colleague.[1] I still do not know whether it managed to reach you, except that you write by means of the most sincere brother, Firmus, that the man who first came after you with the sword has been driven off with the pen so that it will be a mark of my humanity and justice to find fault with the one making an accusation, not with someone giving a response.[2] From that slimmest indication alone I somehow guess that you have read that letter of mine. In it, of course, I deplored the existence of such great discord between you, since fraternal charity rejoiced over so great a friendship wherever rumor had carried the news of it.[3] I did not do this to reprimand you, my brother, for I would not dare to say that I knew of any fault of yours in this regard. But I say this in grief over the misery of human beings, for in maintaining friendships by mutual love, no matter how great it is, their permanence is so uncertain. But I had wanted to learn from your reply whether you granted me the forgiveness I had asked for, and I want you to inform me of this more clearly, even though the somewhat more cheerful tone of your letter seems to indicate that I have obtained this as well, at least if it was sent after you read mine—something that is not clear from it.

2. You ask or rather you command with the confidence of love that we play-fully exercise on the field of the scriptures without causing injury to one another.[4] As far as I am concerned, I prefer to do this seriously rather than play-fully. But if you chose to use this word on account of a certain facileness, I admit that I am looking for something more from the goodness of your abilities, from such learned and leisured wisdom, and from long, studious, and gifted applica-

---

1. He refers to Letter 68 from Jerome to which Augustine replied in Letter 73.
2. See Letter 81.
3. See Letter 73, 3, 6-8, where Augustine speaks of the destruction of the friendship between Jerome and Rufinus.
4. See Letter 81.

tion. And with the Holy Spirit not only giving, but also dictating these answers to you, in these important and laborious questions you ought to help me, who am not like someone playing on the field of the scriptures, but like someone gasping for air in the mountains. But if on account of the cheerfulness that ought to exist among friends holding a discussion, you thought that you ought to say, "Let us play," whether the site of our conversation is open and level or steep and difficult, teach me, I beg you, how we may be able to attain the result of not incurring the suspicion of childish boastfulness, as if we were seeking to make our name famous by accusing illustrious men.[5] For at times something perhaps upsets us that has not met with our approval, if not due to our less careful attention, at least due to our slowness to understand, and at times we try to defend our contrary view and state it with a somewhat more carefree freedom. But if out of the need for refutation something harsh is said, we surround it with gentler language in order that it may be more tolerable in order that we may not be judged to unsheathe a sword coated with honey.[6] Or perhaps the way to avoid both defects or suspicion of a defect is to argue with a more learned friend with such an attitude that we necessarily approve of whatever he says and are not permitted to oppose him even a little for the sake of investigating the matter further.

3. Then indeed without any fear of giving offense we can play as if on a field, but I wonder whether if we are not mocking each other.[7] For I admit to Your Charity, I learned to show this reverence and respect only to those books of the scriptures that are now called canonical so that I most firmly believe that none of their authors erred in writing anything. And if I come upon something in those writings that seems contrary to the truth, I have no doubt that either the manuscript is defective or the translator did not follow what was said or that I did not understand it. I, however, read other authors in such a way that, no matter how much they excel in holiness and learning, I do not suppose that something is true by reason of the fact that they thought so, but because they were able to convince me either through those canonical authors or by plausible reason that it does not depart from the truth. Nor do I think that you, my brother, hold anything else. In fact, I say, I do not think that you want your books to be read like those of the prophets or apostles, for with regard to their writings it is wicked to doubt that they are free from all error. May God keep this far from your pious humility and from the truthful estimation you have of yourself. If you had not been endowed with it, you, of course, would not say, "Would that we deserved your embraces and that by conversation with each other we either learned something or taught something!"[8]

---

5. See Letter 68, 2.
6. See Letter 72, 1, 2.
7. Augustine plays on "*luditur*: play" and "*illuditur*: mock."
8. See Letter 68, 2.

2, 4. If from a consideration of your life and character I believe that you said this without pretense and without falsity, how much more just it is that I believe that the apostle Paul had thought nothing other than what he wrote where he said of Peter and Barnabas, *When I saw that they were not living correctly in relation to the truth of the gospel, I said to Peter in the presence of all, "If you, though you are a Jew, live as a Gentile and not as a Jew, why do you force the Gentiles to live like Jews?"* (Gal 2:14). After all, about whom may I be certain that he does not deceive me in writing or in speaking, if the apostle was deceiving his children? He was again bringing them to birth until Christ, that is, the truth, should be formed in them.[9] And, though he began by saying to them, *But as for what I am writing to you, look, before God, I do not lie* (Gal 1:20), he, nonetheless, was not writing truthfully. He was, rather, deceiving them by some diplomatic pretense, when he said that he saw that Peter and Barnabas were not living correctly in relation to the truth of the gospel and that he resisted Peter to his face for no other reason than that he was forcing Gentiles to live like Jews.[10]

5. "But it is, after all, better to believe that the apostle Paul did not write something in accord with the truth than that the apostle Peter did something wrong." If this is so, let us say—God forbid!—that it is better to believe that the Gospel lies than that Christ was denied by Peter[11] and that the Book of Kings lied rather than that so great a prophet, who was chosen by the Lord God in so exceptional a way, committed adultery in lusting after and taking away the wife of another man and committed so horrible a murder in killing her husband.[12] On the contrary, certain of and secure in its truth, I shall read the holy scripture, which has been placed at the highest and heavenly peak of authority, and I shall learn from it that human beings were truthfully either praised or corrected or condemned rather than everywhere hold the words of God suspect, because I am afraid to believe that human actions need at times to be reprimanded, even in certain persons of a praiseworthy excellence.

6. Because they cannot twist them to some other meaning, the Manichees claim that very many sections of the divine scriptures are false, by which their wicked error is refuted with the utterly lucid clarity of its statements. And yet, they do not attribute the same falsity to the apostles who wrote them, but to some persons who have corrupted the manuscripts. Because they, nevertheless, were unable at any point to prove this either by more or older exemplars or by the authority of the original language, from which the Latin books were translated, they go off, defeated and put to shame by the truth, which is well known to all. Do you not understand in your holy wisdom how great a loophole would lie open

---

9. See Gal 4:19 and Jn 5:6.
10. See Gal 2:11-14.
11. See Mt 26:69-75.
12. See 2 Sm 11:4-17.

for their malice, if we should say that the letters of the apostles were not falsified by others, but that the apostles themselves wrote what is false?

7. "It is not credible," you say, "that Paul blamed in Peter what Paul himself had done."[13] I am not now investigating what he did; I am asking what he wrote. It most of all pertains to the question that I raised that the truth of the divine scriptures, which were entrusted to us in order to build up our faith, not by just any persons, but by the apostles themselves, and which were for this reason accepted as having the canonical peak of authority, should remain true and indubitable in every respect. For, if Peter did what he ought to have done, Paul lied in saying that he saw him not living correctly in relation to the gospel. For whoever does what he ought to do certainly acts correctly. And he who says that he did not correctly do something that he knows he ought to have done does not speak the truth about that person. But if Paul wrote the truth, it is true that Peter did not then live correctly in relation to the gospel. He, therefore, did not do what he ought to have done, and if Paul himself had already done something of the sort, I would rather believe that, after having been corrected, he could not have neglected to correct his fellow apostle than that he could have said something that was a lie in his letter—or in any other letter! How much more then in that letter in which he earlier said, *As for what I am writing to you, look, before God, I do not lie* (Gal 1:20).

8. I myself believe that Peter was acting so as to force the Gentiles to live as Jews. For I read that Paul, who I do not believe lied, wrote this. And for that reason Peter was not acting correctly. For it was against the truth of the gospel that those who believed in Christ should have thought that they could not be saved without those old sacraments. For the people of Antioch who came to the faith from the circumcision maintained this; Paul battled against them with perseverance and fierceness. When Paul circumcised Timothy[14] or fulfilled his vow at Cenchreae[15] or when, after being admonished by James, he undertook the celebrations of those rites of the law with those who have taken a vow,[16] he did not do this in order to bring people to believe that those sacraments confer Christian salvation, but so that he would not be thought to condemn, like the idolatry of the Gentiles, those rites that God had commanded in the earlier times, as was fitting, to foreshadow things to come.[17] This is, after all, what James said to him, namely, that it was reported concerning him that he taught the abandonment of Moses.[18] And it is, of course, wrong that believers in Christ should abandon his

---

13. See Letter 75, 3, 4, and Jerome, *Commentary on Paul's Letter to the Galatians* 2, 11-13: PL 26, 339.
14. See Acts 16:3.
15. See Acts 18:18.
16. See Acts 21:26.
17. See Col 2:17.
18. See Acts 21:26.

prophet, as if they despised and condemned his teaching. Christ himself says of him, *If you believed in Moses, you would also believe in me; after all, he wrote concerning me* (Jn 5:46).

9. Consider, after all, I beg you, the words of James. He says, *You see, brother, how many thousands there are in Judea who have come to believe in Christ, and these are all zealous for the law. But they have heard concerning you that you teach the abandonment of Moses for those Jews who are living among the Gentiles, telling them that they need neither to circumcise their children nor to live according to the tradition. What then is to be done? A crowd must, of course, assemble. For they have certainly heard that you have come. Do, therefore, what we tell you. We have four men who are under a vow; take these men, purify yourself along with them, and pay their expenses so that they may shave their heads. In that way all will know that what they have heard concerning you is false, but that you yourself follow and keep the law. But with regard to the Gentiles who come to believe, we have given a decree, judging that they should observe nothing of the sort, except to abstain from what has been sacrificed to idols, from blood, and from fornication* (Acts 21:20-25). It is, in my opinion, clear that James gave this warning precisely so that they would know that those reports were false that these men who had come to believe in Christ from the Jews, but were still zealous for the law, heard about him. For he wanted to avoid their thinking that what Moses gave to the patriarchs had been condemned by the teaching of Christ as sacrilegious and as not having been written by the command of God. For this rumor was spread about concerning Paul, not by those who understood the spirit with which Jewish believers ought at that time to have observed these sacraments, namely, in order to emphasize the authority of God and the prophetic holiness of those sacraments, not in order to obtain salvation, which was already revealed in Christ and attained through the sacrament of baptism. But this rumor was spread about concerning Paul by those who wanted those sacraments to be observed as if without them there could be no salvation in the gospel for those who believe. For they saw that he was a most energetic preacher of grace and especially opposed to their aims, since he taught that a human being is not made righteous through those rites, but through the grace of Jesus Christ. After all, those shadows in the law were given for the sake of announcing in advance that grace. And for this reason they tried to stir up hatred and persecution against him, and they accused him of being an enemy of the law and of God's commandments. He could not have more fittingly avoided the odiousness of that false accusation than by his observing those rites that he was thought to condemn as sacrilegious and by thus showing that the Jews were not at that time to be kept from them, as if they were wicked, and that the Gentiles were not to be forced to observe them, as if they were necessary.

10. For, if he really rejected them in the way it was reported concerning him and undertook to observe them in order to conceal his thought by an action that

was mere pretense, James would not have said to him, *And all will know what they have heard about you is false* (Acts 21:24), but he would have said, "And all will suppose this," especially since the apostles had already decreed in Jerusalem that no one should force the Gentiles to live as Jews.[19] But they did not decree that no one should forbid the Jews to live as Jews at that time, although Christian teaching would not now force even them to do so. Hence, if after this decree of the apostles Peter carried out that pretense in Antioch in order to force the Gentiles to live as Jews, something that he himself was now not forced to do, although he was not forbidden to do so for the sake of showing reverence for the words of God that were entrusted to the Jews,[20] why is it surprising that Paul constrained him to state openly what he remembered that he decreed at Jerusalem along with the other apostles?

11. But if, as I prefer to think, Peter did this before that council of Jerusalem, even so it is not strange that Paul wanted him not timidly to hide, but confidently to state what he already knew that he likewise held, either because he had compared with Peter his understanding of the gospel[21] or because he heard that Peter was admonished by God on this subject in the calling of the centurion, Cornelius,[22] or because he saw Peter eat with Gentiles before those whom he feared had come to Antioch.[23] Nor do we deny that Peter already held the same view that Paul did. He did not, therefore, at that time teach Peter what was true on this subject, but accused his pretense by which he was forcing the Gentiles to live as Jews. He rebuked him for no other reason than that all those rites were being practiced as a pretense, as if what those were saying who thought that believers could not be saved without circumcision of the foreskin and the other observances that foreshadowed what was to come was true.[24]

12. And he, therefore, circumcised Timothy precisely so that it would not seem to the Jews and especially to his family on his mother's side that the Gentiles who had come to believe in Christ despised circumcision, as idolatry ought to be despised. After all, God commanded that circumcision be performed, but Satan persuaded people to commit idolatry. And he did not circumcise Titus so that he would not give occasion to those who said that believers cannot be saved without that circumcision and so that they would not in order to deceive the Gentiles spread it about that Paul also held this view. He himself clearly enough indicates this where he says, *But Titus who was with me, since he was a Greek, was not forced to be circumcised. This question arose on account of the intrusion of false brethren who entered in for the purpose of*

19. See Acts 15:28.
20. See Rom 3:2.
21. See Gal 2:2.
22. See Acts 10:9-16.
23. See Gal 2:12.
24. See Col 2:17.

spying on our freedom in order to bring us back to slavery. We have not yielded in submission to them even for a moment in order that the truth of the gospel might be preserved for you (Gal 2:3-5). Here it is clear that Paul understood what they were looking for, namely, how he did not do what he had done in the case of Timothy, something that he could have done with that freedom in order to show by it that those sacraments ought neither to be sought as if they were necessary nor condemned as if they were sacrilegious.

13. But we must, of course, avoid in this discussion saying, as the philosophers do, that no actions of human beings are midway between a correct action and a sin, actions that are counted neither among correct actions nor among sins.[25] And we must avoid being pressured on the grounds that to observe the ceremonies of the law cannot be indifferent, but must be either good or bad. In that way, if we say that their observance is good, we too would be forced to observe them, but if we say that it is evil, we would believe that the apostles did not observe them sincerely, but as a pretense. I myself do not fear for the apostles the example set by philosophers when they say something true in their discussions as much as that example set by lawyers of the courts when they lie in the trying of the cases of others. If you thought it proper to introduce a comparison in the explanation of the Letter to the Galatians to support the pretense of Peter and Paul,[26] why should I fear in your writings the mention of philosophers? They are worthless, not because everything they say is false, but because they have put their trust in many false theories and, when they are found to speak the truth, they are strangers to the grace of Christ, who is the truth itself.

14. But why should I not say that those commandments about the old sacraments are not good, since human beings are not made righteous by them? For they are figures that foretell the grace by which we are made righteous. And yet they are not bad, because they were commanded by God as appropriate to that time and those persons, since even the statement of the prophet supports me by which God says that he gave to that people commands that were not good?[27] For he perhaps did not say, "Evil," but only, "Not good," that is, not such that human beings would become good by them or such that they would not become good without them. I wish that Your Sincerity would kindly inform me whether, when any holy Easterner comes to Rome, he fasts as a pretense on every Sabbath, except for the day of the Easter vigil. But if we say that such fasting is wrong, we will condemn not only the Roman church, but also many churches close to it and those somewhat more remote where the same custom is observed and continues. But if we think that it is wrong not to fast on the Sabbath, we will accuse so many churches of the East and the far greater part of the Christian world with great

---

25. See Letter 75, 4, 16.
26. See Jerome, *Commentary on the Letter of Paul to the Galatians* 2:11-13: PL 26, 340.
27. See Ez 20:25.

rashness. Do you agree that we should say that it is something indifferent that is, nonetheless, commendable in a person who does this, not as a pretense, but in accord with the observance of the community? And still we do not read on this in the canonical books that Christians received such a commandment. For how much better reason do I not dare to call that wrong which by the Christian faith I cannot deny that God commanded, though by that faith I learned that I was not made righteous by that command, but by the grace of God through Jesus Christ our Lord![28]

15. I say, therefore, that God gave circumcision of the foreskin and other such rites through the testament that is called old to his first people in order to signify those things that were to come, which had to be fulfilled by Christ, and when those prophecies were fulfilled, those rites remained only to be read of by Christians for the understanding of the prophecy that came first, but not to be observed as necessary, as if we still had to await the coming of the revelation of the faith that these rites signified. But although they ought not to have been imposed upon the Gentiles, they ought not to have been removed from the customs of the Jews, as if they were to be despised and condemned. Later, bit by bit and little by little, the preaching of the grace of Christ, of course, grew more widespread, and the faithful would know that they are made righteous and are saved by it alone, not by those symbols foreshadowing the realities that were earlier still in the future, but were at that time coming and present. Thus, with the calling of those Jews at the time of the presence of the Lord in the flesh and during the apostolic times, all that observance of the symbols would be brought to an end. It was sufficient as a commendation of it that this observance would not be avoided as detestable and like idolatry, but that it would not develop further. Otherwise, it might be thought to be necessary, as if salvation came from it or could not exist without it. This is what the heretics thought who, while they wanted to be both Jews and Christians, could be neither Jews nor Christians.[29] You were, nonetheless, so kind as to warn me with the greatest good will that their opinion must be avoided, though I had never thought otherwise. Out of fear Peter did not fall into agreement with that opinion, but into a pretense of agreement with it. Hence, Paul wrote of him with complete truth that he had seen that he was not walking correctly in relation to the truth of the gospel, and he said to him with complete truth that he was forcing the Gentiles to live as Jews. Paul, of course, forced no one to do this; yet he truly observed those ancient rites where there was need with a view to show that they were not to be condemned. He, nonetheless, constantly preached that the faithful were saved, not by them, but by the grace of the faith that had been revealed, and in that way he did not force anyone to practice them as if they were necessary. Thus I believe, however, that the apostle Paul truth-

---

28. See Rom 3:24.
29. For example, the Ebionites or Nazareans; see Letter 75, 4, 13.

fully observed all those practices, and I do not, nonetheless, force or allow a Jew who has become a Christian to practice those rites in a sincere manner, just as you, who thought that Paul practiced them as a pretense, do not force or allow such a person to pretend to practice them.

16. Or do you want me also to say that this is the essence of the question, in fact of your view, that after the coming of the gospel of Christ Jewish believers act correctly if they observe the commandments of the law, that is, if they offer the sacrifices that Paul offered, if they circumcise their sons, if they keep the Sabbath, as Paul with Timothy and as all Jews observed them,[30] provided that they do this as a pretense and a deception? If that is so, we are slipping, not into the heresy of Ebion or of those who are commonly called Nazareans or into some old heresy, but into some new heresy that is more destructive insofar as it arises not from an error, but from an aim and desire to deceive. You might, I suppose, answer, in order to clear yourself of this view, that the apostles at that time acted laudably in pretending so that they would not scandalize the many weak persons who came to believe from among the Jews and who did not yet understand that those practices were to be rejected. But now the teaching of Christian grace has been solidly established in so many nations, and the reading of the law and the prophets has also been solidly established in all the churches of Christ, and we read of these practices in order to understand them, not to observe them. And whoever would want to observe them as a pretense is insane. Why, then, am I not permitted to say that the apostle Paul and other Christians of the true faith ought at that time to have truly shown reverence for those old sacraments by observing them for a little while so that those observances filled with prophetic meaning, which the most devout patriarchs practiced, might not be thought despicable by their descendants, as if they were sacrilegious and diabolical? For, when the faith had come that was foretold earlier by those observances and was revealed after the death and resurrection of the Lord, they lost the life, as it were, of their function. And yet, like dead bodies of parents, they had to be carried as if to their burial, not as a pretense, but with respect, but were not to be immediately abandoned or thrown to the abuse of their enemies, as if to the teeth of dogs. Hence, any Christian of the present time, even though formerly a Jew, who wants to observe them in a like manner, as if disturbing ashes already at rest, will not be devoutly accompanying or carrying the body, but wickedly violating its burial.

17. I admit, of course, that in the passage of my letter in which I said that Paul had undertaken the observance of the sacraments of the Jews when he was already an apostle of Christ in order to teach that they were not dangerous for those who wanted to observe them, as they had received them from their parents through the law,[31] I had failed to add, "At least at that time when the grace of the

---

30. See Letter 75, 4, 13.
31. See Letter 40, 4, 4.

faith was first revealed." For at that time this was not dangerous. But with the advance of time those observations ought to have been abandoned by all Christians; otherwise, if they were practiced then, people would not distinguish what God commanded his people through Moses from what the unclean spirit instituted in the temples of the demons. Hence, my negligence in not adding this is to be blamed rather than your reprimand. Still, long before I received your letter, I wrote to Faustus the Manichee how I interpreted the same passage, though only briefly, and there I did not omit this.[32] And Your Grace can read it there if he deigns to do so, and your dear friends by whom I have just sent these writings will, in whatever way you wish, serve as a guarantee for you that I had dictated it before. And believe me from my heart, something that, in speaking before God, I demand by the law of love, that I never thought that Jews who have become Christians ought even now to observe those old sacraments with any devotion or any other disposition and that it is in any way permissible for them to do so. For I always held that idea about Paul from the time his letter became known to me, just as you do not think that at this time anyone could observe those sacraments as a pretense, though you believe that the apostles did this.

18. Hence, just as you say the opposite and just as, despite the protests of everyone, as you write, you state frankly that the ceremonies of the Jews are dangerous and deadly for Christians and that whoever observes them, whether coming from the Jews or from the Gentiles, has plunged into the pit of the devil,[33] so I absolutely agree with this statement of yours and add: "Whoever observes them, whether coming from the Jews or from the Gentiles, not only sincerely, but also as a pretense, has plunged into the pit of the devil." What more do you ask? But just as you distinguish the pretense of the apostles from the rule of life in the present time, so I distinguish the truthful way of life of the apostle Paul in all these matters at that time from any observation in the present time of the Jewish ceremonies, although not done out of pretense, because at that time it deserved approval and now is detestable. Thus, we read: *The law and the prophets lasted until John the Baptist* (Lk 16:16), and that *the Jews sought to kill Christ because he not only did not observe the Sabbath, but also called God his father, making himself equal to God* (Jn 5:18), and that *we have received grace in place of grace* (Jn 1:16), and that *the law was given through Moses, but it became grace and the truth through Jesus Christ* (Jn 1:17), and that it was promised through Jeremiah that God would give a new testament to the house of Judah, not according to the testament that he established with their fathers.[34] I do not, nonetheless, think that the Lord himself was circumcised by his parents only as a pretense. Or if he did not forbid it on account of his age, I do not think that he

32. See *Answer to Faustus, a Manichean* 19, 17.
33. See Letter 75, 4, 14.
34. See Jer 31:31.

said as a pretense those words to the leper, who was certainly not healed by that observance commanded by Moses, but by the Lord himself: *Go and offer for yourself the sacrifice that Moses commanded as testimony for them* (Mk 1:44).[35] Nor did he go up to Jerusalem for the feast day as a pretense, but was so far from going up in order to be seen by people that he did not go up openly, but in secret.[36]

19. The same apostle, after all, said, *Look, I, Paul, say to you: If you are circumcised, Christ will be no benefit for you* (Gal 5:2). He, therefore, deceived Timothy and brought it about that Christ brought him no benefit. Or did the circumcision not have this effect because it was done as a pretense? But Paul did not write or say, "If you are sincerely circumcised," or "not as a pretense," but he said without any exception, *If you are circumcised, Christ will be no benefit for you.* Just as you want to find a place here for your view so that you want to understand, "as a deception," so I demand without any impudence that you also allow us to understand here that he said, *If you are circumcised,* to those people who wanted to be circumcised because they thought that they could not be saved in Christ in any other way. To whoever, then, is circumcised with this disposition of mind, with this desire, with this intention, Christ is of absolutely no benefit, as he elsewhere openly states, *For, if righteousness comes through the law, Christ has died in vain* (Gal 2:21). And the passage you quoted says the same thing, *You who would be made righteous by the law are severed from Christ; you have fallen from grace* (Gal 5:4). And so, he blamed those who believed that they were being made righteous by the law, not those who observed those matters of the law to honor him who commanded them, while understanding both that they were commanded in order to foreshadow the truth and how long they ought to last. For this reason he says, *If you are led by the Spirit, you are no longer under the law* (Gal 5:18); from this it is clear, as you see, that he does not have the Holy Spirit who is under the law—not apparently, as you think our ancestors wanted to be, but really, as I understand it.

20. It strikes me as an important question what it is to be under the law in the sense in which the apostle blames it. For I do not think that he said this on account of circumcision or those sacrifices that were then offered by the patriarchs, but are not now offered by Christians, and other things of this sort, but on account of this very command that the law gives, *You shall not desire* (Ex 20:17, Dt 5:20, or Rom 7:7.12). We certainly admit that Christians ought to observe this and proclaim it especially by the light of the gospel. The apostle says that the law is holy and that the commandment is holy, just, and good.[37] Then he adds, *Has what is good, then, become death for me? Heaven forbid! But in order that sin might be seen as sin, it produced death for me through the good in order that it*

35. See Lv 14:2-32.
36. See Jn 7:10.
37. See Rom 7:12.

might become sinful or sin beyond all measure through the commandment (Rom 7:14). But his words here, *That it might become . . . sin beyond all measure*, are the same as he says elsewhere: *The law entered in in order that sin might abound. But where sin abounded, grace was also superabundant* (Rom 5:20). And elsewhere, since he was previously saying about the economy of grace that it makes one righteous, he says as if asking a question, *Why, then, was there the law?* and he immediately replies to this question: *It was given for the sake of transgression until there came the offspring to whom the promise was made* (Rom 3:19). He, therefore, says that those whom the law makes guilty are under the law as condemned, because they do not fulfill the law. For, because they do not understand the benefit of grace for carrying out the commandments of God, they place their confidence in their own strength in their proud arrogance. For *the fulfillment of the law is love* (Rom 13:10). But *the love of God is poured out in our hearts*, not by ourselves, but *by the Holy Spirit who has been given to us* (Rom 5:5). But a sufficient explanation of this matter perhaps deserves a longer discussion and one in a volume of its own. If, then, the words of the law, *You shall not desire* (Ex 20:17), holds a sinner guilty under the law if human weakness is not helped by the grace of God and makes one a transgressor rather than sets the sinner free, for how much better reason was that circumcision, which was commanded for the sake of what it signified, and those other observances, which had to be abolished as the revelation of grace became more widely known, unable to make anyone righteous! They were not, nonetheless, to be avoided like the diabolical and sacrilegious rites of the Gentiles, even when the grace had itself begun to be revealed that had been foretold by such foreshadowing of what was to come. Rather, they were to be permitted for a little while, especially for those who had come from that people to whom they were given. But afterward, as if they had been buried with honor, they were to be definitively abandoned by all Christians.

21. What, I ask you, do your words mean: "Not as a matter of expediency, as our ancestors intended"?[38] This is either what I call a useful lie, that is, this expediency is the duty, as it were, of lying for a good cause, or I do not see what else it is —unless by the addition of the term "expediency" a lie ceases to be a lie. And if that is absurd, why do you not openly say that one should defend a useful lie, unless perhaps the term bothers you because the word for "duty" is not much used in ecclesiastical books, though our Ambrose was not afraid of it? He wanted certain books of his full of useful instructions to be called *Duties*.[39] Or if anyone who lies out of duty is to be blamed, is one to be approved if he lies out of expediency? I ask you, May the person who has this idea lie whenever he

---

38. See Letter 75, 3, 14 at the end.
39. Ambrose, *Duties* (*De officiis*), a work most probably written over many years between 377 and 391. See PL 16, 25-194.

chooses? After all, there is an important question here whether good men may ever lie or whether Christians may. For to them it was said, *Let your speech be: "Yes, yes," and "No, no,"* (Mt 5:37) *in order that you may not fall under the judgment* (Jas 5:21),[40] and to those who hear with faith it is said, *You will destroy all those who speak lies* (Ps 5:7).

22. But this, as I said, is another question and an important one; let a person who thinks this way choose what he wishes when he lies, provided, nonetheless, that he believes with unshaken faith and maintains that the authors of the holy scriptures and especially of the canonical ones were absolutely free from lies when they wrote. Otherwise, the ministers of Christ, of whom it was said, *Here it is now required of ministers that they be found faithful* (1 Cor 4:2), would think that they learned from faith, as if it were an important lesson, to lie for the ministry of the truth. After all, the term "faith" is so called in the Latin language because what one says is what happens.[41] Where what one says is what happens, there is no place for lying. The faithful minister, the apostle Paul, undoubtedly presents us with faithfulness in writing, because he was a minister of the truth, not of falsity. And for this reason he wrote the truth, namely, that he saw that Peter was not living correctly in relation to the gospel and resisted him to his face because he was forcing the Gentiles to live like Jews.[42] But Peter himself accepted to his own benefit with the piety of holy and loving humility what Paul did with the freedom of love. And in that way he offered to those who would come after him a more exceptional and holier example than the example Paul offered them. For Peter offered them an example that they might not reject being corrected even by their juniors, if they perhaps had in any way abandoned the path of truth, while Paul offered an example that they might confidently venture to resist their elders for the sake of defending the truth of the gospel, as long as brotherly love was preserved. After all, though it is better for someone making a journey to go astray in no way than in some way, it is, nonetheless, much more admirable and praiseworthy willingly to accept one who gives correction than boldly to correct one who goes astray. In Paul we praise righteous freedom and in Peter holy humility, and in my limited judgment we need to defend such praise against the slanders of Porphyry[43] rather than to give him greater opportunity for his abusive talk.

3, 23. You demand of me that I show at least one person whose opinion in this matter I have followed, since you have mentioned by name so many who preceded you in the position you are defending. You ask that, if I reprimand your

40. The CSEL edition omits the quotation from James, which is found in the early editions.
41. See Cicero, *Duties* (*De officiis*) I, 7, 23: "*credamusque quia fiat quod dictum est appellatam fidem.*"
42. See Gal 2:14.
43. Porphyry was a Neoplatonic philosopher and student of Plotinus; he wrote a work, *Against the Christians*, which is no longer extant.

error in this matter, I allow you to err with such persons,[44] none of whom, I confess, have I read. But though they number about almost six or seven, you also weaken the authority of four of them. For you say that the Laodicean, whose name you do not give, has recently left the Church. You call Alexander an old heretic, and I read in your more recent writings that you have found fault with Origen and Didymus, and not just slightly, nor on unimportant issues, although you earlier praised Origen marvelously.[45] I think that you will not allow yourself to be in error along with these, though you might say this in the sense that they did not err in this view. For who is there who is willing to err with anyone? There are three who remain: Eusebius of Emesa, Theodore of Heraclea, and John, whom you mention a little later, who has long ruled the church of Constantinople in the capacity of bishop.[46]

24. On the other hand, if you investigate or recall what our Ambrose thought on this issue,[47] what our Cyprian likewise thought,[48] you will perhaps find that we are not without those whom we follow in what we defend. And yet, as I said a little before, I owe this complete obedience only to the canonical scriptures, and by it I follow them alone in such a way that I have no doubt that their authors erred in them in absolutely no way and wrote nothing in them in order to deceive. Hence, when I seek a third in order to set my three against yours, I could, I think, easily have found one, if I had read extensively. But instead of all these, in fact above all these, the apostle Paul, nonetheless, comes to my rescue. I take refuge with him; I appeal to him from all the commentators on his letters who think otherwise. In questioning him, I plead and demand: When he wrote to the Galatians that he saw Peter not living correctly in relation to the gospel and resisted him to his face, because he was forcing the Gentiles to live like Jews by that pretense, did he write the truth or did he lie with some sort of lie of expediency? And I hear him a little earlier in the beginning of the same account crying out to me with words of piety, *But as for what I write to you, look, before God, I do not lie* (Gal 1:20).

25. May any who think otherwise pardon me; I myself believe such a great apostle who swears in his own letter and in defense of his own letter rather than anyone, however learned, who argues about someone else's letter. Nor am I afraid that it may be said that I defend Paul in that way because he did not pretend to hold the error of the Jews, but because he really held that error.[49] For he neither acted out of pretense when with the freedom of an apostle he honored those old sacraments, as was fitting at that time when there was need. After all, he put into

---

44. See Letter 75, 3, 6.
45. See Letter 75, 3, 4.
46. See Letter 75, 3, 4.
47. See Ambrosiaster, *Commentary on the Letter of Paul to the Galatians* 2:1-14: PL 17, 349-350.
48. See Cyprian, Letter 71, 3: CSEL 82, 773.
49. See Letter 75, 4, 17.

practice those rites that were instituted, not by the wiles of Satan to deceive people, but by the providence of God to foretell prophetically the realities to come. Nor did he really hold the error of the Jews. Rather he not only knew, but constantly and energetically preached that they were in error who thought that those sacraments should be imposed on the Gentiles or were necessary for anyone's salvation.

26. But I said that he became like a Jew for the Jews and like a Gentile for the Gentiles, not with the wiles of a liar, but with the feeling of compassion.[50] You seem to have paid little attention to the sense in which I said this. Or perhaps I was unable to explain it sufficiently.[51] For I did not say this because he did those things as a pretense out of compassion, but because he did not do as a pretense those things that he did like the Jews, just as he did not do as a pretense those that he did like the Gentiles, things which you also mentioned. And in that respect you also helped me, something that I admit not without gratitude. For I had asked you in my letter how he was thought to have become for the Jews like a Jew since he took up the sacraments of the Jews as a pretense, though he became for the Gentiles like a Gentile and did not, nonetheless, take up the sacrifices of the Gentiles as a pretense.[52] You replied that he became for the Gentiles like a Gentile because he accepted the uncircumcised into the faith and because he permitted without discrimination the eating of foods that the Jews condemn.[53] Here I ask whether he did this also as a pretense, and if that is utterly absurd and false, the same thing, therefore, holds with regard to those actions in which he adapted to the tradition of the Jews with a wise freedom, not a servile necessity—or, what is more unworthy, with a false rather than a faithful ministry.

27. After all, for the faithful and those who have come to know the truth, as he himself bears witness, unless here too he is being deceitful, *every creature of God is good, and nothing should be rejected that is received with thanksgiving* (1 Tm 4:4). And so, for Paul, not only as a man, but also as a most faithful minister, who not only knows, but also teaches the truth, every creature of God among the foods is, of course, good, not as a pretense, but really. Why then did he become like a Gentile for the Gentiles, without taking up as a pretense any of the sacred rites and ceremonies of the Gentiles, but by holding and teaching the truth about foods and the uncircumcised? And why could he become for the Jews like a Jew only by taking up as a deception the sacraments of the Jews? Why did he preserve the truthful faithfulness of a minister for the wild olive tree that was grafted on, while he stretched out some sort of veil of ministerial deception for the natural branches that were not located apart from, but on the tree?[54]

---

50. See Letter 40, 4, 6.
51. See Letter 75, 4, 17.
52. See Letter 40, 4, 6.
53. See Letter 75, 4, 17.
54. See Rom 11:17.

Why having become like a Gentile for the Gentiles does he teach what he believes and believe what he does, but having become like a Jew for the Jews he holds one thing in his heart and brings forth another in his words, deeds, and writings? But God forbid that we should think that! For to both of them he owed love from a pure heart and a good conscience and unfeigned faith.[55] And for this reason he became all things for all human beings in order to gain them all,[56] not with the wiles of a liar, but with the feeling of compassion, that is, not by committing as a pretense all the sins of human beings, but by showing the concern of compassionate healing for all the evils of others, as if they were his own.

28. When, therefore, he did not reject even for himself the observance of those sacraments of the old testament, he was not deceiving anyone out of compassion; rather, he did not deceive anyone at all. And in this way, by teaching that they were commanded by the Lord God up to a certain time in God's plan, he distinguished them from the sacrilegious rites of the Gentiles. But then he become for the Jews like a Jew, not out of the wiles of a liar, but out of the feeling of compassion. For he wanted to set them free from that error by which they either did not want to believe in Christ or thought that they could be cleansed from their sins and be saved by the old rites of their priests and by the observances of their ceremonies. He did this as if he himself were caught in the same error, loving, of course, his neighbor as himself[57] and doing for others these things that he would want to be done for himself by others,[58] if he needed this. For, when the Lord taught this, he added, *For this is the law and the prophets* (Mt 22:40).

29. He commanded this same feeling of compassion in the same Letter to the Galatians when he said, *If anyone is caught in some sin, you who are spiritual people, instruct such a person in the spirit of gentleness, looking out for yourself so that you too are not tempted* (Gal 6:1). See if he did not say: Become like that person in order that you may gain him, not, of course, that one should pretend to commit the same sin or that one should pretend to have it, but that one should consider in the sin of the other what could have happened to oneself as well. And in that way one should compassionately help the other as one would have wanted the other to help him, that is, not with the wiles of a liar, but with the feeling of compassion. In that way Paul became all things for all in order that he might gain all,[59] for the Jew, for the Gentile, for any human being found in some error or sin, not by pretending to be what he was not, but by being compassionate because he could have been such, for he knew that he himself was human.

---

55. See 1 Tm 1:5.
56. See 1 Cor 9:22.
57. See Mt 22:39.
58. See Mt 7:12.
59. See 1 Cor 9:22.

4, 30. Please, I ask you, consider yourself a little, yourself, I mean, in relation to me, and recall or, if you have a copy, reread your words in that rather brief letter that you sent me by the hands of our brother and now our colleague, Cyprian. Consider the genuine, the brotherly, the full affection with which you added the following, after you had seriously complained that I had done you certain wrongs, "In this you do injury to our friendship; in this you violate the laws of our relationship; [I write these things] so that we do not seem to fight like children and give material for argument to our respective followers or detractors."[60] I feel that you not only spoke these words from the heart, but also from a heart kindly disposed to show concern for me. Then you add what, even if you had not added it, would have been obvious; you say, "I write these things because I desire to love you in a sincere and Christian manner and not hold back anything in my mind that differs from what is on my lips." O holy man, you whom I love with sincere heart, as God sees my soul, this very same thing that you expressed in your letter and that I do not doubt that you have shown to me, this very same thing, I believe, the apostle Paul showed in his letter, not to each human being, but to the Jews and the Greeks and all the Gentiles, his children, whom he begot in the gospel and whom he labored to bring to birth.[61] And afterward he showed this to so many thousands of later faithful Christians, on whose account that letter was committed to memory in order to show that he did not hold back anything in his mind that differed from what was on his lips.

31. Certainly you also became like me, not by the wiles of a liar, but by the feeling of compassion, when you thought that you should not leave me in that sin in which you thought I had fallen, just as you would not have wanted to be left there if you had fallen in that way. Hence, I am grateful for your mind so kindly disposed toward me, and I at the same time ask that you not be angry at me because I have made known to you my concern when some things in your works disturbed me. For I want all to do with regard to me what I have done with regard to you, namely, that whatever they find in my writing that is blameworthy they neither hide in a deceitful heart nor criticize in front of others, while they are silent before me. For I think that this rather does injury to our friendship and violates the rules of our relationship. For I do not know whether friendships should be considered Christian in which the common saying, "Flattery begets friends, but truth gives birth to hatred,"[62] is more valid than the proverb of the Church, *Wounds from a friend are more trustworthy than the spontaneous kisses of an enemy* (Prv 27:6).

32. Hence, let us rather teach, with as much insistence as we can, our dearest friends who most sincerely foster our labors that they may know that it is

---

60. Letter 72, 2, 4.
61. See Gal 4:19.
62. Terrence, *Andrea* 68.

possible that among friends one contradicts the words of another, though love is, nonetheless, not diminished and though the truth, which is owed to friendship, does not give birth to hatred. It makes no difference whether what is contradicted is true or whether, whatever it may be, it is said with a sincere heart, without holding back anything in the mind that differs from what is on the lips. And so, let our brothers, those who live with you and to whom you bear witness that they are vessels of Christ,[63] believe that it was done against my will and that no small sorrow lies in my heart over the fact that my letter came into the hands of many before it was able to come to you, to whom it was written. How this happened would, however, take a long time to recount and, unless I am mistaken, it is unnecessary, since it is enough if the brothers at least believe me in this matter that it was not done with the intention that they supposed and that it was absolutely not done by my desire or plan or with my consent or even with my thought. If they do not believe this, and I say it with God as my witness, I have nothing more to do. Heaven forbid, nonetheless, that I myself should believe that they suggest these ideas to Your Holiness with an evil intention of stirring up hostilities between us. May the mercy of God keep such hostilities from us. But it is easy to suspect human failings in a human being without any intention of doing harm. For, if they are vessels of Christ made for not a dishonorable but an honorable purpose and placed in a grand house for a good work,[64] it is right for me to believe this of them. But if, after this testimony of mine has come to their knowledge, they choose to believe as they did, you yourself also see that they are not behaving correctly.

33. I had, of course, written that I did not send to Rome a book written against you.[65] I had written this because I did not connect the term "book" to that letter, and for this reason I had thought that you had heard of something or other absolutely different. Nor did I send this letter to Rome, but to you, and I did not think that it was against you, because I knew that I had written it out of the sincerity of friendship either to admonish you or to correct you or to be corrected by you. Apart from the brothers with whom you live, I beg you yourself by the grace by which we have been redeemed that you do not think that I have out of an insidious flattery mentioned in my letter all your good gifts, which were given you by the goodness of the Lord. But if I have sinned against you in any way, forgive me. As for that story that I quoted from the work of some poet or other with more ineptitude perhaps than literary flourish, do not apply it to yourself more than I said. For I immediately added that I had not said this in the sense that you might recover the eyes of your heart—heaven forbid that you ever lost them!—but that you might bring to bear the healthy and vigilant eyes you have. I thought that I

---

63. See Letter 72, 1, 2.
64. See 2 Tm 2:20-21.
65. See Letter 67, 2, 2.

should mention this only on account of imitating Stesichorus' παλινωδίαν,[66] if we wrote something that we ought to destroy by a later writing, not on account of his blindness, which I neither ascribed to your heart nor fear for it. And again I beg you to correct me with confidence where you see that I need this. For, though in accord with the terms of honor which the usage of the Church has introduced, the episcopacy is greater than the priesthood, Augustine is still less than Jerome in many ways, although one should not reject or disdain correction, even from any inferior.

5, 34. You have already persuaded me with regard to your translation of the benefit of wanting to translate the scripture from the Hebrew texts, namely, that you may bring out into the open whatever the Jews passed over or corrupted. But I ask that you be so good as to indicate which Jews you mean. Is it those by whom the scriptures were translated before the coming of the Lord? And if it is, which one or ones of them? Or is it these later ones who can be thought to have either removed some passages from the Greek manuscripts or corrupted them so that they might not be refuted by those testimonies concerning the Christian faith? I do not find any reason why those earlier translators would have wanted to do this.[67] Also send us, I beg you, your translation of the Septuagint, which I did not know you had published. I also desire to read your book that you mentioned on the best sort of translation and to know how one must combine in a translator knowledge of the languages with the conjectures of those who deal with the scriptures by expounding them. For, even if they have the one true faith, they necessarily produce diverse opinions because of the obscurity of many passages, though that variety of opinions is by no means in conflict with the unity of the same faith. Thus one commentator can explain the same passage in different ways in accord with the same faith because the obscurity of the texts allows this.

35. But I desire your translation of the Septuagint in order that we may be free, as much as possible, from the ignorance of the Latin translators, whoever they might be who have attempted this, and in order that those who suppose that I am jealous of your useful labors may at long last understand, if possible, that I did not want your translation from the Hebrew to be read in the churches for fear that, by introducing something new opposed to the authority of the Septuagint, we might disturb the people of God to their great scandal, for their ears and hearts are accustomed to that translation that even the apostles approved. Hence, if in Jonah that plant is in Hebrew neither an ivy nor a gourd plant, but something else that supports itself by its own trunk without any stakes, I would prefer that we read "gourd plant" in all the Latin translations.

36. I think that I have replied sufficiently, in fact perhaps more than sufficiently to your three letters; of these I received two by means of Cyprian and one

---

66. See Letter 40, 4, 7.
67. See Letter 72, 19.

by means of Firmus. Write back what you think good for instructing us or others. I, however, will make a more diligent effort, to the extent that the Lord helps me, that the letters which I write to you come into your hands before they come to those of anyone else who might circulate them more widely.[68] For I admit that I do not want to happen with your letters to me what you most justly complain happened with my letter to you. May we, nonetheless, enjoy not only mutual love for each other, but also a freedom of friendship so that you do not pass over in silence before me, nor I before you, what mutually disturbs us in our correspondence. That is, may we do this in fraternal love with a spirit that is not displeasing in the eyes of God. But if you do not think that this is possible between us without a harmful offense to love itself, let us not do this. For that love that I want to have with you is certainly greater, but this smaller love is something better than no love at all.

---

68. See Letter 72, 3, 5.

Letter 83

In 404 or 405 Augustine wrote to his lifelong friend, Alypius, who was now the bishop of Thagaste, Augustine's hometown, concerning the possessions of Honoratus, a priest from Thiave, who died in the monastery of Thagaste. The faithful of Thiave claimed his money as their own. Augustine tells Alypius that the disturbance of the faithful of Thiave must be settled immediately and offers him his own resolution of the problem (paragraph 1). He warns that bishops must avoid giving scandal and should avoid even the appearance of greed (paragraph 2). Augustine points out that the problem with Honoratus could have been avoided if he disposed of his goods before entering the monastery (paragraph 3). Augustine suggests the rule that the possessions of a cleric should belong to the church where he was ordained if he dies without selling or giving them away. He reports that he sought the advice of another bishop who was horrified at the first decision of Augustine and Alypius (paragraph 4). Augustine begs Alypius to sign and send on the letter he has drafted in the name of both of them so that they can avoid further harm to the faithful of Thiave (paragraph 5). He agrees to pay half of what the people are claiming if Alypius really thinks that it is just, when his monastery has such a sum (paragraph 6).

To his most blessed and venerably most dear and most beloved brother and fellow bishop, Alypius, and to those brothers who are with you, Augustine and the brothers who are with me send greetings in the Lord.

1. The sadness of the church of Thiave does not permit my heart to rest until I hear that they have been restored to their original relation with you, something that must be done quickly. For, if the apostle had tried to do so much because of one man, when he said, *Lest such a person be swallowed up by greater sadness* (2 Cor 2:7), where he also said, *For fear that we should be taken over by Satan, for we are not unaware of his wiles* (2 Cor 2:11), how much more ought we to act with vigilance for fear that we should have to grieve over this in a whole flock and especially in those who have now entered the Catholic peace and whom I can in no way abandon. But since the shortness of time has not permitted us to carefully work out together a well-considered statement on this, I ask Your Holiness to accept what I have decided in thinking about it for a long time since our parting. And if you also like it, let the letter that I wrote to them in the name of both of us be sent on without delay.

2. You said that the faithful of Thiave should have half of their inheritance[1] and that I should somehow or other provide them with the other half. I, however, think that, if we provide[2] them with whole of it, it would be the case that people

---

1. The dispute concerned the property of the priest, Honoratus, who died without a will.
2. I have followed the reading in one manuscript of *"provideretur"* in place of *"auferetur,"* which is found in the CSEL.

said that we labored so greatly, not for money, but for justice. But when we grant them half and in that way compromise with them at some point, people will see quite clearly that our concern has been only financial, and you see what damage results. For to them we will give the impression that we have taken the half belonging to them, and to us they will give the impression that they have suffered a wrong and an injustice in receiving a half, while the whole of it belonged to the poor. For your words, "We must be careful that, when we want to correct a doubtful matter, we do not inflict more serious wounds," will have the same validity if they are granted a half. For on account of a half, of course, those whose entrance into monastic life we want to foster are going to delay the selling of their property through those periods in which they excuse themselves in order that they might be dealt with in accord with this example. Finally, if there is so great a scandal of a whole people over a doubtful matter, would it be a surprise that they think that their bishops, whom they hold in high esteem, are tainted with filthy greed, if the appearance of wrongdoing is not avoided?

3. For, when anyone enters a monastery, if he enters with a sincere heart, he does not think about that problem, especially after having been warned how wrong it is. If, however, he is pretending and is seeking his own interests, not those of Jesus Christ,[3] he surely does not have love. And what good does it do him if he distributes all he has to the poor and hands his body over to be burned?[4] Besides this, as we have already said, that problem can be avoided hereafter and handled with the one entering the monastery if he cannot be admitted to the society of the brothers before he strips himself of all those impediments and enters free from business concerns since those possessions have ceased to be his. But we can only avoid this death for the weak and so great an impediment to the salvation of those for whom we have labored so greatly in order to gain them for the Catholic peace, if they understand with absolute clarity that we are by no means after their money in such cases. And they will never understand this unless we leave for their use that property that they thought always belonged to the priest, because, even if it was not his, they ought to have known this from the beginning.

4. It seems to me, then, that this rule should be observed in matters of this sort: whatever belongs to the man who is ordained a cleric anywhere, by whatever law he owns such things, should belong to the church in which he is ordained. Now that property we are dealing with belongs to the priest, Honoratus, by the same law so that, having been ordained elsewhere, but still living in the monastery of Thagaste, if he died with some property not sold nor transferred to someone by a public gift, only his heir would enter into possession of it, just as Brother Aemilian came into possession of those thirty silver pieces of Brother Privatus.

3. See Phil 2:21.
4. See 1 Cor 13:3.

These precautions, then, should be taken in advance; if, however, they were not taken, it is necessary for them to observe those laws that have been established in civil society for acquiring or not acquiring possession of such things, in order that we may avoid, as far as possible, not only all wrongdoing, but even the appearance of wrongdoing,[5] and that we may preserve our good reputation, which is quite necessary for our ministry. Let Your Wisdom consider how damaging the appearance of wrongdoing can be. Leaving aside the sorrow of those people that we experienced, for fear that I myself might be deceived in some way, as often happens when I err by being more inclined to my own view, I recounted the whole case to our brother and colleague, Samsucius,[6] without as yet telling him what I now think, but rather including what the two of us thought when we were opposing those people. He was deeply horrified and was amazed that we had that idea, disturbed by nothing else but the appearance of wrongdoing, which is most inappropriate not only for our life and conduct, but for the life and conduct of anyone.

5. Hence, I beg you not to delay in sending on with your signature the letter that I wrote to them under both of our names. And if you see with great clarity that my proposal in it is just, let the weak not now be forced to learn what I do not as yet understand, but in this case let us observe in their regard to the words of the Lord, *I have many things to say to you, but you cannot now bear them* (Jn 16:12). While sparing, of course, such weakness, he also said this about paying the tribute, *Therefore, the children are exempt, but for fear that we cause them scandal* (Mt 17:26), and so on, when he sent Peter in order that they might pay the two drachmas, which were then demanded. For he knew another law in accord with which he owed nothing of the sort, but he paid the tribute in accord with that law by which we said that the heir of the priest, Honoratus, would have come into possession of his goods if he died before he gave away or sold his possessions. And yet, with regard the very law of the Church the apostle Paul spares the weak and does not exact the wages they owe him, certain in his conscience that he would demand them with full justice. But he avoided nothing other than the suspicion that disturbs the good odor of Christ and held himself back from that appearance of wrongdoing, in those regions where he knew this was necessary,[7] and perhaps before he had experienced the sorrow of the people. But let us, though slower, at least after we have experienced this sorrow, correct what we ought to have foreseen.

6. Finally, because I fear every eventuality and recall what you proposed at our departure, namely, that the brothers of Thagaste should consider me as owing half of that sum, if you clearly see that this is just, on that condition at least

5. See 1 Thes 5:22.
6. Samsucius was the bishop of Turris in Numidia.
7. See 1 Cor 9:1-23.

I will not refuse to pay it when I have it, that is, when so great an amount is obtained by the monastery of Hippo that this can be done without difficulty, that is, that, when so great a sum has been removed, our brothers receive a part no less than equal in proportion to the number of members of the community.

Letter 84

Sometime between 397 and 411 Augustine wrote to Novatus, who was the Catholic bishop of Sitifis in Mauretania Sitifensis, from 403 to 440. Augustine firmly refuses to send Novatus' blood brother, the deacon, Lucillus, back to Sitifis, arguing that the needs of the Church must take precedence over brotherly affection and friendship (paragraph 1). Lucillus' knowledge of Punic makes him necessary for the church of Hippo where there is need for clerics with that language, which is common in Sitifis (paragraph 2).

To his most blessed, venerable, and lovable brother and fellow priest, Novatus, and to those brothers who are with him, Augustine and those brothers who are with me send greetings in the Lord.

1. I too am aware of how hardhearted I seem, and I can scarcely bear with myself because I do not send and surrender to Your Holiness my son, the deacon Lucillus, who is your blood brother. But when you yourself also begin to grant to the needs of churches located far from you some of your most dear and beloved sons whom you have educated, then you will feel the stings of desire by which I am pierced because certain people bound to me by the closest and deepest friendship are not also physically present with me. For, in order that I might send your blood relative away, despite all that blood brotherhood can do, it does not surpass the bond of friendship by which Brother Severus[1] and I are bound to each other, and you, nonetheless, know how rarely it happens that I see him. And the reason for this is not my will or his. Rather, for the sake of the world to come, in which we will live with each other inseparably, we set the needs of our mother, the Church, before the needs of our own time. How much more rightly, therefore, ought you to tolerate for the benefit of mother Church the absence of that brother, with whom you have not tasted the Lord's supper for nearly as long a time as I have not with my most dear fellow citizen, Severus, who speaks to me now hardly at all or at times by means of very short messages, and more of them are filled with other cares and concerns than carry to me something from our meadows with the sweetness of Christ.

2. At this point you may perhaps say, "So what? Will my brother not be useful to the church among us? Or do I long to have him with me for some other reason?" Clearly, if you thought that his presence was as beneficial there as I think that it is here for gaining and governing the flocks of the Lord, no one would rightly blame, not my hardness of heart, but my injustice. But since the

---

1. Severus was the Catholic bishop of Milevis in Numidia.

preaching of the gospel suffers much in our territories for the lack of the Punic[2] language, while in your area the use of the same language is common, do you think that we ought to look after the salvation of the people of the Lord in such a way that we send a man with this ability off there and remove him from here, where we long for his abilities with great desire of the heart? Pardon me, therefore, because not merely contrary to your desire, but also contrary to my feelings, I am doing what the burdensome care of a pastor constrains me to do. The Lord, to whom you have entrusted your heart, will grant you that your labors are such that you will be rewarded for this benefit. For in that way you have rather granted to the most ardent thirst of our territories the deacon, Lucillus, and you will give me no small gift when you will not further burden me with any request on this matter. Otherwise, I will seem to be only more hardhearted in the eyes of Your Benevolence, who are venerable for me and holy.

---

2. I have followed the conjecture by Antoine Arnauld, "*Punicae linguae*," in place of "*Latina lingua*," which is found in the CSEL.

Letter 85

Between 405 and 408 Augustine wrote to Paul, bishop of Cataqua in Numidia.[1] Augustine reprimands Paul for his manner of living that has seriously wounded the church of Hippo (paragraph 1) and urges him to live the sort of life appropriate to his holy calling (paragraph 2).

To his sincerely most beloved lord, brother, and fellow priest, Paul,[2] who will be blessed by all our prayers, Augustine sends greetings in the Lord.

1. You would not call me so hardhearted if you did not think that I was also a liar. For what else do you believe of my heart when you write such things but that I hold against you the sin of discord and detestable hatred, as if in so evident a matter I do not take care lest, while preaching to others, I myself am found to be rejected?[3] Or as if I wanted to remove the straw from your eye, while leaving the beam in my own?[4] It is not what you think. Look, I say it again, and I call God as my witness that, if you would want for yourself those things that I want for you, you would already be securely living in Christ and you would be bringing joy to his whole Church in the glory of his name. Look, I wrote that you are not only my brother, but my colleague. For it is not possible that any bishop of the Catholic Church, whoever he may be, not be a colleague of mine, provided that he has not been condemned by an ecclesiastical court. But there is no reason that I should not be in communion with you except that I cannot flatter you. For I am especially indebted to you because I brought you to birth in Christ Jesus through the gospel, reproaching you truthfully with the sting of salutary love. And I rejoice that with God's help many have been drawn into the Catholic Church through you, while I must also bewail the fact that more are driven from it. For you have so wounded the church of Hippo that, unless the Lord delivers you from all your worldly concerns and burdens and calls you back to a genuine episcopal manner of life, such a wound cannot be healed.

2. But since you do not cease to become more and more involved so that after renouncing them you insert yourself even into those affairs that you renounced, something that cannot in any way be defended even in terms of human laws, and since you are said to live in that ostentation for which the frugality of your church cannot suffice, why are you looking for communion with me since you never

---

1. See Letter 92, which Augustine wrote to Boniface, the successor of Paul as bishop of Cataqua. From Letter 92 the present letter can be dated as prior to September 408.
2. Paul was the Catholic bishop of Cataqua in Numidia.
3. See 1 Cor 9:27.
4. See Mt 7:4 and Lk 6:41.

wanted to listen to my admonition? Or is it in order that people, whose complaints I cannot endure, may impute to me whatever you do? But you have no reason to suspect that those people who were always opposed to you even in your earlier life are your detractors. It is not so, nor is it surprising that much escapes your notice. But even if this were true, they ought to have found nothing in your conduct with which they might rightly find fault and because of which they might blaspheme against the Church. You perhaps still think that I say these things because I did not accept your excuse. On the contrary, I say them for fear that I could not excuse my sins before God if I kept silent with you about these things. I know that you have a heart, but even a slow heart is secure when it is in heaven, and a clever heart is nothing while it is on earth. The episcopacy is not the art of living a life of deception. The Lord God will teach you what I am saying, for he has closed off for you all the roads for which you wanted to make use of him in order that he might direct you onto that road for which he has placed upon you so holy a burden in order that you may walk on it.

Letter 86

Between 406 and 409 Augustine wrote to Caecilian, the governor of Africa. He briefly praises the anti-Donatist edict issued by Caecilian and urges him to implement the edict in Hippo and the surrounding territory.

To his excellent lord and son, Caecilian,[1] who is truly and rightly honorable and to be embraced in the love of Christ, Augustine the bishop sends greetings in the Lord.

The splendor[2] of your administration, the reputation of your virtues, and also the praiseworthy concern and faithful sincerity of your Christian piety are gifts of God, and you rejoice that they have been given to you by him from whom you hope for better ones in accord with his promise. These gifts have stirred me to share with Your Excellency the turmoil of my concern by addressing this letter to you. For to the extent that we rejoice that you have shown concern for the Catholic unity through the other parts of Africa with a wonderful effectiveness, to that extent we are saddened that the region of Hippo Regius and the areas near it bordering on Numidia have not yet merited to be helped by the force of your official decree, my excellent lord and son, who are truly and rightly honorable and to be embraced in the love of Christ. For fear that this may be ascribed to the negligence of myself, who have the burden of bishop in Hippo, I thought that I should not keep silent before Your Magnificence. If you would deign to listen to how presumptuous the audacity of heretics has been in the area of Hippo either from my brothers and colleagues who could tell Your Highness of these things or from the priest whom I sent to you with a letter, you would undoubtedly with the help of the Lord our God make provision that the tumor of sacrilegious vanity may be healed by instilling fear rather than cut away by taking vengeance.

---

1. Caecilian was a Catholic layman and the legate for Numidia of the proconsul of Africa.
2. I have followed the reading *"claritas"* in the PL rather than *"castitas,"* which is found in the CSEL.

Letter 87

Between 405 and 411 Augustine wrote to Emeritus, the Donatist bishop of Caesarea in Mauretania Caesariensis.[1] Augustine explains that he has heard that Emeritus is a good man with a good mind and urges against him the argument that the presence of unknown sinners cannot defile the members of the Church (paragraph 1). Nor can known sinners be a hindrance to the good people in the Church (paragraph 2). It is not the presence of a sinner in a community, but joining in the commission of the sin or the approval of the sin that makes a person sinful (paragraph 3). The earlier Donatists did not act consistently when in order to preserve their unity they did not expel Optatus (paragraph 4). The Donatists cannot plead that they did not know the crimes of Optatus and at the same time hold as excommunicated the whole world, most of which has never heard of what happened in Africa (paragraph 5). The principal question is why the schism came about (paragraph 6). Augustine appeals to Paul's words to justify the action of the earthly powers to suppress the Donatists (paragraph 7). The Catholics appeal to the Roman authorities, not in order to persecute the Donatists, but in order to defend themselves from them (paragraph 8). The Catholics want the Donatists to be united with them in order that they may have life in the Church of Christ (paragraph 9). The principal question, once again, is why the Donatists began the schism (paragraph 10).

To his lovable and beloved brother, Emeritus, Augustine sends greetings.

1. When I hear that someone endowed with a good mind and educated in the liberal arts—though the salvation of the soul is not found in them—holds another view than the truth demands on a very easy question, the more I am surprised, the more I am eager to know the man and to converse with him or, if I am unable to do this, I desire to touch his mind and be touched in turn by him, at least by letters, which speed over long distances. As I hear that you are such a man, I also grieve that you have been torn away and separated from the Catholic Church, which is spread throughout the whole world, as was foretold by the Holy Spirit.[2] But I do not know why you are separated from the Church. For it is certain that the sect of Donatus is unknown to a great part of the Roman world, not to mention the barbarian nations as well, to which the apostle said that he was under obligation[3] and with whose Christian faith our communion is united. And it is certain that they absolutely do not know when or for what reasons this schism has arisen. And unless you admit that all those Christians are innocent of the charges that you hurl at Africa, you are forced to say that you are all guilty of the evil actions of all your people and are all defiled, since there are hidden

---

1. Emeritus was a participant at the Council of Carthage in 411; Augustine debated with him in Caesarea on 20 September 418.
2. See Ps 2:8.
3. See Rom 1:14.

among you, to put it mildly, some misguided souls. For you do not expel someone from your communion, or you only expel him after he has done that action because of which he had to be expelled. You do condemn someone who remains unknown for some time and is afterwards exposed and proven guilty, do you not? I ask, then, whether he did not contaminate you during that time when he remained unknown? You will answer, "In no way." He would, then, contaminate no one at any time, even if the sin was always unknown. For we often find out about the commission of some sins by people who are now dead, and it does not harm those Christians who were in communion with them when they were living. Why, then, have you cut yourselves off by your sacrilegious schism from communion with countless Eastern churches, which have never known and still do not know what you either teach or pretend was done in Africa?

2. It is another question, after all, whether those charges you make are true, charges that we in fact prove to be false by much more plausible proofs, and we claim that those charges that you hurl at us were better proven then against your people. But, as I said, this is another question to be undertaken and examined when there is need. Let your vigilant mind now consider this: No one can be contaminated by the unknown crimes of unknown people. Hence, it is evident that you have separated yourselves by a sacrilegious schism from communion with the world that does not know and never has known the charges, whether true or false, that you direct at Africa. And yet, it should not go unmentioned that even evil persons we know cause no harm to the good people in the Church, if there is lacking the authority to keep them from communion or if some reason for preserving the peace prevents this. For who are the ones who in the prophet Ezekiel merited to be sealed before the destruction of the wicked and to escape unharmed, when the wicked were destroyed,[4] if not, as is most clearly shown there, those who grieve and groan over the sins and injustices of the people of God that are committed in their midst? But who groans and grieves over what he does not know? For the same reason Paul the apostle tolerates false brethren. After all, he does not say of persons he does not know, *For all seek their own interests, not those of Jesus Christ* (Phil 2:21), and he, nonetheless, shows that they were with him. What sort of people are they who preferred to offer incense to idols or to hand over the books of God rather than to die but those who *seek their own interests, not those of Jesus Christ*?

3. I pass over many testimonies of the scriptures in order not to make this letter longer than necessary, and I leave many points for you to consider with your learning. But see, I beg you, what is sufficient: If so many unjust persons in the one people of God do not make *those who testified against them* (Neh 9:26) to be as bad as they were, if a multitude of false brethren[5] do not make the apostle

---

4. See Ez 9:4-6.
5. See Gal 2:4 and 2 Cor 11:26.

Paul, who was living in the one Church with them, one of those who *seek their own interests, not those of Jesus Christ*, it is evident that a person does not become the same as a bad person with whom he approaches the altar of Christ, even if the bad person is not unknown, provided one does not approve of that person and separates himself from him by a good conscience by disapproving of him. It is evident, then, that to be an accomplice of a thief is nothing other than to steal with him or to accept his theft with a consenting heart. We say this in order to remove countless superfluous questions about the actions of human beings that do not undermine our argument.

4. But unless you also hold this position, you all will be just as Optatus[6] was in your communion, since you were not unaware of him. May God keep this from the conduct of Emeritus and such others among you who I have no doubt are far removed from the deeds of that man. After all, our objection against you is only the crime of schism, which you have also made into heresy by wrongly continuing in it. But regarding how great this sin is considered in the judgment of God, read the passage I have no doubt that you have read. You will find that Dathan and Abiram were swallowed by the earth's opening up and that all the rest who sided with them were consumed by a fire coming from the midst of them.[7] The Lord God branded that crime with an immediate punishment as an example of what we should avoid in order that, when he spares such sinners with great patience, he might show what sort of punishment he is reserving for the last judgment. Nor do we, after all, blame your arguments if at that time when Optatus is reported to have raged with his pestilential power, when he was accused by the groaning of the whole of Africa with your groans included, at least if you are the sort of person that your reputation declares you to be, something that God knows that I both believe and desire. We do not blame you, if you did not want to excommunicate him at that time for fear that he would drag with him many other excommunicated people and would split your communion with the madness of schism. But this is precisely what condemns you, Brother Emeritus: Though you saw that it is so great an evil that the sect of Donatus be divided that you thought that Optatus should be tolerated in your communion rather than that such a split be accepted, you remain in that evil that was committed by your predecessors in dividing the Church of Christ.

5. Here perhaps because of the lack of an answer, you will attempt to defend Optatus. Do not, brother, do not, I beg you. It is not fitting for your character, and even if it is perhaps fitting for someone else's, if anything can be fitting for evil persons, it is certainly not fitting for Emeritus to defend Optatus. But it is perhaps fitting for you not to accuse him. Granted that it is so. Take the middle path, and say: *Each person carries his own burden* (Gal 6:5). *Who are you to*

---

6. Optatus was the infamous Donatist bishop of Thamugadi in Numidia. See Letter 53, 6.
7. See Nm 16:31-35.

judge another's servant? (Rom 14:4). Even if by the testimony of the whole of Africa, in fact even by that of all lands, wherever the reputation of Gildo[8] spread, Optatus was also known at the same time,[9] you have never dared to pronounce judgment on Optatus for fear that you would rashly pronounce judgment on persons whom you did not know. Can we and ought we—merely on the basis of your testimony—rashly pass judgment concerning persons whom we do not know? Is it not enough that you condemn actions you do not know unless we also pronounce judgment on actions we do not know? After all, you do not defend Optatus, even if he is in danger because of misguided hatred, but you defend yourself when you say, "I do not know what sort of man he was." How much more is the Eastern world ignorant of the sort of people those lesser known Africans were whom you accuse! And yet, from those churches whose names you have in your books and read aloud, you are separated by a wicked schism. If your bishop of Thamugadi, who was most infamous and notorious, was unknown to his colleague at that time—I do not mean in Caesarea, but in Sitifis— how was the church of the Corinthians, of the Ephesians, of the Colossians, of the Philippians, of the Thessalonians, and of the Antiochenes, the church of Pontus, of Galatia, of Cappadocia, and of the other parts of the world, which were built up in Christ by the apostles, able either to know the African traditors, whoever they were, or to deserve condemnation by you because they were not able to know them? And yet, you are not in communion with them, say that they are not Christians, and try to rebaptize them. What am I to say? What complaint am I to put forth? Or what outcry am I to make? If I am speaking with a man of intelligence, I share with you the sharpness of this indignation. For you see, of course, what I might say if I wanted to say it.

6. Or did your predecessors perhaps hold a council among themselves and condemn the whole Christian world apart from themselves? Has your assessment of the situation been reduced to the point that the council of the Maximianists, who split off from your splinter group, has no validity against you, because they were very few compared to you, while your council has validity against the nations, which are the heritage of Christ, and against the ends of the earth, which are his possession?[10] I wonder whether a person has any blood in his body who does not blush at this. Reply to these points, please; I heard, after all, from some people whom I could not fail to believe that you would reply if I wrote you. I had already sent one letter, though I do not know whether you received it or replied to it and I perhaps did not receive your reply. Now I again ask that you not delay to reply to these questions what you think.

---

8. Gildo was Count of Africa from 395 to 397 and sided with Optatus of Thamugadi.
9. Optatus was known as "Gildonius" because of his association with Count Gildo.
10. See Ps 2:8.

But do not wander off into other questions; for the beginning of a well-ordered investigation starts with this question: Why was the schism produced?

7. For, when earthly authorities persecute the schismatics, they defend themselves by that rule which the apostle states, *One who resists authority resists the governance of God. But those who resist bring condemnation upon themselves. For rulers cause no fear for a good work, but for an evil work. Do you want to be without fear of the authority? Do good, and you will have praise from him. For he is God's minister for your good. But if you do evil, fear. For he does not carry the sword for no reason. He is, after all, God's servant to carry out his wrath in punishing the wrongdoer* (Rom 13:2-4). The whole question, then, amounts to whether schism is not something evil or whether you did not produce a schism, that is, whether you resist the authorities for a good work, not for an evil work, because of which you will receive condemnation. Hence, in his great providence God did not say merely, *Blessed are those who suffer persecution,* but added, *On account of justice* (Mt 5:10). I desire, then, to know from you if it is justice that you did in that act of schism, in which you also remain, in accord with what I said above. Is it wrong to condemn the whole world without a hearing, either because it had not heard what you heard or because your beliefs or accusations without certain proofs have not been made known to it? And is it wrong for this reason to want to rebaptize so many churches of the Lord that were founded by the preaching and labor of the apostles, when he was still here in the flesh? If so, why are you permitted either not to know your evil African colleagues who are living at the same time and administering the sacraments at the same time or even to know them, but to tolerate them so that the sect of Donatus is not divided, whereas those situated in the farthest corner of the world are not permitted to be ignorant of what you either know or believe or have heard or make up concerning Africans? What a great perversity it is to cling to one's own wickedness and bring accusations against the severity of the state!

8. "But," you claim, "it is not permitted that Christians persecute even bad people." Granted; it should not be permitted. But is it right to raise this as an objection to the authorities that were established precisely for this purpose? Or shall we do away with the apostle? Or do your books lack those lines that I quoted? "But," you will say, "you ought not to be in communion with such people." What follows then? Were you not in communion with Flavian, once the vicar for Africa, a man of your sect, because, in obedience to the laws, he put to death the guilty persons he had found. "But," you will say, "you stir up the Roman emperors against us." On the contrary, you stir them up against yourselves, for you have dared to tear apart with your schism the Church of which they are members, as was foretold so long before. For it was said of Christ, *And the kings of the earth will adore him* (Ps 72:11). And you still stubbornly dare to rebaptize. But our people seek protection from the established authority against the illicit and private acts of violence, acts over which you yourselves, who do

not do such actions, sorrow and groan. Our people do this, not in order to persecute you, but to defend themselves. The apostle Paul acted in the same way against the Jews who were conspiring to kill him, before the Roman empire was Christian, so that he was also given the protection of armed guards.[11] But at whatever occasion those emperors know the evil of your schism, they set up against you whatever they choose in accord with their concern and authority. For it is not without reason that they carry the sword; they are, after all, God's servants to carry out his wrath in punishing wrongdoers.[12] Finally, even if some of ours do these actions without Christian moderation, we are displeased, but we still do not leave the Catholic Church on account of them if we cannot cleanse it before the last day when the straw will be separated from the wheat,[13] since even you did not leave the sect of Donatus on account of Optatus when you did not dare to expel him.

9. But you say after all, "Why do you want us to be united with you if we are criminals?" Because you are still alive and can be corrected if you would want to. For, when you are united to us, that is, to the Church of Christ, the heritage of Christ, whose possession is the ends of the earth,[14] you are corrected so that you have life from the root. For the apostle speaks in this way of the branches that were broken off, *God, after all, is able to reinsert them* (Rom 11:23). Change, then, in that respect in which you were in dissent, though the sacraments that you have are holy, since they are the same in all. Hence, we want you to change from your misguided ways, that is, so that your cut-off branches may be again attached to the root. For the sacraments, which you have not changed, are approved by us as you have them. Otherwise, when we want to correct your wickedness, we would do a sacrilegious injury to those mysteries of Christ, which were not spoiled in your wickedness. For even Saul had not spoiled the anointing he had received, the anointing to which King David, the devout servant of God, showed such great respect.[15] For this reason we, who want to restore you to the root, do not rebaptize you; we, nonetheless, accept as valid the form of the branch that has been cut off, if it has not been changed. Though the branch is whole, it still can in no way bear fruit without the root. One question concerns the persecutions that you say you suffer from such great gentleness and mildness on the part of ours, though your people actually do as private citizens forbidden acts that are worse; another question concerns baptism since we do not ask where it exists, but where it is beneficial. For wherever it is, it is the same, but the one who receives it is not always the same wherever he is. And so, we detest the private sinfulness of human beings in the schism, but we reverence the

---

11. See Acts 23:12-24.
12. See Rom 13:4.
13. See Mt 3:12.
14. See Ps 2:8.
15. See 2 Sam 1:1-16.

baptism of Christ everywhere. For, if deserters carry off with them the standards of the emperor, once they have either been punished by condemnation or corrected by pardon, the standards are received back intact, if they remained intact. And if anything needs to be more carefully investigated concerning this matter, it is another question, as I said. For in these areas we ought to do what the Church of God does.

10. The question is whether yours or ours is the Church of God. Hence, we must ask from the beginning why you began the schism. If you do not write back, I have, I believe, an easy case before God. For I sent to a man who I heard is, apart from the schism, a good and liberally educated person a letter that attempts to restore peace. It is up to you to see what you should reply to God, whose patience should now be praised, but whose judgment is to be feared in the end. But if you write back with the same care with which you see I have written to you, the mercy of God will be with you in order that at some point the error that divides us may perish out of the love of peace and by reason of the truth. Remember what I said about the Rogatists who are said to call you Firmians, just as you call us Macarians.[16] Nor have I said anything about your bishop of Rusicca; he is reported to have had an agreement with Firmus about the safety of his people so that the gates were opened for him and the Catholics were handed to him for slaughter and countless other things. Stop, then, exaggerating by these familiar arguments the actions of human beings, whether rumored or known for facts. For you see what I pass over in silence regarding your people in order that the discussion may focus on the origin of the schism where the whole case rests. May the Lord God inspire you with thoughts of peace, my lovable and beloved brother. Amen.

---

16. Rogatus was the Donatist bishop of Cartenna in Mauritania Caesariensis; disgusted with the conduct of the Circumcellions, he broke away from the Donatists with several other bishops to form the sect of the Rogatists. See Letter 93, 3, 11. Firmus was an African chief who revolted in 372; he was supported by the Donatists and persecuted the Rogatists. For Macarius, the imperial commissioner who persecuted the Donatists, see Letter 44, 4.

Letter 88

Between 406 and 411 the Catholic clerics of Hippo wrote to Januarius, the
Donatist bishop of Casae Nigrae in Numidia and Donatist primate of Africa.
They begin by denouncing the violence of the Circumcellions. They include a
copy of the letter of Anulinus, the proconsul of Africa, to the emperor,
Constantine, to remind Januarius of the beginnings of the schism (paragraph 1).
The letter forwarded to Constantine the Donatist appeals for a hearing (paragraph 2). The clerics tell of how Constantine granted the Donatists an episcopal
hearing in Rome where Caecilian, the Catholic bishop of Carthage, was
acquitted and of how the Donatists again appealed to the emperor who granted
them another episcopal hearing in Arles where Caecilian was again acquitted
(paragraph 3). A letter to the proconsul of Africa from the two emperors is
included to show how the Donatists continued to badger the imperial court for
redress (paragraph 4). Hence, the clerics point out that the Donatists have themselves to blame for the orders of the emperor first issued against them (paragraph
5). The Donatists should not complain that laws have recently been promulgated
against them by the emperor since their clerics and the Circumcellions have
disturbed the peace of Africa with their violence against the Catholics (paragraph 6). The Catholic bishops did not appeal to the emperor after such violence,
but proposed a council, which was rejected by the Donatist bishop. Hence, when
the violence did not subside, the Catholic bishops appealed to the emperor who
issued the recent laws (paragraph 7). Januarius refused to hold a conference with
the Catholics, and the violence of the Circumcellions increased; yet, the
Donatists complain about being persecuted while they kill some Catholics and
try to blind others with acid and lime (paragraph 8). The clerics describe their
own gentle treatment of Donatists held in their custody, though they admit that
some Catholics have not acted with such restraint (paragraph 9). They urge the
Donatists to hold a conference among themselves to correct such violent
behavior (paragraph 10) and then to meet with the Catholics to debate which side
has the truth (paragraph 11). If the Donatists refuse to give the Catholic clerics a
hearing, the latter ask that they at least write back and quiet down from their acts
of violence (paragraph 12).

The Catholic clergy of the area of Hippo Regius send greetings to Januarius.

1. Your clerics and Circumcellions rage against us in a persecution of a new
kind and of unprecedented cruelty. If they were repaying evil with evil, they
would even so be acting against the law of Christ. But now, after having considered all your actions and ours, we find that we are suffering what scripture says,
They have repaid me with evil for good (Ps 35:12), and in another psalm, *With
these who hated peace, I was peaceful; when I spoke to them, they attacked me
without reason* (Ps 120:7). After all, since you have attained so advanced an age,
we think that you know very well that the sect of Donatus, which was first called

351

the sect of Majorinus at Carthage,[1] accused on its own initiative Caecilian, then bishop of the church of Carthage, before the illustrious former emperor, Constantine. But lest Your Reverence has perhaps forgotten this or you are pretending not to know of it or even perhaps do not know it, which we do not think to be the case, we insert in our letter a copy of the report of Anulinus, then proconsul, to whom the sect of Majorinus then appealed in order that the charges that it was bringing against Caecilian might be sent on by the same proconsul to the emperor already mentioned.

"Anulinus, Ex-Consul, Proconsul of Africa, sends greetings to our august emperor.

2. Having received and reverenced your heavenly writings, your devoted servant has taken care to communicate them in an official manner to Caecilian and his subordinates, who are called clerics. I have exhorted them to establish unity by the agreement of all and, since they seem to be set free by the graciousness of your majesty from all public service, I exhorted them to devote themselves to the things of God, while preserving with due reverence the holiness of the Catholic law. But after a few days there came forward certain persons with a large crowd of people joined to them who thought that they must speak against Caecilian, and they presented to your humble servant a sealed document on parchment and a booklet without a seal, and they asked me earnestly to send them on to the sacred and venerable court of Your Divine Majesty. With Caecilian retaining his status, your humble servant has taken care to forward these documents along with the proceedings of these same actions attached to them so that Your Majesty can decide all these issues. Two booklets have been sent on, one on parchment with the title: 'The Book of Catholic Church with the Charges against Caecilian Submitted by the Sect of Majorinus,' and the other attached to the same parchment without a seal. Given on April 15th in Carthage, to our lord, Constantine Augustus, consul for the third time."

3. After this report that was sent to him the emperor commanded that the two sides come to an episcopal hearing to be held in the city of Rome. The church records indicate how the case was heard and terminated there and how Caecilian was judged innocent. Now after the peaceful and balanced judgment of the episcopal court all stubbornness of strife and animosity ought, of course, to have been extinguished. But your predecessors again went back to the emperor, and they complained that the judgment was not correctly rendered and that the whole case was not heard. Hence, he granted that another episcopal hearing be held in Arles, a city of Gaul, where many bishops of your sect returned to communion

---

1. Majorinus, who was the counterpart of Caecilian, was the first bishop in the schism that was later called Donatism.

with Caecilian after your vain and diabolical schism was condemned.[2] But others, who were most stubborn and contentious, appealed to the same emperor. Afterwards, he himself was compelled to terminate the case of the bishops after hearing the two sides, and he first established a law against your side such that your places of assembly were claimed for the imperial treasury. If we wanted to include the proofs for all these matters, we would have made this letter excessively long. This point, nonetheless, must not be passed over, namely, how the case of Felix of Aptungi was examined and terminated in a public court at the insistence of your people before the emperor. Your fathers said that this Felix was the source of all the evils in the council of Carthage presided over by Secundus of Tigisi. For by his letter, of which we have made a copy below, the previously mentioned emperor bears witness that your people constantly made accusations and appeals before him on this case.

"The Emperors, Caesar Flavius Constantine Maximus and Caesar Valerius Licinian Licinius, send greetings to Probian, the Proconsul of Africa.

4. Since Verus, the vicar of the prefects in our Africa, a most excellent man, was at the time impeded because of ill health, Aelian, your predecessor, who was acting in his stead, rightly believed that, among other things, he should recall for his examination and jurisdiction the question or animosity that is seen to have been stirred up concerning Caecilian, the bishop of the Catholic Church. For, after he had brought before him Superius, the centurion, and Caecilian, the magistrate of the people of Aptungi, Saturninus, the former curator, Celebius the younger, the curator of the same city, and Solus, the civil servant of the same city, he gave them a hearing in accord with the law. As a result, when the objection was raised against Caecilian that the episcopacy, it seems, was conferred upon him by Felix, who, it seems, according to the objection had handed over and burned the sacred books, he determined that Felix was innocent of this. Secondly, since Maximus claimed that Ingentius, the decurion of the city of Zicca, had falsified the letter of Caecilian, the former duumvir, we saw clearly from the proceedings that were attached that the same Ingentius was put on the rack and was not subjected to torture because he claimed that he was the decurion of the city of Zicca. Hence, we want that you send this same Ingentius with a suitable escort to my imperial court, that is, of Constantine Augustus, in order that in the presence and hearing of those who are presently pleading this case and who do not cease to appeal day after day, it can be seen and can become known that they are stirring up hatred for Caecilian, the bishop, without reason and want to rise up with force against him. For in that way it will come about that,

2. Thirty-three bishops met at Arles in 314 and confirmed the decision made the previous year in Rome under Pope Melchiades.

with such strife removed, as it ought to be, the people will practice their own religion with due reverence and without any disagreement."

5. Since you see that these are the facts, why is it that you stir up hatred against us concerning the orders of the emperors that are established against you? After all, it was rather you who did all this before. If the emperors ought to issue no orders in these cases, if this concern ought not to belong to the Christian emperors, who urged your predecessors to forward the case of Caecilian to the emperor through the proconsul? Who urged you again to accuse before the emperor a bishop against whom you had already somehow pronounced sentence, despite his absence? And who urged you, once he had been pronounced innocent, to devise before the same emperor other slanders against Felix who ordained him? And now what else but the judgment of Constantine the Great remains valid against your sect, the judgment that your predecessors chose, that they forced from him by their constant appeals, and that they preferred to the judgment of the bishops? If you are dissatisfied with the imperial judgments, who first forced the emperors to issue them against you? For you now cry out against the Catholic Church over these decrees that are issued against you by the emperors. It is just as if those men wanted to cry out against Daniel who, after he was set free, were sent to be devoured by the same lions, by whom they first wanted him to be devoured.[3] For scripture says, *There is no difference between the threats of a king and the anger of a lion* (Prv 19:12). His slanderous enemies forced Daniel to be thrown into the lions' pit; his innocence conquered their malice. He was raised up out of there unharmed; they were thrown there and perished. In a similar way your predecessors hurled Caecilian and his companions to be devoured by the anger of the king, and now after those innocent men were set free, you suffer from the same kings the same punishments that your predecessors wanted them to suffer. For scripture says, *One who prepares a pit for the neighbor will himself fall into it* (Sir 27:29).

6. You have, then, no reason to complain about us, and the gentleness of the Catholic Church, nonetheless, would have remained completely at peace, unruffled even by these decrees of the emperors, if your clerics and Circumcellions had not disturbed and destroyed our peace by their monstrous wickedness and mad acts of violence and forced that those decrees be recalled and put into effect against you. For, before these more recent laws, about which you are now complaining, had come to Africa,[4] they laid ambushes for our bishops on their journeys, struck our fellow clerics with the cruelest blows, inflicted upon lay people most serious wounds, and set their buildings on fire. Because a certain priest chose the unity of our communion of his own free will, they seized him

---

3. See Dn 6:16-24.
4. These laws were promulgated against the Donatists in February 403.

from his home, beat him cruelly for his choice, rolled him in a filthy stream, dressed him with weeds, and put him on display in parading their crime, to be sorrowed over by some and to be laughed at by others. They led him off where they wanted and released him only after twelve full days.[5] Hence, Proculeian[6] was summoned by our bishop to a municipal hearing, but he only pretended to investigate the case. And when he was again summoned, he stated for the records that he would say nothing more. And today those who did this are your priests, still terrorizing us and persecuting us to the extent they can.

7. Our bishop did not, nonetheless, complain to the emperors about these injuries and persecutions that the Catholic Church endured at that time in our area. Rather, a council was held,[7] and it decided that you should assemble peacefully where you might, if possible, have a conference among yourselves and, once your error had been removed, brotherly love might rejoice over the bond of peace. Let the records themselves inform Your Reverence about what Proculeian first replied in the conference, namely, that you would first hold a council and see what you ought to reply, and then about what he stated for the records, after he was again summoned on account of his promise, when he rejected a peaceful conference. Then, when the savagery of your clerics and the Circumcellions, which was well known to all, did not subside, the case was heard, and Proculeian was pronounced a heretic along with Crispinus.[8] And because of the gentleness of the Catholic Church he was not permitted to suffer the fine of ten pounds of gold, which the emperors established against the heretics,[9] and yet he thought that he should appeal to the emperors. Did not the preceding wickedness of your people and the same appeal of this man make it necessary that his appeal should receive such a response? And, even after the rescript, because of the intercession of our bishops before the emperor, he was not, nonetheless, penalized by the same fine of gold. But from our council[10] the bishops sent a legation to the imperial court to obtain that the same fine of ten pounds of gold, which was established against all heretics, would not be imposed on all the bishops and clerics of your sect, but only upon those in whose territories the Catholic Church suffered some acts of violence from your people. But when the legation came to Rome, the horrible and quite recent scars of the Catholic bishop of Bagai[11] moved the emperor to issue the sort of laws that we now have. And when these laws arrived in Africa, after you began to be

---

5. See Letter 105, 2, 3. The priest in question, Restitutus, died as a result of his mistreatment. After his murderers confessed and were condemned to death, Augustine interceded on their behalf to spare them. See Letters 133 and 139.
6. Proculeian was the Donatist bishop of Hippo Regius.
7. The council was held at Carthage on 25 August 403.
8. Crispinus was the Donatist bishop of Calama in Africa Proconsularis.
9. See *Answer to Cresconius* III, 46, 50-47, 51, and Possidius, *The Life of Augustine* 12.
10. The council was held on 26 August 404; I have followed the reading *"concilio,"* found in the early editions, rather that *"consilio,"* found in the CSEL.
11. The bishop was Maximian, a convert from Donatism.

urged not, of course, to something evil, but to something good, what ought you to have done but send word to our bishops that, as they had invited you, so you invited them to a conference in order that the truth might better be seen as the result of a conference?

8. You, however, not only did not do this, but your people now commit worse evils against us. They not only beat us with clubs and kill us with the sword, but they have also thought up an incredible crime and hurl lime mixed with acid into our eyes in order to put them out. Moreover, they pillage our homes, and they fashion for themselves huge and terrifying weapons. And armed with them, they run off in different directions, threatening and breathing slaughter, robbery, fires, and blindness. Compelled by these events, we first complained to you that Your Reverence should consider how many of your people, in fact all of you, who say that you suffer persecution under the supposedly terrifying laws of the Catholic emperors, remain secure in your possessions and those of others, while we suffer from your people such unheard-of evils. You say that you are suffering persecution, and we are being killed by your people armed with clubs and swords. You say that you are suffering persecution, and our homes are destroyed by the pillaging of your armed people. You say that you are suffering persecution, and our eyes are put out by your people armed with lime and acid. Moreover, even if they bring any forms of death upon themselves by their own doing, they want these deaths to bring odium upon us and glory to you. What they do to us, they do not blame upon themselves, and what they do to themselves, they blame upon us. They live like robbers; they die like Circumcellions; they are honored like martyrs. And yet we have never heard that robbers have blinded those whom they have plundered. Robbers remove from the light of day those whom they kill; they do not remove the light of day from those whom they leave alive!

9. If we ever hold your people in our hands for a time, with great love we keep them uninjured; we speak with them and read to them everything by which this error that separates brother from brother is refuted. We do what the Lord commanded through Isaiah, the prophet, when he said, *You who are fearful, listen to the word of the Lord. Say, "You are our brothers," to these who hate you and who curse you, in order that the name of the Lord may receive honor and may be seen by them in joy and in order that they may be put to shame* (Is 66:5). And in that way we bring some of them who consider the evidence of the truth and the beauty of peace, not to baptism, which like the mark of the king they had already received as deserters, but to the faith, which they lacked, and to the love of the Holy Spirit and to the body of Christ. For scripture says, *Cleansing their hearts by faith* (Acts 15:9); scripture likewise says, *Love covers a multitude of sins* (1 Pt 4:8). But if either because of a great hardness of heart or shame they cannot bear the insults of those with whom they hurled so many false charges and plotted so many evils against us or rather because of the fear that they may now suffer along with us what they were previously doing to us, they refuse to

return to the unity of Christ, then, just as they were held without injury, they are released by us without injury. We also instruct our lay people, as much as we can, that they should hold them uninjured and bring them to us to be rebuked and instructed. But some of them hear us and do this if they can; others deal with them as they deal with robbers because they really suffer from them as they suffer from robbers. Some repel their blows that threaten their bodies by striking them so that they are not first struck by them; some bring them before judges after they have been arrested and do not spare them despite our intercessions, since they have a great fear of suffering terrible evils from them. In all these cases they do not abandon the actions of robbers, and they demand for themselves the honor of martyrs!

10. This, then, is our desire that we bring before Your Reverence by this letter and by the brothers whom we sent: First, that if possible, you confer peacefully with your bishops in order that the error itself may be destroyed, not the human beings in whom it is found, that human beings not be punished, but corrected, and that you now come together since you earlier scorned their gathering. How much better it is that you do this among yourselves, so that you might forward what you have done signed and sealed to the emperor rather than that this be done before temporal authorities, who cannot but obey the laws established against you. For your colleagues who set sail said before the prefects that they came for their case to be heard. And they named our holy father, the Catholic bishop, Valentine, who was at the time in the imperial court, saying that they wanted to be heard along with him. The judge, who was passing judgment according to the laws that had been established against you, was not able to grant them this request, and that bishop had not come for that purpose nor had he received some such mandate from his bishops. How much better, then, could the emperor himself, who was not subject to the same laws and who had it in his power to make other laws when the report of your conference was read out to him, pronounce judgment on the whole case, although it had long since been declared ended. But we want you to confer, not in order that the case may be brought to an end once again, but in order that it may be shown to those who do not know it that it has already been brought to an end. Suppose that your bishops are unwilling to do this. What do you lose from it? You in fact rather gain. After all, your desire is made known so that your lack of confidence about your case is not reasonably blamed. Or do you perhaps suppose that it is not permitted to hold a conference, though you are not unaware that Christ the Lord conferred even with the devil concerning the law[12] and that not only the Jews, but also the philosophers of the Gentiles conferred with Paul the apostle about the sects of the Stoics and Epicureans?[13] Or do these laws of the emperor perhaps not permit

---

12. See Mt 4:1-10.
13. See Acts 18:14.

you to meet with our bishops? Look, summon again your bishops who are in the territory of Hippo where we suffer such great evils from you. How much more permissible it will be—and pleasant for us—that your letters reach us through your people rather than their weapons!

11. Finally, through these same brothers of ours whom we sent to you, write back to us. But if you also refuse to do this, at least give us a hearing along with your people, from whom we suffer such mistreatment. Show us the truth for which you say that you suffer persecution, though we suffer such cruelty from your people. After all, if you prove that you are not in error, you will perhaps grant that we need not be rebaptized by you, thinking that, since we were baptized by those whom you have not condemned by any tribunal, you should offer us what you offered to those whom Felix of Musti and Praetextatus of Assuri[14] baptized over a long time, when you were trying to remove them from their basilicas by judicial orders, because they were in communion with Maximian, with whom they were condemned expressly and by name in the Council of Bagai.[15] We prove all these facts from the judicial and municipal records, where you also introduced the acts of your council, since you want to show to the judges that you drove those who split off from you from their basilicas. And you, nonetheless, who have split off from the offspring of Abraham, in whom all the nations are blessed,[16] do not want to be driven from your basilicas, not by judges, as you did to those split off from you, but by the very kings of the earth, who in fulfillment of the prophecy[17] worship Christ, though when you accused Caecilian before those kings, you left after having lost your case.

12. But if you refuse either to give us a hearing or to teach us, come, or send with us to Hippo men to see your armed soldiers, although no soldier has added to the number of his weapons lime and acid for the eyes of the barbarians. If you also refuse to do this, at least write to them that they should no longer do these actions in order that they may settle down from the slaughter, robbery, and blinding of our people. We do not want to say: Condemn them. For it is up to you to see how they whom we are now proving to be thieves in your communion do not defile you, while those whom you were never able to prove to be traditors defile us. From all these options choose what you want. But if you hold our complaints in contempt, we will not be sorry for having wanted to act in a peaceful way. May the Lord help his Church so that you are rather sorry for having held our lowliness in contempt.

---

14. Felix and Praetextatus were Maximianists, that is, in schism from the Donatists, and when they were received back by the Donatists, those whom they had baptized in schism were not required to be baptized again.
15. The council of Bagai in Numidia met on 24 April 394.
16. See Gn 22:18.
17. See Ps 72:14.

Letter 89

Between 405 and 411 Augustine wrote to Festus, a Roman official and Catholic layman in Africa. He explains to Festus the great reasonableness with which the Catholic Church works not only for her own defense against heretics, but also for the correction of them (paragraph 1). He points out the falsity of the Donatists' claim to be suffering persecution and martyrdom, since it is not suffering alone that makes a martyr (paragraph 2). The Donatists complain about the imperial laws that are brought to bear upon them, though they first appealed to Emperor Constantine against Caecilian and persisted in their position after having lost their case (paragraph 3). Furthermore, the Donatists regard the whole Christian world as guilty for not having known about the traditors in Africa, though no one is guilty because of an unknown sin (paragraph 4). Augustine argues that the validity of baptism does not depend upon righteousness of the minister of the sacrament, but upon Christ (paragraph 5). The Donatists resist the medicine of the Church either by wild savagery or by quiet lethargy, while the Church shows them her maternal love (paragraph 6). Nor does the Catholic Church receive into herself Donatist converts just as they were, but as transformed (paragraph 7). Finally, Augustine urges Festus to cooperate with him in dealing with the Donatists around Hippo (paragraph 8).

To his most beloved, honorable, and venerable lord, Festus, Augustine sends greetings in the Lord.

1. In defense of their error and damnable schism and doctrine, which has been proven false in every way, human beings are so presumptuous that they do not cease to plot against and threaten so boldly the Catholic Church, which seeks their salvation. How much more just and necessary it is, then, that those who defend the truth of Christian peace and unity, which is evident to all, even to those who pretend not to see it and who attack it, work constantly and vigor-ously, not only for the defense of those who are already Catholic, but also for the correction of those who are not as yet! For if stubbornness tries to maintain an insuperable strength, what great strength ought that constancy have that both knows it pleases God and certainly cannot be displeasing to prudent human beings in that good that it does perseveringly and without flagging?

2. But what is more unhappy and more perverse in the conduct of the Donatists, who boast that they suffer persecution, than not merely their failing to be ashamed over the coercion of their wickedness, but also their wanting to be praised for it? They either do not know out of an amazing blindness or pretend that they do not know out of a damnable fanaticism that it is not the punishment, but the reason for suffering it that makes true martyrs. And I would say this against those who were only wrapped in the fog of heretical error—for which sacrilege they would pay the penalties they fully deserve–and have not dared to

injure anyone out of any violent madness. But what should I say against these whose pernicious perversity is either repressed by a fear of fines or is taught by exile how the Church is spread everywhere, as it was predicted that she would be,[1] the Church that they prefer to attack rather than recognize? And if those things that they suffer through a most merciful discipline are compared to those deeds that they commit out of a mindless fury, who would not see which of us should rather be called the persecutors? After all, by the very fact that bad children live wicked lives, even if they do not lay their hands on their parents in violence, they persecute more grievously their loving parents than when a father or a mother compels them all the more to lead a good life without any pretense to the extent that they love them more.

3. There exist the most solid proofs in public records, which you can read if you wish; in fact, I beg and exhort you to read them. They prove that their predecessors who first split away from the peace of the Church dared on their own initiative to accuse Caecilian[2] by means of Anulinus, the proconsul,[3] before the emperor Constantine. And, of course, if they had won in that case, what was Caecilian going to suffer from the emperor except the sentence he pronounced against those men after they had lost? But if, for example, after they brought their accusations and won their case, Caecilian and his colleagues were expelled from the sees they held or were punished more severely, because they also continued in their rebellion—for the imperial authority could not have ignored the convicted who continued in opposition—then these people would have spread about word of their foresight and solicitous concern for the Church as something worthy of praise. But now, since they lost because they could not prove the charges they brought, if they suffer anything in return for their wickedness, they call it persecution. Nor do they hold in check such great fury of the wicked, but even seek the honor of martyrs, as if the Catholic Christian emperors carry out anything else against their most stubborn wickedness than the judgment of Constantine, before whom they were on their own initiative the accusers of Caecilian and whose authority they preferred to all the overseas bishops. For they brought a case belonging to the Church, not to them, but to Constantine. And after he granted them an episcopal court in the city of Rome in which they first lost, they again brought the accusation before him. And they appealed to him from a second episcopal court granted them in Arles, and having lastly been condemned by him, they remained in their perversity. I think that, if the devil himself were so often defeated by the authority of a judge whom he had chosen on his own, he would not be so impudent as to persist in that case!

---

1. See Ps 2:8.
2. Caecilian was the Catholic bishop of Carthage at the time when the Donatist schism began.
3. See Letter 88, 1, 2.

4. But these judgments are regarded as human, and they say that the judges can be circumvented, deceived, and even corrupted. Why, then, do they still accuse the Christian world and why do they blacken its reputation by some charges against the traditors? For the Christian world, of course, could and ought to have believed only the judges who had been chosen rather than the litigants who lost their case. Those judges have to present their own case, whether good or bad, before God. But what did the Church spread throughout the whole world do? She is judged to be in need of rebaptism by these Donatists for no other reason than that in that case in which she could not judge what was true, she thought that she should believe those who were able to judge rather than those who, though they lost, did not yield. Oh the great crime of all the nations, which God promised would be blessed in the offspring of Abraham[4] and which he has shown us as he promised! With one voice they ask, "Why do you want to rebaptize us?" And they are told, "Because you do not know who surrendered the sacred books in Africa, and on that point on which you were ignorant you chose to believe the judges rather than the accusers." If no one is made guilty by the crime of another, how does a crime committed by anyone in Africa become that of the whole world? If no one is made guilty by a crime he does not know, how could the whole world come to know the crime of the judges or of the guilty? You who have a heart, be the judges. This is the justice of heresy: Because the whole world does not condemn a crime that it does not know, does the sect of Donatus condemn the whole world without a hearing? But surely it is enough for the world to hold onto the promises of God and to see that there is fulfilled in itself what the prophets predicted so long before. It is enough to recognize the Church in the same scriptures in which Christ is recognized as her king. For, where we find such predictions about Christ as we read were fulfilled in the gospel, there we read predictions about the Church that we now see are fulfilled throughout the whole world.

5. But perhaps someone among the wise will be upset because the Donatists often say of baptism that it is then the true baptism of Christ when it is conferred by a righteous person. And yet, on this point the whole world has the most evident truth of the gospel, where John says, *He who sent me to baptize with water said to me, "He upon whom you see the Spirit descending like a dove and remaining over him is the one who baptizes with the Holy Spirit"* (Jn 1:33). For this reason the Church is secure and does not place her hope in a human being for fear that she may fall under that condemnation where it says, *Cursed is everyone who places his hope in a human being* (Jer 17:5). Rather she places her hope in Christ who took up the form of the servant in such a way that he did not lose the form of God.[5] Of him scripture said, *He is the one who baptizes.* Hence, it is not

---

4. See Gn 22:16.
5. See Phil 2:6-7.

any human minister of Christ's baptism, whatever burden of guilt he may bear, but it is the one upon whom the dove descended who baptizes. But such great absurdity follows upon those people who think these foolish thoughts that they find no place where they may escape from it. For they admit that baptism is valid and true when some criminal whose crimes are hidden baptizes in their sect, and for this reason we say to them, "Who baptizes in that case?" and they have no answer but, "God." For they cannot say that an adulterer sanctifies anyone. We reply to them, "If, then, when a human being who is obviously righteous baptizes, it is he who sanctifies; but when a human being who is a hidden sinner baptizes, then it is not he, but God who sanctifies; those who are baptized ought to hope to be baptized by hidden sinners rather than by obviously good persons. For God sanctifies much better than any righteous human being. But if it is absurd that anyone about to be baptized should want to be baptized by a hidden sinner rather than by an obviously chaste person, it, of course, remains that, no matter who comes along from among human ministers, baptism is valid because he upon whom the dove descended is the one who baptizes."

6. And yet, though such clear truth strikes the ears and hearts of human beings, such a great whirlpool of bad habit pulls down certain people that they prefer to resist all authorities and reasons rather than to agree. But they resist in two ways: either by wild raging or by being lazy. What, then, does the medicine of the Church do here, as she seeks the salvation of all out of her motherly love, caught up as it were among those who are manic and those who are lethargic? Ought she or can she scorn them or leave them? She is necessarily bothersome to both, because she is an enemy to neither. For the manic cases do not want to be restrained, and the lethargic do not want to be stirred up. But loving concern continues to chastise the manic and to stimulate the lethargic, but to love them both. Both are offended, but both are loved; both are bothered. As long as they are ill, they are angry, but once healed, both are grateful.

7. Finally, we do not, as they think and as they boast, receive them such as they were, but entirely changed, because they do not begin to be Catholics unless they have ceased to be heretics. For their sacraments are not opposed to us, since they are common to them along with us, because they are not human, but divine. Their peculiar error, which they have swallowed wrongly, must be removed, not the sacraments, which they similarly received. They carry and have these sacraments for their own punishment to the extent that they have them more unworthily, but they do, nonetheless, have them. After having abandoned their error and having corrected the wrong of schism, they cross over from heresy to the peace of the Church, which they did not have and without which what they had spelled their destruction. But if when they cross over they are pretending, this is not now a matter for our judgment, but for God's. And yet, though some are thought to be pretending because they crossed over to us out of fear of authority, they are later in some temptations shown to be the sort of persons who are better

than certain others who were Catholics at an earlier date. It is not true that nothing is accomplished when it is accomplished with violence. Nor is the wall of hardened habit stormed by merely human threats, but faith and mental intelligence are also instructed by divine authorities and arguments.

8. Since this is so, Your Graciousness should know that your people, who are in the territory of Hippo, are still Donatists and that your letter achieved nothing with them. There is, however, no need to write why it had no effect. But send one of your domestics or friends to whose reliability you can entrust this. Let him first come, not to those areas, but to us, without their knowing this, and after having first discussed with us a plan, let him do, with the Lord's help, what seems necessary to do. For, in doing this, we do not act only on their behalf, but also on behalf of our people who have already become Catholics, for whom their proximity is so dangerous that we absolutely cannot ignore it. I could, of course, have written this briefly, but I wanted you to have a piece of our writing by which you yourself not only might know the reason for my concern, but also might have something to reply to anyone who dissuades you from working vigorously for the correction of your people and who slanders us because we want such things. If I did that needlessly, because you had already learned such things or have yourself thought of them, or if I was a burden because I thrust upon you, who are so busy with public concerns, a long letter, I ask your pardon, provided that you do not, nonetheless, reject what I have suggested or asked for. May the mercy of God protect you in that way.

Letter 90

In the summer of 408 or 409 Nectarius, a pagan and city official of Calama in Numidia, wrote to Augustine on behalf of his fellow citizens. Nectarius pleads out of love for his native city that Augustine pardon the citizens of Calama for violating the imperial laws against the celebration of pagan feasts and for having injured many Christians during the celebration. He urges Augustine to act like a bishop, that is, to seek only the salvation of human beings, to obtain God's pardon for the sins of others, and to punish only the guilty and these without corporeal punishments.

To Bishop Augustine, his excellent lord and rightly revered brother, Nectarius sends greetings.

I pass over the greatness of the love for one's fatherland, since you know this. For it is the only love that rightly surpasses love for one's parents.[1] For, if there were any limit or end for good men in caring for the fatherland, we would rightly deserve to be excused from our services to her. But because my love for and gratitude to my city grows day by day, I want to leave my fatherland intact and flourishing insofar as my life is near its end. For this reason I rejoice first of all that I have initiated this discussion with a man learned in all the disciplines. In the colony of Calama there are many things that we rightly love, either because we were born in her or because we are seen to have offered her great services. This city has, my most excellent and rightly revered lord, fallen into disgrace by no slight mistake on the part of its people. If we should indeed measure this by the rigor of civil law, the people ought to be chastised by a rather severe punishment.[2] But a bishop is permitted only to procure salvation for human beings and to be involved in a case only for the better outcome and to earn pardon before the almighty God for the sins of others. Hence, with as much supplication as I can muster, I beg that, if the case deserves to be defended, the innocent may be defended and punishment be kept from the innocent. Grant this favor that you clearly see is being asked for in accord with your nature. With regard to the losses taxes can easily be gathered. We only beg that there be no bodily punishments. May you live closer to God, my excellent lord and rightly revered brother.

---

1. See Cicero, *The Republic* (*De republica*) fragment IV, 7, 7.
2. Honorius reaffirmed the prohibition of the celebration of pagan festivals on 23 November 407. The pagan citizens of Calama, nonetheless, celebrated the feast of Flora on 1 May 408 and the following days during which they stoned the church, did bodily harm to many servants of God, killed one of them, forced Possidius the bishop to hide, and plundered Christian property. Augustine journeyed to Calama to console the Christians and to see to the correction of others; upon returning to Hippo he found the present letter from Nectarius.

Letter 91

In the summer of 408 or 409 Augustine replied to the previous letter from Nectarius, a city official of Calama in Numidia. Augustine commends Nectarius for his love of his earthly fatherland and urges him to think of his heavenly fatherland (paragraph 1). He argues that a city truly flourishes through virtuous conduct (paragraph 2). He points out that Cicero taught that a city flourished because of virtues and claims that such virtues are found in the Church (paragraph 3). Roman comedies do not present models of conduct worthy of imitation (paragraph 4). Cities cannot be said to flourish if they are filled with impiety and shamefulness (paragraph 5). Augustine urges Nectarius to see to the removal of the idols and explains the Christian use of gentleness in punishing idolatry (paragraph 6). To Nectarius' words of advice about how a bishop should act, Augustine agrees that he tries to act in accord with them (paragraph 7). He then briefly describes the vicious crimes perpetrated by the pagans upon the Christians in Calama on 1 June 408 and the following days (paragraph 8). Augustine spells out how the pagans of Calama should be punished mercifully and in moderation in the interest of their salvation and in accord with their guilt (paragraph 9). Finally, Augustine describes how he dealt with the Christians and the pagans of Calama during his recent visit and prays for the conversion of Nectarius (paragraph 10).

To his excellent lord and rightly honorable brother, Nectarius, Augustine sends greetings.

1. I am not surprised that, even though your limbs grow cold with age, your heart is warm with love for your fatherland, and I praise you for this. I am not unwilling, but even happy to hear that you not only hold it in memory, but also show by your life and conduct that for good men there is no limit or end in caring for the fatherland.[1] For this reason we would like to have you yourself as such a citizen of a certain heavenly fatherland, in the love for which we face danger in accord with our limitations and are at labor among those whom we help to attain it. If you were a citizen of it, you would judge that there ought to be no limit or end in caring for some small portion of it, even while you are journeying away from it on this earth. And you would become better to the extent that the city is better to which you offer the services you owe her, for you will find no end of rejoicing in her eternal peace, if you set for yourself in the present time no end for your labors.

2. But until that comes about—after all, one must not give up hope that you can attain that fatherland or even now plan with greatest wisdom to attain it, the fatherland to which your father who begot you in this life has gone on

---

1. See Letter 90.

ahead[2]—until, then, this comes about, pardon us, if on account of our fatherland, which we desire never to leave, we bring sadness to your fatherland, which you desire to leave flourishing. If we should argue with Your Wisdom about its flourishing, we need not fear that it would be difficult to persuade you or that it would not readily occur to you how a city ought to flourish. That most illustrious poet of your literature mentioned certain flowers of Italy, but we do not know in the case of your fatherland so much of the men by whom that land flourished as of the wars by which it burned,[3] in fact, not just with wars, but with flames. Nor did it burn, but blazed. Now, if so great a crime goes unpunished without any suitable correction of the criminals, do you think that you will leave your fatherland flourishing? O flowers productive not of fruits, but of thorns! Consider, then, whether you prefer that your fatherland flower with piety or with impunity, with correct moral conduct or with carefree audacity. Consider these, and see whether you surpass us in the love of your fatherland; see whether you desire her to flourish more and more truly than we do.

3. Look for a little while at those books, *The Republic*, from which you have imbibed that attitude of a most devoted citizen that there is no limit or end for good men in caring for the fatherland. Look, I beg you, and see the great praises with which that book speaks of frugality and self-control as well as of fidelity toward the bond of marriage, and of chaste, honorable, and good morals. For, when a city excels in these, it is truly to be said to flourish.[4] But in the churches, which are growing throughout the world, these virtues are taught and learned as if in holy schoolrooms for the people,[5] and especially the piety by which the true and truthful God is worshiped. This God not only commands that we undertake all these actions by which the human mind is instructed and prepared for the society of God in order to dwell in the eternal and heavenly city, but also gives the means to carry them out. This is the reason why he both foretold that the images of the many false gods would be torn down and commanded that they be torn down.[6] For nothing renders human beings unfit for society in terms of the wickedness of their life as much as the imitation of such gods as are described and commended in their literature.

4. Finally, those most learned men, who investigated or even described the character that they thought the earthly state or city ought to have in discussions among friends rather than established and formed it by public actions, proposed for imitation men whom they considered outstanding and praiseworthy rather

---

2. Nectarius' father was a convert to Christianity.
3. Augustine alludes to Virgil, *Aeneid* VII, 643: "By these men the land of Italy already flourished, by these wars it burned."
4. Cicero, *The Republic* (*De republica*), fragment IV, 7, 7.
5. See *City of God* II, 6.
6. See Lv 26:30, Ez 6:4 and 30:13, Hos 20:2, 1 Kgs 15:11-13, 2 Chr 23:17, 31:1, 33:15, and 34:3-4.

than their gods in order to train the character of the youth. And that young man in the play of Terence,[7] who looked on a painting on the wall where there was pictured the adultery of the king of the gods and who kindled the lust that seized him by the goads of such an authority, would in no way have fallen into that sin out of passion or have plunged himself into it by committing it, if he had preferred to imitate Cato rather than Jupiter. But how would he do that since he was forced to worship in the temples of Jupiter rather than Cato? Perhaps we ought not to take these events from a comedy that reveals the corruption and sacrilegious superstition of the wicked. Read or recall how wisely the same books explain that the descriptions and actions portrayed in the comedies can only be accepted if the morals of those who accept them are in harmony with them. In that way the authority of the most illustrious men, who are outstanding in the state and are discussing the state, confirms the view that very wicked men become worse by the imitation of the gods, not, of course, true gods, but false and fictitious ones.

5. But, you may object, the wise must understand and interpret far differently all those things that were written long ago about the life and conduct of the gods. True, we have recently heard that such sound interpretations are read out to the people gathered in the temples. I ask you, is the human race so blind to the truth that it does not see such clear and evident matters? In so many places Jupiter is painted, molded, chiseled, sculpted, described, read about, enacted, sung, and danced as committing such great adulteries! How much better it would be that at least on his Capitoline Hill it were read that he forbids such acts! Are cities said to flourish if these sins full of shame and impiety thrive among the people with no one forbidding them, if the gods are worshiped in the temples and laughed at in the theaters? Do they flourish when people offer sacrifices to them and the flock of even the poor is laid waste? Do they flourish when actors perform and dance these actions and when the patrimonies of the wealthy are poured out? These flowers clearly do not come from the fertile land, nor from some richness of character; rather, that goddess Flora[8] is found to be a worthy mother of these flowers. Her games and stage plays are celebrated with such wild and uncontrolled shamefulness that anyone can understand what sort of demon it is who cannot be placated in any other way than if there perishes in them, as if in sacrifice, not birds, not animals, not finally human blood, but much more sinfully a human sense of shame.

6. I said this on account of what you wrote, namely, that to the extent your lifetime is near its end you desire to leave your fatherland sound and flourishing.[9] Let all the vain insanity of idols be destroyed; let human beings be

---

7. See Terence, *The Eunuch*, Act 3, Scene 5, 584-591.
8. The feast of Flora celebrated the coming of spring with an unrestrained licentiousness. See *The City of God* II, 27.
9. See Letter 90.

converted to the true worship of God and to chaste and pious morals. Then you will see your fatherland flourishing, not in the opinion of the foolish, but in the truth of the wise, when this fatherland of your birth in the flesh will be a portion of that fatherland into which we are born, not by the body, but by faith. There all God's saints and faithful people will flourish for endless eternity after the wintery labors of this life. We, therefore, hold it close to our heart neither to lose Christian gentleness nor to leave in that city a destructive example for others to imitate. May God be there to help us to do this, if he is not seriously angry at those people. Otherwise, the gentleness that we desire to preserve and the discipline that we strive to use in moderation can be interfered with, if God chooses something in secret, whether he judges that this great evil must be punished more severely or whether he becomes even more fiercely angry and wants it to go unpunished in this world, since those people were neither corrected nor converted to him.

7. Your Wisdom prescribes for us in some sense the norm for a bishop to follow, and you say that your fatherland has fallen by no slight mistake of its people. "If we should indeed measure this by the rigor of civil law, the people ought to be punished by a rather severe punishment. But a bishop," you say, "is permitted only to procure salvation for human beings and to be involved in a case only for the better outcome and to earn pardon before the almighty God for the sins of others."[10] We try to observe this norm unconditionally so that no one is punished by a more severe penalty, either by us or, at our intercession, by anyone else. And we desire to procure salvation for human beings, which is found in the happiness of living correctly, not in the security of doing evil. We strive also to merit pardon, not only for our sins, but also for those of others, something that we can in no way obtain except for those who have been corrected. You also add on and say, "With as much supplication as I can muster, I beg that, if the case deserves to be defended, the innocent may be defended and punishment be kept from the innocent."[11]

8. Listen for a moment to crimes that were committed, and distinguish for yourself the guilty from the innocent. Contrary to the most recent laws,[12] on the first of June, a feast day of the pagans, there was celebrated with such insolent audacity the sacrilegious solemnity with no one forbidding it. A most arrogant mob of dancers passed on the same street in front of the doors of the church, something that was not done even in the time of Julian.[13] When the clergy tried to prevent this utterly forbidden and shameful action, the church was stoned. Then, after almost eight days, when the bishop recalled to the minds of the magistrates the very well-known laws and while they are arranging, as it were, to implement

---

10. Letter 90.
11. See Letter 90, end.
12. On 24 November 407 Honorius had reaffirmed the prohibition of obscene pagan celebrations.
13. That is, Julian the Apostate who reigned from 361 to 363 and who revived the pagan feasts.

what the laws commanded, the church was again stoned. The following day, when our people wanted to state their views for the municipal records in order to strike fear into the wicked, their civil rights were denied. And on the same day a hailstorm was sent in return for the stonings in order that they might be frightened at least by God, and when that was over, they immediately inflicted a third stoning and finally tried to burn down the church buildings and the people in them. They killed one servant of God who lost his way and ran into them, while some hid where they could and others fled where they could. Meanwhile, the bishop, who was shoved and crammed into a certain place, was hiding where he heard the voices of those who were seeking his death and blaming themselves because they had committed so great a crime uselessly, since they had not found him. They carried out these actions from almost four in the afternoon through a good part of the night. None of those whose authority could have had some weight tried to quiet things down; no one tried to help, except one stranger who rescued many servants of God from the hands of those who were trying to kill them and who recovered many stolen objects from the looters. He made it clear how easy it would have been entirely to prevent those actions or to stop them once they were begun, if citizens, especially the leaders, had forbidden that they be done and carried out.

9. Hence, in that whole city you perhaps cannot separate the innocent from the guilty, but only the less guilty from the more guilty. For they are guilty of a small sin who were afraid, especially of offending those who they knew had the most power in that town and who were enemies of the Church, and did not dare to offer help. But they are all guilty who contributed to the commission of these actions, even if they did not do them or instigate them, but just willed them. They are more guilty who did those actions, and they are most guilty who instigated them. But with regard to instigation let us admit that we have a suspicion, not the truth, and let us not discuss those points that absolutely cannot be found out except by the torture of those who are questioned. Let us also pardon those fearful ones who thought that they should pray to God for the bishop and the servants of God rather than offend the powerful enemies of the Church. Why do you think that those who remain should be restrained by no discipline, and why do you think that you should set before others an unpunished example of such savage madness? We do not desire to feed our anger by avenging past actions, but we act with mercy in looking out for the future. Bad persons have ways in which they may be punished by Christians, not only gently, but also to their benefit and salvation. They have their life and bodily integrity; they have the means to live; they have means to live badly. Let the first two remain untouched so that those who repent may live. This is what we desire; this is what we seek with all the energy we have. With regard to the third, God will punish very mercifully, if he wills that it be cut back as something decayed and harmful. But if he either wills something more or does not permit even this, he has within him

the reason for this deeper and certainly more just plan. We must use care and do our duty as far as we are allowed to see it, as we beg him to approve our intention of looking out for all and of allowing nothing to happen that does not benefit us and his Church, something he knows far better than we do.

10. Recently, when we were at Calama in order that in so grave a sorrow our people might either be consoled in their affliction or be calmed in their anger, we dealt with the Christians as much as we could, something we judged to be necessary at that time. Then we admitted to our presence those pagans also, the origin and cause of so great an evil, who were asking to see us. We took this opportunity to admonish them as to what they should do if they are wise, not merely for removing their present worry, but also for seeking their perpetual salvation. They heard a great deal from us, and they themselves asked much from us. But heaven forbid that we should be the sort of servants who are pleased to be asked for things by those who do not ask them of our Lord. Hence, you clearly see, given the alertness of your mind, that, while preserving gentleness and Christian moderation, we must strive so that we either frighten the rest from imitating their perversity or desire the rest to imitate their correction. The losses that were inflicted are either endured by Christians or restored by Christians. We desire that the gain of souls, for the acquisition of which we yearn even at the risk of our blood, may be more abundant in that place and may not be impeded elsewhere by that example. May the mercy of God grant that we may rejoice over your salvation.

Letter 92

Sometime prior to 408 Augustine wrote to Italica, a Catholic laywoman who had recently lost her husband. He reminds her that she will again have her husband in eternal life where he has preceded her (paragraph 1). In the light of that life we will be closer to those we love than we can ever be in this life (paragraph 2). Then he turns to the view of some unidentified thinkers who held that God will then be seen by our bodily eyes just as he is now seen by the eyes of the mind (paragraph 3) and argues against the absurdity of such a view, which implies that God is a body (paragraph 4). Augustine insists that it is impossible to see God with bodily eyes (paragraph 5). Finally, he asks Italica to show his letter to the proponents of this view and to inform him about any reply they make (paragraph 6).

To his excellent lady and rightly most outstanding and honorable daughter in the love of Christ, Italica, Augustine, the bishop, sends greetings in the Lord.

1. Not only from your letter, but from the report of its carrier, I learned that you were urgently demanding a letter from me, since you believe that you could derive great consolation from it. It is up to you, then, to see what you may derive from it; I, nonetheless, ought not to have denied or to have postponed it. But may you be consoled by your faith and hope and the love that is poured out in the hearts of the faithful by the Holy Spirit,[1] of whom we have already received something as a down payment,[2] in order that we may know how to desire the full amount. After all, you ought not to think that you have been abandoned, since in your interior self you have Christ present in your heart through faith.[3] Nor should you be sad in that way like the pagans who do not have hope,[4] since because of his most true promise we hope in this life, which we will leave, that we will come to that other life from this life. We are confident that we have not lost those of ours who have departed, but have sent them on ahead, where they will be dearer to us to the extent that they will be better known and where they will be lovable without any fear of our losing them.

2. But here, even if you knew your husband very well, because of whose death you are called a widow, he, nonetheless, knew himself better than you did. And why is this except that, though you saw his bodily face, which he himself, of course, did not see, the more certain knowledge of us is within where no one knows what belongs to a human being but the spirit of the human being who is in him.[5] But when the Lord comes and brings light to things hidden in the darkness

---

1. See Rom 5:5.
2. See 2 Cor 1:22 and 5:5.
3. See Eph 3:16-17.
4. See 1 Thes 4:12.
5. See 1 Cor 2:11.

371

and reveals the thoughts of the heart,[6] then nothing in our neighbor will be hidden from us, nor will it be possible that we disclose something to our friends, but hide it from strangers where there will be no stranger. But who will explain in words or who will even touch upon with our weak mind the nature or greatness of the light itself that will illumine all these things that are now hidden in our hearts? That light is, of course, God himself, because *God is light, and no darkness is present in him* (1 Jn 1:5), but he is the light of minds that have been purified, not of these eyes of the body. The mind, therefore, will then be suited to see that light, something that it is not as yet suited for.

3. But the eye of the body is not now able, nor will it then be able to see this. Everything, of course, that can be seen by the eyes of the body must be in some place and is not whole everywhere, but occupies a smaller place with a smaller part of itself and a larger place with a larger part. The invisible and incorruptible God is not like that; *he alone has immortality and dwells in inaccessible light; no human being has seen him or can see him* (1 Tm 6:16). For he cannot be seen by a human being by means of the eyes by which a human being sees bodies with the body. For, if he were also inaccessible for the minds of the devout, scripture would not say, *Draw near to him and be enlightened* (Ps 34:6), and if he were invisible to the minds of the devout, scripture would not say, *We shall see him as he is* (1 Jn 3:2). For pay attention to that whole sentence in the Letter of John; he says, *Beloved, we are children of God, and it has not yet become manifest what we shall be. We know that, when he has appeared, we shall be like him, because we shall see him as he is* (1 Jn 3:2). We shall see him, then, to the extent that we shall be like him, because even now we do not see him to the extent that we are unlike him. We shall, then, see him because of that on account of which we shall be like him. But who is so completely out of his mind as to say that we either are or shall be like God because of our body? This likeness, then, is found in the interior self *which is being renewed from day to day in the knowledge of God according to the image of God the creator* (Col 3:10). And we become more like him to the extent that we advance more in the knowledge and love of him, because, *even if our exterior self is being corrupted, our interior self is being renewed from day to day* (2 Cor 4:16), in such a way, of course, that however great our progress is in this life, we are still far from that perfection of likeness that is suited for seeing God, as the apostle says, *face to face* (1 Cor 13:12). If we wanted to understand from these words the face of the body, it will certainly follow that God also has such a face and that there is a space between our face and his, when we see him face to face. And if there is a space, there is, of course, a limit and definite shape to his members, and other things absurd to say and wicked to think, by which the merely natural human being, who does not

---

6. See 1 Cor 4:5.

perceive what pertains to the Spirit of God,[7] is deluded by most deceptive vanities.

4. For some of those who spread about such nonsense, as has been able to reach my ears, say that we now see God by the mind, but will then see him with the body, so that they claim that even the wicked will see him in the same way. See how much worse they have become when without a limit to fear or shame their uncontrolled language wanders about here and there with impunity. Before they said that only Christ granted to his own flesh that it might see God with the eyes of the body; then they added that all the saints would see God in the same way, once they received back their bodies in the resurrection. Now they have given this possibility even to the wicked. Let them, of course, give as much as they want to whom they want, for who would dare to oppose human beings who give from what is their own? For *one who speaks a lie speaks from what is his own* (Jn 8:44). But with people who hold to sound doctrine, do not venture to make use of something of your own; rather, when you read, *Blessed are the clean of heart for they shall see God* (Mt 5:8), understand that the wicked will not see him, for the blessed and the clean of heart are not wicked. Likewise, when you read, *We see now through a mirror in an enigma, but then we shall see face to face* (1 Cor 13:12), understand that we will then see face to face by means of that by which we now see through a mirror in an enigma. But each of these is a function of the interior self, whether we still walk by faith on this journey, in which we use a mirror and an enigma, or whether in that fatherland we contemplate God by sight, the vision which scripture calls, *face to face.*

5. Let the flesh drunk with its carnal thoughts hear this: *God is spirit, and for this reason those who worship God must worship him in spirit and in truth* (Jn 4:24). If they must worship him in spirit and in truth, how much more must they see him in spirit and in truth! For who would dare to state that the substance of God is seen as a body, since he refuses to be worshiped as a body? But they think that they speak cleverly and that they corner us, as it were, with their question: "Could Christ grant to his flesh the ability to see the Father with bodily eyes, or could he not?" For, if we reply that he could not, they cry out that we detract from the omnipotence of God, but if we grant that he could, they draw the conclusion of their argument from our reply. How much more tolerable are those foolish people who claim that the flesh is going to be changed into the substance of God and will be what God is so that they at least in that way make the flesh suited for seeing God, not unlike him by so great a difference. I believe these people drive this nonsense away from their faith and perhaps from their ears. And if, nonetheless, they are pressed in a like manner concerning this point by the question whether God can or cannot do this, do they detract from his power if they reply that he cannot, or will they admit that this will be the case if they grant that he

7. See 1 Cor 2:12-14.

can? In the same way, then, in which they might escape from this snare of others, let them escape from their own.

Next, why do they maintain that this gift was given only to Christ's bodily eyes and not also to the other senses? Will God, then, be a sound so that he can also be heard by his ears? Will he be a scent so that he can be perceived by his sense of smell? Will he be a liquid so that he can be drunk? And a solid mass so that he can be touched? "No," they say. What then? Is God able to do the former and unable to do the latter? If they say that he is unable, why do they detract from the omnipotence of God? If they say that he is able and unwilling, why do they grant this only to the eyes, but begrudge it to the other senses of Christ's body? Or are they going to be as foolish as they want? How much better it is that we do not set limits to their foolishness, though we do not want them to be foolish at all!

6. Many arguments can be produced to refute this madness. But if these people ever trouble your ears, read these pages to them for a while, and do not hesitate to write back, as you can, what they reply. Our hearts are cleansed by faith for this purpose,[8] for the vision of God is promised to us as a reward of faith. And if that vision will be attained by the eyes of the body, the mind of the saints is trained to no purpose for attaining it; in fact, a mind that thinks so perversely is not trained in itself, but is entirely absorbed in the flesh. For where will it dwell with more tenacity and determination than where it presumes that it will see God? How wrong this surely is, I leave to your intelligence rather than undertake to explain it in a long discourse. May your heart always dwell in the protection of the Lord, my excellent lady and rightly most outstanding and honorable daughter in the love of Christ. With the respect due to your merits I greet in return your children, who are honorable along with you and most beloved to me in the Lord.

---

8. See Acts 15:9.

Letter 92A

At the same time as the preceding letter, Augustine wrote to Cyprian, a priest of Hippo on his way to Rome, asking him personally to deliver Letter 92 to Italica. He explains the purpose of the previous letter and asks Cyprian to write to him, if Italica does not, about the views of those who claim that God is seen with the eyes of the body.

To his rightly most sincere lord, holy brother, and fellow priest, Cyprian, Augustine sends greetings in the Lord.

I have written a letter to our blessed daughter, Italica, and I ask that you be so kind as to deliver it to her yourself. In it I said something against the opinion of those who can hope for nothing from God except what they perceive from bodies, though they do not dare to say that God has a body. They, nonetheless, in fact say this in another way when they maintain that he can be seen by bodily eyes, which he created only for seeing bodies. But in my opinion these people know neither what a body is nor how remote from a body is the spirit who is God. On the occasion, therefore, on which I thought I should console her in some way, I did not want to pass over that place where the true consolation of the pilgrimage of us all is found. But let Your Holiness not hesitate to write me what those who hold that view, which we have tried to refute in a few words, say against my position, if her modesty perhaps keeps her from taking up this sort of conflict, which stems from the pride of others. Or at least may Your Charity make those who hold this view and do not cease from spreading and teaching these ideas here and there write back to me in reply to what I have written. In that way I will deal with them from that point on about what in your holy wisdom you clearly see along with me must be done on this issue. For it is not without reason that the rational soul that has fed on such phantasms is closed off and completely prevented from perceiving that highest and immutable good, if its hope is fixed upon it so that it presumes that it [can with the eyes of the body see] it. I thank Your Charity that you sent me to read those things I asked for.

Letter 93

In 407 or 408 Augustine wrote to Vincent, the Rogatist bishop of Cartenna in Mauretania Caesariensis. Augustine had, he believes, received a letter from Vincent, whom he had known from his early days in Carthage and who is now the successor of Rogatus, who had split away from the Donatists. He points out the benefit for many derived from the use of secular power to check and correct the Donatists (paragraph 1). In fact, even some of the Circumcellions have become sincere Catholics (paragraph 2). Though the use of fear does not benefit everyone, the Church should not give up all use of it (paragraph 3). God himself teaches us with both severity and gentleness (paragraph 4). Augustine turns to scriptural passages that support the use of force against the schismatics (paragraph 5) and shows how the same actions are good or bad depending on their motives (paragraphs 6 and 7). It is not always praiseworthy to suffer persecution, but only when one suffers on account of justice (paragraph 8).

Though the New Testament reveals no instance of an appeal to secular power for the Church, the old testament books foreshadow such action (paragraph 9). Both Catholics and Donatists favor the laws passed against the pagans, and the Donatists may very well outdo the pagans in wickedness (paragraph 10). The Rogatists are, Augustine admits, less violent that the Donatists, though that may be due to their smaller numbers (paragraph 11). The Donastists went so far as to appeal to Julian the apostate for help against the Maximianists (paragraph 12). The Donatists repeatedly appealed to the emperor and still refused to abide by his decision (paragraph 13). The judgment that the Donatists demanded from Constantine, which turned out to be against them, holds against the present Donatists and Rogatists (paragraph 14). Augustine insists that, even if Caecilian were guilty as charged, his sin could not defile the rest of the Church and justify schism (paragraph 15).

The implementation of the imperial laws has brought about the conversion of many schismatics (paragraph 16). These results led Augustine to change his mind about the use of force against the schismatics (paragraph 17). Those brought into the Catholic unity through fear are now often grateful for such coercion (paragraph 18). Augustine argues that he was right not to oppose his fellow bishops on the use of force (paragraph 19). Augustine invokes Paul's admonition that we should do good if we want to be free from fear of civil authorities (paragraph 20). Though scripture promised the spread of the Church throughout the whole world, the nine or ten remaining Rogatists are confined to Cartenna (paragraph 21).

Given that the Christian faith has been proclaimed almost to the ends of the earth, it is ridiculous to claim that a person can be cleansed from his sins only in Cartenna (paragraph 22). Augustine rejects the Rogatist claim to being Catholic on the basis of their observance of all the commandments and sacraments (paragraph 23). The Rogatists have less claim than the Donatists to be the Church of Christ (paragraph 24). The Rogatists' argument to be the true Church can be turned against them (paragraph 25). Though the Rogatists might claim to be holier because of the fewer numbers, Augustine insists that they cannot claim to be the Church that scripture foretold would be very numerous (paragraph 26). So too, they cannot appeal to the few who were saved with Lot (paragraph 27).

If one looks for the Church in the scriptures, no one can justifiably separate himself from communion with the Church spread through all the nations (paragraphs 28 to 30). Augustine argues against the use Vincent made of a text from Hilary of Poitiers (paragraph 31 and 32). He argues that sinners present in the Church do not harm the elect, using the parables of the weeds amid the grain, the chaff amid the wheat, and the bad fishes in the net with the good ones (paragraphs 33 and 34). Augustine warns Vincent against taking anything from writers of the Church and using it against the canonical books (paragraphs 35 and 36). Augustine explains various texts from Cyprian that seem to favor the Donatist position (paragraphs 37 to 42). He also points to the writings of Tychonius, a Donatist, who actually defended the Catholic Church (paragraphs 43 and 44). Augustine argues that, if the sins of others defile anyone in the Church, then the Church perished long before Cyprian (paragraph 45).

Though the Donatists have the sacraments, they lack the Spirit who is the source of unity (paragraph 46). Augustine distinguishes between the baptism of John and the baptism of Christ (paragraph 47) and explains why Paul baptized people whom John had baptized, though one should not baptize again those baptized by a heretic or a drunkard (paragraph 48). After all, even among the few Rogatists there are probably some drunkards (paragraph 49). Augustine concedes that the imperial laws against the Donatists can be misused (paragraph 50) and invites Vincent to come over to the Catholic Church which he holds to be the true Church (paragraph 51). It involves no shame to be corrected (paragraph 52), and the Church welcomes those who repent (paragraph 53).

To his most dear brother, Vincent, Augustine sends greetings.

1, 1. I received a letter that seems probably to be yours, for someone who is clearly a Catholic Christian brought it, and he would, I think, not dare to lie to me. But even if it is perhaps not your letter, I thought that I ought to reply to the one who wrote it. I am now more eager for and in search of quiet than back then when you knew me as a young man at Carthage, when Rogatus, whose successor you are, was still alive. But the Donatists are excessively restless, and I think that it is not useless that they be held in check and corrected by the authorities established by God. After all, we rejoice over the correction of many who so sincerely hold and defend the Catholic unity and are happy that they have been set free from their former error so that we look upon them with great satisfaction. Given the force of habit they would, nonetheless, by no means have been changed for the better, if they were not struck with this fear and turned their worried mind to a consideration of the truth. Otherwise, they would perhaps suffer these temporal troubles with a fruitless and vain endurance, not for righteousness, but for the misguidedness and presumption of human beings, and they would afterwards find before God only the well-deserved punishments of the wicked, who scorned his gentle warning and fatherly scourges. And so, after having become docile because of this thought, they found among all the nations the Church, which was promised, not in human lies and fables, but in God's books, and they saw it presented before their own eyes, and they did not doubt that Christ, who was foretold in those books, is now above the heavens, even though he is not seen. Ought I to have begrudged salvation to these people and called my colleagues back from such fatherly care, as a result of which we see many blame their former blindness? They believed that Christ had been exalted above the heavens, even though they did not see this, but they denied his glory spread over all the earth, even though they saw it, though the prophet combined both of them in one sentence with such great clarity. He said, *Be exalted, O God, above the heavens, and may your glory be over all the earth* (Ps 108:6).

2. If, then, we scorned and endured these people who were once our fierce enemies and who were attacking our peace and quiet with various sorts of violence and ambushes, so that we devised and did nothing at all that might be able to frighten and correct them, we would really have repaid evil with evil. For, if anyone sees his enemy out of his mind due to dangerous fevers run toward a cliff, would he not repay evil with evil if he allowed him to run in that way rather than if he took care to catch him and tie him up? And yet, he would seem most troublesome and hostile to him at the very time when he was most beneficial and merciful. But once he had recovered his health, he would obviously thank him more profusely to the extent that he had felt that the man had spared him the less. Oh, if I could show you how many sincere Catholics we now have from the Circumcellions![1] They condemn their former life and wretched error, because of which they thought that they did for the Church of God whatever they did in their restless rashness! They would, nonetheless, not have been brought to this healthy position if they were not bound, like men out of their minds, by the chains of these laws that you find displeasing. What about that other form of the most grave disease of those who do not, of course, have this turbulent audacity, but are weighed down by long-standing apathy and say to us, "What you say is, of course, true; we have no answer to make, but it is hard for us to abandon the tradition of our parents"? Were they not to be disturbed for their salvation by the penalty of temporal chastisement in order that they might emerge, as it were, from their sluggish sleepiness and wake up in the salvation of the Church's unity? How many of them are now rejoicing with us and blame the former burden of their destructive activity! How many of them admit that we ought to have been troublesome to them for fear that they would perish in that way from the disease of long-standing habit as if from a deadly sleep.

---

1. The Circumcellions were the bands of Donatists who wandered from one shrine of a martyr to another and often wreaked violence and destruction upon the Catholics.

3. But these measures, after all, do not benefit certain ones. Should we, then, neglect the art of medicine because some have an incurable plague? You pay attention only to those who are so hard that they do not accept even this discipline. For of them scripture said, *In vain have I scourged your children; they have not accepted discipline* (Jer 2:30). I think, nonetheless, that they were scourged out of love, not out of hatred. But you ought also to pay attention to the many over whose salvation we rejoice. For, if they were frightened and did not learn anything, it would seem like a wicked tyranny. Again, if they learned something and were not frightened, they would be lazy about moving to take the path to salvation, since they were hardened by their long-standing habit. For, as we well know, when they were given reasons and the truth was shown to them by the testimonies of God, many replied to us that they desired to pass over into the communion of the Catholic Church, but feared the violent hostilities of the wicked. They, of course, ought to have scorned these hostilities for the sake of righteousness and eternal life, but we must support and not despair over the weakness of such persons until they become strong. Nor should we forget that the Lord himself said to the weak Peter, *You cannot now follow me, but you will follow me afterwards* (Jn 13:36). But when the doctrine of salvation is combined with a beneficial fear, not only so that the light of the truth drives out the darkness of error, but also so that the force of fear breaks the chains of bad habit, we rejoice, as I said, over the salvation of many who bless us and thank God. For, having fulfilled his promise that the kings of the earth would serve Christ,[2] he has in this way cured the sick, in this way healed the weak.

2, 4. Not everyone who is merciful is a friend, nor is everyone who scourges an enemy. *Better are the wounds from a friend than the spontaneous kisses of an enemy* (Prv 27:6). It is better to love with severity than to deceive with leniency. It is more beneficial to take bread away from a hungry man if, when sure of his food, he would neglect his salvation, than to break bread with a hungry man in order that he might be led astray and consent to injustice. And someone who ties down a crazy person and who rouses a lazy person loves them both, though he is a bother to both. Who can love us more than God? And he, nonetheless, does not cease not only to teach us with gentleness, but also to frighten us for our salvation. He often adds to the gentle salves by which he comforts us the most biting medicine of tribulation; he trains even the pious and devout patriarchs with famine. He afflicts the rebellious people with more severe punishments.[3] Though he was asked three times, he does not remove from the apostle the thorn in his flesh, in order that he may make virtue perfect in weakness.[4] Let us also love our enemies because this is just, and God commanded it in order that we

---

2. See Dn 7:27.
3. See Gn 12:10, 26:1, 41:54, 42:1, and 43:1.
4. See 2 Cor 12:7-9.

might be *children of our Father who is in heaven, who makes his sun rise over the good and the evil and sends rain upon the just and the unjust* (Mt 5:45). But just as we praise his gifts, so let us bear in mind his scourges upon those whom he loves.

5. You think that no one ought to be forced into righteousness, though you read that the head of the household said to his servants, *Whomever you find, force them to come in* (Lk 14:23), though you read that he who was first Saul and afterwards Paul was forced to come to know and to hold onto the truth by the great violence of Christ who compelled him,[5] unless you perhaps think that money or any possession is dearer to human beings than this light that we perceive by these eyes. Laid low by the voice from heaven, he did not recover this light that he lost suddenly, except when he was incorporated into the holy Church. And you think that one should employ no force upon a man in order that he might be set free from the harmfulness of error, though you see that God himself, than whom no one loves us more to our benefit, does this in the most obvious examples and though you hear Christ saying, *No one comes to me unless the Father has drawn him* (Jn 6:44). This takes place in the hearts of all who turn to him out of fear of God's wrath. And you know that at times a thief scatters grain to lead cattle away and that a shepherd at times calls wandering cattle back to the herd with a whip.

6. Did not Sarah rather punish the rebellious serving girl when she was given the power? And she, of course, did not cruelly hate her since she had previously made her a mother by her own generosity; rather, she was subduing pride in her in a way conducive to her salvation. But you are not unaware that these two women, Sarah and Hagar, and their two sons, Isaac and Ishmael, symbolize spiritual and carnal persons. And though we read that the serving girl and her son suffered ill treatment from Sarah, the apostle Paul, nonetheless, says that Isaac suffered persecution from Ishmael, *But as at that time the one who was born according to the flesh persecuted the one who was born according to the Spirit, so it is now* (Gal 4:29). Thus those who can may understand that the Catholic Church suffers persecution from the pride and wickedness of carnal persons, whom it tries to correct by temporal troubles and fears. Whatever, then, the true and lawful mother does, even if it is felt to be harsh and bitter, she does not repay evil with evil, but applies the good of discipline to expel the evil of iniquity, not out of harmful hatred, but out of healing love. Since the good and the evil do the same things and suffer the same things, they must be distinguished, not by their actions and punishments, but by their motives. Pharaoh wore down the people of God with hard labor;[6] Moses punished with hard chastisements the same people when they acted sinfully.[7] What they did was similar, but they did not similarly

---

5. See Acts 9:3-7.
6. See Ex 5:6-18.
7. See Ex 32:25-38.

will to do good. Pharaoh was inflated with tyranny; Moses was inflamed with love. Jezebel killed the prophets; Elijah killed the false prophets.[8] I think that the merits of the agents were different and that the merits of the slain were different.

7. Also look at the time of the New Testament when the very gentleness of love was not only to be preserved in the heart, but was also to be manifested in the light of day, when Christ ordered the sword of Peter back into its scabbard and showed that it ought not to be drawn from its scabbard, not even for Christ.[9] We read, nonetheless, not only that the Jews beat the apostle Paul,[10] but also that the Greeks also beat the Jew Sosthenes in defense of Paul.[11] Does not the similarity of their action in some sense link both of them together, though the dissimilarity of their motive separates them? In fact, *God did not spare his own Son, but handed him over for all of us* (Rom 8:32). And it is said of the Son himself, *He loved me and handed himself over for me* (Gal 2:20). And it is said of Judas that Satan entered into him in order that he would hand over Christ.[12] Since, therefore, the Father also handed over his own Son and Christ handed over his own body and Judas handed over his Lord, why in this act of handing over is God loving and the man guilty, if not because in the one action that they did there is not one motive on account of which they did it? There were three crosses in the one place: on one a thief who would be saved, on another a thief who would be condemned, on the middle one Christ who would save the one and condemn the other.[13] What is more alike than those three crosses? What is more unlike than these three who hung on them? Paul was handed over to be imprisoned and chained,[14] but Satan is certainly worse than a prison guard. Paul himself, nonetheless, handed over to him a man *for the destruction of the flesh in order that his spirit may be saved on the day of the Lord Jesus* (1 Cor 5:5). And what do we say here? Look, a cruel man handed Paul over to someone comparatively gentle, while the merciful Paul handed a man over to someone crueler. Let us learn, my brothers, to distinguish the minds of the agents in their similar actions so that we do not, with our eyes closed, criticize unfairly and accuse the good-hearted in place of the guilty. So too, when the same apostle said that he handed over certain people *to Satan in order that they might learn not to blaspheme* (1 Tm 1:20), did he repay evil with evil, or did he rather judge that it was a good deed to correct the evil, even by means of an evil?

8. If it were always praiseworthy to suffer persecution, it would have been enough for the Lord to say, *Blessed are they who suffer persecution*, without

---

8. See 1 Kgs 18:4-40.
9. See Mt 26:52.
10. See Acts 16:22-23.
11. See Acts 18:17.
12. See Jn 13:2.
13. See Lk 23:33 and Jn 19:18.
14. See Acts 16:23-24.

adding, *on account of justice* (Mt 5:10). So too, if it were always blameworthy to persecute, it would not be written in the holy books, *I will persecute him who slanders his neighbor in secret* (Ps 101:5). At times, then, the one who suffers persecution is unjust, and the one who persecutes is just. But it is clear that the evil have always persecuted the good and the good have always persecuted the evil: the former by harming them unjustly, the latter by showing concern for them through discipline; the former savagely, the latter in moderation; the former in the service of desire, the latter in that of love. For a torturer does not worry about how he slashes, but a surgeon considers how he cuts. After all, the surgeon aims at health, the torturer at infection. Wicked men killed the prophets, and prophets killed wicked men. The Jews flogged Christ,[15] and Christ flogged the Jews.[16] The apostles were handed over by men to a human power, and the apostles handed over men to the power of Satan. In all these actions what do we consider but who acted for the truth and who for iniquity, who acted for the sake of harm and who for the sake of correction?

3, 9. Neither in the Gospels nor in the Letters of the apostles is there found a case in which something was asked for from the kings of the earth in defense of the Church against the enemies of the Church. Who would deny this? But this prophecy was not yet fulfilled: *And now, kings, have understanding; you who judge the earth, be warned; serve the Lord in fear* (Ps 2:10-11). For what is said a little before in the same psalm was still being fulfilled, *Why have the nations raged and the people plotted in vain? The kings of earth have arisen, and the princes have gathered together against the Lord and against his anointed one* (Ps 2:1-2).[17] If, nonetheless, past actions in the books of the prophets were symbols of those to come, that king who was called Nebuchadnezzar symbolized both times: both that of the Church under the apostles and that of the Church at present. During the times of the apostles and the martyrs there was fulfilled what was symbolized when the previously mentioned king forced good and righteous people to worship the idol and cast them into the flames when they refused. But now there is being fulfilled what is symbolized a little later by the same king when, after having been converted to honor the true God, he decreed in his kingdom that whoever blasphemed against the God of Shadrach, Meshach, and Abednego would face appropriate punishments.[18] The earlier time of that king, therefore, signified the earlier times of non-believing kings, under whom the Christians suffered instead of the unbelievers, but the later time of that king signified the times of the later kings, who were now believers under whom the non-believers suffered instead of the Christians.

15. See Mt 27:26, Mk 15:15, and Jn 19:1.
16. See Jn 2:15.
17. The Latin for "anointed one" is, of course, "*Christus*" so that the Latin seems more clearly to speak of Christ.
18. See Dn 3:1-21, 91-96.

10. But clearly with those who are misled by the wicked and go astray under the name of Christ, we use a tempered severity, or rather gentleness, in order that Christ's sheep may not perhaps wander astray and need to be recalled to the flock in such a way. Thus by the threats of exile and fines they may be warned to consider what they suffer and why and may learn to prefer the scriptures they read to the rumors and slanders of human beings. After all, who of us and who of you do not praise the laws passed by the emperors against the sacrifices of the pagans? And in that case a more severe penalty was surely established, for that impiety was, of course, a capital offense. But with regard to rebuking and stopping you the idea was that you should rather be admonished to withdraw from error than be punished for a crime. For one can perhaps say of you what the apostle said of the Jews: *I bear witness to them that they have zeal for God, but not in accord with knowledge. For, not knowing the righteousness of God and wanting to establish their own, they were not subject to the righteousness of God* (Rom 10:2-3). What else do you also want but to establish your own righteousness when you say that only those whom you were able to baptize are made righteous? In this statement, then, of the apostle that he spoke about the Jews, you differ from the Jews because you have the Christian sacraments that they still lack. But with regard to his words, *Not knowing the righteousness of God and wanting to establish their own*, and, *They have zeal for God, but not in accord with knowledge*, you are absolutely on a par with them, with the exception of those among you, whoever they are, who know the truth and out of passion for their error fight against the truth, which they too know perfectly well. The wickedness of these people may, of course, surpass idolatry. But since it is not easy to prove them guilty, for this evil lies hidden in their heart, you are all restrained with a milder severity, like people who are not extremely distant from us. And I would, in fact, say this either about all heretics who receive the Christian sacraments and dissent from the truth or unity of Christ or about all the Donatists.

11. But with regard to yourselves, who are not only generically called Donatists after Donatus, but also are specifically called Rogatists after Rogatus, you certainly seem to us less fierce, since you do not run wild with the savage bands of Circumcellions, but no wild animal is called tame if it injures no one because it lacks teeth or claws. You say that you do not want to act savagely; I suspect that you cannot. For you are so few in number that you would not dare to attack the multitudes opposed to you, even if you wanted to. But let us suppose that you do not want to do what you cannot. Let us suppose that you understand the sentence of the Gospel where it is written, *If someone wants to take your tunic and to take you to court, give him your coat as well* (Mt 5:40), and let us suppose that you hold this idea in the sense that you think that you should resist those who persecute you, not only with no injury, but not even by means of the law. Rogatus, your founder, certainly either did not have this understanding or did not live according to it. For he fought with the fiercest persistence, even in

legal arguments, for some possessions that were, as you claim, yours. Suppose that he were asked, "Who among the apostles ever defended his property in a public court when it was a question of the faith?" just as you asked in your letter, "Who among the apostles ever claimed the property of another when it was a question of the faith?" He would, of course, find no example of this action in the divine writings. But he would perhaps find some valid defense, if he held onto the true Church and did not impudently try to keep possession of something in the name of the true Church.

4, 12. But with regard to either obtaining or carrying out the commands of earthly authorities against heretics or schismatics, those from whom you separated yourselves were certainly the most fierce, both against you, to the extent we were able to hear, and against the Maximinanists, as we prove also by certain documents from various proceedings. But you were not yet separated from them when they said in their petition to Julian, the emperor, that in his eyes only justice has a place. And yet, they surely knew that he was an apostate and saw that he was so committed to the practice of idolatry that they either identified justice with idolatry or they could not deny that they had lied in a disgraceful fashion, when they said that in his eyes only justice has a place, for they saw that in his eyes idolatry occupied a large place. Granted that it was an error in speech, what do you say about the action itself? If one should ask for nothing just from the emperor, why did they ask from Julian what they thought was just?

13. Or ought one to petition the emperor only in order that each person might recover his own goods and not to accuse someone in order that he might be coerced by the emperor? Meanwhile, in seeking the restoration of one's own goods one departs from the example of the apostles, because none of them is found to have done this. But when your predecessors accused Caecilian, who was then bishop of the Church of Carthage, with whom they refused to be in communion as if he were a criminal, before the emperor Constantine through Anulinus, the proconsul, they were not seeking the recovery of their lost property, but were slanderously attacking an innocent man, as we view the matter and as the very outcome of the judicial proceedings reveals. What could they have done more outrageous than that? But if, as you incorrectly suppose, they handed over a man who was really a criminal to be tried by earthly authorities, why do you raise as an objection against us what your leaders first presumed to do? For we would not blame them because they did this, if they had not done it with a heart filled with hatred and bent on harm, but with the desire for improvement and correction. We, nonetheless, blame you without any hesitation because you think it a crime that we make some complaint to a Christian emperor about the enemies of our communion, though the list of charges presented by your predecessors to Anulinus the proconsul, which were to be sent on to Constantine the emperor, was entitled as follows: "The Charges of the Catholic Church against

the Crimes of Caecilian Submitted by the Sect of Majorinus."[19] But we blame them more for this because, on their own initiative, they accused Caecilian before the emperor, whereas they ought, of course, first to have convicted him before their colleagues across the sea. The emperor himself, after all, acted in a far more orderly fashion in referring to bishops a case against bishops that was brought to him. Nor did they want to be at peace with their brothers after they were defeated. But they again came to the same emperor and again brought charges before an earthly king, not only against Caecilian, but also against the bishops assigned to them as judges. And again they appealed to the same emperor against another decision of the bishops. Nor did they think that they should yield either to the truth or to peace when the emperor himself heard the case between both sides and pronounced judgment.

14. But what else would Constantine have decided against Caecilian and his companions, if they lost the case to your predecessors who accused them, but what he decided against those very men who, after they had on their own initiative brought accusations against them and could not prove the accusations that they wanted to, refused to submit to the truth, even when they lost their case? That emperor was the first to determine in this case that the possessions of those who lost their case and who were stubbornly opposed to unity should be confiscated. But if the emperor, for example, decreed something of the sort against the communion of Caecilian, had your predecessors brought accusations and won their case, you would want to be called guardians of the Church, defenders of peace and of unity. But when those who on their own initiative brought accusations could prove nothing against them and refused to submit to the embrace of peace offered them by which they might be corrected and welcomed back, the emperors issued such decrees, and your people decry the infamous crime and claim that no one should be forced into unity and that no one should repay evil with evil. What else is this than what someone wrote of you, "All we want is holiness."[20] And now it would not be hard or difficult to consider and see that the judgment and sentence of Constantine has force against you, for, when your predecessors accused Caecilian so many times before the emperor and did not prove their case, it was promulgated against you, and the other emperors, especially the Catholic Christian ones, necessarily follow it as often as your obstinacy necessarily forces them to take some measures.

15. It would be easy to consider these ideas so that at some point you would say to yourselves: "If Caecilian was either innocent or could not be proven guilty, how did the Christian people, who are spread so far and wide, sin in this affair? Why was the Christian world not permitted to remain ignorant of what his

---

19. Majorinus was the first Donatist bishop of Carthage; when he died in 313, he was succeeded by Donatus from whom the Donatists took their name.
20. See below, 10, 43, where this line is attributed to Tychonius.

accusers could not prove? Why are those people whom Christ sowed in his field, that is, in this world, and whom he ordered to grow amid the weeds until the harvest,[21] said not to be Christians? Why should so many thousands of believers in all the nations, whose multitude the Lord compared to the stars of the sky and the sand of the sea, those whom he promised would be blessed in the offspring of Abraham[22] and whom he has blessed as he promised, not be said to be Christians, because in this case in which they were not present for the hearing, they preferred to believe the judges who judged at their own risk rather than the litigants who lost? Surely no charge taints one who knows nothing of it. How could the faithful spread throughout the world have known of the crime of the traditors, when, even if their accusers knew of it, they were, nonetheless, unable to prove it to them? Their very ignorance quite easily proves them innocent of this crime. Why then are innocent people accused of false charges on the grounds that they did not know the crimes of others, whether they were true or false? What place remains for innocence if it is a crime of one's own not to know the crime of another? But if ignorance itself proves that the peoples of so many nations are innocent, how great a crime is it to be separated from communion with so many innocent persons? For the actions of guilty persons that cannot be shown to the innocent or believed by the innocent do not defile anyone, if, even when known, those actions are endured on account of fellowship with the innocent. For the good should not be abandoned on account of the evil; rather, the evil should be tolerated on account of the good. In this way the prophets tolerated those against whom they said so much, nor did they abandon participation in the sacraments of that people. In this way the Lord himself tolerated the guilty Judas up to his fitting end and permitted him to share the sacred supper with the innocent. In the same way the apostles tolerated those who preached Christ out of hatred, which is a vice of the devil himself.[23] In the same way Cyprian tolerated the greed of his colleagues,[24] which he called idolatry in accord with the apostle.[25] Finally, whatever was done at that time among the bishops, even if some of them perhaps knew of it, it is now not known by all of them, provided one side is not listened to rather than the other.[26] Why then do not all love peace?" You could very easily think of these matters, or perhaps you do also think of them. But it would be better that you love earthly possessions and consent to the truth out of fear of losing them than that you love the most empty glory of human beings, which you think you lose if you consent to the truth.

---

21. See Mt 13:24-30.
22. See Gn 22:17-18.
23. See Phil 1:15-18.
24. Cyprian, Letter 55, 27: CSEL 3/2, 644-645.
25. See Col 3:5 and Eph 5:5.
26. See Eph 6:9, Rom 2:11, and Col 3:25.

5, 16. Now you see, therefore, if I am not mistaken, that one ought not to consider the fact that anyone is constrained, but whether that to which one is constrained is good or bad. I do not say that a person can be good against his will. I say, however, that by fearing what he does not want to suffer, he abandons the stubbornness that holds him back or is compelled to recognize the truth he had not known. Thus out of fear he either rejects the error for which he was fighting or seeks the truth that he did not know, and he now willingly holds what he did not want to hold. It would perhaps be superfluous to say this with any words if it were not shown to us by so many examples. We see that, not these or those human beings, but many cities were Donatist and are now Catholic, and they intensely hate the diabolical division and ardently desire unity.[27] They, nonetheless, became Catholic on the occasion of this fear, at which you are displeased, through the laws of the emperor, from Constantine, before whom your people first accused Caecilian on their own initiative, up to the present emperors, who decreed that the judgment of that man whom your predecessors chose, whom they preferred to the bishops as judges, should be most justly observed against you.

17. I yielded, therefore, to these examples, which my colleagues proposed to me. For my opinion originally was that no one should be forced to the unity of Christ, but that we should act with words, fight with arguments, and conquer by reason. Otherwise, we might have as false Catholics those whom we had known to be obvious heretics. But this opinion of mine was defeated, not by the words of its opponents, but by examples of those who offered proof. For the first argument against me was my own city.[28] Though it was entirely in the Donatist sect, it was converted to the Catholic unity out of fear of the imperial laws, and we now see that it detests the destructiveness of this stubbornness of yours so that no one would believe that it was ever a part of it. And it was the same with many other cities, which were reported to me by name, so that I might recognize by the very facts that one could correctly understand the words of scripture as also applying to this case, *Give a wise man a chance, and he will become wiser* (Prv 9:9). For how many, as we know for certain, already wanted to be Catholics, because they were convinced by the clearest truth, but because they feared offending their own people, they daily postponed doing so! How many were bound, not by the truth, in which you never had much confidence, but by the heavy chain of inveterate habit, so that those words of God were fulfilled in them, *A difficult servant will not be corrected by words, for, even if he understands, he will not obey* (Prv 29:19)! How many thought that the true Church was the sect of Donatus because security made them uninterested, reluctant, and lazy to gain knowledge of the

---

27. The mass conversions of Donatists took place after the laws issued against the Donatists in February 405.
28. That is, Thagaste.

Catholic truth! For how many did the rumors of slanderers close the entrance way when they spread it about that we offer something else on the altar of God! How many believed that it made no difference on which side one is a Christian and, therefore, remained on the side of Donatus, because they were born there, and no one forced them to leave it and cross over to the Catholic side!

18. The fright over these laws, in the promulgation of which kings serve the Lord in fear,[29] benefited all these people so that some now say, "We already wanted this, but thanks be to God who gave us the opportunity of finally doing it and cut away time for delaying." And others say, "We already knew that this was true, but we were held back by some sort of habit. Thanks be to the Lord who has broken our chains and has brought us to the bond of peace." Still others say, "We did not know that the truth was here, nor did we want to learn of it, but fear made us concentrate on coming to know it. For we were afraid that we would suffer the loss of temporal goods without any gain of eternal ones. Thanks be to the Lord who shook us free of our negligence by the goad of fear in order that we at least might be worried and seek what we never cared to know in our security." Others say, "We were deterred from entering by false rumors, and we would not have known they were false if we did not enter, nor would we have entered if we were not forced. Thanks be to the Lord who removed our fearfulness by his scourge and has taught us by experience how vain and empty were the reports that deceitful rumors spread about his Church. For this reason we now believe that those charges were also false that the authors of this heresy raised, since their successors have made up false charges and worse ones." Others say, "We, of course, thought that it made no difference where we professed faith in Christ, but thanks be to the Lord who has gathered us back from our schism and has shown us that it is fitting that the one God be worshiped in unity."

19. Should I, then, have set myself against my colleagues to speak against them in order to impede these gains for the Lord so that the sheep of Christ, who were wandering astray in your mountains and hills, that is, in the swellings of your pride, would not be gathered into the flock of peace where there is *one flock and one shepherd* (Jn 10:16)? Should I really have spoken against this providential care so that you would not lose the possessions you call yours and so that you might securely outlaw Christ? Should I have done this so that you might create your testaments by Roman law and so that you might break by your slanderous charges the testament established by divine law with the patriarchs, where it is written, *In your offspring all nations will be blessed* (Gn 26:4)? Should I have done this so that in buying and selling you might freely make contracts and so that you might dare to divide for yourselves what Christ bought when he was sold? Should I have done this so that what any of you has given to anyone is valid and so that what the God of gods has given to his children, whom he called from

---

29. See Ps 2:11.

the rising of the sun to its setting,[30] is not valid? Should I have done this so that you are not sent into exile from the land of your body, while you try to make Christ an exile from the kingdom purchased by his blood, *from sea to sea and from the river to the ends of the world* (Ps 72:8)? On the contrary, let the kings of the earth serve Christ, even by issuing laws in Christ's favor! Your predecessors denounced Caecilian and his companions to the kings of the earth to be punished for crimes that were not true. Let the lions turn around to crush the bones of the slanderers, and let not Daniel himself, who was proven innocent and set free from the lions' pit where they are perishing, intercede for them.[31] After all, one who prepares a pit for his neighbor will himself fall into it with greater justice.[32]

6, 20. While you are still living in this flesh, rescue yourself, my brother, from the wrath to come for the stubborn and proud. When the terror of temporal authorities attacks the truth, it is a glorious trial for the brave and the righteous, but a dangerous temptation for the weak. But when the authorities proclaim the truth, it is a useful admonition for misguided, but intelligent people, and a useless affliction for the mindless. *There is,* nonetheless, *no authority except from God. But one who is opposed to an authority is opposed to God's governance. For princes are not a terror for good conduct, but for bad. Do you want to have no fear of authority? Do good, and you will have praise from it* (Rom 13:1-3). For, if an authority favoring the truth corrects someone, that person who was corrected receives praise from it. Or if an authority hostile to the truth rages against someone, the person who is crowned as victor receives praise from this. But you are not doing good in order that you need have no fear of authority, unless it is perhaps good to sit and not to speak ill against one brother, but against all your brothers located in all the nations, to whom the prophets, Christ, and the apostles bore witness. For we read, *In your offspring all the nations will be blessed* (Gn 26:4), and we read, *From the rising of the sun to its setting a clean offering will be made to my name, because my name has been glorified among the nations, says the Lord* (Mal 1:11). Notice the words, *Says the Lord*; it does not say: "Says Donatus," or "Rogatus," or "Vincent," or "Hilary," or "Ambrose," or "Augustine," but, *Says the Lord.* And we read, *And in him will be blessed all the tribes of the earth; all the nations will proclaim his greatness. Blessed be the Lord, the God of Israel, who alone works wonders, and blessed be the name of his glory forever and for age upon age. And all the earth will be filled with his glory; so be it; so be it* (Ps 72:17-19). And you reside in Cartenna, and with the ten Rogatists who remain you say, "Let it not be so; let it not be so."

21. You hear the gospel say: *"It was necessary that all that was written about me in the law and the prophets and the psalms be fulfilled."* Then he opened up

---

30. See Ps 50:1.
31. See Dn 6:13-24 and 14:39-42.
32. See Prv 26:27.

their mind so that they understood the scriptures, and he said to them, "Because it was written in that way, it was also necessary that Christ suffer in that way and rise from the dead on the third day and that repentance and the forgiveness of sins in his name be preached through all the nations, beginning from Jerusalem" (Lk 24:44-47). You also read in the Acts of the Apostles of how this gospel began from Jerusalem, where the Holy Spirit first filled those one hundred and twenty,[33] and went from there to Judea and Samaria and to all the nations, as he told them when he was about to ascend into heaven, *You will be my witnesses in Jerusalem and in the whole of Judea and Samaria and up to the ends of the earth* (Acts 1:8), *for their voice went out into the whole world and their words to the ends of the earth* (Ps 19:5 and Rom 10:8). And you contradict the testimonies of God supported with such great strength and revealed with such great light, and you try to bring Christ's heritage to reject them. For, when repentance is preached, as he said, in his name in all the nations, unless anyone roused by this preaching in any part of the world whatsoever seeks out and finds Vincent of Cartenna hiding out in Mauritania Caesarienis or one of his nine or ten companions, he cannot have his sins forgiven. What would this poor dead skin, swollen with pride as it is, not dare? To what point would the presumption of flesh and blood not hurl itself? Is this your good deed on account of which you have no fear of the authorities? Do you set such a stumbling block for the son of your mother,[34] that is, a weak and little one, on account of whom Christ has died,[35] one not yet ready for the food of his father, but still needing to be fed by the milk of his mother?[36] And you set Hilary's[37] books against me, in order that you may deny the Church, which is growing in all the nations to the end of the earth, the Church which God promised with an oath contrary to your unbelief! And though you would have been most wretched if you opposed it when it was promised, you speak against it even now when the promise is being fulfilled.

7, 22. But as a learned historian you have found something important that you think you should bring forward against the testimonies of God. For you say, "If one considers all the parts of the world, in comparison to the whole world the part in which the Christian faith is known is small." You either do not want to consider or you pretend that you do not know to how many barbarian nations the gospel came in so short a time that even the enemies of Christ cannot doubt that in a short while there will occur what he replied to his disciples who were asking about the end of the world: *And this gospel will be preached in the whole world as a testimony to all the nations, and then the end will come* (Mt 24:14). Go now,

---

33. See Acts 1:15.
34. See Ps 50:20.
35. See 1 Cor 8:11.
36. See 1 Cor 3:2.
37. See below, 9, 31, where Augustine discusses the passage from the *Synods (De synodis)* by Hilary of Poitiers.

cry out, and argue as much as you can: "Even if the gospel is preached among the Persians and Indians, where it has been, of course, long preached, unless whoever hears it comes to Cartenna or in the neighborhood of Cartenna, he absolutely cannot be cleansed from his sins." Are you afraid to be laughed at, if you do not use this cry? And do you not ask to be wept over, if you use it?

23. But you think that you say something clever when you explain that the name "Catholic" comes not from the communion of the whole world, but from the observance of all God's commandments and all the sacraments. You suppose that we rely on the testimony of this term for proving that the Church is found in all the nations and not on the promises of God and so many and such clear prophecies of the truth, even if the Church might perhaps be called "Catholic" for the reason that it really holds the whole truth, of which some particles are also found in the different heresies. But this is the whole of which you try to convince us: that only the Rogatists have remained who should correctly be called Catholics on the basis of the observation of all God's commandments and of all the sacraments and that you are the only ones in whom the Son of Man will find faith when he comes.[38] Pardon us, but we do not believe this. For it may be that you dare to say that you should be considered to be, not on earth, but in heaven, in order in you may be found the faith that the Lord said that he would not find on earth. The apostle, nonetheless, warned us, for he commanded that even an angel from heaven who brings us another gospel than we have received should be anathema.[39] But how can we be confident that we have received Christ so clearly from the words of God, if we have not received the Church from them with equal clarity? Whoever adds any needless complications contrary to the simplicity of the truth, whoever pours out any clouds of clever falsehood, let him be anathema, just as he will be anathema who proclaims that Christ neither suffered nor rose on the third day. For we have received in the truth of the gospel: *It was necessary that Christ suffer and rise from the dead on the third day* (Lk 24:46). So too he will be anathema who proclaims the Church apart from the communion of all the nations, because we have received from that same truth immediately afterwards: *And that repentance and the forgiveness of sins be preached in his name through all the nations, beginning from Jerusalem* (Lk 24:47). And we ought to maintain with unshaken faith: *Let anyone who proclaims to you another gospel than what you have received be anathema* (Gal 1:9).

8, 24. But if we do not listen to any Donatists, when they substitute themselves for the Church of Christ, because they bring forth no testimony in their favor from the books of God in order to teach this, how much the less, I ask you, ought we to listen to the Rogatists who will not try to interpret in their own favor

---

38. See Lk 18:8.
39. See Gal 1:8.

even that passage where it is written, *Where do you pasture your flocks, where do you make them lie down in the south?* (Sg 1:6). If in that passage "south" should be interpreted as Africa where the sect of Donatus is found, because it is under a hotter region of the sky, the Maximianists will surpass all of you, since their schism arose in Byzacena and Tripoli.[40] But the Arzuges quarrel with them and claim that it rather refers to them. Mauritania Caesariensis, nonetheless, is closer to the eastern than to the southern part; since it does not want to be called Africa, how will it boast of being called "the south"? I do not mean in relation to the rest of the world, but in relation to the sect of Donatus, from which the sect of Rogatus is a tiny fragment broken off from a larger fragment. But apart from great impudence who tries to interpret something expressed in an allegory in his own favor, unless he also has perfectly clear testimonies that cast light on the obscure passages?

25. But how much more emphatically we say to you what we usually say to all the Donatists: Suppose that some people can have a just reason, something that is not possible, for separating their communion from communion with the whole world and for calling their communion the Church of Christ, because they have for just reasons separated themselves from communion with the whole world. How do you know that in the Christian people spread so far and wide, before you separated yourselves, some others have not separated themselves for a just reason in most remote lands, from where a report of their righteousness could not come to you? How can the Church exist in you rather than in those who perhaps separated themselves earlier? Thus it turns out that, since you do not know this, you are uncertain in your own eyes, and it is necessary that this be the result for all who use, not God's testimony, but their own, in defense of their communion. Nor can you say, after all, "If this had happened, we could not fail to know it," when in Africa herself, you could not say, if you were asked, how many sects have split off from the sect of Donatus, especially since those who do this think that they are more righteous to the extent that they are fewer, and they are, of course, to that extent less known. And for this reason you are not certain that, before the sect of Donatus separated its righteousness from the sinfulness of the other human beings, some few righteous persons and, for this reason, scarcely known, somewhere far from the southern region of Africa, did not perhaps separate themselves earlier in the region of the north with a fully just reason. And you are not certain that this sect is not rather the Church of God, like the spiritual Zion, which anticipated all of you with its righteous separation and much more presumptuously interprets in its favor the words of scripture, *Mount Zion, in the northern part, the city of the great king* (Ps 48:3), than the sect of

---

40. That is, the provinces of Byzacena (Byzacium in Greek) and Tripoli, to the south and east of Carthage. The Arzuges were Donatist dissents in Byzacena and Tripoli.

Donatus interprets in its favor, *Where do you pasture your flocks, where do you make them lie down in the south?* (Sg 1:6).

26. And you, nonetheless, are afraid that, when you are forced into unity by the imperial laws, the name of God may for a longer time be blasphemed by the Jews and pagans, as if the Jews do not know how the first people of Israel wanted to destroy even by war those two and a half tribes that received lands beyond the Jordan, when they thought that they had separated themselves from the unity of their people.[41] But the pagans can speak ill of you even more because of the imperial laws that the Christian emperors issued against the worshipers of idols. And yet, many of them have been corrected and have been converted to the living and true God and are being converted every day. But clearly if both the Jews and the pagans thought that the Christians were as few in number as you are, who claim that you alone are Christians, they would not stoop to speak ill of us, but would never stop laughing at us. If your small number is the Church of Christ, are you not afraid that the Jews might say to you, "Where do you find what your Paul interpreted as referring to your church where scripture says, *Rejoice, you who are sterile, you who bear no children; burst forth and cry out, you who have no labor pains, for the children of the abandoned woman are more numerous than those of the woman with a husband* (Is 54:1 and Gal 4:47), where he showed the numerical superiority of the Christians over the Jews?" Is this what you are going to say to them: "We are more righteous precisely because we are few," and do you not notice that they will reply, "However many you say that you are, you are not, nonetheless, those of whom scripture said, *The children of the abandoned woman are more numerous*, if you have remained so few in number."

27. At this point you are going to appeal to the example of that righteous man in the flood who was alone found worthy of being saved along with his family.[42] Do you, therefore, see how far you still are from righteousness? We, of course, are not going to call you righteous until you are down to seven with yourself as the eighth, unless, as I was saying, someone else seized this righteousness before the sect of Donatus and along with his seven companions, after having been provoked by some just cause, separated himself somewhere far away and rescued himself from the flood of this world. Since you do not know whether this happened and you have not heard of it, just as many Christian peoples living in distant lands have not heard of the name "Donatus," you are uncertain about where the Church is to be found. For it will be in that place where there first occurred what you afterwards did, if there could be any just reason for which you could have separated yourselves from communion with all the nations.

9, 28. We, however, are certain that no one could have justly separated himself from communion with all the nations, precisely because each of us seeks

41. See Jos 22:9-12.
42. See Gn 7:1-23.

the church, not in our own righteousness, but in the divine scriptures, and each of us sees that it exists as it was promised. For she is the church of which scripture says, *Like a lily in the midst of thorns, so is my beloved in the midst of daughters* (Sg 2:2). They could be called "thorns" only because of their evil conduct, and they could be called "daughters" only because of their sharing in the sacraments. She, after all, is the one who says, *From the ends of the earth I have cried out to you when my heart was troubled* (Ps 61:3). In another psalm she says, *Weariness grips me because of sinners who abandon your law* (Ps 119:53), and, *I saw the faithless, and I wasted away* (Ps 119: 158). She it is who says to her spouse, *Where do you pasture your flocks, where do you make them lie down in the south lest I should perhaps become like a veiled woman behind the flocks of your companions* (Sg 1:6). This is what scripture says elsewhere, *Make known to me your right hand and those learned of heart in wisdom* (Ps 90:12). In these who are brilliant with light and fervent with love you find rest as if in the south lest perhaps as a veiled woman, that is, one who is hidden and unknown, I should rush, not into your flock, but into the flocks of your companions, that is, of the heretics. And he calls these heretics companions, as he called those daughters thorns because of their sharing the same sacraments. Of these scripture says elsewhere, *But you who are one of heart with me, my guide, my friend, you who ate with me sweet foods, in the house of the Lord we walked in harmony. May death come upon them, and may they descend alive into hell* (Ps 55:14-16), just like Dathan and Abiram, the authors of the wicked schism.[43]

29. She it is who receives the immediate reply, *If you do not know yourself, O most beautiful among women, go out in the paths of the flocks, and pasture your kids in the tents of the shepherds* (Sg 1:7). Oh! Reply of the most lovable spouse! *If you do not know yourself,* he says, because, of course, *A city placed upon a mountaintop cannot be hidden* (Mt 5:14), and for that reason you are not veiled so that you should rush into the flocks of my companions. For I am *a mountain prepared on the height of the mountains to which all the nations will come* (Is 2:2). *If you,* then, *do not know yourself,* not in the words of slanderers, but in the testimonies of my books. *If you do not know yourself,* because scripture has said of you, *Stretch out further your ropes, and strengthen your mighty fences; again and again reach out to the right and to the left. For your offspring will inherit the nations, and you will dwell in cities that were abandoned. There is nothing for you to fear, for you will prevail. Do not be ashamed that you were disgraced. For you will forget your shame forever; you will not remember the ignominy of your widowhood. I, after all, am the Lord who created you; "Lord" is his name. And he who rescues you will be called the God of Israel and of all the earth* (Is 54:2-5). *If you do not know yourself, O most beautiful among women* (Sg 1:7), for scripture said of you, *The king desired your beauty* (Ps 45:12), because it said

43. See Nm 1:7.

of you, *In place of your fathers sons have been born to you; you will establish them as princes over the whole earth* (Ps 45:17). *If you do not know yourself, go out* (Sg 1:7). I do not cast you out, but, *Go out*, in order that it may be said of you, *They went out from us, but they did not belong to us* (1 Jn 2:19). *Go out in the paths of the flocks*, not in my paths, but *in the paths of the flocks*, and not of one flock, but of flocks that are divided and straying. *And pasture your kids*, not like Peter to whom it is said, *Pasture my sheep* (Jn 21:17), but, *Pasture your kids in the tents of the shepherds*, not in the tent of the shepherd, where there is one flock and one shepherd.[44] For she knows herself so that this does not happen to her, because this has happened to those who have not known themselves in her.

30. She it is of whose few numbers scripture says in comparison with the many evil persons, *Straight and narrow is the way that leads to salvation, and few are they who walk on it* (Mt 7:14). And again she it is of whose great number scripture says, *Your offspring will be like the stars of the sky and like the sand of the sea* (Gn 22:17 and Dn 3:36). The same holy and good believers are, of course, few in comparison with the evil and are many by themselves, *Because the children of the abandoned woman are more than those of the woman with a husband* (Gal 4:27), and, *Many will come from the east and from the west and will recline with Abraham, Isaac, and Jacob in the kingdom of heaven* (Mt 8:11), and because *God presents to himself an abundant people who are zealous for good works* (Tt 2:14), and many thousands *whom no one can count* are seen in the Apocalypse *in every tribe and tongue, in white robes and with palms of victory* (Rev 7:9). She it is who is at times obscured and as if clouded over because of a multitude of scandals, *when sinners bend their bows to shoot in the dark moon those who are upright of heart* (Ps 11:3). But even then she stands out in her strongest members. And if some distinction is to be made in these words of God, perhaps there was a point in saying of the offspring of Abraham that they will be *like the stars of the sky and like the sand at the shore of the sea* (Gn 22:17), namely, that we understand by the stars of the sky the fewer, stronger, and more brilliant, but in the sand on the seashore the great multitude of the weak and carnal, who at times seem at rest and free because of the tranquility of the weather, but at other times are overwhelmed and churned up by the waves of tribulations and temptations.

31. Such was that time of which Hilary wrote, because of which you thought that you should attack so many divine testimonies, as if the Church perished from the whole world.[45] You can in this way say that so many churches in Galatia had ceased to exist at the time when the apostle said, *O you foolish Galatians,*

---

44. See Jn 10:16.
45. Hilary of Poitiers said in his work, *Synods (De synodis)* 65: PL 10, 522, "With the exception of Eleusius and the few with him, the ten provinces of Asia, where I find myself, do not really for the most part know God."

who has bewitched you? and, *Though you began with the spirit, you end up in the flesh* (Gal 3:1.3). For you in that way slander a learned man who severely reprimanded the fainthearted and timid whom he was bringing to birth once again until Christ would be formed in them.[46] After all, who does not know that at that period many people of poor judgment were deceived by obscure language so that they thought that the Arians believed what they themselves believed? But others yielded out of fear and pretended to agree with them, *not acting correctly in relation to the gospel* (Gal 2:14), and you would have refused to pardon them when they were later corrected, as they were in fact pardoned. You, of course, do not know the books of God. Read, after all, what Paul wrote about Peter[47] and what Cyprian also thought about that,[48] and do not be displeased at the gentleness of the Church, which gathers together the scattered members of Christ and does not scatter those gathered together. And yet those who were the strongest at that time and were able to understand the insidious words of the heretics were in fact few in comparison with the others, but some even bravely suffered exile for the faith, while others remained unknown in the whole world. And in that way the Church, which is growing in all the nations, is preserved in the grain sown by the Lord and will be preserved up to the end until it contains absolutely all the nations, even the barbarian ones. For the Church is found in the good seed, which the Son of Man sowed and which he foretold would grow among the weeds up to the harvest. But the field is the world, and the harvest is the end of the world.[49]

32. Hilary, then, either reprimanded the weeds, not the grain, of the ten provinces of Asia or thought that the grain itself, which was in danger due to some failing, would be reprimanded with greater benefit the more severely he rebuked them. After all, the canonical scriptures also contain this practice of reprimanding in order that a word seemingly said to all might reach certain individuals. For, when the apostle says to the Corinthians, *How do certain ones among you say that there is no resurrection of the dead?* (1 Cor 15:12), he, of course, shows that they were not all such people, but he, nonetheless, bears witness that such people were not outsiders, but were among them, and he warned shortly afterwards that those who did not share such ideas should not be misled by them. He says, *Do not be misled. Bad conversations ruin good morals. Be sober, you who are righteous; do not sin. For some are lacking knowledge of God; I speak to put you to shame* (1 Cor 15:33-34). But when he says, *Since, after all, there is jealousy and strife among you, are you not carnal and do you not live in a merely human fashion?* (1 Cor 3:3), he seemingly speaks to all, and you see how serious what he says is. Hence, if we did not read in the same Letter, *I always thank my*

---

46. See Gal 4:19.
47. See Gal 2:11-14.
48. See Cyprian, Letter 71, 3: CSEL 3/2, 773.
49. See Mt 13:24-30.38-39.

God for you because of the grace of God that has been given to you in Christ Jesus, because in every way you have become enriched in all speech and in all knowledge, just as the testimony of Christ has been confirmed in you, so that nothing is lacking to you in any grace (1 Cor 1:4-7), we would think that all the Corinthians were carnal and merely natural, not perceiving those things that pertain to the Spirit of God, full of strife, jealous, living in a merely human fashion. And so, *the whole world has been placed in the power of the evil one* (Jn 5:19), on account of the weeds, which are spread throughout the whole world, and Christ *is propitiation for our sins, not only for our sins, but also for those of the whole world* (1 Jn 2:2), on account of the wheat, which is spread throughout the whole world.

33. *But the love of many grows cold* (Mt 24:12), on account of the abundance of scandals to the extent that the name of Christ has attained more and more glory and there are gathered into the communion of his sacraments even the evil and the persistently and utterly perverse, but like the chaff they will not be removed from the threshing floor of the Lord until the last winnowing.[50] These do not choke off the Lord's wheat, which is meager in comparison with them, but great in itself. They do not choke off the wheat plants of the Lord, which in comparison with them are few, but are many by themselves. They do not choke off the elect of God who will be gathered together at the end of the world, as the Gospel says, *from the four winds, from one end of the heavens to the other* (Mt 24:31). For this is their cry: *Save me, O Lord, because even a saint falters, for truthfulness has decreased among the children of men* (Ps 12:2), and of these the Lord also says, "Amid the abundance of sinfulness *he who perseveres up to the end will be saved*" (Mt 24:12). Finally, the following words inform us that not one person, but many are speaking in the same psalm where it says, *You, O Lord, will keep us and guard us from this generation forever* (Ps 12:8). On account of this abundance of sinfulness, which the Lord foretold would exist, this passage was also written, *When the Son of Man comes, do you suppose he will find faith on earth?* (Lk 18:8). For the doubt on the part of him who knows all things prefigured our doubt in him when, because of many from whom she hoped for much, the Church was often disappointed because they were found to be other than they were believed to be and was so troubled over her members that she was unwilling readily to believe anything good of anyone. We must, nonetheless, not doubt that those people whose faith he is going to find on earth will grow along with the weeds through the whole field.

34. She, therefore, is the Church which swims along with the bad fishes within the Lord's net,[51] from whom she is always separated in heart and morals and from whom she departs *in order that she may be presented to her husband as glorious,*

---

50. See Mt 3:12 and 13:30.
51. Mt 13:47.

having neither spot nor wrinkle (Eph 5:27). But she awaits bodily separation on the seashore, that is, at the end of the world,[52] correcting those whom she can, tolerating those whom she cannot correct; she does not, nonetheless, abandon unity on account of the sinfulness of those whom she does not correct.

10, 35. Do not, therefore, my brother, desire to gather slanderous statements from the writings of bishops, whether our bishops, like Hilary, or those belonging to the unity itself before the sect of Donatus was separated, like Cyprian and Agrippinus,[53] against so many, such clear, and such indubitable testimonies of God. After all, writings of this sort are, first of all, to be distinguished from the authority of the canonical books. For we do not read them as if a testimony is drawn from them so that we are not permitted to hold a contrary view, if those writers perhaps somewhere held some view other than the truth demands. We ourselves are, of course, included in that number so that we do not disdain to accept the apostle's words as also spoken to us: *And if on some point you think differently, God will also reveal that to you. Let us, nonetheless, continue in that to which we have come* (Phil 3:15-16), that is, in that way, which is Christ.[54] The psalm speaks of that way as follows: *May God be merciful to us and bless us; may he make his face shine upon us in order that we may know your way on earth, your salvation in all the nations* (Ps 67:2-3).

36. Then, if you are pleased with the authority of Saint Cyprian, the bishop and glorious martyr, which, as I said, we distinguish from the authority of the canon, why are you not pleased that he preserved by love and defended by argument the unity of the whole world and of all the nations? Why are you not pleased that he judged most arrogant and proud those who wanted to separate themselves from her as if they were righteous? He mocked them for claiming for themselves what the Lord did not grant even to the apostles, namely, that they should pull out the weeds beforetime or that they should try to separate the chaff from the wheat, as if it were granted to them to remove the chaff and clean up the threshing floor.[55] Why are you not pleased that he showed that no one can be defiled by the sins of others, the reason which all the authors of an impious rebellion take as their sole reason for separation? Why are you not pleased that on that very issue on which they held another view he decreed that his colleagues who thought differently were not to be judged or removed from the right to communion? Why are you not pleased at what he says in that very letter to Jubaianus, which was first read out in that council whose authority you say that you follow for rebaptizing?[56] For, though he admits that in the past those who were baptized

---

52. See Mt 13:47-49.
53. Cyprian was bishop of Carthage from 248/249 to 258. Agrippinus was a bishop of Carthage before Cyprian and held views similar to his.
54. See Jn 14:6.
55. See Mt 13:28-30.
56. See Cyprian, Letter 73: CSEL 3/2, 778. The council was held in Carthage in 256.

elsewhere were admitted to the Church without being rebaptized and thinks that they were for this reason without baptism, he, nonetheless, sees such a great benefit and blessing in the peace of the Church that on its account he believes that they should not be excluded from offices in the Church.

37. On this point you see with the greatest ease, for I know your fine mind, that your case is completely overthrown and wiped out. For, if by admitting sinners to the sacraments, the Church, which had existed in the whole world, has, as you claim, perished—for you broke away on those grounds; it had as a whole perished earlier when, as Cyprian says, they were admitted into her without baptism. And in that way even Cyprian did not have the Church in which he might be born. For how much greater reason did your author and father, Donatus, at a later time not have the Church! But if at that time when people were admitted to her without baptism, there was still the Church that gave birth to Cyprian and also gave birth to Donatus, it is evident that the righteous are not infected by the sins of others when they share with them in the sacraments. And for this reason you do not have any excuse by which you might excuse the separation by which you departed from the unity, and there is fulfilled in you that prophecy of the holy scripture: *A bad son says that he is righteous, but he does not excuse his going out* (Prv 30:12, LXX).

38. But one who does not dare to rebaptize even heretics on account of their sacraments equal to ours does not equal the merits of Cyprian, just as whoever does not force pagans to live as Jews does not equal the merits of Peter. But the canonical scriptures contain not merely that failure on Peter's part, but also his correction. Cyprian, however, is found to have held other ideas concerning baptism than is contained in the norm and practice of the Church, not in canonical writings, but in his own and in those of a council. He is not, however, found to have corrected this view; it is, nonetheless, not inappropriate that we should think with regard to such a man that he corrected his view, and it was perhaps suppressed by those who were all too pleased by this error and did not want to be without so great a patron. And yet there are some who claim that Cyprian certainly did not hold this view, but that it was made up and attributed to him by bold liars. For the integrity and knowledge of the writings of one bishop, however illustrious, could not be preserved in the same way as the canonical scripture is preserved by translations in so many languages and by the order and sequence of the Church's liturgical celebration. And yet, there were not lacking in opposition to the scripture those who composed many documents in the name of the apostles, in vain, of course, because that scripture is so highly commended, so frequently used in celebrations, and so very familiar. But the attempt of impious audacity has shown even from this case what it could do against writings that are not founded upon canonical authority, since it did not fail to challenge those writings that were supported by so solid a basis of familiarity.

39. We, nonetheless, do not deny that Cyprian held this view. We have two reasons: because his writing has a certain character all its own by which it can be recognized and because his writing rather shows that our case against you is more invincible and undermines with great ease the grounds for your breaking away, namely, so that you would not be defiled by the sins of others. For in the writings of Cyprian we see that sinners participated in the sacraments when people were admitted to the Church who according to your opinion and, as you claim, according to Cyprian's did not have baptism, and yet the Church did not perish. Rather, the Lord's grain remained scattered through the whole world in its special dignity. And for this reason if, when upset, you take flight to the authority of Cyprian as if to some harbor, you see there the rocks upon which your error is dashed. But if you now do not dare to take flight to him, you are shipwrecked without putting up any fight.

40. On the other hand, Cyprian either did not at all hold the view that you report that he held, or he corrected it afterwards by the rule of truth, or he covered over this view like a birthmark on his most pure heart with the richness of his love, while he both most amply defended the unity of the Church that was growing through the whole world and most perseveringly maintained the bond of peace. For it is written, *Love covers over a multitude of sins* (1 Pt 4:8). There is also added to this the fact that, if there was anything in him that needed to be corrected, the Father pruned him like a most fruitful branch with the knife of martyrdom. The Lord says, *For the Father will prune the branch that gives fruit in me in order that it may bear greater fruit* (Jn 15:2). Why, if not, because in clinging to the vine as it spread out, he did not abandon the root of unity? For, even if he handed over his body to be burned, but did not have love, it would have done him no good.[57]

41. Consider a little longer the letter of Cyprian in order that you may see how inexcusable he showed a person to be who chose to break away, as if for the sake of his own righteousness, from the unity of the Church, which God promised and has brought to fulfillment in all the nations. You will better understand how true is that statement I mentioned shortly before: *A bad son says that he is righteous, but he does not excuse his going out* (Prv 30:12, LXX). He puts in a certain letter of his to Antonian a specific point quite pertinent to the issue we are dealing with, but it is better that we include his words. He says, "Certain bishops, our predecessors, here in our province thought that they should not grant reconciliation to fornicators and that they should completely exclude a place of repentance for adulterers. They did not, nonetheless, withdraw from the college of their fellow bishops or shatter the unity of the Catholic Church either by the hardness or the stubbornness of their censure so that one who did not grant reconciliation to adulterers broke away from the Church because others granted such reconciliation. While the bond of harmony remained and the sacrament of the Catholic Church continued undivided, each

---

57. See 1 Cor 13:3.

bishop arranges and orders his own actions, for he will give an account of his conduct to the Lord."[58] What do you say to this, Brother Vincent? You, of course, see that this great man, a bishop of peace, and the bravest of martyrs, worked for nothing with greater intensity than to avoid breaking the bond of unity. You see him in labor, not only that little ones conceived in Christ might be born, but also so that those already born might not die, torn from the bosom of their mother.

42. But consider also the very point that he mentioned against the impious authors of schism. If those who granted reconciliation to penitent adulterers were in communion with adulterers, were those who did not do this defiled by companionship with them? But if, as the truth maintains and as the Church rightly holds, reconciliation was rightly granted to penitent adulterers, those who completely excluded a place of repentance for adulterers certainly acted impiously in denying health to members of Christ and in withholding the keys of the Church from those who knocked and in contradicting with harsh cruelty the most merciful patience of God. For his mercy allowed them to live precisely in order that they might be healed by doing penance when they offered the sacrifice of a contrite spirit and a troubled heart.[59] Nor did so great an error and impiety on their part defile these merciful and peaceful men who participated with them in the Christian sacraments and tolerated them within the nets of unity until they might be separated after being brought to the shore.[60] Or if it did defile them, the Church was already at that time destroyed by being in communion with evil persons, nor did she exist to give birth to Cyprian himself. But if the Church has remained, as is certain, it is certain that no one can be defiled by the actions of evil persons in the unity of Christ, if he does not consent to them lest he be polluted by partaking in their sins and if on account of the society of the good he tolerates the evil, like chaff on the Lord's threshing floor up to the last winnowing.[61] Since that is so, where are the grounds for your breaking away? Are you not bad sons? You yourselves say that you are righteous, but you do not excuse your going out.

43. Now I could also mention those ideas that Tychonius,[62] a man of your communion, put in his writings, a man who wrote in fact against you in defense of the Catholic Church. He uselessly removed himself from communion with the Africans on the grounds that they were traditors, and by this one fact Parmenian[63] held him trapped. What could you answer except what the same

58. See Cyprian, Letter 55, 21: CSEL 3/2, 778.
59. See Ps 51:19.
60. See Mt 13:47-49.
61. See Mt 3:12 and 13:29-30.
62. Tychonius was a learned Donatist whose rules for the interpretation of scripture Augustine incorporated into his own work, *Teaching Christianity*.
63. Parmenian was the Donatist bishop of Carthage at the time of Julian the Apostate. Augustine wrote three books against him in his work, *Answer to the Letter of Parmenian*.

Tychonius said and what I recalled a little before: "All we want is holiness."[64] For that Tychonius, a man, as I said, of your communion, writes that a council of two hundred and seventy bishops was celebrated at Carthage and that in that council for seventy-five days, after having put aside all past norms, the position was worked out and decreed that they should be in communion with the traditors guilty of a grave sin, as if they were innocent, if they refused to be baptized again.[65] He says that Deuterius, a bishop of Macrina, also of your communion, mixed together the assembled people of the traditors with the church and that, according to the statutes of that council celebrated by two hundred and seventy of your bishops, he established unity with the traditors and that Donatus was continually in communion with that Deuterius after this action, and not only with this Deuterius, but also with all the bishops of Mauretania for forty years, and he said that they were in communion with the traditors without rebaptism up to the persecution brought by Macarius.[66]

44. But you say, "Who is this Tychonius to me?" He is that Tychonius whom Parmenian silences when he writes back and threatens him not to write such things. But he does not refute what he writes; rather, he presses him with one point, as I mentioned above, namely, that, though he says such things about the Church spread throughout the whole world and claims that the sins of others stain no one in its unity, he removed himself from the contagion of the Africans, as if they were traditors, and become a member of the sect of Donatus. Parmenian, however, could have said that Tychonius had made up all these lies, but as the same Tychonius reminds us, there were still many alive who could prove that all these facts were most certain and well known.

45. But I will say nothing of these. Argue that Tychonius lied; I take you back to Cyprian, whom you mentioned. According to the writings of Cyprian, if anyone in the unity of the Church is stained by the sins of others, the Church already perished before Cyprian, nor was there a Church from which Cyprian himself could have come to be. But if it is sacrilegious to think that and if it is certain that the Church still remains, no one in its unity is stained by the sins of others. In vain do you, evil sons, say that you are righteous; you do not excuse, you do not acquit your going out.[67]

11, 46. "Why then," you ask, "do you seek us? Why do you so welcome those whom you call heretics?" See how easily and briefly I answer. We seek you because you were lost in order that we may rejoice over you once you have been found, you over whom we grieved because you were lost. We call you heretics,

---

64. See above 4, 14.
65. This Donatist council was held in 335 and presided over by Donatus.
66. Macarius was an imperial commissioner sent to deal with the Donatist schism; in 347 he fought with Donatus, the Donatist bishop of Bagai, and defeated his forces with great loss of life to the Donatist side.
67. See Prv 24:35, LXX, and above 10, 37.

but only before you return to the Catholic peace, before you strip off the error in which you were entangled. When, however, you cross over to us, you, of course, first leave what you were so that you do not cross over to us as heretics. "Then baptize me," you say. I would do so if you had not been baptized or if you had been baptized with the baptism of Donatus or of Rogatus and not of Christ. It is not the Christian sacraments, but your wicked schism that makes you a heretic. On account of the evil that comes from you one must not deny the good that has remained in you. You have that good to your own harm if you do not have it in that source from which there comes the good you have. For from the Catholic Church come all the Lord's sacraments that you possess and confer in the same way as they were possessed and conferred even before you left her. You do not, nonetheless, lack them because you are not in her from whom there comes what you have. We do not change in you those things in which you are with us, for you are with us in many things. And of such things scripture says, *For they were with me in many things* (Ps 55:19). But we correct those things in which you are not with us, and we want you to receive here those things that you do not have there where you are. You are, however, with us in baptism, in the creed, in the other sacraments of the Lord. But in the spirit of unity and in the bond of peace, finally, in the Catholic Church herself, you are not with us. If you accept these, what you have will not only then be present, but they will then benefit you. It is, therefore, not the case, as you suppose, that we welcome your people, but by welcoming them we make our people those who leave you in order that they may be welcomed by us, and in order that they may begin to be ours, they first cease to be yours. We do not force to join us the agents of the error we detest, but we want those people to join us in order that they may not be what we detest.

47. "But the apostle Paul," you say, "baptized after John."[68] Did he baptize after a heretic? Or if you perhaps dare to call that friend of the bridegroom[69] a heretic and say that he was not in the unity of the Church, I wish that you would also put this in writing. But if it is absolutely insane either to think or to say this, Your Wisdom must consider why the apostle Paul baptized after John. For, if he baptized after an equal, you ought all to baptize after one another. If he baptized after someone greater, you also ought to baptize after Rogatus. If he baptized after someone less great, Rogatus ought to have baptized after you since you baptized as a priest. But if, though those by whom it is conferred are unequal in merit, the baptism that is now conferred has equal validity in those upon whom it is conferred, because it is the baptism of Christ, not of those who are its ministers, I think that you already understand that Paul gave to certain people the baptism of Christ, because they were baptized with the baptism of John, not with that of Christ. That baptism was called the baptism of John, as the divine scrip-

68. See Acts 19:1-5.
69. See Jn 3:29.

ture bears witness in many passages, because even the Lord said, *From where does the baptism of John come? From heaven or from human beings?* (Mt 21:25 and Lk 20:4). But the baptism that Peter conferred was not Peter's, but Christ's, and that which Paul conferred was not Paul's, but Christ's. And the baptism that they conferred who at the time of the apostles proclaimed Christ, not with the right intention, but out of envy,[70] was not theirs, but Christ's. And the baptism that they conferred who at the time of Cyprian seized estates by insidious frauds and increased their capital by compound interest was not theirs, but Christ's. And because it was Christ's, though it was not conferred on them by ministers of equal merit, it, nonetheless, equally benefited those upon whom it was conferred. For, if anyone is baptized better to the extent that he is baptized by someone better, the apostle is not correct in giving thanks that he baptized none of the Corinthians except Cripsus, Gaius, and the house of Stephanas.[71] For they would have been better baptized to the extent that Paul was better, if they were baptized by him. Finally, when he said, *I planted; Apollo watered* (1 Cor 3:6), he seems to convey that he preached the good news, but that Apollo baptized. Was Apollo better than John? Why, then, did Paul not baptize after Apollo, though he baptized after John, except that this baptism by whomever it is conferred is Christ's, but that baptism by whomever it was conferred was, nonetheless, John's, though he prepared the way for Christ?

48. It seems invidious to say, "Baptism is conferred after John's baptism, and it is not conferred after that of heretics." But it can also seem invidious to say, "Baptism is conferred after John's baptism, and it is not conferred after that of drunkards." For I do better to mention this vice, which they in whom it rules cannot hide, and who, even if blind, does not know how many drunkards there are everywhere? And still the apostle put this too among the works of the flesh, saying that those who do them will not inherit the kingdom of God, and in the same passage he also listed heresy. He said, *The works of the flesh are evident; they are fornication, impurity, licentiousness, idolatry, sorcery, enmity, strife, jealousy, anger, dissension, heresy, envy, drunkenness, carousing, and the like. I warn you, as I warned you before, that those who do such things shall not inherit the kingdom of God* (Gal 5:19-21). Though baptism was again conferred after the baptism of John, baptism is not again conferred after the baptism of a heretic for the same reason that baptism is not again conferred after that of a drunkard, though it is conferred after that of John. For both heresy and drunkenness are among those works that keep those who do them from inheriting the kingdom of God. Does it not strike you as intolerably improper that, though baptism is again conferred after the baptism of that man who, not drinking wine with sobriety, but not drinking wine at all, prepared the way for the kingdom of

70. See Phil 1:15-17.
71. See 1 Cor 1:14.

God, baptism is not again conferred after the baptism of a drunkard, who will not inherit the kingdom of God? What answer will you give here except that the former baptism, after which the apostle baptized with the baptism of Christ, was the baptism of John, but this baptism, by which the drunkard baptized, is the baptism of Christ? Between John and a drunkard there is as great a difference as possible; between the baptism of Christ and the baptism of John there is not as great a difference as possible, but there is, nonetheless, a great difference. Between the apostle and a drunkard there is a great difference; between the baptism of Christ that the apostle conferred and the baptism of Christ that the drunkard conferred there is no difference. In the same way between John and a heretic there is as great a difference as possible, and between the baptism of John and the baptism of Christ that a heretic confers there is not as great a difference as is possible, but there is a great difference. For the essence of the sacraments is recognized as the same, even when there is a great difference in the merits of human beings.

49. But pardon me; I was mistaken when I wanted to convince you about the drunkard who baptizes; it had slipped my mind that I was dealing with a Rogatist, not with just any sort of Donatist. For you can perhaps in your few colleagues and in all your clerics find not a single drunkard. For you are the people who hold the Catholic faith, not because you are in communion with the whole world, but because you observe all the commandments and all the sacraments. In you alone he will find faith when the Son of Man will come when he will not find faith on earth. For you are not earth, nor are you on the earth, but like heavenly people you dwell in heaven! You neither fear nor pay attention to the words: *God resists the proud, but gives grace to the humble* (Jas 4:6). Nor does the passage of the gospel touch your heart where the Lord says, *When the Son of Man comes, do you think he will find faith on earth?* (Lk 18:8). Immediately, as if he foreknew that some people would proudly claim this faith for themselves, *he told this parable to certain persons who considered themselves righteous and scorned the rest: Two men went up to the temple to pray, the one a Pharisee and the other a publican* (Lk 18:9-10) and so on. Now you yourself answer for yourself the questions that follow. Look, nonetheless, more carefully at the few of you to see whether no drunkard confers baptism among you. For this plague so widely lays waste to souls and rules over them with such great freedom that I would be greatly surprised if it has not also penetrated your little flock, even though you boast to have already separated the sheep from the goats before the coming of the Son of Man,[72] the one good shepherd.[73]

12, 50. But hear from my lips the voice of the Lord's grain that labors among the chaff up to the last winnowing on the threshing floor of the Lord, that is,

---

72. See Mt 25:32-33.
73. See Jn 10:11.16.

throughout the whole world, for God has called the earth from the rising of the sun to its setting,[74] where even the children praise the Lord.[75] Whoever persecutes you as the result of the opportunity provided by this imperial law, not out of a desire to correct you, but out of a hatred for you like enemies, does not have our approval. And, nonetheless, no earthly possession can be rightfully owned by anyone save by God's law, by which all goods belong to the righteous, or by human law, which lies in the power of the kings of the earth, and for that reason you would wrongly call possessions yours that you do not own as righteous persons and that you are commanded to surrender in accord with the laws of the kings of the earth. And you would say to no point, "We have labored to acquire them," since you read in scripture, *The righteous will eat the labors of the wicked* (Prv 13:22). But anyone, nonetheless, who as a result of the opportunity provided by this law that the kings of the earth who serve Christ have promulgated for your correction, covets out of greed your own personal property has our disapproval. Whoever, then, holds the goods of the poor or the basilicas of congregations that you held in the name of the Church, which is the true Church of Christ, not through justice, but through greed, meets with our disapproval. Whoever welcomes someone whom you cast out for some scandal or grave sin in the same way as they are welcomed who have lived among you without serious sin, except for the error that separates you from us, meets with our disapproval. But you cannot easily prove these points, and if you should prove them, we tolerate some whom we cannot correct or punish. We do not abandon the Lord's threshing floor on account of the chaff,[76] nor do we destroy the Lord's nets on account of the bad fishes,[77] nor do we desert the Lord's flock on account of the goats that will be separated in the end,[78] nor do we move from the Lord's house on account of the vessels that were made for dishonor.[79]

13, 51. But it seems to me that if you, my brother, do not consider the vainglory of human beings and scorn the reproaches of the mindless, who are going to say, "Why do you now destroy what you were first building up?" you will undoubtedly cross over to the Church that I understand you hold to be the true Church. Nor do I have to look far for testimonies to this view of yours. In the beginning of the same letter of yours, to which I am now replying, you indeed set forth these words. You said, "Since I know very well that you were for a long time separated from the Christian faith and were once dedicated to literary studies and a lover of quiet and goodness and since you were later converted to the Christian faith, as I know from the reports of many persons, and devoted your

---

74. See Ps 50:1.
75. See Ps 113:3.
76. See Mt 3:12.
77. See Mt 13:47-48.
78. See Mt 25:32-33.
79. See 2 Tm 2:20.

energy to questions of God's law," and so on. Surely, if you sent that letter to me, these are your words. Since, then, you admit that I was converted to the Christian faith, and since I was not converted either to the Donatists or to the Rogatists, you undoubtedly affirm that the Christian faith exists apart from the Rogatists and apart from the Donatists. This faith, then, as we say, is spread though all the nations which are blessed according to the testimony of God in the offspring of Abraham.[80] Why, then, do you hesitate to maintain what you think, if not because you are ashamed either not to have formerly held another view than you now hold or to have defended another view, and while you are embarrassed to correct your error, you are not embarrassed to remain in your error, something over which you ought, of course, to be more embarrassed.

52. This is a point about which scripture is not silent, *There is a shame that leads to sin and there is a shame that brings grace and glory* (Sir 4:25). Shame leads to sin when someone is embarrassed to change a wrong opinion for fear that one will be thought to be unstable or will be thought to have long been in error because of one's own judgment. In that way they go down alive into hell,[81] that is, aware of their own perdition; Dathan, Abiram, and Korah, who were swallowed when the earth opened up, prefigured these people far in advance.[82] But shame brings grace and glory when one is embarrassed over his own sinfulness and changes for the better through repentance. You are reluctant to do this, because you are overwhelmed by that destructive shame. You are afraid that human beings who do not know what they are saying might raise as an objection to you that statement of the apostle: *For, if I again build up those same things that I tore down, I make myself a transgressor* (Gal 2:18). If this could also have been said to those who, once corrected, preach the truth that they attacked when they were in error, it would have been said to Paul himself first of all, for in him the churches of Christ glorified God when they heard that he was preaching the good news of the faith that he once ravaged.[83]

53. Do not suppose that anyone can pass without repentance from error to the truth or from any sin, whether big or small, to correction. But it is an extraordinarily brazen error to want to speak ill of the Church, which, as is clear from so many testimonies of God, is the Church of Christ, for the reason that she treats those who abandon her in one way, if they correct this by repentance, and in another way those who were not previously in her and at that time first receive her peace. She humbles the former more to a greater degree, while she welcomes the latter more gently, loving both, working to heal both with her maternal love. You perhaps have a longer letter than you wanted. It would, however, have been

---

80. See Gn 22:18.
81. See Ps 55:16.
82. See Nm 16:31-33.
83. See Gal 1:23.

much shorter, if I had only you in mind in replying. But now, even if it does you no good, I do not think that it will fail to benefit those who take care to read it with fear of God and without human respect. Amen.

Letter 94

On 15 May 408 Paulinus and Therasia wrote from Nola to Augustine in Hippo. Paulinus first thanks Augustine for his letter and explains that he did not receive it immediately, but only during his trip to Rome where he met the courier (paragraph 1). He praises Melania the Elder's great virtue and courage at the loss of her only son, Publicola (paragraph 2) and then turns to praise for Publicola himself (paragraph 3). Paulinus asks Augustine to be his teacher and spiritual doctor and to teach him to die to this world (paragraph 4) and goes on to explain how one dies to this world through conformity with the death and resurrection of Christ (paragraph 5). The status of the blessed in heaven raises a question about how they and the angels praise God in heaven (paragraph 6). Paul's words about the tongues of angels leads Paulinus to beg for an explanation from Augustine (paragraph 7). Finally, Paulinus complains about the hurry of Quintus, the courier, who has forced him to write to Augustine in such haste (paragraph 8).

To their holy, most blessed, venerable, and beloved lord, father, brother, and teacher, Bishop Augustine, who is singularly of one mind with us, Paulinus and Therasia,[1] sinners, send greetings in the Lord.

1. Your word is always a lamp for my feet and a light for my paths.[2] Thus, whenever I receive a letter from Your Holiness, who are most blessed, I feel that the darkness of my ignorance is dispelled, and I see more clearly once the eye drops, as it were, of your explanation have been poured onto the eyes of my mind, since the night of ignorance has been banished and the fog of doubt has been swept away. I experienced that this benefit was often granted me through the gifts of your letters on other occasions, but especially by this booklet of your recent letter, whose bearer was the deacon Quintus, a man blessed by the Lord and our brother, a man as pleasing to me as he is worthy. After a long time he gave us the blessing of your lips when I had come to Rome according to my yearly custom after the Pasch of the Lord for the veneration of the apostles and martyrs. But since I was unaware of the time he spent at Rome unbeknownst to me, I thought that he was fresh from your presence, and I believed that he came directly from you to me at that time, when I first saw him and when he offered me the full odor of your sweetness in your words fragrant with the chastity of heavenly perfume. I admit, nonetheless, to Your Reverence, with whom we are of one heart, that I could not read the volume at Rome as soon as I received it. For there were such crowds there that I could not carefully examine your gift and enjoy it as I desired, namely, by reading it through without interruption once I began to read it. And so, as often happens when one confidently awaits a banquet

---

1. Paulinus was the future bishop of Nola in Italy; Therasia was his wife.
2. See Ps 119:105.

that has already been prepared, I reined in the hunger of my mind, as keen as it was, and with the certain hope of attaining satiety, I easily restrained, until I left the city, my hunger that longed for the honey of your letter. After all, I held in hand the food for my desire in the volume I would devour, and it was for me most sweet on my lips and in my heart when I ate it later. And I devoted to this work the whole day that we had to take as a stopover on the journey in the town of Formia, and in that way, free from all remaining concerns and from the overwhelming crowds, I feasted on the spiritual delights of your letter.

2. What, then, should I, a lowly and earthly man, reply to this wisdom that is given to you from above, a wisdom that this world does not know and that no one knows except one wise with the wisdom of God and eloquent with the word of God? And so, since I experience Christ speaking in you, I shall praise your words in God,[3] and I shall not be afraid of the terror of the night.[4] For in the spirit of the truth you have taught me a salutary restraint in controlling the mind concerning fading mortal affairs. You saw that the blessed mother and grandmother, Melania,[5] wept with that restraint over the death in the flesh of her only son, with a silent grief, but not with a sorrow unwatered by a mother's tears. As a spirit closer or more equal to her soul, you, of course, understood more profoundly her moderate and grave tears, and from your heart like hers you contemplated better from an equal status the motherly heart of that woman perfect in Christ with all the courage of a manly mind. You saw that she was first moved in accord with a natural love, but was also was pierced for a greater reason and wept not so much over that human fact that she had lost in the present world her only son, who had died according to our mortal condition, as that he had been almost carried off by worldly vanity since he continued to desire the dignity of a senator. She would have thought that he had been taken according to the holy desire of her prayers that he should pass from the glory of this life to the glory of the resurrection in order to receive together with his mother eternal rest and a crown, if in the life of this world, following the example of his mother, he preferred sackcloth to the toga and a monastery to the senate.

3. The same man, nonetheless, as I believe I reported to Your Holiness even before, died, made rich by these works, so that, if he did not bear the dignity of his mother's nobility in his clothing, he did display it in his mind. For he was, according to the words of the Lord, so *meek* in conduct *and humble of heart* (Mt 11:29) that he is not undeservedly thought to have entered into the rest of the Lord,[6]

3. See Ps 56:11.
4. See Ps 91:5.
5. Paulinus refers to Melania the Elder; at the age of twenty-two she was widowed and left with her son, Publicola, whom she left with a tutor, while she went off and founded a monastery in Palestine. After thirty years she returned to Italy to strengthen her niece, Melania the Younger, in her plan to lead a life of asceticism. On that occasion she visited Paulinus. She returned to Jerusalem where she died 8 June 410.
6. See Heb 3:11.18 and 4:1.3.10-11.

for there is posterity for the man of peace (Ps 37:37), and the meek will inherit the earth,[7] pleasing God in the land of the living.[8] For he certainly realized those words of the apostle, not only in meekness with a silent love, but in religion with clearly seen actions. Thus, though he was a colleague of the high and mighty of this world in rank and honor, he did not, like the glorious of the earth, think proud thoughts, but as a perfect imitator of Christ he associated with the lowly,[9] and he also continued to show mercy and lend all day long.[10] For this reason his offspring has become powerful on the earth[11] among those who, like the mighty gods of the earth, have been raised very high,[12] in order that the holy merit of the man might be revealed from the most blessed visitation of his family and home. Scripture says, *The generation of the righteous will be blessed; glory*, not the fading sort, *and riches*, not the sort that pass, *will be in his home* (Ps 112:2-3), which is built in the heavens, not by the labor of hands, but by the holiness of works. But I cease to report more things about the memory of a man as beloved by me as he was devoted to Christ, since I recall that I reported not a few things about him in a previous letter and that I cannot say anything better or more holy of the blessed mother of this son and of Melania, the common root of holy branches, than Your Holiness has deigned to utter and speak about her. For I, a sinner with impure lips,[13] could not say anything worthy of her, since I am far distant from the merits of her faith and the virtues of her soul. But you, a man of Christ, a teacher of Israel in the Church of the truth, are better prepared by the grace of God's providence and more worthy to praise so manly a soul in Christ, since you saw, as I said, by a spirit closer to hers her mind strengthened by God's power and can praise with a more worthy eloquence her piety blended with virtue.

4. You have graciously asked me what the blessed will do in the next world after the resurrection of the body. But I consult you as a teacher and spiritual doctor about the present state of my life in order that you may teach me to carry out what God wills and to walk in your paths after Christ and to die this death of the gospel by which we anticipate the death of the flesh by a voluntary departure, withdrawing, not by death, but decision, from the life of this world, which is full of temptations, or is all a temptation, as you at times have said to me. Would, then, that my paths might be directed after your footsteps in order that at your example I might remove the old shoes from my feet[14] and break my chains and exult in freedom to run the road,[15] in order that I might attain that death by which

---

7. See Mt 5:4.
8. See Ps 116:9.
9. See Rom 12:16.
10. See Ps 37:26.
11. See Ps 112:2.
12. See Ps 47:10.
13. See Is 6:5.
14. See Ex 3:5, Jos 5:16, and Acts 7:33.
15. See Ps 19:6.

you have died to this world in order to live for God in Christ, who lives in you. I recognize both his death and his life in your body, heart, and lips. For your heart does not savor things of the earth,[16] nor do your lips speak of the works of human beings;[17] rather, the word of Christ abounds in your heart,[18] and the spirit of truth[19] is poured out on your tongue, bringing joy to the city of God by the force of a river from on high.[20]

5. But what virtue produces this death in us but love, which is as strong as death?[21] For it so cancels and destroys for us this world that it produces the effect of death through the love of Christ toward whom we have turned in turning away from this world, and in living for him, we die to the elements of this world.[22] As if no longer living in their sight and vision, we judge that our portion is the death of Christ. We do not attain his resurrection from the dead in glory unless we imitate his death on the cross by the mortification of our members and of senses of the flesh so that we do not now live by our own will, but by his, for his will is our sanctification.[23] And he died for us and rose so that we might now live not for ourselves, but for him who died for us and rose[24] and gave to us the guarantee of his promise by his Spirit,[25] just as he located the guarantee of our life in the heavens in his own body, because he is the head of our body. For this reason the Lord is what we await, and with him and in him and through him is our stability,[26] which he has produced. He was conformed to the body of our lowly condition in order that he might conform us to the body of his glory and place us with him in the heavens. For this reason those who are worthy of eternal life will also be in the glory of his kingdom in order that they may be with him, as the apostle says,[27] and may remain with him, as the Lord himself said to the Father, *I want that, where I am, they may also be with me* (Jn 17:24).

6. This is, undoubtedly, what you have in the psalms: *Blessed are they who dwell in your house; they will praise you for ages upon ages* (Ps 84:5). I think, however, that this praise will be produced by the voices of those singing in chorus, even if the bodies of the risen saints will be transformed so that they are as the body of the Lord appeared after the resurrection. In that resurrection, of course, the living image of human resurrection shone forth so that the Lord himself, who also rose in the body in which he had suffered, might be a mirror for

---

16. See Phil 3:19
17. See Ps 17:4.
18. See Col 3:6.
19. See Jn 14:17 and 15:26.
20. See Ps 46:5.
21. See Sg 8:6.
22. See Col 2:20.
23. See 1 Thes 4:3.
24. See 2 Cor 5:15.
25. See 2 Cor 1:22 and 5:5.
26. See Ps 39:8.
27. See 1 Thes 4:3.

the contemplation of all. He, of course, who also rose in the same flesh in which he died and was buried, often spoke and manifested the functions of all the members revealed to the eyes and ears of human beings. But if the angels, who are simple and spiritual creatures, are also said to have tongues by which they, of course, sing spiritual praises to the Lord their creator and do not cease from offering him thanks, how much more will the bodies of human beings, even if spiritual after the resurrection, still with all the members of the glorified flesh remaining along with forms and numbers through all their members, have tongues in their mouths and bring forth sounds with their tongues that speak, by which they might bring forth through words the praises of God or their senti- ments and feelings of joy. Perhaps the Lord will also grant it to his saints in the ages of his kingdom that they may sing with better tongues and voices to the extent that they have gone on to a more blessed bodily nature by a blessed trans- formation so that, now located in spiritual bodies, they may perhaps speak, not with human languages, but with those heavenly and angelic ones, such as the apostle heard in paradise.[28] And he perhaps testified that those languages were ineffable for human beings because among other kinds of rewards new tongues are now being prepared for the saints. Human beings of this world are not yet allowed to use them in order that, as immortal, they may speak with these tongues suited to their glory. Of these it was said, *For they will cry out and sing a hymn* (Ps 65:14), undoubtedly in the heavens where they will be with the Lord[29] and *will delight in the abundance of peace* (Ps 37:11), rejoicing before the throne, setting before the feet of the Lamb their libations and crown, and singing to him a new song,[30] once they have been added to the choirs of angels, powers, dominations, and thrones,[31] in order that they may sing an endless song along with the cherubim and seraphim and the four animals and say, *Holy, holy, holy, Lord God of hosts* (Is 6:2-3; Rv 4:8), and the rest that you know.

7. This, then, is what I ask, I, a needy and poor fellow, that silly and little one of yours, whom you, as someone truly wise, are accustomed to put up with. Teach me what you know or think on this question. For I know that you have been enlightened with the spirit of revelation[32] by the very leader and source of those who are wise[33] so that, just as you knew the past and see the present, so you also judge about the future.[34] What do you think about these everlasting voices of creatures who live in the heavens or even above the heavens in the sight of the

---

28. See 2 Cor 12:4.
29. See 1 Thes 4:16.
30. See Rv 4:6.10 and 5:9.
31. See Col 1:16.
32. See Eph 1:17.
33. See Wis 7:15, Prv 18:4, and Sir 1:5.
34. See Wis 8:8.

Most High? With what organs are those voices expressed?[35] For, though in saying, *If I should speak with the tongues of angels* (1 Cor 13:1), the apostle showed that they have some speech proper to their nature or, so to speak, their kind, that is higher than human senses and languages to the extent that the nature and location of the angels is superior to mortal inhabitants and their earthly abodes, he perhaps, nonetheless, spoke of the tongues of angels in place of kinds of words and languages. In that way, in speaking of the variety of gifts, he lists kinds of tongues among the gifts of grace,[36] indicating, of course, by this sign that individuals were given the gift of speaking the language of many nations. But the voice of God, which was often sent forth from the cloud to holy people, shows that there can be speech without a tongue, since a tongue is, of course, a small, but important member of the body.[37] But perhaps because God located the function of speech in this member, he called the words and languages of even the incorporeal nature of the angels a tongue, just as scripture often assigns to God the names of various members in accord with the kinds of his actions. Pray for us, and teach us.

8. Our most dear and most charming brother, Quintus, is in as much of a hurry to return from us to you as he was slow in coming to us from you. This letter, which has more erasures than lines, also indicates his persistence in demanding a letter, and the excessive haste of the previously mentioned man with his demands has produced these impromptu words. He came to us on May 14th to ask for a reply, and he wanted to leave on the 15th before noon. See, then, whether I praise him or blame him with such testimony. After all, he will undoubtedly be considered more worthy of praise than of blame, since he was fully justified in hurrying off to your light from the darkness, which is what we are in comparison to you.[38]

---

35. The incorporeality of the angels was not common doctrine until some centuries later; see Augustine's reply to Paulinus' question in Letter 95, 8.
36. See 1 Cor 12:10.28.
37. See Jas 3:5.
38. See 1 Pt 2:9.

Letter 95

At the end of 408 or the beginning of 409, Augustine replied to the previous letter of Paulinus and Therasia. Augustine tells his friends of the consolation he finds in their love for him (paragraph 1). He points out that, though he had asked them for their views on eternal life, they had replied that there was need for concern about the present life as well. Augustine agrees that this life is filled with temptations (paragraph 2) and illustrates this point with the seemingly incompatible scriptural commands about judging others (paragraph 3). He continues to express his worries about judging or not judging others and the harm that is done either way (paragraph 4). At least, the life to come will lack all the ignorance and difficulty we find in the present life (paragraph 5). Augustine explains that he knows some things about how one ought to live in order to attain eternal life, but he asks his friends to write him with further guidance (paragraph 6). They had asked him about the nature of the spiritual bodies we will have in the resurrection, and Augustine briefly replies that our bodies will be like Christ's (paragraph 7). He also discusses the scriptural evidence as to whether angels have or do not have bodies (paragraph 8). Finally, he asks Paulinus to reread his letter and answer his question about Christian leisure (paragraph 9).

To his dearest and most sincere lord and lady, Paulinus and Therasia, his holy, beloved, and venerable brother and sister, fellow disciples under the Lord Jesus, our teacher, Augustine sends greetings in the Lord.

1. When our brothers who are very close to us, whom you are accustomed to long for and greet as you are longed for and greeted, regularly see you, our happiness is not so much increased as our unhappiness is consoled. For we do not love the causes and necessities by which one is forced to undertake voyages across the sea; on the contrary, we hate them and try to avoid them as much as we can. I, nonetheless, believe that somehow or other they cannot be avoided, given our merits. But when they come to us and see us, what scripture says is realized, *In proportion to the multitude of sorrows in my heart your exhortations have brought joy to my soul* (Ps 94:19). You will recognize that I say this with complete truth with respect to the joy that Brother Possidius[1] has with you, when you hear from him how sad a cause has compelled him to travel,[2] and yet if any of us should cross the sea for the sole purpose of enjoying your presence, what would be more just than this cause, what could be found more worthy? But our chains, by which we are bound to serve the weaknesses of the infirm, would not tolerate that we should leave them by our physical presence, except when some

---

1. Possidius was a close friend of Augustine, the bishop of Calama, and Augustine's first biographer.
2. Possidius went to Rome to denounce the damage and killings committed by the pagans of Calama against the Church; see Letters 91 and 104.

people force this more imperiously to the extent that they are more dangerously ill. Whether we are being tested or rather punished in these cases, I only know that *he does not treat us in accord with our sins nor does he repay us in accord with our iniquities* (Ps 103:10), when he mixes such great consolations with our sorrows and acts with a marvelous medicine so that we do not love the world and so that we do not grow faint in the world.

2. I asked from you in a previous letter what you think the eternal life of the saints will be, but you replied to me that we still, of course, also need to be concerned about the state of the present life,[3] and you answered quite well if it were not for the fact that you chose to consult me about what you either are ignorant about along with me or know along with me or perhaps know better than I do. For you also said with complete truth that, before we face the dissolution of our flesh, we must willingly die the death of the gospel, "by which we anticipate the death of the flesh by a voluntary departure, withdrawing, not by death, but decision, from the life of this world."[4] This is a simple action and does not waver back and forth with the turmoil of doubt because we resolve that we ought to live in this mortal life so that we in a sense prepare ourselves for immortal life. But the question that troubles people like me in their active life and research is this: How should one live either among those or on account of those who have not yet learned to live by dying, not by the dissolution of the body, but by a certain disposition of the mind that turns itself away from the snares of the body. For in most cases it seems to us that, unless we adapt ourselves to them a little with regard to the things from which we desire to pull them away, we will be able to do nothing with them in terms of their salvation. And when we do this, the delight from such things sneaks up on us too so that we often find delight even in saying silly things and in listening to those who say them, and we do not just smile, but are overwhelmed and carried off by laughter. And in that way we weigh down our souls with certain loves that are not merely dusty, but even muddy, and we raise them up to God with more labor and with less eagerness to live the life according to the gospel by dying the sort of death the gospel speaks of. But if one is at some point successful, there is immediately heard, "Good going, good going!" This does not come from human beings, nor does any human being have such knowledge of the mind of another, but in a certain inner silence it is shouted out from somewhere or other, "Good going, good going!" On account of this kind of temptation so great an apostle admits that he was struck by an angel.[5] There you see why *the whole of human life on earth is a temptation* (Jb 7:1), when one is tempted even in the very action by which he tries to conform himself as much as possible to the likeness of the life of heaven.

---

3. See Letter 94, 4.
4. Letter 94, 4.
5. See 2 Cor 12:7.

3. What shall I say about punishing or not punishing? For we want all of this to contribute to the salvation of those who we judge should be punished or not punished. What a deep and dark question it is what the limit in punishing should be, not only in terms of the quality and quantity of the sins, but also in terms of the particular strength of minds—what anyone might endure or what he might refuse—for fear not only that he might not make any progress, but also that he might give up! Of those who fear an impending punishment, which human beings generally fear, I do not know whether more are corrected than take a turn for the worse. What shall I say about the fact that it often happens that, when you punish someone, that person perishes, but if you leave him unpunished, someone else perishes? I myself admit that I sin daily in these matters and do not know when or how I might observe the words of scripture, *Reprehend sinners in front of all in order that the others may have fear* (1 Tm 5:20), and the words, *Rebuke him between yourself and him alone* (Mt 18:15), and the words, *Do not judge anyone prematurely* (1 Cor 4:5), and the words, *Do not judge in order that you may not be judged* (Mt 7:1). For in this last place he did not add, "Prematurely." And there are also the words, *And who are you who judge another's servant? He stands or falls for his own lord. But he will stand. For God is able to make him stand* (Rom 14:4). By this he affirms that he is speaking of those who are with the Church, and he again commands that they be judged when he says, *For what concern of mine is it to judge concerning those who are outside? Do you not judge concerning those who are within? Remove the evil person from your midst* (1 Cor 5:12-13). And even when it seems that one should judge, what a great worry and fear there is as to the extent one should judge! For there is the fear that there might occur what the apostle is understood to warn us to avoid in his second letter to those same people, *that someone of this sort may not be overwhelmed by excessive sorrow* (2 Cor 2:7). And so that someone may not suppose that he need not worry much about this, he says there, *in order that Satan may not take possession of us, for we are not ignorant of his designs* (2 Cor 2:11). What grounds for fear there are in all these areas, my dear Paulinus, holy man of God! What grounds for fear! What darkness! Do we not think that scripture said of this: *Fear and trembling have come over me, and darkness has covered me. And I said, "Who will give me wings like a dove, and I shall fly away and be at rest? See, I have gone far in flight, and I have remained in the desert"* (Ps 55: 6-8)? Still even in the desert itself the psalmist perhaps experienced what he added, *I was waiting for the one who might save me from my fearfulness and the storm* (Ps 55:9). Indeed, human life on earth is, therefore, a temptation.[6]

4. What does this mean? Does it not mean that the divine words of the Lord are merely touched upon by us rather than thoroughly studied by us as long as in many more passages we are seeking what we should hold rather than hold some-

---

6. See Jb 7:1.

thing settled and definite? And though this caution is filled with worry, it is much better than rashness in making assertions. If someone does not think in accord with the flesh, something that the apostle says is death,[7] will he not be a great scandal for another who still thinks in accord with the flesh in a case where it is most dangerous to say what you hold and most troublesome not to say this, but most deadly to say something other than what you hold? What then are we to do? At times we find[8] things that we do not approve in the words or writings of those who are within the Church, and, thinking that it pertains to the freedom of brotherly love, we do not conceal our judgment. And when we are believed to do this, not out of good will, but out of hatred, how much we are sinned against! And likewise, when we suspect that those who reprehend our views want to harm rather than to correct us, how much we sin against others! Certainly this gives rise to enmities, very often even between very dear and very close friends, when *beyond what is written anyone is puffed up in favor of one against another* (1 Cor 4:6), and when they bite and devour one another, we must fear that they may be consumed by one another.[9] *Who*, then, *will give me wings like a dove, and I will fly away and be at rest?* (Ps 55:7). For, whether the dangers in which anyone is involved seem more serious than those not previously experienced or whether they are truly such, any fearfulness and storm of the desert seems to me less bothersome than that which we either suffer or fear amid crowds.

5. Hence, I highly approve your view that we should be concerned about the state of this life—or rather about its course rather than about its state. I add another point, namely, that we should seek and hold onto this latter before that former question about what that state will be like toward which this course carries us. For this reason, then, I have asked what you think, as if, having held to and kept the right rule of this life, you are already fully secure, though I feel that I labor amid dangers in so many cases and especially in these that I mentioned as briefly as I could. But because all this ignorance and difficulty, it seems to me, arises from the fact that amid a great variety of conduct and amid hidden choices and weaknesses of human beings we work for the benefit of the people, not an earthly and Roman people, but a people of the heavenly Jerusalem, I wanted to speak with you more because of what we will be than because of what we now are. For, though we do not know what goods will be there, we are, nonetheless, certain about no small matter, namely, that these evils will not be there.

6. With regard, then, to living this temporal life in the way by which we are to come to eternal life, I know that the desires of the flesh must be reined in, that we should grant to the delights of the bodily senses only as much as is enough for sustaining and living such a life, and that we must endure all temporal troubles

---

7. See Rom 8:5-6.
8. The CSEL edition indicates a lacuna here; PL has "*credimus*: we believe." I have conjected "*invenimus*: we find."
9. See Gal 5:15.

patiently and bravely for God's truth and the eternal salvation of ourselves and of the neighbor. I also know that we must be concerned about our neighbor with all the zeal of love in order that he may correctly live this life for the sake of eternal life. I also know that we must prefer spiritual things to carnal ones, immutable things to mutable ones, and that a human being can do all these things more or less to the extent that one is helped more or less *by the grace of God through Jesus Christ our Lord* (Rom 7:25). But why that person is helped in that way and this one is helped in another or is not helped at all, I do not know; I do, however, know that God does this with the highest justice, which is known to him. But on account of those issues that I mentioned above about how we should live with human beings, teach me, I beg you, if you have discovered anything with clarity. But if these problems disturb you as they disturb me, discuss them with some kind doctor of the heart, whether you find one there where you live or when you go to Rome every year, and write me what the Lord discloses to you by means of him when he talks to you or when you converse.

7. But since you have repeatedly asked me what I thought about the resurrection of bodies and the future functions of the members in that incorruptibility and immortality, listen briefly to what, if it is not enough, could with the Lord's help be further discussed. We must hold most firmly that point on which the statement of the holy scripture is truthful and clear, namely, that these visible and earthly bodies, which are now called natural, will be spiritual in the resurrection of the faithful and righteous. But I do not know how the character of a spiritual body, unknown as it is to us, can be either comprehended or taught. Certainly there will be no corruption in them, and for this reason they will not then need this corruptible food that they now need. They will, nonetheless, be able to take and really consume such food because of their power, not out of need. Otherwise, the Lord would not have taken food after the resurrection, and he offered us an example of bodily resurrection so that the apostle says of him, *If the dead will not rise, neither has Christ risen* (1 Cor 15:16). When he appeared with all his members and used their functions, he also displayed the places of his wounds.[10] I have always taken these as scars, not as the actual wounds, and saw them as the result of his power, not of some necessity. He revealed the ease of this power, especially when he either showed himself in another form or appeared as his real self to the disciples gathered in the house when the doors were closed.

8. From this there arises a question concerning whether the angels have bodies suited to their functions and dealings with human beings or are merely spirits. If we say that they have bodies, the passage comes to mind, *who made the angels his spirits* (Ps 104:4). But if we say that they do not have bodies, there is more of a worry about how scripture said that they were presented to the bodily

---

10. See Jn 20:24-27, Lk 24:15-43, and Mk 16:12-14.

senses of human beings without a body, when they were welcomed as guests, had their feet washed, and were given food and drink.[11] For one can more easily see that the angels were called spirits in the same way that human beings are called souls, as scripture says that so many souls went down into Egypt with Jacob[12]—for they were not without bodies—than one can believe that all those actions were done without bodies. Furthermore, the Apocalypse ascribes a certain stature of an angel[13] with those dimensions that can only belong to bodies with the result that what is seen by human beings is not ascribed to deception, but to the power and ease of spiritual bodies. But whether angels have bodies or anyone can show how without having bodies they could do all those things, in that city of the saints, nonetheless, where those redeemed by Christ from this generation will also be united with the thousands of angels for eternity,[14] bodily words will not disclose their hidden minds. For in that divine society no thought will be able to be concealed from a neighbor, but there will resound in the praise of God a harmony, expressed not only by the spirit, but also by the spiritual body.[15]

9. That is what I think for the time being. If you now hold or have been able to learn from teachers something more conformed to the truth, I await with great eagerness to learn it from you. Reread, of course, my letter, for you were forced to reply to it in a great hurry because of the deacon's haste.[16] I do not complain about this, but rather remind you that you should now include what you omitted then. And look at it again and see what I asked to learn from you as to what you think with regard to Christian leisure for absorbing and discussing Christian wisdom and with regard to your leisure, which I thought you enjoyed, though your incredible occupations have been reported to me. (In another hand:) Mindful of us, live happily, you saints of God, who are our great joys and consolations.

---

11. See Gn 18:2-9 and 19:1-3.
12. See Gn 46:27.
13. See Rv 10:1-3.
14. See Ps 12:8 and Heb 12:22.
15. See Letter 94, 7.
16. See Letter 94, 8.

Letter 96

In the beginning of September of 408, Augustine wrote to Olympius, a Catholic layman, newly appointed to the highest ministerial post of the imperial court (*magister officiorum*). Augustine congratulates Olympius on the attainment of his high office (paragraph 1). He then commends to Olympius the petition of Boniface, bishop of Cataqua, who has come into possession of ecclesiastical property that was acquired by his predecessor, Paul, through fraud and tax evasion and who is seeking a remission of the back taxes so that the church can own the property with a clear conscience (paragraph 2). Hence, Augustine asks Olympius to support Boniface's petition and even suggests that he might obtain the lands from the emperor in his own name and give them to the church (paragraph 3).

To his most beloved lord and son, Olympius, who is to be embraced with honor among the members of Christ, Augustine sends greetings.

1. Whatever you may have become in your career in this world, we, nonetheless, write with confidence to our dearest and most sincere fellow servant and Christian, Olympius. For we know that this is for you more glorious than all glory and more lofty than every loftiness. Rumor has, of course, brought us the news that you have attained a higher honor; whether or not this is true had not yet been confirmed for us when we obtained this opportunity for writing you. But since we know that you learned from the Lord not to think proud thoughts, but to associate with the humble,[1] we are confident that you will welcome our letter no differently than usual, no matter to what height you have attained, my dearest lord and son who are to be embraced with honor among the members of Christ. We have no doubt that you will wisely use temporal happiness for eternal gains in order that, the more power you have in this earthly state, the more you will use it for that heavenly city, which has brought you to birth in Christ, and you will be more richly repaid in the land of the living[2] and in the true peace of joys that are secure and that last without end.

2. I commend to Your Charity the petition of my holy brother and fellow bishop, Boniface,[3] in the hope that what was impossible before might perhaps now be possible. For, though he could perhaps without any question logically have himself retained what his predecessor had obtained, though under another name, and had already begun to possess in the name of the Church, we do not want him to have this worry on his conscience that he was in debt to the treasury.

---

1. See Rom 12:16 and 11:20.
2. See Ps 115:9 and 27:13.
3. Boniface was the recently ordained bishop of Cataqua in Numidia.

After all, this fraud did not cease to be fraud because it was committed against the government. And after that Paul, to whom we referred, became a bishop, he was going to renounce all his possessions on account of the immense amount of taxes he owed. Having received a pledge by which a certain amount of silver was owed to him, he bought, as if for the Church, these small fields from which he might support himself, under the name of a family that was very powerful at the time, in order that, when according to his custom he did not pay his taxes from them, he would suffer no problems from the tax collectors. But when Boniface was ordained for the same church at Paul's death, he was afraid to take possession of these fields, and though he could have asked the emperor for the pardon of the back taxes alone, which his predecessor had contracted from these small possessions we mentioned, he preferred to confess to the whole situation, since Paul bought those fields from his own money at an auction, when he was in debt to the government for taxes. Boniface did this in order that the Church might own them, if possible, not by the hidden injustice of a bishop, but by the evident generosity of a Christian emperor. But if it cannot be done, it is better that the servants of God endure the hard work of poverty than that they obtain the means to live with fraud on their conscience.

3. We beg that you be so kind as to give this petition your support, for he did not want to claim the benefit that was first obtained for fear that he would preclude for himself the possibility of a second petition. For the reply was not in accord with his desires. But now, since you have the same kindness as usual, but are greater in power, we do not give up hope that, with the Lord's help, this petition can easily be granted in accord with your merits. For, even if you asked for those places in your own name and yourself gave them to the previously mentioned church, who would find fault? Or who would not very highly praise your petition made, not in the service of earthly desire, but in that of Christian piety? May the mercy of the Lord our God protect you, my lord and son, and make you happier in Christ.

Letter 97

At the end of 408, Augustine again wrote to Olympius at the imperial court in Ravenna. Augustine thanks Olympius for replying to his letter (paragraph 1). He asks Olympius to make it known that the laws concerned with the destruction of idols and the correction of heretics were promulgated by the emperor, not by Stilicho (paragraph 2). He assures Olympius that he is acting in union with his fellow bishops in urging Olympius to implement the imperial laws and in asking Olympius to deliberate along with the bishops about the best means of implementing them (paragraph 3). Finally, Augustine expresses his concern for the weakness of some of those who were converted at the occasion of the imperial laws, but are now suffering persecution (paragraph 4).

To his illustrious lord and son, Olympius, who is rightly outstanding and worthy of much honor in the love of Christ, Augustine sends greetings in the Lord.

1. As soon as we heard that you were deservedly raised to your lofty position, though we did not yet have a fully certain report, we believed nothing else concerning your attitude toward the Church of God, whose son we rejoice to know you truly are, than what you soon disclosed to us by your letter. But now we also read the letter by which you of your own accord were so good as to send, despite our slowness and hesitance, your exhortation filled with good will in order that the Lord, by whose gift you are the man you are, might at last come to the aid of his Church through our humble instruction and your religious obedience. And we write to you with greater confidence, my excellent and rightly outstanding lord and son, who are worthy of much honor in the love of Christ.

2. And many brothers, holy colleagues of mine, went off, when the Church was severely disturbed, almost in flight to the most glorious imperial court. Either you have already seen them, or you have received their letters from the city of Rome when they found some opportunity. Though I was unable to share in some planning with them, I could not, nonetheless, pass up the chance to greet Your Charity, a charity which you have in Christ Jesus the Lord, by means of this brother and my fellow priest, who was forced to go to those parts somehow or other, even in the middle of winter, because of the urgent need for the safety of his fellow citizens. I also want to advise you to speed up your good work with much diligence and concern in order that the enemies of the Church may know that those laws which were sent to Africa concerning the destruction of idols and the correction of heretics, when Stilicho[1] was still alive, had been established by the will of the most pious and faithful emperor.[2] They deceitfully boast or rather

---

1. Stilicho was Olympius' predecessor in the post of *magister officiorum*.
2. The emperor was Honorius.

choose to think that these laws were established without his knowledge or against his will, and for this reason they cause the minds of the ignorant to be very upset and dangerous and deeply hostile toward us.

3. I have no doubt that this advice, which I give to Your Excellency in asking this or rather suggesting it, is in accord with the will of all my colleagues throughout Africa. I think that, wherever the occasion first arises, you can most easily and ought quickly, as I said, to inform those foolish people whose salvation we are seeking, though they oppose this, that it was the son of Theodosius[3] rather than Stilicho who had taken care to send the laws that were sent for the defense of the Church of Christ. For this reason, of course, the priest I mentioned who carried them, since he was from the region of Milevis, was ordered by his venerable bishop, my brother, Severus,[4] to pass through Hippo Regius, where I am. Along with me Severus heartily greets Your Most Sincere Charity. For, since we happened to be at the same time suffering great tribulations and disturbances of the Church, we were looking for an opportunity to write to Your Excellency, and we did not find any. I, in fact, sent you one letter concerning the business of my holy brother and colleague, Boniface, the bishop of Cataqua,[5] but at that time there had not yet come upon us the more serious problems that would trouble us more deeply. To suppress or to correct these problems in a way that would bring help by a better plan in accord with the way of Christ, the bishops who have set sail on this account[6] will more suitably deal with the great kindness of your heart; for they were able to come to a decision that was more carefully thought out in a common plan to the extent that the limitations of time permitted. You must in no way, nonetheless, delay that action by which the province might know the mind of that most gentle and most religious emperor toward the church, but even before you see the bishops who have left here, I suggest, beg, plead, and demand that in your most excellent vigilance you hasten to do as soon as possible what you can for the members of Christ who are suffering very great tribulation. For the Lord offered us no small consolation amid these evils in that he willed that you have more power than you had when we already were rejoicing over your many and great good works.

4. We are very pleased at the firm and stable faith of certain persons, and these not few in number, who have converted to the Christian religion or to the Catholic peace at the occasion of these very laws. For their everlasting salvation we are delighted even to face dangers in this temporal life. For this reason, after all, we now endure the more serious attacks of hatred, especially from men who are excessively and cruelly perverse, and some of the converts endure them most

---

3. Theodosius was Honorius' father and predecessor as emperor.
4. Severus was bishop of Milevis in Numidia from 396 to 426.
5. That is, Letter 96.
6. These bishops were Restitutus and Florentius, who by the decree of the Council of Carthage on 13 October 408 were sent to the emperor to protest the actions of the pagans and heretics.

patiently along with us. But we fear very much for their weakness until they learn and have the ability, with the help of the most merciful grace of the Lord, to scorn the present age and the day of man with a greater strength of heart. Let the memorandum that I sent to my brother bishops be presented to them by Your Excellency when they arrive, unless, as I suspect, they are already there. We have such great confidence in your most sincere heart that, with the help of the Lord our God, we want you not only to be a source of help, but also to share in our deliberations.

Letter 98

Toward the end of 408, or possibly as late as 413, Augustine wrote to Boniface, the Catholic bishop of Cataqua in Numidia, who had asked Augustine various questions about baptism. He asked, for example, how the faith of an infant's parents can benefit the child, though the sins of its parents cannot harm it after baptism. Augustine replies that the power of baptism is such that an infant, once reborn in Christ, can no longer be harmed by the sin of another and that the infant only contracted the guilt of original sin from Adam because it was not yet living a life of its own, but was one in Adam and with Adam, when Adam sinned (paragraph 1). When the infant is presented for baptism, the water is applied as the external sign of grace, and Holy Spirit works internally, removing sin, reconciling to God, and giving rebirth in Christ. But once baptized, the infant cannot be harmed by the sin of another (paragraph 2). The parents who subject their baptized infants to sacrilegious rites sin against them, but do not make them sinful.

Augustine explains a passage from Cyprian that might be taken in the opposite sense (paragraph 3) and also explains why an infant allegedly spat out the eucharist after having been offered to demons, namely, to admonish its parents for their sinful actions (paragraph 4). Augustine explains that, even if parents present their children for baptism for the wrong motives, the Holy Spirit still works through the Church to bring forth children of God (paragraph 5). Nor do the parents have to be the ones to present an infant for baptism (paragraph 6).

Boniface had also asked whether the sponsors do not lie when they respond for the infant and claim that the infant believes, though they cannot predict whether the child will believe or not when he grows up (paragraph 7). Augustine complains that Boniface wants a brief answer to a difficult question (paragraph 8), but then draws a parallel with our way of saying on Easter or on any Sunday that the Lord has risen today, where we speak of the sacrament as a reality. So too, as baptism is the sacrament of faith, we can say that a baptized infant has faith on account of the sacrament of that reality (paragraph 9). Thus an infant becomes a believer, not by assenting to the faith, but by receiving the sacrament of the faith (paragraph 10).

To his fellow bishop, Boniface, Augustine sends greetings in the Lord.

1. You ask me "whether parents harm their baptized little ones when they try to heal them by sacrifices to the demons. And if they do not harm them, how does the faith of their parents help them, when they are baptized, if their infidelity cannot do them any harm." To this I reply that the power of that sacrament, that is, of the baptism unto salvation, is so great in the holy structure of the body of Christ that someone who has been once born through the carnal pleasure of others and has been once reborn through the spiritual will of others cannot thereafter be held bound by the bonds of another's sinfulness, if he has not consented

to it by his own will. For the Lord says, *And the soul of the father is mine, and the soul of the child is mine. The soul that sins will die* (Ez 18:4). But a soul does not sin when its parents or anyone else performs for it the sacrilegious rites of the demons, while it knows nothing of this. The soul of the infant, however, contracted from Adam the sin that is removed by the grace of that sacrament, because it was not yet a soul living a separate life, that is, another soul of which it might be said, *And the soul of the father is mine, and the soul of the child is mine.* Now, therefore, after it has become a human being in itself, having become another individual from its parent, the child is not held bound by the sin of another without its own consent. The child contracted the guilt because it was one with Adam and in Adam from whom the child contracted it when the sin that was contracted was committed. But one person does not contract sin from another when each is living his own proper life and there is reason to say, *The soul that sins will die.*

2. But that the child can be reborn through the act of another's will when it is presented to be consecrated to Christ is the work of the one Spirit because of whom it is reborn when it is presented. For scripture does not say, "Unless one is reborn from the will of the parents or from the faith of the godparents or of the ministers," but, *Unless one is reborn of water and the Holy Spirit* (Jn 3:5). The water externally presents the sacred sign of grace, and the Spirit internally produces the benefit of grace, removing the bond of sin and reconciling to God the good of nature; the two bring the human being who was born of Adam to rebirth in the one Christ. The Spirit, then, who brings the child to rebirth is shared in by the adults who present the child and by the little one who is presented and reborn. And so through this society formed by one and the same Spirit the will of the sponsors benefits the little one who is presented. But when adults sin against the little one, offering it and trying to bind it by the sacrilegious chains of the demons, there is no soul common to both of them so that they can also have the sin in common. For one does not have a share in sin through the will of another in the same way as one shares in grace through the unity of the Holy Spirit. For the one Holy Spirit can be in this person and that one, even if they do not know each other, so that through the Holy Spirit grace is common to both. But the human spirit cannot belong to this person and that one so that, though one sins and the other does not, the sin is, nonetheless, common to both through the human spirit. And for this reason a little one, who had been born once from the flesh of his parents, can be reborn by the Spirit of God so that the little one may be released from the bonds of sin contracted from its parents. But someone who has once been reborn by the Spirit of God cannot be reborn from the flesh of his parents so that the bonds of sin that were removed are again contracted. And so the little one does not lose the grace of Christ that it has once received except by its own sinfulness, if he becomes so bad when he comes of age. For he then will also

begin to have his own sins, which cannot be removed by rebirth, but need to be healed by some other remedy.

3. Parents or any other adults are, nonetheless, rightly called spiritual murderers when they try to subject their children or any little ones to the demons by sacrilegious rites. For they do not, of course, commit homicide upon them, but they become killers to the extent they can. They are rightly told when we forbid them to do this crime: "Do not kill your little ones, for the apostle even says, *Do not extinguish the Spirit* (1 Thes 5:19), not because that Spirit can be extinguished, but because they are rightly called his extinguishers to the extent it lies in their power, when they act in such a way that they want him to be extinguished. In this sense one can correctly understand what the most blessed Cyprian wrote in his letter on *Those Who Have Fallen Away*, when, in accusing those who sacrificed to idols during the time of persecution, he said, "And so that nothing would be lacking to the mountain of sin, even infants who were offered or handed to them by the hands of their parents lost as little ones what they had obtained in the first days after their birth."[1] He said, "They lost it," insofar as it pertained to the crime of those who were forcing them to lose it. They lost it in the mind and will of those who committed so great an outrage upon them. For, if they had lost it in themselves, they would have, of course, remained destined for damnation by the divine sentence without any defense. And if Saint Cyprian thought that, he would not immediately have added a defense of them, when he says, "Will they not say when the day of judgment comes, 'We did nothing, nor have we of our own accord rushed to pagan defilement after having abandoned the food and drink of the Lord. The infidelity of others has destroyed us; we have found our parents to be our killers. They denied us the Church as our mother and the Lord as our father so that we were taken captive by the deceit of others when, as little ones unable to look out for ourselves and in ignorance of so great a crime, we were made partakers in crime by others.' "[2] He would not have added this defense if he did not believe it to be fully just and that it would benefit these little ones in God's judgment. For, if it is truly said, "We have done nothing," and, *The soul that has sinned will die* (Ez 18:4), then they will not perish under God's just judgment because by their sin their parents destroyed them insofar as they could.

4. In the same letter he reports the following event. A certain infant was left to a nurse by its parents who were driven into flight, and the same nurse forced the infant to partake in sacrilegious worship of demons. Later, when the eucharist was offered to the child in church, it spit it out with unusual gestures. Now, it seems to me that God did this so that the adults would not think that they did not sin against the little ones by that sin, but would understand rather that they were admonished in a miraculous way through that somehow significant gesture of

---

1. Cyprian, *Those Who Have Fallen Away (De lapsis)* 9: CSEL 3/1, 243.
2. Ibid.

the body of speechless infants. They were admonished about what they ought to have done who after that unspeakable offense rushed to those sacraments of salvation, from which they ought rather to have abstained in penance. When divine providence does something of the sort through infants, we should not believe that the infants did this with knowledge or reason. Nor should we stand in awe of the wisdom of donkeys because God wanted to restrain the madness of a certain prophet by the speaking of a donkey.[3] Moreover, if the sound of something like a human voice comes from an irrational animal, something that we should attribute to a miracle of God, not to the heart of a donkey, the Almighty could show through the soul of an infant, not a soul in which there was no reason, but one in which it was still asleep, by a gesture of its body what they who sinned against themselves and against the little ones should have been concerned about. In any case, since the infant does not return to his parent so that it becomes one human being with him and in him, but is simply another human being, who has its own flesh and its own soul, *the soul that sins will die.*

5. Do not let it disturb you that some do not bring their little ones to receive baptism with that faith for the purpose of being reborn for eternal life, but because they think that they retain or recover their temporal health by this remedy. For they do not fail to be reborn because they are presented by these people with this intention. After all, through them the necessary actions of the minister and the words of the mysteries are celebrated without which the little one cannot be consecrated. But the Holy Spirit who dwells in the saints, from whom that one dove sheathed in silver is formed by the fire of love,[4] produces his effect even through the service, at times not merely of those who are simply ignorant, but also of those who are damnably unworthy. Little ones are, of course, presented to receive spiritual grace, not so much from those in whose hands they are carried, though they do also receive it from them if they are good believing people, as from the universal society of the saints and believers. For they are correctly understood to be presented by all who are pleased that they are presented and by whose holy and undivided love they are helped to come into the communion of the Holy Spirit. The whole Church, our mother, which exists in the saints, does this, because the whole Church gives birth to each and every one. For, since the sacrament of Christian baptism is one and the same sacrament, it has such power, even among heretics, and suffices for the consecration of the infant to Christ, although it does not suffice for the reception of eternal life. This action of consecrating, of course, makes the heretic guilty who has the mark of the Lord outside the flock of the Lord, and sound doctrine warns that he should be corrected, but not that he should be consecrated in a like manner. How much better that in the Catholic Church the grains of wheat are carried in order to be

---

3. See Nm 22:28.
4. See Ps 68:14.

purified, even through the ministry of the chaff, in order that they may be brought through the threshing floor to the society of the mass of believers!

6. I do not, however, want you to be misled into thinking that the chain of guilt contracted from Adam can only be broken if the little ones are presented by their parents in order to receive the grace of Christ. For you write that way when you say, "Just as the parents were the sources of their condemnation, so they are justified through the faith of their parents." After all, you see many infants who are not presented by their parents, but even by strangers of any sort, just as slaves are at times presented by their masters. And sometimes little ones are baptized when their parents are dead, presented by those who were able to show them such mercy. At times even those whom their parents cruelly exposed are taken up to be raised by persons of any sort, at times by consecrated virgins, and are presented by them for baptism. And they certainly neither had any children of their own nor plan to have any, and for this reason you see that they do nothing else in this case but what is written in the gospel when the Lord asked who had been a neighbor to that man who was wounded by robbers and left half dead in the road, for he was told, *The one who showed mercy to him* (Lk 10:37).

7. You thought that you proposed a very difficult question in the last question of your series, that is, because of that habitual intention of yours most carefully to avoid a lie. You said, "If I set a little one before you and I ask whether, when he grows up, he will be chaste or will not be a thief, you will undoubtedly reply, 'I do not know.' And if I ask whether at that tender age the child has any good or evil thoughts, you will say, 'I do not know.' If, then, you do not dare to promise anything certain about his future conduct nor about his present thoughts, why is it that, when infants are presented for baptism, the parents reply on their behalf as responsible for them and say that they do what infants at that age are incapable of thinking or what is hidden from us, if they can. For we ask those who present the children and say, 'Does he believe in God?' And concerning the child at that age at which it does not know whether God exists, they reply, 'He believes.' And they reply in that way to each of the rest of the questions that are asked. For this reason I am surprised that the parents reply on these matters so confidently on behalf of the little one that they say that the child does such important and good acts, about which the minister questions them at the moment when the child is baptized. And yet, if I add at the same time, 'Will he who is being baptized be chaste or not be a thief?' I do not know whether anyone will dare to say, 'He will or will not be one of these,' as he will undoubtedly reply to me that he believes in God and is converted to God." Then, in bringing what you wrote to an end, you go on to say, "I ask you, then, please, reply briefly to these questions, not so that you state what the practice of the Church demands, but so that you give reasons."

8. Having read and reread this letter of yours and having considered it to the extent that the limitations on my time permitted, I was reminded of my friend,

Nebridius.[5] Since he was most diligent and keen at investigating obscure questions, especially ones pertaining to the doctrine of religion, he deeply disliked a brief reply to a profound question. And he tolerated very poorly anyone who made such a demand, and he stopped such a man with anger on his countenance and in his voice, if the person in question could be treated in such a way, since he considered beneath his dignity someone who asked such questions, because he did not know that on such an important topic so much could have been said and ought to have been said. But with you I am not angry in the same way as Nebridius used to be in such a case. You are, after all, a bishop busy with many concerns, as I am. For this reason you neither easily find time to read something lengthy, nor do I find such time to write something of the sort. For he was at that time a youth who refused to listen to brief answers to such questions and asked many questions in conversation with us; as a man of leisure he asked questions of a man of leisure. But you, well aware of who is making demands upon whom, bid me to reply briefly on so important an issue. Look, I am doing the best I can; may the Lord help me that I may be able to do what you ask.

9. We, for example, often speak in such a way that, when Easter is drawing near, we say that the Passion of the Lord is tomorrow or the next day, though he suffered so many years before, and his Passion took place only once. For example, we say on the Lord's day, "Today the Lord has risen," though so many years have passed since he rose. Why is no one so silly as to accuse us of lying when we speak that way, if not because we name these days in accord with a likeness to those days on which these events took place? Thus we call it the very day, though it is not, but it is like it in terms of the recurrence of the seasons, and we say that the event happened on that day on account of the celebration of the mystery, which did not take place on that day, but long before. Has not Christ been sacrificed once in himself, and yet in the mystery he is sacrificed for the people, not only during all the solemnities of Easter, but every day, and a person certainly does not lie if, when asked, he replies that Christ is being sacrificed? For, if the sacraments did not have some likeness to those events of which they are sacraments, they would not be sacraments at all. But because of this likeness they generally receive the name of the realities themselves. Just as, then, in a certain way the sacrament of the body of Christ is the body of Christ and the sacrament of the blood of Christ is the blood of Christ, so the sacrament of the faith is the faith. To believe, however, is nothing else than to have faith. And for this reason when the answer is given that the little one believes, though he does not yet have the disposition of faith, the answer is given that he has faith on account of the sacrament of the faith and that he is converted to the Lord on account of the sacrament of conversion, because the response itself also pertains

5. Nebridius was a close friend of Augustine; he died soon after Augustine's return to Africa. See *Confessions* IX, 3, 6 and Letters 3 to 14.

to the celebration of the sacrament. In the same way the apostle says of baptism, *We were buried together with Christ through baptism into death* (Rom 6:4). He did not say, "We signified burial," but, *We were buried*. He, therefore, called the sacrament of so great a reality by the word for the same reality.

10. And so, even if that faith that is found in the will of believers does not make a little one a believer, the sacrament of the faith itself, nonetheless, now does so. For, just as the response is given that the little one believes, he is also in that sense called a believer, not because he assents to the reality with his mind, but because he receives the sacrament of that reality. But when a human being begins to think, he will not repeat the sacrament, but will understand it and will also conform himself to its truth by the agreement of his will. As long as he cannot do this, the sacrament will serve for his protection against the enemy powers, and it will be so effective that, if he leaves this life before attaining the use of reason, he will by this help for Christians be set free from that condemnation which entered the world through one man,[6] since the love of the Church commends him through the sacrament itself. One who does not believe this and thinks that it is impossible is, of course, an unbeliever, even if he has the sacrament of faith; that little one is by far better off, for, though he does not as yet have faith in his mind, he does not, nonetheless, set any obstacle of his mind against it. Hence, he receives the sacrament in a salutary manner. I have answered, I think, your questions not sufficiently for the less gifted and more argumentative, but perhaps more than sufficiently for peace-loving and intelligent people. Nor have I presented to you the most solid custom of the Church in order to excuse myself; rather, I gave as good an account as I could of her most salutary custom.

---

6. See Rom 5:12.

Letter 99

Late in 408 or early in 409 Augustine wrote to Italica, a Roman widow. Augustine thanks her for her three letters, but complains that neither Italica nor anyone else has informed him of the turmoil around Rome, of which only rumors have reached him (paragraph 1). He tells Italica that charity demands that a Christian share the sorrows as well as the joys of another member of Christ and prays that the Lord may comfort her now, as he will reward her hereafter (paragraph 2). Finally, he sends greetings to Italica's children and explains his inaction regarding a house that his predecessor left to the church (paragraph 3).

To the most religious servant of God, Italica, who is truly holy and praiseworthy among the members of Christ, Augustine sends greetings in the Lord.

1. I had received three letters from Your Goodness when I replied with this one: one that was still demanding a letter from me, another that indicated that mine had already arrived, and the third that contained your most benevolent concern for us regarding the house of the illustrious and outstanding young man, Julian, which is next door to us. When I received it, I did not put off replying immediately, because the administrator of Your Excellency wrote that he could immediately send it to Rome. We were deeply saddened by his letter because he did not care to inform us of the events that are occurring there in the city or at least around the city,[1] in order that we might have certitude about those events regarding which we do not want to believe an unconfirmed rumor. A letter of the brothers that was previously sent reported things that were much less serious, though they were troublesome and painful. I was, of course, more amazed than I can express that our holy brothers, the bishops, did not write, even when given so great an opportunity by your men, and that even your letter has not reported to us anything about such great tribulations of yours. They are, of course, also ours by reason of the feelings of love. But you perhaps thought that you should do nothing, since you considered that it does no good or since you did not want to sadden us with your letter. In my opinion, it does some good just to know these things. First, because it is unjust to want to rejoice with those who rejoice and not to want to weep with those who weep.[2] Secondly, because *tribulation produces patience and patience produces tested virtue and tested virtue produces hope, but hope will not be disappointed, because the love of God has been poured out in our hearts through the Holy Spirit who has been given to us* (Rom 5:3-5).

2. Heaven forbid, therefore, that we should refuse also to hear those things that are bitter and sad concerning our dear friends. For somehow what one

---

1. Augustine refers to the events leading up to the sack of Rome by Alaric's Goths in 410.
2. See Rom 12:15.

member suffers becomes less if other members suffer along with it.[3] Nor does the lessening of the evil come about through sharing the disaster, but through the consolation of love. Thus, though some suffer through enduring the evils and others suffer with them through knowing them, the tribulation becomes shared by those who share the tested virtue, hope, love, and Spirit. But the Lord consoles all of us; he both foretold these temporal evils and promised eternal goods after them. Nor should one be discouraged when he fights if he wants to receive a crown after the battle, since he who prepares ineffable gifts for the victors helps the strength of those who are doing battle.

3. Let not my replies to you take from you the confidence of writing to us, especially since you have calmed my fear with an excuse that seems quite probable. We greet in return your little ones and pray that they grow up in Christ, for they see now in this age how dangerous and harmful is the love of this world, and may they be corrected in their small and flexible ways when they are shaken by these grave and painful events. With regard to that house, what should I say, except that I am grateful for your most benevolent concern? For they do not want the care that we can give. Nor was it left to the church by my predecessor, as they have incorrectly heard, but it is included among its oldest possessions and was next door to the other old church, as this one with which we are dealing was next to the other.

---

3. See 1 Cor 12:26.

Index of Scripture

(prepared by Michael Dolan)

(The numbers after the scriptural reference refer to the section of the work)

15:16	95, 7
15:26	55, 6, 10
15:33-34	78, 5; 93, 9, 32
15:51	55, 14, 26
15:53	55, 2, 3; 55, 13, 23
15:53-54	55, 6, 10

2 Corinthians

2:7	83, 1; 95, 3
2:11	83, 1; 95, 3
3:3	29, 4
4:16	92, 3
5:6	55, 14, 26
5:17	36, 10, 23
6:14	78, 5
7:5	78, 8
9:15	58, 2
11:29	40, 4, 6; 78, 6

Galatians

1:8	53, 1, 1
1:9	93, 7, 23
1:10	22, 2, 7
1:18	75, 3, 8
1:20	40, 3, 3; 82, 2, 7; 82, 2, 24
2:1-2	75, 3, 8
2:2	75, 3, 8
2:3-5	82, 2, 12
2:11-14	75, 3, 8
2:12	40, 4, 5; 75, 3, 8
2:14	28, 3, 4; 40, 3, 3; 82, 2, 4; 93, 9, 31
2:18	93, 13, 52
2:20	93, 2, 7
2:21	82, 2, 19
3:1.3	93, 9, 31
3:16	76, 1
4:4-5	75, 4, 14
4:11	55, 7, 13
4:27	93, 9, 30
4:29	93, 2, 6
4:47	93, 8, 26
5:2	75, 4, 14; 82, 2, 19
5:3	75, 3, 5
5:4	75, 4, 14; 82, 2, 19
5:6	55, 2, 3; 75, 4, 17
5:13	23, 1
5:18	75, 4, 14; 82, 2, 19
5:19-21	29, 6; 93, 11, 48
5:22-23	29, 6
6:1	82, 3, 29
6:5	87, 5
6:14	55, 14, 24
6:15	75, 4, 17

Ephesians

2:6	55, 2, 3

3:17-18	55, 14, 25
4:2-3	44, 5, 11
4:3	40, 1, 1; 43, 8, 23; 61, 2
4:32	48, 3
5:18	36, 7, 15
5:19	48, 3
5:27	93, 9, 34
6:13	75, 1, 2
6:14-17	75, 1, 2

Philippians

1:23-24	55, 14, 25
2:7	33, 5
2:13	55, 10, 19
2:20-21	78, 8
2:21	43, 8, 23; 87, 2
3:2	79
3:8	40, 4, 6
3:12-13	55, 14, 26
3:15-16	93, 10, 35
3:19	29, 11; 55, 5, 9

Colossians

2:16	36, 8, 20
3:2	55, 2, 3
3:3-4	55, 2, 3
3:4	55, 6, 10
3:10	92, 3
3:13	48, 3

1 Thessalonians

3:12	43, 1, 1
5:19	98, 3

1 Timothy

1:5	55, 21, 38
1:20	93, 2, 7
4:1-5	55, 20, 36
4:3	75, 4, 15
4:4	47, 4; 82, 3, 27
4:12	22, 2, 7
5:20	95, 3
6:16	92, 3

2 Timothy

2:17	55, 3, 4
2:24	49, 1
2:24-26	53, 3, 7
2:26	43, 1, 1
3:8-9	55, 16, 29
4:3	35, 3

Titus

1:11	34, 4; 35, 3
1:15	55, 20, 36

2:14   93, 9, 30
3:10   43, 1, 1

Hebrews

6:20   40, 4, 6; 75, 4, 15

Saint James

3:2   73, 3, 9
4:6   55, 10, 18; 93, 11, 49
5:12   23, 1

1 Peter

4:1-3   29, 10
4:8   88, 9; 93, 10, 40
5:5   55, 10, 18
5:8   78, 5

1 John

1:5   92, 2
2:2   93, 9, 32
2:19   93, 9, 29
3:2   64, 1; 92, 3
4:16   73, 3, 10

Revelation

2:1-3   43, 8, 22
2:7   43, 8, 22
4:5   43, 8, 22
4:8   94, 6
7:9   93, 9, 30
22:11   78, 9

Index

The first number in the Index is the Letter number.
The number after the colon is a paragraph number.

removing the straw from your eye . . . while
leaving the beam in my own, 85:2
Ezekiel, the prophet, 87:2
on the sins of children and parents, 44:12

Fabian, 53:2
Fabius: defeating Hannibal, 72:3(2)
fainthearted, *See* weak.
faith, 55:26; 82:22; 98:9
See also Christianity
baptism as sacrament of, 98:9–10
Catholicism as one true, 20:3
differing between spouses, 23:4
eternal rest, as obtaining, 36:25(11)
sacraments and, 98:9–10
as shield, 48:3; 75:2
strong, 97:4
unfeigned, 55:38
weak, 97:4 *See also under* weak
false prophets:
Elijah killing, 44:9
false witness: in Ten Commandments,
55:22(12)
family (ies): religious differences in, 33:5
Famous Men, book by Jerome, 40:2(2), 9(6)
"fantasies," 7:1, 4
farm animals, 55:11
farmer(s), 55:15
God the Father as, 52:2
tenant, in Mappala, rebaptism of, 66:1
fasting, 36:2–32; 48:3
alogia, 36:9(5), 11–12
Ambrose on, 36:32(14)
avoiding, from Easter to Pentecost,
36:18(8)
commands in Bible regarding, 36:25(11)
diverse customs regarding, 82:14
of Elijah, forty days, 36:27(12)
Eucharistic, 54:6(5)–9(7)
feast days, as not practiced on, 36:18(8)
forty days, 36:2, 16; 55:28 *See also* Jesus;
Moses (under fasting, below)
guidelines for, 36:25(11)–27(12)
humility, as signifying, 36:30(13)
Jesus, forty day fast of, 36:13(6)
Lent, 54:5(4), 6(5)
Lord's Day compared to Sabbath regarding,
36:8–13(6)
Manichees, errors in regard to, 36:27(12),
29
of Moses, forty days, 36:13(6), 16, 27(12)
prayer with, angel referring to, 36:18(8)
Priscillianists, errors in regard to, 36:28
and the Sabbath, 36:2–13(6)
as sacrifice, 36:18(8)
"Urbicus" ("the city fellow"), Augustine
refuting treatise, 36:2–32
week, days of, 36:30(13)–31
father

See also parents
Lord as, 98:3
fatherland:
heaven as, 92:4
love for, 90; 91:1–2
Faustus the Manichee, 82:17
fear:
freedom from (foretastes of), 10:2–3
of government, 93:20(6)
of punishment, 95:3
salvation, as catalyst for, 93:3, 16(5)–18
See also force; punishment; secular
power
of secular authority, 93:20(6)
Fear (the god), 17:2
feasts, feast days:
See also food
alogia, 36:19
in cemeteries, to "honor" martyrs, 22:2–6
drunken banquets in churches, 29:1–11
fasting not practiced on, 36:18(8)
Jesus in Jerusalem for, 82:18
pagan, 90
feet:
sayings regarding, 17:2
"the Lord rescues his feet from the
snare," 48:3
washing of, 55:32, 33
Felician of Musti, 51:2, 4–5; 53:6(3);
70:1–2; 76:1
Felix and Hilarinus, letter from Augustine to:
on the scandal of Boniface and Spes,
77:1–2
Felix of Aptungi, 43:3(2)–4, 12–13(4); 53:2;
88:3–5
Felix of Musti, 88:11
Felix of Nola: Boniface and Spes sent to
burial place of, 78:1
Felix the Manichee, 79
fervent in spirit, 48:3
Festus, letters from Augustine to:
on dealing with Donatists, 89:1–8
Fever (the god), 17:2
fidelity, marital, 91:3
fiery furnace, the, 36:16; 93:9(3)
fifty:
fifty days, 55:28–31(7)
symbolism of number, 55:29(16)–31(17)
fighting, 68:2; 73:1(1); 99:2
fine arts: lack of interest in, 1:2
fire, 48:2
Dathan and Abiram consumed, 87:4
of love, 98:5
refinement by, 55:31(7)
schism, punishment for, 51:1
Firmus, 87:10
first day, the, 55:17
fish: bad among the good, 93:33–34, 50(12)
five caves of the nation of darkness, 7:4
flattery, 28:6(4); 82:31

preaching from, 93:15
healing: gift of, 78:3
heart:
    a clever heart, 85:2
    doctor of, 95:6
    hardness of, 88:9
    Raise up the eyes of your heart, 76:1
    a slow heart, 85:2
heaven, 55:17–19
    See also eternal life; eternal rest
    the bosom of Abraham, 78:6
    glory of Christ over, 93:1(1)
heavenly bodies: differences among, 14:3
heavenly trumpet, 1:2
Hebrew (language)
    See also languages
    scripture translations from, 28:2(2);
        71:3(2)–6(4); 75:20(6)–21; 82:34–35
heirarchy of being, 18:2
Helen of Troy, 40:7; 68:1
Hellespont touche, 26:6 (poem of Licentius)
hemorrhoids, 38:1
Heraclea: Theodore of, 75:4(3); 82:23
Hercules, 17:2; 50
heresies, heretics
    See also individual groups and names
    bishops sent to emperor regarding, 97:3
    caelicolae, 44:13(6)
    Cerinthus and Ebion, 75:13
    conversion of, forcible, 93:17 *See also*
        under fear, force
    correction of, 89:1; 97:2–3; 98:5
    "deceitful spirits," paying attention to,
        55:36(20)
    Donatists called, *See* Donatists.
    Ebonism, 82:16
    false Catholics, 93:17
    laws concerning, 97:2
    Mani, 75:14
    Manichees as, 36:29 *See also* Manichees
    Marcion, 75:14
    Minaei, 75:13
    Nazaraeans, 75:13
    punishment for, 88:7
    as quarrelsome, 55:29(16)
    schism as, 87:4; 89:7
    secular authority against, 93:12
    "who wanted to be both Jews and
        Christians," 82:15
Hermogenian, Augustine's letters to:
    on the Academics, 1:1–3
Hilarinus, Felix and, letter from Augustine to:
    on the scandal of Boniface and Spes,
        77:1–2
Hilary of Poitiers, 75:20(6); 93:31–32
    on Asia, 93:31–32
    Synods as by, 93:21
Hippo
    See also specific topics
    people's dependence on Augustine, 22:9

Proculeian as Donatist bishop, *See*
    Proculeian.
Profuturus as priest of, *See* Profuturus.
Valerius as bishop of, 21:1–6
holiness:
    "All we want is holiness," 93:14, 43
    of scriptures, 28:3(3)–5
holocausts, 47:3
Holy, holy, holy, 94:6
Holy Spirit, the:
    in baptism, 98:2, 5
    coming of, celebrated, 54:1(1)
    Donatist(s) as lacking, 93:46(11)
    as dove, 89:5
    filling one hundred and twenty, 93:21
    finger of God signifying, 55:29(16)
    Gentiles, descending on, 75:7
    glorification of Jesus, coming after,
        55:30
    grace through, 98:2
    Mosaic law and, 82:19
    sevenfold gift of, 24:4; 55:10(6)
    in the Trinity, 11:2–4
Holy Week: criminal suits ceased during,
    34:2
honey: sword coated with, 82:2
honor, 32:5
honorable: use of word, 23:1
Honoratus (Donatist bishop), letters from
    Augustine to:
    discussing schism, 49:1–3
Honoratus of Thaive, 83:1–6
Honorius, the emperor, 97:2
hope:
    death as source of, 36:31
    of eternal life, 92:1
    pagans as without, 92:1
    placing, in humans vs. Christ, 89:5
    scandal, despite, 78:1
    in sorrow, 55:26
    of this world and the world to come,
        55:10(6)
horse(s), 47:5
hostility:
    patience with, 73:10
human being(s)
    See also people; persons
    being mistaken about someone, 20:2
    creation of, 14:4
humility, 22:7(2)
    fasting as signifying, 36:30(13)
    of Paulinus, 31:6
humor, 95:2
    Maximus accused of joking, 17:1–2
Hyginus, 53:2
Hymenaeus, 55:4(3)
Hypanis, 26:6 (poem of Licentius)
hypocrisy, 22:7(2)
Hyrcania, 26:6 (poem of Licentius)

idleness, *See* laziness.

proverbs:
  sword coated with honey, 72:2
  "The tired ox puts down his foot with more
    force," 68:2
Psalms, 75:20(6)
  Expositions of the Psalms, 75:20(6)
  harp in, 55:12(7)
  law and the prophets and, 93:21
  singing, 55:34
publican(s):
  fasting, regarding, 36:7(4)
  and pharisee, parable of, 93:49
Publicola, Roman senator: death of, 94:2–3
Publicola, letters to Augustine from:
  on various questions for Augustine,
    46:1–18
puffed up, 95:4
Punic language, 17:2
  Lucillus' knowledge of, 84:2
  names of Christian martyrs, 16:2; 17:2
punishment:
  as correction, 93:8 *See also* correction
  fear, use of, 93:3
  just, 9:9; 91:6
  problems and benefits of, 95:3
purity, 93:48
  food, Jewish beliefs regarding, 36:17
Purpurius (bishop of Limate), 43:6(3)

Quintian, letters from Augustine to:
  on Aurelius, urging reconciliation with, 64:1–4
Quintus, 94:1, 8

rain: on the just and unjust, 55:8(5); 93:4(2)
ram (Aries), 55:14(8)
raven set, 7:6(3)
reading: truth found in, 19:1
reason: images resulting from, 7:4–7
rebaptism, 23:1–8; 34:2–6; 43:21(8);
  44:7(4)–8, 12; 89:4
  Christian standards regarding,
    93:46(11)–48
  Crispinus reprimanded for, 66:1
  Cyprian regarding, 93:36
  Donatist practice of, 23:1–8; 34:2–6;
    43:21(8); 44:7(4)–8, 12
  Jubaianus, letter from Cyprian to, 93:36
  of matricidal young man, 34:2–6
  Maximinianists (returning) exempt from,
    88:11
  Paul baptizing after John, 93:47–48
  of Primus, 35:2
rebirth:
  baptism (infant) and, 98:1–10
religion
  See also Catholicism; Christianity; faith
  differences of, in same family, 33:5
renewal, 92:3
repentance, 93:52
reproaches, *See* correction.
Republic, The, 91:3

reputation:
  of bishops, 83:2
  Boniface and Spes, 78:5
  of cleric(s), 78:6
  of monks, 78:6, 9
rest:
  complete, 48:2
  in death, 36:31
  eternal, *See* eternal rest.
  good works, as reward for, 55:25
  souls as loving, 55:18(10)
  spiritual, 22(12); 55:22
Restitutus, 97:3
  murder of, 88:7
resurrection of Christ, 36:31; 55:2; 94:5–6
  appearance to disciples after, 95:7
  celebrated, 54:1(1)
  the Lord's Day, 55:23(13)
  Lord's Day as preferred to Sabbath,
    36:12
  the power to lay down his life and to take
    it up again, 55:16(9)
  the third day, 93:21, 23
resurrection of the body, 55:3(2)–4(3); 94:6;
  95:7–8
  life after, 55:31(7)
Revelation, Book of, 43:22
  See also Apocalypse
riches, *See* possessions; wealth.
righteousness:
  baptism and, 93:10
  establishing, 93:10
  eternal rest, as obtaining, 36:25(11)
  of God, 93:10
  grace, as only by, 82:14
  law, as coming through, 82:19
  parable regarding pride over, 93:49
  persecution not proof of, 44:7(4)
  Rogatists as far from, 93:27
  scribes and Pharisees lacking, 36:8
Ripheans, the, 26:6 (poem of Licentius)
rites
  See also under Law; sacraments
  of Gentiles, 82:20
  old sacraments, 82:15
River Jordan, 55:14(8)
  and circumcision of Moses, 23:4
robbers:
  Circumcellions contrasted to, 88:8–9
  man wounded by (Good Samaritan), 98:6
  Paul on, 29:5
rock: Christ as, 55:11
Rogatist(s), 87:10; 93:11, 23, 26, 49
  in Cartenna, 93:21–22(7)
  Catholicism, claim of, 93:23
  Donatists, compared to, 93:11
  Rogatus as founder, 93:11
  Vincent (Rogatist bishop of Cartenna),
    letter from Augustine to,
    93:1(1)–53